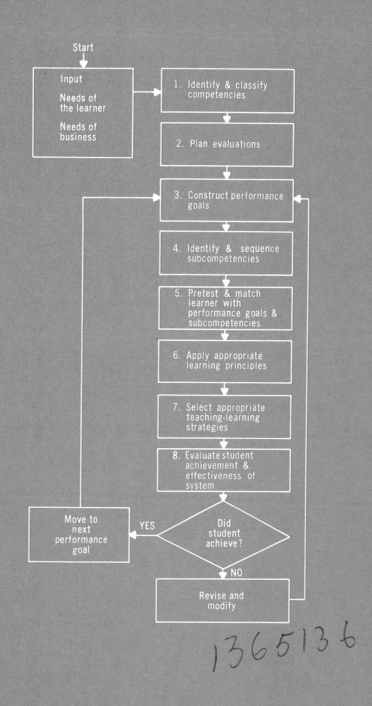

Start

| Input |
| Needs of the learner |
| Needs of business |

1. Identify & classify competencies

2. Plan evaluations

3. Construct performance goals

4. Identify & sequence subcompetencies

5. Pretest & match learner with performance goals & subcompetencies

6. Apply appropriate learning principles

7. Select appropriate teaching-learning strategies

8. Evaluate student achievement & effectiveness of system

Did student achieve?

YES — Move to next performance goal

NO — Revise and modify

1365136

# A Teaching-Learning System for Business Education

# A Teaching-Learning System for Business Education

**Estelle L. Popham**
Professor Emeritus, Department of Business Education
Hunter College of the City University of New York
New York, New York

**Adele Frisbie Schrag**
Professor of Business Education
Division of Vocational Education
Temple University
Philadelphia, Pennsylvania

**Wanda Blockhus**
Professor of Business
San Jose State University
San Jose, California

GREGG DIVISION McGraw-Hill Book Company

NEW YORK   ST. LOUIS   DALLAS   SAN FRANCISCO   AUCKLAND   DÜSSELDORF
JOHANNESBURG   KUALA LUMPUR   LONDON   MEXICO   MONTREAL   NEW DELHI
PANAMA   PARIS   SÃO PAULO   SINGAPORE   SYDNEY   TOKYO   TORONTO

**Sponsoring Editor:** Sheila Whitney Furjanic
**Editing Supervisor:** Linda Stern
**Designer:** Carol Basen
**Art Director:** Frank Medina
**Production Supervisor:** Gary Whitcraft

65017
P827

## Credits

Page 402: Material from Henrietta Fleck, *Toward Better Teaching of Home Economics,*
reprinted with permission of Macmillan Publishing Company, Inc., copyright
© 1968 by Macmillan Publishing Company, Inc. All rights reserved.

Page 422: Material from Joseph S. DeBrum in *Encyclopedia of Education,* reprinted
with permission of Macmillan Publishing Company, Inc., copyright © 1971 by
Macmillan Publishing Company, Inc. All rights reserved.

Page 405: Material from Sally R. Campbell, *Consumer Economics in an Age of
Adaptation,* reprinted with the consent of Sears, Roebuck and Co. © Sears,
Roebuck and Co., 1971.

**Library of Congress Cataloging in Publication Data**

Popham, Estelle L
    A teaching-learning system for business education.

    Bibliography: p.
    Includes index.
    1. Business education. I. Schrag, Adele Frisbie,
date. joint author. II. Blockhus, Wanda,
date. joint author. III. Title.
HF1106.P65        650'.07        75-14140
ISBN 0-07-050504-7

**A Teaching-Learning System for Business Education**

2 3 4 5 6 7 8 9 0  DODO  7 8 4 3 2 1 0 9 8 7 6

# Preface

*A Teaching-Learning System for Business Education,* designed for teacher-trainees, teacher educators, and in-service teachers, differs from the traditional methods book in two ways: first, it implements the concept of competency-based education. Second, it concentrates on student achievement and the effectiveness of the teaching-learning system for each student.

## Focus of Text

The competency—an essential task performed by a worker or consumer at a stated standard—forms the core of competency-based education. The business teacher selects competencies needed by effective entry-level workers, consumers, and citizens and proceeds to implement the teaching-learning system. For example, the teacher will construct performance goals for competencies, create tests to evaluate student learning, choose learning activities appropriate to the goals and for the student, and identify problems interfering with a student's achievement. The importance of preplanning evaluations, of employing appropriate teaching strategies, and of encouraging the student to participate actively in the learning process is also emphasized and discussed in depth.

## Order of Presentation

The text is divided into three parts. Part 1 provides an overview of business education. The historical and legislative backgrounds of business education are presented, and the relationship between career education and business education is discussed, with emphasis placed on the importance of career education to the business education field. Part 1 also focuses on the business educator as a professional and includes such topics as certification, professional associations, and professional activities.

A competency-based teaching-learning system is developed in Part 2. The reader utilizes selected tasks as input into the learning system. The system's eight steps are discussed fully in terms of both theory and practical application.

**Step 1: Identifying and classifying competencies.** Behaviors in the cognitive, affective, and psychomotor domains and the levels within each domain are analyzed to assist the reader in identifying and classifying competencies. Special attention is devoted to the affective domain, an area that often presents difficulties for many teachers.

**Step 2: Planning evaluations.** The necessity of planning evaluations before writing performance goals in order to provide both the teacher and the student with an accurate idea of the expected outcome of learning is fully developed. The appropriate uses of both norm-referenced and criterion-referenced evaluations are explored, along with procedures for planning evaluations that accurately measure achievement of competencies. An added feature is the evaluation continuum, a chart that illustrates the relative values of different kinds of tests, such as multiple choice, essay, and role playing, and suggests the kinds of tests applicable to the different domains and levels of learning.

**Step 3: Constructing performance goals.** The text provides the reader with concrete opportunities to analyze the various components of performance goals and use the analysis in the construction of goals.

**Step 4: Identifying and sequencing subcompetencies.** The reader learns to analyze the competency for subcompetencies that are prerequisites for the achievement of a particular performance goal and arranges the subcompetencies, by means of sequencing charts, in the order in which they should be achieved.

**Step 5: Pretesting and matching learner with performance goals and subcompetencies.** The importance of tailoring educational experiences to the needs of the student is further stressed in the discussion of pretesting students and selecting materials best suited to individual students.

**Step 6: Applying appropriate learning principles.** Fourteen learning principles helpful to effective student achievement are discussed and applied to various subject areas in subsequent chapters.

**Step 7: Selecting appropriate teaching-learning strategies.** The relative advantages and applications of large-group, small-group, and individual instruction are examined in light of teachers' preferences and purposes. As an aid for the future teacher, a wide variety of learning activities is classified according to type of student interaction: reading; writing; listening, speaking, and discussing; and performing and observing. The teacher is guided in the selection of useful learning activities and resources that will develop communication skills as well as other specific competencies.

**Step 8: Evaluating student achievement and the effectiveness of the system.** The text discusses realistic means of evaluating both student achievement and the effectiveness of the system. The teacher makes modifications in the application of the teaching-learning system according to the needs of individual students.

In Part 3, the entire teaching-learning system is applied to the areas of typewriting, shorthand, business communication, accounting, business data processing, business mathematics, clerical training, consumer education, basic business, and marketing and distribution. Each chapter utilizes research in the field to develop a comprehensive approach to teaching the subject area. Suggested competencies are converted to performance goals in conjunction with which other components of the system, including teaching-learning strategies, are developed.

## Intended Audience

Not only is *A Teaching-Learning System for Business Education* a practical "how to" manual for undergraduate and graduate teacher-trainees, it is also a valuable reference source for practicing business education teachers and curriculum specialists. Prospective teachers will find the text an invaluable resource to be referred to frequently as they prepare for their first teaching experiences. By following the steps outlined in the teaching-learning system, they will be able to plan entire courses in a competent, efficient manner. Practicing teachers and curriculum specialists will find the book an effective tool as they adjust courses to keep pace with the growing demands of educational accountability. Above all, as an increasing number of colleges and universities recognize the need for competency-based teacher education, *A Teaching-Learning System for Business Education* will provide the basis for emerging competency-based teacher education programs.

## Acknowledgments

The authors extend special recognition and thanks to the following individuals for their assistance: Phillip Atkinson, Hunter College, New York, New York; Jean Hooven, Penn Ridge High School, Perkasie, Pennsylvania; Sister Celeste Koreckyj, Saint Basil Academy, Jenkintown, Pennsylvania; Andrea Rudnitsky, Graduate Student, University of California, Los Angeles, California; Marie C. Schrag, Oakland County Schools, Pontiac, Michigan; Judith Tidikis, Sun Valley High School, Penn Delco School District, Pennsylvania; Philomena Rosica, Sun Valley High School, Penn Delco School District, Pennsylvania; Marian Stone, Cinnaminson Township High School, Cinnaminson, New Jersey; and Robert Schultheis, Southern Illinois University, Edwardsville, Illinois.

ESTELLE L. POPHAM
ADELE FRISBIE SCHRAG
WANDA BLOCKHUS

# Contents

# How to Use This Book

In order to use *A Teaching-Learning System for Business Education* successfully, you must study this text in a specific manner. In traditional methods books, chapters can be read in random order, but in a text featuring a competency-based system the random selection of chapters cannot be employed.

## Text Organization

Read first, Part 1 provides you with the history and current philosophy of business education. Part 2 presents the teaching-learning system in concise, logical steps. Because all steps in the system are interrelated and interdependent, Part 2 must be read in sequence and must be mastered before you move on to Part 3.

In Part 3, the system is applied to such subjects as typewriting, shorthand, and general business. The chapters in this part, unlike those in the first two parts, may be read in any order. For example, you might wish to study only the chapters on typewriting, shorthand, and the clerical program. Keep in mind, however, that chapters in Part 3 should be undertaken only after the system (Part 2) has been mastered.

## Special Features

The text contains several important features that aid the reader in learning the teaching-learning system. A model of the entire system is illustrated on the inside covers of the book. The model is also presented at the beginning of each chapter in Part 2 where the steps discussed in the chapter are color highlighted. The highlighted models contribute to an understanding of how every step in the system relates to and depends on the other steps.

Performance goals for each chapter in Parts 2 and 3 guide you in preparing for an evaluation by your methods instructor at the end of the chapter. In all cases, assume that the statement "using this book" precedes the actual goal.

In keeping with the learning principles presented within the system itself, Parts 2 and 3 feature numerous "recycles" which direct you to the original discussion of the topic at hand if reinforcement is necessary.

Self-assessments within every chapter in Part 2 enable you to evaluate your own progress as you master each step in the system. After checking your answers with those at the end of the chapter, you should recycle to the original discussions of questions answered incorrectly.

In Part 3, learning activities at the end of each chapter give you practice in applying the teaching-learning system to your own subject areas. The learning activities are keyed to the performance goals appearing at the beginning of the chapter and are a means of enriching your experiences after each goal has been met.

Carefully chosen lists of selected readings appear at the end of each chapter for the reader who wishes to engage in further research. Citations in parentheses next to quoted material in the text refer the reader to the Selected Readings for full bibliographical information.

The text is supplemented by a comprehensive index. In addition, a separate resources section at the end of the text gives up-to-date addresses and information about organizations and publications of interest to business teachers.

## Study Suggestions

Read the Preface for an overall view of the text. As you study each of the chapters in the book, the following suggested procedure will help you make the best use of your study time.

Read the performance goals. Study the system model. Skim the entire chapter and take note of the self-assessments or learning activities.

Carefully read the chapter, recycling when necessary and referring to the Selected Readings as indicated. Answer the self-assessments, recycling when necessary. Complete an evaluation based on the performance goals, as directed by your instructor.

Complete the learning activities, referring to related performance goals when necessary. Study the Selected Readings at the end of the chapter to obtain source material for further research. Refer to the Resources at the end of the book to identify any resources that will help you in studying or applying the teaching-learning system.

*A Teaching-Learning System for Business Education* is research-oriented. Throughout the book, references are made to research findings which identify competencies needed, indicate the effectiveness of teaching-learning strategies, and pinpoint needed curricular changes. As you internalize this accumulated body of research, you will recognize the need for further research and hopefully develop a continuing interest in personally contributing to research.

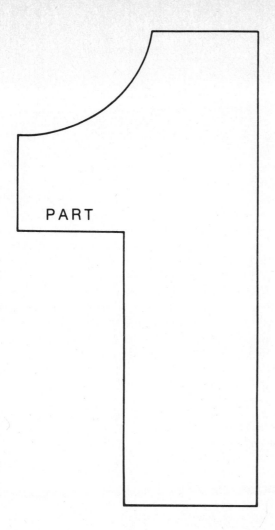

PART

# An Overview of Business Education

# CHAPTER 1

# Emerging Patterns of Business Education

Education is in ferment. All education is reexamining itself and restructuring its programs. Business education, too, is undergoing scrutiny and transformation, and it has become imperative that both students preparing to teach and teachers long accustomed to traditional practices understand the emergent concepts of the field.

## Facets of Business Education

When asked the question, What *is* business education?, a business executive replied, "Education to produce goods and services." A radical retorted, "The avenue to enormous profits." One teacher responded, "Economic concepts necessary for living in a business economy," but another teacher answered, "Learning skills to enter a business or distributive job." A person on the street said, "Shorthand and typing, that's it." These answers bring to mind the parable of the blind men and the elephant. Depending on which part of the elephant he touched, each man defined the elephant as a wall, a spear, a snake, or a rope. Their ideas about the elephant were limited by their own perceptions and experience.

This chapter focuses on the whole picture of business education as well as its many facets—what it is now and what it is becoming. This overview and Chapter 2 set the stage for the teaching-learning system.

Business education prepares students for entry into and advancement in jobs within business, and equally important, it prepares students to handle their own business affairs and to function intelligently as consumers and citizens in a business economy. In educating *for* business, business education is vocational education for business majors. Education *about*

5

business is general education for all students. Figure 1.1 illustrates the two facets of business education.

## General Education Aspects of Business Education

Although business education has specialized goals, it also supports the objectives of all education. A primary aim of general education is to develop basic skills in reading, writing, and arithmetic. In many inner-city schools and indeed in many other schools, this objective is met only to a limited degree or not at all. Some students enter high school lacking reading, writing, and simple arithmetic skills. Many of these students

Figure 1.1   Facets of Business Education

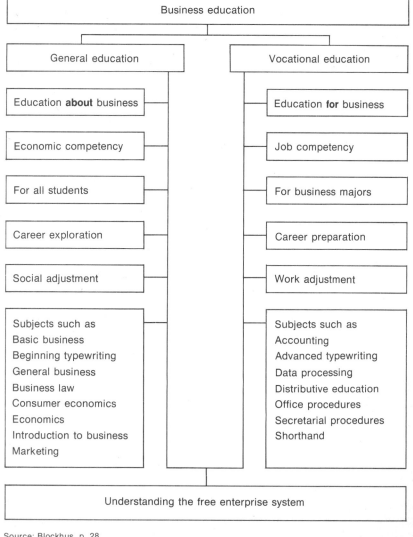

Source: Blockhus, p. 28.

are willing to acquire these basic skills as they are acquiring other competencies. In business classes they learn to appreciate the importance of reading and computational skills in a job-related setting. Thus, business education has a special responsibility to promote these basic skills because of their relevance to later school and job success.

Development of social skills is another general education goal. There are few better settings for improving interpersonal interaction than a classroom operated as a model office, a cooperative-work-experience program, or a group debate on unionism. Business students are often in situations in which they can develop social skills requisite not only for the business world but also for other social situations.

Two popular business courses fall especially into the province of general education. Typewriting at the personal-use level of competency has become general education, and today practically every student learns to type in some school program. The course entitled "General Business" or "Basic Business" is also general education; it provides capabilities for functioning in our business system and develops personal, social, and economic competencies for consumers, workers, and citizens.

## Vocational Business Education

To the student with a career objective, business education is vocational, that is, education to enter or advance in a job. It includes development of technical competencies to required business standards. In addition, the learner acquires an understanding of the business system commensurate with the level of instruction. The third component is adjustment to the work environment as students begin to understand how their skills are used in business; how workers relate to each other and to supervisors; how work is assigned and controlled; what constitutes acceptable business appearance, decorum, and speech; how jobs are interrelated; what time and quality standards are adhered to; and how responsibility relates to job success. This aspect of job training starts in elementary business courses through businesslike classroom organization and management, through helping students organize their work before starting an assignment, through developing standards of business behavior and performance, and through establishing early communication with the business community by utilizing films, speakers, field trips, and individual or group investigations of the business environment.

The initial exposure to business is usually followed by intensified learning experiences structured in a business environment—work in a model office or store, apprenticeship in the school office, cooperative work experience under the joint supervision of business and the school, and the like. In a capstone experience, specific competencies and business behaviors are merged in simulated or real business experiences that bridge the gap between school and business.

A look at the need for both office and distributive workers justifies vocational education in these two areas. Two graphs from the *Occupational*

*Outlook Handbook—1974-1975 Edition* show the number of clerical and sales workers in 1972 and also the projected needs through 1985.

Figure 1.2 shows that more clerical workers were employed in 1972 than any other occupational group and that sales workers comprised the seventh largest group among the ten charted. Sales workers, of course, are only one category of workers in the marketing and distributive field and therefore the chart gives an incomplete picture of that field.

Figure 1.3 is of even greater importance to the business teacher, for it indicates the training needs that will result from replacement of workers and the growth of business by 1985. Again, the need will be greater for clerical workers than for any other occupational group, over 16 million workers. Over three million sales workers will be needed.

Enrollments in vocational education are indicators of business education's ability to meet these needs. Figures are available for advanced vocational programs that receive federal funding. The U.S. Office of Education figures indicate that 2,499,095 students were enrolled in office education programs in 1973. This accounts for about one-fifth of all the enrollment in vocational programs (12,072,445) and is greater than the enrollment in any other vocational program. In that same year, 738,547 distributive education students were enrolled, about one-sixteenth of the total enrolled in vocational programs. (*Summary Data* . . . , p.1)

Programs were offered in office education in accounting and computing; business data processing systems; filing, office machines, clerical; information communication; materials support, transporting, storing, and recording; personnel, training, and related; stenographic, secretarial; supervisory and administrative; typing and related; and other office occupations. Programs in distribution included advertising services, apparel and accessories; automotive; finance and credit; floristry; food distribution; food services; general merchandise; hardware, building materials, home furnishings; hotel and lodging; industrial marketing; insurance; international trade; petroleum; personal services; real estate; recreation and tourism; and transportation. (*Trends in Vocational Education,* Table 4) These programs are evidence that business education is being extended far beyond the secondary school into other institutions.

## Historical Background

The earliest form of business education was apprenticeship training. An experienced bookkeeper who needed an assistant would train an apprentice. Gradually that apprentice would become a bookkeeper and eventually find it necessary to take an apprentice as well.

As business grew, however, more bookkeepers were needed than could be supplied by this method. Itinerant tutors began traveling around the country giving instruction in bookkeeping and penmanship.

Early private Latin grammar schools, primarily for preparation of boys for college, sometimes also included bookkeeping, penmanship, and

Figure 1.2   Employment in major occupational groups, by sex

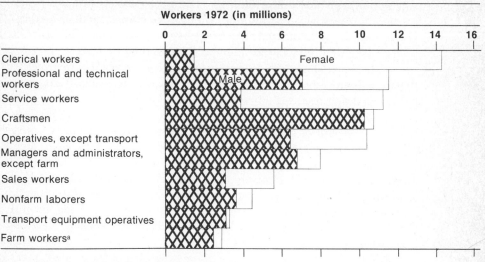

Source: *Occupational Outlook Handbook: 1974-1975*, p. 18
[a]Includes self-employed and unpaid family workers.

commercial arithmetic in their curricula as a result of demands for commercial training. In 1749, a new school organization was introduced at Franklin's Academy in Philadelphia. Instead of including commercial courses in an otherwise academic setting, the school was organized into three divisions, one of which was limited to commercial courses in bookkeeping, arithmetic, history of commerce, and other such courses.

Figure 1.3   Training needs are determined by
           replacement plus growth

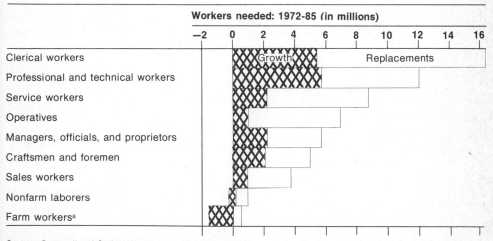

Source: *Occupational Outlook Handbook: 1974-1975*, p. 21
[a]Employment decline more than offsets openings created by deaths and retirements.

The first public high school, the English Classical School for Boys (1821) in Boston, included preparation for commercial careers in a curriculum generally aimed at preparation for college. Six years later the Massachusetts Legislature mandated the establishment of a public high school in every community having as many as five hundred families.

With the expansion of American business, more workers were needed than apprenticeship, tutors, or high schools were preparing. Recognizing the expanding need for office workers, entrepreneurs established private business schools to supply necessary training, sometimes organizing not one but a chain of separate business schools. Bartlett's Business College (1832) in Philadelphia was the first to use the name "business college," and Dolber's Commercial School (1835) in New York was the first institution devoted exclusively to commercial education. The Bryant-Stratton business colleges formed the largest chain, with fifty schools under its management. During this period teachers were usually chosen for their abilities in business positions. They devised their own teaching materials, and there were few textbooks.

Two factors contributed greatly to the expansion of commercial education during the Civil War and Reconstruction periods—the invention of the typewriter in 1868 by Christopher Latham Sholes, and the concomitant increase in the use of shorthand to record materials to be typewritten. To encourage women to enroll in his New York business school to prepare for positions as "type-writers," Silas S. Packard offered free tuition, and his school became the first to teach stenography and typewriting. When the first women were graduated, they drew lots for their first office positions from among those available. The invasion of women into the office had begun; soon the federal government was recruiting women for its offices.

## Public Business Education

Business entered the public high school by taxpayer demand during the last part of the nineteenth century. Parents insisted that the public schools provide the business education they would otherwise have to buy for their children in private business colleges. Many school districts introduced business courses, usually shorthand, typewriting, and bookkeeping. The comprehensive high school, with its curriculum expanded beyond the college preparatory curriculum, was born and still flourishes. In 1890 a public high school devoted exclusively to commercial education was established in Washington, D.C. Other large cities followed this pattern, later abandoned in most places in favor of the comprehensive high school.

With the inclusion of business education in the public high school, business teachers had to meet professional standards for certification. At first, concessions were made because college-trained teachers were not available. This circumstance undoubtedly contributed to the derogatory attitude of teachers of academic subjects toward the first high school business teachers. Of course, business teachers meet the same standards as other teachers today.

An event that had a significant influence on high school business education was the publication of Conant's *The American High School Today* (1959). The prestigious former president of Harvard University included in his 21 recommendations for the comprehensive high school five items directly related to vocational education: Counsellors should be sympathetic to the elective programs which develop marketable skills. Students' programs should not be labeled as college preparatory, vocational, or commercial. Diversified programs should be available for developing marketable skills. Regular vocational courses should not be used as a convenient dumping ground for students with low academic ability. Incentive in the form of special recognition for outstanding achievement should be given to students who elect meaningful nonacademic sequences. (Conant, pp. 44–76)

## Business Education Legislation

Business education has been and is being greatly influenced by federal legislation. The major pieces of legislation are dealt with here.

SMITH-HUGHES ACT. The first federal legislation making funds available for vocational education was the Smith-Hughes Act (1917). It allocated money for the organization and maintenance of part-time vocational schools and classes for employed persons, for the study of requirements for business jobs, and for the development of courses of study based on these requirements. Smith-Hughes funds could not, however, be used for regular high school business courses.

GEORGE-DEEN ACT. Distributive education benefited from the next piece of federal vocational legislation. The George-Deen Act (1937) provided funds for teachers, supervisors, and directors, and for the training of teachers of distributive subjects. Again funds were limited to part-time and evening schools offering instruction to workers employed in distributive occupations.

GEORGE-BARDEN ACT. The George-Barden Act (1946) continued and increased funds for distributive education.

VOCATIONAL EDUCATION ACT. Aid for high school business education was first legislated in the Vocational Education Act of 1963. For the first time the definition of vocational education was amended to include business and office occupations along with distributive education, home economics, trade and industrial education, and agricultural education. Health and technical occupations were later included. Under the VEA, distribution of funds is based on a state plan submitted by the agency having jurisdiction over vocational education in each state. Local school districts administer the program in conformity to the approved state plan. There is usually a state director of vocational education who directs the activities of state supervisors in each vocational field. Local supervisors are usually appointed in highly populated areas.

Federal funds (which must be matched by state and local money) are allotted for:

- Public high school vocational programs.
- Full-time programs for high school graduates and dropouts. (Reimbursable programs include institutions below the baccalaureate level.)
- Full- or part-time adult education programs.
- Programs specially designed for training the handicapped.
- Construction of area vocational schools and other facilities.
- Ancillary services such as teacher education, administration, development of innovative teaching materials, and evaluation.

One of the important outcomes has been the construction of vocational schools whose primary purpose is to provide youth and adults with instruction leading to employment and/or to upgrade them in the jobs in which they are already employed. Vocational schools may be self-contained units offering both general education and vocational education or area vocational schools to which students from several schools offering only general education components are transported for vocational education.

One-tenth of the annual funds are used for research and demonstration grants. A central facility, the Center for Vocational and Technical Education is located at The Ohio State University. It is concerned with research and leadership development in all areas of vocational education. The Center serves as a clearing house for projects carried out in other locations. Money is also available from the separate states for pilot or demonstration projects.

Under the act the various occupations covered are defined. Funds are available for initial preparation, refresher training, and upgrading of individuals leading to employment and advancement. One of its most significant provisions is for education beyond high school and after initial employment.

Vocational business teachers now share common elements and responsibilities with other vocational education groups. The Policies Commission for Business and Economic Education, sponsored jointly by the National Business Education Association, Delta Pi Epsilon, and the Business and Office Education Division of the American Vocational Association, recognized the need for cooperation and issued the policy statement "This We Believe About the Expanding Leadership and Planning Role of Business Educators in Developing a Total Vocational Program in Cooperation with Other Vocational Educators and General Educators." According to the statement, business educators can cooperate with their new cohorts in analyzing manpower needs; in planning curricula that involve cooperation with the other vocational disciplines; in incorporating common elements of vocational education in the preparation of teachers, supervisors, and administrators; in developing standard instruments for evaluating vocational programs and assessing student performance; in cosponsoring cross-disciplinary research; in assisting with planning a total program of career information and guidance; in working with business, industry, and school administrations; and in developing instructional media and materials to enhance the total vocational program.

**VOCATIONAL EDUCATION AMENDMENTS.** Five years after the Vocational Education Act, the Vocational Education Amendments of 1968 were passed, which consolidated all previous vocational legislation and provided funding on a permanent basis. Its purpose was to maintain, extend, and improve existing programs, develop new programs as needed, provide part-time employment for youths who need earnings from such employment to continue their education on a full-time basis, and train those who discontinued their formal education before they were adequately prepared for a vocation or who required retraining because of technological changes. Now, all ages are covered by the act—youth in school, youth out of school, unemployed adults, and underemployed adults. Federal fiscal aid of $565 million was authorized for 1973 and each year thereafter.

Unquestionably the Vocational Education Act of 1963 and the amendments of 1968 constitute a milestone in vocational business education. They have influenced its development and direction more than any other recent single factor. It is apparent that future legislation will change vocational business periodically. The provisions of the 1963 act expire in 1975, and every business teacher must recognize the importance of following the changes in legislation that supplants it. The business education profession has, of course, a responsibility to participate in recommending desirable alterations.

## Growth of Postsecondary Education

In addition to the newly created area vocational schools intended for both high school and postsecondary students, independent business schools and community colleges have become increasingly important as institutions preparing people for careers. In addition to postsecondary schools, special programs for students with special needs have been developed outside the purview of the public secondary school.

**INDEPENDENT BUSINESS SCHOOLS.** The independent business school, formerly called the private business college, which played such a prominent role in the development of business education, continues to prosper. In 1971, there were 1300 independent business schools, with 440,000 enrollees. Chains of independent business schools, some of them owned by large corporations, are again becoming common. Although independent business schools charge tuition, they are very popular because students progress at their own rates and, in many institutions, can enter at frequent specified times during the year. The curricula are stripped of nonrelevant subject matter, and rapid progress can usually be made.

**COMMUNITY AND JUNIOR COLLEGES.** The community college is publicly supported. The junior college is usually privately supported. The growth of the former has been phenomenal. A number of independent business schools are qualifying for junior college status. In 1970, there were more than a thousand junior and community colleges, with more than two million students. One of every three students begins his or her college career in a two-year college. The purpose of these colleges is either to provide academic education to be completed at a senior college or to provide career training. Typical vocational business programs offered at the community college level are accounting, advertising and display (in cooperation with the graphic arts department), office management, records management, secretarial science (educational, legal, and medical), and word processing.

SENIOR COLLEGES AND GRADUATE SCHOOLS. Professional programs are executed at senior colleges and graduate schools. Management programs in office administration, finance, marketing, and systems and procedures are examples of such offerings. Courses for the preparation of business teachers at all levels are given in senior colleges and graduate programs.

SPECIAL PROGRAMS. Federal money is available for vocational business and office education of students with special needs who cannot cope with regular programs. A great deal of attention is being given, too, to the training of unemployed and underemployed adults. Programs for students with special needs are offered at many different levels in educational institutions and also in informal settings in economically disadvantaged neighborhoods. The Manpower Development Training Act is an example of this type of program. It has been replaced by the Concentrated Employment Training Act of 1974.

Not to be overlooked in any survey of business training is the part played by business itself. Most large corporations supply well-equipped classrooms and maintain a permanent instructional staff for employees preparing for advancement.

## The Career Education Movement

Career education is having and will continue to have a profound effect on business education. The career education concept was initiated by U.S. Commissioner of Education Sidney P. Marland in 1971. It is a method of restructuring the focus of education so that what is taught in the classroom has a clear, demonstrable bearing on the learner's future plans—whether an immediate job or further education is the student's aim. A *career* is a person's life work and might include several jobs in one or more occupations. An *occupation* is a work role, such as typist or computer programmer. A *job*, on the other hand, is a position of employment at a particular company or institution in an occupation. The position of statistical typist at Enterprise Industries is a job. It is apparent then that career education is a much broader term than occupational education or job training. It embraces the total educational process from kindergarten through adulthood.

Career education acquaints students with the options open to them in present or future careers along with the special obligations and requirements of careers that interest them. It includes acquisition of both the vocational and the academic competencies required in the careers of their choice. Before students leave school, they are assured the opportunity to gain marketable competencies necessary for an entry-level job. At later periods they gain additional competencies as needed. The school is the constant, and the learner spins off from school and spins back into school as needed.

Career education includes both academic and vocational education. It promotes the relevance of all education by showing that each subject contributes to the self-fulfillment of leading a productive life. Career education enlists the efforts not only of all teachers in the entire school system but also those of the family, employers, government, and organized community groups.

The U.S. Office of Education defines career education as:

The total effort of public education and the community aimed at helping all individuals to become familiar with the values of a work-oriented society, to integrate these values into their personal values systems, and to implement these values into their lives in such a way that work becomes possible, meaningful, and satisfying to each individual. *(Career Education—A Handbook* . . . , p. 8)

Funds from the Vocational Education Amendments of 1968 are used to define objectives at every level and to develop exemplary models in career education, with special attention to materials for early school experiences. The pilot work in developing a Comprehensive Career Education Matrix, which was done at The Center for Vocational and Technical Education, includes eight elements and expected outcomes which are presented here:

| *Elements* | *Outcomes* |
|---|---|
| 1. Career awareness | Career identity |
| 2. Self-awareness | Self-identity |
| 3. Appreciations and attitudes | Self-social fulfillment |
| 4. Decision-making skills | Career decisions |
| 5. Economic awareness | Economic understanding |
| 6. Skill awareness and beginning competencies | Employment skills |
| 7. Employability skills | Career placement |
| 8. Educational awareness | Educational identity |

As shown in Figure 1.4, these outcomes are achieved in three stages: career awareness, career exploration, and career preparation.

In the elementary school, students are introduced to occupational work information (OWI). Multimedia packets such as OCCUPACS provide, in a school-based setting, simulated work experiences, with the emphasis placed on children working with concrete objects. The packets are the vehicles used to get at other factors: attitudes toward work, self-examination, and the feelings which are expressed when a child works with concrete objects. (Peterson, pp. 6–7)

During the middle school or junior high school years students explore several occupational fields and become more familiar with the various occupations, focusing on occupational work adjustment (OWA) during classroom instruction, hands-on experiences, and field observations.

In senior high school, students explore in depth one chosen occupational field, or begin specialized training for a particular job, and also acquire the specific talents and skills required to function in our changing society through occupational work exploration experiences (OWEE). The final phase is job placement or further education followed by job placement. It is hoped that career education at the high school level will improve the present situation, for "in 1970, not counting enrollment in homemaking, only about one high school student in six was enrolled in occupational preparation." (*Career Education: Implementation*, p. 1)

Figure 1.4 also clearly indicates the important role of postsecondary education in preparing for the world of work. In the technical institute or community college, preparation for higher-level specialized or technical jobs is secured. The graduate of the four-year college is presumed to be able to enter a profession, although more people are being graduated from four-year colleges than can find jobs. By 1980, eight out of ten jobs in this country will not require a baccalaureate degree. (*Career Education: Implementation*, p. 1)

The figure also shows continuing career education required for upgrading present jobs or entering new ones throughout the worker's entire career.

## The Job Cluster Concept

It is neither possible nor necessary for teachers to analyze all of the more than 23,000 different jobs that have been identified in the United States or attempt to prepare students to enter an inordinate number of them. A U.S. Office of Education classification system categorizes all jobs into 15 job clusters in each of which common elements are present. Requirements for these clusters rather than for specific jobs can be studied and prepared for. These clusters are: (1) business and office; (2) marketing and distribution; (3) communications and media; (4) construction; (5) manufacturing; (6) transportation; (7) agribusiness and natural resources; (8) marine science; (9) environmental control; (10) public services; (11) health; (12) hospitality and recreation; (13) personal services; (14) fine arts and humanities; and (15) consumer and homemaking-related.

Each broad occupational cluster is comprised of several occupational areas. For instance, the cluster of business and office occupations can be broken down into stenographic and secretarial, typing and related, general office clerical, information and communication, materials support, accounting and computing areas. Each occupational area, in turn, can be broken down into numerous specific jobs. For example:

• *Stenographic and secretarial area:* stenographer, word processor, administrative secretary, executive secretary, legal or medical secretary.

- *General office clerical area:* clerk-typist, file clerk, office machine operator, switchboard operator, receptionist.
- *Business data processing area:* programmer, console operator, keypunch operator, tape librarian, systems analyst.

Statistics show that today's high school graduate is likely to change jobs at least five times before retirement. Usually, a worker moves within the job cluster for which the worker has been trained; but as the employee gains experience and further education, he or she may enter a completely new occupation. For example, a person may have an entry job as a clerk, later become a stenographer, and then be promoted to a secretaryship. With the aid of experience and further education the person might then move into supervision or administration outside the secretarial field but still within the business and office job cluster. There are common elements in all of the jobs mentioned; they all involve a career in business office occupations.

Office or business competencies may also be transferred to another field. For instance, a worker in a business office can effectively use the same office abilities in the health job cluster as a medical secretary or as an accountant in a fine arts museum. Business education may, then, be directly related to part of job preparation for every one of the 15 job clusters.

Figure 1.4   Components and placement of the elements of career education

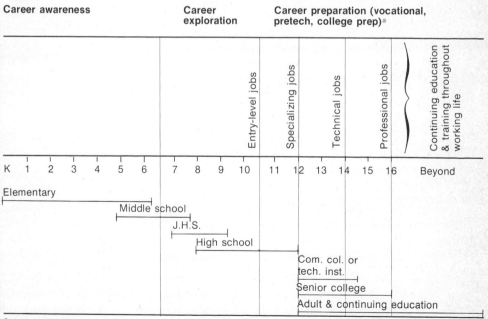

Source: Adapted from U.S. Department of Health, Education, and Welfare, DHEW Publication No. OE 72-39
[a]Career education at the high school level is a common core within each career cluster, plus elective modules preparing for specific job entry and/or further education.

## Impact of Career Education

Although career education is a relatively new approach to education, programs are being developed all over the country. Following the leadership provided by the U.S. Office of Education and The Center for Vocational and Technical Education, a number of states and local districts have restructured their educational programs around the career education themes. For instance, in the spring of 1971, Arizona's legislature voted $2 million in order to launch K-12 career education in 15 selected public schools and in 1972–1973 raised the appropriation to $3.8 million. Part of the money was spent on publicizing the program in the community through a booklet called *Career Education: Leadership in Learning.*

In one county, part was spent in developing a comprehensive information retrieval system hooked up to participating schools. It is possible for any student to interrogate the computer and receive information from three data files (occupational file, college file, and scholarship and financial aid file) upon which career decisions can be based. Some of the appropriations are used for training teachers to use career information within their subject matter fields. A common thread runs through all projects in the Arizona plan: the need to orient the educational staff to career education, to revise teaching methods, and to change attitudes toward school and work by relating learning activities to students' life goals.

The states of Washington, Ohio, Oregon, New Jersey, Georgia, North Dakota, and Wyoming are among those that have developed curricula and have completed or are currently field-testing them, usually starting with the lower grades. The Wyoming plan extends through the fourteenth grade. Curriculum guides are being developed, workshops are being held for teachers, and specialized programs are being developed for emerging occupations in technical areas in the job clusters in which they are needed.

In other words, career education is here to stay, and business teachers are obligated to participate to the fullest possible extent.

## Importance of Career Education to Business Education

Another look at the expected outcomes of career education (page 15) will show that they must be at the heart of business education. According to Fruehling,

> Three of the eight themes of the Comprehensive Career Education Matrix are being handled very well by business teachers—economic understanding, employment skills, and career placement. The other five themes—career awareness, self-awareness, appreciations and attitudes, decision-making skills, and educational awareness—have received varying amounts of attention. (Fruehling, p. 30)

Because these five aspects are key goals in career education, business teachers will have to give more attention to developing the nontechnical requirements in the areas of human relations, work adjustment, and decision making by providing learning activities in which students plan together, work together, and interact with each other and with the teacher. The business teacher is involved in three ways in implementing the goals of career education—in the classroom itself, within the business department, and in working with other teachers outside business education.

The business teacher has a responsibility to assume a leadership role in contributing the guidance material about business careers in offices and distribution that is so essential to the below-high-school-level teacher planning to develop career awareness. The business teacher also has an obligation to join others in helping to organize materials that initiate economic understandings.

Within the classroom the teacher must develop a greater awareness of career opportunities within each class. For instance, the shorthand teacher must not only meet words-a-minute and mailability standards but also provide specific and accurate information about jobs in the secretarial field and career ladders that possibly reach into middle management. This step implies that the classroom teacher will increasingly utilize community resources.

Within the business department, the teacher may be involved in curricular changes. Greater emphasis will be placed on cooperative work experience programs or new organization patterns that create new learning environments within the classroom. Simulations will be used more frequently so that technical competencies can be applied in a worklike environment at the same time that work adjustment is improved and students learn to make decisions about work priorities, methods, and standards. Innovations may result in completely new curricula that enable learners to adapt to the rapid changes that are occurring in business technology, or isolated courses may be combined into integrated blocks of learning materials.

## Summary

Business education is education *about* business and education *for* business. It has had a long history of successfully preparing office workers for the technical aspects of their jobs and of contributing to the development of economic understandings requisite for consumers and citizens. Two influences have emerged, however, which force a modification of traditional business education.

The first is the inclusion of business education in federal legislation and funding of vocational education, first in the distributive education area and eventually in office education. The legislation provided for area vocational schools and extended business education beyond the secondary school into adult education and retraining. It enabled each state to develop a state plan and to provide supervision at the state level. It provided funding for business courses leading to employment at several levels. It allotted funds for research and development at both the national and state levels. Since funding must be renewed at regular intervals, periodic reassessment that affects business education is inevitable. Inclusion of business with the other vocational fields necessitates a willingness on the part of business educators to cooperate with others in common efforts to improve vocational education.

Even more important is the development of the concept of career education. Each one of its eight expected outcomes (career identity, self-identity, self-social-fulfillment, career decisions, economic understanding, employability skills, career placement, and educational identity) is an achievable goal in business education. How they can be made to permeate each business subject is the province of this text.

## SELECTED READINGS

BLOCKHUS, WANDA, "Basic Business Education in the Future," *Delta Pi Epsilon Journal*, Vol. 13, No. 4, August, 1971, p. 28.

BURNSIDE, O. J., JR., "Proposed Vocational Education Legislation: Challenging Opportunities for Business Educators," *Business Education Forum*, May, 1974, pp. 5–8.

*Career Education: A Handbook for Implementation*, U.S. Office of Education, Washington, D.C., 1972.

*Career Education: Leadership in Learning*, Department of Education, Phoenix, Arizona, (undated).

*Comprehensive Career Education Matrix*, Center for Research and Development, Columbus, Ohio, 1971.

CONANT, JAMES B., *The American High School Today*, McGraw-Hill Book Company, 1959.

FRUEHLING, DONALD L., "A Call for Leadership in Career Education," *Business Education Forum*, May, 1974, pp. 29–30.

NOLAN, C. A., *et al.*, *Principles and Problems in Business Education*, South-Western Publishing Company, Cincinnati, Ohio, 1967.

*Occupational Outlook Handbook—1974–75 Edition*, Bulletin 1785, Bureau of Labor Statistics, U.S. Department of Labor, 1974–75.

PETERSON, MARLA, "Simulated Career Development Experiences for Elementary School Children," *Business Education Forum*, February, 1972, pp. 6–7.

*Summary Data Vocational Education: Fiscal Year 1973*, Vocational Education Information No. 1, Bureau of Occupational and Adult Education, Division of Vocational and Technical Education, USOE, Washington, D.C.

"This We Believe About the Expanding Leadership and Planning Role of Business Educators in Developing a Total Vocational Program in Cooperation with Other Vocational Educators and General Educators," Policies Commission for Business and Economic Education, copies available NBEA, 1906 Association Drive, Reston, Va.

TONNE, HERBERT A., AND LOUIS NANASSY, *Principles of Business Education*, 2d ed., Gregg Division of McGraw-Hill Book Company, New York, 1970.

*Trends in Vocational Education: Fiscal Year 1972*, Vocational Education Information II, Center for Adult, Vocational, Technical, and Manpower Education, Division of Vocational and Technical Education, USOE, 1972.

WANOUS, S. J., "A Chronology of Business Education in the United States," *Business Education Forum*, April, 1969, pp. 36–44.

# CHAPTER 2

# Professionalism

Today teaching is widely accepted as a profession along with law, medicine, and the ministry, and teachers are expected to be professional. What is professionalism? It is behavior, attitudes, aims, or qualities that characterize a profession or a professional person. It is an attitude of willingness to work, to share, and to disagree when disagreement leads to progress. It is commitment to self, to students, and to the profession.

What is a profession? By first defining the earmarks of a profession, we can then apply the criteria to business teachers or to accountants, engineers, physicians, ministers, lawyers, or other groups. Criteria commonly accepted for a profession include the following:

1. A common body of knowledge attainable through a long, sequential process with continuous learning throughout the career.
2. Controlled admission to the profession, usually involving educational requirements and/or examination.
3. Sincere interest in the service to be rendered and in the welfare of society over personal gain.
4. High degree of autonomy for individual members and for the profession as a whole.
5. A code of ethics.
6. A strong professional association which enables the profession to meet its goals and advance the welfare of its members.

Although it is possible to argue the degree to which teaching (or any other calling) meets each criterion, such an argument loses sight of the real issue: the appropriate conduct and attitude of the teacher. What sets teaching apart from other occupational groups? What does the teacher do or refrain from doing which makes him or her unique? This chapter focuses on these issues.

The professional business teacher shares certain characteristics and responsibilities with all other teachers. Leighbody describes what constitutes a professional by enumerating characteristics associated with true professional status. (Leighbody, p. 295) Those characteristics are paraphrased below:

The professional worker

1. Takes full responsibility for his or her efforts and actions.
2. Continually seeks self-improvement.
3. Contributes to the skill and knowledge of the profession.
4. Respects the confidence of others.
5. Adjusts grievances through proper channels.
6. Meets professional obligations.

The professional worker *does not*

7. Require close supervision or direction.
8. Regard himself or herself as an employee.
9. Work by the hour nor expect to be paid by the hour.
10. Advance at the expense of others.

The professional worker is

11. Loyal to fellow workers and avoids rumors and hearsay.
12. Sensitive to the problems of fellow workers.
13. Proud of his or her profession.
14. Motivated by the desire to render service.

## What Professionalism Means

Each of the characteristics of the professional worker applies to the teacher and to the student preparing for a professional career. By becoming committed to and involved in the activities of the profession, a student can get a head start on peers who say they are too busy as students but will become involved later. As a matter of fact, people find time to do those things which are important to them; a student who feels that professionalism is important will find time to meet obligations, just as a busy teacher also finds time to meet professional commitments.

A student can meet professional obligations, just as a teacher does, by activities such as the following: joining professional associations as a student member; reading business education and other education periodicals regularly; attending professional meetings, workshops, and conferences; and, whenever appropriate, contributing to conference or workshop programs or to periodicals. A student can belong to business education or other associations on the local campus and serve in some capacity. All organizations need willing people to do myriad tasks. The student can develop leadership abilities by serving as a committee member, committee chairperson, or officer. A student who has frequently served as secretary for groups should volunteer for another job such as program director or fund raiser in order to broaden personal experience. Throughout the professional career, teachers will be working on committees or task forces, and work on student committees will provide invaluable experience. Although the student, like the professional, should be motivated by the desire to render service, student activities will help to perfect personal skills. Incidentally, professional activities as a student enhance placement qualifications.

## Certification

One of the earmarks of a profession is controlled admission to practice. In teaching, that admission is the teaching credential, the license or certification to teach in public schools. Certification is granted by the individual state and historically has been granted on the basis of specified educational credits and sometimes teaching experience, work experience, or a city or state test. Credentials have ranged from provisional certification for minimum qualifications to permanent or life credentials for maximum qualifications.

Emphasis in certification is now changing to teacher competencies, that is, a candidate's possession of specified knowledge, skills, and attitudes. Cotrell and his associates provided the first major research in identifying teacher competencies in vocational and technical education including agriculture, business and office education, distributive education, health occupations, home economics, technical education, and trade and industrial education.

While there may be general agreement on the desirability of using teacher competencies as the basis for certification, the implementation becomes complex. After a state legislature enacts legislation calling for competency-based certification, a state board of education faces some tough decisions. Although research provides some answers, more research is needed. Consideration must be given to questions such as these: What is the relationship between a competency in subject matter and creating an environment which stimulates students to learn? between competency in subject matter and interacting with students? Is the ability to type or to take shorthand at a certain level requisite to the ability to teach the subject? Some competencies are appropriately measured by performance tests and others by process tests, but specifically what kinds of tests? Assuming a teacher needs the ability to diagnose and treat learning difficulties, how can this competency be assessed? How is the role of the student teacher and/or intern affected as competency-based certification is implemented? Must each candidate be tested individually? Some states handle the last question by approving programs in colleges and universities within the state; if a candidate has completed an approved program, he or she is granted a credential, whereas others must pass a competency test.

The Policies Commission for Business and Economic Education issued a policy statement calling for competency-based teacher education programs and competency-based certification which states that:

- Business teacher certification standards should be sufficiently uniform in the 50 states so that business teachers who qualify in any one state are eligible for certification in the other 49 states.
- Prospective business teachers should be required to obtain firsthand knowledge of business activities and requirements for employment.
- Prospective business teachers should be encouraged to participate in professional business education organizations prior to their initial certification.
- Business teacher education programs should include supervised professional laboratory experiences.
- Business teacher certification should be on a renewal rather than a permanent basis, with renewal on the basis of professional growth and development.
- Prospective business teachers should be encouraged to participate in youth organization work during teacher-preparation programs so that organization and supervision of youth organizations will be understood by the time of initial certification.

Continuous study and growth are characteristics of the professional. Certification provides entrée into the field of teaching, but true professionals will continue their professional growth throughout their entire careers.

## Interfacing With Others

In a professional role, the teacher interfaces with administrators, other teachers, support staff, parents and other citizens, business people, and, of course, students; and the teacher is expected to exhibit satisfactory interpersonal relationships with each. In a kaleidoscope the teacher might be likened to a red pebble, with the other colors representing people with whom the teacher has contact. As the kaleidoscope is turned, the red pebble may combine to create other colors or forms, yet it remains distinctly itself. Even though the teacher assumes other roles in the course of a day—club adviser, vocational counselor, or after-school grocery shopper or gardener—the teacher is still a teacher and is recognized as such. The Policies Commission for Business and Economic Education issued a statement concerning the multiple roles of the business educator. These statements deal with the business educator as teacher; developer of instructional materials and media; supervisor of educational activities; job placement adviser; educational consultant; consultant to labor and management groups in business, industry, and agriculture; school-community relations participant; guidance resource person; administrator; research participant; member of the teaching profession; and coordinator of cooperative education programs.

An example of how one role is dealt with follows:

As a supervisor of educational activities, the business educator:

    a. *Serves* as a master teacher supervising less-experienced teachers.

b. *Serves* as an adviser to student clubs and other co-curricular activities.
c. *Supervises* out-of-class practice efforts of students.
d. *Serves* as a member of the supervisory staffs of local, state, and national boards and agencies.
e. *Supervises* paraprofessional personnel.
f. *Supervises* student teachers.

Because teachers are professionals, they are obliged to behave in a professional manner in their multiple roles both at school and elsewhere. In relationships with administrators, the teacher should keep in mind that the administrator once was a teacher and understands the problems faced by teachers. The administrator has certain responsibilities which depend on all segments of the school carrying out individual tasks. For instance, the administrator is responsible for preparing certain reports which depend on input from teachers. By providing that input properly and promptly, the teacher is behaving responsibly toward the administration. If teachers encounter an administrator who seems capricious or unfair, they should concentrate on the requirements of the position and not on the person. The teacher will not agree with all the decisions of even the most able and likeable administrator. Teachers who accept this fact as a part of the world of work will save unpleasantness for themselves and for the administrator as well. Above all, a beginning teacher should not go into a school and expect to remake it the first year.

Departments as well as school districts work under budgetary constraints, and the teacher should therefore use materials and supplies judiciously. These should not be wasted. Before disposing of materials, teachers should ask themselves whether they could be put to another use. For example, some schools use "ruined" spirit duplicator paper for rough-draft typing. In addition to the economic motivation to recycle supplies, there is also the ecological need. Since many teachers use the same equipment, it is the responsibility of each person to return equipment promptly and, if repairs are needed, to notify the appropriate person. It is not uncommon for four or five teachers to use the same classroom in a day's time, and therefore it is thoughtful as well as necessary for each to leave the room in a presentable manner. A room which has been rearranged during an hour should be put back in order at the end of the hour. Litter, if any, should be disposed of in trash cans, books put away, shades or blinds adjusted, and good housekeeping practiced. An orderly room not only sets the stage for learning but also shows respect for other people.

Departments whose members function with harmony and goodwill create pleasant places in which to work. In associations with coworkers, other teachers, paraprofessionals, secretaries, custodians, and so on, an understanding and acceptance of individual differences, needs, and desires goes a long way toward achieving the kind of professional climate expected in a school. As a member of a school faculty, the teacher owes loyalty to the school. Gossip should be avoided and confidences kept. All is not perfect within any school because imperfect people are involved, but with all involved contributing their best efforts, the direction of change will be positive.

Because of the subject matter taught, business teachers have more contact with business people in the community than do other teachers. Business teachers depend on the business community for job research, for current information on methods and procedures, and for data on new equipment. Business firms, in turn, depend on business teachers to utilize the shared information to prepare students better as workers and citizens. The business teacher should participate in activities of the larger community—activities such as service clubs, civic projects, and advisory councils. The business teacher should make presentations before business groups and in turn invite business people into the schools. Both business firms and schools profit from mutual cooperation.

Students are a teacher's reason for being. A high moment between a teacher and a student is the exhilaration of a student's comprehending an idea, taking it for his or her own, and then using it to produce a new idea. The same setting that can produce such a moment of joy can also produce intense emotion at the other end of the scale. Teachers and students experience both extremes, but the successful teacher experiences more joy than grief. One thing great teachers share in common is a respect for and appreciation of people. They accept the learner as a unique human being and they see themselves as capable of aiding learners by unleashing their high potential.

## Professional Associations

A strong professional association is an earmark of a profession. Organizations for teachers at national, state, and local levels which have professional goals and which are of particular interest to business and distributive educators include the following.

### National Business Education Association

Existing exclusively to serve the needs of the business teacher, supervisor, and administrator, the National Business Education Association (NBEA) promotes better business education through a unified association. Members simultaneously hold membership in one of five regional associations: the Eastern Business Teachers Association or the Southern, North-Central, Mountain Plains, or Western Business Education Associations. The membership includes educators in secondary schools, vocational-technical schools, independent business schools, community and junior colleges, colleges and universities, state and local administration, and continuing education. Undergraduate business education students are encouraged to join at reduced membership rates which entitle them to the same benefits as regular members. The national office of NBEA, located in Reston, Virginia, provides liaison with other professional associations and with the United States Congress, state legislative bodies, the U.S. Office of Education, and other federal agencies. NBEA is a department of the National Education Association, which is discussed later.

*Business Education Forum,* the official magazine of NBEA published from October through May, is devoted specifically to the interests of business educators. Subject areas such as the secretarial program, marketing and distribution, data processing, bookkeeping and accounting, and research are regular topics in the *Forum,* as are other important subjects of interest to teacher education, administration and supervision, curriculum, and guidance personnel.

Treatment of a major problem or significant development in the field of business education provides the thrust for the annual *National Business Education Yearbook.* Leaders in the profession serve as yearbook editors and, along with contributing experts, present a scholarly approach to the topic, examining its various aspects and significant implications.

NBEA holds an annual convention, the site of which is rotated among the five regions; each region except that in which the national convention is held also holds an annual meeting.

The international affiliate of NBEA is the United States Chapter of the International Society for Business Education (ISBE). Membership in ISBE embraces educators and business people from the Middle East, Europe, and both North and South America. Members of the United States Chapter receive news bulletins and the *International Review of Business Education,* published at ISBE headquarters in Switzerland. ISBE holds an international congress in a different country each year.

Institutional membership in the National Association for Business Teacher Education (NABTE) is held by colleges and universities with business teacher education programs. NABTE publishes the annual *NABTE Review,* which carries scholarly articles of special interest to teacher educators. Educators from NABTE schools have the opportunity to pursue topics of mutual interest at NABTE meetings, which are part of the NBEA convention program.

The chart in Figure 2.1 depicts the organization of the National Business Education Association.

## American Vocational Association

The American Vocational Association (AVA) is dedicated to the principle that vocational, technical, and practical arts education must be available to all persons of all ages in every community. The divisions and departments shown below are indicative of the scope of AVA:

- *Divisions:* Agricultural Education, Business and Office Education, Distributive Education, Industrial Arts, Home Economics, Trade and Industrial, Technical Education, New and Related Services (Guidance, Health Occupations, Manpower Development Training and Research)

Figure 2.1

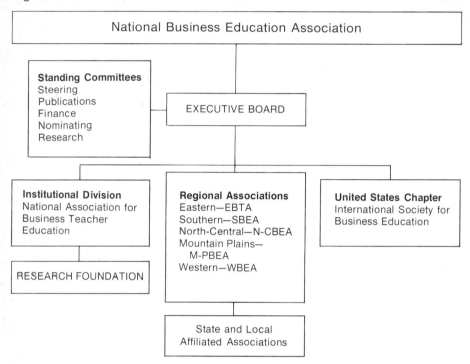

- *Departments:* Adult, Secondary, Post-Secondary, Supervision and Administration, Research and Evaluation, Teacher Education, Special and Related

A division is provided for each occupational area with a membership of 500 or more; within divisions, there are specialized organizations. For example, four organizations within the Distributive Education Division serve the membership: (1) National Association of State Supervisors of Distributive Education (NASSDE), (2) Council for Distributive Teacher Education (CDTE), (3) National Association of Distributive Education Teachers (NADET), and (4) National Association of Distributive Education Local Supervisors (NADELS).

The *American Vocational Journal* goes to members monthly during the school year and contains information on new developments, news of the profession, research, equipment, materials, and services. The annual AVA convention brings together members and representatives from business, industry, labor, agriculture, and government who are interested in improving the nation's program of training for occupational competency. Other services include program development, an annual trade show, practical publications not available elsewhere, a placement service, and insurance.

## National Education Association

The National Education Association (NEA), the largest professional organization in the world, has over 1.5 million members including teachers, administrators, counselors, school secretaries, and student members from all levels and all disciplines. The more than thirty departments of NEA include the National Business Education Association and other associations for vocational education and colleges for teacher education. The Student NEA, an affiliate, represents the preprofessional on the national level; any student enrolled in and interested in education may become a member. Student Action for Education provides secondary students with career exploration experiences and information.

NEA is supported and governed by the nation's teachers. The association works to attain and maintain for teachers a significant role in determining educational policies, in developing solutions to educational and professional problems, and in securing benefits, compensation, and other recognition in keeping with teachers' professional responsibilities. The NEA Code of Ethics pronounces the educator's commitment to the student, the public, the profession, and professional employment practices.

Objectives are achieved through research; publications; press, radio, and television; field services; conventions; legislative lobbying; professional negotiations; investigative reports; and sanctions. Members receive the NEA journal *Today's Education* and the tabloid *NEA Reporter*.

## American Federation of Teachers

The activities of the American Federation of Teachers (AFT) are more like a labor union's than those of a professional association, although AFT does perform certain functions characteristic of a professional association. The AFT, an affiliate of the American Federation of Labor, includes members who are teachers, counselors, and librarians but excludes administrators. Membership is concentrated in large urban centers.

Members receive a monthly tabloid called *The American Teacher*, which features federation news and educational articles. A teacher who joins a local unit automatically becomes a member of the national and state federation if there is one in the state and, indirectly, of the AFL-CIO Industrial Union Department. The AFT is pledged to support labor unions and in return receives financial assistance, political influence, and other assistance from the AFL-CIO.

Collective bargaining and strikes are the major means by which the AFT pursues its objectives, tactics increasingly accepted by NEA. In 1970 more than a million teachers were covered by collective-bargaining agreements executed by AFL or NEA affiliates.

## Honorary Societies

The purposes of Delta Pi Epsilon, a national honorary graduate fraternity in business education, include research, leadership, scholarship, service, and cooperation. Membership in Delta Pi Epsilon is invitational from one of more than seventy chapters and is based on qualifications set by the National Council. Publications include chapter newsletters, research bulletins, the *Business Education Index* and the research-oriented *Delta Pi Epsilon Journal.* The *Index* provides citations by subject and author for business education articles selected from over thirty periodicals and yearbooks, an invaluable service to the profession. Chapter and inter-chapter meetings focus on professional topics, Chapters conduct research initiated locally or by the National Research Conferences. Delta Pi Epsilon presents a research award annually to a researcher for the most outstanding research in business education; the purpose of the award is to encourage and recognize doctoral research in business education.

Pi Omega Pi, a national business teacher undergraduate honor society, celebrated its golden anniversary in 1973. Its members are teachers and prospective teachers of business subjects and its purposes include fellowship, scholarship, civic responsibility, ethical standards, and service. Chapters in thirty-three states engage in activities such as producing publications for the profession, sponsorship of local conferences or handling specific functions for regional business education meetings, participation in campuswide activities, receptions for new students or retiring faculty members, and other service projects. A national convention is held biennially. Members receive the *Here & There* newsletter seven times a year, and a yearbook is also available.

## Other Teacher Organizations

Other organizations for teachers include groups interested in specialized areas such as consumer education, data processing, business law, educational research, marketing, and business communications. The organizations vary in programs and size from fewer than a hundred to the prestigious American Education Research Association, which has over ten thousand members. Such organizations include the American Business Communications Association, American Council on Consumer Interests, Society of Data Educators, the American Economic Association, and the American Marketing Association.

## Youth Organizations

An obligation and reward of the professional business teacher might include sponsorship of a local chapter of a youth organization. Such youth organizations include Future Business Leaders of America, Phi Beta Lambda, Distributive Education Clubs of America, and the Office Education Association.

FUTURE BUSINESS LEADERS OF AMERICA—PHI BETA LAMBDA. Members of Future Business Leaders of America and its college division, Phi Beta Lambda, are students enrolled in business subjects in public or private schools irrespective of whether such education is federally reimbursed. Formerly sponsored by NBEA, independent status was chosen in 1969 under the name Future Business Leaders of America—Phi Beta Lambda, Inc. Both groups have their own national officers and organizations, activities, and leadership conferences. Competitive events are conducted on the local, state, and national levels, including best chapter project, unique chapter project, public and extemporaneous speaking contests.

DISTRIBUTIVE EDUCATION CLUBS OF AMERICA. Members of Distributive Education Clubs of America (DECA) are students enrolled in reimbursable programs in marketing and distribution. Individual student membership in DECA is achieved through membership in the local DECA chapter. DECA has divisions for high school, junior college, college, alumni, and professionals. Members participate in competitive events including best chapter display, best merchandise manual, best job application and interview, public speaking contest, essay contest, and best state newspaper and newsletter. (See also Chapter 18, Marketing and Distribution.)

OFFICE EDUCATION ASSOCIATION. The Office Education Association (OEA), an independent youth organization for students enrolled in reimbursable high school and postsecondary office occupations education programs, was founded when the Vocational Education Act of 1963 made business and office education eligible to receive federal funds. OEA is designed to develop leadership abilities, interest in the American business system, and competency in office occupations within the framework of vocational education. Members participate in competitive events such as job application contests, job manual contests, verbal communications contests, parliamentary procedures contests, chapter displays, and chapter activities.

## Professional Activities

Participation in professional associations provides an opportunity for personal growth and for shaping the future of business education. One avenue of participation is through attendance at professional meetings such as local workshops and conferences and, whenever possible, state, regional, or national conventions. Such attendance affords an opportunity to hear leaders in the field, to share ideas with fellow teachers, and to see the latest educational materials and equipment. Friendships initially made in a teacher education program are nurtured over the years at professional meetings.

In addition to attendance, teachers also have the obligation to plan for and participate in meetings. Anyone who has ever worked on a conference or convention knows the enormous amount of work that goes into a large meeting; many people are needed to do a variety of jobs, from seeing that audiovisual equipment is available and operative to introducing speakers and serving as recorders. Future teachers and teachers should contact the person in charge of a conference or convention and volunteer to help out wherever services are needed. Invariably personal satisfaction comes from contributing time and energy to the success of a conference or convention.

## Professional Reading and Writing

The in-service and prospective teacher should scan the literature which comes from professional associations and read in detail those articles which are relevant to his or her teaching area or interest. Publications such as the *Business Education Forum, AVA Journal,* and *Delta Pi Epsilon Journal* have already been mentioned. In addition to publications from professional associations, there are excellent magazines supplied free to teachers who write to the publishers on school stationery asking to be put on the mailing list. *Business Education World* is published bimonthly during the school year by the Gregg and Community College Division of McGraw-Hill Book Company; the *Balance Sheet* is published monthly during the school year by South-Western Publishing Company. The *Journal of Business Education,* an independent professional magazine, is available by subscription and is published monthly during the school year.

A teacher or prospective teacher who has an idea for an article should identify an appropriate periodical, write the article to conform to the periodical's editorial policy, and submit it for publication. A great deal of information about the publication policy of a periodical can be learned simply by examining recent issues. How long are articles? Are the articles primarily research-oriented? methodology-oriented? news items? theoretical statements? written in first person? illustrated? Are authors primarily classroom teachers? college professors? textbook authors? Even periodicals which primarily solicit manuscripts will occasionally publish provocative unsolicited articles.

## Graduate Study

Teachers usually continue their education beyond the bachelor's degree and, even after obtaining advanced degrees, go back to school from time to time to keep up with the latest developments. A plus benefit is the fact that school districts usually pay additional salary as units beyond a bachelor's degree, up to a specified maximum number, are completed. Bachelor's degrees held by teachers usually are the B.A. (bachelor of arts) or B.S. (bachelor of science). Degrees may be taken in education or business, each of which has advantages. Master's degree candidates must complete one or two years of advanced study beyond the bachelor's degree. Some institutions require a thesis as part of a master's program. The two most common master's degrees are the M.A. (master of arts) and M.S. (master of science); however, business teachers might also have the M.B.A. (master of business administration) or a specialized teaching master's degree.

At one time, the doctor of philosophy (Ph.D.) was the only doctor's degree awarded by universities. Today, universities offer the Ph.D., the doctor of education (Ed.D.), the doctor of business administration (D.B.A.), and the doctor of arts in teaching (D.A.). Some universities require individual research only of candidates for the Ph.D.; other universities require research of both Ed.D. and D.B.A. candidates. Because hundreds of institutions now offer doctorates, it is impossible to generalize concerning requirements. Much depends upon the institution offering the degree. It is possible for a candidate to select from among programs leading to the Ed.D., D.B.A., and Ph.D., all of which may be offered by the same department in a given university. The quality of a degree depends upon the institution conferring it, and the requirements may be diverse. Generally, a doctorate requires two or three years of study beyond the master's degree, rigorous subject-matter examinations, and submission of a dissertation approved by a committee within the university. At one time the Ph.D. candidate demonstrated reading facility in two foreign languages; this, too, is changing. In fact, some universities permit individual departments to stipulate language requirements, and it is not unusual for those in business or business education to be required to take advanced statistics and computer science in lieu of two foreign languages.

## Research

The professional has an obligation to advance knowledge through the scientific method of inquiry. Some business teachers can participate in research more actively than others, but all should understand research methods and be able to interpret research findings which relate to their teaching field and to apply the findings if desirable. Major research strategies include descriptive, experimental, action, and historical research.

Descriptive research is concerned with accurate assessments of the present status of phenomena in the field. Descriptive research goes beyond routine fact gathering and tabulating; it also provides the basis for predictions and reveals relationships among variables. Surveys, case studies, and correlation studies are all descriptive research. Examples of descriptive studies include Brown, "The Relationship Between Supervisor and Student Evaluations of Teaching Effectiveness of General Business Teachers"; Pyke, "Patterns of Organization and Characteristics of Student Teaching and Internship Programs in Business Teacher Education"; and Ristau, "The Development of a Business Education Model for Methods and Procedures in a Planning, Programming, and Budgeting System."

In experimental research the investigator seeks to ascertain whether a condition occurs by the manipulation of an experimental variable under controlled conditions. Experimental and control groups are identified, with one treatment given the control group and a particular treatment given the experimental group. Nonexperimental variables that might contaminate the experiment are identified and controlled. The experiment is then conducted in an attempt to determine the effect of one treatment versus another. Examples of experimental studies include Butts and Prickett, "The Effect of Audio Tutorial and Programmed Instruction Laboratories on Achievement in Accounting"; Missling, "A Comparison of the Traditional Plan to Three Selected Flexible Modular Plans in

First-Semester High School Typewriting With Straight Copy Achievement and Production Achievement as Criteria"; and Weaver, "An Experimental Study of the Relative Impact of Controllable Factors of Difficulty in Typewriting Practice Materials."

Historical research looks to the past in order to gain information on a problem. The researcher utilizes primary sources whenever possible, sources such as eyewitness accounts or actual objects which can be examined. If primary source material is not available, then secondary source material is used, such as information from a person who did not directly observe the event, object, or condition. Such information might be found in newspapers, periodicals, or other written accounts. Historical studies include Furtado, "An Interpretative History of Distributive Education, 1936–1972, As Seen by Selected National Leaders"; and Phillips, "The Evolution of Federal Vocational Education Legislation with Special Reference to Business Education (1862–1963)."

## Future of the Profession

Crises in national life, in education, and in the classroom come and go, but the profession will continue as long as dedicated men and women believe in business education and devote themselves wholeheartedly to it. The profession will continue to grow as capable young people are attracted to it.

A professional has the obligation to single out and talk to promising young people about entering the profession. As teachers work with students over a period of time, they see students who they feel could become excellent teachers. Maybe a student has a certain temperament, a certain enthusiasm, a certain zest for living, and a certain finesse with people that indicates the kind of person likely to make a fine teacher. When teachers in secondary schools, community colleges, and colleges observe such students, they should encourage them to consider teaching. They should talk realistically about teaching, both its advantages and pitfalls as well as the economic considerations and employment outlook. Many master teachers entered the profession because their own teachers served as models and encouraged them.

## Summary

Professionalism is behavior, attitudes, aims, or qualities that characterize a profession or a professional person. It is commitment to self, to students, and to the profession. Earmarks of a profession include a common body of knowledge, controlled admission, interest in service over personal gain, autonomy for members, code of ethics, and a strong professional association. The professional worker meets his professional obligations, which include continuous learning, contributing to the advancement of the profession, and participation in professional affairs.

In the past, certification has been granted on the basis of educational credits and perhaps teaching or work experience. Emphasis is now changing to teacher competencies and the possession of specified knowledge, skills, and attitudes.

The teacher fulfills many roles in the course of a workday, such as developer of instructional materials and media, supervisor of educational activities, job placement adviser, consultant, school-community relations participant, guidance resource person, administrator, and researcher in addition to teacher. As a professional, the teacher is expected to exhibit satisfactory interpersonal relationships in each role.

Professional associations for business education teachers include the National Business Education Association, the American Vocational Association, and the National Education Association. Delta Pi Epsilon and Pi Omega Pi are honorary societies for business and distributive teachers. Youth organizations include Future Business Leaders of America and its college division, Phi Beta Lambda; Distributive Education Clubs of America; and the Office Education Association. Besides membership in professional associations, other activities of the professional include participation in conventions and conferences, professional reading and writing, graduate and even postgraduate study, and research.

## SELECTED READINGS

BANGS, F. KENDRICK, "Our Commitment to Research," *Balance Sheet,* May, 1968, p. 397.

BLYTH, MARY M., "If You Read the FORUM, You Know," *Business Education Forum,* January, 1974, p. 3.

BOGGS, LOHNIE J., ET AL., "Needed Research in Business Education," *DPE Research Bulletin No. 3,* Delta Pi Epsilon, St. Peter, Minn., 1972.

BROWN, BETTY JEAN, "The Relationship Between Supervisor and Student Evaluations of Teaching Effectiveness of General Business Teachers," unpublished doctoral dissertation, University of Tennessee, Knoxville, Tenn., 1971.

BUTTS, FRANKLIN EUGENE, AND GARY L. PRICKETT, "The Effect of Audio Tutorial and Programmed Instruction Laboratories on Achievement in Accounting," unpublished doctoral dissertation, University of Northern Colorado, Greeley, Colo., 1969.

CALHOUN, CALFREY C., AND MILDRED HILLESTAD, *Contributions of Research to Business Education,* Yearbook No. 9, National Business Education Assn., Washington, 1971.

————, AND JOHN M. SHEPPARD, "Building Research Competencies in Business Education," *National Business Education Quarterly,* Spring, 1969, p. 3.

COTRELL, CALVIN J., ET AL., *Model Curricula for Vocational and Technical Teacher Education: Report No. I, Performance Requirements for Teachers,* The Ohio State University Center for Vocational and Technical Education, Columbus, Ohio, December, 1971. (Grant OEG 3-7-000158-2037)

DORROS, SIDNEY, *Teaching as a Profession,* Charles E. Merrill Publishing Co., Columbus, Ohio, 1968.

EYSTER, ELVIN S., "The Role of Business Education Associations," *Journal of Business Education,* April, 1969, p. 270.

FURTADO, LORRAINE T., "An Interpretative History of Distributive Education,

1936–1972, As Seen by Selected National Leaders," unpublished doctoral dissertation, Michigan State University, 1973.

HAMPTON, DONALD F., "Involvement: Essential for Professional Growth," *Balance Sheet,* May, 1969, p. 398.

HUFFMAN, HARRY, "Focus on NBEA'S Professional Leadership Role," *Business Education Forum,* January, 1971, p. 7.

JEFFREY, WILLIAM T., "Professionalism—What's in It for Me?" *Business Education Forum,* October, 1972, p. 62.

LEIGHBODY, G. B., "What Makes a Professional, Professional?" *Phi Delta Kappan,* April, 1953, p. 295.

LIEBERMAN, MYRON, *Education as a Profession,* Prentice-Hall, Inc., Englewood Cliffs, N.J., 1956.

MISSLING, LORRAINE, "A Comparison of the Traditional Plan to Three Selected Flexible Modular Plans in First-Semester High School Typewriting with Straight Copy Achievement and Production Achievement as Criteria," unpublished doctoral dissertation, University of North Dakota, 1970.

OLIVERIO, MARY ELLEN, "Business Education: Needs and Innovations," *Delta Pi Epsilon Journal,* February, 1971, p. 2.

PHILLIPS, JEAN DAVIS, "The Evolution of Federal Vocational Education Legislation with Special Reference to Business Education (1862–1963)," unpublished doctoral dissertation, The Ohio State University, 1971.

PLEVYAK, PAUL P., "Professionalism—Are We Losing It?" *Balance Sheet,* February, 1972, p. 5.

PYKE, WILLIE BRASWELL, "Patterns of Organization and Characteristics of Student Teaching and Internship Programs in Business Teacher Education," unpublished doctoral dissertation, Northern Illinois University, 1972.

RAHE, HARVES, *Index to Research in Business and Office Education,* Gregg and Community College Division, McGraw-Hill Book Company, New York, 1974.

RISTAU, ROBERT ARTHUR, "The Development of a Business Education Model for Methods and Procedures in a Planning, Programming, and Budgeting System," unpublished doctoral dissertation, University of Wisconsin, 1970.

RYANS, DAVID G., *Characteristics of Teachers,* American Council on Education, Washington, 1960.

SCHULTHEIS, ROBERT A., "Research Priorities for Business Education," *Delta Pi Epsilon Journal,* February, 1971, p. 1.

SHELL, WALTER L., "Memo to Graduate Students: Why You Should Write a Thesis," *Balance Sheet,* November, 1969.

STINNETT, T. M., AND ALBERT J. HUGGETT, *Professional Problems of Teachers,* The Macmillan Company, New York, 1963.

TATE, DONALD J., "The Many Voices of Business Education," *Business Education Forum,* November, 1969, p. 2.

WEAVER, DAVID H., "An Experimental Study of the Relative Impact of Controllable Factors of Difficulty in Typewriting Practice Materials," unpublished doctoral dissertation, Syracuse University, 1966.

WEST, LEONARD J., *Research on Teaching Business and Commercial Subjects,* City University of New York, Division of Teacher Education, New York, 1972.

WOELLNER, ELIZABETH, AND M. AURILLA WOOD, *Requirements for Certification—Teachers, Counselors, Librarians, Administrators,* University of Chicago Press, Chicago, Illinois, (issued annually).

WOOLSCHLAGER, RUTH B., "The State of the Profession," *Delta Pi Epsilon Journal,* May, 1971, p. 15.

PART

2

**The
Teaching-Learning
System**

## PERFORMANCE GOALS

**1. Describe** the rationale for competency-based education and the inputs necessary to establish a competency-based program.

**a. Define** the following terms in your own words, according to the meanings presented in this chapter.

1. competency
2. task
3. subcompetency
4. feasibility study

**2. Describe** how the teaching-learning system presented in this chapter facilitates the implementation of a competency-based program.

**a. Define** the following terms in your own words, according to the meanings presented in this chapter.

1. teaching-learning system
2. learning
3. teaching
4. feedback

**3.** Given five cognitive and affective tasks, correctly **convert** each task to a competency and **identify** each as to the dominant domain and level, justifying your decision in one sentence.

**a. Convert** a task to a competency.

**b. Identify** the dominant domain of a competency.

**c. Identify** a competency in the cognitive domain as to level—*knowledge, comprehension, application, analysis/synthesis,* or *evaluation.*

**d. Identify** a competency in the affective domain as either *low-level responding* (receiving, responding, or valuing) or *high-level responding* (organizing or internalizing).

**4.** Given six tasks, **identify** the skills involved in each as motor skills and/or cognitive skills, justifying your decision in one sentence.

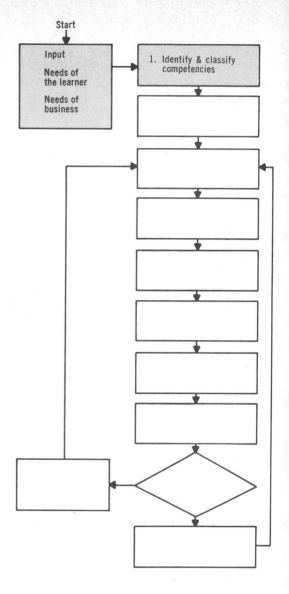

# CHAPTER 3

# Identifying and Classifying Competencies

The competency-based education movement is an important trend in business education, indeed all education, today. The basic component of competency-based education is the *competency*. A competency is a *task* (specific activity performed by a worker or consumer) that is performed to a certain standard. Competency-based education is not a competitive educational concept. Rather it encourages each student to develop to his or her own full capacity. In other words *competency-based education* is the term used to describe education that prepares the worker or consumer to perform essential tasks at stated standards.

An example of a task is playing the guitar. Playing well enough to perform as one of three guitarists in a rock group is one competency. Playing well enough to be a folk guitar soloist is another competency. Playing well enough to be a member of a 30-piece orchestra is a third competency. While the task of playing the guitar is basically the same for each of these three competencies, close examination reveals that each competency may attach more or less importance to specific skills.

The rock guitarist who plays with two other guitarists has to play by ear. He or she must also be able to play one basic part well (melody, for example) and, at the same time, harmonize with the other two guitarists. The folk guitar soloist also has to play by ear, but may have to play a combination of melody, rhythm, and background chords. In addition, it is important for the soloist to be able to perform without the aid and moral support of other performers. The orchestra guitarist does not have to worry about playing alone. However, he or she must be able to read music and follow the leader's directions.

One competency is not necessarily better than another. The task of guitar playing remains recognizably the same in all of these competencies; yet each individual competency places heavier emphasis on some skills and techniques than others. One competency may even require a skill or technique not needed in other similar competencies. A folk guitar soloist may be required to sing; an orchestra guitarist may not.

In order for a student to achieve any given competency successfully, it may be necessary for the student to first achieve the subcompetencies that make up that competency. *Subcompetencies* are the many things a person must be able to do in order to perform a task up to the standard of a specific competency.

For instance, "File cards" is an office task. The standard is "250 cards, alphabetically, in an hour." The competency is "File 250 cards alphabetically in an hour." To achieve this competency, the worker must possess such subcompetencies as: (1) index and code cards correctly; (2) sort cards into alphabetic order; and (3) store cards correctly.

The learner may already possess all three of these subcompetencies and be able to achieve the competency immediately. If, however, any of the subcompetencies has not been attained, it should be mastered before the learner attempts to file 250 cards.

Figure 3.1 shows how a competency results from combining a task with a standard of performance. The figure also shows the relationship between a competency and a subcompetency.

How will the teacher's use of subcompetencies help the student achieve? Together the teacher and student can analyze a competency, asking, "What must the student be able to do to attain this competency?" Each student works toward attaining only those subcompetencies needed. At the same time, if the student attempts to perform a competency and is unable to complete it successfully, close analysis will reveal the specific subcompetencies that remain to be mastered.

Today, many state departments of education and many teacher education departments in colleges are recommending the development of competency-based educational curricula. However, before a competency-based education program can be established, much research within each subject is needed in order to identify tasks. Some formal research has been done in the business occupations area, but more work is needed in this area as well as in the basic business and consumer fields. In order to implement a competency-based education program, the business teacher should make use of a teaching-learning system.

A *teaching-learning system* circumscribes the progression from the identification of a competency to the learner's acquisition of that competency. "Teaching-learning system" is comprised of three familiar words—"teaching," "learning" and "system." *Learning* is changing behavior. When a student who enters a computer programming class not knowing how to write a program finally prepares a program from which the computer produces specified data, the student has learned. *Teaching* facilitates the changing of behavior. A *system* is a group of independent components which form a unified whole to serve a particular function. A *teaching-learning*

Figure 3.1

*system's* function is to enable a student to learn; its components include identifying competencies to be learned, constructing student goals, identifying subcompetencies the student needs, checking the student's present levels of performance, employing learning principles, selecting teaching-learning strategies, and evaluating student achievement and the effectiveness of the system. The competency-based system developed here is founded upon the needs of the learner and of business—both inputs of the system. The teacher must utilize data from these inputs.

### Needs of the Learner (Input A)

A student's basic needs determine his or her reactions in class. Only after identifying these individual needs can the teacher really understand student behaviors. Then the teacher can take steps to mold a course around the requirements of the particular students who are enrolled, not just around the needs of the "average" class.

Some learners are highly motivated; others are indifferent or even, in some cases, belligerent. As Schultheis noted, "The business teacher of today is faced with a greater proportion of students variously described as slow learners, disadvantaged youth, or students with learning disabilities which interfere with their achievement in business courses." (Schultheis (1), p. 6) Unless the teacher gains insight into the background of each learner, the learning system will not be effective for all learners. Teachers may find themselves assigned to classes in which large numbers of students cannot comprehend what they read. The students' achievement records indicate that they have failure patterns. Their attitudes toward school range from negative to apathetic. What is the teacher to do? The teacher can initiate small, informal group discussions in which students reveal their aspirations, their special interests, and their general levels of enthusiasm. Some teachers solicit information about the life goals of their students and the reasons students are taking a particular course. The most effective method of getting to know an individual student is through direct teacher-student interaction, frequently difficult to implement in the traditional classroom situation.

The teacher must find opportunities to learn as much as possible about the individual student. The teacher must also determine whether each student possesses the basic competencies necessary for reaching an objective. If the learner is not able to read and comprehend the material, a reading assignment is an ineffective learning experience for that student. The teacher must substitute other types of activities from which the student is more likely to benefit.

Ideally, the teacher should be able to locate school remedial learning programs to which a student can be referred. While this suggestion seems idealistic because many remedial reading programs are overcrowded, the classroom teacher should still consult with the specialists if only to bring a student with deficiencies to their attention. Once a teacher has identified a student needing help, the teacher ought to arrange a conference with a guidance counselor. Very often, concerted efforts of multiple teachers and other professionals can be coordinated by guidance counselors.

The beginning teacher must make every effort to identify each learner's problems early in the school year if the teacher is to direct the student toward goals *which are attainable.* Because the teacher's role is to facilitate learning, the teacher cannot dismiss a student who reveals learning problems with "Karen's whole record shows she cannot learn." The teacher must determine, if possible, why the present pattern exists and structure a plan to enable that student to begin achieving, even though slowly.

A student's needs are influenced by many factors. Important among these are: socio-economic status, value system, previous academic accomplishments, special aptitudes and interests, and communication skills.

## Socio-Economic Status

Knowledge about the socio-economic status of each student should help the teacher to avoid treating all students alike. A student from a low-income family who has been urged to quit school and earn money and a student from a family of professionals who has been encouraged to become a doctor or a lawyer are likely to react differently to a learning exercise. Students are unique; they should be treated as individuals.

The teacher should consider questions such as: (1) What type of family background does the student come from? Is he or she likely to have parental support (financial and/or moral) for education? (2) What type of neighborhood or community does the student come from? Is the student likely to have either a positive or negative attitude toward school or the subject area because of this background? (3) Are the student's family members employed? Can the student learn from their employment? (4) Is the student non- or minimally English-speaking?

## Value System

A teacher who understands a student's self-image, feelings about the course, and future expectations can better identify elements of the course work that are relevant to that particular student. The teacher can then help the student to realize that the subject is an essential stepping-stone in the achievement of the student's own goals.

The teacher should ask: (1) What is the student's self-image and what factors in the student's background contribute to that self-image? (2) What are the student's aspirations? Is he or she career-oriented? Is the student's immediate goal preparing for an entry-level job? for college? (3) Did the student elect to take this course or has the student been pressured into it by parents, guidance counselors, or others?

## Previous Academic Accomplishments

Knowledge of previous academic accomplishments is useful in helping students overcome learning difficulties and in selecting competencies that are realistic in terms of the learner's abilities. However, the teacher should guard against the temptation to classify each student as good, average, or poor. The teacher who prejudges a student and communicates those preconceived expectations to the student either verbally or by attitude may inadvertently elicit the expected behavior from the student. This type of prejudgment gives the student who has done well in the past an unfair advantage, and the student who has not, a disadvantage.

The teacher should answer the following questions: (1) If the student's record is poor, what are the possible reasons for nonachievement? (2) Is the student a slow learner? If so, how can the teacher structure the present learning situation to enable the student to achieve expected outcomes? (3) Is the student a fast learner who is capable of reaching higher levels of competencies than those mastered by most other students?

## Special Aptitudes and Interests

Knowing a student's particular aptitudes, abilities, and accomplishments will enhance the teacher's perception of the student as a discrete personality. The teacher will be able to help the student apply course learning to areas of special interest. In addition students may become more involved in subject matter once they perceive it as relevant to their other interests.

The teacher might ask: (1) Does the student have artistic, musical, dramatic, or athletic aptitudes? (2) Has the student achieved recognition from peers because of a special aptitude?

## Communication Skills

"Approximately eleven hours of a person's waking time are spent in some form of communication," according to Andrews. "On the average 9 percent is spent in writing; 16 percent in reading; 30 percent in speaking; and 45 percent in listening." (Andrews, p. 2)

Obviously, all students should develop all four skills, but for the business student communication skills become doubly important. Writing and reading are emphasized in most business programs, but results are often disappointing. Since more time is spent in either speaking or listening than in reading and writing together, it is evident that these two skills are of major importance in a competency-based business education program. The learner must acquire skill in speaking in order to achieve the good interpersonal relations needed in transmitting information and in discussing problems with peers, supervisors, and other business contacts both on the telephone and face to face.

Consider for a moment the often neglected skill of listening. Andrews further states that "Tests of listening comprehension have shown that without training, employees listen at only 25 percent efficiency." (Andrews, p. 2) Nichols and Stevens maintain that

The school program, with its many opportunities for youngsters to speak and make formal reports, has provided much practice in speaking . . . On the other hand, it has usually been assumed that children know how to hear everything that is said to them. . . . In other words, we are "educationally deprived" as far as listening is concerned . . . for the improvement of communication in our school curriculums has been seriously out of balance. The eye has occupied the favored position, with the visual skills of reading and writing getting the chief attention. Meanwhile the aural skills of speaking and listening have been kept in the background. (Nichols, p. 7)

The teacher should consider: (1) Does the student have a sight problem? Does the student have a reading problem that impedes learning? (2) Is the student able to write legibly? Can the student write without errors in English mechanics? Can the student express ideas effectively in writing? (3) Can the student express ideas orally? Is the student comfortable talking with other people? (4) Does the student have a hearing problem? Can the student follow oral directions? Is the student used to listening? Is the student able to develop and state a concept from listening to an oral presentation?

## Needs of Business (Input B)

Because the primary goals of business education are often vocational, the needs of business are vital in planning new educational programs and revising existing programs.

## Employment Trends

Each business teacher must be aware of employment trends for various occupations both nationally and for the specific localities in which graduates may seek employment. One way to gather this information is to consult published labor statistics at the national and regional levels. (Recycle to Chapter 1, p. 9.) This information can be supplemented by interviews with local employers, conversations with former students, and structured questionnaires to be completed by local business people.

Questionnaires are generally short, often only one page, and request information such as the numbers of beginning employees hired as typists, stenographers, clerks, and programmers in a given year. In addition, a request is made for an estimate of the number of beginning workers to be hired for each of those jobs during the following year. After tabulation of this data, the business department may reexamine its programs to determine if they are geared to meet these trends.

## Evolution of New Jobs

Information must be collected on the changing of competencies required of people employed in specific jobs. In many cases, new competencies or subcompetencies are required as a result of technological changes. For instance, the competency of typing a usable letter does not change; but if an office acquires a new typewriter with an automatic erasing mechanism, the typist must master the new subcompetency of operating the erase key.

The availability of automatic typewriting equipment has led to the establishment of word processing centers in many companies. (See Chapter 10 for a more detailed description.) Competencies that were previously performed by secretaries are now divided between corresponding secretaries who spend their time transcribing dictation on this new equipment and administrative secretaries who perform the nontyping duties.

This type of change in competency requirements affects school programs. However, before program changes are made, the school may need to make a feasibility study. A *feasibility study* is an analysis of the need for in-school training in terms of costs, number of jobs, availability of teaching personnel, probable enrollment, and ease of learning competencies on the job. (For specific directions for conducting a feasibility study, see Butler in Selected Readings at the end of the chapter.)

Some schools provide released time for teachers to conduct such studies, particularly when information gathered from other sources indicates the need for major changes in existing school programs.

## Competency Description

Business is the source of information about tasks performed by workers and the range of levels to which they must be developed for various positions in different industries and localities (performance standards). Often this information includes attitudes a person should exhibit to get and hold a specific job. All of this information is used to develop a competency description. A *competency description* is a summary of a specific activity including the expected behavior, activities performed, the order in which these activities are carried out, equipment needed, and the range of performance standards. Since the same competency may be performed in several office jobs—for example, general clerks, typists, stenographers, and office clerks are all required to type—the same competency description can form the basis for the learning activities of many students working toward different occupational goals. That is, there may be a common core of competencies required for several office jobs.

Recently, there has been a major thrust in research to identify tasks performed by business employees. Data from these findings is used to illustrate the learning system. Seven studies, five of them in office education and two in distributive education, provide guidance for the teacher planning and developing a competency-based program. (These studies, by Perkins, Lanham, Huffman and Brady, Erickson, Crawford, Huffman and Gust, and Ertel, are discussed later in this chapter.) Since the studies of office tasks represent those performed in selected offices across the United States and the distribution studies are reflective of different parts of the country, the business teacher may use the findings confident that they are likely to apply in any business community. One note of caution is needed, however, for the constantly accelerating changes in technology may be affecting these tasks. For this reason, any teacher using the data will want to reevaluate it periodically within the local business community. For the teacher with limited time and school funds, reevaluation may have to be conducted informally through work with local advisory committees and personnel representatives, and with school graduates.

If the necessary data is not available from research, the business teacher must develop his or her own competency descriptions as input to the learning system. Teachers confronted with establishing competency descriptions will want to consult Butler and Mager. (See Selected Readings at the end of this chapter.) Once the needs of the learner and the needs of business have been identified, the business teacher is ready to apply these inputs to the learning system.

### Self-Assessment 3-1 (Answers on p. 64)

Answer the self-evaluation questions below. Then, check your responses.

1. A competency-based education program is founded on
   a. the various jobs performed in business.
   b. identification of the occupational clusters.
   c. identification of tasks and standards of performance.
   d. determination of the abilities an experienced worker needs.

2. A competency is
   a. a task developed to a required standard.
   b. a job or occupation.
   c. a task performed by a beginning worker.
   d. one behavior developed to a high level.
3. A task is
   a. the activity in the occupational cluster.
   b. a specific activity performed by a worker or consumer.
   c. one segment of a job.
   d. the result of competency on a job.
4. A subcompetency is
   a. a low-level standard of performance.
   b. something a person must be able to do in order to perform a task up to the level stated in the competency.
   c. a behavior that can never be bypassed.
   d. one input to the learning system.
5. Learning is
   a. a change in the behavior of the student.
   b. the ability to perform a task.
   c. the ability to pass a test.
   d. the ability to perform while being observed.
6. A competency-based teaching-learning system is
   a. the scientific application of principles of learning.
   b. a system which assures the learner of success.
   c. the progression from the identification of a competency to the learner's acquisition of that competency.
   d. the establishment of performance goals for all competencies to be achieved.

## The Teaching-Learning System Model

The system employed in this text is a progressive teaching-learning system. A model of the system is illustrated in Figure 3.2 and explained in this part (Chapters 3 to 8). In Part 3 (Chapters 9 to 18) the teaching-learning system is applied to various subject areas.

The system is comprised of eight steps; work progresses in the direction of the arrows. Thus, when one step is completed, the next step is begun. At step 8 evaluation takes place. The student and teacher assess how successful they and the teaching-learning system have been; revisions of the system are planned. This process is called *feedback*.

If the evaluation indicates that the student has achieved the specific goal and is ready to begin work on another goal, the feedback is positive. The student is ready to return to step 1 and begin work on another competency. On the other hand, if the evaluation reveals that the student has not attained the goal, the feedback is negative. The teacher and student must determine what has gone wrong and make revisions. Evaluation of the system is presented in Chapter 8 with detailed suggestions for procedures to follow when the system proves ineffective for a

Figure 3.2   A teaching-learning system for business education

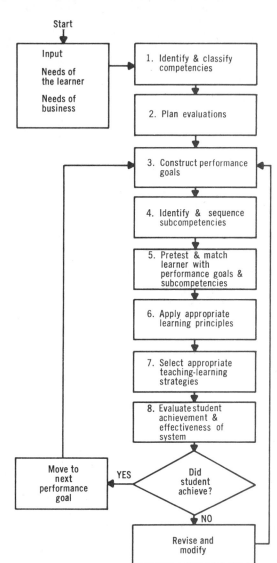

student. The student then returns to the step in the learning system where the learning problem originated and proceeds again through the remaining steps. This process of returning to a previous step in the learning system is known as *recycling*. The term "Recycle" appears throughout the text whenever the material being presented is related to a previous discussion that is essential to understanding. The student who needs to refresh his or her memory on the previous discussion should return to the pages indicated and study them.

## Identifying Competencies

In the first step of the teaching-learning system, the teacher analyzes the subject area, using inputs to isolate and identify competencies to be attained by the students. In many cases, multiple competencies must be combined in order to prepare a student to perform effectively on the job or as a consumer. If these combined competencies can be stated as one overall competency, that competency may be referred to as a *terminal competency*. "Perform as an operator of punched-card equipment from the issuing of instructions to the receiving of correctly prepared output" is a terminal competency. It is a combination of ten competencies, two of which are "Operate the sorter, interpreter, collator, and accounting machine so that output is usable for the next steps in the system and free from errors" and "Screen reports and instructions for obvious errors and refer them to supervisor if they cannot be corrected." Each of the ten competencies has several subcompetencies.

The identification of terminal competencies, competencies, and subcompetencies is somewhat relative. What is considered a competency for one learning situation may be considered only one of many subcompetencies for another more complex learning situation.

Recent research is an invaluable aid in identifying competencies in business and consumer areas. Perkins made the first major effort to study tasks performed in the office. He constructed a list of 599 office tasks, categorized them into thirteen classifications, and sent questionnaires to more than 300 business firms and government agencies to determine the frequency with which each of the tasks was performed. He then ranked the tasks in order of frequency within each of the following categories: (1) typing; (2) operating office machines and equipment; (3) taking dictation and transcribing; (4) mailing; (5) filing; (6) telephoning and communicating; (7) performing clerical operations; (8) securing data; (9) using mathematics; (10) performing financial and recordkeeping operations; (11) performing editorial operations; (12) meeting and working with people; and (13) miscellaneous. While Perkins's study identifies office tasks, it does not include standards of performance. Therefore, the tasks cannot be considered competencies.

Perkins's study influenced other research attempts to identify specific office tasks. The major study in the office education field, *A New Office and Business Education Learning System (NOBELS)*, involves a series of research projects designed to identify tasks upon which to build a competency-based education program. Before *NOBELS*, attention had not been directed toward descriptions of specific steps in performing office tasks.

The key to developing competencies lies in the choice of the verb used to describe accurately what the worker *does*. The preliminary *NOBELS* study, *Taxonomy of Office Activities,* provided a framework for later research. It identified verbs used to describe the multiple behaviors required in performing office tasks. This study contributed to three related studies

Figure 3.3  Classification of tasks performed
by beginning office workers

| Major category of task | % of 300 jobs for which task was reported |
|---|---|
| 1. Communicating with others (interpersonal relations) | 90 |
| 2. Sorting, filing, and retrieving | 71 |
| 3. Typewriting | 49 |
| 4. Checking, computing, and verifying | 47 |
| 5. Collecting and distributing | 21 |
| 6. Operating business machines | 18 |
| 7. Operating automatic data processing equipment | 14 |
| 8. Taking dictation | 10 |
| 9. Supervising, planning, and training | 3 |
| 10. Analyzing procedures and flow charting | 3 |

Source: Adapted from Erickson, *Basic Components of Office Work—An Analysis of 300 Office Jobs,* p. 22.

by Lanham, Erickson, and Huffman and Gust. Lanham and his colleagues used the identified verbs in analyzing almost five thousand tasks performed by office workers.

Another contributor to *NOBELS* was Erickson who conducted an in-depth analysis of 300 beginning-to-intermediate office jobs. (Erickson, pp. 6–19) He identified almost a thousand office tasks, classified them into ten categories, and then determined the percentage of the 300 jobs in which each category of task is required. (See Figure 3.3.)

These findings provide further insight into office tasks. They emphasize the importance of communications in preparing students for work in the office (Category 1). Also, they emphasize the importance of nonmechanized (Categories 2, 4, and 5), as well as mechanized work activities (Categories 3, 6, and 7). Finally, they reveal that even for jobs at the beginning-to-intermediate levels some supervisory and management competencies are required.

While this study was confined to one urban area, its findings are sufficiently representative to make it a useful guide for the business teacher to identify competencies which students should acquire.

Communication was defined in the study as "Exchanging oral and written information with persons outside the company or with company personnel; interacting and working in harmony with other office workers toward a specific accomplishment of goal." (Erickson, p. 6)

Some specific communication tasks identified by Erickson can be restated as: (1) receive incoming telephone calls; (2) greet visitors to the office; (3) discuss job procedures and problems with other personnel; (4) communicate with others orally and in writing; (5) use the telephone effectively; (6) screen decisions; (7) act with tact, courtesy, and calmness; (8) record messages skillfully; (9) cope with pressures of simultaneous tasks and contacts; (10) cope with verbal abuse; calm difficult persons; (11) exercise judgment and discretion; (12) use message forms; (13) use good diction; (14) explain the same thing in different ways; and (15) explain procedures requiring special or technical skills and knowledges without using specialized or technical language.

A close analysis reveals that some of Erickson's "tasks" are actually competencies because they include standards of performance. Others must be converted to competencies through the application of standards.

Schultheis explains that there is actually no such thing as a single business standard for each competency, but rather a wide range of acceptable standards. This range has five different variables. First, entry-level standards vary from industry to industry for the same job title. Second, entry-level standards vary within the firms of any industry. Standards for entrance into entry-level positions in a large firm may be much higher than standards for entry-level positions in a smaller firm that cannot afford formal recruiting or many fringe benefits. Third, standards also vary within any firm depending upon the needs of a department or supervisor. Absolute accuracy regardless of speed may be required of a stock clerk, while high speed and less accuracy may be the standard for a clerk-typist.

Fourth, standards vary according to the relationship between demand for and supply of workers. When the demand outstrips the supply, personnel directors express requirements in terms of the type of employees they would like to hire, not in terms of actual minimum standards for employment. Fifth, standards vary with geography, because supply and demand vary with geography. The standards in a small town may be lower than those in a nearby metropolitan area or vice versa. Teachers should keep the mobility of graduates in mind when they decide on classroom standards (Schultheis (2), pp. 23–31).

Just as the identification of tasks begins with input from the needs of business, so does the identification of standards. Regardless of whether the identification of tasks comes from research such as the Erickson study or from teacher-made competency descriptions, the teacher should use the range of business standards in the local community, when it is possible to identify them, as a basis for standards of performance.

The actual wording of the standard of performance in the competency may be as simple as "accurately" or "correctly" when there is only one acceptable way to do something. Often, however, there are many ways to do something and the desired behavior must be explicitly described in the standard of performance. It might be appropriate to develop several different competencies with progressively more stringent standards if there seems to be a wide range of acceptable standards in the business world. Competencies with less difficult standards could be used as subcompetencies leading to ones with more difficult standards. (See the discussion of subcompetencies in Chapter 4.)

In Figure 3.4 four of Erickson's tasks are converted to competencies through the addition of standards of performance.

Another phase of *NOBELS* resulted in the Huffman and Gust study

Figure 3.4   Selected tasks converted to competencies

| Task | Standard | Competency |
|------|----------|------------|
| Receive incoming telephone calls. | Efficiently and courteously. | Receive incoming telephone calls efficiently and courteously. |
| Use message forms. | To record all necessary data accurately. | Accurately record messages on message forms. |
| Use good diction. | By pronouncing and enunciating all words correctly. | Use good diction by pronouncing and enunciating all words correctly. |
| Cope with pressures of simultaneous tasks and contacts. | Remaining outwardly calm while efficiently completing tasks and handling contacts. | Cope with pressures of simultaneous tasks and contacts by remaining outwardly calm while efficiently completing tasks and handling contacts. |

which identified tasks essential to second-level office work, jobs that require on-the-job experience and/or specialized training or education beyond that usually given in two-year colleges. Two purposes of this study were (1) to identify emerging trends in office work and (2) to develop plans for preparing present students and in-service workers for the emerging office. This study was based on the changes in offices resulting from technology. Almost seven hundred representatives from organizations such as the Association for Systems Managers, the Administrative Management Society, and the American Records Management Association contributed data.

While the researchers recognize the needs for programs geared toward the preparation of students of average or below-average ability for entry-level office jobs, they emphasize the need for greater concern for preparing above-average students for entry into or for promotion to higher-level jobs.

Thirty-eight essential tasks performed by second-level office workers were identified. Three are reported here, each with the percentage of respondents who regard the task as an emerging office activity:

1. Ability to communicate via data communication devices and to know the limitations and methods of utilization, and to be able to choose from available equipment for particular operations (80 to 90 percent).
2. Ability to input data in on-line, real-time systems to obtain information for report preparation, office work, production, and exception reporting (70 to 80 percent).
3. Ability to ascertain what information should be programmed into an integrated information system (70 to 80 percent).

The first major effort to study tasks in the marketing field was done by Crawford, who identified almost a thousand tasks performed in distributive jobs in advertising, communications, display, human relations, mathematics, merchandising, operations and management, products and/ or services, technology, and selling. Although they are referred to as competencies in the study, in many cases no standard of performance provides clues as to how well an activity should be performed. Here again it is the responsibility of the teacher to convert each task into a competency by identifying the standard of performance required.

Selected communication tasks identified by Crawford are presented in Figure 3.5. While these are reported for department store workers, they are applicable to all employees at all levels. Each task has been analyzed in terms of what the student should be able to do to demonstrate the task. In addition, a standard of performance has been added to each task to convert it into a competency.

In another distributive research study, Ertel identified the tasks performed by retail employees working in department stores, variety stores, and general merchandise stores. The objective of his study was to determine which major types of tasks are actually performed in occupations employing noncollege-bound youth and to identify major categories of knowledge most likely to prepare them for that work.

One common thread runs through all research cited: the dominant need for communication abilities among business workers—for higher- as well as lower-level workers. (See Chapter 11.) More training programs for in-service employees are offered in the communication area, either by employing companies or by educational institutions, than in any other area.

## Figure 3.5 Crawford's tasks converted to competencies

| Communication task[a] | Standard of performance | Competency |
|---|---|---|
| 1. Knowledge of when to keep communications confidential. | Refrain from releasing information evaluated as confidential. | Discriminate between confidential and nonconfidential information and refrain from releasing that evaluated as confidential. |
| 2. Knowledge of how to address other people in a businesslike manner whether they be customers, fellow employees, supervisors, or management. | Correct forms of address for customers, coworkers, supervisors, and management. | Use correct forms of address for customers, coworkers, supervisors, and managers. |
| 3. Understanding that valuable information can be gained by reading manufacturers' hangtags, labels, and directions. | Use correct information from manufacturers' labels and directions. | Use correct information from manufacturers' hangtags, labels, and directions in discussions with customers and coworkers. |
| 4. Skill in interpreting store policies to customers. | Correctly and in understandable language. | Interpret store policies to customers correctly and in understandable language. |

[a]Communication tasks taken from Crawford, *A Competency Pattern Approach to Curriculum Construction in Distributive Teacher Education.*

### Self-Assessment 3-2 (Answers on p. 64)

Add a standard of performance to each of the following tasks to form a competency.

1. Operate transcription equipment.
2. File business papers.
3. Keep log of work to be done and work completed.
4. Act courteously with fellow employees.
5. Cope with work pressures.

## Classifying Competencies

Once competencies have been stated, the teacher must classify the types of learning involved. This step is necessary because competencies in different categories are developed in different ways. Learning may be classified into the following categories (or *domains*): cognitive, affective, and psychomotor.

## Domains

*Cognitive* behaviors involve the recall of specific information, the application of information, and the processes of analysis and decision making. *Affective* behaviors, frequently hidden from observation, are values which a learner places upon what is being learned, including attitudes toward learning. *Psychomotor* behaviors are those requiring muscular (or motor) movements. Often all three types of behavior must be combined to produce a competency such as that of a proficient typist who prepares a usable manuscript from rough draft.

First, the typist must be able to read rough draft symbols for meaning, set up a manuscript page, proofread and make corrections—all cognitive behaviors. Second, the typist must make correct muscular movements in striking keys and reaching for the shift keys and space bars—psychomotor behaviors. Third, the typist's affective behaviors are revealed by the pride taken in producing a corrected, usable manuscript.

Any cognitive or psychomotor behavior is accompanied by affective behavior. Affective behaviors are usually the direct result of cognitive or psychomotor behaviors acquired by the learner during a successful or an unsuccessful learning experience. A student who succeeds in a learning activity is frequently motivated to try harder and learn more. The opposite may also be true; a student who is unsuccessful in a given subject may acquire a distaste for it.

Because of their importance, teachers should give top priority to the development of desirable affective behaviors, particularly when students have been previously conditioned by negative learning experiences.

A *skill* is a habit or fixed way of making many complex responses (usually at the subconscious level) to a variety of stimuli. A skill may be either cognitive or psychomotor. The typist skilled in the production of a finished manuscript from the rough draft has formed multiple habits. Striking keys and using parts of the typewriter without conscious thought is psychomotor behavior or motor skill. Reading rough draft copy;

deciding when to delete, when to capitalize, when and how to punctuate; and proofreading are cognitive skills. A *motor (psychomotor) skill* is the habit of making complex motor responses without giving conscious thought to the movements involved. A *cognitive skill* is the habit of making complex mental responses without conscious thought. The student who punctuates correctly without thinking about rules of punctuation is performing a cognitive skill; responses are made without conscious thought. Habits such as reading a shorthand transcript for meaning, using English grammar correctly in preparing a shorthand transcript, punctuating, spelling, and solving problem situations in reading shorthand notes are also cognitive skills.

Any competency includes behaviors in one, two, or all three domains. For example, the accounting competency "Operate the ten-key adding machine for simple additions with work correct" involves: manipulating the machine (psychomotor), using the machine to get the desired data (cognitive), and revealing by behavior that the worker is agreeable to performance (affective). The accounting competency "Record data from business forms in correct journals with correct data" involves: writing legibly in journal form (psychomotor), deciding the relationship of transaction to accounting equation (cognitive), and showing appreciation of neatness and correctness by performance (affective). The consumer competency "Make an accurate shopping list for purchases before going to the store" involves: writing down the list (psychomotor), deciding what purchases are to be made (cognitive), and appreciating the necessity for making a list before going to the store (affective).

Even though all domains are involved in most competencies, one domain is always the most important. This domain is referred to as the *dominant domain*. For instance, typewriting involves the psychomotor domain, but when a typist produces office work, the dominant domain is cognitive. The typist thinks about content and makes decisions about placement and English mechanics, performing the psychomotor skill automatically.

Two teachers might perceive the dominant domain for a competency differently. In typewriting, one teacher might argue that the psychomotor domain is dominant because of the manipulation of the machine. In this situation students would probably be expected to attain high copying speed. Another teacher might believe that the dominant domain is cognitive and require many applications of typewriting to the preparation of business papers. In each case the teacher makes a judgment about dominant domain in order to determine the kinds of behaviors the student must develop to perform the stated competency.

Figure 3.6 analyzes five competencies according to dominant and secondary domain. Two key points are illustrated by the figure: (1) the affective domain is involved in every competency and (2) at least two domains are involved in each competency, one of which is judged to be more important or dominant. When the competency is dominantly affective, as in the competency "Tolerate routine work without displaying frustrations," some cognitive or psychomotor behaviors must be involved since the student is doing something that could lead to frustration.

Generally speaking, no competency expected at the end of a program in business education is dominantly psychomotor. Motor skill is only a means of performing the much more complicated process of creating a usable product.

## Levels Within Domains

Competencies may be further classified into various levels within the domains. The teacher should plan for each student to attain competencies at the highest possible level.

It is not always necessary for people to recall basic facts; these can be found in library sources. Emphasis today is on preparing students for unpredictable situations in which they must assess situations, forecast probable outcomes, and make judgments.

COGNITIVE DOMAIN. Figure 3.7 illustrates Bloom's taxonomy (classification system) of cognitive behaviors and a statement of the behavior to be exhibited by a student at each level. (For other classification systems within this domain, see Gagne and Tuckman in Selected Readings at the end of the chapter.)

An example from accounting illustrates the various levels of the cognitive domain. The student learns the terms "assets," "liabilities," and "equity" (*knowledge*). The student classifies accounts into these categories (*comprehension*). Eventually the student applies these learnings by constructing a balance sheet and recording changes in the accounting equation (*application*). Later the student compares items on statements from two different periods *(analysis/synthesis)* and ultimately makes decisions about business operations based on this data (*evaluation*). Analysis/synthesis and evaluation are the highest levels of cognitive learning.

## Figure 3.6 Analysis of competencies by dominant and secondary domains

| Competency | Dominant domain | Secondary domains |
|---|---|---|
| 1. Tolerate routine work without displaying frustrations. | Affective | Cognitive: Individual must know what steps are involved in performing work. Psychomotor: Motor skill may also be involved. |
| 2. Mentally add, subtract, multiply, and divide simple numbers accurately. | Cognitive | Affective: Individual values mental addition, and so on. |
| 3. Follow oral instructions accurately. | Cognitive: Individual must listen and comprehend instructions. | Affective: Individual appreciates need for careful listening. |
| 4. Regularly differentiate between logical and illogical answers. | Cognitive: Thinking is involved. | Affective: Individual appreciates need to differentiate between logical and illogical; also displays positive attitude toward checking and correcting work. |
| 5. Read and interpret word problems accurately. | Cognitive | Affective: Individual appreciates need for careful reading. |

Figure 3.7   Levels of cognitive domain
analyzed for observable behaviors

| Level of cognitive domain[a] | Observable behavior |
|---|---|
| HIGH  Evaluation | Judges which data or actions are appropriate for a given situation. |
| Analysis/Synthesis | Gathers facts from multiple sources and determines possible courses of action. |
| Application | Uses previously learned facts in a new situation. |
| Comprehension | Reveals understanding of material by explaining it in own words. |
| LOW  Knowledge | Recalls facts and terms and discriminates among items. |

[a] Taken from Bloom, et al, *Taxonomy of Educational Objectives: The Classification of Educational Goals, Handbook I: Cognitive Domain*, pp. 62-187.

The following guidelines may assist the teacher in classifying cognitive competencies according to level. *Evaluation* requires a decision or judgment. *Analysis/synthesis* implies carefully considering and weighing all facts in terms of a situation. *Application* involves using the previous learnings in new situations. *Comprehension* involves demonstrating understanding of material without necessarily relating the material to other data. *Knowledge* requires recalling facts, terms, and principles in the form in which they were learned.

In the accounting example, every student should reach the application level. Some students will reach the analysis/synthesis level, and others, the evaluation level.

In any subject, some students will not be capable of reaching the analysis/synthesis or evaluation levels in the cognitive domain. For example, all students might be required to operate the spirit duplicator (application); however, only a few students will achieve the decision-making level of selecting the most efficient means of duplicating programs for a school event in terms of the constraints of time and cost (evaluation).

The only purpose for acquiring and comprehending facts is the application of facts to other learning; thus, practically all cognitive learning must be developed to at least the application level.

This principle applies to cognitive skills as well as other cognitive learning. Because a cognitive skill is the habit of making complex mental responses without giving conscious thought to the thinking pattern, these skills always occur at the application level.

Figures 3.8 and 3.9 show sample competencies in general business and business communication that are in the cognitive domain. The figures include the level to which the competencies should be developed and the reason for choosing the level.

AFFECTIVE DOMAIN.   Just as Bloom classified cognitive behaviors into levels, he and other researchers classified affective behaviors. The five levels presented in Figure 3.10 illustrate the observable and nonobservable behaviors of a student in the affective domain. Four of these five levels

## Figure 3.8   Cognitive general business competencies classified by level

|  | Competency | Level of cognitive domain | Reason (Student behavior) |
|---|---|---|---|
| HIGH ↑ | Using given facts, decide on the best course of action, and defend decisions logically. | Evaluation | Makes and defends decision. |
|  | Regularly differentiate between logical and illogical answers. | Analysis/Synthesis | Analyzes answers logically. |
| ↓ LOW | Mentally add, subtract, multiply, and divide simple numbers accurately. | Application | Applies previously learned knowledge. |

involve responding and can be classified as either high-level responding and low-level responding.

The lowest level *(receiving)* involves mere observation of the behavior of others. The student is passive. As the student reaches the next level *(responding)* some reaction is evident to the observer. The student is at the lowest level of responding. As the student responds, he or she is probably analyzing the worth of the activity and formulating an attitude *(valuing)*, although it is impossible for the teacher to recognize that this stage has been reached. From this point, the student enters high-level responding by planning to exhibit the desired behavior *(organizing)* and eventually by consistently exhibiting the behavior *(internalizing)*.

Attitudes are reflected by the way in which people react to others or interact with others. A salesperson frustrated by having shown a customer ten items only to have the customer say "I'm sorry, but none of these is exactly what I want" may reveal a negative attitude by a facial expression or snide remark. The frustration is apparent, for the salesperson has not learned to control visible reactions. Exhibiting hostility in a trying situation is part of the salesperson's behavior pattern. This behavior illustrates that negative as well as positive behavior may be exhibited at the highest level.

Determination of a standard of performance in the initial formation of an affective competency poses special problems for the teacher. The teacher must decide just which observable behavior will reflect the desired affective task and how well that behavior must be performed. Because there is no correct answer for each task and standard of performance, this decision largely depends on the teacher's interpretation of the meaning of the particular affective task. For instance, one affective task that was identified by Crawford is "Awareness that certain thoughtlessly used terms or words can be misinterpreted by the listener."

One teacher may decide that a student has correctly demonstrated performance by refraining from using thoughtless words or terms while being observed interacting with a customer in a role-playing situation.

Another teacher may decide that the student has correctly demonstrated performance when the student has identified thoughtlessly used words or terms that have been misinterpreted by a listener in a case problem situation or during a role-playing situation. Either of these approaches may be correct, depending upon the interpretation of the teacher. It is important, however, that the teacher decide which standard of performance will constitute demonstration of the desired behavior and specify that standard in the competency.

Figure 3.9  Cognitive communication competencies classified by level

| | Competency | Level of cognitive domain | Reason (Student behavior) |
|---|---|---|---|
| | **Reading** | | |
| HIGH ↑ ↓ LOW | Read for instructions to be followed correctly. | Application | Follows instructions. |
| | Read for facts which are relevant to questions posed. | Comprehension | Uses ideas in answering oral or written questions. |
| | **Writing** | | |
| HIGH ↑ | Compose effective correspondence from data supplied by selecting that needed. | Evaluation | Decides which data to use and which to omit. |
| ↓ LOW | Apply rules for English mechanics (spelling, punctuation, grammar, and usage) correctly. | Application | Uses previously learned rules. |
| | **Speaking** | | |
| HIGH ↑ | Make decisions as to content before speaking. | Evaluation | Selects data to use in speech. |
| | Give verbal instructions for job logically so that they are clear to receiver. | Analysis/Synthesis | Organizes steps of instructions before expressing verbally. |
| | Interact with teacher and peers by organizing ideas into logical sequence before speaking. | Analysis/Synthesis | Thinks before speaking so that thoughts expressed are well organized. |
| ↓ LOW | Give verbal responses to specific questions. | Application | Applies previously learned knowledge. |
| | **Listening** | | |
| HIGH ↑ | Accept or reject ideas expressed on basis of effectiveness of presentation. | Evaluation | Decides whether to accept or reject, depending upon persuasion. |
| | Listen to speaker and formulate a concept which can be expressed. | Analysis/Synthesis | Analyzes what is being said in order to determine how it relates to situation. |
| ↓ LOW | Listen to directions so that they may be followed. accurately. | Application | Applies directions in work situation. |

Figure 3.10   Levels of the affective domain analyzed for observable and nonobservable behaviors

| Levels of affective domain[a] | Observable and nonobservable behaviors |
|---|---|
| **HIGH**  **High level of responding** | |
| Internalizing | Observable: Reveals by consistent, automatic responses to situations that affective behavior is a part of general behavior pattern. |
| Organizing | Nonobservable: Recognizes value of behavior and establishes some system of exhibiting desired behavior. |
| **Low level of responding** | |
| Valuing | Nonobservable: Sees the value of this attitude or trait and recognizes how it can be important. |
| Responding | Observable: Reacts by answering questions, participating in discussions, working with others, and following instructions. |
| **LOW**  Receiving | Nonobservable: Begins to think about behavior to be developed. |

[a]Taken from Krathwohl et al., *Taxonomy of Educational Objectives: The Classification of Educational Goals, Handbook II: Affective Domain.* p. 95.

Only by repeated observations of each student can the teacher determine whether a student exhibits a specified behavior consistently. Repeated observations are also necessary to determine learning needs in the affective domain in order to establish goals for individual students. However, most attitudes are the result of years of accumulated experiences; they are not easily changed. A teacher who is able to get a student who enters the class with a negative attitude to respond positively, even at a low level, accomplishes much. However, each student must be aware of the need for perfecting the affective behaviors and responding at high levels, particularly for those affective behaviors valued by business.

A few examples of predominantly affective competencies needed in general business are: consistently work with others without exhibiting jealousy or hostility; tolerate routine work; move from task to task freely without wasting time; and identify errors of others without exhibiting a smug attitude. Examples of predominantly affective communication competencies are: appreciate the importance of communication (reading, writing, speaking, and listening) by making a conscious effort to communicate effectively; willingly extend reading and listening beyond minimum requirements; respect the ideas of others by listening to them and analyzing ideas expressed; willingly share ideas with others; phrase requests and instructions courteously; and use effective techniques in persuading others to react as desired.

These affective competencies should be exhibited in high-level responding. Because an individual may exhibit both positive and negative behaviors at high-level responding, the teacher's role is to structure learning experiences that provide for positive affective behaviors, a difficult task.

Affective behaviors dominate many competencies required of beginning and experienced workers. Unless the teacher consciously plans for the development of desirable affective behaviors, their acquisition is left to chance. The importance of affective behaviors to success in a competency-based program dictates the inclusion of these competencies along with those in the cognitive and psychomotor domains.

PSYCHOMOTOR DOMAIN. Tuckman's classification system is employed in Figure 3.11 to illustrate the various levels of the psychomotor domain. These levels or steps in the acquisition of a motor skill are divided into three major categories: acquisition, application, and communication. All students should ultimately be able to perform at levels within the application or communication category.

Tuckman's classification system is especially useful in helping the teacher pinpoint a student's progress in developing a motor skill. For example, the student learning the keyboard of the typewriter begins at the reacting level of the acquisition category and should move through the other levels of the acquisition category until he or she attains as high a level of the application category as possible. Each level in Figure

Figure 3.11   Levels of the psychomotor domain analyzed for observable typewriting behaviors

| | Levels of psychomotor domain[a] | Observable typewriting behaviors |
| --- | --- | --- |
| | **Communication** | |
| HIGH | Transmitting | Uses typewriter as a tool of communication. |
| | **Application** | |
| | Adapting | Performs automatically while consciousness is involved in solving problems of material arrangement, proofreading, and error correction. |
| | Manipulating | Performs automatically as material is typed on various business forms. |
| | Anticipating | Performs automatically while experimenting in various applications for typewriting—tabulations, letters, manuscripts, and other business forms. |
| | **Acquisition** | |
| | Habituating | Performs correctly without conscious attention and with precision and speed. |
| | Coordinating | Experiments with reaches until a smooth pattern is formed. |
| | Modifying or adjusting | Imitates teacher model in order to modify movements to fit correct pattern. |
| LOW | Reacting | Makes reaches and strikes keys according to instructions given or model provided. |

[a]Taken from Tuckman, "A Four-Domain Taxonomy for Classifying Educational Objectives," pp. 36–38.

3.11 is explained in terms of typewriting, the primary psychomotor activity in business education. However, the operation of various other office machines, such as adding machines, electronic calculators, duplicating machines, and copiers, also involves psychomotor behavior.

Cognitive learning is always involved while the learner is performing at levels within the acquisition category. For example, the learner in typewriting must know the machine parts to be manipulated, the correct keystroke, and the correct hand positions (cognitive learnings at the knowledge and comprehension levels). To these cognitive learnings, the learner adds the physical movements of reaching for and striking the keys (psychomotor behavior in the acquisition category).

This text will be concerned with the broader category designations—acquisition, application, and communication—rather than with the more specific levels within categories. Hereafter, the main categories will be referred to as "levels."

## Self-Assessment 3-3 (Answers on p. 64)

The following competencies should be possessed by entry-level workers. Identify the dominant domain of each competency as cognitive, affective, of psychomotor:

1. Schedule appointments correctly.
2. Consistently take pride in work.
3. Always be willing to help others.
4. Compile data for reports from multiple source documents and prepare accurately.
5. Read and follow instructions.
6. Punctuate all correspondence accurately.
7. Use correct grammar in all verbal communications.

Identify the dominant domain and the level of that domain for each of the following competencies.

8. Routinely check and correct all work before submitting to superior so that work is error free.
9. Define a familiar term so that a co-worker understands it.
10. Punctuate all correspondence according to the rules followed by the company.
11. Accept constructive criticism graciously.
12. Collect evidence needed to answer a question and outline it for employer.
13. Work with superiors, peers, and subordinates without friction.
14. Maintain a neat and orderly work station at all times.
15. Answer the telephone with no sign of irritation in voice.
16. Use adding machine and/or electronic calculator efficiently.
17. Maintain a file which can be used effectively for storing and retrieving materials.
18. Decide on order of instructions to be given, so that directions can be followed efficiently.

Classify each of the following as (a) cognitive skill, (b) motor skill, or (c) neither.

**19.** Read and comprehend business letters and reports, and abstract them for employer.

**20.** Read typed copy for sense before reading for mechanical errors.

**21.** Work with others without creating friction.

**22.** Accurately punctuate all correspondence being typed.

**23.** Manipulate the ten-key electronic calculator without looking at machine.

**24.** Add columns on invoice manually locating errors.

## Summary

An important and fast-growing trend in business education today is the competency-based education movement. A basic component is the competency, which is a task (specific activity done by a worker or consumer) that is performed to a certain standard.

Input in two forms—the needs of the learner and the needs of business—helps the teacher to implement a learning system by which intelligent consumers and employable workers may be developed. The needs of each individual learner are influenced by five factors: socio-economic status, value system, previous academic accomplishments, special aptitudes and interests, and communication skill. The needs of business include employment trends, evolution of new jobs, and competency descriptions.

A number of studies dealing with competencies and tasks have been conducted. *NOBELS (New Office and Business Education Learning System)* studies have contributed a great deal to the field. A study by Huffman and Brady identifying verbs to be used in describing competencies provided the framework for later *NOBELS* studies. These verbs were used by Lanham in interviews in which about five thousand office tasks were identified. Erickson then classified the types of tasks performed by beginning office workers into ten categories. Huffman and Gust in an extension of the *NOBELS* study solicited the opinions of business management about the nature of the emerging office. Independently, Crawford and Ertel similarly identified tasks performed in distributive occupations. All of these studies emphasize the importance of communication skills.

Once identified, competencies must be classified according to dominant domain—cognitive, affective, and psychomotor—as well as to the specific level within each domain. Level of cognitive learning to be achieved depends upon the desired competency. However, most affective behaviors essential for success should be developed to the highest level so that the behavior is a consistent response in the individual's behavior pattern. The levels of the psychomotor domain are actually steps through which a learner moves in acquiring a motor or muscular skill. They are useful for the teacher evaluating a student's development of a motor skill.

The classification of competencies by domain and level enables the teacher to assist the student in planning for learning or behavior changes and in establishing strategies helpful in acquiring the desired behaviors.

## Answers to Self-Assessments

The answers to self-assessments on pages 46, 54, and 62 appear below. If your responses differ from the responses given here, please recycle yourself to the self-assessments and study the preceding material for a second time.

### 3-1 (p. 46)

1. c  2. a  3. b  4. b  5. a  6. c

### 3-2 (p. 54)

1. Standard: to produce usable correspondence; competency: operate transcription equipment to produce usable correspondence.

2. Standard: so that they can be found easily; competency: file business papers so that they can be found easily.

3. Standard: with the log correct and up to date at any given point; competency: keep log of work to be done and completed so that it is always correct and up to date.

4. Standard: at all times; competency: act courteously with fellow employees at all times by treating them with respect.

5. By not showing frustration. Cope with work pressures by not showing frustration.

### 3-3 (p. 62)

1. cognitive  2. affective  3. affective  4. cognitive  5. cognitive  6. cognitive  7. cognitive  8. affective: high-level responding  9. cognitive: application  10. cognitive: application  11. affective: high-level responding  12. cognitive: analysis/synthesis  13. affective: high-level responding  14. affective: high-level responding  15. affective: high-level responding  16. cognitive: application  17. cognitive: application  18. cognitive: evaluation  19. a (Reading is a cognitive skill, but abstracting requires conscious thought.)  20. a  21. c (affective)  22. a (if done without conscious thought)  23. b  24. a (if done without conscious thought)

## SELECTED READINGS

ANDREWS, ANN, "All Within Earshot," *From Nine to Five,* Vol. 2, No. 21.

BLOOM, BENJAMIN, ET AL., *Taxonomy of Educational Objectives: The Classification of Educational Goals, Handbook I: Cognitive Domain,* David McKay Company, Inc., New York, 1956.

BUTLER, F. COIT, *Instructional Systems Development for Vocational and Technical Training,* Educational Technology Publications, Inc., Englewood Cliffs, N.J., 1972.

COOK, J. MARVIN, AND HENRY H. WALBESSER, *Constructing Behavioral Objectives: Book I,* Maryland Book Exchange, College Park, Md., 1972.

CRAWFORD, LUCY G., *A Competency Pattern Approach to Curriculum Construction in Distributive Teacher Education,* Vol. 1–4, USOE Grant No. OEG 6-85-044, Virginia Polytechnic Institute, Blacksburg, Va., December, 1967.

ERICKSON, LAWRENCE W., *Basic Components of Office Work—An Analysis of 300 Office Jobs,* Monograph 123, South-Western Publishing Company, Cincinnati, 1971.

ERTEL, KENNETH A., *Clusters of Tasks Performed by Merchandising Employees in Three Standard Industrial Classifications of Retail Establishments,* Report No. 20, Project No. E.E. 7-0031, University of Idaho, Moscow, Idaho, 1968.

GAGNE, ROBERT M., *The Conditions of Learning,* Holt, Rinehart & Winston, Inc., New York, 1965.

HARROW, ANITA, *A Taxonomy of the Psychomotor Domain,* David McKay Company, Inc., New York, 1972.

HUFFMAN, HARRY, MARY MARGARET BRADY, ET AL., *A Taxonomy of Office Activities for Business and Office Education,* The Center for Research and Leadership Development in Vocational and Technical Education, Ohio State University, Columbus, Ohio, 1968.

_____ AND DALE D. GUST, *Business Education for the Emergent Office,* USOE Grant No. OEG 0-0-080414-3733 (083), Center for Vocational and Technical Education, Ohio State University, Columbus, Ohio, June 1970.

KRATHWOHL, DAVID R., ET AL., *Taxonomy of Educational Objectives: The Classification of Educational Goals, Handbook II: Affective Domain,* David McKay Company, Inc., New York, 1964.

LANHAM, FRANK W., ET AL., *Development of Performance Goals for a New Office and Business Education Learning System (NOBELS),* Final Report, Project No. 8-0414, USOE Grant No. OEG-0-0-080414-3733 (083), Center for Research and Leadership Development in Vocational and Technical Education, Ohio State University, Columbus, Ohio, April 1970.

MAGER, ROBERT F. (1), *Analyzing Performance Problems,* Fearon Publishers, Palo Alto, Calif., 1970.

_____(2), *Developing Attitude Toward Learning,* Fearon Publishers, Palo Alto, Calif., 1968.

_____(3), *Preparing Instructional Objectives,* Fearon Publishers, Belmont, Calif., 1962.

_____AND KENNETH M. BEACH, JR., *Developing Vocational Instruction,* Fearon Publishers, Palo Alto, Calif., 1968.

NICHOLS, RALPH G., AND LEONARD A. STEVENS, *Are You Listening?,* McGraw-Hill Book Company, New York, 1957.

PERKINS, EDWARD A., *Clusters of Tasks Associated with Performance of Major Types of Office Work,* USOE Project No. 7-0031, ED 018-665, Pullman, Wash., 1968.

POPHAM, JAMES W., AND EVA L. BAKER (1), *Establishing Instructional Goals: Systematic Instruction,* Prentice-Hall, Inc., Englewood Cliffs, N.J., 1970.

_____(2), *Planning Instructional Sequence,* Prentice-Hall, Inc., Englewood Cliffs, N.J., 1970.

SCHULTHEIS, ROBERT A. (1), "Research Priorities for Business Education," *The Delta Pi Epsilon Journal,* Vol. 13, February 1971, pp. 1–16.

_____(2), "Standards in Business Education for 'Disadvantaged' Youth," *Business Education Review,* February, 1970, pp. 23–31.

SIMPSON, ELIZABETH J., "The Classification of Educational Objectives, Psychomotor Domain," *Illinois Teacher of Home Economics,* Vol. 10, No. 4, Winter 1966–67, University of Illinois, Urbana, Ill., 1970.

TUCKMAN, BRUCE W., "A Four-Domain Taxonomy for Classifying Educational Tasks and Objectives," *Educational Technology,* No. 12, December 1972, pp. 36–38.

WALBESSER, HENRY H., *Constructing Behavioral Objectives,* The Bureau of Educational Research and Field Services, University of Maryland, College Park, Md., 1970.

*Writing Performance Goals: Strategy and Prototypes,* Center for Vocational and Technical Education, Ohio State University, and Gregg Division, McGraw-Hill Book Company, New York, 1971.

## PERFORMANCE GOAL

Using the five competencies constructed for performance goal 3 of Chapter 3 (page 38), correctly **decide** upon one type of measurement—product or process—and at least three types of evaluations for each competency, according to the information in this chapter.

**a. Decide** whether product or process measurement (or both) is appropriate for a given competency.

**b. Decide** which type of written test (matching, multiple choice, completion, short answer, or essay) or performance test (individual performance, role playing, simulation, on-the-job training, or actual employment) is appropriate for a product evaluation.

**c. Decide** whether essay, individual performance, role playing, simulation, on-the-job training, or actual employment is appropriate for a process evaluation.

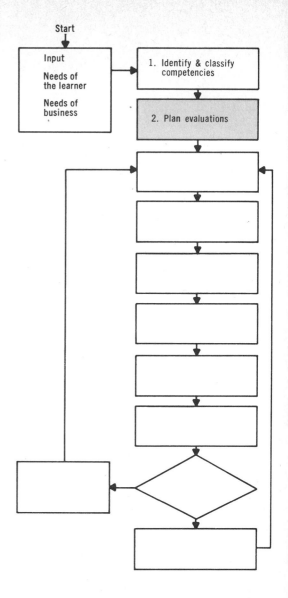

# CHAPTER 4

# Planning Evaluations

After the student and teacher have decided upon the competency a student is to acquire, the teacher constructs a performance goal for the competency. A *performance goal* is a statement of what the student should be able to do at the end of a learning sequence. Performance goals have a twofold purpose: First, they outline the specific activity the student will learn to perform. Second, after the activity has been learned, the performance goal serves as a guide for measuring the student's actual performance. Performance goals not only define the activity to be learned, they also describe how the learned activity will be evaluated. Therefore, before performance goals can be written, the teacher must plan and/or construct specific evaluations for each competency that has been identified. Evaluations are discussed here; performance goals are covered in Chapter 5.

The process of constructing an evaluation to measure a specific competency is referred to as "developing a criterion-referenced measure," because the stated competency provides the criterion against which the teacher measures achievement. A *criterion-referenced measure* is an assessment of a student's performance in terms of a specific standard. Such a measure concerns itself with the results of the instruction and is a quality control not only of the student's learning but of the effectiveness of the instruction.

The other major type of measure, which differs from the criterion-referenced measure, is the norm-referenced measure. A *norm-referenced measure* conveys information about the capability of a student compared with that of other students. It does not convey information about achievement but only about the way in which a student's performance compares to that of the student's peers. Direct comparisons among students are frequently made by teachers who employ norm-referenced measures—"Joe doesn't think as logically as Bill" or "Mary was second from the top in the test, and poor Ben was second from last."

The same types of test questions can be used for both criterion- and norm-referenced measures. The major difference between them lies in emphasis. Criterion-referenced measures are individual-oriented and non-competitive. The student's achievement is not measured against the achievement of others or against some arbitrary norm. A learning goal has been selected for the individual student, and the criterion-referenced measure evaluates whether the learning goal has been achieved. There are no tricky questions; the test item accurately reflects the criterion. The purpose of the criterion-referenced measure is (1) to determine whether a student has achieved a specific performance goal and, if not, (2) to determine what additional subcompetencies are needed. A criterion-referenced measure, moreover, is used to evaluate the teaching-learning system itself and to give the teacher some insight into how the system can best be implemented or revised.

Norm-referenced measures, by contrast, classify, or rank, students according to the degree of achievement. Tests are developed specifically to provide a range of results, so that students can be ranked from highest to lowest. Norm-referenced measures are used in competitive situations: for example, to determine which five out of thirty applicants will be hired as accounting clerks. On the other hand, if the ability to perform a certain task at a specific standard of performance—launch a lifeboat in time to save a drowning person—is an absolute requirement of a situation, criterion-referenced measures are applicable. A person must be able to perform successfully regardless of how poorly any other individual performs.

Only criterion-referenced measures are presented here. Chapter 8 discusses instances in which norm-referenced measures are appropriate in a competency-based program.

### Forms of Evaluation

Teachers often ask, "How may I as a teacher know when a student has achieved a specified competency?" The answer is to prepare tests that evaluate the presence or absence of the competency. *Evaluation* is the process of assessing both student achievement and effectiveness of the teaching-learning system.

Two principles of evaluation guide the teacher who wishes to apply the system—the evaluation is designed to measure a specific competency, and the evaluation is planned and/or constructed before the performance goal is written and before any teaching or learning takes place. The teacher should never be heard saying: "Tonight I must make up a test for tomorrow." The test is planned and often even constructed before the student begins working toward the goal.

Some critics react negatively to this approach, saying that such a process leads to teaching for a test. Actually, if the test measures the goal the student is seeking, it is desirable that the teaching be directed toward the goal and thus toward the test. Since the teacher identifies specific behaviors that a student should be able to perform at the end of a learning process, all instructional efforts are directed toward attaining those behaviors. No mystery should surround the evaluation, for both teacher and student must be aware of what the student is striving to accomplish.

## The Evaluation Continuum

Several kinds of tests can be used to measure competencies in any of the three domains. It is important for criterion-referenced measures to be constructed thoughtfully to reflect precisely what the teacher wishes to evaluate.

In Figure 4.1 the various types of tests are arranged along a continuum from "contrived" to "actual" performance. While all good measures must take place under controlled conditions, some tests are more "actual" in that they approximate a real life situation. The most contrived test is a true-false exam; the most actual test is a real life employment or consumer situation.

In any test situation, the student is asked to do something. What the student does results in the *product*, the end result of the student's actions. The procedure the student uses to achieve the product is the *process*.

In a multiple choice test, the product is the answer to the question, and the process is the thinking required of the student in selecting the answer. For this type of test, only the product may be evaluated. The teacher cannot determine the process the student used.

In a more actual situation, such as a simulation, the product may be a typed letter or the sales check prepared to record a sale of merchandise. The processes for these situations are the typing of the letter and the thinking and writing necessary to prepare the sales check.

On the evaluation continuum (Figure 4.1), written tests (contrived), from matching through essay, are used for product evaluation. Performance tests (actual), from individual performance through actual employment or consumer activity, are used for either product or process evaluation. Essay tests may measure process provided the student defends or substantiates a stated position. In preparing students for on-the-job performance or day-to-day consumer activity, the teacher is first concerned with product evaluation in the form of contrived tests that measure knowledge and comprehension of basic facts. Later, as the student perfects each step in the creation of the product, the teacher becomes more concerned with process evaluation. Finally, when the student is actually employed or performing day-to-day consumer activities, the primary concern is once again product evaluation. If a typist turns out perfectly typed letters within the required time limit, the employer is not really concerned with the typist's methods.

## Written Tests

Traditionally, pen-and-pencil tests have been the predominant measures of all student performance. While they are often used as norm-referenced

Figure 4.1 Continuum reflecting the progression from contrived to actual test situations

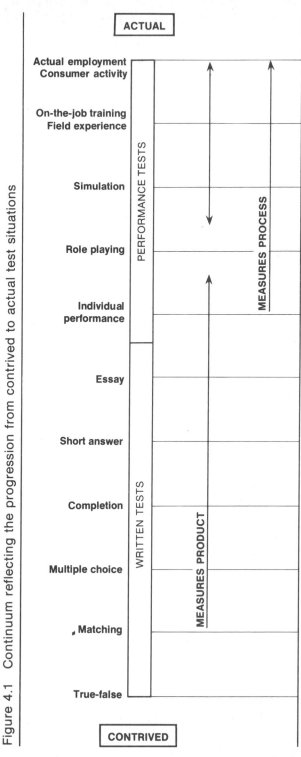

Developed with the aid of Carl J. Olson, Educational Consultant, Educational Foundation, American Society for Plastic and Reconstructive Surgery.

measures, if correctly written, most are also suitable criterion-referenced tests.

TRUE-FALSE. Meaningful true-false items are difficult to write because many statements are neither completely true nor completely false. The teacher often simply copies sentences directly from the textbook to use as test questions. When this is done, the student need only recognize the sentence. Therefore the test measures recognition only, which is the lowest level of cognitive behavior.

---

A contract to perform an illegal act is void.  T_____  F_____

---

Most on-the-job competencies should be performed above the recognition level, making the true-false measure inadequate, unrealistic, and inappropriate for use as a criterion-referenced measure. On the continuum, therefore, the true-false test is not included among recommended evaluations.

MATCHING. Matching tests, which are appropriate criterion-referenced measures, provide several problems or questions and a list of possible answers. The same list of answers is used for all the problems in one matching exercise, and the student is asked to choose from the list the answer that most correctly satisfies each problem.

---

In the space provided in Column 1, write the number of the phrase in Column 2 that best completes each statement.

COLUMN 1

____a. An equal exchange of assets and liabilities

____b. An unequal exchange of assets with no change in liabilities resulting in an increase in total assets

____c. An equal exchange of liabilities with no change in assets

____d. An unequal exchange of assets and liabilities resulting in an increase in total liabilities

____e. An unequal exchange of assets and liabilities resulting in a decrease of total assets

____f. An unequal exchange of assets and liabilities resulting in an increase in total assets

____g. An unequal exchange of assets and liabilities resulting in a decrease in total liabilities

____h. An unequal exchange of assets resulting in a decrease in total assets and with no change in liabilities

COLUMN 2

(1) increases owner's equity
(2) does not affect owner's equity
(3) decreases owner's equity

71

Matching items are best suited to large units of subject matter. It is desirable to find items that are sufficiently homogeneous to require discrimination on the part of the student.

Several suggestions for writing matching items should be kept in mind: (1) Include more answer options than questions, or many fewer options than questions. If there are exactly as many answers as questions, the student will be able to find the answers by process of elimination. Take care, however, not to make the list too long, or the student will spend too much time hunting for correct responses. (2) Write short statements for the response column and arrange them systematically. (3) If only one response is to be used for each question, make sure that no other responses match the question. (4) Use the same grammatical construction for each item because variations in grammar may provide clues. (5) Be sure the entire test item appears on a single page.

MULTIPLE CHOICE. Multiple choice items measure the ability to discriminate between almost correct answers and entirely correct answers. A stem, which may be an incomplete statement or question, is followed by at least three alternatives, one of which completes the statement or answers the question correctly.

---

An unequal exchange of assets and liabilities resulting in an increase in liabilities will

a. decrease assets                    c. increase liabilities
b. increase owner's equity            d. decrease owner's equity

---

In constructing multiple choice questions, several points must be considered: (1) Include in the stem as much of the content of the question as possible. Then the student will have the answer in mind before reading the alternative responses. (2) Eliminate the words "always" and "never"; they may give away the answer. (3) Write alternative responses that are logical choices for the student who has not mastered the material. (4) Make all possible answers approximately the same length. (5) Avoid giving clues to the correct answer through variations in grammatical construction.

COMPLETION. Completion items usually consist of a direct question that can be answered by a single word or brief phrase, or an incomplete sentence that can be completed by a single word or brief phrase.

---

Give the maturity value for each of the following notes:
1. $850 150-day note at 6% _____ .
2. $575 20-day note at 7% _____ .

---

The following suggestions should be kept in mind when constructing completion questions: (1) Word all questions to avoid ambiguity, and construct a scoring key that includes all acceptable answers. (2) Make statements as definite as possible. For example, if the desired answer is a date, indicate that the missing word is a year. (3) Minimize the need for students to answer with a unique word or phrase from the textbook. It is best to require responses that indicate understanding of a concept rather than recall of specific obscure words. (4) Do not give away answers by varying the lengths of answer lines or giving grammatical hints.

SHORT ANSWER. In short answer items, students are required to supply a complete sentence or two in answer to a question. They may be asked to define, list, state, or name something. They may also be asked to manipulate figures or locate answers from multiple business forms. These items are easier to construct than completion items because there is no need to structure sentences that require a single-word answer. Also, although both short answer and completion items require the student to recall factual information, short answer items provide an opportunity for the student to combine related facts rather than just recall isolated facts.

---

List the steps in computing the maturity value of an interest-bearing note and illustrate each step with computations for a $1,000 60-day note at 7½%.

---

The teacher should make sure that these items are worded clearly and carefully so the student knows precisely what to do.

ESSAY. Essay items require the student to organize thoughts and express them in paragraph form. The following suggestions help the teacher in constructing essay items: (1) Be as specific as possible in giving directions so that the student knows the purpose of the essay. (2) Limit the questions so that the student has enough time to answer all of them. (3) Prepare an answer key for each essay.

---

Listen to a taped speech on inflation. Develop any two concepts on the basis of the presentation and present them in writing, defending your decision by referring to points made by the speaker.

---

The greatest problem with the use of essay questions is the difficulty of developing a teacher's key against which to evaluate the essay. For the sample essay item here, prior to giving the test the teacher would listen to the tape several times in order to construct a list of points against which students' papers could be checked. While the essay is more difficult to assess than matching, multiple choice, short answer, or completion items, it is the only written evaluative test that enables the teacher to determine a student's ability to engage in critical thinking.

## Performance Tests

Performance tests appear on the continuum (Figure 4.1) beginning with individual performance and continuing through to actual employment. They can measure either product or process. A *product performance test* demands that the student produce something tangible such as a sales check, a typed report, or a trial balance. A *process performance test* is used to evaluate a series of continuous actions such as correct fingering in touch typewriting or interaction with other people during a discussion.

The only way the teacher may evaluate the process performance is by observation.

Product performance evaluations require the active participation of the student in a structured situation. It is the real life atmosphere in which the student functions that makes performance tests realistic measures of a student's ability to perform. A report of petty cash transactions completed during a week's work in a simulated office provides more accurate proof of the student's ability to handle a petty cash register than do multiple choice questions on steps in handling petty cash.

Process performance evaluations utilize the technique of controlled observation in order that each student evaluated is judged according to the same criteria. In *controlled observation* trained observers (both student and teacher) use criteria sheets to evaluate students' specific behaviors. Process performance tests are especially useful in evaluating student interaction and work habits, and activities such as manipulating a cash register or a photocopy machine.

To formulate an appropriate performance test for any given situation the teacher should ask: (1) What *competency* or *subcompetency* is being evaluated? (2) Which *type of performance* is being evaluated—process or product? What is the expected *result* of the performance? What *specific*

## Figure 4.2 Construction of performance tests

| Question | Situation 1 | Situation 2 |
|---|---|---|
| 1. Competency or subcompetency | Reconcile a bank statement. | Use the cash register correctly while ringing up different items on customer's order. |
| 2. (a) Type of performance; (b) result of performance; (c) test used. | (a) Product performance; (b) individual performance test; (c) reconciled bank statement. | (a) Process performance; (b) individual performance test; (c) criteria sheet completed during control. |
| 3. Teacher preparations | Teacher must prepare (a) checkbook stubs and canceled checks; (b) bank statement; (c) instructions to the student. Also, teacher must do test to make sure it measures performance and is correctly prepared. | Teacher must prepare (a) a cash register; (b) items of merchandise marked with department number and price; (c) tax table; (d) instructions to the student; and (e) checklist (Figure 4.3). |
| 4. Criterion | Correct reconciliation on provided form. | All steps on criteria sheet performed "slow but accurate" or "perfect." |
| 5. Instructions to student | "Enclosed is a bank statement for the ABC Company and the canceled checks for April. Reconcile this bank statement with your checkbook, correcting all errors and following the reconciliation form on the back of the statement." | "You will be observed using the cash register while you ring up a customer's order of 10 items. Use the cash register correctly according to the criteria on the checklist" (Figure 4.3). |
| 6. Checklist | Not needed. | See checklist, Figure 4.3. |

## Figure 4.3 Checklist of criteria for situation 1 in figure 4.2

**Name**_____ **Date**_____

**Observation No.** (circle one)     1   2   3   4   5

**Subcompetency:** Depress the correct keys on the cash register to ring sale of 10 items, some with sales tax.

**Student Process Performance**

| Perfect | Slow but correct | Incorrect | |
|---|---|---|---|
| _____ | _____ | _____ | **a.** Clears cash register. |
| _____ | _____ | _____ | **b.** Totals if not clear. |
| _____ | _____ | _____ | **c.** Examines tape for end. |
| _____ | _____ | _____ | **d.** Gets items ready for ringing. |
| _____ | _____ | _____ | **e.** Enters department number for each item. |
| _____ | _____ | _____ | **f.** Enters amount for each item using tax symbol when needed. |
| _____ | _____ | _____ | **g.** Subtotals taxable items. |
| _____ | _____ | _____ | **h.** Depresses subtotal of tax items. |
| _____ | _____ | _____ | **i.** Computes tax correctly. |
| _____ | _____ | _____ | **j.** Depresses total key. |

**Comments:** _____

_____

_____

**Signature of Evaluator**

*performance test* should be used (individual performance, role playing, simulation, on-the-job training, or field experience)? (3) What *preparations* must be made by the teacher? (4) What criterion will be used in evaluating the student's performance? (5) What *instructions* must the student receive? (6) Is a *criteria sheet* needed? What should it contain?

In Figure 4.2, two testing situations are evaluated in light of these six questions. Figure 4.3 shows the checklist for Figure 4.2, Situation 2. The most important determination to be made for each competency is whether product or process must be evaluated. In addition, the teacher must choose, from among the various kinds of performance tests, the test that is most appropriate for the particular competency and student. These specific tests, which include individual performance, role playing, simulation, on-the-job training, field experience, actual employment, and consumer activity, appear "actual" on the continuum in Figure 4.1.

INDIVIDUAL PERFORMANCE. The most contrived performance test is the individual performance test. It requires the least amount of coordination and staging on the part of the teacher, and the student does not often sustain the performance for more than one class period. Individual performance is used to test one or more students on various specific activities. The activities may be subcompetencies of a larger competency the student is trying to achieve. In Situation 1 of Figure 4.2 the competency "Reconcile a bank statement" is being evaluated by means of an individual performance test.

---

Enclosed is a bank statement for the ABC Company and the canceled checks for April. Reconcile this bank statement with your checkbook, correcting all errors and following the reconciliation form on the back of the statement.

---

ROLE PLAYING. Role playing requires students to put themselves in the position of participants in real life situations. They are asked to act and react spontaneously as they interact with other role-playing participants for a short time, at most a class period.

---

Next week you will role play an interview for a position as a clerk-typist with a personnel director who will visit your class. Prior to this evaluation, work with a classmate to develop a checklist of possible questions and answers and role play sample interviews.

---

While role playing has traditionally been used as a learning activity, it may also be used to evaluate student performance of a particular competency. Because interaction must be observed, role playing is appropriate for process, but not product performance evaluation.

SIMULATION. Simulations place students in real life situations for longer periods of time than do role-playing evaluations. Usually, students will be "employed" in a simulated business, although simulations can be used equally effectively for consumer activities.

---

In a simulated office, act as a cashier for a period of two weeks, handling the exchange of money with other office workers.

---

In a simulation, students contend with realistic work input, working conditions, and quantity and quality standards. Simulations are ideal for evaluating process since the teacher observes the students interacting with each other. In addition, in simulation tests the products that are created by the students can also be evaluated by the teacher, just as they might be evaluated by an employer. Constructive criticism about the process a student is using may ultimately improve the product as well as the process.

ON-THE-JOB TRAINING. A form of evaluation that is very close to the actual end of the continuum is on-the-job training. In most on-the-job training situations, the employer and the teacher work together to evaluate both product and process performance.

For one week, work three hours a day as a typist in a participating office. Arrive promptly; be neat and courteous; efficiently complete all work assigned to you. You will be evaluated by the supervisor and teacher-coordinator according to the enclosed criteria.

On-the-job training is usually used as a learning activity where the student may acquire competencies available only in actual situations. However, on-the-job training can also be a testing situation in which several competencies already acquired can be evaluated most effectively by a teacher-coordinator and cooperating supervisor, both of whom will be trained in controlled observation.

FIELD EXPERIENCE. Field experience is very close to actual experience. It parallels on-the-job training and is especially suitable for evaluation in consumer subjects.

For one week, do all of the food shopping for your family, keeping a record of expenditures. Plan menus; construct a shopping list; choose a place to shop and be able to defend your choice; make use of sales and seasonal buys; analyze information on package labels; and select the sizes, grades and quality of merchandise that promote the most economical use of your money. You will be evaluated by your teacher according to the enclosed criteria.

ACTUAL EMPLOYMENT AND CONSUMER ACTIVITY. Actual employment and consumer activity are included in the evaluation continuum because evaluation is an ongoing process, continuing after the learner has left school. Employers and consumers are usually more concerned with product than process, although both may be evaluated at this level. These evaluations provide feedback for needed improvement and additional learning. Their greatest value, however, lies in their use by the school for modifications and revisions of the teaching-learning system.

## Selecting an Appropriate Evaluation

It is the teacher's responsibility to select an evaluation that is appropriate for each competency. While the ultimate decision is up to the teacher, there are guidelines to help in making this choice. Figure 4.4 shows the range of evaluations that are appropriate for various levels within the three domains.

## Cognitive Domain

Terminal competencies in the cognitive domain generally require performance at the application level or above. Learning at the lower levels— knowledge of basic facts and terms, and comprehension of principles and concepts—is not usually an end product. Rather, learning at these levels must eventually be applied to higher-level learning in order to be productive. Since, once they enter the business world, students will hardly ever be called upon to exercise mastery of low-level learning alone, it

Figure 4.4 Continuum reflecting test situations appropriate for evaluation of performance at various levels of the three domains

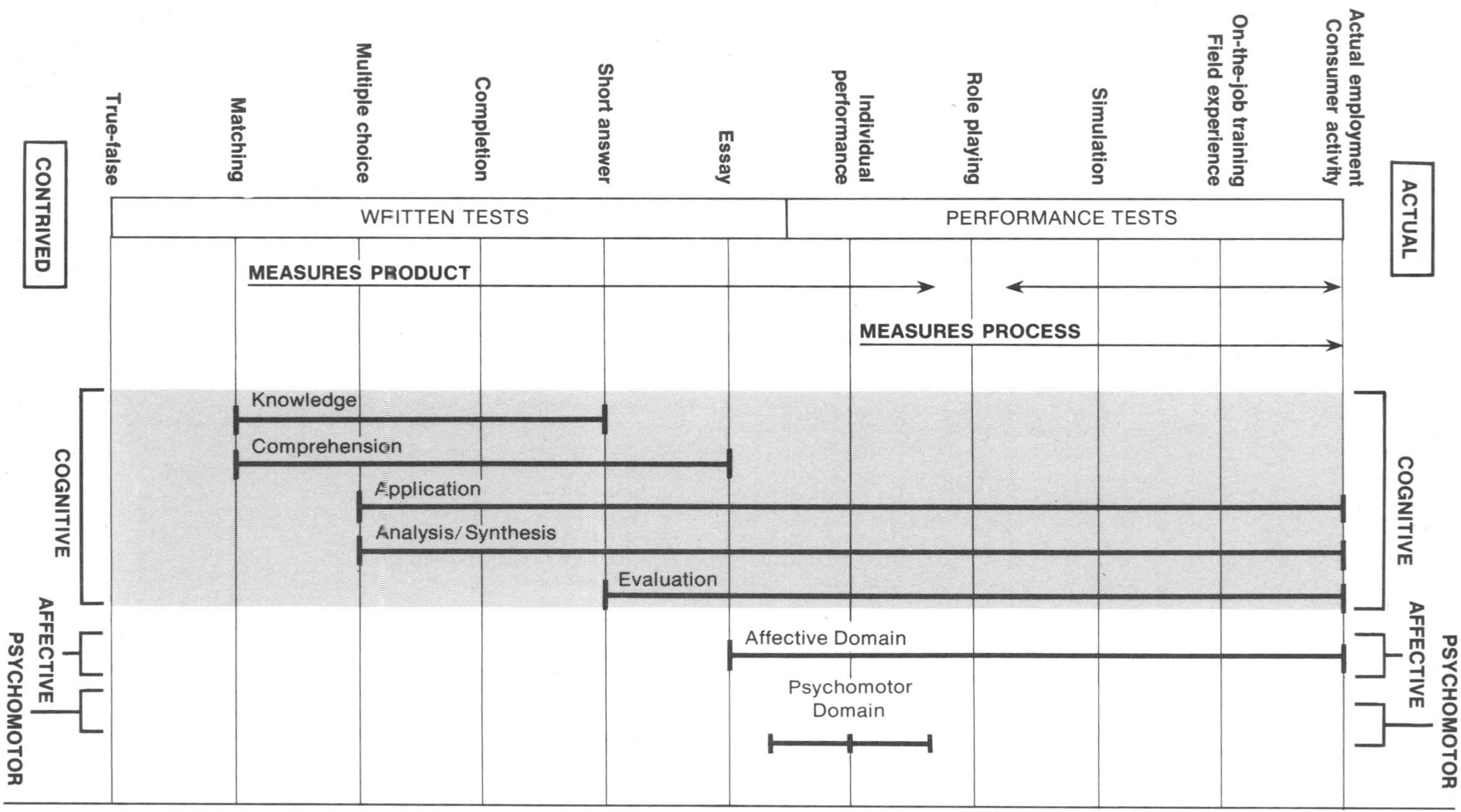

Developed with the aid of Carl J. Olson, Educational Consultant, Educational Foundation, American Society for Plastic and Reconstructive Surgery.

is wise for the teacher to limit testing of these low-level competencies to the initial stages of learning and to encourage the student to acquire cognitive competencies at the higher levels of learning.

Matching, multiple choice, completion, and short answer tests are appropriate for measuring both the knowledge and comprehension levels of the cognitive domain. At the comprehension level, essay items may also be used.

At the application and analysis/synthesis levels of the cognitive domain, matching tests are no longer suitable. Multiple choice, completion, short answer, and essay questions, and product evaluations of individual performance or simulation tests should be used. In addition, process evaluations of role playing, simulation, on-the-job training, field experience, actual employment and consumer activity may be employed. In other words, the only tests on the evaluation continuum that are inappropriate for application and analysis/synthesis are true-false and matching items.

At the highest level of the cognitive domain, evaluation, the only suitable written tests are short answer and essay tests. Also, all of the product and process performance tests shown on the continuum are appropriate for this level.

When process performance tests are used to evaluate cognitive competencies, they often involve observation of an individual's interaction with other people in problem-solving situations. If a teacher provides situations in which a group is able to demonstrate problem-solving competencies at the analysis/synthesis and evaluation levels, these competencies may be measured by an adaptation of Erickson and Kourilsky's instrument. A modification of that instrument is shown in Figure 4.5. Both the decision of the group and the problem-solving process in which the group is engaged are measured.

Items 5, 6, and 7 evaluate the group's solution (product), and Items 1, 2, and 3 evaluate application of problem-solving techniques (process). Before using the instrument, both participants and observers (peers only or peers with a teacher) should train themselves in the instrument's use by self-evaluating taped problem-solving situations. Although the situation is somewhat contrived because the performers are aware of the criteria against which they will be evaluated, repeated application of the instrument in multiple problem-solving situations enables a group to work toward the desired behaviors. Immediately after the discussion, the group should have access to the evaluations made by the observers so that any criteria not met can be identified and plans can be made to meet them in another group discussion.

## Affective Domain

Affective behaviors determine how enthusiastically a student strives to attain a new competency—whether the student tackles it immediately or at all. Affective behaviors are often by-products of cognitive and

Figure 4.5   Evaluation of group's
problem-solving competencies

| Competency or subcompetency | Nature of response | | |
|---|---|---|---|
| | Positive | Neutral | Negative |
| 1. Clear definition of prob-lem. | 1  2  3 | 4 | 5  6  7 |
| 2. Logical and systematic in-vestigation of the prob-lem. | 1  2  3 | 4 | 5  6  7 |
| 3. Objective analysis of problem by presentation of evidence. | 1  2  3 | 4 | 5  6  7 |
| 4. Adequate diagnosis of problem—reasoning. | 1  2  3 | 4 | 5  6  7 |
| 5. Solution—availability of al-ternatives. | 1  2  3 | 4 | 5  6  7 |
| 6. Solution—degree of relat-edness to previous find-ings. | 1  2  3 | 4 | 5  6  7 |
| 7. Solution—reflection of group's potential. | 1  2  3 | 4 | 5  6  7 |

Source: Kourilsky and Erickson, "Interaction Process Analysis Applied to Economics and General Business Courses," p. 29.

psychomotor behaviors rather than the direct outcome of planning for affective behaviors.

Indisputably, the most accurate measure of a student's affective behaviors is multiple controlled observations. How the student acts does not always reveal the feelings behind the act, but people are judged by their actions rather than their good intentions. For this reason, the essay has limited value in measuring affective behaviors. If used *in addition to* controlled observations, it gives the teacher a clue as to why a student evaluates a situation differently than the teacher does. For example, the competency "Value another's opinion by accepting it even when it differs from yours" can be measured by controlled observation. The teacher may *also* be interested in using an essay to determine why the student would accept an opinion which differs from his or her own. The teacher can construct a situation in which a student must decide whether or not to accept an opinion and then must defend the action. The essay has value in this situation as long as the teacher does not simply assume that the student would act under pressure as described in the essay answer.

Before affective competencies can be evaluated, the teacher must structure observation instruments for the behaviors to be observed. For instance, the teacher asks what observable behaviors should be exhibited to reveal that the student "tolerates routine tasks." Possible observable behaviors are working quietly without disturbing others, not complaining, and not exhibiting frustrations when bored with a task. These behaviors are illustrated in a criteria sheet in Figure 4.6. All such criteria sheets should be made available to the learner early in the learning situation so that he or she knows exactly the behavior to be displayed and the basis upon which the evaluation will be made.

Most teachers hold a conference immediately following an observation so that the student is aware of deficiencies and can make conscious efforts to acquire the desired behaviors. By using the same forms for multiple observations, the teacher is able to trace the student's progress over a period of time.

## Figure 4.6  Criteria sheet for controlled observation

**Name of student observed**_____

**Competency:**   Tolerate routine tasks by displaying
the following behaviors.

| | | Behavior | |
|---|---|---|---|
| | Dates observed | Acceptable | Needs attention |
| 1. Works quietly without wasting time visiting with neighbor. | | | |
| 2. Does not exhibit frustrations by making verbal protests or complaints. | | | |
| 3. Remains calm and attentive to work. | | | |
| 4. Consults with others only when necessary to resolve a problem. | | | |

Figure 4.7　Evaluation of student's interaction
with one other person

---

**Date**_____

**Name of student observed** _____

**Competency:**　Act courteously in all situations with teacher and other students.

|  | Always | Usually | Seldom |
|---|---|---|---|
| 1. Phrases requests for teacher assistance courteously. | _____ | _____ | _____ |
| 2. When asked by another student, gives instructions courteously. | _____ | _____ | _____ |
| 3. Requests assistance from other individual students courteously. | _____ | _____ | _____ |

---

The checklist and the instruments shown in Figures 4.7, 4.8, 4.9, and 4.10 may be used for controlled observation of individual performance, role playing, simulation, on-the-job training, field experience, actual employment, and consumer activity.

An instrument such as the one shown in Figure 4.7 is appropriate to evaluate interaction with one other person. In Figure 4.7 the competency being evaluated is "Act courteously in all situations with teacher and other students."

Erickson and Kourilsky, and Barnlund and Haiman developed and tested instruments which are especially useful in evaluating group interaction during discussions of various kinds—planning, executing, evaluating, and reporting a committee assignment. These instruments may be used in measuring communication competencies, such as appreciating the importance of communications, reading and listening beyond minimum requirements, respecting the ideas of others, sharing ideas, and using effective techniques of persuasion. All of these competencies may be exhibited during a discussion.

The first concern in measuring affective behaviors during the communication process of a group focuses on the entire group rather than the individual performers within the group. For evaluation of each group, Figure 4.8 is used to cover such points as: Is it a group, or is it an association of individuals? Does each person contribute? Is the group organized so that each person performs a specific task? Does each person contribute to the plan as well as to the execution of the plan?

The instrument is given to the group at the time of its organization so that each member knows what elements are to be evaluated. After discussing the instrument, the group may decide to revise the form, adding or deleting items. At any rate, each person knows that this evaluation focuses the group's process.

Sometimes an individual will want to know his or her own rating as a member of an interacting group. A Barnlund and Haiman instrument is useful for the evaluation of an individual's performance.

Figure 4.8   Evaluation of interpersonal
environment of the group

| Competency or subcompetency | Nature of response | | |
|---|---|---|---|
| | Positive | Neutral | Negative |
| 1. Cooperative as opposed to competitive situation. | 1  2  3 | 4 | 5  6  7 |
| 2. Degree of permissiveness (freedom to speak one's mind) | 1  2  3 | 4 | 5  6  7 |
| 3. Flexibility in adherence to rules and regulations | 1  2  3 | 4 | 5  6  7 |
| 4. Effective leadership (each performs given task) | 1  2  3 | 4 | 5  6  7 |
| 5. Optimum utilization of member resources | 1  2  3 | 4 | 5  6  7 |

Source: Erickson and Kourilsky, "Interaction Process Analysis Applied to Economics and General Business Courses," p. 29.

Though the instrument shown in Figure 4.9 is suggested for use following a panel discussion, it can easily be adapted to any discussion situation involving students. Since evaluations might be influenced by subjective reactions, ratings should be done by more than one student, even as many as five. To protect the identity of the observer, the teacher may collect the evaluations and schedule a feedback session with the individuals who comprised the discussion group.

Figure 4.9   Analyzing an individual's
interaction with the group

| Category of interaction | Participant | | | | |
|---|---|---|---|---|---|
| | Sue | Leroy | Sara | José | Lili |
| 1. Expresses support; releases tension. | | | | | |
| 2. Agrees or accepts conclusion. | | | | | |
| 3. Gives information. | | | | | |
| 4. Gives opinion or idea. | | | | | |
| 5. Gives argument or reason. | | | | | |
| 6. Defines or clarifies remark. | | | | | |
| 7. Offers procedural help. | | | | | |
| 8. Asks for procedural help. | | | | | |
| 9. Asks for clarification. | | | | | |
| 10. Answers argument; refutes; criticizes. | | | | | |
| 11. Asks for opinion. | | | | | |
| 12. Asks for information. | | | | | |
| 13. Disagrees; objects; blocks. | | | | | |
| 14. Expresses antagonism, tension. | | | | | |

Source: Adapted from Barnlund and Haiman, *The Dynamics of Discussion*, p. 400.

Another instrument enables peers to express reactions to a group discussion. The instrument serves two purposes: (1) to enable the observers to evaluate the group according to the criteria and (2) to provide members of the group with evidence about the impression their discussion created. Figure 4.10 illustrates an instrument appropriate for this type of evaluation. The peer observers benefit; they are developing critical thinking abilities by making judgments in terms of the stated criteria.

No teacher would use all of these criteria sheets and evaluation instruments for controlled observations in every situation. Sometimes a group will focus on individual reactions by choosing the instrument in Figure 4.9. At another time, members of the group might decide to concern themselves with group environment (Figure 4.8). Or they might want to have a general reaction to both process and product. Two groups of observers could use the instrument in Figure 4.10—one group evaluating for process, and one group, for product.

In addition to the criteria sheets presented here, the teacher can find numerous rating sheets, questionnaires, and self-inventories in other resource materials. It is important to be alert for developments in this relatively new area, evaluations for the affective domain.

Increasing attention, largely of a nonscientific nature, is being given to the evaluation of affective behaviors, along with the evaluation of cognitive and psychomotor behaviors, by business itself. The teacher can adapt instruments used in actual business situations to measure affective behaviors in role playing, simulations, and on-the-job training. An evaluation of students in a supervised cooperative work experience situation is illustrated in Figure 4.11.

### Figure 4.10 Affective judgments of observers of discussion

**Instructions:** Check the point on each of these scales that represents your honest opinion. (Do not sign your name.)

1. How satisfied are you with the conclusions or decisions reached?
   **very satisfied      moderately satisfied      very unsatisfied**

2. How productive was this discussion in terms of new ideas?
   **very valuable      moderately valuable      waste of time**

3. How orderly and systematic was the group in its overall approach?
   **too regulated      just right      too chaotic**

4. Was the atmosphere of the group conducive to effective communication?
   **too cooperative      just right      too competitive**

5. Was the responsibility for leadership properly distributed?
   **too concentrated      just right      too diffused**

6. How do you feel about the character of our leadership?
   **too autocratic      just right      too laissez-faire**

7. Did the group evidence willingness to extend reading and listening beyond minimum requirements?[a]
   **great effort      moderate effort      no effort**

Source: Kourilsky and Erickson, "Interaction Process Analysis Applied to Economics and General Business Courses," p. 29.
[a] Added for use here.

Figure 4.11  Evaluation of supervised cooperative work experience

**Name of student observed** _____

|  | Evaluation of worker's performance | | | |
|---|---|---|---|---|
| **Quality of work** | Careless; frequently makes mistakes. | Usually does passable work. Sometimes must be told to do a better job. | Usually does usable work. Seldom makes mistakes. | Consistently does good work. Errors rare. |
| **Quantity of work** | Slow; output frequently below requirements. | Turns out only the required amount of work. | Fast; more than is expected. | Exceptionally fast; unusually high output. |
| **Job knowledge** | Limited knowledge of job. Needs to be told repeatedly what to do. | Adequate knowledge of job. Regularly requires supervision and instruction. | Well informed on job and related work. Rarely needs assistance or instruction but asks for it when needed. | An expert at the job. Makes the most of knowledge and experience. |
| **Dependability** | Requires frequent followup, even in routine duties. | Generally carries out instructions but occasionally needs following up. | Carries out instructions and does what is expected. Needs little followup. | Inspires confidence; works efficiently and independently. |
| **Attitude** | Cooperates only when necessary. Unwilling to try out new ideas. Creates poor impression. | Usually cooperates with some reluctance to accept suggestions and try new ideas. | Meets others halfway and goes out of way to cooperate. Usually ready to try new ideas. | Exceptionally good team worker. Goes out of way to cooperate. Always ready to try new ideas. |
| **Initiative** | Does only as much as told; takes no interest in doing more than enough to get by; cannot see what has to be done. | Does only enjoyable jobs, requires constant supervision to keep going. | Able to get started and maintain interest without undue urging. Does other obviously related jobs. | Has ability to get started without pressure. Makes effort to get the most out of activities participated in, high degree of interest in job. |
| **Maturity** | Very immature. Lack of self-confidence and poise. | Seems immature at times and lacks self-confidence. | Mature and shows poise and self-confidence. | Very mature. Very confident and has assured manner. Very polite. |
| **Emotional stability** | Has chip on shoulder and has bad temper. Requires kid-glove handling. | Occasionally flares up and displays unpredictable temper. Unstable. | Calm and collected under most circumstances. Fairly even tempered; looks at both sides of a situation. | Even tempered, level-headed, rarely impulsive. Seems a stable individual. |
| **Judgment & insight** | Frequently acts without obtaining facts. Judgment unsound in many instances. | Occasionally makes questionable decisions usually caused by not obtaining all the facts or being influenced by personal feelings. | Handles problems encountered in a practical down-to-earth manner. Usually uses good judgment. | Judgment seldom questionable. Considers all the facts and reaches sound conclusions. |

**Comments:** _____

**Signature of evaluator:** _____  **Date:** _____

Adapted from evaluation forms developed by the Distributive Education Associations of Wisconsin and Milwaukee.

On the checklist (Figure 4.11) only the first three items involve the evaluation of the quality and quantity of work produced and the worker's ability to apply cognitive learnings in work situations. All other items evaluate affective behaviors and highlight their importance to business and the necessity for their inclusion in the evaluation of school performance.

Because the value system accepted by a consumer is a crucial part of his or her consumer decisions, the teacher will want to search out measures in the affective domain from available consumer materials to use in evaluating controlled field experiences. (See Chapter 16, Consumer Education.)

### Psychomotor Domain

Virtually no evaluation of psychomotor behaviors is made at the end of a program in business education, since at that time motor skills are employed simply as a means to an end. However, at the acquisition level of the psychomotor domain, multiple process performance evaluations must take place. While the teacher is usually the observer of techniques, each student must also assume the role of a self-evaluator.

For example, the typewriting teacher observes techniques such as whether the student looks up when typing and how the student strikes the keys. To evaluate these techniques, the teacher selects specific criteria to use in making controlled observations. Because of individual needs, a teacher may observe one student for some techniques and another student for other techniques. The teacher directs attention to each behavior the student needs to develop and apprises the student of the results of each observation.

When the learner applies basic skills to the production of business or personal papers, he or she has reached the application level of the psychomotor domain. At this level, product evaluation is employed, and the learner is beginning to use typewriting as a means to an end.

### Analyzing Competencies to Select Evaluations

Before deciding upon the appropriate instrument to use, the teacher must analyze the competencies in terms of dominant domain and level, decide whether to use product or process evaluation or both, and consult the continuum in Figure 4.4 to determine the specific evaluation that is appropriate for the situation. Figure 4.12 shows how to make such an analysis for a selected list of competencies.

### Building a Test File

Because evaluation is vital to the teaching-learning system, it is imperative that each teacher build a test file. In it will be specific items for each type of evaluation; complete tests which have been used, evaluated, and

Figure 4.12   Choosing evaluations for various competencies

| Competency | Domain & level | Result of performance | | Evaluation |
|---|---|---|---|---|
| | | Product | Process | |
| Tolerate routine tasks without displaying frustrations. | Affective: high-level responding | | x | Individual performance, simulation, or on-the-job training. |
| Follow oral instructions accurately. | Cognitive: application | x | x | Essay; individual performance, simulation, on-the-job performance, or field experience. |
| Read and interpret word problems accurately. | Cognitive: analysis | x | | All written tests except matching. |
| View facts given to decide the best course of action and defend decision logically. | Cognitive: evaluation | x | x | Essay; role playing, simulation, on-the-job training, or field experience. |
| Use typewriter controls consistently.[a] | Psychomotor: application | | x | Individual performance. |
| Respect the ideas of other discussants. | Affective: high-level responding | | x | Individual performance. |

[a]Considered a subcompetency by most.

modified; and tests collected from teachers' manuals, professional journals, and publishers.

It is a good idea to put each question to be used on a teacher-constructed written test on an index card; after the test has been given, the teacher may evaluate the items to determine which questions were ambiguous and should be reworded or discarded, which were too easy or too difficult, and which did not measure what they purported to measure. It is a simple task to remove items and reword questions. The file of cards is always up to date and can be used as a source in future evaluations.

## Self-Assessment (Answers on p. 88)

Indicate the type of measurement (product or process) and suitable evaluations for each of the ten competencies below.

1.   Work effectively as a member of a team by carrying an equal share of the burden. (Affective: high-level responding)

2.   Proofread and correct all completed work. (Cognitive: analysis)

3.   Use sources effectively in collecting and reporting data. (Cognitive: analysis)

4.   Handle visitors to office effectively by getting name and data, and providing visitor with material to read while waiting. (Affective: high-level responding)

**5.** Accept assistance willingly when a deadline makes it impossible to complete the work assigned. (Affective: high-level responding)

**6.** Handle all incoming telephone calls efficiently by routing them to the person who can give information. (Cognitive: analysis)

**7.** Possess adequate knowledge of own job, sources of data, and channels through which work must be routed and use that knowledge effectively. (Cognitive: application)

**8.** Follow oral instructions accurately. (Cognitive: application)

**9.** Establish work priorities so that the most important work is done first. (Cognitive: evaluation)

**10.** Act courteously with fellow employees. (Affective: high-level responding)

## Summary

Before the teacher constructs a performance goal for each competency, he or she plans the evaluation to be used in measuring whether or not a student has achieved a stated competency.

Evaluations may be either criterion-referenced or norm-referenced. A criterion-referenced test measures whether the learner meets a stated standard. A norm-referenced evaluation measures how one learner achieves in comparison with other students. In a competency-based program only criterion-referenced evaluations are appropriate.

Evaluations may measure either product (what the student produces) or process (the efficiency of the techniques used in creating a product) or both.

Either written or performance tests may be used. Written tests include matching, multiple choice, completion, short answer, or essay items. Performance tests include individual performance, role playing, simulation, on-the-job training, field experience, actual employment, and consumer activity.

Before the teacher can select an appropriate evaluation instrument, he or she must consider the domains into which the required learnings fall (cognitive, affective, or psychomotor) and the levels within these domains into which each competency is to be developed. A continuum showing appropriate tests to measure competencies within the domains is shown in Figure 4.4, which should be consulted before the teacher chooses the evaluation to be used in each case.

## Answers to Self-Assessment

**1.** Process performance: controlled observation of individual performance, simulation, or on-the-job training.

**2.** Product performance: evaluation of product created during individual performance, simulation, or on-the-job training.

**3.** Product performance: written tests using completion, short answer, or essay; evaluation of product produced during individual performance, simulation, or on-the-job training.

**4.** Process performance: controlled observation of role playing, simulation, or on-the-job training.

**5.** Process performance: controlled observation of simulation or on-the-job training.

**6.** Process performance: controlled observation of individual performance, role playing, simulation, or on-the-job training.

**7.** Product performance: any written tests except matching; evaluation of product produced by any performance test.

**8.** Product or process performance: all performance tests, for both evaluation of product and observation of process.

**9.** Product or process performance: essay test; all performance tests, for both evaluation of product and observation of process.

**10.** Process performance: controlled observation of simulation or on-the-job training.

## SELECTED READINGS

BAKER, EVA L., AND W. JAMES POPHAM, *Expanding Dimensions of Instructional Objectives*, Prentice-Hall, Inc., Englewood Cliffs, N.J., 1973.

BARNLUND, DEAN, AND FRANKLYN HAIMAN, *The Dynamics of Discussion*, Houghton Mifflin, Boston, 1960.

BUTLER, F. COIT, *Instructional Systems Development for Vocational and Technical Training*, Educational Technology Publications, Inc., Englewood Cliffs, N.J., 1972.

EBEL, ROBERT L., *Essentials of Educational Measurement*, Prentice-Hall, Inc., Englewood Cliffs, N.J., 1972.

GLASER, R., AND R. C. COX, "Criterion-referenced Testing for Measurement of Educational Outcomes," *Instructional Process and Media Innovation*, Rand-McNally & Company, Chicago, 1968.

GLASER, R., AND D. J. KLAUS, "Proficiency Measurement: Assessing Human Performance," *Psychological Principles in System Development*, Holt, Rinehart & Winston, New York, 1962.

HARDAWAY, MATHILDE, *Testing and Evaluation in Business Education*, South-Western Publishing Company, Cincinnati, 1966.

*Item Writer's Handbook: Techniques for Test Construction*, unpublished internal document prepared for CTB/McGraw-Hill, Del Monte Research Park, Monterey, Calif.

KOURILSKY, MARILYN, *The Use of the Adversary Approach in Teaching Economics*, Monograph 122, South-Western Publishing Company, Cincinnati, 1970.

KOURILSKY, MARILYN, AND LAWRENCE ERICKSON, "Interaction Process Analysis Applied to Economics and General Business Courses," *Business Education Forum*, October, 1969, pp. 28–30.

*Making the Classroom Test: A Guide for Teachers*, Educational Testing Service, Princeton, N.J., 1961.

*Multiple-Choice Questions: A Close Look*, Educational Testing Service, Princeton, N.J., 1963.

POPHAM, W. JAMES (ED.), *Criterion-Referenced Measurement: An Introduction*, Educational Technology Publications, Englewood Cliffs, N.J., 1971.

POPHAM, W. JAMES, *Evaluating Instruction*, Prentice-Hall, Inc., Englewood Cliffs, N.J., 1973.

_____ AND EVA L. BAKER, *Classroom Instructional Tactics*, Prentice-Hall, Inc., Englewood Cliffs, N.J., 1973.

## PERFORMANCE GOALS

**1.** Using any three of the five competencies constructed for performance
goal 3 of Chapter 3 (page 38), including at least one affective and one cognitive, **analyze** to discover the components of a performance goal (see Figure
5.3 on page 95). From the components,
**construct** for each competency a
performance goal which meets all of
the criteria stated in this chapter.

**a. Identify** the dominant domain and
level of each competency.

**b. Decide** on a product and/or process
evaluation and **select** the appropriate
test for each.

**c. Decide** on an appropriate verb
using Figure 5.1 on page 92 as a reference.

**d. Decide** on the conditions under
which performance will take place.

**e. Decide** on the criterion or criteria
by which performance will be judged.

**2. Analyze** the performance goal
constructed for performance goal 1
above for subcompetencies and
**sequence** the subcompetencies logically, using Figure 5.4 on page 98 as a
model.

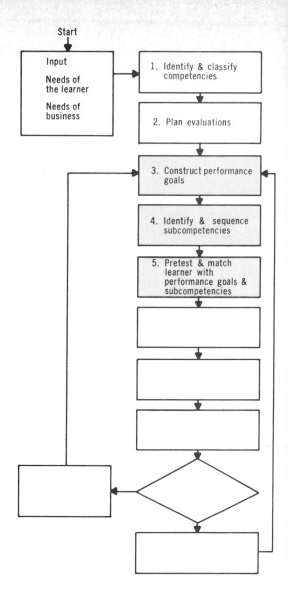

Start

Input

Needs of
the learner

Needs of
business

1. Identify & classify
   competencies

2. Plan evaluations

3. Construct performance
   goals

4. Identify & sequence
   subcompetencies

5. Pretest & match
   learner with
   performance goals &
   subcompetencies

# CHAPTER 5

# Constructing Performance Goals

After the competencies have been identified and analyzed for dominant domain and level and the evaluations planned, the teacher is ready to construct performance goals. A *performance goal* states a measurable behavior, the product to emerge from the performance, the conditions under which performance will be conducted, and the criterion (standard) on which performance will be judged.

Performance goals give the student a concrete idea of what is expected and how the result of the performance will be evaluated. Goals that are vague and incapable of being measured—such as "Develop an appreciation of data processing"—are meaningless to both student and teacher. The student should know precisely what is expected. The same goal given above might read "Determine the greatest effect data processing is likely to have on your life and give reasons for your choice."

## Components of Performance Goals

Constructing a performance goal involves four steps: (1) determining the actual behavior to be performed so that a verb may be selected to convey the action and the level of the dominant domain; (2) determining the result of the performance—a product created or a process to be observed; (3) deciding on the relevant conditions under which performance will take place; and (4) deciding on the criterion against which performance will be evaluated.

## Determining the Behavior and Selecting the Verb

Competencies demand different behaviors; there is a great difference between the actions of a student who is to "read a handwritten rough

Figure 5.1 Verbs used at different levels of the cognitive and affective domains

## Cognitive domain

Simple and low level ⎯⎯⎯⎯⎯⎯⎯⎯⎯⎯⎯⎯⎯⎯⎯⎯⎯⎯⎯⎯⎯⎯⎯➤ Complex and high level

| Knowledge | Comprehension | Application | Analysis/Synthesis | Evaluation |
|---|---|---|---|---|
| define | compute | apply | analyze | assess |
| identify | describe | classify | arrange | conclude |
| list | differentiate | connect | construct | decide |
| name | distinguish | demonstrate | create | defend |
| recognize | match | interpret | design | determine |
| state | order | relate | detect | judge |
| | organize | translate | develop | predict |
| | select | use | estimate | |
| | sequence[a] | | explain | |
| | | | formulate | |
| | | | infer | |
| | | | sequence[a] | |
| | | | weigh | |

## Affective domain

Low-level responding ⎯⎯⎯⎯⎯⎯⎯⎯⎯⎯⎯⎯⎯⎯⎯⎯⎯⎯⎯⎯➤ High-level responding

| | |
|---|---|
| exhibit (specific behavior sought) | consistently exhibit (specific behavior sought) |
| demonstrate (specific behavior sought) | consistently demonstrate (specific behavior sought) |

[a]"Sequence" is appropriate at both the comprehension and analysis levels, depending upon the degree of intellectualzing involved.

draft and prepare a mailable transcript" and the actions of another who is to "treat all customers courteously." The teacher preparing to construct performance goals needs assistance in selecting verbs which convey the behavior to be performed and also denote the level of the dominant domain involved. As stated earlier, virtually no competency associated with job performance is dominantly psychomotor. Motor movements are performed as a means to an end; the worker is actually concentrating on other aspects of the performance. For this reason the teacher constructing performance goals generally works with either the cognitive or affective domain.

## Cognitive Verbs

The verbs in Figure 5.1 are suggested to guide the teacher in selecting appropriate verbs for competencies at the various levels of the cognitive domain and the affective domain.

The teacher using the verbs examines the competency first and classifies it as to domain and level. Figure 5.2 illustrates how the verbs are selected.

Because cognitive competencies performed on the job are at the application level or above, a concerted effort is made throughout this text to use competencies at the application, analysis/synthesis, and evaluation levels. Thus, the teacher is guided in creating realistic goals.

Figure 5.2   Selection of verbs for various competencies

| Competency | Domain & level | Verb |
|---|---|---|
| Consider the alternatives and make a decision which you defend. | Cognitive: evaluation | **Assess, defend, decide** |
| Gather evidence and list the alternatives which are appropriate. | Cognitive: analysis | **Explain, analyze, develop** |
| Use English grammar correctly in presenting a speech. | Cognitive: application | **Apply, demonstrate** |

## Affective Verbs

An affective competency such as "Tolerate routine tasks without portraying frustration" should be developed to high-level responding so that the worker demonstrates this competency consistently. The teacher planning for the performance recognizes that the action must be demonstrated or exhibited and the appropriate verbs are "demonstrate" or "exhibit." (See Figure 5.1.) If the teacher plans to require the student to perform at a high level, the adverb "consistently" precedes the verb. The teacher recognizes that a student who demonstrates the behavior during multiple observations has acquired the behavior as part of the total behavior pattern.

## Psychomotor Verbs

Since performance goal verbs are selected for the dominant domain only, it is not likely that special performance goals for the psychomotor domain will be needed. For example, the competency "Demonstrate the ability to convert rough, handwritten copy, into an acceptable typewritten manuscript with no errors" is primarily a cognitive competency. The typist's attention is focused upon deciphering the copy, interpreting proofreader's symbols, and correcting errors. The actual manipulation of the typewriter, for a person accomplished enough to be typing a rough draft, is simply the application of a motor skill.

For the beginning typewriting student who is concentrating primarily on acquiring a motor skill, the psychomotor domain may be the dominant domain of competencies to be achieved. To construct a performance goal, the teacher must use a verb that specifies the motor activity to be performed by the student (*strike, stroke, type, operate, manipulate*). There is no need to be concerned with the level of the verb. Whenever the psychomotor domain is dominant, the activity being performed by the student is at the lowest level, reacting. Such a goal might read "Given a drill comprised of left- and right-hand home keys, **type** 60 strokes in 1 minute." However, even in the learning of motor skills such as typing and operating various machines, the student moves quickly from strict concentration on the motor skill itself toward the incorporation of that skill in other areas. At this point the student is performing at the application level of the cognitive domain. Competencies and performance goals should reflect this situation.

## Determining the Result of Performance

The result should be identified at the time the evaluation is selected and planned. The teacher who plans a product evaluation knows a product will emerge from the performance. The teacher who plans a process evaluation with a controlled observation is aware that the process, evaluated by using a criteria sheet during controlled observation, will be the result.

## Determining the Relevant Conditions

Considerable teacher decision making is involved at this step. The teacher should ask: (1) What materials will be given to the student before the performance? The performance goal will state, for example, "Given 15 business forms . . ." (2) Will the student be observed? by whom? The performance goal may state "While being observed by three classmates . . ." or "While being observed by the teacher . . ." (3) Must the student perform within a time limitation? Some teachers prefer to establish time limits; others do not. It is a matter of individual philosophy. The performance goal might state "Within 10 minutes. . . ."

## Determining the Criterion

While it is not unusual to see performance goals using a criterion of "85 percent correct," such a standard does not approximate the standard of performance business requires. It is most unusual to find an office in which 85 percent accuracy is acceptable, and no consumer who functions at 85 percent accuracy in transactions can be considered wise. The criterion must *approximate* an acceptable business or consumer standard. The criterion for the performance goal is the standard the student will meet at the end of learning experiences; it should be realistic. (Recycle to Chapter 3, pp. 51–53.)

## Examples of Performance Goals

In Figure 5.3, five competencies are analyzed in terms of the dominant domain and level, result of performance, verb, conditions of performance, and criterion. Competencies selected for illustration are likely to be required of an entry-level worker and a student completing training should be able to perform them.

After the teacher has analyzed a competency for the five components of a performance goal as shown in Figure 5.3, the goal may be constructed.

Figure 5.3 Components of performance goals

| Competency | Dominant domain & level | Result of performance | | Verb | Conditions of performance | Criterion |
|---|---|---|---|---|---|---|
| | | Product | Process | | | |
| 1. Locate and correct errors in all work. | Cognitive: application | 15 error-free forms. | | **Demonstrate** | Given 15 business forms, some of which have errors. | All work error free. |
| 2. Take dictation and transcribe into mailable correspondence. | Cognitive: application | Mailable letters, carbons, and envelopes. | | **Demonstrate** | Given tape with new matter dictation of four 100-word letters at 80 wam. | According to criteria for mailability at a minimum of 10 wam. |
| 3. Determine priorities for all work, doing most important work first. | Cognitive: evaluation | Priority list and completed work. | | **Assess** | Given an in-basket of incoming mail, boss's schedule, mail schedule, and a written description of an office situation; within 60 minutes. | High-priority work completed and a list of other items arranged in descending order of priority according to guidelines in the written instructions. |
| 4. Understand how the job you perform relates to jobs performed in other departments. | Cognitive: analysis | Short answer test. | | **Analyze** | While working in a simulated or real office for no less than two weeks; given 10 questions on how your job relates to jobs in departments from which you receive work and to which you route. | Answered correctly. |
| 5. Tolerate routine work without showing frustration. | Affective: high-level responding | Criteria sheet for controlled observation. | Observation in simulated office or real office. | **Demonstrate** | While being observed by teacher with no forewarning as you perform routine tasks. | Without exclaiming or complaining aloud or attracting attention to yourself. |

## COMPETENCY 1
Locate and correct errors in all work.

### PERFORMANCE GOAL
Given 15 business forms, some of which have errors, **demonstrate** the ability to locate and correct errors by producing 15 error-free forms.

1. *Demonstrate* followed by the specific ability states the action.
2. *15 forms* is the product.
3. *Given 15 business forms, some of which have errors* is the condition.
4. *Error-free* is the criterion.

## COMPETENCY 2
Take dictation and transcribe into mailable correspondence.

### PERFORMANCE GOAL
Given tape with new-matter dictation of four 100-word letters at 80 wam, **demonstrate** the ability to transcribe the dictation by transcribing the letters, each with carbon and envelope, at a minimum of 10 wam with all work mailable.

1. *Demonstrate* followed by the specific ability states the action.
2. *Letters, each with carbon and envelope*, provides the product.
3. *Given tape with new-matter dictation of four 100-word letters at 80 wam* provides the conditions.
4. *All work mailable* and *at a minimum of 10 wam* are the criteria.

## COMPETENCY 3
Determine priorities for all work, doing most important work first.

### PERFORMANCE GOAL
Given an In basket of incoming mail, boss's schedule, mail schedule, a written description of the office situation, and 60 minutes, **assess** the priorities and complete all high-priority work and list all other work in descending order of priority according to guidelines given in written description.

1. *Assess* indicates the action involved.
2. *Completed high-priority work* and *priority list* are the products.
3. *Given an In basket of incoming mail, boss's schedule, mail schedule, a written description of the office situation,* and *60 minutes* are the conditions.
4. *Complete high-priority work* and *list all other work in descending order of priority according to guidelines given in description* are the criteria.

## COMPETENCY 4
Understand how the job you perform relates to jobs performed in other departments from which you receive work and to which you route your completed work.

### PERFORMANCE GOAL
After having worked in a simulated or real office for no less than two weeks' time and given a short answer test comprised of ten questions on how the job you perform relates to jobs performed in other departments from

which you receive work and to which you route completed work, **analyze** each question in terms of your situation by answering each question correctly.

1. *Analyze* provides the action.
2. *Ten answered questions* is the product.
3. *After having worked in a simulated or real office for no less than two weeks' time* reveals the conditions.
4. *Correctly according to how the job you perform relates to jobs in other departments* supplies the criterion.

COMPETENCY 5
Tolerate routine work without showing frustration.

PERFORMANCE GOAL
While being observed by the teacher using a criterion sheet and with no forewarning, **demonstrate** your tolerance for routine work by not exclaiming or complaining aloud or attracting attention to yourself.

1. *Demonstrate* provides the action.
2. *Completed observation* and *completed criterion sheet* provide the results of performance.
3. *While being observed by the teacher using a criterion sheet and with no forewarning* states the conditions.
4. *By not exclaiming or complaining aloud or attracting attention to yourself* is the criterion.

## Identifying and Sequencing Subcompetencies

Almost every performance goal involves the mastery of several subcompetencies. Some subcompetencies may be learned in any order before they are combined in the achievement of a performance goal. (Recycle to Chapter 3, p. 40.) Others must be learned in a specific sequence. If attaining one subcompetency depends on the mastery of another, the subcompetencies must be arranged in proper sequential order and are said to be linear.

Figure 5.4 shows a performance goal for which subcompetencies have been identified and sequenced. It is clear from the figure that not all subcompetencies must feed directly into each other and then directly into the performance goal. Such branching subcompetencies are independent of each other and are still necessary for the achievement of the same performance goal.

Subcompetencies 1, 2, 3, and 4 in Figure 5.4 feed directly into each other, as do subcompetencies 10, 11, and 12. However, subcompetencies 5, 6, 7, 8, and 9 are not dependent on each other. Each of these five subcompetencies is a prerequisite to subcompetency 10, and subcompetency 4 is a prerequisite to each of these five. After a student completes subcompetency 4, he or she may choose to complete 5, 6, 7, 8, and 9 in any order. The student must, however, complete all five of these subcompetencies before proceeding to subcompetency 10.

Figure 5.4   Sequencing of subcompetencies

**Performance goal**

Given fifteen source documents including checks, invoices, credit memorandums, purchase requisitions, purchase orders, statements of account, and the appropriate journals, **demonstrate** the ability to journalize by recording each transaction in the appropriate journal.

**Subcompetencies**

**12**  Identify source documents and appropriate journal into which each is entered.

**11**  Discriminate among source documents such as checks, invoices, credit memorandums, purchase requisitions, purchase orders, statements of account, time cards, approval of payment notices, and inventory cards, identifying each one correctly.

**10**  Using various journals, journalize transactions involving cash receipts, cash payments, sales on account, purchases on account, and sales and purchases returns and allowances.

| | | | | |
|---|---|---|---|---|
| **9**  Journalize correctly transactions involving sales and purchases returns and allowances in general journal. | **8**  Journalize correctly sales on account. | **7**  Journalize correctly purchases on account. | **6**  Journalize correctly cash payments for merchandise, services, expenses, and other payments made. | **5**  Journalize correctly cash receipts resulting from sales, accounts receivable, or investments. |

**4**   Journalize in general journal by debiting and crediting for cash receipts, cash payments, cash withdrawals, and cash investments.

**3**  Record changes in the accounting equation for (**a**) equal exchange of assets with no change in liabilities, (**b**) equal exchange of liabilities with no changes in assets, (**c**) unequal exchange of assets with increase in total assets, (**d**) unequal exchange of assets with decrease in total assets, (**e**) unequal exchange of liabilities with increase in total liabilities, (**f**) unequal exchange of liabilities with decrease in total liabilities, (**g**) unequal exchange of assets and liabilities resulting in increase in assets, (**h**) unequal exchange of assets and liabilities resulting in decrease in assets, (**i**) unequal exchange of assets and liabilities resulting in increase in liabilities, (**j**) unequal exchange of assets and liabilities resulting in decrease in liabilities.

**2**   Correctly identify each of 10 accounts as asset, liability, or equity.

**1**   State the fundamental accounting equation.

## Pretesting and Matching

The difference between the competencies or subcompetencies a student already has at the beginning of the learning process and those the student has acquired by the end is *achievement*. The teacher cannot determine individual student achievement without first determining the level of each learner at the beginning of the learning process. Pretesting accomplishes this task. *Pretesting* is the measuring of competencies and subcompetencies a student possesses before the student tackles a stated performance goal. The pretest measures the competencies a student should possess at the end of the learning process. In fact, some teachers use the identical test for the pretest and the posttest. Others construct similar tests covering identical competencies. If a student cannot perform a specific competency at the beginning of the learning process and has acquired it by the end of the learning process, the student has achieved.

In addition to helping the teacher determine student achievement, pretests serve another important function. They help the teacher and the student select specific performance goals and subcompetencies needed by the student. This selection process has an important consideration. In one type of learning situation, *individually prescribed learning,* each student is working toward his or her own goals. These goals are not necessarily the same as those toward which other students are working. When individually prescribed learning is employed, those competencies and subcompetencies being evaluated by the pretest *will not* be the same for all students. In another type of learning situation, *individually paced learning,* each student is working toward the same goals, but at his or her own rate. When individually paced learning is employed, the competencies and subcompetencies being evaluated by the pretest will be the same for all students. Both individually prescribed and individually paced learning are discussed further later in this chapter.

Regardless of the type of learning situation being employed, if a student demonstrates on the pretest that he or she already possesses a competency or subcompetency, that student should go on to other competencies or subcompetencies. Once the teacher and the student determine which specific subcompetencies the student has yet to achieve, the teacher can construct en route goals for each of these subcompetencies. An *en route goal* is a performance goal created for any subcompetency that a student needs to attain. It is not necessary for the teacher to construct en route goals for *each* subcompetency; they need to be constructed only for those subcompetencies needed by individual students.

In the accounting example in Figure 5.4, the beginning accounting student may be unable to perform subcompetency 1; for that student, subcompetency 1 should be used as the basis for an en route goal. Another student may demonstrate the ability to handle subcompetencies 1 and 2; for that student, subcompetency 3 may be used as the basis for an en route goal.

In addition to helping teachers and students select competencies and subcompetencies toward which each individual student must work at the beginning of the learning process, sequenced subcompetencies assist the teacher and the students in identifying subcompetencies which inhibit students from succeeding at a specific performance goal. Once a student has gone through the teaching-learning system and has failed to achieve a given performance goal, the teacher's responsibility is to determine which of the subcompetencies are unmastered and to convert these to en route goals for the student.

## Individually Prescribed Learning

*Individually prescribed learning* describes the type of learning situation in which each student selects performance goals which meet his or her individual needs, interests, and abilities. It is generally facilitated by teacher-prepared instructions as well as readings, problems, and other learning activities or learning packets selected by the teacher. A *learning packet* (also called a *minipac, module,* or *individual learning packet*) is a kit containing a performance goal and subcompetencies, appropriate learning activities, and multiple opportunities for self-evaluation.

Individually prescribed learning is a reality in business education, since many schools are committed to the approach and encourage students to participate in selecting goals which relate to special vocational interests. One student may select goals involving machine operations and related clerical tasks, while another may select goals leading to accounting-related positions. No prerequisites restrict a student in selecting performance goals; if a student does not possess the essential subcompetencies, en route goals are structured for their attainment.

## Individually Paced Learning

Any teacher who hesitates about wholehearted commitment to individually prescribed learning can experiment with individually paced learning. *Individually paced learning* (or *individual progress method*) describes the type of learning situation in which a flexible time schedule is employed to enable students to achieve a given performance goal at their own individual learning rates. Some students learn more quickly than others and can, therefore, attain a goal sooner. Although the faster learner may accomplish considerably more during a year, the slower learner is not penalized but progresses toward the same goals at a slower pace.

The teacher who believes in providing for the needs of students through individually prescribed learning or providing for varying learning rates through individually paced learning will invariably elect to organize several small groups within the larger class group. (See Chapter 7 for a fuller discussion.)

## Self-Assessment (Answers on p. 102)

1.   Analyze each of the competencies below for the components of a performance goal (see Figure 5.3) and construct a performance goal for each competency. Be sure your verbs are consistent with the domain and level of each competency.

   a.   Use sources and reference books to obtain needed data to answer questions correctly.
   b.   Help others whenever work is up to date.
   c.   Check contents of incoming mail and determine all papers to be retrieved from file in order to process work.
   d.   Identify correctly the various tasks performed in a given office, who performs them, and which papers should be routed to each worker.
   e.   Maintain an accurate record of petty cash at all times.

2.   Analyze the performance goal constructed for 1e for subcompetencies and sequence the subcompetencies to illustrate their relationships, using Figure 5.4 as a model.

## Summary

A performance goal states a measurable behavior, the product to emerge from performance, the conditions under which performance will be conducted, and the criterion against which performance will be judged.

Performance goals tell the student exactly what is expected and how well the competencies should be performed. Before constructing the goal, the teacher analyzes the competency for dominant domain and level, and selects and plans the evaluations to be used. Then the teacher (1) determines the actual behavior and selects the verb; (2) determines the result of the performance; (3) decides on the conditions; (4) decides on the criterion.

Subcompetencies are identified as the components required to achieve a performance goal. In some cases it makes no difference whether one subcompetency is attained before another. In other cases achieving one subcompetency depends on mastering a previous one. Then, it is necessary to sequence subcompetencies into logical order so that learning can proceed from simple to complex. Any subcompetency a student needs then becomes an en route goal. If a student reveals during pretesting that some subcompetencies are already mastered, the student is routed to the next subcompetency needed for achievement.

To identify student status at the beginning of a learning process, the teacher pretests on evaluations which include the same behaviors as the posttest. Achievement is the difference between the student's performmance on the pretest and the posttest. When individually prescribed learning is used, each student works on performance goals consistent with individual needs, interests, and abilities; and the competencies and subcompetencies

101

evaluated by the pretest are not the same for each student. When individually paced learning is used, each student works toward the same goals at his or her own rate; and the competencies evaluated by the pretest are the same for all students.

## Answers to Self-Assessment

1.   Your performance goals should contain the components revealed in the following answers:

    a.   Given five problems requiring the use of some of the 20 source books listed, **decide** which source to use and locate the answers to the problems and write them with care to assure that the most recent documents are used, the data is correctly transferred, and the sources of the answers are correctly stated.

    b.   While being observed by peers and your teacher in a work situation, **demonstrate** your willingness to assist others in their work as soon as your work is completed.

    c.   Given an In basket as well as a file of office materials, **arrange** all related papers and attach them to the pieces of incoming mail to which they refer, discarding those not applicable.

    d.   Given an In basket and a description of tasks and jobs performed by others in the office, **classify** all papers as to a given worker and mark the worker's job number on the top sheet with no important papers omitted.

    e.   Given a petty cash book and a record of incoming and outgoing transactions, **demonstrate** the ability to keep an accurate petty cash record by entering each receipt and payment in the appropriate column, with the petty cash book balanced correctly and reimbursed ready for payments during the next period.

2.   Your items may vary from these; however, you should have identified the major subcompetencies needed for attainment of the goal. Check to determine what you missed and why.

---

Given a petty cash book and a record of incoming and outgoing transactions, **demonstrate** the ability to keep an accurate petty cash record by entering each receipt and payment in the appropriate column, with the petty cash book balanced correctly and reimbursed ready for payments during the next period.

### Subcompetencies

Balance petty cash book, putting lines and amounts in correct places, and bringing forward correct balance.

Enter reimbursement check correctly in petty cash book.

Complete request form for check to reimburse fund in correct amount needed.

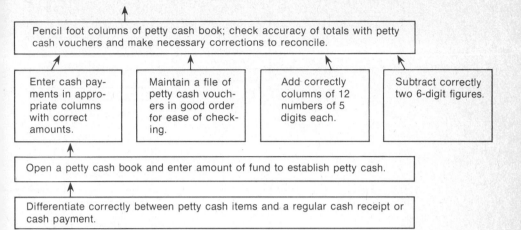

## SELECTED READINGS

COOK, J. MARVIN, AND HENRY H. WALBESSER, *Constructing Behavioral Objectives: Book 1,* Maryland Book Exchange, College Park, Md., 1972.

———*How to Meet Accountability with Behavioral Objectives and Learning Hierarchies,* Bureau of Educational Research and Field Services, University of Maryland, College Park, Md., 1973.

KEMP, JERROLD E., *Instructional Design: A Plan for Unit and Course Development,* Fearon Publishers, Belmont, Calif., 1971.

KIBLER, ROBERT J., ET AL., *Behavioral Objectives and Instruction,* Allyn and Bacon, Inc., Boston, 1970.

MAGER, ROBERT F. (1), *Analyzing Performance Problems,* Fearon Publishers, Palo Alto, Calif., 1970.

———(2), *Developing Attitude Toward Learning,* Fearon Publishers, Palo Alto, Calif., 1968.

———(3), *Preparing Instructional Objectives,* Fearon Publishers, Belmont, Calif., 1962.

MAGER, ROBERT F. AND KENNETH M. BEACH, JR., *Developing Vocational Instruction,* Fearon Publishers, Palo Alto, Calif., 1968.

PETER, LAURENCE J., *Prescriptive Teaching System: Individual Instruction,* McGraw-Hill Book Company, New York, 1972.

POPHAM, JAMES W., AND EVA L. BAKER (1), *Establishing Instructional Goals: Systematic Instruction,* Prentice-Hall, Englewood Cliffs, N. J., 1970.

———(2), *Planning Instructional Sequence,* Prentice-Hall, Inc., Englewood Cliffs, N. J., 1970.

WALBESSER, HENRY H., *Constructing Behavioral Objectives,* Bureau of Educational Research and Field Services, University of Maryland, College Park, Md., 1970.

STEDMAN, RON, MARIE SCHRAG, AND JACK HUMBERT, *The National Association of Distributive Education Teachers Accountability Kit or How to Survive the 70s,* Monroe County Community College, Monroe, Mich., 1974.

*Writing Performance Goals: Strategy and Prototypes,* Center for Vocational and Technical Education, Ohio State University, and Gregg Division, McGraw-Hill Book Company, New York, 1971.

## PERFORMANCE GOAL

Using the performance goal analyzed for the subcompetencies in Chapter 5, **decide** which learning principles apply, substantiating each by a simple statement defending its use.

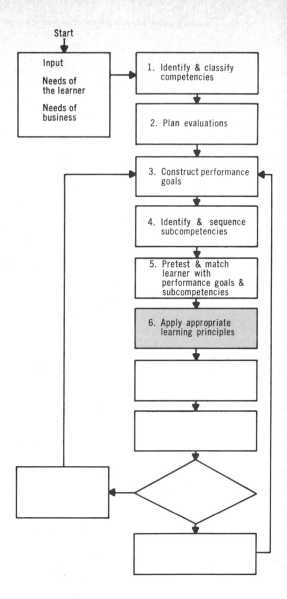

# CHAPTER 6

# Applying
# Learning Principles

Today, the learner is the focal point in the classroom; the teacher's role is changing rapidly. One role of the teacher remains unchanged, however, that of applying principles of learning in all instructional activities. This chapter focuses on step 6 of the teaching-learning system, "Apply appropriate learning principles." No discussion of learning principles is complete until the roles of the learner and the teacher have been identified.

Both the teacher and learner are involved in the learning process, although their roles are quite different. Previously, the teacher was the central figure in the classroom; what the teacher did and felt determined the learning environment. The teacher planned in terms of "Today, *I* am going to———." The student was the receiver of knowledge; the teacher, the dispenser of information. In many classes, the student was passive.

Now the emphasis has changed. The attention is on the learner and what the learner is gaining from each educational experience. With the impact of technological developments, the teacher is both the director and facilitator of learning. Once goals are established, the teacher may call upon a vast spectrum of resources—learning laboratories equipped with computer terminals, filmstrips, learning packets, and other media—to assist the learner.

Because learning is the process of changing behavior, the student must be involved in the learning process. Frequently, however, the teacher cannot assess the student's actual degree of involvement. The teacher evaluates paper-and-pencil tests or products emerging from a student's performance. The teacher who does not accurately measure the behaviors of the student entering the learning system may erroneously conclude that the student has learned; in fact, this may not be true. The student may have had the competencies at the beginning and simply had no opportunity to reveal them. Thus, in order to make an objective judgment of achievement, the teacher must be aware of each student's prior competencies.

Perhaps one of the most difficult facts for any teacher to accept is that well-structured learning experiences do not necessarily assure student learning. Students learn in different ways. Some learn better by discussing and doing than by listening, and vice versa. The teacher's role is to plan multiple learning experiences so that the teacher and student, working together, may identify those learning experiences most appropriate for each individual. Through repeated self-evaluation, the learner can decide whether additional learning experiences are necessary.

Having differentiated between the role of the teacher and that of the learner, the teacher is prepared to act as director and facilitator of learning.

## Principles of Learning

How does the learner learn? What affects students during the learning process? Learning theories give insight into processes by which learning experiences are organized and structured. Much research is being conducted in this area. Nevertheless, theorists are frank about admitting that they are just approaching the threshold in providing answers to the question of how a student learns.

The following fourteen principles of learning apply to the acquisition of cognitive, affective, and psychomotor competencies. The first seven principles apply to all learning, while principles 8 through 14 apply specifically to the acquisition of psychomotor and cognitive skills.

---

PRINCIPLE 1
The learner must perceive what is to be learned as relevant.

---

The term "relevant" enters any discussion of education today. Psychologists provide evidence that there is a greater positive effect on learning when a student perceives that information, attitudes, or motor skills are valuable, than when the student fails to perceive the relevancy of material studied. This principle illustrates the vital importance of affective behaviors in the learning process. The business teacher should determine a student's attitude toward a course and his or her perception of its value and practical use. Many students enter a learning situation enthusiastically. On the other hand, a teacher is also likely to encounter apathetic learners. Frequently, the teacher may identify several students whose behaviors challenge the teacher to motivate them. Or, the teacher may also identify students with whom he or she is unable to communicate effectively.

What can a teacher do to reach these students? Perhaps the learner has had no opportunity to recognize the value of the goal involved. A teacher's attempts at persuasion are likely to be ineffective. The only way of changing the student's attitude may be to develop a situation in which the student recognizes the value of this learning. One major argument for cooperative work experience is that it alerts the student to the need for acquiring certain behaviors.

Sometimes the teacher can reach a student by permitting the individual to select a particularly appealing goal, even though the goal may not be one the teacher values. For example, a learner who sees no reason to bother with accuracy in making accounting entries may be stimulated by an auditing problem in which he or she must identify and correct errors. Appointing such a student class auditor may not only give the student status but may also have a positive effect upon the individual's attitude toward records and the accuracy needed in recording.

A teacher who analyzes pretests is able to pinpoint competencies already possessed as well as those the learner needs to develop. In this way, the student recognizes what is needed in order to succeed. Any subcompetency decided upon may be meaningful, especially if the student views the goal as valuable. Also, many teachers find that learners respond better if they select their own performance goals, instead of having goals assigned. Implicit here is the idea that all performance goals offered must be vital in terms of competencies needed by business people and consumers. Such an approach emphasizes the ladder concept: one student may opt for performance goals leading to a job within one occupation, while another student may strive to attain goals required in a more difficult job. An example may be taken from data processing. One student may select performance goals that enable him or her to become proficient in the operation of the sorter, collator, or accounting machine. Another student may not develop as high a standard of performance on this equipment, but may elect to specialize in operating the computer. Still another student may select additional goals that enable him or her to program business applications for the computer.

Arguments are offered against high degrees of specialization; however, the teacher who involves students in selecting meaningful goals is stimulating positive attitudes toward learning that may carry over to other subject areas.

---

PRINCIPLE 2
Learning results from the learner's interaction with his or her total environment.

---

Too often the teacher mistakenly believes that the experiences provided within the classroom are the sole factors responsible for learning. First, each learner has other environments with which to interact. The learner's *internal environment* is created by past experiences and involves self-perception, acquired knowledge, attitudes, and skills, as well as methods of dealing with problem situations. Second, the learner is confronted by several *external environments*—home, neighborhood, peer group, and school— in relation to which patterns of response have been developed.

A student who has a positive self-image and a pattern of successful adjustment to external environments will react quite differently from the student whose self-image is negative and who has learned from experience that his or her reactions differ from teachers' expectations. Thus, the teacher who finds a student not responding as expected needs to learn more about the individual in order to determine what environmental factors are conditioning the learner to respond as he or she does. What can the teacher do to improve the student's self-image?

Teachers react differently toward unmotivated students. Frequently, a teacher subconsciously exhibits negative attitudes toward a student whose behaviors reveal lack of accomplishment. The wise teacher must understand that student apathy, or even rebellion, is not directed against the teacher personally. The student who displays apathy or hostility probably needs the teacher's attention and praise far more than the student whose pattern of success is well established. Unfortunately, a year may be too short a time in which to change a student's self-image, particularly when negative attitudes of other teachers or guidance counselors contribute to this self-image. Only a concerted effort of all school personnel with whom a student comes into contact can assure behavior changes. Research conducted among students who were tutored by classmates reveals a positive influence on learning. This may be one way to reach students who seem to erect barriers between themselves and the teacher. Also, the discovery that learning is possible often serves as a motivating factor.

One positive attitude change revealed by Levin affected student absences. He found that students who were developing basic competencies for clerical work in an individually prescribed learning situation were absent less than half as often as students who were developing the same competencies in a conventional classroom. Apparently, an individually prescribed learning situation was a more favorable environment than the conventional class situation.

---

### PRINCIPLE 3
Learning is facilitated when the learner can associate new behaviors with previously learned behaviors.

---

This is related to step 3 of the teaching-learning system, "Pretest and match learner with performance goals and subcompetencies." The teacher who determines where the student is in the learning process can more effectively help the student build upon learnings to reach present goals.

Transfer of learning is implied in this principle, since what has been learned with respect to one task can be utilized in the learning of other tasks. Transfer of learning is positive when mastery of one task facilitates mastery of another. An example of positive transfer is the shorthand student whose first attempt to transcribe is grammatically correct. The mastery of English grammar enables the student to use correct grammar in typing from the symbols in the shorthand notebook.

Negative transfer occurs when mastery of one task inhibits mastery of another task. For example, negative transfer occurs when a shorthand student substitutes the phonetic spelling used in shorthand for correct spelling in transcriptions. Negative transfer of attitudes is familiar to all teachers. A student conditioned to failure is likely to exhibit a negative attitude even in encounters with new teachers. The student transfers the previously learned attitude to a new learning situation, but the transfer is negative. In such a case, the teacher must help the student win acceptance among peers and work on attainable goals.

---

**PRINCIPLE 4**
Learning proceeds more effectively when the learner is an active participant in the learning process.

---

Interaction with the learning environment is essential if the student is to develop healthy, positive attitudes toward learning. Students who interact with learning materials and peers as well as with the teacher generally develop healthier attitudes toward the learning process than those who passively listen to the teacher talk.

Piaget's studies of learners reveal that merely subjecting a learner to external experiences does not compel the individual to restructure his or her thinking. Learning did not necessarily take place. It is the teacher's responsibility to manipulate the learning situation to require active learner involvement. Many business subjects are activity-based. Students in typewriting are involved as they compute spacing for a table, decide upon the arrangement on the page, type the table, or prepare a manuscript. They are compelled to think about what is being done and to perform. A basic business teacher who arranges for student discussions on provocative questions and then withdraws from the activity in order to observe students interacting is promoting this learning principle.

---

**PRINCIPLE 5**
Learning is more effective when the learner knows the immediate goal to be met.

---

Essentially, application of the system is based on this principle. The student should know not only the specific performance expected, but also precisely how attainment of the goals will be evaluated. Use of pretests, performance goals, and subcompetencies contribute to the student's knowledge of what must be attained. Individuals are able to eliminate irrelevant material and concentrate completely on essentials. They are likely to be more secure, and security generates greater confidence and a positive attitude. In contrast, when a teacher says that a test "will cover chapters three through five" the students are totally unaware of what specific learnings should have been attained. They may be insecure, and their insecurity may contribute to inability to perform.

---

**PRINCIPLE 6**
Learning proceeds faster when the learner is aware of the progress being made toward the stated goal.

---

Knowledge of results improves performance and stimulates more positive attitudes toward learning. Once a student knows that he or she has performed successfully (knowledge of results) the student develops confidence which reinforces the behavior exhibited. When the same stimulus is encountered later, the student is likely to respond in the same manner. Most learning involves the formation as well as the strengthening of habits; each time the student responds and knows immediately that the response is correct, the habit is being strengthened. An incorrect response can also reinforce a good habit, provided the learner becomes immediately aware that the response is not correct. The individual can then search for other ways to elicit a correct response. Two guiding rules emerge from this principle: (1) The teacher must provide some way of enabling each learner to make correct responses at some time; and (2) a student must know immediately whether a response is right or wrong so that an incorrect habit will not be formed.

This principle is further emphasized by Skinner, who believes that both the attitudes of students and the entire atmosphere of the class can be improved when the teacher responds to students' successes rather than their failures. (Skinner, p. 15) A combined teacher-student decision on appropriate goals for competencies a student lacks is only the first step. Next, the teacher must make certain that the en route goals selected are attainable by the student. Providing easy en route goals to stimulate success helps students attain competencies needed for successful performance.

Immediate knowledge of results is part of the feedback process, an integral part of the learning system. Feedback may be accomplished by frequent self-evaluation. Students who have access to models or answers either on a transparency or in a student guide may check their own work immediately upon completing it. In finding the work correct, the student strengthens the learned habit. If the work is incorrect, the student either seeks teacher assistance or independently investigates why the work is incorrect. If the student were to continue performing incorrectly, a poor habit would emerge which would have to be broken later so that the correct habit could be substituted.

---

PRINCIPLE 7
**Learning proceeds more effectively when the learner participates in a continuously expanding pattern of behaviors.**

This principle is analogous to the ripple effect created by a stone dropped into a pool of water. The learner cannot perceive all of the behaviors essential to performance of a competency at once. First, the learner acquires the simpler behaviors; then, the more complex. The term "spiral learning" is sometimes used to illustrate this principle. A task is first performed in its simplest form. Once that phase is perfected, the task is practiced in a more complex form. Business educators are fortunate in that most learning materials, including textbooks, are developed according to this principle. A teacher who analyzes performance goals for subcompetencies is applying this principle. Unless the learner perfects subcompetencies, he or she is unlikely to be successful in achieving the performance goal.

## Principles of Skill Building

Learning principles which apply only to the acquisition of cognitive and psychomotor skills are frequently referred to as principles of skill building. Actually, the only motor skills for which the business teacher has responsibility are those involved in typewriting and machine operations. Other motor skills essential to successful performance in business involve handwriting and eye movements, both of which have been acquired before the student enters the business classes. However, the business teacher may need to improve the learner's cognitive skills or punctuation, use of the English grammar in speaking and writing, and arithmetic operations, if they are inadequately developed. Whether teaching accounting, business mathematics, data processing, retailing, shorthand, typewriting, or office procedures, the business teacher will find multiple opportunities to apply these principles.

---

PRINCIPLE 8
In order to respond, the learner must have the requisite behavior in his or her repertoire.

---

This principle may be explained in terms of the multiple behaviors a student needs in order to succeed in beginning shorthand. The student must be able to read from the printed page, listen, hear sounds and connect them with syllables or words, spell syllables, and pronounce words accurately. Obviously, the non-English-speaking student taking English-language shorthand experiences learning difficulties. Although such a student can read, understand, and speak in a foreign language, the student does not possess these competencies in the English language. It is totally unrealistic for these students to be asked to read shorthand symbols in English or take and transcribe dictation into acceptable English until they have acquired the appropriate behaviors. Such students are headed for frustration and failure unless the teacher identifies the areas in which help is needed and provides remedial work from the first day of instruction.

Students from environments in which speech patterns differ from those used by the teacher or the person dictating on the tapes are bound to encounter learning difficulties, for they do not possess the specified behaviors needed for success. Similarly, students who have hearing or sight impairments not identified by the teacher will encounter difficulties which will retard their learning.

With the common practice of scheduling students into any subject requested, more and more teachers encounter situations in which the learner does not have the required behaviors in his or her repertoire. This is especially true in shorthand. The teacher must find some means of handling these students, many of whom are motivated and qualified in other ways. Again the learning system provides the teacher with a solution. Pretesting shorthand students by dictation of a short letter to be written in longhand will alert the teacher to hearing and sound-hearing problems as well as linguistic problems and deficiencies in handling grammar and punctuation. Results enable the teacher to evaluate special needs and construct specific en route goals to assist a student in overcoming pronunciation and enunciation problems, sound-hearing problems, and other language problems identified by the pretest. Thus, a student with poor hearing must be referred to the school nurse and guidance counselor.

---

PRINCIPLE 9
At the initial learning stage, individual tasks must be learned to a high level before they are combined to form effortless performance.

---

All psychomotor skills are developed through achievement of subcompetencies which become progressively more difficult. Although the ultimate goal in shorthand is taking dictation of unfamiliar material and transcribing it correctly, the beginner cannot emulate the pattern of the expert. The teacher must identify all subcompetencies which comprise this pattern and plan for student evaluations on each goal. A student who can perform each subcompetency should achieve the stated goal.

An example of motor skill development combined with cognitive behaviors is the typewriting student who must develop in succession (1) stroking of individual keys, (2) letter-by-letter stroking at the concentrated thought level, (3) typing of sentences at the subconscious level, relying on muscular sensations (feeling the correct pattern), and finally (4) typing while solving problems of setting up manuscripts, letters, rough draft revisions, and tabulations. While the student who converts hand-scribbled rough draft into a well-placed correct manuscript appears to be working effortlessly, expert performance is possible only because each of the competencies essential to the ultimate performance has been mastered.

Learning to a high level simply means being able to perform consistently the behavior desired. The teacher should construct en route goals which require students to exhibit behaviors at the level at which they will be performed in the evaluation. For example, if the expert stenographer is able to take dictation and transcribe it into a mailable letter, the following subcompetencies can be identified: (1) take dictation; (2) read symbols accurately and convert them by transcribing on the typewriter; (3) use letter forms correctly; (4) type accurately from shorthand notes and use English correctly; and (5) proofread carefully. Unless each of these subcompetencies is attained to a predesignated standard, the learner cannot be expected to achieve the ultimate performance goal.

---

PRINCIPLE 10
In motor skill learning, the results are better when the learner understands the relationships between the subcompetencies and the competency to be achieved.

---

A typist who knows that the tabulator must be used repeatedly in preparing an outline will not object to isolated drill to achieve an en route goal on tabulation. A shorthand student who realizes that appositives must be identified before transcription can be punctuated correctly will understand why a drill on appositives is important.

---

PRINCIPLE 11
Isolated practice on unmastered components of a complete skill may be preferable to practice on the final task.

---

In determining the kinds of practice, the needs of individual learners must be considered. Generally, no kind of practice meets the needs of all students. Principle 9 is closely related to this idea. Once a student's needs are identified, the student should have specific practice that will lead to attainment of any subcompetency identified as an en route goal. If a student cannot achieve an attempted performance goal, it is the teacher's role to analyze the reason for the failure and schedule practice on unmastered subcompetencies.

---

PRINCIPLE 12
In the early stages of skill learning, practice distributed over short periods is more effective in building skill than longer practice periods.

---

Short practice periods eliminate the possibility of fatigue. Beginning shorthand and typewriting students frequently complain that their muscles hurt. Tension in the muscles results in symptoms of fatigue. Concentrating on tightened muscles prevents the learner from giving thought to the task being performed. Thus, the practice is ineffective. Short practice periods, each on one element of a drill, may be followed by some change of activity in order to rest the muscles of the learner. For this reason, shorthand teachers plan varied activities for the learner—reading from bookplates, reading from transparencies or the chalkboard, spelling and pronouncing outlines, and taking dictation.

---

PRINCIPLE 13
In motor learning, early stages are characterized by excessive movement which disappears as the skill is perfected; ultimately, effortless performance results.

---

The teacher of a motor skill should be aware that beginners cannot perform with the economy of motion of an expert. The right kind of practice will eventually enable the learner to make smoother movements. Everyone who has engaged in skill building—bicycle riding, skiing, tennis, or typewriting—is aware that movements are modified by watching an expert and by practicing. Simply listening to a teacher describe motor skills will not enable a student to acquire the skills.

---

PRINCIPLE 14
While high skill levels require performance without conscious attention, varying levels of attention and consciousness are essential during the skill-building process.

---

Conscious attention at the beginning stages of skill learning is valuable only if the learner can discriminate between correct-incorrect movements; thus, the student must be supplied with the knowledge of the results. The typewriting learner who seeks the key before striking it and then checks to see whether the result is correct is performing at the conscious level. The shorthand learner who writes an outline for the first time and checks it with a model in the book is performing at the conscious level. Each is checking to determine that the movements made produced the desired result. As the level of skill is developed, the learner performs with less and less conscious attention to the results. At the highest level of skill development, the learner performs the movements without any conscious effort, while focusing on problem-solving activities such as setting up the page, punctuating difficult passages, and checking the spelling of new words.

## Self-Assessment (Answers on pp. 114–115)

Using this chapter as a resource, determine which of the learning principles apply to each of the situations below and defend your choice of each principle in one sentence:

1.   A student in your room is apathetic and, despite your attention, makes no effort to do any work at all.
2.   In your consumer economics class, you are trying to plan learning activities for students whose computational abilities need sharpening.
3.   A beginning typewriting student needs constant observation because he uses incorrect fingering.

## Summary

The role of the teacher is changing from that of dispenser of information to that of director and facilitator of learning. Rather than prepare lengthy presentations and tell the students what to remember, today's teacher is involved in seeking relevant learning experiences that involve the student in the learning process. Because the teacher is accountable for student learning, the teacher must seek to identify, by means of pretests, the changes in behaviors emerging from use of the learning experiences. Despite the changing role of the teacher, tested principles of learning still apply to any learning situation. These principles include those basic to all types of learning, as well as those particularly applicable to acquisition of cognitive and motor skills. Teachers should apply principles of learning in terms of the goals or en route goals involved.

## Answers to Self-Assessment

1.   The student may not believe the material is relevant (principle 1). The student may have problems outside class which affect behavior (principle

2). The student may be unaware of how the work relates to something he or she already knows (principle 3). The goal may seem remote to the individual (principle 5).

**2.** Involve the learner actively by giving answers for practice work and demanding a response of some nature—written or oral (principle 4). Explain the purposes of drills to student (principle 5). Plan to make the student aware of progress through self-evaluations (principle 6). Plan work so that difficulty increases as student succeeds (principle 7). Provide many opportunities for students to practice computations (principle 8). Plan so that each necessary computational skill is perfected before student is asked to compute accurately for material to be graded (principle 9). Student must know why he or she is being selected for drill (principle 10). Learning activities may depend upon the student's needs (principle 11).

**3.** The student is involved in making responses when he types (principle 4). The student should be made aware of the reason for achieving the en route goal (principle 5). Praise the student when fingering is correct (principle 6). Plan and observe many drills so that correct fingering becomes perfected and habitual (principle 7). Unless the student masters fingering correctly, he will be unable to type accurately and quickly (principle 11). Do not be concerned about awkward finger movements at this stage (principle 12). Do not correct the student for looking at his or her fingers; conscious attention is needed at this point (principle 13).

## SELECTED READINGS

BILODEAU, EDWARD A., *Acquisition of Skill*, Academic Press, New York, 1966.

BRUNER, JEROME S., *The Process of Education*, Harvard University Press, Cambridge, Mass., 1960.

GAGNE, ROBERT M., *The Conditions of Learning*, 2d ed., Holt, Rinehart & Winston, Inc., New York, 1970.

———, *Categories of Human Learning*, Academic Press, New York, 1964.

GLOCK, MARVIN D. (ED.), *Guiding Learning*, John Wiley & Sons, New York, 1971.

GUTHRIE, J. T., *The Psychology of Learning*, Harper & Row, New York, 1935.

HILGARD, E. R. (ED.), *Theories of Learning and Instruction: Sixty-third Yearbook, Part I*, National Society for the Study of Education, Chicago, 1964.

LEVIN, HERBERT A., "An Analysis of Selected Characteristics of Students in a Clerical Skills Laboratory Compared to Students in a Conventional Clerical Skills Program," unpublished doctoral dissertation, Temple University, Philadelphia, Pa., 1973.

PIAGET, J., *The Origins of Intelligence in Children*, International Universities Press, New York, 1952.

SKINNER, B. F., "The Free and Happy Student," *Phi Delta Kappan*, Vol. 60, September 1973, p. 15.

TRAVERS, ROBERT M. W., *Essentials of Learning*, The Macmillan Company, New York, 1967.

WEST, LEONARD J., *Acquisition of Typewriting Skills*, Pitman Publishing Corporation, New York, 1969.

## PERFORMANCE GOAL

**Select** a teaching-learning strategy for the performance goal that was analyzed for subcompetencies in Chapter 5 and defend your decision in terms of the material presented in this chapter.

**a. Identify** an appropriate organizational pattern (large-group, small-group, and/or individual instruction).

**b. Determine** at least two learning activities you would like to use.

**c. Select** at least two resources.

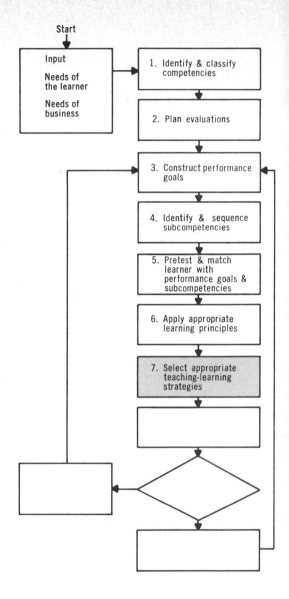

# CHAPTER 7

# Selecting Teaching-Learning Strategies

The only true measure of the effectiveness of any teaching-learning strategy is, "Did it result in the student achieving the identified goal?" Educators are sometimes said to be more concerned with methods of teaching than with the results of learning. By placing the emphasis of this book first on learning relative to predetermined goals and evaluations, and second on teaching, the philosophy is clearly established.

A *teaching-learning strategy* is the implementation of an organizational pattern, learning activities, and resources to assist students in achieving their goals as efficiently as possible. An *organizational pattern* is the right mix of large group, small group, and/or individual instruction. *Learning activities* are the educational exercises completed by the learner. Listening to a lecture, watching a film, participating in role playing, and writing an essay are all examples of learning activities. *Resources* are the learning materials and media used to implement and/or supplement learning activities.

The word "learning" is an integral part of the term "teaching-learning strategy" because the student should always be involved in the selection and implementation of strategies. Unless the student shares the responsibility for learning with the teacher, the student cannot attain the goal efficiently.

Optimum teaching-learning strategies for one student are not necessarily the best ones for another student. Thus, the teacher's role is to work with the student in selecting and implementing strategies that assist each student to learn. Should a student not learn after participating in one teaching-learning strategy, an alternate organizational pattern, learning activities, and/or resources are planned to enable that student to achieve the goal.

Although the right choice of a teaching-learning strategy depends on the goal as well as the student's interests and needs, research reveals several basic contributions that can assist the teacher in selecting appropriate strategies: (1) No one strategy is the most effective for all learners. (2) Some learning, although not necessarily that desired, will take place despite the strategy employed. The learning may be positive or negative and may relate to the affective domain as well as to the cognitive and psychomotor domains. (3) Students learn better when they are involved in multiple learning activities—listening to a teacher presentation, reading a textbook, performing a task, discussing the applications of principles, and solving problems by applying acquired information.

The teacher should master the use of a variety of organizational patterns, learning activities, and resources, in order to have the widest possible repertoire from which to select and implement teaching-learning strategies. Because the teacher must select strategies with which he or she feels comfortable, the beginning teacher must become familiar with various strategies at a comfortable pace. Ultimately, the teacher must be able to coordinate teaching-learning strategies with the learning principles applicable to a particular learning situation.

## Patterns of Organization

The first concern in the selection of a teaching-learning strategy is how students should be grouped. The three basic organizational patterns are large-group instruction, small-group instruction, and individual instruction. Some learning activities can be performed within all three settings, while other activities depend on the utilization of one specific pattern. For example, students in a consumer education class who are asked to develop guidelines for the purchase of a car can do so in large-group, or small-group settings or on an individual basis. The emphasis will be different in each situation. Perhaps different levels of competency will be achieved with the help of different organizational patterns. Another activity involving the discussion of guidelines developed by students could, of course, only be realized in a large- or small-group situation.

### Large-Group Instruction

The terms "large" and "small" are somewhat relative; there is no fixed number of students that constitutes a large group. Both an ordinary classroom situation involving 25 students and an auditorium of 200 students can be considered large groups.

Large-group instruction sometimes enables a teacher to avoid duplication of effort. For instance, general instructions or background material for a course can be more economically presented at one time to one large group than five times to five different sections. A large group could conceivably include several ordinary-size classes brought together for basic information. For instance, all general business or accounting students may be assembled in an auditorium to hear a guest speaker or typewriting classes may monitor a televised demonstration by a champion typist. If awards are made for outstanding performances in individual business classes, other students can be motivated by a presentation before all business classes, indeed before the entire student body.

Typically, teachers do not have to be encouraged to use large-group instruction within ordinary-size classes. It is usually easiest for the beginning teacher to teach each class as an entire group because this organizational pattern presents the fewest obvious variables. Since all students are directed toward one objective, the teacher may feel more in control of the learning situation. However, both the beginning and experienced teacher should keep in mind that the number of people involved in large-group instruction restricts the kinds of learning activities that may be used successfully. In addition, large-group instruction assumes that all students are ready to work toward the same goal at the same time. Frequently, this is a completely false assumption.

## Small-Group Instruction

A large group may be broken into smaller units which provide (1) a greater opportunity for interaction among individuals, (2) the chance for students who feel lost in a large group to extend themselves and establish a positive self-image, and (3) the option of grouping together students with similar abilities, interests, and learning problems.

The beginning teacher may feel uneasy at first about utilizing the small-group organizational pattern. It may appear that the general activity and discussion in the classroom is not under the teacher's control. The teacher may feel that the class is becoming too fragmented because the aims of each group are different. The increased variables involved in this organizational pattern require concentrated preplanning by the teacher. With such planning, the teacher will soon discover the students assuming active roles. Also, the teacher accustomed to a classroom in which only one person speaks at a time may be disturbed by the noise level of small groups. While the noise may be high at first, it will subside as students adjust to working with each other. Most teachers circulate among the groups to assure that students are working on the prescribed goals.

Small-group instruction is especially useful when working with students whose listening and speaking skills need special attention that cannot be given in a large group. Small-group interaction and the stimulation generated by working together not only develops better communication but also motivates the learner. Students are made to feel that their opinions matter. They listen to each other, and each is important to the group effort.

Small-group activities can be structured so that students with similar learning problems work together in developing subcompetencies adapted to their needs, although not to the needs of the larger group. For instance, students in accounting who cannot prepare a worksheet may be separated from the large group for additional instruction, perhaps from overhead projection of a transparency or a filmstrip to illustrate the steps in preparing the worksheet. When each student within the smaller group accomplishes the primary purpose for which the group was established, the group is disbanded and students join other groups.

## Individual Instruction

Individuals working alone comprise the third organizational pattern. There are two types of individual instruction—individually paced learning and individually prescribed learning. (Recycle to p. 100.) With individually paced learning, students work toward the same goal; however, each student works at his or her own pace. With individually prescribed learning, each student not only works at an individual pace, but with the teacher's help, chooses a specific goal toward which to work. The goals chosen by various students often differ from each other, although they are each related to the course content.

Because students learn at different rates, perceive the value of learning differently, and have different approaches to learning, no two students can be expected to be at the same point at any given time. Both individually paced and individually prescribed learning allow for these differences by enabling students to work at their own rates. Students become frustrated when they cannot keep up with the group; such frustration may lead to apathy toward learning. When given the opportunity to be involved in individual instruction, however, frustrated students often find they can and do learn. Success is a strong motivator and may lead to future successes.

Keuschner, as reported by Howes, presents several reasons for selecting individually prescribed learning. It is more democratic, encouraging students to prepare themselves for the decision making required in later life as well as in school. It encourages critical thinking by requiring students to question, criticize, and discuss points of view about the goals toward which they should be working and about the content they are studying. It demands self-direction, teaching students to act independently and on their own initiative. Perhaps even more importantly, it helps students develop a positive feeling about themselves. If students participate in making the wrong choice, at least they are assuming responsibility for their own learning.

Because the teacher who is experienced in teaching large and small groups needs special training before being given responsibility for either form of individual learning, schools planning to utilize this organizational pattern must train their teachers. An example of one school's efforts is shown in Figure 7.1.

Figure 7.1  Model of an individualized learning system—Training Pac 1

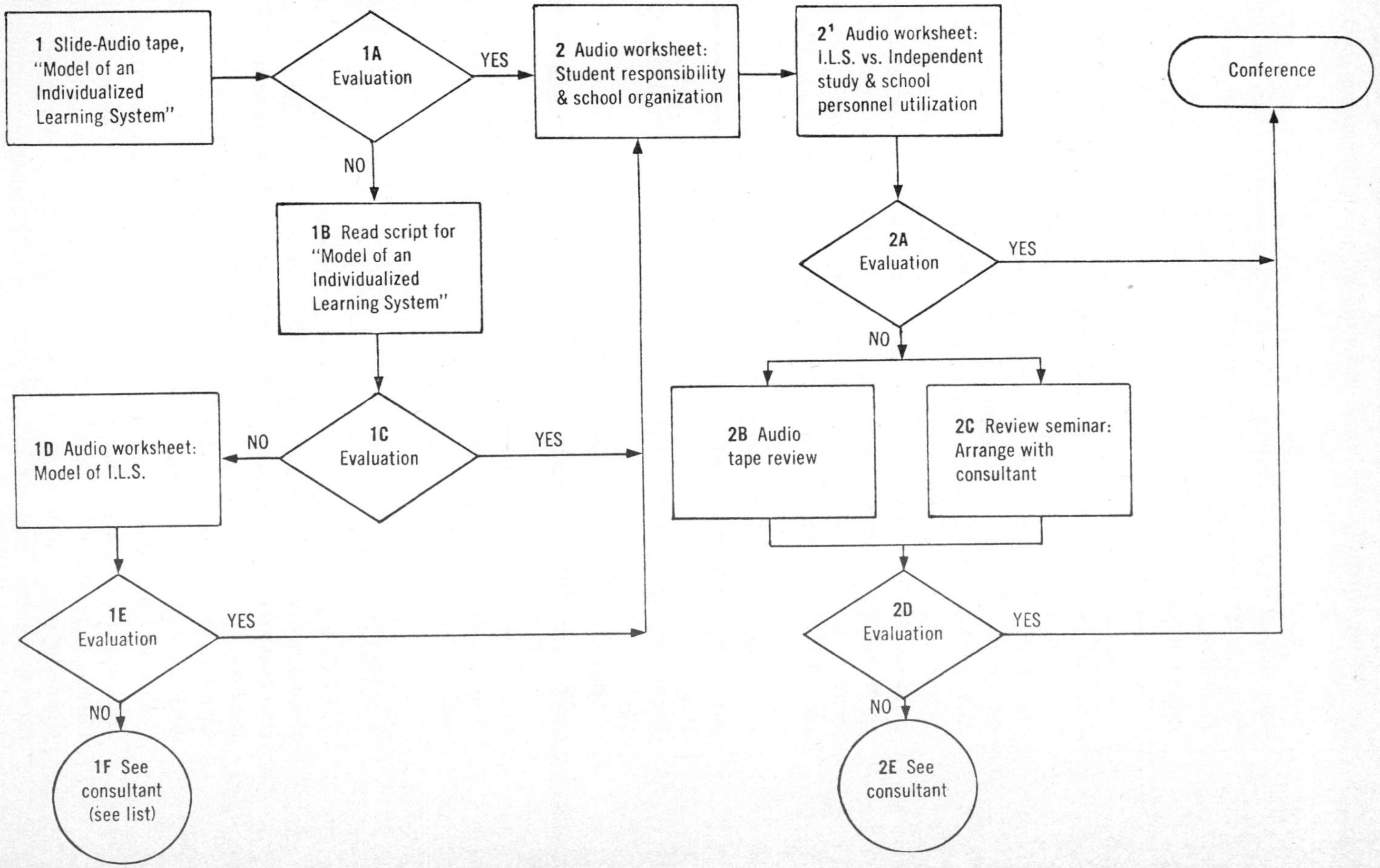

Source:  Coatesville Area High School, Coatesville, Pennsylvania

Teachers who volunteer for training in individual learning agree to utilize the carefully structured individually paced learning packets (referred to as *pacs*) which have been developed according to the systems approach. Thus, the teachers undergo much the same type of learning experiences they later employ in their own classrooms. The goal of the first pac, the model for which is illustrated in Figure 7.1, is for the teacher completing the packet to describe the individual instruction system employed at Coatesville Area High School. First (1), the teacher listens to an audio tape and uses the self-evaluation (1A). If results of the self-evaluation are satisfactory, the teacher listens to the audio worksheets (2) and ($2^1$) and engages in the self-evaluation (2A). If the self-evaluation is satisfactory, the participant arranges for a conference with the instructional technology specialist to determine the next packet to begin work on. On the other hand, a person who does not succeed on self-evaluation (2A) moves to the next learning activities (2B, 2C).

Another teacher who completes self-evaluation (1A) unsatisfactorily, proceeds to the script to read about the model (1B). Afterward, he or she evaluates progress. If the teacher is not successful on this attempt, there is another activity available. Should the participant still not attain the goal, consultants are available to diagnose the difficulties. The pac is so designed that a teacher moving through it may skip any activity not needed and proceed to the next step until the final evaluation (2D) is reached, at which point the formal evaluation is taken. The many learning activities permit a person who learns quickly to accomplish Pac 1 quickly and begin Pac 2. However, no teacher moves to Pac 2 until the goal for Pac 1 has been reached.

Students involved in an individual instruction program follow the same types of activities as those used by the teachers in Figure 7.1. Student decisions figure prominently in the Coatesville Area High School, for each student taking a course has the option of selecting either a class taught traditionally (large- and small-group instruction) or one employing individual learning.

## The Right Mix

The choice of an organizational pattern is influenced by the role in which the teacher perceives himself or herself. Teachers have individual teaching styles with which they feel comfortable. Similarly, students have individual learning styles. The teacher who seeks maximum learning for all students will merge organizational patterns to achieve the mix appropriate for both an individual teaching style and individual learning styles.

Teachers should keep in mind the strong points and limitations of each organizational pattern when they are determining the right mix. Large-group instruction enables a teacher to avoid duplication of effort when the presentation is of value to the entire group, but it does not provide for the needs of individual students. Small-group instruction provides an opportunity for students with similar interests and/or learning problems to work together. It is also a good organizational pattern for the mastery of communication skills because there is more opportunity for interaction. But, like large-group instruction, it does not always provide for individual needs. Individually prescribed and individually paced learning are organized especially to meet the needs of individual students, but they provide little opportunity for students to interact with peers. Unfortunately, some enthusiasts for individual instruction overlook the values to be derived from the right mix and eliminate groups altogether.

## Self-Assessment 7-1 (Answers on p. 148.)

1. Selection of teaching-learning strategies is based upon
   a. organizational patterns.
   b. individually prescribed and individually paced learning.
   c. a combination of organizational pattern, learning activities, and learning resources.
   d. the teacher.
2. In a typical classroom, the teacher should consider employing
   a. combinations of large-group, small-group, and individual instruction.
   b. predominantly small-group instruction with provision for some large groups.
   c. generally large-group instruction except for slower students.
   d. only individual instruction because of student differences.
3. Individually prescribed instruction is desirable because it
   a. holds each learner to identical standards with the rest of the group.
   b. permits students to participate in decisions concerning what they will learn.
   c. allows for learning only those things the student is interested in.
   d. reduces the teacher's responsibility for student learning.
4. Research on student learning indicates that
   a. there is one strategy best suited for each individual.
   b. large-group instruction is superior to small-group instruction.
   c. no one strategy is most effective for all learners.
   d. students will meet goals despite the strategy employed.
5. If a student fails on an evaluation of a required subcompetency in a group working toward the same performance goal, he or she should
   a. move with the class to next subcompetency.
   b. work individually or in a group with those who also failed on subcompetency.
   c. work permanently in a small group of students labeled as slower than class.
   d. seek the assistance of a classmate.

## Learning Activities and Resources

A wide variety of learning activities may be classified according to types of interaction required of the student. Figure 7.2 shows selected learning activities that have been divided into four classifications: (1) reading, (2) writing, (3) listening, speaking, and discussing, and (4) performing and observing. As a rule, no student will engage in all possible learning activities to achieve any one goal, but most students profit from a variety of learning activities. Publishers are meeting the student need for variety by offering complete programs that include such diversified learning resources as textbooks, workbooks, tests, filmstrips, records, transparencies, cassettes, film loops, games, and simulations.

## Reading

Each business teacher has the opportunity to utilize a variety of learning activities that involve the student in reading. Among the possibilities are the reading of textbooks, programmed materials, transparencies, and computer printouts.

TEXTBOOKS. The most commonly used learning activity is the reading of a textbook; however, textbooks are being published in new forms. Because some learners progress best by working on small units, the traditional textbook is in some cases being supplanted by several paperbacks or by modules. A *module* (packet or pac) is a self-contained instructional unit designed to achieve either a performance goal or a subcompetency. A module may involve the student in reading only or may combine reading with other types of student interaction, such as listening and discussing, for learners who need multiple types of interaction. After the teacher and student select a specific goal, the student chooses the appropriate modules to assist in achieving the goal.

TRANSPARENCIES. Textbooks can and should be supplemented constantly with reading materials from multiple sources. One such source is transparencies. A small group of students who need to review punctuation rules and their application may view a transparency, discuss the rule, and test its application before applying the rule in punctuating sentences. Correct models of letters may be placed on a transparency and read by the student who is self-evaluating a transcript for form and content.

Transparencies are, without a doubt, vital for many business classes. Some of the chief advantages of the use of transparencies in virtually any class follow: (1) The overhead projector is easy to operate with only three controls: an on/off switch, a knob to focus, and one to raise or lower the image. (2) The teacher faces the class and can control the sequences and timing of the presentation depending on pupils' reactions. (3) The teacher controls the projector, and can initiate and encourage

Figure 7.2 Selected learning activities classified by type of student interaction

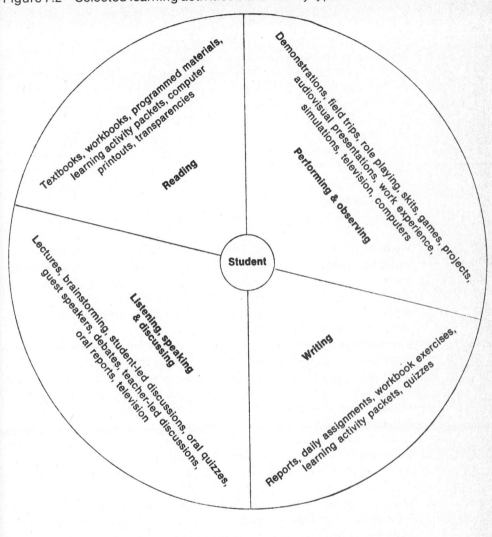

classroom interaction. (4) The teacher can build ideas from simple to complex by using overlays and masks. (5) The group can see the transparencies without darkening the room. (6) Good transparencies are commercially available. The teacher may also prepare individual transparencies. (7) The teacher's time is conserved. Once prepared, the transparency can be used over and over again. Information which might ordinarily be put on the chalkboard can be presented in less time and, often, more legibly. (8) Any student who needs to view transparencies more than once in order to understand the process being illustrated may handle the transparencies and study them as long as necessary.

Transparencies can be made by writing or drawing directly on acetate with a felt pen or wax pencil. Marks made by water-base felt pens can be removed by rubbing with a dry cloth. Marks made with permanent ink felt pens can usually be erased with a solvent such as lighter fluid. Many teachers prefer to use permanent ink on transparencies which they plan to save for more than a year.

Transparencies can also be made by running special transparent film and a master copy through a copy machine. This indirect heat process is fast and efficient and especially useful for transferring typewritten matter to acetate. However, the teacher who limits use of transparencies to projecting words is not capitalizing on the potential value of this medium. Diagrams projected in this way provide the student with a close-up of the operation of a typewriter or an office machine. With the use of overlays, steps in the preparation of multiple carbons or the changing of a ribbon may be portrayed.

One word of caution is necessary. Any teacher who plans to use a transparency with typed words on it—titles, captions, or text—should use a typewriter with large case letters. If one is not available, the printing should be done by hand rather than typed; projection of a transparency prepared from regular-sized typed letters is not clearly visible to those some distance from the screen. Examination of commercially prepared transparencies will reveal that large case type has been used so that the image will be clear from afar.

PROGRAMMED MATERIALS. This is another reading source frequently used to assist individual students in learning. Material is presented in small segments, requiring the student to supply an answer or a word to complete the sense, and providing immediate feedback in the form of the correct answer. *Linear programming* presents material in small units or frames. An immediate response is required of the learner, who checks to determine whether the response is correct or incorrect. All students follow the same path through the program. *Branching programming* contains larger units of textual material followed by multiple choice questions. The answers direct the student to various parts of the material, depending upon the student's responses. Programmed materials appear in various formats—answers printed upside down, on the next page, or in a column designed to be uncovered by sliding an opaque mask.

COMPUTER PRINTOUTS. A printout, or its graphic presentation on a television screen, may replace or supplement the textbook as source reading material. Use of the computer is often associated with individually prescribed learning. The learner is seated at a computer terminal equipped with a telephone that is connected to a computer. Typed (hard) copy is received from the computer terminal. The learner reads the copy and responds to the questions by typing the response on the terminal's keyboard. The computer then analyzes the response and directs the student to the next step.

SELECTION OF READING RESOURCES. Because of the heavy reliance on reading materials, each teacher must ascertain: (1) the reading level of each student so that appropriate materials may be used, and (2) the reading level of textbooks or other materials so that students and materials may be matched.

There is a wealth of evidence to indicate that one of the primary causes of student failure is inability to read required materials. For instance, during a project in Oakland County, Michigan, seven out of ten students were found to have reading comprehension scores below the eleventh-grade level, some even below the "survival level" of sixth grade. When the project researchers completed a computer analysis of the reading difficulty of textbooks used in classes in these schools, they found that much of the material was considerably beyond the reading comprehension levels of the students. This research led to affirmative action. The Oakland researchers met with publishers to explore the possibility of publishers providing objective data about the reading levels of textbooks that teachers consider for adoption. Two states, Michigan and California, now require a statement of readability from publishers before textbooks may be considered for adoption in their schools (Butz).

The findings of the Oakland study have alerted teachers to the need for seeing that reading materials are compatible with the reading abilities of individual students. A teacher who knows that a certain student reads at the eighth-grade level will not require the student to read a textbook that has an average reading level of eleventh grade without devising a plan for assisting the student in comprehending the material. Most schools have a record of student reading levels from various norm-referenced tests, and teachers have access to these scores as well as to their interpretations.

THE CLOZE TECHNIQUE FOR DETERMINING READABILITY OF MATERIALS. Any teacher can use the Cloze technique to measure the compatibility of reading materials with individual student ability. The steps to be followed are outlined here.

1. Randomly select reading material in six to nine passages and delete every fifth word, except the first word in each passage. Stop when 20 words have been deleted.

2. In place of each word deleted, substitute an underscore _____ .

3. Have the material typed and instruct students to place in each blank a word that makes sense. No guessing or time restrictions permitted.

4. Analyze the answers and give credit for each substitution that approximates the original meaning. Determine a raw score for each student and convert that raw score to a percent by dividing the actual number of correct answers by the possible number of correct answers. For instance, if the student had 15 of the 20 answers correct, the score is 75 percent.

5. Determine the level at which the student comprehended the material by using the following formula: A score of 0–30 percent is Frustration Reading Level; a score of 31–49 percent is Instructional Reading Level; and a score of 50–100 percent is Independent Reading Level. (Brown)

This technique tells the teacher whether the material used is appropriate for reading assignments for a particular student. A student whose reading is at the Independent Level can read the material without question. A student whose reading is at the Instructional Level can use the material but not without related learning activities to assist in understanding the unreadable portions. The material should not be used as a resource for a student whose reading is at the Frustration Level.

## Writing

Learning activities that involve the student in writing include reports, daily assignments, workbook exercises, modules (learning packets and pacs) and quizzes. Teachers who view written communications next in importance to oral communications provide a variety of learning activities in which students can express themselves in written form. Reports which require book research may encourage students to plagiarize, while written reports of committee work, observations made on field trips, and reports on topics students have researched in person give students more opportunities for creative writing.

Because a detailed discussion of the learning activities that involve the student in writing is given in Chapter 11, no further discussion of those learning activities is presented here.

## Listening, Speaking, and Discussing

Listening, speaking, and discussing are combined in this section because many of the learning activities that involve the student in either listening or speaking also involve the student in some type of discussion. There are, however, special learning activities that can aid the student in developing the ability to listen, both for directions and for ideas.

LISTENING FOR DIRECTIONS. How frequently the typewriting teacher gives careful instructions to set the margins at certain points and to double space the assignment, only to have one student after another ask, "Where did you tell us to set our margins and the line spacer?"

One activity that can improve listening involves the combining of written and verbal instructions. Instructions recorded on a transparency are flashed on the screen from the overhead projector and are read aloud by the students. The transparency is removed, and the students answer questions about the instructions. Should some students be unable to respond correctly, the transparency may be flashed again for rereading.

Another activity involves listening to a recording of directions on a tape. The student may listen to it as many times as necessary until he or she can follow the instructions correctly. Eventually, the student will have only one opportunity to listen to the tape before following the directions. As part of both of these activities, the learner should be encouraged to develop the habit of taking notes during the directions.

A few additional oral alertness activities can improve the student's ability to follow verbal instructions accurately.

- Take a half sheet of paper, fold it into four sections, and write your initials on the lower lefthand section. (General)
- Insert a full sheet of paper. Type your name five single spaces from the top at 25. Single space five times, type the make of typewriter you are using at 40, double space three times, and type the name of your school at 15. (Typewriting)
- On a sample deposit slip write "1" where you write your name, "2" where you list currency, "3" where you write the amount of the third check being deposited, "4" where you write the number of the bank on which the second check has been drawn, and "5" where you write the total. (Accounting or Basic Business)
- Report this week to Jim, who is the bank manager. Your responsibilities are to accept all deposits from students and to prove cash every day. If you have any difficulties, Jim will help you. On Friday you are to check your totals with him and then work with him as he moves to the loan department, for which you will be responsible next week. Outline in writing your responsibilities for this week and next. Where will you go for help? (Simulation)

LISTENING FOR IDEAS.    In the classroom, students can be trained in this area by having to write down the main points presented during a speech after the speaker has finished. If students compare their statements, they begin to sharpen their listening techniques. Writing helps to focus the listener's attention.

Another means of developing listening abilities is through playing tapes or records after the students have been prepared for the experience and know what they are listening for. Students answer specific questions and receive immediate reinforcement when they discover whether answers are right or wrong. Students can tell if their listening abilities are improving. Replays of the tape may be necessary for those students who need repeated exposures before being able to answer the questions correctly.

Two additional learning activities are listening to lectures by the teacher and listening to guest speakers. Because lecturing tends to preclude student participation, it should be used sparingly. However, when lecturing is used, there are a number of practical tips that will help to maximize its usefulness as a learning activity: (1) Limit the lecture to a maximum of fifteen minutes whenever possible. (2) Design the lecture to meet a specific en route or performance goal. (3) Know the material and organize it thoroughly. (4) Train students to take notes. At first give them a duplicated outline to follow; later emphasize strongly—"Point 1," "Point 2," and so on—and, finally, use normal lecture procedures and provide for immediate student responses. (5) Use attention-getting devices. Anecdotes, questions and illustrations, humor, and visual aids are proven techniques. (6) Direct the lecture to students as individuals, not as a mass. (7) Be realistic about what the class will absorb and retain. (8) Avoid reading your lecture. (9) Avoid extending the lecture beyond the pupils' attention span. (10) Avoid assuming that students have understood all you said. (11) Avoid using lecture extensively.

GUEST SPEAKERS. When a guest is invited to speak before a class, the teacher should plan with the group prior to the presentation. One technique is to hold a preliminary group discussion in order to find out what the listeners would like to learn from the speaker.

Often the guest may be a successful alumnus who has agreed to share some of the interesting aspects of his or her job. To provide for student participation, Robert Hoppock suggests handing the group a list of suggested questions rather than taking class time to develop the entire list. Questions can be added or deleted, and the list agreed on can be used by the students in questioning the interviewee, who has the privilege of not answering questions by saying "Next question, please."

After using an instrument like the one in Figure 7.3 at one conference with an alumnus, the class may decide to invite another speaker. The teacher can ask the first speaker to suggest additional interviewees.

## Figure 7.3 Format for questioning during alumni conferences

**Questions for Group Conferences with Employed Alumni**

What school did you attend? Did you graduate? Drop out? When?

What was your first job?
How did you get it?
What three things did you like most about it? Least?
How long were you there?
Why did you leave?

What was your next job? (Same questions. Repeat for subsequent jobs.)

Regarding your present job,
What time did you go to work this morning?
What was the first thing you did?
How long did it take?
What did you do next? (Repeat through the entire day.)
Did you do anything yesterday that was different from what you did today? How about the day before yesterday? Last week? Last month?
What else do you do on your job? Of all of these jobs, which ones take most of your time?
What three things do you like most about your job? Least?

What is the usual starting salary in jobs like yours?

What qualifications do you need to get the job?
Age? Sex? Height? Weight? Other physical qualifications? Marital status? Tools? License? Aptitude? Unions? Discrimination? Veterans? Capital?

Preparation (Minimum? Desirable? Time?)
Cost? Content? Approved schools? Preferred subjects?

Supply and demand for workers? Outlook for the future? Advancement?

Hours? Regular? Overtime? Evening? Sundays? Holidays?

Steady or seasonal? Hazards? Chances for marriage?

Anything we should have asked? You want to ask us? Thanks.

Source: Developed by Robert Hoppock, Professor Emeritus, New York University.

TEACHER-LED DISCUSSION. Many times a teacher will elect to lead a class discussion in order to develop a concept, discuss its implications, or to solve a problem. In this role, the teacher serves as the manipulator of the group in eliciting responses from students and stimulating them to interact with each other. Most developmental and problem-solving discussions led by the teacher demand active participation; therefore, the teacher must be skillful in (1) setting the stage, (2) asking questions which utilize the developmental approach, (3) guiding student participation, (4) stimulating disagreement, (5) appraising progress, (6) handling arguments, and (7) leading into summaries and conclusions. Considerable practice is needed to become an expert in discussion techniques. An ideal way to implement teacher self-evaluations is to have discussions videotaped. The teacher may replay the tape and evaluate his or her own performance using the criteria in Figure 7.4. In this way, any teacher can pinpoint ways to improve behaviors during teacher-led discussions.

Figure 7.4 may also be employed in evaluating another teacher or student teacher who is leading a discussion. No one displays every competency during the first attempt. A teacher using the criteria should select one or two areas needing improvement and concentrate on perfecting them. Gradually, a teacher is able to demonstrate every competency in leading discussions. The criteria to be used by the teacher in evaluating ability to lead a discussion are shown in Figure 7.4.

A more scientific way to gain insight into a teacher's actual behavior during a discussion is to use the Flanders' Interaction Analysis in Figure 7.5. The instrument is used extensively in teacher education as well as in in-service training programs. Before the teacher or student teacher begins leading a discussion, he or she records a statement of the behaviors to be exhibited. During the teacher-led discussion one or more trained observers record at three-second intervals the behavior the teacher is demonstrating at that moment. The recorded observation continues for 15 minutes. Very often the teacher observed requests a tape (video or sound only) be made. A personal assessment of behaviors may be made during replay of the tape and study of the profile prepared by the observers. Often a teacher using the prepared profile and reviewing the tape recognizes that the behaviors demonstrated were not those intended. Constant use of the instrument during observations enables teachers eventually to demonstrate intended behaviors.

BRAINSTORMING. Teachers may employ this technique in problem-solving situations. The teacher or leader presents the problem, and the group members contribute suggestions for solutions. Four basic rules apply in brainstorming: (1) The teacher or leader makes no judgments or comments on each idea as it is recorded on a flip chart or chalkboard. (2) Use of imagination is encouraged; the more creative the suggestion, the more others are encouraged to think. (3) A large number of solutions is the goal, to make it more likely that one or more idea will be appropriate. (4) Finally, "hitchhiking" or building on the idea of another is encouraged.

**131**

## Figure 7.4   Self-evaluation for teacher-led discussions

**Setting the stage**

The teacher
1. Elicits responses from students by using any of the following: (a) demonstration, (b) role playing, (c) a film or filmstrip, (d) a preplanned field trip, or (e) a reading assignment.

**Asking questions**

The teacher
2. Asks questions based upon common learning experiences to focus student attention on important points or issues.
3. Asks questions that require thought rather than "yes" or "no" responses.
4. Encourages students to defend their statements.
5. Devises techniques to bring nonparticipating students into the discussion without embarrassing them.

**Guiding student participation**

The teacher
6. Involves as many students as possible, using small groups when the need arises.
7. Provides assistance for students who need it.
8. Permits deviation from the topic only when some benefit is derived.

**Simulating disagreement**

The teacher
9. Challenges students by disagreeing or introducing a dissenting point of view.
10. Stops disagreement whenever it distracts students from main purpose of discussion.
11. Never leaves unresolved a point on which there has been disagreement.

**Appraising progress**

The teacher
12. Does not permit misinformation to remain in discussion.
13. Utilizes questions or thoughtfully worded statements to stimulate students to reconsider statements which were not entirely accurate.
14. Avoids taking discussion away from students when it lags, but injects questions to keep discussion alive.
15. Records important points as they are developed.
16. Terminates discussion when goal has been met and calls for summary.

**Handling conflicts**

The teacher
17. Terminates conflicts which are distracting by suggesting assignments to obtain correct facts.
18. Utilizes conflict of values as an opportunity to make students aware of the need for respecting the values another holds.

**Guiding summary and/or conclusions**

The teacher
19. Utilizes students for summary whenever possible.
20. Avoids summarizing and injecting own opinions.
21. Involves as many students as possible in formulating summary.
22. Uses students to synthesize summaries of all points and draw conclusions.

When all ideas are recorded, the leader begins involving participants in evaluating ideas and discarding those not appropriate and retaining those which are feasible.

STUDENT-LED GROUP DISCUSSIONS.   Encourage student interaction with no intervention from the teacher. The teacher is responsible for supplying

Figure 7.5    Summary of catagories of
              Flanders' Interaction Analysis

| | | |
|---|---|---|
| **Teacher talk** | **Indirect influence** | 1.[a] **Accepts feeling:** accepts and clarifies the feeling tone of the students in a nonthreatening manner. Feelings may be positive or negative. Predicting or recalling feelings is included.<br>2. **Praises or encourages:** praises or encourages student action or behavior. Jokes that release tension, but not at the expense of another individual; nodding head, or saying "um hm?" or "go on" are included.<br>3. **Accepts or uses ideas of students:** clarifying, building, or developing ideas suggested by a student. As teacher brings more of his or her own ideas into play, shift to Category 5.<br>4. **Asks questions:** asking a question about content or procedure with the intent that a student answer. |
| | **Direct influence** | 5. **Lecturing:** giving facts or opinions about content or procedures; expressing his own ideas, asking rhetorical questions.<br>6. **Giving directions:** directions, commands, or orders with which a student is expected to comply.<br>7. **Criticizing or justifying authority:** statements intended to change student behavior from nonacceptable to acceptable pattern; bawling someone out; stating why the teacher is doing what he is doing; extreme self-reference. |
| **Student talk** | | 8. **Student talk—response:** talk by students in response to teacher. Teacher initiates the contact or solicits student statement.<br>9. **Student talk—initiation:** talk by students, which they initiate. If "calling on" student is only to indicate who may talk next, observer must decide whether student wanted to talk. If he did, use this category. |
| | | 10. **Silence or confusion:** pauses, short periods of silence, and periods of confusion in which communication cannot be understood by the observer. |

Source: Edmund J. Amidon and Ned A. Flanders, *The Role of the Teacher in the Classroom*, p. 14.
[a]No scale or rank is implied by the numbering of items. Each number is classificatory; it designates a particular kind of communication event. To write these numbers down during observation is to enumerate—not to judge a position on a scale.

guidelines for structuring the discussion groups, identifying the goal of the discussion, setting the time limit, preparing a report (oral and/or written), and evaluating the performance of the participants. Figure 7.6 outlines the points to be considered in preplanning student-led group discussions.

After the discussion is planned, certain simple procedures should be followed for structuring the small groups.

• Divide the class into groups of approximately five students. Rotate students in groups so that those who do not ordinarily work together will have an opportunity to do so, and to break up groups of friends who may have seated themselves together deliberately.
• Arrange chairs in a circle if there is to be no outside observer of affective behavior. If affective behaviors are to be observed, arrange chairs in a semicircle. The teacher should be careful not to sit at the front.
• Establish a five-minute time period for group to select moderator and recorder/reporter.

Responsibilities of the moderator include (1) stating the purpose of

**133**

### Figure 7.6　Checklist for preplanning a discussion

1. Decide on subcompetencies or competencies to be developed (cognitive and/or affective).
2. Select and distribute checklists to be used. Recycle to Chapter 4, pp. 79–84.
3. Prepare and distribute outline of what is expected from students, including such things as:
   a. group conclusion
   b. summary of main points, ranked in order of importance
   c. group recommendations
   d. selection of representative to give oral report
   e. sample format for oral and/or written report
4. Establish time limits for:
   a. preplanning (discussion requiring research needs adequate time)
   b. selection of moderator and recorder/reporter
   c. discussion itself (decide when warning is to be given)
   d. preparation and presentation of report

the discussion, (2) setting guidelines for the time of each speaker and the points at which interruption for questions or comments may be made, (3) asking key questions if the discussion lags, and (4) summarizing the main points briefly.

Responsibilities of the recorder/reporter are (1) recording main points of the discussion, (2) making a brief oral report to the class after studying notes and conferring with the moderator, and (3) preparing a short written report containing a statement of the purpose of the discussion and a summary of the outcomes. This report should be approved by the moderator.

Since meaningful discussion can never develop in a pool of ignorance, each member of the group must prepare for the interaction by such activities as researching a topic in the library, watching a film, interviewing people who can make a helpful contribution, or just analyzing his or her own thoughts on the topic.

Often, the purpose of a student discussion is the preparation of a group report. In such cases, the teacher frequently chooses not to observe the group's deliberations (process evaluation), but evaluates the report as the effort of the group (product evaluation). Reports should follow guidelines given to the students at the time they undertake an assignment. A small group organized to perform a special function, such as the preparation of a report, is known as a committee. A committee works on specialized assignments and shares its findings with the larger group. In committees strong students help weaker ones, and the content of the course is enriched by reports based on the independent research of members of committee. A creative teacher finds various ways to employ committee organization.

Group discussions are considerably more effective in enabling students to achieve high levels of cognitive and affective behaviors than are the traditional teacher-centered classes. Although group discussions are time consuming, the learning gained through participation is likely to be retained far longer than that spoon-fed by a teacher.

## Performing and Observing

An old Chinese proverb says, "I hear, I forget; I see, I know; I do, and I understand." Learning activities that involve either performing or observing the performance of others include role playing, skits, debates, panel discussions, field trips, demonstrations, projects, television, computers, games, and simulations and work experience. Both performing and observing require active participation and provide the common experiences upon which a group might base discussions.

ROLE PLAYING.   Rather than discuss how a person should act in a specific situation, students act and react spontaneously as they interact with each other. According to Price, et al., *role playing* is a method of human interaction that involves realistic behavior in an imaginary situation.

It (1) presents alternative courses of action, (2) develops better understanding of problems, (3) develops better understanding of the other people's points of view, (4) prepares student for meeting future situations, (5) increases spontaneity and encourages creative interaction, (6) gives students practice in what they have learned, (7) illustrates principles from the course content, (8) maintains and/or arouses student interest, (9) stimulates discussion, (10) develops more effective problem-solving ability, and (11) develops desirable attitudes. (Price, p. 5)

Role playing offers many ways of achieving an affective competency such as "Consistently display tact in dealing with others." For instance, students may be presented with a case study involving a cooperative office work experience student whose supervisor assigns considerably more work than can be performed during work hours. Two students may volunteer to play the parts of the supervisor and student solving their problem. In role playing, both the performers and the observers have specific responsibilities. The performers present their solution, either spontaneously or after a planning session, while the nonperformers develop criteria for evaluation. After the role play and discussion, members of the class should be able to develop a principle to be followed in meeting similar office situations (evaluation level of the cognitive domain).

An interesting variation is to have two groups volunteer for role playing. One team performs while the second team waits outside the room. After both performances and their evaluations, each team is responsible for defending its solution before the group. If one solution is unacceptable, the group can be asked for a preferable solution. This gives the players a chance to demonstrate what they have learned from the evaluation and discussion. Another variation has the players switch roles in the middle of the presentation.

A common role-playing situation is the initial job interview, with one team of actors depicting the correct way and the other team, the wrong way, of handling one's self. An adult guest may serve as interviewer.

SKITS.   Because students enjoy dramatizing, *skits,* which are short, usually humorous, dramatic presentations, are useful in illustrating the right and wrong ways of greeting a caller, confronting a supervisor or coworker, shopping, and so on. Skits frequently provide valuable common learning experiences for a group prior to discussion.

FIELD TRIPS.    Field trips supply a wealth of information that can be used in discussions. Students should always be apprised of what they are to observe. In this way, they become active observers and are able to take notes on things seen and heard. A group of no more than fifteen can adequately observe a demonstration or a piece of equipment and report to the class on what has been seen. The teacher is responsible for detailed planning with both students and representatives at the visiting place. To preplan the teacher should do the following:

1.  Contact the office or business to be visited for permission to bring students.
2.  Clarify to the business representative exactly what students are to see and the purpose of the trip.
3.  Give the specific number of students to expect.
4.  Suggest that the company provide a briefing session prior to the tour so that students will be adequately prepared for observing.
5.  Make specific arrangements concerning the time of arrival and departure.
6.  Arrange with authorities at the school for permission to make the trip and follow school policy about getting parents' permission, arranging for transportation, and notifying other teachers whose classes may be missed.
7.  Hold a planning session with all students to identify the purpose of the trip and prepare a list of what they should look for. Better yet, make committee or individual assignments of specific responsibilities for enlarging the scope of the learning. For instance, one committee may be responsible for finding out what employment tests are used while another investigates opportunities for employees to obtain further education.
8.  Discuss what the group saw and listen to reports of special assignments.

To communicate effectively with those who have not taken the same field trip, many teachers ask each student to prepare a summary. These reports may be collected, combined, duplicated, and distributed to those who missed the trip—an excellent opportunity for experience in writing.

DEMONSTRATIONS.    Students learn more by seeing than by hearing, and the demonstration combines both seeing and hearing. Either a student or the teacher may be the demonstrator. Specific steps in the demonstration include: (1) explanation and demonstration by demonstrator, (2) imitation by observer, (3) evaluation by demonstrator and observer, (4) redemonstration if necessary, (5) observer imitation, (6) reevaluation by demonstrator and observer. Steps are repeated as many times as necessary for individual learners who need recycling; usually not for an entire group. Demonstrations may be done directly in front of the class or shown on film, filmstrips, television, videotape, or transparencies.

A teacher planning demonstrations must consider several facts.

1.  Demonstrations from the front of the room are frequently ineffective; therefore, the teacher should demonstrate to a small group or to an individual so that each person can see each step of the operation.
2.  Since teachers of many business subjects find themselves doing the identical demonstration many times for different students, consideration should be given to videotaping a demonstration.
3.  Demonstrations should not be considered a one-time method of presenting material. It may be necessary to repeat them for students whose performance indicates that they cannot imitate the demonstration.

AUDIO-VISUAL PRESENTATIONS. Films, filmstrips, and slide-sound presentations involve the learner in observing. The teacher will want to form a pattern when selecting audio-visual materials and may be guided by the following suggestions:

1.  Decide whether the film, filmstrip, or slide/sound presentation selected contributes toward the goal sought.
2.  As you preview the audio-visual, jot down specific guides to present to the viewer. Duplicate these guides and present to the students a few minutes before the viewing takes place.
3.  If you decide the material does not serve the purpose for which it was rented, return it unused.
4.  Evaluate the effectiveness of the audiovisual with students immediately to determine if they were able to absorb the points you identified.
5.  Arrange for viewings out of class for students who need them.
6.  Once an audio-visual is identified as valuable, prepare a documentation of it on a small card, complete with the topic, source, goal for which it is to be used, and a listing of points to be observed. A reference file of this type is indispensable.

Some teachers involve students in filming or in taking slides which can be synchronized with sound on tapes. See Blockhus in Selected Readings for hints on developing slide/sound presentations. This technique may be helpful for conveying to a large group what was seen on a field trip by a small group.

PROJECTS. Many students enjoy learning through projects. A *project* is a planned learning activity that requires students to go outside of the traditional classroom and interact with representatives of the business community. (For a description of project plan as used in distributive education, see Chapter 18.) A group of typewriting students trying to achieve a performance goal based on a time standard in producing envelopes might volunteer to address envelopes soliciting funds for a local charity. Retailing students might integrate buying, selling, managing, and financial competencies by operating a school store. A consumer class might make a comparative survey of the cost of food in various areas of a city for use by the local consumer council. An accounting class might volunteer to handle the accounting activities of a school cafeteria. Another example is Junior Achievement, sponsored by business people who guide students in organizing a corporation, manufacturing a product, advertising and selling the product, and liquidating the enterprise at the end of the school year.

THE COMPUTER.    Computers (hardware) have three functions as learning resources. First, computers are used by students as tools in problem solving. The *terminals* (typewriters connected to the computer by telephone lines) may be located in the same building with the computer or hundreds of miles away. Second, computer-managed instruction (CMI) utilizes the computer for pretesting, testing, and maintaining student records; and for dial access systems through which a student dials for a particular lecture, film, or performance (software). (See p. 158 for an example of CMI output of a student record.) The student then views the film or listens to the tape at either a television screen or through earphones. The computer activates the tape or film to run.

Third, computer-assisted instruction (CAI) utilizes the computer for supplying drills and/or tutorial programs (software) to students sitting at terminals. CAI of tutorial programs is considerably more expensive than any other computer learning resource because it requires thousands of hours for a teacher to produce a usable tutorial program. Progressive community colleges now use tutorial CAI to teach accounting, data processing, and even typewriting. As progress is made in its development, software (teaching programs) is likely to be applied to other subjects as well. Federal funding offers schools the opportunity to experiment in tutorial program construction, which frees the teacher to work with individual students. Experiments have proved it to be an effective learning resource for many students.

TELEVISION.    Experiments utilizing television as an instructional resource have achieved mixed results. There is sufficient evidence that when television is integrated with other learning resources, results are effective. As with other resources, though, students must know the purpose of the experience and have an awareness of what they are to look and listen for.

When television presentations are combined with some type of student-teacher interaction, students respond more favorably than when no teacher contact is available during the presentation or immediately thereafter. Students may interrupt the presentation by contacting the teacher who monitors the group watching the television. If the monitor deems the question worthy of interruption, he or she simply signals the teacher-presenter by telephone and poses the student's question for the presenter to answer. Some monitors have students write down questions which are screened at the end of the presentation. Immediately following television presentations to large groups, small-group discussions provide feedback of what the students derived from the presentation. Also, the discussion serves as a reinforcer.

Television permits the teacher to bring into the classroom discussions by outside specialists, lectures by prominent figures, or demonstrations of new office equipment. Its use is unlimited, and the true potential of instructional television has only begun to be realized in business classes.

SIMULATIONS. Simulations are not only a means of evaluating students (recycle to Chapter 4, p. 76), they are also valuable learning activities. A *simulation* is a reproduction of a real situation, containing elements which the author identifies as necessary to the goals. Twelker explains that simulations include the important aspects of reality and eliminate the unimportant ones (Twelker, p. 133). According to Sabin, they provide an opportunity for students to experience the type of input, working conditions, and quantity and quality standards that would be encountered in an actual employment situation. At the same time, they provide several advantages: (1) There is fast feedback. The time factor can be shortened so that students can quickly see the consequences of their actions. (2) The teacher has control over the variables and can introduce peripheral elements that exist on the job after students have begun to develop confidence. (3) There is a low risk factor; the teacher can minimize the consequences of failure. (4) The cost of operating a simulation can be less per student than that incurred with on-the-job training. Simulations can be used in a wide variety of business subjects, including accounting, data processing, basic business, and distributive education. They are often based upon costs and other quantitative data because of the desirability of presenting students with hard data on which to base their actions and decisions. Simulations may be either obtained from publishers or designed and duplicated by the classroom teacher.

One area in which simulations are frequently used is office education. Sabin explains the distinction among the three different kinds of simulations. These three kinds of simulations are common to a variety of business subjects in addition to office education.

There are three significant kinds of office simulations. The first is the model office, and this is the form that is currently attracting the greatest attention. A model office is typically based on a real operation, it contains a number of work stations that reflect a realistic office organization, and it permits a realistic flow of work. As input comes into this office (in the form of orders, payments, inquiries, and so on), it generates a flow of work through the various job stations so that at each stage some form of output is produced. While the individual jobs within the model office may be limited in scope, the fact is that all the jobs, taken in aggregate, cover the full range of objectives for a well-trained office worker from A to Z. Therefore, the office education student who rotates through all of the jobs in the model office and performs them satisfactorily demonstrates beyond question that he has achieved the behavioral objectives that were established for him.

The second kind of simulation focuses on just one of those job stations. Although it does not typically allow for interaction, it does permit you to simulate the way input comes in on the job, the conditions under which the job will be performed, and the standards of quality and quantity that would be applied on the job.

The third kind of simulation does not attempt to simulate a total job; it deals only with the decision-making process that the student must go through in resolving problems that will occur on the job. These may be problems that involve a management decision, they may be human relations problems that can occur between people on staff, or they may involve problems of communication with people outside the company. They may be presented in the form of case problems or as role-playing situations. In either case, the student must go through a certain process of analysis to arrive at a decision—which is the output in this instance. (Sabin, pp. 5-7)

GAMES. Like simulations, games are becoming increasingly popular as learning activities. Blucker describes a game as "a contest conducted according to a set of rules and undertaken in pursuit of educational (or learning) objectives as well as for enjoyment" (Blucker, p. i).

One commercially prepared accounting game involves teams of students in problem-solving situations which result in net income or net loss to a hypothetical business. Each team analyzes input data and makes decisions, which are recorded onto punched cards. After these cards are fed into the computer and analyzed, the results are returned to the teams in the form of printouts showing profit or loss to the business. The winning team is the one that makes the most profit for the business. If the teacher chooses, teams restudy their decisions in order to identify those that were detrimental to the business.

While both games and simulations may involve students in decision making and may in many ways approximate reality, there are several basic differences between games and simulations:

1. The input for a simulation should approximate real life input; the input for a game is often the result of chance.
2. A simulation requires students to perform as they would in real life; a game involves symbolic performance (often the movement of a pawn on a board).
3. The outcome of a simulation is feedback for each individual participant; the outcome of a game is usually some degree of winning or losing.

WORK EXPERIENCE. This method of instruction consists of programs that use the cooperative efforts of the school and community to direct students in developing occupational understanding from direct participation in the work environment.

There are three basic types of work experience education: exploratory work experience, general work experience, and vocational work experience.

The student who participates in exploratory work experience has an opportunity to sample and observe a wide variety of jobs. The object is to help students determine their own suitability (or lack of it) for the jobs studied.

General work experience provides maturing experiences for students through supervised employment and in-school instruction. Employment need not be related to the student's occupational goals. The object of general work experience is to help students become productive, responsible individuals.

Vocational work experience may also be referred to as *supervised cooperative work experience.* Occupational preparation is provided through a cooperative arrangement between the school and employer. On-the-job experience, in an occupation that is directly related to the vocational objectives of the student, is coordinated and supervised by a teacher from the cooperating school. In-school instruction is directly related to on-the-job experience and to occupational goals. The purpose of vocational work experience is to help students in developing and refining occupational competencies, adjusting to the employment environment, and advancing to higher-level positions.

## Learning Activities to Develop Communication Skills

While it is understood that any learning activity selected must contribute to the attainment of the stated goal, many learning activities serve a dual purpose by also contributing to students' communication competencies. The importance of communication competencies is substantiated by the available task analyses. (Recycle to Chapter 3, p. 49–53.)

The teacher planning learning activities for a student who is striving to operate a duplicating machine may recommend reading the instructional manual, and listening to and observing a demonstration of the machine's operation. Two communication skills are involved—reading and listening. The student is strengthening both skills while working toward the goal of machine operation.

Relatively few students enroll in separate business communication courses. Those who do not may be insensitive to the importance of communication unless the teacher of each business subject establishes activities which strengthen skills in reading, writing, speaking, listening, and discussing whenever possible. Responsibility must be fixed in all courses for achieving predetermined performance goals for reading, writing, speaking, and listening.

Figure 7.7 illustrates the learning activities the teacher of each business course may employ to involve students in all of the communication areas. Reading is placed first in the figure because each business teacher has multiple opportunities to utilize reading activities. Students read for the purpose of following instructions, gaining ideas, and comprehending content. In courses where the student is to follow a procedure (for instance, typewriting, data processing, accounting, business mathematics), the student must *read intensively* in order to follow directions. In subjects in which the textbook serves as the major source of content, students must *read intensively* to gather knowledge of facts and terms and to comprehend ideas. In some courses students will *read extensively,* beyond the textbook and assigned enrichment readings, even scanning a wide range of materials.

Figure 7.7  Learning activities to strengthen communication skills

| Subject | Reading | Writing | Speaking & Discussing | Listening |
|---|---|---|---|---|
| **General Business & Consumer Education** | Extensive: Textbooks and transparencies, articles from newspapers and magazines. | Extensive: Research conclusions, essays, and tests. | Extensive: Large-group, small-group, outsiders. General discussions, panel discussions. Debates. Role playing. | Extensive: To ideas of others, to form concepts. |
| **Accounting** | Intensive: Textbooks, transparencies, and problems. | Limited: Analysis of rough data and tests. | Limited: Instructor and peers. Possibly small group discussion for recycled students. | Intensive: To instructions. |
| **Shorthand** | Intensive: Letters to learn how business is conducted. EDL pacing materials. | Limited: English mechanics. Composition of replies to dictated material. | Limited: Instructor and peers. | Intensive: To instructions. To reader while student proof-reads work. To dictation. (Must have high level of aural acuity.) |
| **Typewriting** | Intensive: Instructions and subject matter about mechanics and machine operation. EDL pacing materials. | Extensive: Composing. Applying rules of English mechanics and typewriter usage. | Limited: Instructor and peers. | Intensive: To instructions. To subject matter about mechanics. To pacing tapes. |
| **Office Practice, Clerical Practice, & Secretarial Practice** | Intensive: Textbooks, workbooks, minipacs, instructions. Extensive: Outside sources about job opportunities. | Extensive: Spelling, punctuation, and other mechanics. Composing messages and simple letters following instructions. Lists. Reports. Memorandums. Tests. | Extensive: Instructor and peers about procedures and human relations problems. Small committee investigations of the business community. Role playing. Receptionist and telephone duties. | Intensive: To instructions. Extensive: To outside speakers and interviewees. To telephone conversations. To ideas of others. To office callers. |

Figure 7.7 (Continued)

| Subject | Reading | Writing | Speaking & Discussing | Listening |
|---------|---------|---------|----------------------|-----------|
| **Simulated Business Office** | Intensive: Procedures, organization charts, incoming correspondence. Proofreading. | Extensive: Messages, lists, letters, reports, procedures. | Extensive: Instructor, supervisor, peers, discussing human relations problems, organization of work, and scheduling. | Intensive: To instruction. To problems in human relations and procedures. To criticism. To telephone callers and visitors. |
| **Business Arithmetic** | Intensive: Instructions. Word problems. Figures. EDL packing materials. | Limited: Tests. Statements justifying decisions. | Limited: Instructor and peers. Little group interaction. | Intensive: To instructions. |
| **Data Processing** | Intensive: Textbooks, problems, punched cards. Flow charts. Computer programs. Computer printouts. | Limited: Composition. Summaries of printouts. | Extent depends on job. Communication with people who will use data, with instructor or computer. Possible small-group discussions of capabilities or learning problems. | Intensive: To instructions. To statements of needs of various departments. To lectures of instructor. |
| **Business Law** | Intensive: Textbooks, cases, problems. | Extensive: Tests and case analyses. | Intensive: Large and small groups. To explain and persuade. | Intensive: To cases and principles. Possibly testimonies in court. |
| **Cooperative Office Work Experience** | Intensive: Company and school manuals and procedures. Correspondence and reports. | Extensive: Messages, letters, memorandums under close supervision. Short reports analyzing experiences for related in-school learnings. | Intensive: Supervisor, teacher-coordinator, and peers. May involve small-group discussions. | Intensive: To directions. To evaluations, and criticisms. Extensive: To other workers, interacting with each other. To case problems in human relations. |
| **Business Communication** | | | **See discussion on page 256.** | |

Writing is placed second in the figure because most business courses provide opportunities for writing practice. While evaluation of student writing consumes teacher time, the benefits of written activities to student learning are indisputable.

Listening and speaking consume the greater part of the time spent in communicating with others. More than half of the office day is spent in listening and/or speaking. Even a greater proportion of the distributive worker's day is spent in these two activities. Also, two basic means of obtaining consumer information are speaking and listening. Speaking and listening are interdependent in discussing, for the student must hear what has been said before responding intelligently.

Consider how many hours the student listens to teachers, talks with other students and teachers, and engages in class discussions. Everybody needs to communicate effectively, yet it is estimated that people listen at only 25 percent efficiency. If one does not listen and grasp the meaning of what is being said, it is difficult to respond intelligently. Students develop listening competencies only by concentrated experiences in listening. Listening, like reading, must often be done *intensively*, particularly by the student seeking facts or instructions. The learner seeking enrichment *listens extensively* and extracts from a mass of material the ideas to be retained after listening to several different speakers.

Subjects involving technical skills offer few occasions for students to develop speaking competencies; other courses offer limitless opportunities. One strong argument for small-group organization is the environment it provides for students to express ideas, refute the ideas of others, and respond to arguments which are irrefutable. While student speaking is sometimes considered time consuming by teachers, the outcomes of an individual's speaking effectiveness and greater self-confidence before large and small groups outweigh teachers' reservations.

Some teachers feel they are abdicating their responsibilities if they are not performing as the dominant figure in a class, but the teacher who is guided by student goals to improve interpersonal reactions provides multiple opportunities for students to communicate with each other as well as with the teacher. Most business teachers attempt to use committees, panel discussions, field trips, debates, and so forth, but need practice in using all of these learning activities effectively. The teacher who uses the ideas for communications in Figure 7.2 and follows suggestions made in this chapter, will develop expertise in involving students in communication skills at every opportunity and will seek learning activities to involve students in communications whenever appropriate.

## Selection of Learning Resources

One of the most difficult tasks for some teachers is selecting appropriate learning resources. In some schools, specialists are available to assist the teacher. In some instances, schools have instructional resource centers in addition to specialists.

## Published Materials

Business education has been more fortunate than many fields in the quality and quantity of supplementary materials accompanying textbooks. Workbooks contain materials which enable students to apply recently learned ideas or concepts. They save both the teacher's and the students' time in preparing forms and in identifying specific areas for practice. Workbooks should be used intelligently, though, so that completion of exercises in a workbook does not become mere busywork. If they relate to the goal toward which the student is working, they are appropriate.

Textbooks or workbooks which contain practice work are frequently accompanied by a teacher's key or teacher's manual (sometimes called source books). The keys contain correct answers for exercises or problems, and the manuals contain suggestions the teacher might follow in using the exercises in the text. Each beginning teacher should inquire of the publisher as to the availability of a key and teacher's manual. Duplicated tests or printed tests may also be available from the publisher; these sometimes are supplied to users of the textbooks. Many of the tests are accompanied by norms to assist the teacher in determining how well his or her students perform in relation to others who have taken the tests. These norms should not be used for grading purposes in a competency-based education program.

While catalogs of leading publishers of business education materials list all available items, learning materials developed by federal grants are also available, usually through the state departments of education in states where the materials were developed. While the staff at the school's instructional resource center can be most helpful, they may not be able to identify all available materials in a given subject area. The best advice is for teachers to read the professional journals regularly. *The Balance Sheet, The Business Education World, Business Education Forum, Journal of Business Education,* and *Journal of Data Education,* as well as others, carry advertisements, reports on current media, and descriptions of new developments. Also, most of the special projects resulting in teaching materials created by teachers, often with federal funds, are offered on microfiche available through the Education Resources Information Center (ERIC) network. Microfiches measure 4½ by 6 inches and each microfiche may contain up to 70 pages of printed material which has been filmed on the fiche. Reading microfiche requires a reading machine. Most libraries have special equipment to produce photocopies of the material.

Vocational educators are fortunate in that all materials in vocational-technical education are disseminated through ERIC. Teachers interested in using the indexes, arranged by subject matter as well as by author, should contact the Vocational Education Division in their state, to ascertain the location of the nearest ERIC microfiche library. Many states have computer facilities capable of conducting searches for certain topics and will send the teacher a printout of the titles and microfiche numbers of materials located in the search. Some states make microfiche available to any teacher who makes a request. It may be read with a microfiche reader in the local school or library.

## Audio-Visual Materials

Films, filmstrips, sound slides, and other audio-visual materials may often be borrowed or rented from the state departments of education or university depositories. Commercial agencies and publishers are also sources for rental or purchase. The addresses of such suppliers are found at the back of the book.

## Selection Guidelines

These criteria guide the teacher in selecting learning activities for students: (1) Is the learning activity appropriate for the goal toward which the student is working? (2) Do the activities selected involve multiple senses of the student? (3) Does the student possess the prerequisite competencies to perform the activities selected? (4) Does the use of the activity justify the cost? (For instance, the use of CAI may be too expensive for a school despite its effectiveness in assisting students to learn.) (5) Is all of the equipment needed by the student and/or teacher available and on location when needed? (6) Is the quality of audiovisuals technically acceptable?

### Self-Assessment 7-2 (Answers on p. 148.)

1. Which of the following items does not apply when selecting a textbook or other reading materials?
   a. reading level of each student
   b. readability of reading material
   c. national reputation of authors
   d. appropriateness for goals being sought
2. Which resource is not appropriate in the development of listening abilities of students?
   a. study guide and/or workbook
   b. teacher-led discussions
   c. tapes
   d. student discussion groups
3. Which learning activity is inappropriate for the goal of "Given two income statements for one company for two different years, **identify** the factors which account for differences in net income and describe how each factor affects income"?

    a. discussion
    b. cooperative work experience in accounting department
    c. committee report
    d. project involving analysis of statements

4. Which learning activity is most appropriate to be used first for the goal of "Given a problem on inventory control, **construct** a flowchart to illustrate each department involved and the flow of each document from its initiation to its being filed"?
    a. discussion
    b. reading assignment
    c. field trip
    d. work experience

5. Which learning activity is *inappropriate* for the goal "**Identify** all factors to be considered in selecting a new home and rank them in order of importance to your family"?
    a. discussion with parents
    b. reading assignment
    c. lecture
    d. small-group discussions with students

6. Which learning activities seem to offer the greatest potential for the goal "From handwritten rough draft copy marked with proofreading symbols, **prepare** a manuscript with two carbons and no uncorrected errors"?
    a. lecture, field trip, discussion, performance at typewriter
    b. role playing, lecture, simulation, and field trip
    c. debate, discussion, film, and performance at typewriter
    d. reading, lecture, demonstration, and performance at typewriter

7. Which learning activities offer the greatest potential for the goal of "Given a problem situation involving conflict between two coworkers in the office, **describe** the best solution to the problem"?
    a. reading, lecture, demonstration, and role playing
    b. role playing, discussion, and skit
    c. role playing, discussion, and group report
    d. field trip, film, group discussion, and work experience

## Summary

The teacher strives to establish the best environment in which learning may take place, choosing and applying different teaching-learning strategies to help students of varying needs achieve different goals. Decisions which confront the teacher who structures teaching-learning strategies involve the organizational patterns, the activities, and the selection of learning resources.

    Learning may take place through large-group instruction, small-group instruction or interaction, or by individualized learning. Individually prescribed learning and individually paced learning are becoming increasingly popular as new instructional materials are developed by publishers and classroom teachers. No single organizational pattern should be used exclusively; students need interactions with other students as well as with the teacher that small-group activities provide. They also need, of course, learning activities which work in terms of their own individual needs.

Learning activities may be classified as reading, writing, speaking, listening, discussing, observing, and performing. A major role of every business teacher is to assess the student's reading, writing, listening, and speaking abilities and to provide learning activities which strengthen these skills as well as assist in achieving subject matter goals. No reading materials—textbooks, workbooks, programmed materials, modules, or study guides—should be selected without evaluation of their readability and the reading levels of students who will use them. Planned opportunities for interaction among students can assist in improving their communication skills. Continuous evaluation of process as well as product is necessary if stated goals in the interaction process are to be reached.

Identifying and selecting learning activities is a time-consuming task, yet an essential one if teachers are to keep abreast of rapid changes in learning resources. The teacher who examines various materials must apply objective criteria. These criteria include the appropriateness of the learning activity for the goal sought, the involvement of multiple senses, the student's ability to use the activity, its cost, the availability of equipment when needed, and the quality of audio-visual materials in terms of readability, visibility, and audibility. Professional journals and ERIC offer valuable information on all types of learning resources as well as publishers of business education materials, who offer not only textbooks and workbooks, but complete modules and learning pacs, keys, teachers' manuals, and multiple audio-visual materials.

## Answers to Self-Assessments

**7-1 (p. 123)**
**1.** c **2.** a **3.** b **4.** c **5.** b

**7-2 (pp. 146–147)**
**1.** c **2.** a **3.** b **4.** b **5.** c **6.** d **7.** b

## SELECTED READINGS

AMIDON, EDMUND J., AND NED A. FLANDERS., *The Role of the Teacher in the Classroom: A Manual for Understanding and Improving Teacher Classroom Behavior,* rev. ed., Association for Productive Teaching, Inc., 1040 Plymouth Building, Minneapolis, Minn., 1967.

BLOCKHUS, WANDA, "Slide/Sound Media in Basic Business Classes," *Business Education Forum,* Vol. 27, No. 2, November 1970, p. 55.

BLUCKER, GWEN, "An Annotated Bibliography of Games and Simulations in Consumer Education," University of Illinois, Urbana, Ill., and Office of the Superintendent of Public Instruction, Springfield, Ill., 1973.

BROWN, CAROL, "The Cloze Technique," from "Reading in Business Education," an unpublished report of the proceedings of a workshop sponsored by Edward Brower and Susan M. Glazer at Rider College, Trenton, N.J., June 1972.

BUTZ, ROY J., Project Director, *Vocational Reading Power Project,* ESEA, Title III, 1971–72. Available through J. Kenneth Cerny, Associate Director of Research, Oakland Schools, Reading and Language Center, 2100 Pontiac Lake Road, Pontiac Lake, Michigan 48054.

COTRELL, CALVIN J., AND EDWARD F. HAUCK (EDS.), "The Learning Systems Approach to Instruction and the Changing Role of the Educator," *Educational Media in Vocational and Technical Education,* The Center for Research and Leadership Development in Vocational and Technical Education, Ohio State University, Columbus, Ohio, 1967.

COTRELL, CALVIN J., ET AL., *Model Curricula for Vocational and Technical Teacher Education: Report No. V, General Objectives Set II,* The Center for Vocational and Technical Education, Research and Development Series, No. 78, Ohio State University, Columbus, Ohio, September 1972.

DALE, EDGAR, AND JEANNE S. CHALL, *A Formula for Predicting Readability,* Bureau of Educational Research, Ohio State University, Columbus, Ohio, 1967.

DAWSON, HELAINE S., *On the Outskirts of Hope: Educating Youth from Poverty Areas,* McGraw-Hill Book Company, New York, 1968.

*Educational Technology,* Vol. 8, No. 1, January 15, 1968.

EISELE, JAMES E., AND ROBERT S. HARNACK, "Improving Teacher Decision-Making and Individualizing Instruction," *The Quarterly,* Vol. 18, No. 4, May 1967, p. 8.

FLANDERS, NED. A., *Analyzing Teacher Behavior,* Addison-Wesley, Boston, 1970.

HARMS, HARM, ET AL., *Methods of Teaching Business and Distributive Education,* South-Western Publishing Company, Cincinnati, Ohio, 1972.

HOWES, VIRGIL M., *Individualization of Instruction: A Teaching Strategy,* The Macmillan Company, New York, 1970.

JOYCE, BRUCE A., *The Teacher and His Staff: Man, Media, and Machines,* National Education Association, Washington, D.C., 1967.

KINGHORN, JOHN RYE, AND JON S. PADEN, "Individualized Instruction Especially Helpful to Non-Conforming Students," *Pennsylvania School Journal,* February 1971, pp. 204–205, 235, 237.

KOURILSKY, MARILYN, *The Use of an Adversary Approach in Teaching Economics,* Monograph 122, South-Western Publishing Company, Cincinnati, Ohio, 1970.

PRICE, RAY G., ET AL., "Basic Business," *Changing Methods of Teaching Business Subjects: National Business Education Association Yearbook,* 1972, pp. 1–10.

SABIN, WILLIAM, "Simulation in the Seventies: An Overview," *Business Education World,* Vol. 52, No. 1, September-October 1971, pp. 5-7.

TORKELSON, GERALD, *What Research Says to the Teacher—Instructional Media,* National Education Association, Washington, D.C., 1967.

TWELKER, PAUL A., "Simulation and Media," in *Educational Aspects of Simulation,* P. J. Tansey (ed.), McGraw-Hill Book Company, London, 1971.

## PERFORMANCE GOAL

Using any one of the three evaluations planned for the performance goal for Chapter 4 on page 66, **describe** whether you are using criterion-referenced or norm-referenced measures or both and defend your analysis in terms of the material in this chapter.

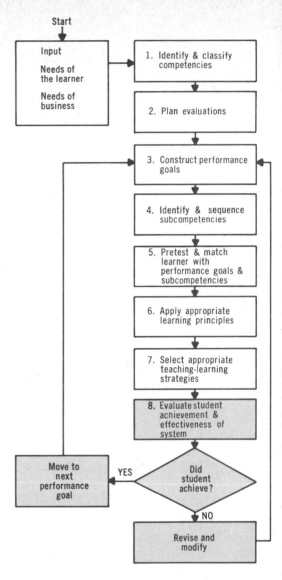

Start

Input

Needs of the learner

Needs of business

1. Identify & classify competencies

2. Plan evaluations

3. Construct performance goals

4. Identify & sequence subcompetencies

5. Pretest & match learner with performance goals & subcompetencies

6. Apply appropriate learning principles

7. Select appropriate teaching-learning strategies

8. Evaluate student achievement & effectiveness of system

Did student achieve?

YES

Move to next performance goal

NO

Revise and modify

# CHAPTER 8

# Evaluating Student Achievement

Evaluation is an integral part of the teaching-learning system. To effectively implement the system, the teacher must continually measure each student's progress toward stated goals as the student moves through the system. Concomitantly, the teacher must use data emerging from student and system evaluations to revamp the system and make it more effective for each student.

The major purpose of evaluation is to determine the progress a student has made toward attainment of a goal. Evaluations also serve several other purposes. Pretests measuring the level of students as they enter learning situations are important for selecting competencies and subcompetencies. Self-evaluations provide immediate feedback. Frequent evaluations of en route goals help the teacher and student assess progress toward the assigned performance goal. End-of-unit or end-of-course evaluations help determine student learning. Performance goal evaluations help the teacher determine the effectiveness of the system. In addition, any type of student evaluation can provide information for the determination of grades.

Figure 8.1 illustrates the use of multiple evaluations of a student moving through the learning activities to achieve one en route goal. As the student completes each evaluation (2a, 3a, or 4b), he or she determines whether to proceed to another en route goal or to recycle to other learning experiences. A student may participate in one successful self-evaluation and need no other learning activity for the particular en route goal. A second student may need to be involved in additional learning activities and self-evaluations.

Because the learning system is designed so that a student is engaged in multiple self-evaluations, to determine readiness for evaluation on any

Figure 8.1   Teaching-learning strategies and
evaluations for one en route goal

**En route goal no. 8:**   In dialogue with another student who plays the role of a
caller, **demonstrate** your ability to record a message on appropriate form with
complete accuracy.

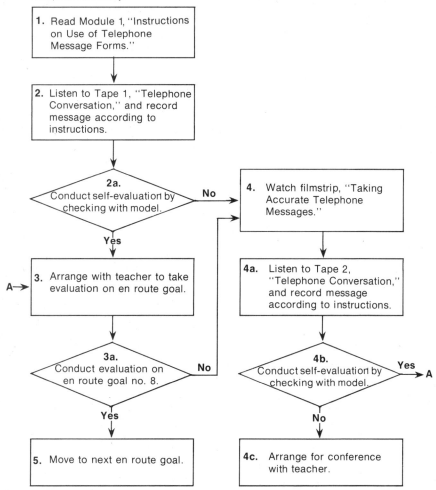

en route goal or performance goal, attention is focused on successes rather
than failures. Such emphasis improves instruction and creates a supportive
environment in which students may seek assistance.

## Using Norm- and Criterion-Referenced Measures

Competency-based education implies criterion-referenced measures because of the emphasis on the learner's achievement; however, some guidance should be given for the use of norm-referenced measures. (Recycle

to Chapter 3, p. 67.) The teacher is bound to make some comparisons among students, perhaps to compare the progress of students in one group with others in schools across the country. Even if the data for the comparison comes from criterion-referenced measures, the actual comparison becomes a norm-referenced measure. The teacher who says, "Ellen completed twenty performance goals this year, five more than any other student in the class," is using criterion-referenced data for a norm-referenced measure. The teacher who says, "Ed is a fine boy, but he does not progress as rapidly as Joe," is using a norm-referenced measure.

Norm-referenced measures are appropriate in:

1. Evaluating reading levels to determine which students need remedial assistance or to select materials suitable to the reading levels of the learners.
2. Comparing student performances on tests for which norms have been established. Examples are the National Business Entrance Tests in Business Fundamentals, Bookkeeping, General Office Clerical, Machine Calculation, Stenography, and Typewriting. (See Selected Readings at the end of this chapter.) Teachers may use the tests to determine how their students compare with those in another class or school. Percentile tables accompany these tests so that a teacher may ascertain how many students who have taken the test perform better or worse than any given student.
3. Using a standardized test to determine the need for work in basic mathematics.

Teachers often use norm-referenced measures in discussing students' performance with other teachers, in plotting scores on a test to determine percentages within each grade category, and in recommending students to employers. Historically, most schools have employed norm-referenced measures in evaluating student achievement. The practice has resulted in ranking students within any group. Such measures provide practically no information about the degree of competency a student exhibits, nor do they reveal what a student can do under given circumstances. In contrast, criterion-referenced measures provide precise information about what a student can do at the end of a course or program. Also, criterion-referenced measures enable the teacher to measure student achievement between pre- and posttests. Norm-referenced measures may reveal that a student achieved a high score on a test, but cannot reveal what was learned in a given class. He or she may have entered the class with competencies developed to such a level that little or no actual learning was necessary to perform at a high level on the test.

Both measures are used by teachers, but someone who is interested in ascertaining precisely what learning takes place employs criterion-referenced measures regularly. When the need does arise to compare performances, norm-referenced measures are used cautiously with the knowledge that there are severe limitations in comparing individuals.

*Accountability,* the justification for education in terms of both time and money spent, has become a major issue in the past few years. The school is accountable to the public which provides funds for its support and must be able to document the degree of actual learning that takes place in a classroom. The concept of accountability pervades the entire educational system. The student is accountable to the teacher, and vice versa. The teacher is responsible to the administrator, and the administrator is answerable to the board of education and ultimately to the community. Teachers who are held accountable find that criterion-referenced measures provide hard data with which to document their effectiveness as teachers.

## Student Achievement

The teacher is responsible for facilitating learning, but the student is also responsible for learning. Personal factors may contribute to achievement or nonachievement. Recent studies show that attributes of other students in the school influence a student's ability to learn, as do characteristics of the student's family.

If a student does not succeed in an evaluation, the teacher, the student, or both may be at fault; but, it is the teacher's responsibility to ascertain the reason. Some of the questions to guide the teacher in analyzing the situation are:

1. Was the goal attainable for the student? Physical or emotional problems may prevent learning, or poor reading ability may be a deterrent.
2. Were all appropriate principles of learning applied during the learning process?
3. Were competencies in which the student is deficient identified correctly? A pretest provides a quick evaluation of a student's ability to meet a performance goal, but does not always identify deficiencies in all subcompetencies. Analysis by the teacher may pinpoint some deficiencies but not all; more study is required.
4. Were the teaching-learning strategies employed appropriate for the goal? for the learner? If the strategies did not employ multiple senses, the student may need exposure to strategies that involve additional senses. If too much listening was demanded, the student's attention span may have been shorter than the demands.
5. Were the evaluative instruments selected appropriate for the goal? Reanalysis of the performance goal and subcompetencies and of the evaluative instruments may reveal that the evaluation does not measure what it was intended to evaluate.
6. Were totally unrealistic time limitations imposed? The student may have failed because he or she needs more time, additional learning activities and more self-evaluations to check progress.
7. Did the teacher's attitude reveal even the slightest glimmer of negativism toward the student? Teacher attitude, a hidden factor in any learning system, may be a crucial element in nonachievement. Several studies reveal there is a direct relationship between student learning and teacher attitude toward the student. A teacher should examine his or her attitudes toward students, particularly toward one who is not achieving.

Studies have found that attitudes are affected by a student's relationships with other students and with the teacher, and may reflect the student's low or high self-image. It is possible that, despite a teacher's efforts to create an effective learning environment, some students will not learn. In general, though, the primary responsibility for student achievement is the teacher's. The teacher who maintains a constructive attitude toward each student will eliminate many hurdles which impede learning.

The teacher has a responsibility toward achieving as well as nonachieving students. He or she must determine whether the system can be improved upon to promote achievement at even higher levels.

Three factors are involved in analyzing student achievement. (1) Has the student achieved goals at the highest level possible? The system is structured to move each student toward increasingly higher-level goals. If a student has not achieved goals at the evaluation, analysis/synthesis, and application levels, he or she should be challenged to do so. The student who has reached goals at these levels in one area should be expected to achieve equally high goals in other related content areas. (2) Does the student's achievement correspond with his or her perception of success? Many students are satisfied with lower-level goals, while others continually strive to achieve goals at higher levels. If a student's perception of success is lower than his or her ability, it may need modification. (3) Is the student's achievement of affective behaviors measured? Since attitude is so important to success in a job or as a member of society, attention must always be directed toward affective performance goals.

## Solutions to Student Learning Problems

What situations confront the teacher, and what actions can resolve the problems? In the situations presented here solutions are based on the teaching-learning system:

- *Situation 1:* The student fails the first test of the performance goal. *Teacher Analysis:* Review the system, examining teaching-learning strategies and application of learning principles; determine whether unmastered subcompetencies were identified early and whether the student met each subcompetency before moving on to the next.
- *Situation 2:* The student fails a second evaluation of performance goal despite recycling through additional learning experiences and retesting on subcompetencies. *Teacher Analysis:* Reexamine the self-evaluations and evaluations used to determine if they actually measure the behaviors expected. Restructure evaluations and provide different teaching-learning strategies with frequent student-teacher conferences and periodic informal evaluations.
- *Situation 3:* Student refuses to begin working on a goal; simply sits and stares into space. *Teacher Analysis:* Try to determine the real reason for lack of interest. Perhaps there is a serious physical or emotional

problem. Convey to the student your sincere interest. The guidance department might be a source of help.

- *Situation 4:* Student exhibits hostile attitude toward you as teacher and acts defiant despite your efforts to assist. *Teacher Analysis:* Seek additional information on the student from the principal, guidance counselors, or other teachers. Does the student exhibit similar behavior in other classes? Reexamine your own attitude toward student. Find ways of helping him or her create a better image in eyes of peers. If student will accept responsibilities, assign important duties for him or her to perform such as leading group discussions, working on a committee to plan field trips, or planning for and introducing guest speakers.
- *Situation 5:* Student works on learning activities but is apathetic and seems to care little whether they are completed or not. *Teacher Analysis:* Talk informally with student to determine which activities he or she believes might be helpful. Perhaps the student considers the activities or even the goal irrelevant. If the goal is vital to later success, perhaps it may help the student to rearrange or add new learning activities, or adopt new strategies.

By no means do these represent all the situations a teacher may encounter; they are simply examples of how the teacher can identify a problem and plan solutions.

## Effectiveness of the System

A major value of data emerging from the teaching-learning system is its use in improving the system. The teacher can utilize data collected in evaluating students to determine the number of students who met each goal on the first attempt and the number who needed successive attempts after system modifications.

This data will pinpoint strengths and weaknesses of the total system and alert the teacher to performance goals which are either too easy or too difficult. They can then also determine whether the teaching-learning strategies are effective or ineffective for the learners, and whether the evaluative instruments actually measure the stated goals.

If examination of the evaluative data reveals that all students achieved the minimum level or above, the system is effective in its present form. A positive judgment may be made of the system. Frequently, however, an examination reveals the system is ineffective for certain students. For these students some adjustment in the system must be made. The continuous evaluation of the system enables a teacher to modify the system so that it works for all students.

## Grades

The recurring theme throughout this book is emphasis on the individual's achievement. Actual practice emphasizes the flexibility of scheduling so that no student is hampered by unrealistic time limitations. Each learner must be free to move toward a goal at a comfortable pace, although it is inevitable that some students need prodding. These students may not be able to achieve the performance goals by the end of the school year. Other students may achieve their goals before the end of the semester or year. They may then work toward higher-level goals or leave the class early. In this situation the teacher is confronted with a dilemma when grades are assigned. One solution that is being tested is a credit–no credit system, or pass-fail system. However, teachers entering a school system usually find that they are required to issue grades. Even if this is the case, they may be able to experiment with grading systems other than the traditional one.

Students and parents expect some type of evaluation of student accomplishment and effort. Also, schools of higher education require a record of student accomplishment in high school, although these reports are not always letter or percentage grades. Admittedly, there is no objective means of determining whether a student is working to capacity or has a positive attitude toward a given subject. Yet teachers make judgments on these factors and will probably continue to do so. Little hope exists that subjectivity in grading can be eliminated. However, objective measures in grading are based on the difference between the related behaviors a student reveals entering a learning process and those at the end of that process. First, then, students may be graded objectively on the number of goals attained in a given class.

Second, an objective judgment can be made on the basis of the goals reached at each of the levels of the cognitive domain, as well as those in the affective domain.

In almost any subject students achieve at different levels, and the judgments made on these two objective measures enable the teacher to assign to each student a grade which reflects the student's accomplishments. For purposes of illustration, it is assumed that for a given subject there are multiple goals in the cognitive and affective domains. The teacher using performance goals as guides may construct a scale such as that in Figure 8.2.

Figure 8.2 shows a domain-referenced grading system; each student receives a grade depending on the number of goals accomplished at different levels of the cognitive and affective domains. Were the teachers

Figure 8.2 Domain-referenced grading system

| | Cognitive Goals | | | Affective Goals | |
|---|---|---|---|---|---|
| Grade | Evaluation | Analysis/Synthesis | Application | High-Level | Low-Level |
| A | 2 | 4 | | 2 | |
| B | 1 | 4 | | 1 | |
| C | | 1 | 4 | | 2 |
| D | | | 2 | | 1 |

Figure 8.3  Computer printout of tasks student is able to do

CAPITAL AREA CAREER CENTER
INGHAM INTERMEDIATE SCHOOL DISTRICT
611 HAGADORN ROAD   MASON, MICHIGAN

CLERK-TYPIST

SUSAN RICH  NO. 10014

COMPLETED SKILL MODULES

*CORRECTING TYPING ERRORS
*PROOFREADING YOUR TYPED BUSINESS PAPERS
*DICTIONARY AND 20000 WORDS
*FINDING ZIP CODES IN A ZIP CODE DIRECTORY
*SELECTING CORRECT ENVELOPES FOR MAILING
*FOLDING AND STUFFING CORRESPONDENCE FOR MAILING
*TYPING A SHORT BUSINESS LETTER (LESS THAN 100 WORDS) IN FULL BLOCK STYLE
*TYPING A BUSINESS ENVELOPE

*SECRETARY AT ASTROLITE CANDY COMPANY
*TYPING AN INTEROFFICE MEMORANDUM
*TYPING A POSTAL CARD
*TYPING COPY FOR PHOTOCOPYING
*TYPING A SPIRIT MASTER FOR SPIRIT DUPLICATION.
*USING THE FLUID DUPLICATOR
*TYPING A MIMEOGRAPH STENCIL
*TYPING A SHORT BUSINESS LETTER (LESS THAN 100 WORDS) IN MODIFIED BLOCK STYLE
WITH NO PARAGRAPH INDEN
TYPING A SHORT BUSINESS LETTER (LESS THAN 100 WORDS) IN MODIFIED BLOCK STYLE
WITH PARAGRAPH INDENTIO
*TYPING A SHORT BUSINESS LETTER (LESS THAN 100 WORDS) IN INDENTED STYLE
*TYPING A SHORT BUSINESS LETTER (LESS THAN 100 WORDS) IN SIMPLIFIED STYLE

Figure 8.4   Capital Area Career Center Certificate of Completion

## CAPITAL AREA CAREER CENTER
611 NORTH HAGADORN ROAD      MASON, MICHIGAN 48854

-- Certificate of Completion --

has successfully completed the attached job skills leading towards
the _____ program and this
certificate is being presented in recognition of this achievement.
Signed, this _____ day of _____ , 19____ .

_____
INSTRUCTOR

_____
DIRECTOR, CACC

capital area career center

_____
ASSISTANT SUPERINTENDENT

of a department to agree upon some domain-referenced system, there would be continuity of grading to a greater extent than exists with the norm-referenced grading. In a subject requiring psychomotor develop- ment, a third category could be added.

In the grading illustration, knowledge and comprehension were omitted because they serve as requisites to the higher-level goals and are not ends in themselves. Some students enter a class with affective behaviors which need modification; they are entitled to credit if they are successful in achieving goals established in this domain.

A distinct difference exists between domain-referenced grading and norm-referenced grading which is prevalent. Domain-referenced grading is based upon specific criteria as well as the level of goals attained.

Although some teachers consider a system with no grades utopian and others recoil at such an idea, schools are experimenting with nongraded evaluations. One school which recognizes that a grade cannot portray what the student is actually able to perform, established an innovative system which the teachers believe states clearly the tasks the student is prepared to perform on the job. The Capital Area Career Center in Mason, Michigan, matches students with goals and gives no grades. Yet, at any point during the year the teacher and student know precisely what the student is able to perform.

In the Capital Area Career Center an entering student selects an occupational area and requests a computer printout of all of the tasks in that area. Students decide which tasks they will try to achieve. At any point the teacher or student may request a computer printout of the list of tasks the student has performed successfully. Such a printout is illustrated in Figure 8.3. A student completing work is presented with a printout of tasks performed and a certificate of completion (Figure 8.4). These two items are then taken to job interviews; employers in the area are aware of the school's program and the individual evaluations. The interviewer uses the data to match the student with a job requiring performance of the tasks in which the student is competent.

## Self-Assessment (Answers on p. 162.)

For 1 through 7, determine whether a or b below best completes the statement.

    a. Criterion-referenced measure
    b. Norm-referenced measure

**1.** A teacher who indicates the number of application-level performance goals a student has attained is using a _____.

**2.** A teacher who says, "Leon is now able to lead a group effectively, because he chaired a discussion on environmental problems in Des Moines which culminated in the identification of six problems the students are concerned with today," is using a _____.

**3.** A teacher who says, "I am emphasizing criterion-referenced measures in all my work, and I have found that Juanita always emerges as the top student in the class no matter what goal she is seeking," is employing a _____.

**4.** A teacher says to a student, "Lynn, do you realize what tremendous progress you have made since the beginning of the semester? You are not only able to construct flow charts, but you are able to construct computer programs which are virtually error free," is employing a _____.

**5.** A teacher who wants to select materials appropriate to the reading levels of students and inquires whether reading scores are available, is planning to use a _____.

**6.** When students in a first-year accounting class are compared by their teacher with other students who have taken a national test, the teacher is employing a _____.

**7.** Members of the Future Business Leaders of America who compete in annual regional contests in shorthand, typewriting, clerical practice, accounting, and business mathematics are engaging in _____.

For 8 through 11 determine the letter of the phrase which best completes the statement or answers the question.

8. Which one of the following is not a purpose of evaluation?
   a. To involve student in self-evaluation.
   b. To measure student attainment of goals.
   c. To evaluate the teacher's effectiveness in using the system.
   d. To compare the student's performance with others in group.
9. Evaluation is the process of collecting data to
   a. Make decisions on student achievement.
   b. Make decisions on the effectiveness of the system.
   c. Make decisions on student achievement and the effectiveness of the system.
   d. Determine grades.
10. Assume that you have employed the teaching-learning system for ten students working toward the same goal and after evaluation find that six out of ten were unable to attain the goal. What would be your first step?
   a. Through feedback gained, design new strategies.
   b. Analyze results of evaluation to determine the precise subcompetencies which were not performed.
   c. Change the performance goal to a simpler one for these six students.
   d. Examine your attitude toward each of the six students.
11. If you were using criterion-referenced measures for the first time, which grading pattern would you choose to use in a traditionally oriented school?
   a. Chart the number of goals completed on a curve to determine which students would receive A, B, C, D, and F, according to total number met.
   b. Pressure the administration for a credit–no credit or pass-fail system.
   c. Preplan a domain-referenced grading system so that a student knows that in order to receive B, two analysis/synthesis-level goals must be achieved, and for a C, four application-level goals must be achieved.
   d. Wait until the end of the learning period and determine how many goals each student achieved at the various levels and then determine the grading system to be used.

## Summary

Evaluation enables the teacher to (1) measure the progress each student makes toward stated goals while moving through the system, and (2) evaluate the system itself and institute changes that make it more effective. Feedback permits intensive scrutiny of all components of the system whenever a student fails to meet a specified goal.

While failure may be the student's own fault, the teacher using the teaching-learning system should first assume that the failure is within the system or in the teacher's attitude toward the student. Modifications of the system to accommodate individual learners frequently enable a student to achieve previously unattained goals. Effectiveness of the system in general is measured by the number of students who meet goals on the first attempt and the number who need successive attempts after system modifications. Continuous evaluation of the system and each of its components is essential if the system is to work for each learner.

The teaching-learning system employs only criterion-referenced measures. Norm-referenced measures are appropriate for use with the system only when they are employed to determine reading levels, compare student performance on national tests, or determine a need for remedial work in mathematics. They are inappropriate for determining grades because they do not portray the achievement of the student or give an assessment of what that student can do.

Grading is an essential ingredient in most schools. The teacher's role is to establish as objective a means of measuring student achievement as possible. One such means is the domain-referenced grading system which focuses on the levels of the cognitive and affective goals attained during the learning period, students achieving higher-level goals earn higher grades.

## Answers to Self-Assessment

After you have answered the questions, check your responses with the appropriate ones below.

**1.** a  **2.** a  **3.** b  **4.** a  **5.** b  **6.** b  **7.** b  **8.** d  **9.** c  **10.** b or d  **11.** c

## SELECTED READINGS

BARNLUND, DEAN, AND FRANKLYN HAIMAN, *The Dynamics of Discussion*, Houghton Mifflin, Boston, 1960.

BUTLER, F. COIT, *Instructional Systems Development for Vocational and Technical Training*, Educational Technology Publications, Inc., Englewood Cliffs, N.J., 1972.

GLASER, R., AND R. C. COX, "Criterion-Referenced Testing for Measurement of Educational Outcomes," *Instructional Process and Media Innovation*, Rand-McNally & Company, Chicago, 1968, pp. 545–550.

GLASER, R., AND D. J. KLAUS, "Proficiency Measurement: Assessing Human Performance," *Psychological Principles in System Development*, Holt, Rinehart & Winston, New York, 1962, pp. 421–427.

*National Business Entrance Tests*, National Business Education Association, Reston, Va.

POPHAM, W. JAMES, ED., *Criterion-Referenced Measurement: An Introduction*, Educational Technology Publications, Inc., Englewood Cliffs, N.J., 1971.

PART

**Applications
of the
Teaching-Learning
System**

## PERFORMANCE GOALS

1. Given a description of students' objectives (vocational and personal) in a typewriting class, determine which competencies are appropriate for each group and **defend** your recommendations in terms of this chapter and your instructor's presentations. Evaluation will be based upon your defense as judged by your instructor.

2. Using one of the 13 vocational typewriting competencies in this chapter, **develop** a teaching-learning system to be evaluated in terms of the standards in subcompetencies a through e.

*Subcompetencies*

a. **Construct** an acceptable performance goal for the competency.

b. **Construct** an actual evaluation which measures the performance goal.

c. **Analyze** the goal for subcompetencies essential to successful achievement of the goal.

d. **Describe** how appropriate principles of learning are involved in achieving the goal and subcompetencies.

e. **Describe** a teaching-learning strategy you would employ, including organizational pattern and the instructional resources, defending each in terms of its appropriateness for the subcompetencies.

3. Given papers produced by three students during production typing activities (letters, rough draft, tabulation, and manuscript), **analyze** the papers for each student to identify all of the subcompetencies needed, as evaluated by your instructor.

4. Using the technique chart from learning activity 1, repeatedly observe a beginning typist, and **decide** upon appropriate remedial drills that meet your instructor's approval.

5. While being videotaped or recorded, **demonstrate** your ability to teach *one* teacher-controlled drill to a small group for five to ten minutes, meeting the criteria on the sheets developed by your group.

# CHAPTER 9

# Typewriting

The teaching-learning system is easily applied when planning and teaching a course in typewriting. Typewriting contributes to the objectives of the entire school. Since it involves performance, the student may learn to produce usable work (something never before achieved in schoolwork) and, encouraged by success, develop affective behaviors that conform to school goals. It is not uncommon for obstreperous, disinterested students to "find themselves" in a typewriting class where *doing,* rather than abstract thinking, is required. The student also learns to perform in an orderly manner: planning before working, starting to work promptly, following directions, and self-evaluating performance.

Typewriting contributes to the development of basic skills of reading, writing, listening to directions, and computing. More important is the relation of typewriting to the objectives of career education, especially the goal "to assure the opportunity for all persons to gain an entry-level marketable skill prior to their leaving school." In many cases, typewriting is that marketable skill and provides, for those who achieve levels of competency required in the employing community, the means to become gainfully employed.

## Needs of Business

It is necessary to know the extent to which typewriting is used in office jobs to justify its inclusion in the vocational office curriculum. Erickson found that typewriting was a basic component of 147 of the 300 jobs he studied and a supportive activity in 20 other jobs. Erickson also found that of the 147 jobs in which typewriting was a basic component, 44 (34 percent) require a worker to type between one-fourth and one-half of the working day, and all these jobs require that at least 5 percent of the day be spent in typing. The ability to type is, then, basic to performance in the office.

The next consideration is: What kinds of typing are done in the office? Perkins, Byrd, and Roley surveyed stenographic-secretarial and clerical workers in the state of Washington and found that the ten commonest typing tasks are as follows (in rank order): (1) cards and envelopes, (2) business letters, (3) memorandums, (4) tables, (5) final copy from rough draft, (6) labels and cards, (7) final copy from unarranged copy, (8) manuscripts or reports, (9) fill-ins, and (10) composing.

Erickson found that handwritten, or combined handwritten and typed rough draft, provided the input for about two-thirds of the typewriting jobs he studied.

## Needs of the Student

Typewriting is a vocational course for some and a general education course for others. Featheringham studied the real-life applications of 750 high school students who had studied or were studying a course in personal typing, ranging from a few still in high school through those who had been graduated more than ten years before. More than four-fifths had a home typewriter at the time of the study. The respondents averaged 2½ hours a week at the typewriter, some using it up to 8 hours a week. The ten commonest personal typing activities were (1) letters and envelopes, (2) manuscripts, (3) speeches, (4) job application forms, (5) labels, (6) personal data sheets, (7) minutes of meetings, (8) tables, (9) postcards, and (10) poems.

Business needs and personal uses of typewriting overlap to quite an extent. Greater proficiency is expected of vocational typists who must use more complex training materials.

Learning to typewrite has also been used as a means of achieving other learnings. For instance, typewriting has proved to be an aid in helping slow learners to read. Seibert taught a group of poor readers typewriting two hours a day for eight weeks and was able to raise their reading level 0.96 grade. She also found significant gains in vocabulary, linguistic comprehension, alphabet recognition, and phonetic association.

Typewriting has also been used to help foreign students who were prevented from entering American colleges by language deficiencies to reach acceptable admission standards. McLeod and First accompanied regular English instruction with a typewriting course, and their students achieved significant gains over their colleagues who studied English alone.

In some instances typewriting has been taught for motivational reasons. For example, an elementary school principal in a Denver school with a mixed ethnic population organized an experimental fifth-grade typewriting class (using electric machines), one of its objectives being: "increasing motivation and enjoyment of school work" (Babbs and Cline, p. 103). The project was so successful that classes were extended to other grades.

Many different types of people of many varying abilities learn typewriting: students in elementary school, middle school or junior high school, senior high school, community colleges, independent business schools, and senior colleges as well as lawyers, teachers, and homemakers in evening school or at the YM-YWCA. The blind learn to type and hold jobs involving typewriting. Other handicapped people learn to type by using special equipment and learning materials.

## Elementary School Typewriting

The usual competencies to be developed in elementary school typewriting are (1) improved reading, spelling, punctuation, and creative writing (general education) and (2) a skill that will be needed throughout life.

Rowe was the first business educator to apply electric machines to elementary school typewriting classes. He conducted demonstration classes which showed that elementary school pupils using electric portables can excel in the subject. Krevolin and Lloyd also conducted numerous experimental classes while developing materials for an elementary school typewriting textbook, and they reached the same conclusion.

Elementary school classes taught touch typewriting by someone competent in teaching both typewriting and English achieve excellent results both in typewriting and in improved communication. If typewriting is used simply as a motivational device and the machines become playthings, and if the teacher is not qualified to teach typewriting as well as communication, the results are often disappointing.

## Middle School or Junior High School Typewriting

Objectives of middle school or junior high school typewriting are (1) learning to type business papers prepared by nonoffice workers, (2) preparing schoolwork both in present classes and during later educational experiences, and (3) improving communication skills. A typed paper frequently receives a higher grade than a handwritten one, although the content is the same. Knowing this, all students are motivated to learn to type assignments. Many students realize, too, that they may not have another opportunity to learn typewriting.

Several studies have been conducted to test the efficacy of junior high school typewriting in achieving the objectives of general education relating to communication. Morrison taught experimental classes in which general education values were emphasized and concluded that typewriting rates of the experimental group were practically as high as those of the group taught by traditional methods; in addition, the experimental group showed greater skill in capitalization, grammar, punctuation, sentence structure, and both quality and rate of composition.

More recently, Bartholome studied the spelling achievement of experimental and control groups of 100 ninth-grade typewriting students. The experimental classes typed spelling lessons during the first 15 minutes of the 75 lessons, while control classes typed warm-up and textbook drills. During the rest of each period, instruction was identical in both groups. At the end of the experiment, the experimental group had a significantly higher spelling average, speed record, and accuracy record. In other words, an objective of improved spelling can be achieved without sacrificing the attainment of speed and accuracy (Bartholome, pp. 28–31).

## High School Typewriting

In a national survey (1967), Robinson found that in more than half the responding high schools, 71 percent of the entire student body take at least one year of typewriting and fewer than 10 percent of the students take one semester only. More than half of the schools offer four semesters of typewriting. In the usual pattern, the typewriting teacher can expect to have one year in which to develop learner competencies (Robinson 5, p. 2).

Most high schools are organized on the semester plan, and the competencies achieved in half a school year form the basis for grades. Terminal performance goals, too, can be developed in terms of semesters. Ideally, though, time limits are eliminated, and the learner moves into and out of a typewriting course when performance goals have been achieved. As a matter of fact, there is a trend in cost-conscious school districts toward permitting all students to elect a personal-use typewriting course, holding them until they meet the standards set for the course, and then clearing them out to make room for other learners. Because equipment costs in typewriting are high, taxpayers approve of such mobility.

## Independent Business Schools and Two- and Four-Year Colleges

Typewriting competencies are often achieved faster in the independent business school than in the high school for three reasons: (1) more hours a day are spent on learning typewriting; (2) students are highly motivated, with the prospect of a job after completion of the program; and (3) independent business schools almost universally utilize individually paced learning. The time required for graduation depends on the learner's ability and effort, not on an artificial time structure.

In the traditional two-year college where the semester or quarter plan is followed, the learner is expected to do in two or three days a week what a high school student does in five and at the end of one semester meet the performance goals expected of a high school student at the end of a year.

There is an even bigger difference between high school and collegiate typewriting. The levels of competency required of the college student are higher both in kind and in quality, for it is assumed that the two- and four-year college students will use typewriting on a higher level than the high school graduate.

Since learners with such varied backgrounds study typewriting, let us ask this question: Can the ability to learn to type be predicted by the same predictive measures that are usually relied on in other subjects? The answer is no if straight copying skill is the only ability being predicted.

Correlations between straight-copy typing and IQ, between straight-copy typing and grade-point averages, and between straight-copy typing and reading level are statistically insignificant. Simple typing can be learned by almost anybody with sufficient motivation. Making application of typing skill to real-life problems, though, requires higher cognitive skills and is related to such measures as IQ, grades, and reading skill. We can accept the mastery learning theory of many educators that 90 percent of all students can learn what we have to teach them if we allow *time* to be the variable. The problem is to establish conditions of learning that are appropriate for all the learners found in typewriting classes.

## Identifying Competencies

Three factors are involved in establishing competencies to be achieved during typewriting instruction: (1) they must be based on tasks performed by actual typists, (2) they must require the student to produce work that is realistic in quality, and (3) they must require the student to produce a reasonable amount of work within a given time period.

In nonvocational courses, the learners type assignments from simple compositions to term papers with footnotes, friendly and business letters, simple tabulations, displays such as announcements and programs, carbon copies, and fill-ins on forms. In vocational courses, the learners type the materials usually prepared by beginning office workers. Figure 9.1 includes 13 competencies that should be taught in beginning typewriting.

In any course, the learner should produce a reasonable amount of usable material within a reasonable period of sustained effort. What is reasonable is determined by the level of the learner, the level of the course, and the length of the course. A person using the typewriter for personal use is usually not under time pressure. Quantity is less important for this typist. On the other hand, the importance of establishing time standards and measuring sustained effort (30-minute timings rather than 10-minute spurt efforts, and timings that include planning and proofreading time) cannot be overemphasized for the vocational student. Unless typists can maintain a steady flow of work over a period of time, they have not achieved success in typewriting.

## Planning Evaluations and Constructing Performance Goals

It is, of course, impossible to include terminal performance goals that fit each typewriting learning situation in this chapter. Only the teacher can write goals that meet specific local needs. However, in Figure 9.2 the competencies from Figure 9.1 are analyzed as to dominant domain to be reached, the verb that may be used in writing the performance goal, and the type of evaluation to be used. Sample goals are given which indicate the standards that might be reached at the end of one year in a high school typewriting course meeting daily for 40 minutes. These goals are based on the 13 competencies listed in Figure 9.1. Copy difficulty

Figure 9.1   Converting typewriting tasks to competencies
by establishing a standard (Recycle to Chapter 4)

| Task | Standard | Competency |
|---|---|---|
| 1. Type from straight copy | Rapidly and accurately, using all machine controls properly | Type from straight copy rapidly and accurately, using all machine controls properly |
| 2. Type letters and envelopes | That are mailable, in semiblock and block style, at a rapid rate | Type mailable semiblocked and blocked letters and envelopes at a rapid rate |
| 3. Type manuscript from rough draft | Rapidly and accurately | Type manuscript from rough draft rapidly and accurately |
| 4. Type memorandums from handwritten copy | In correct format, are usable, and at a rapid rate | Type usable memorandums at a reasonable rate |
| 5. Proofread for typographic errors, spelling, punctuation, grammar, or typewriter usage | So that errors are detected in a reasonable time | Proofread letters within a reasonable time, locating all errors in spelling, punctuation, grammar, or typewriting usage |
| 6. Type tabulations with columnar headings | In proper format, with no uncorrected errors, within a reasonable time | Type tabulations with columnar headings in proper format, with no uncorrected errors, within a reasonable time |
| 7. Punctuate sentences containing parenthetical expressions, introductory clauses, apposition, two independent clauses, series, and compound adjectives | With practically no errors | Punctuate sentences containing parenthetical expressions, introductory clauses, appositives, independent clauses, series, and compound adjectives with practically no errors |
| 8. Fill in printed forms on the typewriter | Properly aligned | Fill in properly aligned, typed information on printed forms |
| 9. Chain feed envelopes and address them | Rapidly, with a high percentage of usable addressed envelopes | Chain feed envelopes rapidly and address them with a high percentage of usable envelopes |
| 10. Type special notations on letters prepared from handwritten copy | Rapidly, using correct format | Type special notations on letters prepared from handwritten copy rapidly, in correct format |
| 11. Compose and type simple business letters | In correct format, including all essential information, with no uncorrected errors, within a reasonable time | Compose and type simple business letters in correct format that contain all essential information and no uncorrected errors, within a reasonable time |
| 12. Clean and maintain a typewriter | To the instructor's standard for approval | Clean and maintain a typewriter to the instructor's standard for approval |
| 13. Demonstrate good work habits | Consistently | Demonstrate good work habits consistently |

is not mentioned, as it is assumed that material will be taken from current typewriting textbooks containing copy of suitable difficulty.

Figure 9.2 Typewriting competencies analyzed for dominant domain, appropriate verb, and type of evaluation

| Competency | Dominant domain & level | Verb | Evaluation |
|---|---|---|---|
| 1. Type from straight copy rapidly and accurately, using all machine controls properly | Psychomotor: acquisition, habituating | **Type** | Product Process |
| 2. Type mailable semiblocked and blocked letters and envelopes at a rapid rate | Cognitive: application | **Demonstrate** | Product |
| 3. Type manuscript from rough draft rapidly and accurately | Cognitive: application | **Demonstrate** | Product |
| 4. Type usable memorandums at a reasonable rate | Cognitive: application | **Demonstrate** | Product |
| 5. Proofread letters within a reasonable time, locating all errors in spelling, punctuation, grammar, or typewriting usage | Cognitive: evaluation | **Decide** | Product |
| 6. Type tabulations with columnar headings in proper format, with no uncorrected errors, in a reasonable time | Cognitive: application | **Demonstrate** | Product |
| 7. Punctuate sentences containing parenthetical expressions, introductory clauses, appositives, independent clauses, series, and compound adjectives with practically no errors | Cognitive: evaluation | **Decide** | Product |
| 8. Fill in properly aligned typed information on printed forms | Cognitive: application | **Demonstrate** | Product |
| 9. Chain feed envelopes and address them with a high percentage of usable addressed envelopes | Cognitive: application. After Psychomotor: acquisition | **Demonstrate** | Process Product |
| 10. Type special notations on letters prepared from handwritten copy, rapidly, in correct format | Cognitive: application | **Demonstrate** | Product |
| 11. Compose and type simple business letters, in correct format, that contain all essential information and no uncorrected errors, within a reasonable time | Cognitive: application | **Demonstrate** | Product |
| 12. Clean and maintain a typewriter to the instructor's standard for approval | Cognitive: application | **Demonstrate** | Process: controlled observation |
| 13. Demonstrate good work habits consistently | Affective: highest level | **Demonstrate** | Process: controlled observation |

1.  Given multiple opportunities, **type** three 5-minute timings at the gross rate of 35 wam with no more than four errors in each.
2.  Given two letters containing a total of 225 words, **demonstrate**

your understanding of letter styles and a reference source by typing one letter in semiblocked style and the other in blocked style, referring to the zip code directory for zip codes, and typing the letters and envelopes all within 20 minutes.

3. Given rough-draft copy, **demonstrate** your ability to type a one-page manuscript within 20 minutes with no more than one uncorrected error. (A small error tolerance may be allowed because of nervousness brought about by test conditions. This decision can be made by the individual teacher.)

4. Given handwritten copy, **demonstrate** your ability to type two interoffice mailable memorandums at a production rate of 10 words a minute, including planning and proofreading time. Standard: correct format and placement, no uncorrected errors.

5. Given a one-page typewritten letter containing errors in typewriting, spelling, punctuation, grammar, and typewriting usage, **decide** what errors have been made by marking the errors within five minutes. Standard: no more than one undetected error. (A small error tolerance may be allowed as in goal 3 above.)

6. Given arranged copy with headings, **demonstrate** your ability to compute margins and type a tabulation with headings by completing a tabulation with nine lines in the body within 10 minutes. Standard: usable copy by instructor's evaluation.

7. Given 28 sentences requiring application of punctuation rules covering parenthetical expressions, introductory clauses, apposition, compound sentences, series, and compound adjectives, **decide** on the correct punctuation of at least 26 of the sentences.

8. Given the necessary information, **demonstrate** your ability to fill in printed business forms with 10 items of information aligned correctly. (No timing)

9. Given 16 envelopes and a list of 15 mailing addresses, **demonstrate** your ability to chain feed and type 15 envelopes according to United States postal regulations. Product and process evaluation.

10. Given 150 words of handwritten copy with special notations (subject line, special attention line, enclosures, postscript, reference notation, and file reference), **demonstrate** your ability to indicate proper placement of these notations by typing two letters and envelopes in mailable form within 15 minutes.

11. Given the information required, **demonstrate** your ability to compose and type a business letter ordering goods, reserving a hotel room, or acknowledging an order within 12 minutes. Standard: all essential information included, no uncorrected errors.

12. Given proper maintenance supplies, **demonstrate** that you can perform the cleaning and maintenance function on your typewriter to the satisfaction of your instructor.

13. During class sessions, **demonstrate** good work habits consistently that will not only allow you to achieve performance goals but will also be useful later. Regular process evaluations.

## Selecting Appropriate Evaluation Instruments

Selecting the evaluation instruments to measure the learner's achievement of such precisely stated performance goals is a simple process. Some teachers choose test material from the textbook used all year. Others select material of comparable difficulty from companion textbooks. The average teacher is not sufficiently skilled in controlling the difficulty of copy to be able to compose tests. He or she is advised to make wise judgments in using copy prepared by experts. (See the discussion of copy difficulty later in this chapter.)

## Components and Areas of Typewriting Learning

There are four basic components of all typewriting ability: (1) technique (touch control and correct operation of machine mechanisms), (2) knowledge of essential typewriting information (such as word division, punctuation, and spacing), (3) straight-copy speed and accuracy, and (4) production ability. Typewriting textbooks provide material which allows students to develop these four abilities as they are achieving specific competencies and subcompetencies.

Because mastery of the four basic components of typewriting ability is already built into the materials that are used within the classroom, the teacher should concentrate on the three broad areas or phases of typewriting learning: keyboard presentation, skill building on straight copy to build basic copying skill, and typewriting applications or production typewriting.

## Keyboard Presentation

The student must learn the use of the typewriter mechanical controls and the proper key-stroke technique in order to master the keyboard. Using the mechanical controls involves both cognitive and psychomotor learnings. Touch typewriting lies within the psychomotor domain.

Most typewriting textbooks present the keyboard in from five to fifteen lessons. The assumption is made that for the 26 letters of the alphabet, there are 26 responses to be learned. West points out that "keyboard learning actually involves hundreds of responses (motion patterns), not merely 26, and the variety of motion paths should make apparent that the letter sequence, not the single stroke, is the proper focus of attention" (West 2, p. 7).

## Skill Building

During this phase, time is given to a limited number of typewriting applications, but in general the focus is on refining stroking motions and improving techniques before emphasis is shifted to production typing. The learner types short timed writings almost from the beginning. First timings are as short as 12 seconds and are gradually increased in length. Emphasis is on correct technique, especially correct key stroke, not on

**173**

perfect copy. The learner is allowed errors when taking timed writings, but error limits are established. For instance, two errors a minute may be allowed on timed writings during the first month, but the number is gradually reduced as copying ability improves.

A typist cannot solve problems until basic stroking facility and necessary cognitive learnings with which to work in arriving at solutions have been achieved. Research tells us, though, that probably teachers have been spending too much time in developing copying facility before production work is introduced and that higher copying speed will develop at the same time that production rate is increased. West suggests that: "An approximate answer is perhaps about 25 gross wpm straight-copy speeds for five minutes on new copy of average difficulty" (West 1, p. 350).

## Production Typing

The goal of all typewriting is, of course, to produce a reasonable amount of usable copy in a reasonable time, to use the typewriter as the writing tool by which written communication is disseminated.

Crawford defines production typewriting as typewriting which, in addition to machine manipulation, includes "following variously specified directions, handling materials, preparing carbon copies, correcting occurrent errors, and appropriately disposing of the finished products" (Crawford, Monograph 97, p. 1). The final product is usable work produced in reasonable quantity over a sustained period of time.

Ideally, usable work and reasonable quantity would be defined in terms of actual office standards. The NOBELS study found, however, that very little office work has been subjected to standard time-data analysis, probably because copy varies widely in difficulty according to many factors discussed later (see page 190), such as length of item, difficulty of the task, syllable and stroke intensity, and vocabulary. Standards as to the quality of work that is acceptable also vary so widely from office to office that they have not been accurately defined. West very properly deplores "the virtual absence of national standards and norms for the genuine objectives of instruction" (West 2, p. 9).

## Identifying Subcompetencies and En Route Goals

After the keyboard has been mastered and minimum copying speed developed, production typewriting is begun. Although subcompetencies are necessary throughout typewriting learning, at the start of production work they are particularly important. Because production involves the amalgamation of all previous typewriting learnings, students in any one class may have a wide variety of special needs. The identification of subcompetencies will provide an organized means of helping individual students meet these needs.

Two points should be made about typewriting subcompetencies. In the first place, although many subcompetencies should be sequenced, others are developed simultaneously. The learner does not master one terminal performance goal in quite the same way that units are completed in courses such as Consumer Education or Office Procedures. Because psychomotor skills are best developed through short, intensive practice sessions, the learner types for a limited time in this area. After working on a module requiring practice in developing copying speed (psychomotor, acquisition level), the learner may complete a module designed to improve English mechanics (cognitive, application level), move to a drill to automatize correct use of machine controls (psychomotor, manipulation level), and from there to production typewriting, in which the previous learnings at lower levels are integrated into typewriting tasks. First efforts are judged by a reasonable error tolerance, for the standard is an evolving one.

The second point is that typewriting authors understand well the importance of subcompetencies, have identified those essential in reaching a performance goal, and have carefully prepared materials for developing them.

However, Robinson stresses the fact that the teacher must also analyze learning materials in order to identify subcompetencies and establish attainable en route goals. Although textbooks contain materials that normally enable the learner to reach the designated competency, a learner may follow the assignments that are designed to develop a competency and still not be able to achieve it. In this case the teacher must identify the subcompetency that has not yet been learned and recycle the learner through the same kind of material until he or she can meet the expected goal. Different diagnoses and different assignments for different students in terms of subcompetencies not yet achieved—that is the responsibility of the typewriting teacher.

## Sample En Route Goals

Figure 9.3 shows en route goals from Part 2 of *Typing 300,* Volume One. Part 2 contains 20 modules, each one representing about 20 minutes' work for the average student. The en route goals are to be met by most students after about 25 days of instruction and may be used in either a teacher-controlled class or in a class organized for individually paced learning. The student who is completing Part 2 will be in the skill-building (preproduction) phase of typewriting learning.

The first en route goal should be evaluated by controlled observation. The teacher constructs or follows an already developed checklist of techniques to be observed, focusing on one or two points at a time. In some classrooms videotapes are made of each learner while typing. These tapes can be used by both the teacher and the learner in assessing areas requiring improvement.

The objective test mentioned in the second en route goal is printed in the workbook. Some teachers prefer to let students preview the questions before studying for the test, while others collect the objective tests from

Figure 9.3   Sample en route goals from *Typing 300*

When you finish Part Two, you should be able to demonstrate the following abilities when you take the test in a-i-m 50, page 54:

1. **Touch Typing**   You will control all letter and punctuation keys by touch. You will use the main operating parts, like the carriage return and tabulator, correctly and by touch. You will return the carriage, indent, even double-indent with the tabulator, all by touch.
2. **Technicalities**   You will score at least 80 percent on an objective test that reviews both Part One and Part Two. The test includes items on word division, names of machine parts, score keeping, spacing after punctuation, etc.
3. **Production**   You will be able to display typed material by centering it vertically on the paper, with individual or groups of lines centered horizontally. You will be able to spread words and to type them in all capitals.
4. **Skill**   You will type at least 50 words in 2 minutes within 4 errors as you copy alphabetic paragraph material whose line endings are not shown—that is, you must listen to the margin warning bell and decide on line endings.

Source: *Typing 300*, p. 36.

the workbook at the beginning of the course and use them at the end of each part. Objective tests on typewriting are also available from other publishers or may be prepared by the teacher. As learners become proficient in composition at the typewriter, the teacher may require that students type the answers to typewriting information tests. It is important to remember that the learning of typewriting information to be used in applying typewriting skill is essential to achieving terminal goals. It must become a regular component of each unit of the course and is included in the performance goals.

Since the application of typewriting to the production of a reasonable amount of usable copy is the terminal performance goal, the third en route goal requires the learner to begin preproduction typing. After only 25 days of instruction, however, exercises requiring applications of skill are not timed nor is an error range stated.

The standard in the fourth en route goal is stated for the C-minus student. The teacher who wishes to assign a grade at any time may convert the rate by using the following table:

- D — 80% of the standard: 20 wam
- B — 120% of the standard: 30 wam
- A — 130% of the standard: 32–33 wam

## Further Breakdown of En Route Goals

The en route goals for each part or unit of typewriting instruction can be further broken down into goals for each lesson or module (20-minute segment). Sample goals from selected modules in *Typing 300* illustrate this breakdown. They also show how standards are raised gradually as the learner increases in ability.

- *Module 20* (after about 10 days of instruction). Goals: To control X and P keys. To type 34 words or more in two minutes within four errors on 26 keys.

- *Module 78* (after about 39 days of instruction). Goals: To type 105 words or more in four minutes within five errors on part of a letter (salutation through complimentary close, page 83). To copy a short letter, arranging it correctly. To type it within seven minutes.
- *Modules 200-202* (after about 20 weeks of instruction). Goals: To learn correct form for a subject line in a letter. To learn how to choose a complimentary closing. To use "bcc" notations correctly. To type 190 or more words of production copy in five minutes within four errors.

Just as the standards for speed and accuracy in typing straight copy are raised progressively during succeeding weeks, the standard for production typing is also an ever higher one. When the student is working under untimed conditions, he or she should be held to a "usable copy" standard requiring that any problem be typed in complete agreement with directions and contain no uncorrected errors on either the original or the carbon copies. Work is unacceptable if it contains uncorrected typographic errors, misspellings, incorrect word division, incorrect punctuation, or other deviations from correct typewriter usage. Erasures on both original and carbon copies must be unobtrusive.

The creative teacher is always on the alert to establish, when necessary, new en route goals to success on the terminal one. For instance, as a way of helping students who have tried and tried and still cannot produce mailable letters because they cannot proofread, the teacher might use this en route goal: "Given the privilege of exchanging with a classmate a series of five letters which you have typed and of correcting all errors found by either reader, **demonstrate** your ability to produce five mailable letters during a 40-minute period."

The pair of students can question each other, teach each other, and learn to work cooperatively until they are self-reliant enough in proofreading to work alone again.

During first efforts at sustained production work, with all mailable letters marked "In" and all unmailable letters marked "Out," the student might work toward this en route goal: "Erasing all errors, **demonstrate** your ability to produce five mailable letters from the six attempted during the 40-minute period."

## Preassessing the Present Level of the Learner

Preassessing the present level of the learner is particularly important in admitting students to advanced typewriting courses, whether they transfer from other schools or from other courses within the same school. Although many schools discriminate against the student whose initial training was at less than high school level while they accept the student who has had a first course in high school, Luchin (see Selected Readings) found that trained junior high school students do as well in high school Typing 2 as do high school students who have had Typing 1. He recommends that both junior high and middle school graduates be admitted to advanced courses on the basis of placement tests. Buchl also found that most high school business education chairmen recommend placement tests rather than previous typewriting grades as the basis for admission to advanced typewriting courses.

The placement test should cover not only speed and accuracy but also the three other components of typewriting ability: technique, typewriting information, and production ability (ability to make typewriting applications upon which later assignments will be built). The test should include measurement of competencies and subcompetencies necessary to complete the performance goals for Typing 1. If a student cannot pass such a test, the teacher should consider rejecting him or her from advanced typing. If the student is admitted, individually prescribed instruction should be used to remedy the deficiencies exhibited.

## Learning Principles Applicable to Typewriting

Learning principles 1, 3, 6, 8, 10, 12, 13, and 14 have special application in typewriting. They are paraphrased and discussed in this section.

### Principle 1: Learning Must Be Perceived as Relevant

The purpose of each drill to be practiced or knowledge to be mastered should be known to the learner: to increase speed or accuracy (different copy for practice on each goal), to improve stroking technique, to improve speed on isolated letter parts before they can be incorporated into a timed letter-writing test, to master punctuation of restrictive clauses, or to improve control of numbers. Performance and en route goals should be available so the student knows exactly what is expected. By relating practice to en route rather than terminal goals, the teacher makes step-by-step learnings meaningful. To help the learner, some textbooks label the purpose of each part of each lesson. Learners may overlook these purposes, though, unless the teacher calls attention to them.

### Principle 3: New Behaviors Should Be Associated With Previously Learned Behaviors

Transfer of learning is not automatic. The textbook and the teacher must teach for transfer. Some examples in typewriting follow. After a student has reached a certain higher level of stroking on a one-minute timing, he or she tries to transfer that higher speed to (1) copy of greater difficulty, (2) a two-minute timing on the same copy, or (3) a specified reduction of errors on the same copy. The student who has achieved a certain level of stroking on straight copy then tries to type a rough draft at 75 percent of that rate.

The area of production typing is closely related to helping the learner transfer straight-copying skill to production typing speed. Correlations of 0.84 were found by Muhich and reported by West between straight-copying speed and production of already arranged letters on which no corrections were made (West 1, pp. 327-354).

When planning time had to be computed for unarranged copy and erasures were made, correlations between copying speed and production rate dropped to 0.28 and 0.47 in Crawford's classes taught by the traditional speedbuilding-on-straight-copy method with production typing introduced near the end of the course (Crawford). In four classes which were taught for production improvement, however, correlations were as high as 0.55 to 0.88. In other words, if the teacher stresses planning time and erasing time and helps the learner become expert in both and if the teacher then times planning time and erasing time in the same way that copying tests are timed, production typing will more nearly approximate straight-copy rates. Production can be taught as well as tested.

Robinson reports:

In separate unpublished studies, Robinson and Beaumont recently measured the amount of straight-copy skill transferred to statistical, rough-draft, and script paragraphs of average vocabulary difficulty at the end of Semester 1 and Semester 4, respectively. (Robinson 4, pp. 42–43)

They found that the relationship between straight-copy accuracy and accuracy on production work is negligible. West found that

Only 10 percent of the factors that determine straight-copy accuracy also influence the quality of production typing. Ninety percent of whatever determines production quality has nothing to do with straight-copy accuracy . . . it is apparent that straight-copy speed contributes more than four times as much to production speed as straight-copy accuracy contributes to production quality.

He then speaks of "the gross impropriety of heavy concern with straight-copy accuracy" (West 1, pp. 331–332).

## Principle 6: Students Should Be Aware of Progress Toward Goals

Knowledge of results is essential. Copy is fitted to a scale that enables the learner to figure rates immediately. If a writing is to be completed in three minutes, the typist consults the scale and knows at once if the goal was met. If the student is to stay within a two-error limit, some proofreading drill may be called for, but he or she usually knows whether there are more than two errors. If a class is typing its first tabulation, all students hold up their completed table so that the teacher can make a visual inspection while walking quickly down the aisles. In one program, the student kit provides proof guide keys with which typists compare their work as they evaluate results.

A word should be said about grading papers early in the course: **don't.** Inspection of papers periodically tells the teacher whether the methods used are right or wrong, but the word "immediate" in reinforcement indicates that next-day knowledge of results is too late. Besides, one of the most important objectives of the course (based on business needs) is to develop typists who are self-evaluators.

### Principle 8: Learners Must Have Requisite Behaviors in Their Repertoires

Probably this principle is the most important one of all. The learner who has not achieved behavior appropriate to one level is not ready to progress to the next one. It is the teacher's responsibility to recycle learning until the required behavior is exhibited. For instance, if the learner cannot make the computations necessary for planning tables, an assignment to type tables is doomed to failure. The teacher must constantly inventory the learner's repertoire before assigning tasks beyond present levels of competency.

### Principle 10: Students Must Understand the Relationship Between Subcompetencies and Competencies

Subcompetencies and en route goals have meaning only insofar as the learner understands their relationship to the ultimate objective. For instance, the student who recognizes the necessity for learning to compute margins for a nine-line three-column table with all errors corrected in 15 minutes will really struggle to meet en route goals involving enough computations to ensure mastery of this performance goal component.

### Principle 12: Distributed Practice Is Superior to Massed Practice

Textbook authors understand this principle and vary copy and change goals before the law of diminishing returns begins to operate. For one thing, the beginner's attention span, far below that of the career typist, is usually no longer than five or ten minutes. Early skill-building drills are interspersed with frequent rest periods and changes of pace. Early production exercises are fairly short too, gradually increasing to 20 or even 30 minutes of sustained effort in completing a variety of tasks. In advanced typewriting, though, it is desirable to schedule massed practice to provide enough time to learn how to plan and execute one kind of production job before going on to the next.

### Principle 13: Early Excessive Movements Are Replaced by Economical Motions

The purpose of practice is to reduce excessive motions so that the time between stimulus-response reaction is shortened and, indeed, sometimes to eliminate the second stimulus so that response leads to another response (R-R not S-R). This practice, known as *chaining*, becomes operative as the learner begins to feel the correct strokes rather than making them by conscious direction. The typist achieves a rhythm pattern, a quite different thing than typing with metronomic rhythm in which every stroke requires exactly the same time. For example, "th" is written faster than "ex." Rhythm or fluency is a flow of writing in which the easy letter combinations are typed at a faster rate than the difficult letter combinations. The learner types some short words at the pattern level and, if no pattern for the entire word has been developed, patternizes part of it and drops back to the letter level for the rest.

Langford experimented with the chaining concept using three groups: a control group using textbook material with little or no attention to response patterns or chaining, a second group using dictation tapes the first ten minutes of each class period three days a week for 18 weeks, and a third group using both the tape recorder and various visual cues. He explained and demonstrated to the experimental groups orally and on tape the process of chaining and the sounds of chained and unchained responses. His conclusions were that (1) chaining can be taught and contributes to statistically significant higher speeds; (2) audiovisual presentations plus teacher demonstrations, with emphasis on the sound of chained and nonchained typing, are most successful; and (3) chaining patterns differ among students and from time to time with the same student, so that the learner should be taught to listen to, evaluate, and perfect his own stroking patterns (Langford, pp. 100–105).

During the period of refinement of movements, constant reminders of the elements of good technique should be kept before the learner by displays in the textbook, on transparencies, or on film, or by teacher demonstration. Admonitions are given on tape or orally to use specific techniques. The teacher's role is not only to identify faulty technique but also to prescribe what to do to correct each deterrent to improvement. Improvement in technique will, *if the right copy is used,* lead not only to improved speed but also to better accuracy.

An analysis of the motions that help and hinder a learner was made by Weaver. He studied the motions that improve speed and those that improve accuracy. (They are not the same.) The motions are different, too, for manual and for electric typewriters. (See Rowe, Lloyd, and Winger for tables compiled as a result of this study.) The tables enable the teacher to prescribe appropriate drills on the sequences of letters at any point in a learner's progress—drills that are useful on the electric but not on the manual typewriter, drills that will improve speed but should not be used for accuracy. Reduction of error comes from the use of "contrived" copy while the typist refines motions that frequently produce errors.

## Principle 14: Varying Levels of Attention and Consciousness Are Needed During the Skill-Building Process

In the early stages of skill building the learner uses all senses (eyes to measure reaches, ears to hear correct stroke, touch to feel the right movements, and voice to sharpen attention). He or she must give such close attention to details of the task that frequent rest periods are required to reduce tension. Later, less and less concentration on details is required. In fact, it can be said that the mastery of typewriting is achieved when the learner can stroke correctly when focusing attention on something else—whether the copy contains an appositive or whether a number should be typed in figures or spelled out, for instance.

## Selecting Teaching-Learning Strategies

Teaching-learning strategies in typewriting are undergoing a great deal of change. Students are becoming increasingly more involved in making decisions that affect the way they learn.

Two research studies in which students were allowed a great deal of freedom or self-direction in learning to type probably have something to say to the teacher who controls the learning process tightly.

Kline, in a self-directed typewriting program, studied both the achievements and the attitudes of middle-school learners who worked in typewriting carrels using programmed materials on records and textbooks. After about eight weeks there were no differences in typewriting speed or error control between the two groups, although videotapes of all students showed that the self-directed learners were significantly poorer in technique. While this study clearly identifies the role of the teacher in developing technique, it also suggests that the student may wisely be allowed to proceed as he or she wishes.

A study by Warner follows the same line of thought. An experimental group of college students practiced on production assignments until *they thought* that they were ready to be tested. When they were given the same tests as the control group, in which every student completed ten production assignments before being given the same tests, there was no significant difference between the groups. Again, this research indicates that students learn just as well when they make their own decisions.

## Organizational Patterns

The organization of a modern typewriting class includes some large-group instruction during the introductory lessons and when new materials are introduced and small groups for special instruction or drill on problems shared by all members of the group. During most of the time, though, each student follows his or her own individually paced learning plan, moving on to new performance goals only after succeeding on present goals. The teacher, in cooperation with the learner, determines learning needs and prescribes appropriate learning resources, which the student checks out from the resource cabinet and uses until the assigned goal is met. It may be that the teacher writes the goals or even supplementary materials, but in most cases they are already available.

It is desirable to maintain an open typewriting laboratory, with a supervisor to protect equipment, so that the learner can work additionally on individual goals and type assignments for other courses. In some situations the student pursues an individually paced learning plan by using computer-assisted instruction.

Does individually paced learning work? Little evidence is yet available, but here are two reports. An independent study of individual instruction in beginning typewriting in University High School, the University of Wyoming, showed no significant difference between a class taught by traditional methods and one in which students had an opportunity to complete eight units of instruction at their own pace, although if they completed three units they received course credit (Lambrecht and Gardiner, pp. 243–244).

Missling studied typewriter achievement in four classes, one using five days a week of 55-minute periods and the others organized into different modular scheduling arrangements. In the traditional class, a textbook was used and tests were scheduled at the completion of each production unit. In the modular classes, using learning packets similar to textbook material, the tests were given when students felt ready for them and asked for them. Straight-copy tests were scheduled at a fixed time in each school. The traditional class achieved higher speed rates and typed more accurately on straight copy than did any of the modular classes. The range of differences in achievement was greater in the modular classes than in the traditional one. Production typing rates for the traditional class were also higher than those of the modular classes, but differences in accuracy were negligible.

Michigan State University has adopted a mixed organization pattern. The first 25 lessons in beginning typewriting have been videotaped under the supervision of Robert Poland and are presented to the whole class, which works together under the supervision of an experienced teacher. After the 25 lessons, the large group is dissolved, and each learner, in cooperation with the teacher, who is always available, is "on his own." The students participate in small-group instruction as needed, but most of the time they work with individually paced learning materials. The learning time in the typewriting program at Michigan State University has been cut one-fourth since the introduction of the plan and the development of the accompanying instructional resources.

Some teachers prefer to teach typewriting traditionally and to keep all learners together. Many of them show just as good results as those using innovative organizational patterns. If a learner is absent, a teacher's aide or a superior student may help him or her catch up with the group during the open laboratory session. (Never underestimate the amount of learning that occurs with student instruction.)

## Teacher-Controlled Drills With Individualized Goals

Specific attention must be given to the use of typing drills as a learning activity. While they should be assigned in terms of each learner's individual needs, it is entirely possible to conduct profitable drills for large groups of students with widely varying abilities. One learner may be using speed copy while another is using accuracy copy. Some learners may stroke 70 wam while others stroke only 40 wam, but each learner is judged on the increase in stroking ability rather than just on stroking ability. Many teachers merge innovative and traditional methods and use individually prescribed goals for teacher-controlled drills as a regular feature of most class sessions. The following drills are suggested for this situation.

GUIDED DRILLS. The learner selects the rate at which to type for a specified time, such as 40 wam, and then divides the copy into four equal parts (10 words every quarter minute). The teacher calls out the quarter, half, and full minutes so that the student can achieve the desired rate. This drill can be used to stretch rates or to achieve better continuity in writing by evening out the amount of copy in a minute, possibly reducing the rate to focus on a new objective.

MATCHING DRILLS. The student who achieves a new speed at a forced rate then tries (a) to maintain that rate for the same time on more difficult copy, (b) to maintain the rate for a longer period, or (c) to maintain the rate and reduce errors. Each student works with a different goal.

VARIABLE LINE DRILL. This drill can be used with any copy—the school newspaper, a history textbook, or a magazine article—when the teacher senses that a change of pace would enliven proceedings. In a drill that is equally effective in typewriting and shorthand, Grubbs recommends that lines of differing lengths (starting with 50 spaces—10 words) be typed at each learner's pace (Grubbs 1, pp. 26-27). The teacher calls "line" every 30 seconds. A student completing a line in half a minute with precision is typing 20 wam accurately and is ready to move the margins for a 60-space line (12 words). When the typist can complete that line with precision, the 70-space line is attempted. The teacher then reduces the time allowed for each line to 20 seconds, and so on.

Figure 9.4 shows the rates that may be computed with various line spacings and also the timing variations that may be used.

SCRIBBLE TYPING. When the teacher cannot get a class to make a sprint in speed timings, Grubbs recommends a "scribble-typing" drill (Grubbs, 2). Using a 50-space line to simplify rate computing (10 words to a line), the teacher gives a succession of one-minute timings in rapid succession. Each time the student rolls the paper back in the machine, so that each retyping is superimposed on the typing just finished. With each repetition on top of the others, the typist tries to exceed the previous rate each time—with the ultimate goal of adding an extra line of 10 words. Looker-uppers are frustrated by this drill as they cannot see what they have done—they know only that they have struck more keys.

Figure 9.4

| Calling "line" each . . . | The rate is . . . | | | |
|---|---|---|---|---|
| | 40-space line | 50-space line | 60-space line | 70-space line |
| 30 seconds | 16 wam | 20 wam | 24 wam | 28 wam |
| 20 seconds | 24 wam | 30 wam | 36 wam | 42 wam |
| 15 seconds | 32 wam | 40 wam | 48 wam | 56 wam |
| 12 seconds | 40 wam | 50 wam | 60 wam | 70 wam |

PRACTICE-SUITED-TO-NEEDS DRILL. A learner's self-inspection of his or her own paper can help that student self-prescribe individual drills. After reaching a specific speed goal, the student can work on one-minute accuracy drills. The student who has an accuracy problem can check one of the charts developed as a result of the Weaver study (see Selected Readings) in order to see just what to practice.

THE PACED LETTER. The paced letter enables every student to finish one complete letter within a timed period regardless of the student's typing speed. Thus, a 20-wam typist is given a letter in which the body contains 60 words, a 24-wam typist is given a 72-word body, and so on. All letters are to be written in the same format. Each letter is divided into four sections with a pacing signal following each section. The teacher uses the following timings: return address and date, 20 seconds; inside address and salutation, 34 seconds; body, 3 minutes; and closing and identification lines, 14 seconds. The teacher also gives a signal at the end of each minute while the students are typing the body so that they can see if they are meeting their goal (Friedrichs, p. 3).

## Suggestions for Improving Cognitive Learnings

At least four areas of typewriting involve cognitive learnings: planning production typing items, learning all of the applications of English usage to typewritten work, proofreading, and composition at the typewriter.

IMPROVING PLANNING OF PRODUCTION ITEMS. In this area, massed practice is preferred to distributed practice. For instance, the learner should practice making computations for typing tables before typing any tables. If the learner makes one computation, types the table, makes another computation, and types another table, the learning time is wrongly distributed; it should be spent on computations, the unknown element, rather than on typing, the known element. Initial instruction is given by the teacher, the textbook, videotapes or television, programmed instruction sheets, sound slides, or transparencies. If necessary, the learner listens again, rereads, reviews, or replays the instructions until the level of cognition required to plan the type of item to be typed is achieved. Then isolated drill in making the necessary computations is given until the learning has been developed into a cognitive skill demonstrable on a test.

Since planning time must be included in all production typing rates, timed drills on planning all types of production work are given until students can meet en route goals in terms of time as well as correctness. For instance, an en route goal might read: Given four simple tables involving words of varying length to be arranged in tables of three to five columns without a title on a half sheet, **demonstrate** your ability to compute the margins and tab stops without error in two minutes.

Guides as to how long it should take to plan an exercise encourage students to reduce planning time. (Students are also constantly reminded to plan before typing.) Some typewriting textbooks specify the planning time that should be given to planning an exercise. **185**

**IMPROVING KNOWLEDGE OF TYPEWRITING USAGE AND ENGLISH MECHAN-ICS.** Since training in typewriter usage and English mechanics proceeds simultaneously with the development of copying skill, the learner's attention is often focused so much on the act of typewriting that he or she cannot concentrate on the subject matter being presented. The typewriter, however, has an advantage over handwriting as the tool for teaching English mechanics. The copy stands out so much more clearly that decisions are easier to make at the typewriter. That factor probably explains why significant gains in general education can be made when the typewriter is the writing instrument.

The secret to developing cognitive skills in English lies in identifying the subcompetencies required but often not yet developed in the learner. For instance, the learner who does not know the difference between a phrase and a clause is not prepared to study restrictive and nonrestrictive clauses. The teacher may find it necessary to add to a collection of learning resources a set of standardized grammar and usage tests and modules of instructional materials from English and business English sources. Here is a place where individualized goals should be set.

Reinforcement is secured if the learner can immediately know whether a response is right or wrong. The student working alone may be given a key containing the correct answers, or learners may work in pairs in checking answers against a teacher's key or a projected transparency. The point is that feedback should be available at once.

An example follows that illustrates how an instant key can be developed for a spelling lesson. The teacher can rather easily program the lesson by using a duplicated sheet for student responses on which each word is correctly spelled at the right margin one double space *below* the line on which the learner attempts to spell the word from dictation.

1. _____
             1. separate
2. _____
             2. benefited
3. _____
             3. determining

As the student throws the carriage to type "benefited," he or she sees whether "separate" is spelled correctly. After "benefited" is typed, the typist throws the carriage to type *determining* and checks the response to *benefited.*

**PROOFREADING.** One of the most important competencies in typewriting is accurate proofreading. This skill does not come automatically though; it must be taught. Here are some suggestions for developing this cognitive skill. Before a group lesson on proofreading, the teacher distributes the following en route goal:

Given a sample page containing errors of various kinds (typographic, spelling, spacing with punctuation marks, omissions, etc.), **demonstrate** your proofreading ability by circling all errors. Standard: not more than one error overlooked.

1. Each student inserts the duplicated page containing errors into the typewriter. The teacher projects a transparency showing correct copy or students follow their own proofguide sheets from their work kits. The teacher reads aloud while each student moves the paper down from line to line by using the left hand to operate the cylinder knob so that the paper bail serves as a visual guide. The student marks each error found. In case of doubt, the learner checks the copy against the model after the oral reading has been finished.
2. The learners insert another duplicated sheet with errors and repeat the procedure.
3. After several attempts to locate all errors, the learners are tested. If they meet the performance goal, they proceed. If not, they are recycled.
4. Another lesson might be given on proofreading twice, once for typographic errors and mechanics and once for content.
5. Students proofread their own typewritten work against proofguide sheets and submit their self-evaluated work to the teacher along with their proofsheets, on which they have recorded their ratings.
6. The teacher provides a definite, reasonable length of time for proofreading exercises so that the learner automatically develops an appreciation of its importance.
7. The teacher spot checks to see whether learners are meeting en route goals.
8. The teacher gives a double penalty for undetected errors, using good judgment in deciding whether this rather drastic measure is necessary.
9. Students work in pairs while proofreading production units, exchanging papers and having the privilege of correcting errors located by the partner, who signs the paper, and receiving the resulting higher grade.
10. The teacher constantly raises standards in performance goals in proofreading. As a terminal goal, of course, production typewriting is graded on an acceptable–not acceptable basis. Nonacceptable items receive *no* credit.

COMPOSING AT THE TYPEWRITER. If the typewriter is to be used in composing, appropriate goals must be established. An example follows:

Given a simple topic, **demonstrate** your ability to compose at the typewriter by preparing a typed rough-draft composition, correcting all errors on the draft in pencil, choosing a title, and typing the corrected composition on which all errors are corrected and the title is centered on a half sheet. Do this in 12 minutes. When the product is read aloud, classmates will agree that it is interesting.

A definite cycle is suggested to develop this skill (Cook et al.). Probably the most difficult problem is to remove the inhibitions that this activity causes when first attempted.

1. The teacher explains the goal and introduces the topic to be written about. The class discusses the topic while students jot down a longhand outline of the points they want to cover.
2. Students type as rapidly as the words come, not even thinking about errors, changing their minds and x-ing out material when new ideas occur.
3. They remove the copies from the machine, read them thoughtfully, making any longhand changes desired, create an appropriate title, and plan carefully a setup that gives attractive side, top, and bottom margins.
4. Learners type from rough draft a usable copy, making any necessary changes.
5. Selected learners read their compositions aloud as the class evaluates content.
6. The teacher checks the paper for technical elements.

## Suggestions for Improving Affective Learnings

It is desirable that all students attend classes regularly. It is imperative that the typewriting student attend class regularly to be able to produce the same output expected of the entire class, which often moves in lockstep. Yet regular attendance is not characteristic of many of today's students. If individually prescribed instruction is provided, the learner who was absent or requires longer than most of the group to reach a goal can work individually to reach unmet goals. Usually attendance improves when the learner becomes successful. He or she may now proceed upward through the domain of affective behaviors—observing successful learners, questioning the desirability of adopting behaviors observed, and beginning to value behaviors that will ensure reaching prescribed goals.

The learner follows the same steps in developing good work habits: observing, questioning, and finally valuing the behaviors of other students who are achieving.

Because of the close proximity of teacher and student in most typewriting classrooms, the relationship between the two can become very meaningful. The teacher learns to know the student. The student then begins to value himself or herself as someone in whom the teacher is interested. Self-images improve as attainable goals are reached. The student feels important and also that the work being typed is important. For optimum results the learner cooperates with the teacher in evaluating learning needs and in selecting performance goals. If a student says to the teacher, "Will you please watch me type and tell me what I should change so that my basic skill will improve," that teacher knows that, for that student, the system is succeeding.

Working conditions in the classroom approximate those found in business. The teacher can start the class promptly, develop orderly routines for passing papers to and from work stations, and, in general, act like an office supervisor. Standards of conduct that are based on acceptable office behavior are required of all students. The teacher must always exhibit courtesy and require similar courtesy from students.

Because of the importance of learning to work together, it is desirable to establish conditions in which learners cooperate. They can proofread together, just as office workers do. Cooperatively, they can develop standards for acceptable work and substitute these standards for teacher-imposed ones.

Students appreciate an atmosphere in which they can concentrate. A disruptive student does not receive the same approbation from peers in a typewriting class that would be accorded in a history class; learners are annoyed if they are disturbed at work.

## Learning Resources

Most publishers are beginning to produce, rather than merely typewriting textbooks, typewriting programs containing a variety of learning resources. A program may be basic (essential) or comprehensive (including supplementary materials that add to the effectiveness of the total presentation but are not required). Essential typewriting resources include the textbook, the teacher's manual and key, and instructional recordings (cassettes or tapes). Some publishers also supply periodic teaching suggestions for using the materials more effectively. A comprehensive program might include such things as transparencies, wall charts, progress charts, progress certificates, rhythm records, placement tests, and end-of-unit tests.

## Textbooks

Typewriting textbooks are usually written by a corps of authors, each contributing special talents. Some of the authors direct doctoral studies in the field regularly; others do independent research.

Materials are carefully tried out before they are published. Probably the authors' greatest contribution is their analysis of the difficulty of practice materials, analysis not possible for the classroom teacher.

It goes without saying that the textbook should fit the objectives of the learner. There are textbooks for elementary school classes, middle-school or junior high school classes, general high school use, vocational classes, personal use, adult education, and for refresher training. There are textbooks by well-known authors and books by unknown writers who market their wares at the paperback counter.

Robinson's survey of typewriting instruction shows that, unfortunately, although most schools provide the typewriting textbooks, almost three-fourths of them provide one book for each typewriter, not a book for each student (Robinson 5, p. 8). This means that homework is out of the question except as the student refers to workbook instructions.

For the teacher who is developing his or her own materials, it will be helpful to know that Robinson has proved that there are three components of copy difficulty: syllabic intensity, average word length, and high-

Figure 9.5

| Classification | Syllabic Intensity | Average Word Length | Percent of High-Frequency Words |
|---|---|---|---|
| Very Easy | 1.2 | 5.0 | 95 |
| Easy | 1.3 | 5.2 | 90 |
| Low Average | 1.4 | 5.4 | 85 |
| Average | 1.5 | 5.6 | 80 |
| High Average | 1.6 | 5.8 | 75 |
| Difficult | 1.7 | 6.0 | 70 |

frequency word levels (Robinson 4, p. 21). Figure 9.5 shows how these elements are simultaneously merged to produce copy that may be classified from "Very Easy" through six levels to "Difficult."

It is apparent that "Very Easy" refers to copy in which almost all of the words (95 percent) come from high-frequency word lists with five letters and only slightly more than one syllable (1.2 syllables) to the word.

## Typewriters

Robinson's survey also showed that in 1967 only 10 percent of school typewriters were electric (Robinson 5, p. 8). Yet Erickson (see Selected Readings), in 1971, reported that only 18 percent of the typewriters used by the office workers he surveyed were manual. How can the schools meet the needs of business if this wide discrepancy between school and office equipment continues to exist?

Elite type is commonly used for office work, but the schools reported a preponderance of pica type, with only about a third reporting that more than half of their typewriters have elite type. Again the difference is frustrating.

If there are several classrooms, it is desirable to have the room for beginners equipped with typewriters all of the same make. Classrooms for advanced students should contain a number of different makes that the graduate will find in the employing community.

The teacher who is fortunate enough to have electric typewriters should *insist* on a master switch that controls the power so that there is less likelihood that a motor will be left on. Care of typewriters is the major responsibility of the teacher. He or she should develop a system by which learners report machines out of order. A duplicated chart on which the position of each typewriter is marked and the number of each machine recorded could be posted so that each learner can record the nature of the repair needed—that is, if the teacher cannot make the repair when called to the learner's desk. The number is usually visible at the right side of the machine if the carriage or element is moved to the extreme left. The teacher checks to see whether the machine is really out of order or whether a minor correction will restore it to working condition. A new chart is posted when the old one becomes too cluttered.

Some schools have contracts with typewriter repair companies who come to the school whenever called and also take the machines into their shops during the summer for cleaning. Other schools call a repairman when needed. The teacher should investigate the cost of a contract and keep careful comparative cost figures to ensure that the least expensive but most efficient repair service is obtained.

Changing a ribbon should be included in the performance goals of a typewriting course. It is suggested that the performance goal include a time limit. One experience will not develop ribbon changing to the standard usually required on the job and the learner should repeat the procedure until the standard is met.

Another performance goal that should be included is that the learner should keep the machine dusted so that it will always pass teacher inspection. Many teachers rotate the responsibility of cleaning the typewriters among the different classes. The disadvantage is that learners clean their typewriters only when told to do so, although they should learn to clean them when they need it. They should also learn to evaluate their work in terms of the quality of the ribbon impression and ask for a new ribbon when one is needed.

## Transparencies

Most typewriting programs include transparencies for large- or small-group instruction. On the *Typing 300* transparencies, the teacher's guide is written in the margins so that it does not project but can be referred to constantly by the teacher. Transparencies can be used for teacher demonstration. A transparency of the keyboard allows the teacher to place his or her hand on the keyboard on the visual and to move the fingers so that their shadow illustrates the reach, the direction, and the release. A transparency can be used to proofread the students' output. In fact, with modern equipment, a teacher can take a student's paper and quickly make a transparency which can be used as the model.

## Tapes, Cassettes, and Records

Recordings supplement teacher-controlled drills or supplant them if individually prescribed learning is adopted. They are excellent ways of pacing students while they practice. They are especially valuable because there is no wasted time.

## Pacing Instruments

There are several mechanical pacers available that provide steady pace at the rate at which they are set. They are valuable when the learner wants to move on to a higher speed level. The learner (individually or in a small group) tries to keep up with the pacer until the desired speed is achieved. Pacers are also helpful to the erratic typist because they can be set to force him or her to type at a slower pace.

The Educational Development Laboratory (EDL) Skillbuilder can be used for controlling the rate at which copy is shown to the typist. A single line of material is shown on the screen, and a device moves across the screen making the copy visible to the typist at a predetermined rate. The typist must keep up with the copy, completing the line as the blockout moves across the page and going on to the next line as it appears along with the blockout device. The EDL Skillbuilder is appropriate for small-group instruction of learners at the same stage of speed development but is to be avoided with a group having widely varying speed rates.

One pacer that is available shows a green light at the middle and a red light at the end of each line so that the learner can pace performance to match the goal if a 70-space line is used.

Another pacesetter has a plastic eye guide that moves down the page of copy at whatever speed is desired, thus providing the learner with a letter-by-letter pacing cue.

## Stopwatches and Timers

A stopwatch is indispensable to the typewriting teacher, for it eliminates any waiting period while the second hand reaches a desired point. Each classroom should have three or four interval times so that individual students or small groups working on a special improvement drill may be timed. A second or third interval timer can also be set to signal portions of a longer timing.

## Programmed Instruction

Teachers can use programmed homework instruction sheets advantageously if textbooks are not permitted outside the classroom or if textbook materials are inadequate. West proved the value of such programs in teaching low-ability vocational high school students how to plan production items. He compared experimental Year 1 and Year 2 students who had used programmed homework instruction sheets with control Year 1 and Year 2 students who had used the textbook only. The results showed no differences in straight-copying skills. Although the control students had faster production rates, the experimental students had about half as many errors in placement on the page. West recommends a revision of vocational typing instruction in which production work is begun earlier and deliberate instruction is given in making placement decisions, followed by a great deal of practice thereafter from unarranged materials without teacher assistance (West 3, pp. 52–53). Programmed instruction materials are also recommended for remedial instruction in spelling, punctuation, and word division.

## Videotapes and Closed-Circuit Television

Preparing an outstanding typewriting lesson requires a lot of time and effort. The teacher who captures such a lesson on videotape for reuse has both conserved time and also improved the quality of instruction.

A second advantage of videotaped lessons is that they can be run or rerun by any student at any time. Also, the technique being shown on a screen is usually easier to see than a teacher's demonstration on a typewriter at the front of the room. Videotaping also has value for analyzing the learner at work.

## Computer-Assisted Instruction

Computer-assisted instruction in typewriting is beginning to be used. For example, nonsecretarial students at Ocean County College, Toms River, New Jersey, have been admitted to such a course for several years. The terminal performance goals include speed of 30 wam with no more than five errors in a five-minute timing, typing of mailable business and personal letters and envelopes, setting up a tabulation problem in columnar form, and typing a manuscript with footnotes properly located. Each student is assigned a logon key which unlocks the program of lessons. When he or she "plugs in," two-way communication is provided between the system and the student, who completes the assignments, queries the computer when necessary, is graded, and is either recycled or progresses to new goals. Results and student reaction have been favorable, although learners miss the pressure of competing with other students. (Source: Personal letter from Jeanette M. Wolcott, assistant professor of computer science.)

## Individual Progress Method

The Gregg Typing Individual Progress Method (IPM) is a new, multimedia approach to the teaching of typing. The teacher may find that IPM maximizes individually paced learning. Students work by themselves with colored slides for visuals and audio cassettes that provide instructions and explanations. Electronic pulses on the cassettes activate the slides, stopping the program so that the student can type the required drills. The student, working at his or her own pace, touches a foot pedal to reactivate the program. IPM can be used in resource centers for students who wish to progress at their own rate. It frees the teacher to circulate among students and provide individual instruction and evaluation as they are needed.

## Evaluation of Student Performance and of the System

The final step in the learning system is the administration of the evaluation instruments that measure the terminal performances that were selected. Can the learners *do* what they are supposed to do after the learning experiences they have had? Have their typewriting behavior and their total behavior *changed* to conform with the performance goals established?

If, at the end of a year of high school typewriting, the students can meet all the thirteen performance goals on pages 171–172, the teacher can relax somewhat; the system works and requires only minor adaptations in terms of newly identified competencies to be achieved, new students to be taught, and new learning resources.

If the answer is no, the teacher modifies the system. For instance, if goal 5, page 172, was not met, the teacher may decide that although en route goals involving visual acuity, knowledge of English mechanics, spelling, and typewriter usage were provided in the textbook, the students were so far below the level for which the textbook was intended that the goal should be changed. Or the teacher may decide to organize small groups for instruction in commonly difficult goals, supplementing the textbook with transparencies covering basic punctuation until the members can meet the goals. Or the teacher may decide that the standards are unrealistic and must be revised. Finally, the teacher may decide that most of the students just do not care enough about the subject to want to meet the standards and that attention should be concentrated on problems in the affective domain.

## Learning Activities

1. Because you will be expected to type with correct technique when working with learners, ask your instructor and a group of peers, using a technique chart which it approves from among numerous charts available, to evaluate your typewriting during a one-minute speed test and to prescribe en route goals for you to follow. After individual practice, ask for reevaluation until you meet the en route goals. (Performance goals 2 and 5)

2. Teach the typewriting keyboard (possibly the first 15 lessons, depending on the textbook) to a beginner (younger brother or sister, friend, even your cooperative mother or father). As a member of a small group compare your results with the performance goals given in *Typing 300* and with those of the rest of the group. Present your conclusions to the entire class. (Adapted from West's *Acquisition of Typewriting Skill* with appreciation to the author.) (Performance goals 2, 3, 4, and 5)

3. Analyze five speed tests from a typewriting class in your college and prescribe the appropriate corrective drills from the Weaver chart on page 15 of the *Instructor's Manual and Visual Key for Typing 75* (Gregg, 1971). (Performance goals 3, 4, 5, and 6)

4. Using typewriting textbooks and professional articles, in a small group develop a list of drills that can be used to develop competency in handling parts of letters, rough draft, tabulations, and manuscript typewriting. Duplicate the list when it has been approved by your instructor for inclusion in every student's kit of teaching materials. (Performance goals 3 and 4)

5. To improve your understanding of acceptable and unacceptable typed materials, procure a set of one day's advanced transcription or typewriting papers that are expected to meet the terminal mailability standard. Number each paper. Evaluate each paper as acceptable or unacceptable on an individual chart on which numbers only are used. After all papers are evaluated, compare evaluations and form conclusions. (Performance goals 2 and 3)

**6.** Demonstrate to the class or to a small group (as your instructor directs) the use of a specific (a) cassette, sound slide, or record, (b) EDL Skillbuilder, filmstrip, transparency, or videotape, (c) pacer or performance analysis instrument, setting the stage by identifying the situation in which you would use the resource chosen (10 minutes). After group discussion, write an evaluation of the resource and a recommendation as to how it is to be used. Duplicate and distribute for inclusion in student kits of teaching materials. (Performance goal 5)

**7.** While working in the organization pattern preferred by your instructor and after choosing a production typewriting unit from an advanced typewriting textbook and writing the terminal performance goal for the unit, construct a detailed plan for the unit. Your instructor will evaluate in terms of identification of subcompetencies required, provision for en route goals, identification of needed learning packets (which are not to be written), relevance of evaluations chosen to measure performance goals, and provision for development of affective behaviors. (Performance goal 2)

**8.** In a small group develop criteria for evaluating the teaching of a group drill with individualized performance goals that meet your instructor's approval. (Performance goal 5)

## SELECTED READINGS

BABBS, LYNDA F., AND RUTH CLINE, "Experimental Typing Project: Denver (Colorado) Elementary School," *Journal of Business Education,* December, 1970, pp. 103–105.

BARTHOLOME, LLOYD W., "The Typewriter as a Tool for Improving Spelling," *Delta Pi Epsilon Journal,* February, 1970, pp. 28–31.

BUCHL, THOMAS V., "Articulation Procedures and Policies for Junior High School Typewriting in Selected Secondary Schools of the United States," unpublished doctoral dissertation, University of North Dakota, Grand Forks, N. Dak., 1970. Also reported in the *Journal of Business Education,* November, 1971, p. 77.

*Business Education Forum.* Every year the November issue focuses on typewriting.

CAULFIELD, PHYLLIS, "A Study of Certain General Education Values of Typewriting in the Junior High School, " unpublished doctoral dissertation, University of Michigan at Ann Arbor, Ann Arbor, Mich., 1957, 186 pp. (See also *Business Education World,* **40:**28–29, June, 1960; *Journal of Business Education,* **35:**35, October, 1959; *National Business Education Quarterly,* **28:**53, October, 1959.)

CRAWFORD, T. JAMES, "The Effect of Emphasizing Production Typing Contrasted with Speed Typewriting in Developing Production Typewriting abliltiy," unpublished doctoral dissertation, University of Pittsburgh, 1956. Summary also available in Monograph 97, South-Western Publishing Company, Cincinnati.

DOUGLAS, LLOYD V., JAMES T. BLANFORD, AND RUTH I. ANDERSON, "Teaching Typewriting," *Teaching Business Subjects,* 3d ed., South-Western Publishing Company, Cincinnati, Ohio, 1973, pp. 95–152.

ERICKSON, LAWRENCE W., *Basic Components of Office Work—An Analysis of 300 Office Jobs,* Monograph 123, South-Western Publishing Company, Cincinnati, 1971.

_____"The Teaching of Typewriting," *National Business Education Yearbook*, 1971, pp. 17–37.

FEATHERINGHAM, RICHARD, "The Validity of Personal-Use Typewriting Courses as Determined by an Analysis of the Practical Application of This Subject over a 15-Year Period," unpublished doctoral dissertation, University of North Dakota, Grand Forks, N. Dak., 1965.

FRIEDRICHS, LLOYD, "The Paced Letter," *Business Education World*, March–April, 1971, p. 3.

GRUBBS, ROBERT L. (1) "Prescription for Effective Shorthand Teaching," *Business Education World*, May, 1961, pp. 26–27.

_____(2) Demonstration at the Business Education Association of New York City and Vicinity, Gregg Shorthand Division, Spring, 1961.

_____ALAN LLOYD, BARBARA NALEPA, JOHN ROWE, DAVID WEAVER, AND FRED WINGER (3) *When to Type What to Increase Typing Skill,* undated four-page brochure, Gregg Division of McGraw-Hill Book Company, New York.

HARMS, HARM, B. W. STEHR, AND E. EDWARD HARRIS, "Typewriting," *Methods of Teaching Business and Distributive Education,* 3d ed., South-Western Publishing Company, Cincinnati, Ohio, 1973.

KLINE, GERALDINE, "An Analysis of the Achievements and Attitudes of Middle-School Students in a Self-Directed Typewriting Program Compared with Students in a Teacher-Directed Program," unpublished doctoral dissertation, University of North Dakota, Grand Forks, N. Dak., 1972. Also reported in the *Journal of Business Education*, March, 1973, page 261.

KREVOLIN, NATHAN, "How Can We Best Implement Elementary School Typing Courses?" *Business Education World,* November, 1965.

LAMBRECHT, JUDITH J., AND MARGE GARDINER, "Individual Instruction in Beginning Typewriting," *The Journal of Business Education,* March, 1971, pp. 243–244 (independent research).

LANGFORD, THOMAS E., "Effects of Three Practice Strategies upon Chaining, Speed, and Accuracy in Typewriting," unpublished doctoral dissertation, Syracuse University, Syracuse, N.Y., 1970. Also reported in the *Balance Sheet,* November, 1971, pp. 100–105.

LUCHIN, DENNIS P., "The Effect of Ninth Grade Typewriting on Student Success in Typewriting II Compared to the Effect of Senior High School Typewriting on Success in Typewriting II," unpublished master's thesis, Kent State University, Kent, Ohio, 1970. Also reported in the *Journal of Business Education,* December, 1970, p. 120.

MACH, KAYE ALLAN, "The Effects of Repetitive and Nonrepetitive Practice on Straight-Copy Speed and Accuracy Achievements in First-Semester Beginning Typewriting," University of North Dakota, Grand Forks, N. Dak., 1971. Also reported in the *Business Education Forum,* October, 1972, p. 44.

MCLEOD, DORIS, AND RAMONA FIRST, "Typewriting Instruction as an Aid to the Learning of English as a Foreign Language," unpublished mimeographed report of research at San Francisco State College, San Francisco, 1963.

MISSLING, LORRAINE, "A Comparison of the Traditional Plan to Three Selected Flexible Modular Plans in First-Semester High School Typewriting with Straight-Copy Achievement and Production Achievement as Criteria," unpublished doctoral dissertation, University of North Dakota, Grand Forks, N. Dak., 1970. Also reported in *Business Education Forum,* October, 1971, page 46, and in the *Business Education Forum,* March, 1972, pp. 70–71.

MORRISON, PHYLLIS CAULFIELD, "A Study of Certain General Education Values in the Junior High School," unpublished doctoral dissertation, University of Michigan, Ann Arbor, Mich., 1957.

PERKINS, E. A., JR., F. R. BYRD, AND D. E. ROLEY, *Clusters of Tasks Associated with Performance of Major Types of Office Work,* USOE Project No. 7-0031, 1968.

ROBINSON, JERRY W. (1) "Effects of Copy Difficulty upon Typewriting Performance," University of California, Los Angeles, unpublished doctoral dissertation, 1966. Also reported in *Delta Pi Epsilon Journal,* 1967, pp. 9–24.

———(2) *Practices and Preferences in Teaching Typewriting* South-Western Publishing Company Monograph 117, Cincinnati, 1967.

———(3) "Psychological Conditions of Problem-Production Skill Building," *Balance Sheet,* January, 1972, pp. 148–149.

———(4) *Strategies for Instruction in Typewriting,* soft-cover publication of South-Western Publishing Company, 1972, pp. 42–43.

———(5) "Profile of Typewriting Instruction in American Secondary Schools," *Practices and Preferences in Teaching Typewriting,* South-Western Publishing Company Monograph 117, 1967, p. 2.

ROWE, JOHN, "An Experiment in Teaching Portable Electric Typewriting to Third and Fourth Grade Students," University of North Dakota, Grand Forks, N. Dak., 1959 (independent study).

———(ed.) "Part III: New Thinking in the Teaching of Typewriting," *National Business Education Yearbook,* 1974, pp. 58–128.

ROWE, JOHN L., ALAN C. LLOYD, AND FRED E. WINGER, *Typing 300,* Gregg Division of McGraw-Hill Book Company, 1972 (also teacher's manual and student guides).

RUSSON, ALLIEN R. AND S. J. WANOUS, *Philosophy and Psychology of Teaching Typewriting,* 2d ed., South-Western Publishing Company, Cincinnati, Ohio, 1973.

SEIBERT, KATHERIN E., "Teaching Slow Readers Using the Electric Typewriter," unpublished report of research under a federal grant, California State Polytechnic College, Pomona, Calif., 1971.

WARNER, DOUGLAS E., "Structured Production Assignments vs. Unstructured Production Assignments in Programmed Intermediate Collegiate Typewriting," unpublished master's thesis, Brigham Young University, Provo, Utah, 1972.

WEAVER, DAVID H., "An Experimental Study of the Relative Impact of Controllable Factors of Difficulty in Typewriting Practice Materials," unpublished doctoral dissertation, Syracuse University, Syracuse, N.Y., 1966. Portions of the study are distributed with the Gregg typewriting materials.

WEST, LEONARD J. (1) *Acquisition of Typewriting Skills,* Pitman Publishing Company, New York, 1969.

———(2) *Implications of Research for Typewriting,* 2d ed., Delta Pi Epsilon Research Bulletin #4, Gustavus Adolphus College, St. Peter, Minn., 1974.

———(3) *Effect of Programmed vs. Conventional Instruction on Proficiency at Office Typing Tasks,* Independent Study, City University of New York, Office of Teacher Education, Research Report 71-S, 1971. Also reported in *Business Education Forum,* October, 1972, pp. 52–53.

———(4) *Research on Teaching Business and Commercial Subjects,* ERIC Ed 051 377

———(5) *Implications of Research for Teaching Typewriting,* 2d ed., Delta Pi Epsilon Research Bulletin No. 41, 1974.

## PERFORMANCE GOALS

**1.** Given data on students in a hypothetical school, including academic records, English grades, and reading levels, **construct** a plan to present to your department for identifying deficiencies of individual students which are likely to affect success in shorthand learning, defending each recommendation made on the basis of material in this chapter and material added by your instructor.

**2.** Select any two letters from sources other than shorthand textbooks and revise the letters to include no more than ten words beyond the first 1,500 on either Silverthorn's or Mellinger's lists, and **demonstrate** your ability to prepare the material for a dictation speed your instructor assigns. Evaluation will be based on a statement of the en route goal appropriate for the dictation, no more than ten words beyond the stated 1,500, and material converted into groups of twenty standard words and marked for ease of dictation.

**3.** After your instructor has approved the letters prepared for performance goal 2, use the two letters in preparing a speed-building drill you select from your readings (giving the source for the drill used). **Demonstrate** your ability to dictate for speed building by preparing a cassette which meets the following criteria: speed goal is stated at beginning of tape; speed-building plan is accurately followed; dictation speeds are accurate when checked by your instructor or a classmate using stopwatch; and your dictation is natural with appropriate pauses.

**4.** Assume you are responsible for submitting a grading plan at a meeting of your business department. Using the material in this chapter and in Chapter 8, **construct** a grading plan which provides for any *one level* of shorthand learning, using either a performance goal presented in this chapter or one you construct. Present your plan in duplicated form for distribution to your class with a written defense in terms of individual differences, flexibility of time for individual needs, and significance of grade in terms of what the individual can perform.

**5.** Select any shorthand lesson between 3 and 19 of any shorthand textbook and prepare a detailed plan for your instructor's approval. After approval, use the plan while microteaching for ten minutes to a small group and **demonstrate** your ability to meet the criteria developed in learning activity 5 for the following: using chalkboard; reading homework; presenting new brief forms and phrases, review brief forms and phrases, new theory, and review theory.

**6.** Select any *two* techniques below and while microteaching for ten minutes **demonstrate** your ability to perform according to criteria on sheets developed in learning activity 5 for the following: reading bookplates without transcript; reading bookplates with aid of transcript; reading homework bookplates with transcript; reading homework bookplates without transcript; writing homework in notebook; and taking dictation in notebook.

**7.** Select any one of the six steps of transcription and while microteaching for 10 minutes, **demonstrate** your ability to meet the criteria developed in learning activity 5.

**8.** Given a report on an observation of a hypothetical student and a copy of the typed transcript the student submitted, **decide** on specific remedial drills for the student and prepare a short directive which may be given to the student for use. Evaluation will be based upon the appropriateness of the drills for the problem.

# CHAPTER 10

# Shorthand

Although more than a thousand rapid writing systems have been invented, only a few have survived the rigorous test of use. They can be classified as vocational and personal-use systems. Recording may be done by hand or machine. The handwritten vocational systems generally taught today are Gregg and Pitman, both of which rely on symbols to represent sounds, enabling writers to attain high speeds of dictation. The new Century 21 Shorthand is also a symbol system. The most widely taught shorthand system is Gregg. Other handwritten systems such as Speedwriting, Stenoscript ABC Shorthand, and Forkner utilize abbreviated longhand and are used for both vocational and personal uses. A personal-use symbol system is Gregg Notehand, designed to improve the student's study habits, improve listening and comprehension, and take usable notes.

A machine system of shorthand, called stenotypy, utilizes English alphabetic characters which are recorded on paper tape by the operator depressing keys. Because the number of keys on the keyboard is limited, certain letters are combined to represent words. Thus the speeds necessary to record legislative and administrative hearings, court trials, and convention proceedings can be reached.

"Verbatim reporting," as it is sometimes called, is the recording of speech up to 250 words per minute—and even faster—in a note system that persons other than the recorder can transcribe swiftly and accurately.

Many two-year colleges, particularly those in urban areas, offer stenotypy to students who want to develop high speeds in shorthand; however, additional specialized training is essential for court and convention reporting. Experimentation with computer transcription of the tapes is already in progress, but the different theories espoused by various writers, phonetic problems, and the inconsistencies of the English language present technical difficulties which must be resolved before "computer compatible" stenotypy is feasible.

## Needs of the Learner

Selection of a shorthand system depends upon the student's objectives (vocational or personal note making), the length of time needed for mastery, the capability of the student, and the memory load. Regardless of the system, the vocational objectives are identical.

Men and women who possess high-level competencies in taking dictation and transcribing it accurately are in constant demand by business. Such jobs often serve as direct pipelines to administrative posts.

Business teachers are concerned with the loss in enrollments between first- and second-year shorthand. Multiple reasons account for this phenomenon. In one year, some students develop basic competencies which permit them to gain entry-level positions as stenographers. Other students who might benefit from a second year of shorthand encounter scheduling difficulties and make priority decisions which rule out shorthand; and still others who are discouraged by slow progress decide against continuing shorthand. Some of these students, especially those in schools allowing anybody to enroll in shorthand, enter with deficiencies in English grammar, reading, listening, and hearing phonetic sounds accurately. Unless such problems are identified at the beginning of shorthand instruction and corrective measures are taken, both student and teacher become frustrated. The solution to losing enrollments is probably to provide a flexible program enabling students to exit from shorthand when they attain competencies for entry-level jobs and to progress toward relevant and attainable individual goals all during their study of shorthand.

Traditionally, shorthand classes have been comprised of women, who are benefiting from affirmative action programs requiring that more women be hired at all levels in business and, if qualified, promoted to managerial and junior executive positions. It is not uncommon today, as sex differences disappear in all job categories, to find men electing shorthand for use as a tool in employment.

The ultimate goal of shorthand is for a student to perform in a business situation by taking dictation at a speed which enables the accurate recording and transcription of notes into mailable letters and reports at a rate commensurate with an acceptable range of office standards.

While it is difficult to identify any one measure which predicts success in the complex process of learning shorthand, research by Frink, Moskovis, Nennich, Skaff, and Varah identifies these multiple abilities which affect shorthand success: the ability to (1) hear phonetic sounds correctly, (2) record sounds heard accurately, (3) read shorthand notes for word sense, (4) use correct grammar in transcript, (5) use correct spelling in transcript, (6) use correct punctuation in transcript, (7) proofread and correct all errors, (8) be motivated, and (9) think critically.

A valuable tool in identifying learning problems is the aptitude test. Three popular ones are: Byers' First Year Shorthand Test, Deemer's ERC Stenographic Test, and Turse Shorthand Aptitude Test. Figure 10.1 identifies the subtests within each of the tests and illustrates similarities

Figure 10.1   Comparison of activities
measured by shorthand aptitude tests

| Subtests | Turse Shorthand Aptitude Test | ERC[a] Stenographic Aptitude Test | Byers' First-Year Shorthand Test |
|---|---|---|---|
| Spelling and word sense | Discriminate between correctly and incorrectly spelled words and spell words from those contracted, abbreviated, or incomplete | Select from five words one which is nearest meaning of key word | Supply right letter from one omitted in text |
| Phonetic association | Spell correctly words presented phonetically | Spell correctly words presented phonetically | Spell correctly words written phonetically |
| Using symbols | Transcribe six shorthand sentences using an alphabetic key to determine meaning of symbol | No subtest | Select a converse pattern from that of image presented |
| Word discrimination | Select word to best complete sentence | Select best word from two or three available | No subtest |
| Retention ability | Listen to dictation, carry dictation in mind, and write dictation while continuing to listen | Write in longhand from sentences dictated | Convert into alphabetic letters the dictation of numbers |
| Manual dexterity (stroking) | Write lines within boxes | Copy Gettysburg address | Record symbols rapidly |

[a]Educational Research Corporation

among the three tests. Each test measures mental dexterity, verbal aptitude, facility in using symbols, and the ability to take dictation. None of them measures motivation, the ability to hear sounds correctly, proofread, punctuate, read, and think critically. In fact, some of the subtests measure areas unrelated to success in learning shorthand. For example, Byers found that hand dexterity and retention ability are weak predictors of shorthand success. (Lambrecht, pp. 42–43; Skaff) Therefore, a teacher may omit these subtests.

Nennich studied beginning shorthand students in selected two-year colleges in an effort to predict success in shorthand. By combining the scores on Cloze (analysis of reading level), spelling, reading rate, and vocabulary tests, she was able to accurately predict shorthand success for two-thirds of the students studied. (This procedure involves a statistical technique which permits manipulation of scores for prediction.) Since the Cloze test alone was a successful predictor for 63 percent of the students, Nennich recommends its use in determining the beginning shorthand student's language problems. (Recycle to Chapter 7, pp. 127–128, for a description of the use of the Cloze test.)

## Needs of Business

Demand for proficient stenographers and secretaries has always exceeded the supply, despite the fact that high schools, two-year colleges, and some four-year colleges offer secretarial programs. The U.S. Bureau of Labor Statistics forecasts a demand for an additional 237,000 stenographers and secretaries for each year through 1980 (*Our Manpower and Training Needs,* p. 43). BLS also reveals that a total of 142,055 stenographers and secretaries were graduated by high schools and two-year colleges in 1970 (*Employment and Unemployment in 1971 . . .,* p. 76). Thus, the annual supply is far short of the demand, even when consideration is given to the numbers of people who re-enter the labor force each year.

The *National Survey of Professional, Administrative, Technical, and Clerical Pay* (pp. 73–75, see Selected Readings) identifies specific tasks for stenographers, as follows:

Stenographer, General—Primary duty is to take and transcribe dictation from one or more persons either in shorthand or by Stenotype or similar machine, involving a normal routine vocabulary. May also type from written copy. May maintain files, keep simple records or perform other relatively routine clerical tasks. May operate from a stenographic pool. *Does not include transcribing-machine work.*

Stenographer, Senior—Primary duty is to take and transcribe dictation from one or more persons either in shorthand or by Stenotype or similar machine, involving a varied technical or specialized vocabulary such as in legal briefs or reports on scientific research. May also type from written copy. May also set up and maintain files or keep records, etc. . . . Performs stenographic duties requiring significantly greater independence and responsibility than stenographer, general. Work requires high degree of stenographic speed and accuracy; a thorough working knowledge of general business and office procedure and of the specific business operations, organization, policies, procedures, files, workflow, etc. Uses this knowledge in performing stenographic duties and responsible clerical tasks.

The job of a stenographer (general or senior) is distinguished from that of secretary in that the secretary normally works in a confidential relationship to one or more employers and performs more responsible and discretionary tasks. The differentiation between the stenographer and secretary is apparent in the description of a secretary.

Secretary—assigned as personal secretary, normally to one individual. Maintains a close and highly responsive relationship to the day-to-day work activities of the supervisor. Works fairly independently receiving a minimum of detailed supervision and guidance. Performs varied clerical and secretarial duties, usually including most of the following (*National Survey . . .,* p. 73):

    a. Receives telephone calls, personal callers, and incoming mail, answers routine inquiries, and routes the technical inquiries to the proper persons;

    b. Establishes, maintains, and revises the supervisor's files;

    c. Maintains the supervisor's calendar and makes appointments as instructed;

    d. Relays messages from supervisor to subordinates;

    e. Reviews correspondence, memoranda, and reports prepared by others for the supervisor's signature to assure procedural and typographic accuracy;

    f. Performs stenographic and typing work.

The need of business for qualified stenographers and secretaries is further stimulated by the emergence of "word processing," a term used to describe a systematic combination of dictators, administrative secretaries, equipment, and correspondence secretaries to handle a firm's communications effectively.

Some schools offer word-processing programs to students who have not met with success in shorthand. In many instances, however, such students cannot be prepared successfully as correspondence secretaries, for they lack competencies involved in written communications. If an organization adopts word processing, successful stenographers and secretaries are usually selected as key people to establish the new system.

Additional evidence of the importance of communications abilities among stenographers and secretaries is presented by NOBELS, which classifies stenographic duties under "communications services" and also includes typewriting and oral communications. (Recycle to Chapter 3, p. 49–50.)

Data from many sources identifies specific tasks performed by employees in the stenographic and secretarial positions as follows:

1. Understand words and their correct use in correspondence.
2. Hear phonetic sounds and record them in symbols or abbreviated longhand.
3. Take dictation from individual.
4. Typewrite from dictation, shorthand notes, and rough drafts.
5. Transcribe the dictation, using correct English and spelling, and prepare various types of letters and business forms.
6. Use specialized vocabulary—technical, medical, and legal for higher-level stenographic positions.
7. Take notes given for instructions and follow the instructions.
8. Communicate verbally with superiors and with fellow workers.
9. Adapt to routine tasks.
10. Analyze incoming mail to identify the name, title, and address.
11. Proofread letters and reports typed.
12. Make corrections in letters and reports.
13. Understand the operation of the business.
14. Understand the organizationl pattern of the business.
15. Understand and follow selected office procedures.
16. Follow an established flow of work.

Little evidence exists as to the standards of performance for the above tasks, and much of what does exist is based upon what employers think they need. Multiple factors affect the standard of performance in taking dictation and transcribing: (1) the kind of dictation material (simple or technical), (2) the dictation competencies of the dictator, (3) the range of dictation speeds required on the job, (4) the number of letters transcribed within one day, and (5) the degree of accuracy required by the person dictating.

Green investigated speeds of office-style dictation. After analyzing speed patterns of 72 dictators, he concluded that a shorthand writer taking dictation at 80 words a minute for a three-minute period could take only 48 percent of all material dictated. A stenographer taking 100 words a minute for three minutes could take 75 percent of all material dictated. (See Figure 10.2.)

Figure 10.3 illustrates the percentages of time dictators spent in the various phases of dictation—60 percent being either groping or thoughtful and the other 40 percent confident or sprinting. He concluded that a stenographer must be able to take a top speed for three minutes and a cruising speed for five minutes. Each teacher recognizes that only the most competent dictators "sprint" at 100 words or above as they dictate; many dictators rarely exceed 70 or 90 words a minute.

## Identifying and Classifying Competencies

All shorthand instruction is geared toward the attainment of those competencies needed on the job. The on-the-job competencies may be stated as follows: (1) Take office-type dictation at speeds varying from 60 to 100 words per minute and transcribe the letters, reports, and/or manuscripts into mailable form at a rate commensurate with office standards. (2) Interact with others in a positive way. (3) Understand organizational structure and its procedures by adapting to office routines that facilitate the total work flow.

Within the shorthand class, the primary concern is to develop Competency No. 1; thus the following discussion omits Nos. 2 and 3, which are discussed in the chapters on communications (Chapter 11) and office procedures (Chapter 15).

The teacher must first determine the kinds of competencies which form a ladder to the terminal competency stated above. Because the learner

Figure 10.2   Analysis of dictation speeds as related to percentage of dictation recorded

| Writing speed for 3 min. | % of dictators from whom all dictation would be recorded | % of dictators from whom all dictation would not be recorded |
| --- | --- | --- |
| 70 wam | 20 | 80 |
| 80 wam | 40 | 60 |
| 90 wam | 60 | 40 |
| 100 wam | 75 | 25 |
| 110 wam | 85 | 15 |
| 120 wam | 95 | 5 |
| 130 wam | 98 | 2 |
| 140 wam | 100 | 0 |

Source: Harold H. Green, "The Nature of Business Dictation," unpublished doctoral dissertation, University of Pittsburgh, 1951.

Figure 10.3  Pattern of dictation of selected dictators

| Phase of dictation | Slow dictators | Average dictators | Rapid dictators | Very fast dictators |
|---|---|---|---|---|
| Groping (15% of time) | 0–30 wam | 0–40 wam | 0–40 wam | 0–50 wam |
| Thoughtful (45% of time) | 40–60 wam | 50–80 wam | 50–90 wam | 60–100 wam |
| Confident (30% of time) | 75–90 wam | 85–105 wam | 100–130 wam | 110–140 wam |
| Sprinting (10% of time) | 100 wam up | 120 wam up | 140 wam up | 150 wam up |

Source: Harold H. Green, ''The Nature of Business Dictation,'' unpublished doctoral dissertation, University of Pittsburgh, 1951.

must progress from a low level toward a high level of learning, it is preferable to speak in terms of levels of learning rather than in semesters or years of study. This is particularly true because students enter the shorthand class with different achievement, attitudes, and learning problems. The concept of learning levels is not new, for in 1960 Reynolds identified three levels of learning for shorthand (Reynolds, pp. 26–39). These are as follows:

1. *Learning Level* — The *introductory* stage of learning as well as the stage of *improvement* in use of the elementary processes.
2. *Application Level* — The point at which the elementary skills are used in production.
3. *Integration Level* — Stage when the learner is able to use the learning successfully to produce usable work.

Each level of shorthand learning is presented in Figure 10.4, together with the competency being sought for that level or sublevel. Each competency is analyzed for tasks involved in the cognitive, affective, and psychomotor domains. For example, the student who is able to perform the competency stated for the introductory stage of the Learning Level must be

1. Able to: (*a*) comprehend and read shorthand outlines (cognitive); (*b*) comprehend and read punctuation marks (cognitive); (*c*) transcribe shorthand outlines and punctuation (cognitive); and (*d*) apply rules of grammar, spelling, and punctuation (cognitive).
2. Willing to respond by transcribing and following rules of grammar, punctuation, and English usage (affective).
3. Able to use hand in writing (psychomotor).

A competency performed at the end of each level (learning, application, integration) involves the performance of tasks from each of the three domains.

**205**

Figure 10.4   Competencies of four levels of learning with tasks involved for each domain

| Competencies | Cognitive | Affective | Psychomotor |
|---|---|---|---|
| **Learning level**<br>Introductory stage<br>  Transcribe longhand from bookplates at a minimum rate of speed and with a limited number of transcription, spelling, punctuation, and grammar errors | 1. Comprehend and read short-hand outlines<br>2. Comprehend and read punctuation<br>3. Transcribe shorthand outlines and punctuation<br>4. Apply rules of grammar, spelling, and punctuation | Willingly respond by reading, transcribing, and applying rules, etc. | Write long-hand |
| **Improvement stage**<br>  Record open-book or closed-book dictation of familiar material and transcribe in good form at a minimum rate with a limited number of transcription, spelling, punctuation, and grammar errors | 1. Construct shorthand outlines<br>2. Apply grammar, punctuation, and spelling in transcript<br>3. Transcribe from own shorthand outlines | Willingly respond by performing | Write long-hand and/or with type-writer as communication tools |
| **Application level**<br>  Record previewed new-matter dictation at a minimum speed and transcribe with a limited number of errors. | 1. Hear new words and construct readable outlines<br>2. Nos. 1, 2, and 3 above | Consistently respond in handling new vocabulary and transcribing | Use type-writer as communication tool |
| **Integration or fusion level**<br>  From new-matter dictation and office-style dictation record material at a rate commensurate with office standards and transcribe mailable letters and reports | 1. Both Nos. 1 and 2 above<br>2. Decide on appropriate word or words so that transcript makes good sense<br>3. Identify and correct all errors<br>4. Use good form in setting up letter | Consistently exercise care in performing all tasks | Use type-writer as communication tool |

## Constructing Performance Goals

Each competency is first analyzed for the dominant domain and level in order that an appropriate evaluation and verb may be selected, then the conditions of performance and the criterion are added as in Figure 10.4 (Recycle to Chapter 4, p. 95.) In choosing the criterion, all shorthand teachers in a department should decide on the acceptable minimum standard based upon the range of standards demanded by offices. Shorthand research as well as handbooks accompanying shorthand textbooks suggest possible standards.

From the data in Figure 10.5, the teacher constructs performance goals for each of the levels, including the two sublevels of the Learning Level. The following performance goals are merely examples, which teachers may modify in terms of the range of standards in local offices.

---

LEARNING LEVEL: INTRODUCTORY STAGE
Given familiar bookplate material from Lessons 4–6, **demonstrate** the ability to transcribe in longhand for three minutes at a minimum of 15 words a minute, with a maximum of 3% transcription errors and no spelling, punctuation, or grammatical errors.

---

LEARNING LEVEL: IMPROVEMENT STAGE
From open- (or closed-) book dictation of familiar material for three minutes, **demonstrate** the ability to record at a minimum of 50 words a minute by transcribing on the typewriter (or in longhand if no machines are available) in double-spaced manuscript form a minimum of 10 words a minute with a maximum of 3% transcription errors and no spelling, punctuation, or grammatical errors. (Open or closed book is up to the teacher.)

---

APPLICATION LEVEL
From previewed, new-matter material of four or more letters totaling approximately 600 words, **demonstrate** the ability to record at a minimum of 70 words a minute and to transcribe into simple mailable letter form with no carbon at a minimum of 15 words a minute.

---

INTEGRATION
From unfamiliar, unpreviewed new-matter material of four or more letters totaling approximately 600 words, **demonstrate** the ability to record at a minimum of 80 words a minute and to transcribe by transcribing complex letters with subject lines, attention lines, tabulations, and special instructions into mailable form with one carbon and one envelope at a minimum of 15 words a minute.

From office-style dictation of six letters of approximately 125 words each, **demonstrate** the ability to record and to transcribe by transcribing the letters into mailable form with one carbon and one envelope each at a minimum of 10 words a minute.

---

Figure 10.5  Competencies of shorthand learners at various levels

| Competencies | Dominant domain & level | Result of performance | Verb | Conditions of performance | Evaluation |
|---|---|---|---|---|---|
| **Learning level**<br>Introductory stage<br>Transcribe longhand from bookplates at a minimum rate of speed with a limited number of transcription, spelling, punctuation, and grammar errors. | Cognitive-application | Product: longhand transcript | **Demonstrate** | Longhand transcription of familiar bookplates for 3 minutes. | 15 words a minute 3% transcription errors; no spelling error, no punctuation error, no grammar error. |
| Improvement stage<br>Record (open- or closed-book) dictation of familiar material and transcribe in good form at a minimum rate with a limited number of transcription, spelling, punctuation, and grammar errors. | Cognitive-application | Product: typed transcript | **Demonstrate** | Dictation of familiar material at 50 words a minute. Timed transcription on typewriter, manuscript style. | 10 words a minute transcription; 3% transcription errors; no spelling, punctuation, or grammar errors. |
| **Application level**<br>Record previewed new-matter dictation at a minimum speed and transcribe at a minimum rate with a limited number of errors. | Cognitive-application | Product: typed transcript | **Demonstrate** | Dictation of 600 words of previewed new matter at 70 words a minute; letter form with no carbon. | 15 words a minute transcription; mailable letters. |
| **Integration or fusion level**<br>From new-matter dictation and office-style dictation record material at a rate commensurate with office standards and transcribe mailable letters and reports. | a. Cognitive-evaluation | Product: typed transcripts | **Demonstrate** | Dictation of 600 words of unpreviewed new matter at 80 words a minute; letter form with carbon and envelope; complex; special instructions. | 15 words a minute transcription; mailable letters. |
|  | b. Cognitive-evaluation | Product: typed transcripts | **Demonstrate** | Dictation of 6 letters of approx. 125 words each in office-style dictation; transcribe with carbon and envelope. | 10 words a minute transcription; mailable letters. |

## Identifying and Sequencing Subcompetencies

Construction of the final performance goal at each level is merely step 1. The teacher must then analyze the goal to identify each subcompetency essential to attainment of the goal.

For performance goal 1 the student who is to meet stated standards while transcribing from bookplates must be able to perform at least ten subcompetencies:

1. Read aloud familiar bookplates, spelling and pronouncing each outline correctly.
2. Read aloud familiar bookplates for 10 seconds accurately and with no hesitation.
3. Read aloud familiar bookplates, reading punctuation in sentences and at the ends of sentences correctly.
4. Read aloud familiar bookplates for 10 seconds, conveying good word sense.
5. Read aloud familiar bookplates correctly for 10 seconds at 60 percent of the individual's reading speed of printed copy.
6. Transcribe in longhand from familiar bookplates for three minutes with no grammatical errors.
7. Transcribe in longhand from familiar bookplates for three minutes with no spelling errors.
8. Transcribe in longhand from familiar bookplates for three minutes with no punctuation errors.
9. Record and transcribe timed dictation of brief forms, brief form derivatives, commonly used phrases, and frequently used words with 90 percent correctly recorded and 90 percent accurately transcribed.
10. Transcribe in longhand from familiar bookplates for three minutes with a minimum of 10 words a minute transcribed, with no more than 3 percent transcription errors, and no spelling, punctuation, or grammatical errors.

The next step is to sequence the subcompetencies so that the learner can proceed from the simple to the difficult ones or, according to individual needs, attack only those not yet mastered but essential to achieving the performance goal.

Figure 10.6 includes the statement of the required competencies, which are sequenced so that they ultimately lead to mastery of the performance goal. Two major classifications of competencies are required at the introductory stage of learning: reading and handwritten or longhand transcription. Subcompetencies 1 through 5 lead to attainment of No. 6, and all involve reading. Numbers 6 through 9 lead to achievement of Nos. 10 and 12 and involve transcription, and No. 5 leads to No. 12, which leads directly to the performance goal for the Introductory Stage. A teacher referring to this model recognizes that any student who cannot perform satisfactorily on No. 5 may lack one or more of subcompetencies 1, 2, 3, or 4.

Because the reading standard on each student's speed in reading is based on printed copy, no student is competing with a faster or slower reader; each one is competing with himself or herself.

Use of the subcompetencies in Figure 10.6 enables a teacher to assess the readiness of each student to progress to the next subcompetency. Any subcompetency which a student cannot perform then becomes an en route goal for that student.

## Using Goals

The primary purpose of establishing levels rather than rigid time segments such as semesters is based on the premise that students progress at varying rates. A student with few problems in grammar, punctuation, capitalization, or sentence structure may speed through in less than half the time required by the student who has problems. The performance goal for each level is stated in terms of the *minimum performance* essential for successful achievement; thus, it is highly possible that some students may never achieve beyond the Application Level and never reach the Integration Level. If the student has the potential to attain the highest level, he or she may schedule shorthand the following year. On the other hand, a student who is ready for graduation except for nonachievement of the goal at the Integration Level has no flexibility of time. Thus, the teacher must make the decision as to whether or not that student should be graduated and approved for a job in the stenographic field. When making the decision, the teacher must keep two facts in mind: first, not all stenographic jobs involve performance at the Integration Level. In fact, some students hired as stenographers may take little dictation during the early days of employment. Second, the employing firm has the responsibility for evaluating an applicant's qualifications. The mere fact that a student has studied shorthand for two years does not mean competency at the Integration Level.

## Identifying Present Level of Learner and Matching Learner With Subcompetencies and Performance Goals

Pretesting a student in advanced shorthand classes is relatively simple, for the teacher has only to identify the present performance level and relate it to the goals and subcompetencies. The problem becomes more complex for the beginning student, even though the teacher has access to results of aptitude tests, interviews, and other data.

Pretesting and analysis of performance on subcompetencies, however, enable a teacher to plan instructional efforts to assist each student.

Effective shorthand teachers utilize the subcompetencies in Figures 10.4 and 10.5 to determine each learner's competencies. For example, the teacher first determines the speed of reading of print for each student. Thus, slow readers may be referred for remedial reading from the first day. As the beginning student progresses, the teacher may find that punctuation is a problem. If so, subcompetency No. 8 (Figure 10.4) becomes an en route goal.

**Figure 10.6** Performance goal for the Introductory stage of learning level sequenced for subcompetencies

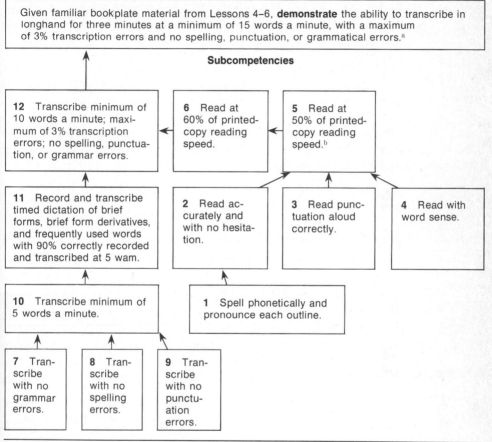

**Performance goal**

Given familiar bookplate material from Lessons 4–6, **demonstrate** the ability to transcribe in longhand for three minutes at a minimum of 15 words a minute, with a maximum of 3% transcription errors and no spelling, punctuation, or grammatical errors.[a]

**Subcompetencies**

**12** Transcribe minimum of 10 words a minute; maximum of 3% transcription errors; no spelling, punctuation, or grammar errors.

**6** Read at 60% of printed-copy reading speed.

**5** Read at 50% of printed-copy reading speed.[b]

**11** Record and transcribe timed dictation of brief forms, brief form derivatives, and frequently used words with 90% correctly recorded and transcribed at 5 wam.

**2** Read accurately and with no hesitation.

**3** Read punctuation aloud correctly.

**4** Read with word sense.

**10** Transcribe minimum of 5 words a minute.

**1** Spell phonetically and pronounce each outline.

**7** Transcribe with no grammar errors.

**8** Transcribe with no spelling errors.

**9** Transcribe with no punctuation errors.

[a]*All* transcription from bookplates in longhand for 3 minutes.
*All* reading from bookplates for 10 seconds aloud.
[b]Teacher identifies reading speed of printed copy for each student.

## Applying Appropriate Learning Principles

Fortunately, shorthand authors prepare instructional materials based on appropriate learning principles. Only those principles which need expanding are discussed here. (Recycle to Chapter 6.)

### Principle 2. Learning a New Behavior Results From the Learner's Interaction With His or Her Total Environment

Because of the need for each learner to be able to read, spell, punctuate, use correct grammar, and hear sounds accurately, the teacher realizes that students who come from diversified environments and several schools may not possess the subcompetencies essential to success in shorthand.

Early identification of each student's deficiencies is imperative, so that teachers can use sequenced subcompetencies to pinpoint a deficiency, diagnose the problem, and either provide remedial work or seek the assistance of other professionals within the school.

### Principle 7. Learning Proceeds More Effectively When the Learner Participates in a Continuously Expanding Pattern of Behaviors

Sequenced subcompetencies for a performance goal enable the teacher to guide the student through expanding patterns of behaviors—a spiral which grows more complex each time a performance is demanded.

### Principle 9. At the Initial Learning Stage, Individual Tasks Must Be Learned to a High Level Before These Movements May Be Combined to Form Effortless Performance

No shorthand learner who is unable to read bookplates with ease can be expected to read his or her own notes.

### Principle 11. Isolated Practice on Unmastered Components of Complete Skill May Be Preferable to Practice on Final Tasks

A student can take dictation of unpreviewed, new-matter dictation and transcribe into complex letters for months and still not achieve success. The primary reason is inability to perform one or more subcompetencies.

### Principle 12. In the Early Stages of Skill Learning, Practice Distributed Over Short Periods Is More Effective than Longer Practice Periods

As the learner begins to write, tightening of the muscles may inhibit success if the activity is pursued too long. As the authors of Gregg shorthand say (Gregg, Leslie, Zoubek, p. 33):

For many reasons it is desirable to alternate classroom activities. Learners very quickly tire of any one activity, and the mere change from the one activity to the next renews their interest and attention briefly.

### Principle 13. In Motor Learning, Early Stages Are Characterized by Excessive Movements; but as the Skill Is Perfected, Excess Movements Disappear and an Effortless Performance Takes Place

Leslie discounts teachers' concern with beautiful shorthand penmanship by the admonition: The attempt to develop it in the ordinary stenographic learner will hamper and inhibit the development of other and more important skills (Leslie, p. 124). Each of the subcompetencies associated with expert performance must be mastered. The expert's motions do not occur automatically; they must be identified and practiced singly before the overall patterns can be produced.

## Teaching-Learning Strategies

The teacher now asks: Which organizational pattern is appropriate? What are the time constraints within which the teacher must operate? Both decisions are interdependent.

## Organization of Groups and Allocation of Time

Shorthand teachers who follow traditional methods generally group the entire class together. Some excellent students are impeded by the large-group instruction; others benefit from each day's instruction; and still others are unable to maintain each day's pace. Individual needs remain unmet. Teachers who choose a modern approach, however, focus on learning activities which enable each student to progress successfully. Moreover, technological developments and a proliferation of teaching materials enable the teacher to plan for both small-group and individual learning. There is an accelerated trend toward providing flexible instructional programs in which the student moves to the next level only when the initial goal is attained. Because shorthand classes often no longer contain average and above-average students, this strategy is used.

Anderson's synthesis of research shows that shorthand students in classes of 21 or more achieved significantly better than those in smaller classes (Anderson, R., pp. 109–110). Competition evidently plays a significant part; yet the basic philosophy behind the learning system is that each student compete with his or her own record. The best of both worlds may be available by utilizing small-group and individually paced instruction in regularly scheduled classes. Suggestions for combining large-group, small-group, and individual organization are presented next. Not all students learn as effectively from the individualized approach as others and some students need the security of a group, particularly at the beginning stage. The teacher must observe students in order to determine which students benefit from the various combinations.

LARGE- AND SMALL- GROUP INSTRUCTION. Some teachers are more comfortable teaching the whole class at one time. The arguments for large-group instruction beyond the first two weeks of beginning shorthand are scant, however, in light of the changing composition of shorthand classes.

SMALL- GROUP INSTRUCTION. A shorthand teacher is soon aware of varying rates of learning. One solution is to divide the class into small groups—perhaps one group of those progressing rapidly; second, those diligently trying but progressing more slowly; and third, those showing evidence of multiple learning problems. At this point, the value of the shorthand laboratory is evident, for instruction to the fastest groups may be presented by taped reading practice followed by dictation while the teacher works with the other two groups. Students may be grouped by the lesson they are studying, the dictation rate for which they are striving, or by learning problems associated with shorthand—punctuation, grammar, and/or reading.

INDIVIDUAL INSTRUCTION. Individually paced learning offers great promise in freeing the teacher to observe and measure individual progress and to diagnose learning problems. However, many students are not sufficiently motivated to work alone and become discouraged without constant teacher attention.

## Teaching Competencies

The following discussion relates to the competencies required of the teacher at the various levels of shorthand learning.

### Learning Level, Introductory Stage

Because beginning students quickly decide whether or not they have the requisites for learning shorthand, the teacher's responsibility is to provide a supportive and helpful environment.

GROUP INSTRUCTION. Whether large or small groups are involved, the teaching activities are similar. The shorthand teacher performs twelve tasks, each of which is presented below with criteria by which teaching competencies can be evaluated.

1. *Planning for Chalkboard or Transparency.* A possible pattern is to divide, mentally, the chalkboard or transparency in half, using the left-hand side for review and the right-hand side for new material. The advantages of using a transparency are twofold. First, the teacher faces the class; second, the size of the outlines is more likely to be similar to the size written by the students.

2. *Using the Chalkboard or Transparency.* Some teachers believe that students progress better when they can see the actual writing of an outline. All new outlines are written, therefore, while the learner watches.

   a. If using the chalkboard, stand to one side so that the class may see the outlines written. The right-handed teacher will have his left side to the board and look at the class over the right shoulder.
   b. After writing an outline, examine it quickly. If a poor one has been written, cross it out and write the correct outline beside it.
   c. Make your outlines sufficiently large and dark that they may be seen from every seat in the class.
   d. Write an oversize outline for a difficult joining and follow it with a natural-sized outline. This enables a student to see exactly how the outline is written.

3. *Presenting New Brief Forms and Phrases.*

   a. Write an outline on chalkboard or transparency and pronounce it. (Some teachers prefer to spell a brief form the first time it is written and instruct students to pronounce it only.)
   b. Have students pronounce word.
   c. Point with soft-tipped pointer while students pronounce word.

d.   Write second outline and pronounce it.

e.   Point to new outline, to previously written outline, and return to one just written.

f.   Write successive outlines and pronounce, following each addition by randomly pointing to previously written outlines, returning more often to the one most recently written.

g.   Point to all outlines while students read in unison.

4.   *Reviewing Brief Forms and Phrases.*

a.   Write outline on chalkboard or transparency and instruct class to read each as it is written.

b.   When all review brief forms and/or phrases are written, point randomly to each as students read in concert. Establish the pace by clipped speech.

c.   Point randomly as students read each outline. Avoid consecutive order so that students will encounter the outline in a different context each time it is read.

Many teachers prefer to alternate this method of reviewing brief forms with random reading of brief forms from the chart inside the back cover of *Gregg Shorthand, DJS.*

5.   *Presenting New Theory.*

a.   Write new theory; for example, in Gregg the disjoined "r" for "rity," spelling and pronouncing each word written. Instruct students to spell and pronounce, in imitation.

b.   Instruct students to spell and pronounce each word in unison as pointer indicates.

c.   Point to each word as students read randomly in concert. Continue process until students read confidently.

6.   *Presenting Review Theory.*

a.   Instruct class to spell and pronounce or to pronounce only each outline as it is written.

b.   When all review outlines are written, point to outlines randomly as students read in concert or individually.

7.   *Demonstrating Correct Reading Techniques.*   The next five competencies involve demonstrations, for which the appropriate steps are employed until each student performs according to the established criteria. (Recycle to Chapter 7.) Demonstrate reading of contextual material from book-plates by reading aloud and spelling (phonetically by shorthand symbols) each word over which a student hesitates, pronouncing afterward.

8.   *Demonstrating Correct Reading Technique with Transcript.*   Demonstrate use of (1) separate transcript or (2) transcript at back of book by reading, hesitating over words which present difficulties, spelling and pronouncing, and continuing reading until the next hesitation. Repeat demonstration several times.

9a. *Demonstrating Correct Techniques for Reading Homework with Transcript.* Read sentence, pausing to spell difficult words, look at transcript for words the student is unable to pronounce or spell, pronounce word and reread sentence until there is no hesitation.

9b. *Demonstrating Correct Techniques for Reading Homework Without Transcript.* Although most teachers prefer that students use transcripts, a teacher who feels that transcripts should not be used may read sentence, pausing to spell difficult words, pronounce word, and reread sentence until there is no hesitation.

10. *Demonstrating Correct Techniques for Writing Homework.*

a. Demonstrate in class, marking the cover of one notebook "Homework" and dating it with the first date this notebook is used. Repeat this demonstration until each student shows correct techniques.

b. Write current date in right-hand corner at bottom of first page, then read material to be written for homework. After reading material without hesitation (as many times as necessary), begin reading aloud and writing the dictated material in the first column of the notebook. Some teachers prefer to have students read what they have written from their notebooks immediately after writing it.

11. *Demonstrating Correct Notebook Techniques for Taking Dictation.* Write "Classwork" on cover of second notebook and date it; then, from homework, read until fluency is achieved. Dictate the first part of the sentence and write, then the next part, and so on until the entire sentence is recorded in the notebook.

12. *Planning a Lesson.* While each teacher's style differs, one who strives to perfect the competencies in Nos. 1 through 11 will develop an individual style of presentation, although the basic plan is retained.

In the Introductory Stage, the teacher varies activities in each day's lesson so that students do not become fatigued. Only two to five minutes are devoted to any one activity.

a. Reading homework from bookplates to evaluate the student's ability to read.
b. Presenting new theory on transparency or chalkboard.
c. Reviewing theory.
d. Presenting new brief forms.
e. Reviewing brief forms.
f. Presenting commonly used phrases.
g. Reviewing phrases.
h. Comparing proportions of outlines.
i. Dictating familiar material to students who have begun writing.
j. Comparing written outlines with bookplates to check proportions and accuracy.
k. Reading selected material from student's notebook.
l. Practicing punctuation, vocabulary, grammar, or spelling.

The plan for teaching Lesson 9, shown in Figure 10.7, illustrates the organization of these activities.

**QUESTIONS POSED BY SHORTHAND TEACHERS.**   Commonly asked questions about how to teach frequently include the following:

*When should writing be introduced?* Results of experiments with early writing versus deferred writing are inconclusive because some students respond well to early writing while others do not. Generally, writing should not be deferred too long, or a student will write without teacher direction. The reason for deferring writing is to allow the learner to see only well-written and well-proportioned outlines.

*How long should a student be required to spell a new outline before simply reading it?* Some students read fluently immediately; others read haltingly and need to spell the outline. A good guide is to have each student spell new outlines before reading them until each demonstrates reading without hesitation. At that point, the student no longer needs to spell unless a difficult-to-read outline is encountered.

*How much prompting should a teacher do?* When group instruction is employed, early reading is almost always done in concert before an individual is asked to read aloud. The focus on the individual comes later; at that point, the teacher immediately prompts a student who hesitates. This practice reduces frustration.

Figure 10.7   Plan for Lesson 9 (Continued on page 218)

---

Lesson 9–1

**I.  Goals**
1.  Read homework at approximately 60% of printed-copy reading rate.
2.  Read review theory, brief forms, and phrases from transparency without hesitation.
3.  Read bookplates for Lesson 6 or 7 fluently.
4.  Practice dictation of material in para. 36, pp. 38–39 at 40 wam.
5.  Read back sentence from dictation.

**II.  Resources**

| Teacher | Student |
|---|---|
| 1.  Lesson plan. | 1.  *Gregg Shorthand, DJS.* |
| 2.  *Gregg Shorthand, DJS.* | 2.  Class notebook. |
| 3.  Transparencies with review words. | 3.  Pen. |
| 4.  Transcript for dictation. | |

**III.  Reading homework**

*Lesson 8*                                                          Student begins reading immediately
1.  Brief form letter: para. 51, pp. 48–49.      upon being seated.
2.  Para. 55, pp. 50–51.
3.  Para. 57, p. 51.                   *7 min.*
4.  Check reading of: Nancy Floyd, Willis          Random reading for ¼ to ½ minute
    Tucker, Sharon Bookman, Ike Rosen,             from textbook.
    Marcia Odlen.

---

Lesson 9–2

| Teacher | Student |
|---|---|
| **IV.  Review** | Reading brief forms chart on |
| 1.  Brief forms         *3 min.* | inside cover of book. |
| | Random reading through brief forms of Lessons 1–8. |

## Figure 10.7 (Continued)

2. Phrases (transparency)   2 min.

        Random reading as called on.

3. Theory (transparency)   3 min.

**V. New work**   5 min.

        Spelling and pronouncing each one.
        Random reading in concert, then
        individually.

**IV. Review**   2 min.

Read from transparency.   Random reading as called on.

**V. New work**   3 min.

Read from board (Review of new theory.) Random reading as called on.

**VI. Dictation**   5 min.

*Lesson 6*
1. Page 38, para. 40: read until fluent.  Concert reading followed by random
        reading.
2. Dictate first sentence at 40 wam.  Reading back from notes.
3. Continue dictation from para. 38.

---

                **Lesson 9–3**

    **Teacher**          **Student**

**V. New work**   3 min.

Read from board (review of new theory). Random reading as called on.

**VI. Dictation**   5 min.

*Lesson 6*
1. Para. 42: read several times and  Reading sentences 1, 2, and 3 as
 dictate in sentences until    dictated.
 completed—40 wam.      Reading back entire letter.

*Lesson 7*
1. Para. 57: read until fluent; dictate in  Reading back.
 small units—40 wam.

**V. New work**   2 min.

Read from board.      Random reading by individuals.

**IV. Review**   2 min.

Read from transparency.   Random reading by individuals.

**V. New work**   3 min.

Read all new work for day.   Spelling and pronouncing each word.
        Reading words.
        Individual reading.
        *Total =*
        *45 min.*

**VII. Homework**

Preparation: Read P. 53, para. 63 and Working individually.
spell each word over on which you
hesitate.

Instructions: Read contextual material until it can be read without hesitation.
Write in notebook: New theory words three times through; para. 63, 65, and 68.

*When should concert reading end and individual reading be used?* A sound plan for the very beginning stages of reading bookplates is:

1. Concert reading of three sentences.
2. Concert rereading of the same sentences.
3. Individual reading by students selected at random for half a minute.

The student must be aware that the purpose of reading bookplates is to read his or her own shorthand notes later.

A student who demonstrates confidence in reading bookplates is ready to read individually. Such a pattern might include:

1. Student reads sentence, spelling each outline he or she is unable to read.
2. Teacher prompts as soon as a student hesitates in spelling difficult-to-read outlines.
3. Student spells and pronounces outline causing hesitancy.
4. Student rereads sentence to gain confidence.

*Should dictation tapes be used at either stage of the Learning Level?* Conclusions from research indicate that no one technique applies to all students equally effectively. Tapes are available for beginning lessons and provide the teacher with a valuable resource provided the student is able to work independently. The use of tapes at the beginning stage frees the teacher to identify individual learning problems; however, the minute tapes are ineffective for any student, the teacher should dictate to that individual or group of students.

*How much penmanship drill should be employed during the learning stage?* Research shows that a student who knows the outline will write it correctly. (Substantiated by Haggblade, Klein, Iannizzi, and Uthe. See Selected Readings.) Therefore, the tendency today is to have students check bookplates and transparencies against their own outlines for proportion and correctness. Formal penmanship drills are usually eliminated in favor of a dictation speed which enables the student to form correct outlines but is not slow enough to permit drawing outlines. Early dictation at 40 words a minute has been found effective provided students check notes with bookplates and identify the best ones as well as the poor ones. Many teachers redictate the material, directing students to improve poorly written outlines.

*How much emphasis should be given to word-list tests?* To emphasize correct outlines even more, many teachers time dictation of brief forms, phrases, frequently used words, and also the transcription of the outline. Dictation of each word at five- or six-second intervals requires students to write quickly without hesitation. Both accuracy of outline and transcript may be self-checked by students viewing a projected transparency, or students may exchange papers and check each other's work. Since the purpose is to evaluate the accuracy of writing, some follow-up must be planned. For example, a student who does not meet the en route goal should be recycled and evaluated later on the same words.

**INDIVIDUAL INSTRUCTION.** Shorthand theory can be learned by individuals working alone with specially prepared instructional materials. Henson and Taylor each developed programmed materials for *Gregg Shorthand Simplified.* Their findings reveal that shorthand theory can be mastered by students working alone. O'Connell reinforced these findings in her study, using the programmed material of Hosler, Condon, Grubbs, and Huffman. (See Selected Readings for all these studies.)

A more recent contribution to shorthand learning is the *Gregg Shorthand Individual Progress Method (IPM),* which consists of a Presentation Book, in which theory is introduced; a Reinforcement Book, in which students practice the new theory and review theory taught earlier; and a series of Self-Checks (see Leslie et al., Selected Readings). Paralleling the Presentation Book is a series of tapes. The tape of each lesson teaches the theory, and a dictation tape contains the material in the Reinforcement Book. The minimum goal for any student is to take new-matter dictation at 60 words a minute and transcribe it accurately. Utilization of the multimedia approach permits the student to listen to the presentation tape and execute the instructions by writing in the Presentation Book. Reinforcement material following the presentation requires the student to practice additional material on new theory and to read, write, and punctuate. Each Self-Check involves the student in transcribing bookplate outlines, writing shorthand from printed words, and transcribing contextual material. Immediate reinforcement is available through the keys for each Self-Check. Although recycling is not a formal part of the structure, each student is told to review the material for which the goal was not achieved. Here the responsibility lies with the individual teacher who checks each learner's daily progress and assists as needed.

Before publication, *IPM* was tested on approximately 300 high school and college students. Strangely, the two-year college students surpassed the four-year college students. Since 60 percent of the two-year students were employed full time, a plausible explanation is that their high motivation may have had a pronounced positive effect upon achievement. This finding relates directly to those of Frink, Moskovis, Skaff, and Varah all of whom reported motivation and interest to be directly related to success in shorthand.

No study has identified the competencies essential to the teacher using *IPM.* While the teacher's role is changed from that of the traditional shorthand teacher, certain elements are identical. Both teachers identify learning difficulties, evaluate regularly, select or develop supplementary learning materials when needed, and provide an environment which motivates the student. Put simply, the teacher using *IPM* has substantially more time for these activities.

**HOMEWORK.** At the learning level the student is involved in three activities—reading bookplates (isolated words illustrating new theory and contextual material), writing contextual material from self or recorded dictation, and reading shorthand outlines and contextual material from his or her own notes.

A learner who has not followed correct homework procedures is unable to read the material when called upon. To assure that correct procedures are used in homework, specific instructions must be provided by live or videotaped teacher demonstrations. Duplicated homework assignments should be prepared and distributed to the beginning students with specific instructions as to their use. In this way, a student will know the precise assignment and those who are absent may keep assignments up to date.

All homework should be related to an identified performance goal or subcompetency. For example, the student reading familiar bookplates aloud for a half minute, spelling and pronouncing all words with accuracy, will know that each word must be spelled at home and then pronounced. On the other hand, the student striving to read familiar bookplates at 60 percent of printed-copy reading speed will practice reading the contextual material until the stated speed is reached.

Suggestions for preparing homework at the learning level are as follows:

1. Students should read the bookplates assigned as many times as necessary to achieve the en route goal.

2. When writing is involved, the student reads as above and then writes the contextual material from self- or recorded dictation. Hanson found that college students who copied homework from shorthand plates achieved better than those who used the textbook only to refer to outlines while recording dictation (see Selected Readings). This suggests that the student should give conscious thought to the word being written in the outline. Without such concentration, writing of outlines may be meaningless. Some teachers prefer to use a workbook as supplementary to the text. While a workbook does not retard progress, Rittenhouse found it had no positive effect on student achievement. Thus, a workbook for homework is a matter of teacher preference.

If homework is goal-related, then it is valuable to the student. During the Learning Level, homework should be read to the teacher, either individually or as a member of a group. Taking five minutes each day for random reading of short sentences checks the mastery of the homework and also motivates the student to do it. Rather than collect homework and file it, most teachers prefer to have each student keep homework notes for later reading as "cold" notes, a competency often required on the job.

## Learning Level (Improvement Stage)

Although still at the Learning Level, the student is trying to record dictation of familiar material and transcribe it. The teacher is involved in the following activities:

**SELECTING DICTATION TAPES OR DICTATING TO STUDENTS.** The teacher selects dictation from tapes which parallel the text, from the text itself, or from other published materials.

Taped dictation provides each student with material appropriate to his or her ability and also frees the teacher to work with individual students. Even though a classroom is not equipped with multiple-channel dictation, many teachers find that portable cassette players serve the needs of small groups. Thus, three or four such players may be used simultaneously by students grouped around the units. Only if no other possible avenue is open should the teacher spend valuable time dictating, and then only to groups whose needs can be met by the same dictation speeds.

The teacher employs the timing guide in Figure 10.8 and follows instructions on the figure for dictating at various speeds.

The following suggestions enable the beginning dictator to avoid all possible pitfalls:

1. Dictate in a natural voice; avoid overenunciation.
2. Dictate in complete thoughts and phrases—for example, pauses in the following are marked with an (X):

Dear Mr. Bennett: We are enclosing our check for $100, (X) in

## Figure 10.8  Guide for dictating multiple speeds

| Groups of | Words per minute | | | | | | | | | | | | |
|---|---|---|---|---|---|---|---|---|---|---|---|---|---|
| 35 | 70 | 87.5 | 105 | 122.5 | 140 | 137.5 | 175 | 187.5 | 210 | | | | |
| 30 | 60 | 75.0 | 90 | 105.0 | 120 | 135.0 | 150 | 165.0 | 180 | 195.0 | 210 | | |
| 25 | 50 | 62.5 | 75 | 87.5 | 100 | 112.5 | 125 | 137.5 | 150 | 162.5 | 175 | 187.5 | 200 |
| 20 | 40 | 50.0 | 60 | 70.0 | 80 | 90.0 | 100 | 110.0 | 120 | 130.0 | 140 | 150.0 | 160 |
| 15 | 30 | 37.5 | 45 | 52.5 | 60 | 67.5 | 75 | 82.5 | 90 | 97.5 | 105 | 112.5 | 120 |

**Time intervals in seconds**

| | | | | | | | | | | | | |
|---|---|---|---|---|---|---|---|---|---|---|---|---|
| 30 | 24 | 20 | 17 | 15 | 13 | 12 | 11 | 10 | 9 | 8 | 8 | 7 |
| 60 | 48 | 40 | 34 | 30 | 26 | 24 | 22 | 20 | 18 | 17 | 16 | 15 |
| 30 | 12 | 60 | 51 | 45 | 40 | 36 | 33 | 30 | 27 | 25 | 24 | 22 |
| 60 | 36 | 20 | 08 | 60 | 53 | 48 | 44 | 40 | 37 | 34 | 32 | 30 |
| | 60 | 40 | 25 | 15 | 06 | 60 | 55 | 50 | 46 | 42 | 40 | 37 |
| | | 60 | 42 | 30 | 20 | 12 | 06 | 60 | 55 | 51 | 48 | 45 |
| | | | 60 | 45 | 33 | 24 | 17 | 10 | 04 | 60 | 56 | 52 |
| | | | | 60 | 47 | 36 | 28 | 20 | 14 | 08 | 04 | 60 |
| | | | | | 60 | 48 | 39 | 30 | 23 | 17 | 12 | 07 |
| | | | | | | 60 | 50 | 40 | 32 | 25 | 20 | 15 |
| | | | | | | | 60 | 50 | 41 | 34 | 28 | 22 |
| | | | | | | | | 60 | 51 | 42 | 36 | 30 |
| | | | | | | | | | 60 | 51 | 44 | 37 |
| | | | | | | | | | | 60 | 52 | 45 |
| | | | | | | | | | | | 60 | 52 |
| | | | | | | | | | | | | 60 |

Example: To dictate at 70 words a minute material counted in groups of 20, place your finger on the line that reads "Groups of 20." Run your finger along that line until you reach 70. Drop down to the first figure below the rule, which is 17. To dictate at 70 words a minute material counted in groups of 20 standard words, dictate each group in 17 seconds. The figures below 17 indicate the point on the watch where the second hand should be at the end of each group of 20 words. These time indications have been carried through the first two minutes.

Source: Charles E. Zoubek, Speed Dictation with Previews in Gregg Shorthand, Diamond Jubilee Series, Gregg Division, McGraw-Hill, N.Y., 1963, pp. X.

payment of your July 12 invoice. (X) We appreciate your prompt-ness in filling our order, (X) and we look forward to sending you many more orders in the year ahead.

3. Dictate at a smooth pace, with the pauses provided to enable the student to record dictation carried in his or her mind.

The teacher will want to involve the students in self-evaluation by asking, "How many recorded all of that?" Should several students not raise their hands, the teacher redictates. Those who were successful on the first attempt try to write more accurate and better-proportioned outlines.

**BUILDING SPEED OF DICTATION.** To achieve the performance goal for the Improvement Stage: "When taking open-book dictation of familiar material for three minutes, the student should record at a minimum of 50 words a minute," subcompetencies must be developed. A student must be able to take dictation for three minutes at a given speed before attempting higher speeds. The one-minute plan is recommended (see Leslie, Zoubek, and Strony). In this, the teacher selects dictation material which is approximately 210 words in length and:

1. Dictates first minute's take at 60, 70, and 80.
2. Dictates the second minute's take at 60, 70, and 80.
3. Combines the first two minutes of dictation and dictates at 60, 70, and 80.
4. Dictates the third minute of dictation at 60, 70, and 80.
5. Combines the three-minute take and dictates at 70 words a minute.

A student who can take three minutes of dictation at 70 words a minute after multiple one-minute speed-building drills should be able to record familiar material which is not practiced at a minimum of 50 words a minute. Other suggested speed-building plans may be used by teachers who seek variety.

**TEACHING TRANSCRIPTION.** The shorthand teacher must be able to *teach* so that students produce acceptable transcripts.

The question of when to introduce new-matter dictation confronts each teacher. Although research conclusions are somewhat mixed, there is sufficient evidence to substantiate the use of vocabulary-controlled, new-matter dictation in the Learning Improvement Stage without retarding the student's ability to take and transcribe the material. McKenna and Persing found that early introduction of new-matter dictation had neither a positive nor negative effect upon the student's abilities to take and transcribe material. Conversely, A. Anderson and Gallion began giving vocabulary-controlled, new-matter dictation as early as the seventh class period and found that students who were given supplemental dictation material of this nature rather than dictation from the textbook achieved higher scores in transcription than did those students to whom no new-matter dictation was given. Obviously much depends upon the kind of new-matter dictation presented as well as upon the ability of the student. Thus, the teacher who desires to use vocabulary-controlled new-matter dictation may do so with confidence that while it may assist some students, it will not retard the progress of others. (See "Determining the Frequently Used Words in Dictation Material," pp. 226–227 of this chapter.)

While decisions as to the best time to introduce transcription vary, much is dependent upon the student's typewriting abilities as well as the availability of typewriters. A student who is able to type for five minutes from straight copy at approximately 25 words a minute with no more than one error a minute is usually ready for transcription at the typewriter if shorthand bookplates can be read fluently.

A teacher plans the introduction of transcription in steps, ranging from easy to more difficult. Each step should have a stated goal. A suggested plan includes the following steps, each a subcompetency of transcription of a mailable letter.

### STEP 1: TRANSCRIPTION AT THE TYPEWRITER FROM BOOKPLATES

1. Assign a specific letter in the text to be read for homework and transcribed later.
2. The next day have students read and reread the letter until they do not hesitate in reading outlines or punctuation.
3. Review spelling of difficult words or problems in capitalization.
4. Instruct students to set a five-inch line and to type the letter in manuscript form at their own speeds.
5. Time the students as they type the letter and continue practice of this nature until the established goal is reached—approximately straight-copy speed.

### STEP 2: TRANSCRIPTION AT THE TYPEWRITER FROM FAMILIAR SHORTHAND NOTES

1. Assign a specific letter for homework with instructions to read and reread the letter until it is read without hesitation. The student pronounces each word and writes it in the homework notebook.
2. Plan more practice on the shorthand note reading when needed.
3. Review problems in spelling, letter form, and punctuation prior to transcribing the letter.
4. Instruct student to use a special letter form or to select a letter style and set the margins. Assist any student who needs help.
5. Time the student transcribing the letter, repeating as many times as needed until the goal is achieved. (The goal may be two-thirds of straight copy speed.)

### STEP 3: TRANSCRIPTION OF FAMILIAR DICTATION MATERIAL
Prior to moving to this step, provide drills in handling materials so that the organization of work flow facilitates reaching the goal

1. Dictate two letters familiar to the students at approximately 40 words a minute. If necessary, redictate while the students check the dictation and make necessary insertions. This may be done the day prior to the transcription, so that the students may resolve all problems before transcription.

2. Have the students transcribe the letters in good letter form at leisure and check spelling and punctuation, using the dictionary, word lists, or punctuation materials.
3. Redictate the letters while students check for errors in transcription, punctuation, grammar, and capitalization; or use a transparency in checking.
4. Evaluate with the students the letters typed to identify problems.
5. Redictate the same or similar letter until students needing additional practice achieve the goal of two-thirds of straight copy speed.

ASSIGNING HOMEWORK. Homework for students at the Improvement Stage of learning differs slightly from the Introductory Stage, for the student is striving to record familiar material at increasing speeds. Homework should involve reading and writing activities and automatization of frequently used words. Thus, a student should be instructed to read a given set of letters until fluency is achieved and then to write each letter once. Some teachers prefer to have students write the letters twice, and there is some thread of evidence that repetition may be beneficial. If possible, students might use dictation tapes while preparing homework. Other kinds of homework beneficial are transcription practice and individualized drills—punctuation and grammar, for instance.

## Application Level

At this point the student is ready to record and transcribe mailable copies of previewed new-matter dictation. Leslie's definition of a mailable letter is simple: "One that can be signed and mailed." Generally, mailable correspondence contains none of the following: omission of important parts of letter (date, title, enclosure, etc.), poor centering (horizontal or vertical), poor erasures, misspelled words, incorrectly divided words, transposition of words, grammatical errors, changes in meanings of sentences, incorrect abbreviations, jagged right-hand margins, or major punctuation errors.

While teachers of this level need all the competencies identified at the Learning Level, they also need the following additional competencies:

DEVELOPING PREVIEWS OF DICTATION MATERIAL. Previews of new vocabulary, difficult outlines, and other outlines selected for automatization are essential in expanding vocabulary and preparing students to take new-matter dictation first with previews and later without.

A duplicated preview sheet is more practical if students are working for different goals, for previews will vary depending upon the letters involved. A student simply retrieves the preview sheets for a given tape from the file and studies at home for the next day's dictation.

Using a transparency for writing new outlines has distinct advantages over the chalkboard, particularly at the Application Level, for time is saved and the transparency may be used many times.

At intervals between takes, students may ask the teacher to write any additional outline needed.

IDENTIFYING LEVEL OF DIFFICULTY IN DICTATION MATERIALS. The difficulty of dictation material must be consistent, so that the student's progress can be attributed to improved performance rather than to these variations. Two factors affect the difficulty of dictation material: (1) the syllabic intensity (average number of syllables per word of dictated copy) and (2) the percentage of frequently used words dictated.

*Syllabic Intensity.* Published dictation material usually has a syllabic intensity of 1.40 (measure employed to assure that all dictation material includes the identical number of syllables in each 20 words dictated). However, many teachers elect to change the pace by dictating additional materials. Some teachers use horoscopes from the newspaper, short stories, jokes, poems, and letters from "Dear Abby." All such material must be adjusted for syllabic intensity.

To analyze material for syllabic intensity, the teacher simply:

1. Counts the syllables on each line and records them in the right-hand margin, indicating the total cumulative syllables at the end of each line.
2. Counts the actual words in the letter.
3. Divides the total syllables in the letter by the number of actual words to get the average number of syllables in each word.

If a letter has 184 syllables and 124 actual words, it has a syllabic intensity of 1.48 (184 divided by 124).

This material (1.48 s.i.) is slightly more difficult than that normally dictated to the students. Some teachers may accept it without revising it; others will revise it to the 1.40 level.

Perry's analysis of more than two thousand business letters revealed an average syllabic intensity of 1.63, and West's reanalysis of Silverthorn's 300,000 words resulted in a revised list of 11,055 different words with an average syllabic intensity of 1.54. (See Perry; West (2), pp. 13-25; and Silverthorn in Selected Readings.)

The teacher must recognize that a student who can record and transcribe dictation of 1.4 syllabic intensity at 80 words a minute is likely to fall short of that goal when given dictation of 1.5 or 1.6 syllabic intensity. As long as both the teacher and student are aware of the danger of overstating a student's performance, however, there is no reason to revise dictation material.

*Determining the Frequently Used Words in Dictation Material.* A second measure of the difficulty of dictation material is its vocabulary. Increasing evidence alerts the shorthand teacher to examine the vocabulary employed in dictation materials. Hillestad, Uthe, and Mickelson found that familiarity of vocabulary relates directly to the difficulty of dictation materials. In fact, Hillestad's and Uthe's studies indicate that the vocabulary used may contribute more to the difficulty of the dictation material than the syllabic intensity. Uthe also found that the number of brief forms helps determine difficulty. The teacher who desires to dictate easier matter will ascertain that the words are from the first 1,500 of the Silverthorn list.

Conversely, the teacher who wishes to test the student's ability to take more difficult dictation material will include substantial numbers of words not among the first 1,500. Mellinger provides the shorthand teacher with an up-to-date source of office communications vocabulary and with categories of words among the first 500, 1,000, and 1,500.

**PREPARING SUPPLEMENTARY MATERIAL FOR DICTATION.** Once the vocabulary has been selected and the words have been counted, it is a simple task to mark dictation material for the standard 28 syllables contained in the 20 words.

The first 28 syllables in a letter to be dictated are counted and followed by a "1"; the second 28, by a "2"; and so on. Dictation material of any syllabic intensity may thus be converted to the common 1.40.

**PLANNING FOR STUDENT DEVELOPMENT OF TRANSCRIPTION SKILLS.** Once students are trying to attain the ultimate goals in transcription, drills become a vital part of the teaching strategy. In addition to the three steps in introduction to transcription at the Improvement Stage of learning, two more are included at the Application Level:

---

STEP 4: TRANSCRIBING PREVIEWED DICTATION MATERIAL WITH CARBON
Plan preliminary drills such as setting margins, typing various letter forms, erasing (crowding and spreading), using a carbon, or developing an efficient flow of work.

---

1. Prepare dictation material on tapes containing two previewed letters. The student records.
2. Have student select letter style and insert the stationery into the typewriter, evaluating the placement of carbon.
3. Time the transcription by putting the beginning time on chalkboard and following it by the time at which each student has completed transcription, proofreading, and corrections.
4. Project a transparency so that the student may evaluate the form and the content of the letter, or play the tape so that the students may evaluate their own transcripts. (Some teachers alternate student evaluation with peer evaluation by having students evaluate each other's work.)
5. Follow procedures above until the individual student achieves the stated subcompetency.

---

STEP 5: TRANSCRIBING PREVIEWED DICTATION MATERIAL WITH CARBON AND ENVELOPE
Follow the same procedures as for step 4 with the addition of the envelope, which is typed while the student is timed on the entire process.

---

**ASSISTING INDIVIDUAL STUDENTS WITH LEARNING PROBLEMS.** Diagnosing student problems is a competency also needed by the transcription teacher. The teacher evaluates not only the transcripts at the stages of the Application Level but also the process used during transcription. Product evaluation is facilitated by use of a form similar to Figure 10.9, so that,

Figure 10.9   Checklist for identifying problems during typewriting transcription

| Week of _____, 19__ | | | | | |
|---|---|---|---|---|---|
| **Name of Student** | | | | | |
| **Reel Number** | | | | | |
| **Identification and correction errors** | | | | | |
| Proofreading | _____ | _____ | _____ | _____ | _____ |
| Erasing | _____ | _____ | _____ | _____ | _____ |
| Corrections | _____ | _____ | _____ | _____ | _____ |
| **Letter style and placement** | | | | | |
| Placement on page—horizontal | _____ | _____ | _____ | _____ | _____ |
| Placement on page—vertical | _____ | _____ | _____ | _____ | _____ |
| Attention line | _____ | _____ | _____ | _____ | _____ |
| Subject line | _____ | _____ | _____ | _____ | _____ |
| Syllabication at end of line | _____ | _____ | _____ | _____ | _____ |
| **Machine manipulation** | | | | | |
| Crowding | _____ | _____ | _____ | _____ | _____ |
| Spreading | _____ | _____ | _____ | _____ | _____ |
| Tabulation | _____ | _____ | _____ | _____ | _____ |
| Ribbon too light | _____ | _____ | _____ | _____ | _____ |
| Keys need cleaning | _____ | _____ | _____ | _____ | _____ |
| **Information** | | | | | |
| Inside address inaccurate | _____ | _____ | _____ | _____ | _____ |
| Salutation inaccurate for inside address | _____ | _____ | _____ | _____ | _____ |
| Complimentary close | _____ | _____ | _____ | _____ | _____ |
| Initials or enclosures | _____ | _____ | _____ | _____ | _____ |
| Names inaccurate | _____ | _____ | _____ | _____ | _____ |
| Numbers inaccurately written | _____ | _____ | _____ | _____ | _____ |
| **English grammar** | | | | | |
| Spelling | _____ | _____ | _____ | _____ | _____ |
| Punctuation | _____ | _____ | _____ | _____ | _____ |
| Capitalization | _____ | _____ | _____ | _____ | _____ |
| Syllabication | _____ | _____ | _____ | _____ | _____ |
| **Shorthand** | | | | | |
| Transcription—incorrect outline | _____ | _____ | _____ | _____ | _____ |
| Context meaning incorrect | _____ | _____ | _____ | _____ | _____ |
| Cannot decipher outline | _____ | _____ | _____ | _____ | _____ |
| Omitted shorthand outline(s) | _____ | _____ | _____ | _____ | _____ |

at the end of a couple of days, both student and teacher have concrete evidence of areas which need correcting. A student whose checklist reveals the same problem day after day needs an en route goal.

Jester's analysis of the transcription process reveals that 38 percent of the transcription time is devoted to typing activities and 62 percent to nontyping activities. The first ten nontyping activities reported account for 53 percent and are reported in the order of the percent of time consumed: (1) Erasing and correcting, 16.8 percent; (2) proofreading and correcting, 7.2 percent; (3) deciphering incorrect shorthand outlines, 6.2 percent; (4) reading shorthand notes for context and meaning, 5.1 percent;

(5) making ready, 3.9 percent; (6) dealing with spelling problems, 3.8 percent; (7) deciphering poor shorthand penmanship, 3.3 percent; (8) supplying and verifying inside address, 3.0 percent; (9) supplying miscellaneous fill-in information (not parts of letters), 2.5 percent; and (10) dealing with tabulations problems, 1.7 percent.

Characteristics of slow transcribers identified by Jester indicate areas which cause problems for many students. Since fast transcribers execute all the activities listed on page 228 faster than slow transcribers, the transcription teacher must plan for controlled observations of process while students are transcribing. An observation chart containing such items as those identified by Jester plus others is helpful. See Figure 10.10.

Once learning problems are identified, the teacher plans remedial drills for each student. Alpha Xi Chapter, Delta Pi Epsilon, published a book (no longer available) of drills especially designed for transcription. The drills can be divided into five categories, namely:

(1) Context drills (fill-in-blank, vocabulary substitution, homonym, office-style dictation, synonyms, states of the Union, computations, composing at the typewriter, and following shorthand directions); (2) spelling and punctuation drills; (3) technique drills (eyes on copy, isolated word, margin setting, margin release, tab bar, shift, and others); (4) drills for building transcription speed; and (5) proofreading drills.

As the teacher observes the transcriber and notes time wasted on setting margins, the drill to speed margin setting is selected for that student. After the student practices the drill, the teacher observes whether the student follows the correct procedures in setting margins.

En route goals and the resulting drills have a distinct place in transcription, for unless the particular problem or problems of the learner are identified and corrected, he or she may transcribe numerous letters and never achieve the desired goal.

Figure 10.10  Process observation checksheet

Date of Observation _____

Name of Student _____

| Activity | Yes | No | Comments by Teacher |
|---|---|---|---|
| 1  Types rhythmically | | | |
| 2.  Keeps eyes on notebook | | | |
| 3.  Syllabicates without hesitation | | | |
| 4.  Handles papers quickly | | | |
| 5.  Handles carbon pack quickly | | | |
| 6.  Wastes no time in erasing and correcting | | | |
| 7.  Utilizes reference sources quickly | | | |
| 8.  Sets up letter form quickly | | | |

Another cause of errors in transcripts is incorrectly written shorthand outlines. Research findings from such studies as Frink, Iannizzi, Haggblade, Minnick, Hillestad, Patrick, and Pullis indicate the need to stress theoretically correctly written outlines even at later stages of shorthand learning. Some teachers find it helpful to have students check their dictation notes to determine causes of errors.

## Integration Level

At the Integration Level, the student is ready to record unpreviewed, complex new-matter dictation of traditional types or in office style and to transcribe mailable copies with carbon copies and envelopes during a sustained period of effort.

All the teacher competencies essential to the Application Level apply here too. In addition, the teacher should be expert in preparing dictation material including memorandums, letters, and reports (with footnotes) and material to be tabulated, plus notations for regular and blind carbon copies, air mail, special delivery, multiple enclosures, attention lines, and subject lines. At this point, the sixth step of transcription is presented.

---

STEP 6: TRANSCRIPTION OF UNPREVIEWED, NEW-MATTER DICTATION OF COMPLEXITY

---

1. Increase length and complexity of dictation to include two-page letters requiring notations on carbons, enclosures, and attention and subject lines.
2. Dictate or provide dictation tapes at appropriate speeds.
3. Time all transcription, including proofreading and correction.
4. Evaluate products with students, diagnose problems, and provide additional practice for students who need assistance.
5. Plan and offer additional dictation for both practice and evaluation until student reaches goal.

At this point, the student integrates multiple learnings from typewriting with those of taking dictation and transcribing correspondence found in the business office. The teacher who also insists on verbatim transcripts will establish another goal at a slower dictation speed. Also, many teachers establish a separate terminal goal for transcripts of office-style dictation so that students will be prepared for any eventuality.

## Planning and Maintaining a Shorthand Laboratory

The rapidly expanding instructional resources available enable any teacher to establish a shorthand laboratory, complete with either multiple-channel dictation equipment or individual cassette players and typewriters. The laboratory is essential if students are to receive instruction geared to their levels of performance. The following guides are helpful in establishing and maintaining such a laboratory.

1. Identify kinds of dictation equipment to meet student needs and to fit the constraints of space and funds.
2. Arrange a multipurpose room for shorthand, typewriting, and office procedures if space is limited, so that equipment may serve multiple purposes.
3. Identify tapes appropriate to textbook or other instructional material employed.
4. For each side of each reel of tape, prepare preview sheets containing selected difficult-to-write words, brief forms derivatives, commonly used phrases, and words to be automatized. Label each preview sheet with number or reel and side and file so that each student may remove the appropriate sheet.
5. Prepare transcripts of each reel and arrange in loose-leaf notebook, identifying each transcript by reel and side (of reel). These transcripts serve as keys in checking student transcripts and may be converted to transparencies for student use.
6. Design forms for use by students in handing in homework. Figure 10.11 enables the student to check the number of errors against the speed of dictation and determine the percentage of errors on the transcript. The resulting figure is then entered on the homework

Figure 10.11    Percentages of error for three-minute takes[a]

| No. of errors | Speed of dictation | | | | | | | | | | | | |
|---|---|---|---|---|---|---|---|---|---|---|---|---|---|
| | 40 | 50 | 60 | 70 | 80 | 90 | 100 | 110 | 120 | 130 | 140 | 150 | 160 |
| 0 | 0 | 0 | 0 | 0 | 0 | 0 | 0 | 0 | 0 | 0 | 0 | 0 | 0 |
| 1 | 0 | 0 | 0 | 0 | 0 | 0 | 0 | 0 | 0 | 0 | 0 | 0 | 0 |
| 2 | 1 | 1 | 1 | 1 | 0 | 0 | 0 | 0 | 0 | 0 | 0 | 0 | 0 |
| 3 | 2 | 2 | 1 | 1 | 1 | 1 | 1 | 0 | 0 | 0 | 0 | 0 | 0 |
| 4 | 3 | 2 | 2 | 2 | 1 | 1 | 1 | 1 | 1 | 1 | 0 | 0 | 0 |
| 5 | 4½ | 3 | 2 | 2 | 2 | 1 | 1 | 1 | 1 | 1 | 1 | 1 | 1 |
| 6 | 5 | 4 | 3 | 3 | 2 | 2 | 2 | 1 | 1 | 1 | 1 | 1 | 1 |
| 7 | | 4 | 3 | 3 | 3 | 2 | 2 | 2 | 1 | 1 | 1 | 1 | 1 |
| 8 | | 5 | 4 | 4 | 3 | 2 | 2 | 2 | 2 | 2 | 1 | 1 | 1 |
| 9 | | | 5 | 4 | 3 | 3 | 3 | 3 | 2 | 2 | 2 | 2 | 1 |
| 10 | | | | 4 | 4 | 3 | 3 | 3 | 2 | 2 | 2 | 2 | 2 |
| 11 | | | | 5 | 4 | 4 | 3 | 3 | 3 | 2 | 2 | 2 | 2 |
| 12 | | | | | 5 | 4 | 4 | 3 | 3 | 3 | 2 | 2 | 2 |
| 13 | | | | | | 4 | 4 | 3 | 3 | 3 | 3 | 2 | 2 |
| 14 | | | | | | 5 | 4 | 4 | 3 | 3 | 3 | 3 | 2 |
| 15 | | | | | | | 5 | 4 | 4 | 3 | 3 | 3 | 3 |
| 16 | | | | | | | | 4 | 4 | 4 | 3 | 3 | 3 |
| 17 | | | | | | | | 5 | 4 | 4 | 4 | 3 | 3 |
| 18 | | | | | | | | | 5 | 4 | 4 | 4 | 3 |
| 19 | | | | | | | | | | 4 | 4 | 4 | 3 |
| 20 | | | | | | | | | | 5 | 4 | 4 | 4 |
| 21 | | | | | | | | | | | 5 | 4 | 4 |
| 22 | | | | | | | | | | | | 5 | 4 |
| 23 | | | | | | | | | | | | | 4 |
| 24 | | | | | | | | | | | | | 5 |
| 25 | | | | | | | | | | | | | |

[a] To find the percent of error in a three-minute transcript, locate the number of errors made and follow across the chart to the speed of the dictation.

form. Figure 10.12 provides a form for student entry of mailable letters and a record of the number of words to be added for each component. The student does all computations, which need only spot-checking by the teacher after the accuracy of the mailable copy has been determined. The same form in a different color may accompany a transcript which a student evaluates as meeting the stated performance goal. Thus a white copy of Figure 10.12 might be used for evaluating practice work and a green form for evaluating a performance goal.

7. For each tape on which mailable letters are required, prepare duplicated copies of inside addresses and other information to be used in transcription. These, too, are filed so that students may retrieve the appropriate address list as needed.

8. Duplicate copies of book lists, including not only required textbooks but also supplementary materials such as those used for individual drills in grammar, spelling, or punctuation. Also, the room should be equipped with multiple copies of dictionaries, secretaries' handbooks, books of word divisions, and the *National Zip Code Directory*.

9. Plan statements of goals for specific levels of shorthand learning and duplicate for distribution to students. Also, analyze each goal

**Figure 10.12  Form for self-evaluation of transcripts**

**Blank School**

**Mailable Letters**

Date _____ , 19_____          Speed of dictation _____

Time of transcription _____          Words a minute transcribed _____

Reel no. _____

| Ltr. No. | Total Body | Date | Inside Address | Comp. Close | Car-bon | Sub-ject | Attn. Line | Ident. Initials | Enclo-sure | Enve-lope | TOTAL |
|---|---|---|---|---|---|---|---|---|---|---|---|
| | | | | | | | | | | | |
| | | | | | | | | | | | |
| | | | | | | | | | | | |
| | | | | | | | | | | | |
| | | | | | | | | | | | |
| | | | | | | | | | | | |

Total mailable words transcribed _____

Add the following points whenever they are used in transcription

| | | | |
|---|---|---|---|
| Date | 5 | Attention Line | 5 |
| Inside Address | 15 | Identification Initials | 3 |
| Complimentary Close | 10 | Enclosure | 3 |
| Carbon (each) | 10 | Envelope (each) | 25 |
| Subject Line | 5 | | |

INSTRUCTIONS: Evaluate your letters and mark as "M" for mailable and "U" for unmailable and list above only those you consider mailable.

Arrange all letters, both mailable and unmailable, in numerical order and staple with this sheet on top and hand in.

for subcompetencies and use as guides in identifying en route goals toward which individuals should work.

## Other Instructional Resources

More shorthand resource materials become available each year, including programmed instructional materials to meet special needs of students as well as possible applications of shorthand to television and computers.

PROGRAMMED MATERIALS.   Since English grammar, spelling, and punctuation are frequently problems among shorthand learners, materials are available to assist in correcting these deficiencies. Perkins found that the programmed punctuation materials he developed were twice as effective in changing student behaviors in punctuation as the traditional teacher review of punctuation rules (Perkins 1, pp. 1–9). Programmed materials are, of course, valuable only for those students who have sufficiently high-level reading skills to employ them successfully.

COMPUTER-ASSISTED INSTRUCTION.   Thus far no shorthand system has been taught by computer-assisted instruction. With the sensitive television screens now available, such teaching is technologically feasible although prohibitively expensive. Students might write directly on a pad and have immediate feedback as to the accuracy of the outlines written.

TELEVISION.   Shorthand was successfully taught by television in the late 1950s; however, despite student achievements, virtually nothing has been done since. Part of the explanation may lie with students, who obviously prefer to work with a live teacher.

## Evaluating Students and the System

While the goals in this chapter are stated with minimum standards, the standards used are for illustration only. Each department must agree upon standards to be used in all shorthand classes. Teachers tend to interpret existing standards differently, for multiple variations influence evaluation: the kind of dictation material used (familiar, practiced, previewed, or unpreviewed); the syllabic intensity; the number of words included, from the most frequently used 500, 1,000, and 1,500; the conditions under which transcription is timed; individual interpretations of mailability; and subjective evaluation of punctuation rules and their applications. Thus, the use of performance goals provides the greatest single opportunity for tightening loosely constructed standards and using a common measure. A performance goal might be written as "Given new-matter dictation of vocabulary among the first 1,500 with a syllabic intensity of 1.4, . . ." While these guides might never be given to students, such precise stipulations would enable the teacher to use materials similar to those used by other shorthand teachers in the department.

Shorthand learning is cumulative because performance is best judged by what a student is able to do at the end of the learning process, not

Figure 10.13   Evaluative procedures for levels of shorthand learning

| Evaluative procedures | Levels of shorthand learning | | | |
| --- | --- | --- | --- | --- |
| | Introductory | Improvement | Application | Integration |
| 1. Timed reading of familiar bookplates evaluated in terms of each student's printed-copy reading rate. | X | | | |
| 2. Timed reading of unfamiliar bookplates evaluated in terms of each student's printed-copy reading rate. | X | X | | |
| 3. Dictation of theory words, brief forms, brief form derivatives, and phrases followed by immediate timed transcription. | X | X | X | |
| 4. Timed transcription of familiar bookplates evaluated according to<br>a. Transcription rate<br>b. Transcription errors<br>c. Spelling errors<br>d. Punctuation errors<br>e. Other grammar errors, tense, capitalization, etc. | X | | | |
| 5. Timed reading of shorthand notes written for homework. | | X | X | |
| 6. Dictation and timed verbatim transcription of familiar bookplate material. | | X | | |
| 7. Dictation and timed verbatim transcription of unfamiliar material (three-minute dictations). | | X | X | |
| 8. Timed verbatim transcription at the typewriter from familiar bookplates. | | X | | |
| 9. Timed verbatim transcription at the typewriter from shorthand material written for homework. | | X | X | X |
| 10. Dictation and timed verbatim transcription of new-matter dictation (three- and five-minute dictations). | | X | X | X |
| 11. Dictation and timed transcription of new-matter simple[a] mailable letters. | | | | X |
| 12 Dictation and timed transcription of complex[b] mailable letters. | | | | X |
| 13. Office-style dictation and timed transcription of complex mailable letters. | | | | X |

[a]No tabulations, one carbon, no enclosures, subject or attention lines, and no envelope.
[b]One or more of the following items in each letter: tabulations, multiple copies (including blind carbons), enclosures, subject line, attention line, and envelopes.

by an average of multiple performances during the learning process. *All* subcompetencies leading to a performance goal are merely guideposts; not bases for grades. To guide the teacher in establishing specific standards to incorporate in performance goals, Figure 10.13 enumerates evaluative procedures appropriate at each level of learning. The teacher may relate them to the subcompetencies on pages 209–211 and plan specific standards. (Recycle to Chapter 8 for ideas for evaluating students.)

PROBING QUESTIONS. Two questions frequently asked by shorthand teachers are: "How many times should a student pass a given dictation and transcription test?" and "How should students be graded?"

Just because a student records dictation given at 90 words a minute and transcribes it according to the set standard, is he or she able to repeat the performance? If not, it cannot be said that satisfactory transcription at 90-word dictation has been achieved. If this goal is reached twice, however, the learner can proceed to a new, higher level with confidence.

GRADING. Grades in shorthand vary not only among schools but among teachers. Once the teachers agree upon the performance goals for a given level of shorthand instruction, that level may be designated the "C" grade. Although grades must be given every six weeks, it is imperative that for a shorthand student the end-of-the-year (or semester) grade should *not* be an average of those for the preceding weeks but a grade which reveals his or her present level of performance. A committee of shorthand teachers can formulate a series of en route goals stated as minimum requirements and use these as a basis of assigning grades at each report period.

## Learning Activities

**1.** Visit a shorthand teacher (high school or two-year college) and collect information on the means employed to collect data on the deficiencies of students entering shorthand and the use of the data. (Goal No. 1.)

**2.** Collect business letters and analyze the vocabulary levels (first 1,500 words and higher groups). Prepare two letters which utilize 50 percent of the words above the most common 1,500 and two letters which utilize vocabulary within the first 1,500. Working in a minigroup, select two letters from each group and convert them to 1.40 syllabic intensity. Dictate them to a peer who is unfamiliar with the letters and who transcribes them. Evaluate the transcripts and report to the minigroup on how well the transcriber performed, the words causing errors, and the reaction of the transcriber to the material. Try to reach consensus as a group as to what role the vocabulary had in the student's performance. (Goal No. 2)

**3.** Practice dictating until you meet the criteria on page 223. Then dictate speed-building material using the one-minute plan on page 222 (or another plan which your instructor may suggest). Practice with another student—one person dictating while the other one records. Evaluate each other's efforts in order to prepare for Goal No. 3.

**4.** Divide your large group into four smaller groups, each one selecting one of the following phases: Learning Level—Introductory; Learning Level —Improvement; Application Level; Integration Level. Using publishers' catalogs and all available resources, compile for your group a complete list of recommended resources. Discuss the list your minigroup prepared with your instructor, and using the instructor's suggestions for improvement, revise the list before duplicating and distributing it to each member of the class.

**5.** Divide the class into minigroups and, using the criteria in this chapter which are compatible with those your instructor suggests, construct criteria which may be used to evaluate performances on Goals Nos. 4, 5, and 6. Offer them for evaluation by your instructor. After you get his or her approval, duplicate copies for the teacher, performer, and observers for use in evaluating each student's performance. Plan to reevaluate the criteria sheets after use and make any modifications which will improve their usefulness. (Goals Nos. 4, 5, and 6)

**6.** Observe any two shorthand students who are at the Application Level or above. Analyze their performances during transcription and evaluate all the products created. Identify subcompetencies which each student lacks and prepare a strategy or test to assist each one to overcome any problem which inhibits success. Present a brief evaluation and recommendation and a report on the outcomes to your group. (Goal No. 8)

## SELECTED READINGS

ALPHA XI CHAPTER, DELTA PI EPSILON, *Drills to Improve Teaching Transcription,* Hunter College, New York, 1971.

ANDERSON, ALBERTA R., "A Comparison of Dictation Speed-Development Materials and Methods in Beginning Shorthand Using the Micromolar Approach," unpublished doctoral dissertation, University of Northern Colorado, Greeley, Colo., 1969.

ANDERSON, RUTH I. (1), "Shorthand," *Changing Methods of Teaching Business Subjects,* National Business Education Yearbook, No. 10, National Business Education Association, Washington, D. C., 1972, pp. 109–110.

————, (2), "Shorthand and Transcription," *Informal Research by the Classroom Teacher,* The American Business Education Yearbook, Vol. 18, 1961, Somerset Press, Somerville, N.J., 1961, pp. 125–138.

BAIRD, STANLEY J., "The Effectiveness of Introducing Regular Dictation of Unpracticed Material Before the Completion of Gregg Shorthand Theory," unpublished doctoral dissertation, Oregon State University, 1967.

BALSLEY, IROL W., "Shorthand," *Evaluation of Pupil Progress in Business Education,* The American Business Education Yearbook, Vol. 17, 1960, Somerset Press, Somerville, N.J., 1960, pp. 185–217.

BYERS, EDWARD E., *First-Year Shorthand Test,* Allied Publishers Incorporated, Portland, Ore., 1959.

DEEMER, WALTER L., JR., *ERC Stenographic Aptitude Test,* Science Research Associates, Chicago, 1947.

DICKINSON, TILLY S., *Semester Shorthand Accomplishment Test,* Simmons College, Boston, 1956.

*Employment and Unemployment in 1971, Special Labor Force Report No. 742,* U.S. Department of Labor, Bureau of Labor Statistics, 1972, p. 76.

FRINK, INEZ, "A Comparative Analysis and Synthesis of Research Findings and Thought Pertaining to Shorthand and Transcription, 1946–1957," unpublished doctoral dissertation, Indiana University, Bloomington, Ind., 1961.

GALLION, LEONA M., "A Comparison of Dictation Speed Development Materials and Methods in Beginning Shorthand," unpublished doctoral dissertation, University of Northern Colorado, Greeley, Colo., 1968.

GREEN, HAROLD H., "The Nature of Business Dictation," unpublished doctoral dissertation, University of Pittsburgh, Pittsburgh, 1951.

GREGG, JOHN R., LOUIS A. LESLIE, AND CHARLES E. ZOUBEK, *Instructor's Handbook for Gregg Shorthand, Diamond Jubilee Series,* 2d ed., Gregg Division, McGraw-Hill Book Company, New York, 1971.

————, (2), *Instructor's Handbook for Gregg Shorthand, Diamond Jubilee Series,* Gregg Division, McGraw-Hill Book Company, New York, 1963, p. 33.

HAGGBLADE, BERLE, "Factors Affecting Achievement in Shorthand," unpublished doctoral dissertation, University of California, Los Angeles, Calif., 1965.

HANSON, ROBERT N., "Visual Stimulus versus Combined Audio-Visual Stimulus for Out-of Class Practice in First-Semester College Gregg Shorthand," unpublished doctoral dissertation, University of North Dakota, Grand Forks, N. Dak., 1966.

HENSON, OLEEN M., "The Development, Utilization, and Effectiveness of Programmed Materials in Gregg Shorthand Simplified," unpublished doctoral dissertation, Temple University, Philadelphia, Pa., 1964.

HILLESTAD, MILDRED C., "Factors which Contribute to the Difficulty of Shorthand Dictation Material," unpublished doctoral dissertation, University of Minnesota, Minneapolis, Minn., 1960.

HOSLER, RUSSELL J., ARNOLD CONDON, ROBERT GRUBBS, AND HARRY HUFFMAN, *Programmed Gregg Shorthand, Experimental Edition,* Gregg Publishing Division, McGraw-Hill Book Co., New York, 1969.

IANNIZZI, ELIZABETH, "Transcription and Shorthand Errors among Elementary and Advanced High School Writers of Simplified and Diamond Jubilee Gregg Shorthand," unpublished doctoral dissertation, New York University, New York, 1967.

JESTER, DONALD D., (1) "A Time Study of the Shorthand Transcription Process," unpublished doctoral dissertation, Northwestern University, Evanston, Ill., 1959.

————, (2), *The Shorthand Transcription Process and Its Teaching Implications,* Monograph 108, South-Western Publishing Company, Cincinnati, 1963.

KLEIN, ABRAHAM, "Variations in the Speed of Writing of Symbol Combinations in Gregg Shorthand," unpublished doctoral dissertation, New York University, New York, 1950.

LAMBRECHT, JUDITH J., "The Validation of a Revised Edition of the Byers' Shorthand Aptitude Test," unpublished doctoral dissertation, University of Wisconsin, Madison, Wisc., 1971.

LANHAM, FRANK W., ET AL., *Development of Performance Goals for a New Office and Business Education Learning System (NOBELS),* Final Report, Project No. 8-0414, USOE Grant No. OEG-0-0-080414-3733 (083), Center for Research and Leadership Development in Vocational and Technical Education, Ohio State University, Columbus, Ohio, April 1970.

LESLIE, LOUIS A., *Methods of Teaching Gregg Shorthand,* Gregg Division, McGraw-Hill Book Company, New York, 1953, p. 124.

————, CHARLES E. ZOUBEK, AND OLEEN M. HENSON, *Gregg Shorthand Individual Progress Method,* Gregg Publishing Division, McGraw-Hill Book Co., New York, 1972.

————, CHARLES E. ZOUBEK, AND MADELINE S. STRONY, *Instructor's Handbook for Gregg Dictation, Diamond Jubilee Series,* Gregg Division, McGraw-Hill Book Company, New York, 1963.

————, CHARLES E. ZOUBEK, A. JAMES LEMASTER, AND OLEEN M. HENSON, *Gregg Dictation and Transcription Individual Progress Method,* Gregg Division, McGraw-Hill Book Company, New York, 1974.

MCKENNA, MARGARET A., "Effect of Early Introduction of New-Matter Dictation in the Teaching of Beginning Shorthand to College Students," unpublished doctoral dissertation, Michigan State University, East Lansing, Mich., 1966.

MELLINGER, MORRIS, *Basic Vocabulary for Written Business Office Communications,* Chicago State College, Chicago, 1970.

MICKELSEN, LEONARD P., "The Relationship Between Word Frequency and the Difficulty of Shorthand Dictation Materials," unpublished doctoral dissertation, University of North Dakota, Grand Forks, N. Dak., 1970.

MINNICK BARBARA J., "An Evaluation of Systematic Repetition of Brief Forms through Specially Constructed Dictation Material for *Gregg Shorthand, Diamond Jubilee Series,*" unpublished doctoral dissertation, University of Tennessee, Knoxville, Tenn., 1967.

MOSKOVIS, MICHAEL L., "An Identification of Certain Similarities and Differences between Successful and Unsuccessful College Level Beginning Shorthand and Transcription Students," unpublished doctoral dissertation, Michigan State University, East Lansing, Mich., 1967.

*National Survey of Professional, Administrative, Technical, and Clerical Pay,* Bulletin 1804, U.S. Department of Labor, Bureau of Labor Statistics, pp. 73–75.

NENNICH, FLORENCE, "A Predictor Index for Use in Elementary Shorthand," unpublished doctoral dissertation, Temple University, Philadelphia, Pa., 1974.

O'CONNELL, MARY MARGARET, "An Experimental Study to Determine the Effectiveness of Programmed Gregg Shorthand Materials," unpublished doctoral dissertation, University of Wisconsin, Madison, Wisc., 1967.

————, AND RUSSELL J. HOSLER, "Predictors of Success in Shorthand," *Journal of Business Education,* December, 1968, pp. 96–98.

*Our Manpower and Training Needs,* Bulletin 1701, BLS Regional Office, U.S. Department of Labor, Bureau of Labor Statistics, 1971, p. 43.

PALMER, ROSE, "A Comparison between Two Groups of Shorthand Writers," unpublished doctoral dissertation, New York University, New York, 1964.

PATRICK, ALFRED L., "An Error Analysis of Selected Brief Forms and Principles in Shorthand Notes of Beginning Gregg Diamond Jubilee Shorthand Students," unpublished doctoral dissertation, University of Tennessee, 1965.

PERKINS, WILMERT E., "The Development and Evaluation of Programmed Punctuation Materials for Secondary School Transcription Classes," unpublished doctoral dissertation, University of California, Los Angeles, Calif., 1959.

_____, (2) "Development and Evaluation of Programmed Punctuation Materials for Transcription," *Delta Pi Epsilon Journal,* November, 1970, pp. 1–9.

_____, (3), *Punctuation: A Programmed Approach,* South-Western Publishing Company, Cincinnati, 1972.

PERRY, DEVERN J., "An Analytical Comparison of the Relative Word-Combination Frequencies of Business Correspondence with Phrase Frequencies of Selected Shorthand Textbooks," unpublished doctoral dissertation, University of North Dakota, Grand Forks, N. Dak., 1968.

PERSING, BOBBYE S., "A Classroom Investigation of When to Begin New-Matter Dictation in Gregg Shorthand," unpublished doctoral dissertation, University of Oklahoma, Norman, Okla., 1966.

PULLIS, JOE M., "The Relationship between Competency in Shorthand Accuracy and Achievement in Shorthand Dictation," unpublished doctoral dissertation, North Texas State University, Denton, Tex., 1966.

RAINEY, BILL G., AND CARLOS E. JOHNSON, "Specific Standards in Office Skills," *Business Education World,* March-April, 1972, pp. 25, 31.

REYNOLDS, HELEN, "Evaluation in the Skill Building Subjects," *Evaluation of Pupil Progress in Business Education,* The American Business Education Yearbook, Somerset Press, Somerville, N.J., 1960, pp. 26–39.

RITTENHOUSE, EVELYN J., "A Study of Certain Factors Influencing Success in the Learning and Achievement of Shorthand," unpublished doctoral dissertation, Michigan State University, East Lansing, Mich., 1968.

SILVERTHORN, JAMES E., "The Basic Vocabulary of Written Business Communications," unpublished doctoral dissertation, Indiana University, Bloomington, Ind., 1955.

SKAFF, LORRINE B., "The Development and Validation of a Predictive Instrument to Measure Student Success in the First Semester of Gregg Shorthand," unpublished doctoral dissertation, Oregon State University, Corvallis, Ore., 1972.

TAYLOR, HELEN W., "Development and Evaluation of Programmed Materials in the Presentation of Theory in Beginning Shorthand Classes," unpublished doctoral dissertation, University of Tennessee, Knoxville, Tenn., 1963.

TURSE, PAUL L., *Turse Shorthand Aptitude Test,* World Book Company, New York, 1940.

UTHE, ELAINE, "An Evaluation of the Difficulty Level of Shorthand Dictation Materials," unpublished doctoral dissertation, University of Minnesota, Minneapolis, Minn., 1966.

VARAH, LEONARD J., "Effect of Academic Motivation and Other Selected Criteria on Achievement of First and Second-Semester Students," *The Delta Pi Epsilon Journal,* Vol. 10, No. 1, November, 1967, pp. 27–29.

WEST, LEONARD J., *Implications of Research for Teaching Typewriting,* 2d ed., DPE Research Bulletin No. 4, Gustavus Adolphus College, St. Peter, Minn., 1974.

_____, (2) "The Vocabulary of Instructional Materials for Typing and Stenographic Training—Research Findings and Implications" *Delta Pi Epsilon Journal,* Vol. 10, No. 3, May, 1968, pp. 13–25.

## PERFORMANCE GOALS

**1.** Using a goal from this chapter which utilizes listening and discussing activities, an instrument from Chapter 4 appropriate for evaluation of the goal, and while working with a small group **demonstrate** your ability to meet the designated criteria.

**2.** Given an in basket including three business letters which are well and poorly written according to the criteria in this chapter, **assess** the letters and rewrite any parts in order to make the writing conform to the criteria for properly written business letters.

**3.** Given a communication subcompetency and working with a small group while being taped, **demonstrate** your ability to plan and present a lesson involving the development of a model students may use for one of the forms of written communication, according to the criteria established in learning activity 4.

**4.** Given a brief description of students in a communication class and access to several tests of English usage, analyze the situation, select the test you deem best as a pretest, and **defend** your selection of the test according to the criteria presented.

**5.** Given completed standardized tests and the established norms and scores of students who have taken the test, **assess** each student's strengths and weaknesses, and for each of three students construct en route goals for subcompetencies they lack, defending each subcompetency selected.

**6.** Given a goal involving verbal communication, gather the data needed and while being recorded or videotaped **demonstrate** your ability to speak before a group according to the criteria developed in learning activity 8.

**7.** While working as a member of a group and given a list of competencies, utilize all available sources and **analyze** and classify instructional resources according to those competencies for which they are appropriate and prepare a handout sheet including the title of the instructional resource, a brief description, and the source. Evaluation will be made on the appropriateness of a given resource for a stated competency.

**8.** Given a performance goal and descriptive data on two students, **construct** a teaching-learning system including an appropriate evaluation, subcompetencies which apply, appropriate principles of learning, organizational patterns, and instructional resources. Evaluation will be made according to the criteria presented in Chapters 3–8 and in this chapter.

# CHAPTER 11

# Business Communication

"Business communication" is defined by Erickson as "exchanging oral and written information with persons outside the company or with company personnel; interacting and working in harmony with other office workers toward a specific accomplishment or goal" (Erickson, p. 6).

Business communication as a separate school subject has been one of the most neglected courses in the business curriculum. Very little attention has been given to defining the communication competencies that are necessary to success in the office and relating them to course content. Perhaps even more serious is the fact that students—and even teachers—have not developed sensitivity to the importance of communication as *the* most important component in office work.

The infrequent articles about business communication appearing in professional journals stress the fact that students do not like present courses and that the subject needs "a shot in the arm." Engerrand substantiates this contention by enrollment figures from a random sample of 20 percent of the public high schools in the U.S. Office of Education's Region 4 (South) when she reports: "As school enrollment increases, courses in communication are more likely to be offered, but the percentage of students enrolled in communication courses progressively decreases—apparently due to the increases in course options in larger schools" (Engerrand 1, p. 120). She says, "About 48 percent of the schools give courses, but only 8 percent of the total school population in grades 10–12 are taking a communications course" (Engerrand 2, p. 34).

A study of business English instruction in the state of Wisconsin reflects a similar situation. A questionnaire returned by 38 high schools in which business English instruction had been given during the two previous school years indicated that in 12 of them "a business English course was not being taught during the year for which data was sought" (Van Rens, p. 51).

The decline in interest in present courses in business communication is antithetical to its demonstrated importance in office work. It is not only desirable but essential that the whole subject of business communication be redesigned within the framework of the learning system so that appropriate standards are established and met in this basic element of office work, whether within a separate course or as separate competencies prescribed in several courses.

Early business communication courses, which were labeled "Business English" and "Business Letter Writing," focused on the technicalities of acceptable writing and on the writing of the types of letters that were commonly used in business. Later, courses called "Business Writing" included the writing of such things as reports, memoranda, procedures, and announcements as well as letters.

Gradually the college teachers of Business Writing expanded their concept of the area to include the behavioral sciences aspects of communication. This extension led to the view that is currently accepted: Business communication at all levels includes reading, writing, speaking to individuals and small groups, and listening.

Business communication as taught at the high school level in the business department may cover a year's work or a semester's work. In two-year colleges it is a one-semester course. In some two-year colleges it is a required subject for all business majors. In others it is a required subject for all secretarial, general clerical, and retailing majors. In still others it is an elective subject for all business students but is especially recommended for secretarial majors. It is not uncommon for two-year colleges to substitute business communication for the required English course in the basic curriculum.

Business communication is usually a required course in independent business schools that emphasize secretarial training. It is frequently offered in senior colleges and is required, along with a separate course in Report Writing, in a number of colleges of business administration.

## Needs of the Learner

All four aspects of business communication (reading, writing, speaking, and listening) are basic education that all students should master. The levels of competency required, though, to get an entry-level job and be promoted in it are relatively high.

As Andrews stated, "Approximately eleven hours of a person's waking time are spent in some form of communication." (Recycle to Chapter 3, p. 44.) All students should develop skills in writing, reading, speaking, and listening, but for the business student they become doubly important. Every business activity involves communication and every business employee becomes involved in this communication.

For a long time we have emphasized writing and reading, with specialized training in both for the business student. However, because each business employee spends more time speaking and listening than reading and writing, these skills are of major importance in a competency-based business education program.

Teachers of business communication at all levels will find the publications of the American Business Communication Association (formerly the American Business Writing Association) helpful. They are *The ABCA Bulletin* and the *Journal of Business Communication,* 317B David Kinley Hall, University of Illinois, Urbana.

## Needs of Business

All research reported in Chapter 3 that was undertaken to determine the competencies needed by office and distributive workers (Perkins, Lanham, Erickson, Crawford, and Huffman and Gust) emphasizes the primacy of communication skills among the requisite competencies for office work. It should be remembered that Erickson reported that some form of communication with others (interpersonal relations) was needed in 90 percent of the 300 entry-level jobs he analyzed. The entry-level worker must not only be able to perform the tasks involved in effective communication but also display affective behaviors required in interacting with others successfully.

The need of business for better communication skills is underscored by the fact that more in-service courses are given in this area than in any other, from induction training through executive development programs.

WRITING.    There are in-service courses in writing technicalities (grammar, spelling, punctuation, and usage) for lower-level workers, so that they can handle their present jobs of transmitting the ideas of others as well as originating simple written materials. These courses may lead to a higher level of employment. There are also courses in letter writing, from the simple order letter to the sales letter employing various psychological appeals, memorandums, procedures, short periodic informal reports, and long formal reports involving research and the interpretation of data.

Improvement of written communication is included in many middle-management in-service programs. The letters written in such programs frequently require an understanding of psychology-based skills in interpersonal relations. Attention is given to the organization of reports so that the important points can be gleaned quickly by the reader. Procedures writing is often included, since presenting the steps to be followed in performing a task in logical order and in simple, clear language is a middle-management responsibility.

READING.    As a result of the increasing employment of persons deficient in reading skills, in-service courses in reading and vocabulary building are often given. Special equipment and materials such as those available from the Educational Developmental Laboratories may be used. By use

**243**

of the Controlled Reader, materials of adult level are projected at a controlled rate as a moving slot forces the reader's attention so that he or she makes fewer eye fixations and fewer regressions, thus broadening the span of recognition. The vocabulary-building tapes present spoken materials whereby new words are learned from their use in context rather than from reference to the dictionary.

Because a manager progressing up the executive ladder becomes inundated by the flood of paperwork to be read, many companies provide courses in speed reading.

LISTENING. Business is beginning to provide in-service courses to improve the listening skills of employees at all levels. Entry-level workers need to *hear* directions clearly with their senses; but, more important, they must listen with their minds and decide what to do with the information. The supervisor needs to give clear directions and *listen* for reactions (either oral or physical). Listening is a requisite skill of all employees, but, Keefe says, "Listening reaches its highest pitch of purpose as an instrument of organizational interaction. The manager listens specifically to build a more effective organization" (Keefe, p. 31). The higher the level of the employee, the more time spent in listening.

An outstanding course for improving employee listening is available from the Xerox Corporation. The learner listens to a series of taped exercises ranging in difficulty from simple to complex and records answers to questions or solutions in a test booklet. There are several checkpoints at which the learner gets feedback as to progress. In a four- or five-hour period, the learner improves the ability to listen to directions, sorts out a specified number of main ideas from a rather garbled presentation, and reorganizes a recording into logical order. The listener learns not to be distracted from the main thrust by an ungrammatical speaker, by someone with a foreign accent, or by someone who is angry, garrulous, or aggressive.

SPEAKING. Most of the communication responsibilities Erickson identified as necessary for entry-level workers involve oral communication: receiving and giving information, scheduling appointments, receiving visitors, referring inquiries to others, discussing job-related procedures with the supervisor or others, and cooperating with others. Business gives formal training in a number of these components with the help of outside resources such as the telephone company. In addition, conversational courses in English are sometimes given to bilingual workers.

OVERALL NEEDS. Surveys made by college teachers of business communication to determine the communication needs of their graduates always find that executives stress the importance of speaking skills, sometimes even stating that they are more important than writing ability.

A look at the written communication responsibilities of a specialized group of business employees—secretaries—gives clues as to their training needs. Treece identified not only the commonest items composed by the

244

secretary but also the commonest problems encountered in composing these materials. Many people do not realize that top-level secretaries originate most of their output. It is unfortunate that Treece did not include the reading, speaking, and listening responsibilities in her study. The commonest items composed are given in rank order: (1) request letters; (2) general administrative letters; (3) responses to requests; (4) interoffice memorandums; (5) executive correspondence; (6) periodic reports; (7) miscellaneous letters; (8) minutes, agendas, and resolutions; (9) informational reports (not periodic reports); and (10) miscellaneous reports.

The commonest difficulties, also in rank order, are (1) avoiding trite expressions, (2) writing without wasting time, (3) building goodwill, (4) conciseness, (5) formal report form, (6) letter placement and layout, (7) making the message clear, (8) making the message accomplish its purpose, (9) planning the type of letter to use, and (10) paragraph construction.

To discover the communication skills needed in business management, the members of a business communication class at the University of Toledo interviewed 34 members of personnel departments, who listed the competencies in Figure 11.1.

Half of the 34 companies have formal communication programs. All corporate presidents responding to another portion of the study believed that some type of communication training should be provided for all management personnel (Zaugg, p. 6).

These responses are especially important to the communication teacher in professional and semiprofessional business administration programs in two- and four-year colleges. They are also helpful to teachers at lower levels, especially if their goals are not only to prepare students to enter business but to progress upward from their initial positions.

CONCLUSIONS. It is necessary for business to train its employees at all levels in all four areas of communication. At the lower levels, workers are trained to speak and write clearly, correctly, and in a way that promotes good interpersonal relations. Much of this initial training is directed toward compensating for previous undereducation. Improvement in communication skills is a very important component of management training.

Figure 11.1  Communication skills needed in management

| Written | % responding | Oral | % responding |
|---|---|---|---|
| Write letters and informal reports | 100 | Perform well in conferences inside company | 91 |
| Write acceptable notices | 91 | Participate in group activities such as committees inside the company | 88 |
| Write formal reports | 76 | Present oral reports within the company | 85 |
| Write acceptable procedures | 71 | Participate in conferences outside the company | 59 |
| Write policy statements | 47 | Speak before outside groups | 38 |

Source: Zaugg, p. 6.

If the schools did a better job in preparing students for business, business itself could cut back on a number of its costly communication programs.

## Identifying Competencies

The communication competencies required of beginning office workers were identified in Chapter 3 and at various other points. In Chapter 7, the opportunities for developing communication competencies in business courses other than the specialized course in business communication were shown in Figure 7.7. In the chapters devoted to teaching the different business subjects, the importance of communication competencies has been stressed, and performance goals based on them have been included. It is, however, highly desirable to include a separate course in Business Communication in the business curriculum. The course that is suggested in this chapter is much more challenging than the traditional one, which was largely remedial in nature, limited almost exclusively to letter writing at the expense of other forms of communication and almost devoid of opportunities for creativity. No wonder enrollments declined.

The course presented here is based on task analysis and is designed to develop competencies in not only writing but also reading, listening, and speaking. It includes the forms of business writing usually executed by the general office worker and omits such specialized writing as sales and collection letters. The student acquires the ability to write letters requesting something, acknowledging something, ordering goods, transmitting materials, accepting or rejecting requests, applying for a position, or persuading another person to act.

In addition to letters, the learners also write memorandums, informal reports, and directions for performing office procedures. They prepare abstracts and summaries of materials either read or heard. They improve discussion techniques, both as speakers and listeners, on committees planning and executing projects. They gain experience in instructing other persons orally in how to perform an office task. They make oral presentations that persuade a group to act in the way they wish, or they convince others to accept their viewpoints. Finally, the reading, writing, and listening competencies are coordinated in the activities performed during the course.

The following communication competencies are organized into three categories—those required to succeed in a business environment, those needed to acquire technical skills, and those needed to find a satisfactory worker role.

SUCCEEDING IN A BUSINESS ENVIRONMENT. In order for a worker to succeed in a business environment, it is important for that person to demonstrate that he or she appreciates as much as business does the importance of communication to office success. The worker should make continuous attempts to improve communication skills, and every communication must reflect sensitivity to the reaction of the reader, listener, or speaker. The following tasks, which reflect the importance of communication, are combined with standards to form competencies:

1. *Task:* Use a "you" attitude in communications.
   *Standard:* At all times.
   *Competency:* Use a "you" attitude in communication at all times.
2. *Task:* Value effective communication.
   *Standard:* By continuously using effective communication and improving your communication skills.
   *Competency:* Value effective communication by continuously using effective communication and attempting to improve your communication skills.

ACQUIRING TECHNICAL SKILLS. It is much easier to determine whether technical skills in reading, writing, speaking, and listening have been developed to a required tangible standard than to assess affective behaviors. The communication tasks requiring technical skills are stated below and, accompanied by the standard to which they are to be developed, translated into competencies.

3. *Task:* Write letters.
   *Standard:* Correct, clear, complete, and convincing.
   *Competency:* Write correct, clear, complete, and convincing letters that request, acknowledge, order goods, transmit, accept or reject, apply for a position, persuade someone to act.
4. *Task:* Write memorandums.
   *Standard:* Correct, clear, and complete.
   *Competency:* Write memorandums that are correct, clear, and complete.
5. *Task:* Write informal reports.
   *Standard:* Correct, clear, concise, and convincing.
   *Competency:* Write informal reports of progress, needs, results, and recommendation that are correct, clear, concise, and convincing.
6. *Task:* Write office procedures.
   *Standard:* That can be followed step by step.
   *Competency:* Write office procedures that can be followed step by step.
7. *Task:* Write abstracts.
   *Standard:* Correct, clear, and concise.
   *Competency:* Write correct, clear, and concise abstracts of written business information.
8. *Task:* Write summaries.
   *Standard:* Correct, clear, and complete.
   *Competency:* Write correct, clear, and complete summaries of group discussions and speeches.
9. *Task:* Instruct a classmate in how to perform an office task.

*Standard:* So that listener can execute the task.

*Competency:* Instruct a classmate so that he or she can execute an office task.

10. *Task:* Speak to a group.

   *Standard:* Until members accept speaker's viewpoint.

   *Competency:* Speak to a group so that members accept the speaker's viewpoint.

11. *Task:* Read, write, speak, and listen as a member of a committee planning, executing, and reporting a project.

   *Standard:* In which each member contributes, respects the worth of others, and works in cooperation with others.

   *Competency:* Read, write, speak, and listen as a member of a committee that plans, executes, and reports a project while contributing, respecting other members, and working cooperatively for a common goal.

FINDING A SATISFYING WORKER ROLE. A twelfth competency relates to finding a satisfying worker role.

12. *Task:* Write or tell the opportunities for using communication skills in the business office.

   *Standard:* While demonstrating ability to locate primary and secondary research sources and to organize the material into a correct, clear, and complete report.

   *Competency:* Write or tell the opportunities for using communication skills in the office while demonstrating ability to locate primary and secondary research sources and to organize the material into a correct, clear, and complete report.

In Figure 11.2, the identified communication competencies are classified by dominant domain and the level to which the competency is to be developed. The verb to be employed is designated and the type of evaluation to be used is identified.

Some written communications (letters of request, acknowledgment, order, and transmittal) require the learner to perform at a lower level of the cognitive domain than do letters accepting or rejecting a request or persuading someone to do something, such as employ the writer. In the first instance the writer can follow a model, being sure to include all essential information and to express himself or herself correctly. In the second instance the writer must make decisions requiring judgment in assessing a situation, the highest level of the cognitive domain.

In Competency 8 (summaries of speeches and discussions), the writer must first operate at the analysis-synthesis level to *analyze* what was said. He or she must then progress upward to the evaluation level and decide on the relative importance of the different points and the order in which to present them.

Although Competency 11 (a committee project culminating in a report) results in a product—a committee report—the teacher may also use this project as the framework for developing better group interaction, evaluat-

Figure 11.2 Analysis of competencies as the basis for writing performance goals

| Competency | Domain & level | Evaluation | Verb |
|---|---|---|---|
| 1. Use a "you" attitude in communications at all times. | Affective: highest level | Process | Consistently demonstrate |
| 2. Value effective communications by continuously using effective communications and attempting to improve your communication skills. | Affective: highest level | Process: controlled observation. Product | Consistently demonstrate |
| 3. Write correct, clear, and complete letters that request, acknowledge, order and transmit goods. | Cognitive: application –Routine following of a guide | Product | Demonstrate |
| 4. Write correct, clear, and complete memos. | Cognitive: application | Product | Demonstrate |
| 5. Write informal reports of progress, needs, results, and recommendations that are correct, clear, concise, and convincing. | Cognitive: evaluation –Decisions | Product | Judge |
| 6. Write office procedures that can be followed step by step. | Cognitive: analysis-synthesis | Process: controlled observation. | Construct |
| 7. Write correct, clear, and concise abstracts of business information. | Cognitive: analysis-synthesis | Product | Analyze |
| 8. Write correct, clear, and complete summaries of speeches and group discussions. | Cognitive: analysis-synthesis, evaluation | Product | Analyze Assess |
| 9. Instruct a classmate so that he can perform an office task. | Cognitive: analysis-synthesis | Process: controlled observation. | Explain |
| 10. Speak to a group so that members accept the speaker's viewpoint. | Cognitive: evaluation | Product | Assess |
| 11. Read, write, speak, and listen as a member of a committee that plans, executes, and reports a project while contributing, respecting other members' viewpoints, and working cooperatively for a common goal. | Cognitive: evaluation Affective: highest level | Product Process | Decide Demonstrate |
| 12. Write (or tell) the opportunities for using communication skills in the office after demonstrating ability to locate and use primary and secondary research sources and to organize the material into a correct, concise, and complete report. | Cognitive: evaluation | Product | Assess |

ing both the reactions of the committee as a group and the behaviors of each member of a group. (Recycle to pp. 79–86 for a discussion of evaluation instruments used in measuring affective behaviors. This recycle is a must.) Measuring the success of interpersonal relationships requires process evaluation by both the teacher and the learners' peers of both the reactions of the committee as a group and the affective behaviors of each member of the group. The instruments described on page 83 are used.

Obviously, en route goals must be set and group interactions evaluated a number of times before most learners will exhibit the desired behaviors consistently.

## Establishing Performance Goals

Performance goals for a one-semester high school course based on Figure 11.2 follow. Two all-encompassing goals (1 and 2) in the affective domain should be worked on continuously by the learner as he or she completes other goals.

1. In all daily business correspondence, **consistently demonstrate** that you have a "you" attitude by using "you" instead of "I," by taking time to listen to the other person's point of view, and by empathizing with the other person.

2. While reading, interviewing business employees, listening to discussions, and writing business communications, **consistently demonstrate** by your affective behaviors and the quality of the communications you produce that you value effective communication and that your behaviors are characterized by continued attempts to improve your communication skills.

3a. Given case problems requiring the writing of four types of letters (request, acknowledgment, transmittal of materials, and orders for goods), **demonstrate** that you can compose and type communications that contain all essential information when evaluated against a checklist, display the ideas effectively, and contain no stereotyped phrases or uncorrected errors. (Three of four mailable).

3b. Given situations in which letters granting a request, refusing a request, persuading someone to act as you wish, and applying for a position are required, **decide** how to present your case and type solutions that (a) display the ideas effectively, (b) show consideration for the reader, (c) state the positive actions expected from the reader, (d) avoid stereotyped phrases, and (e) contain no uncorrected errors in spelling, punctuation, or grammar. (Three of the four items to meet the standards of the instructor)

4. Given situations in which it is necessary to communicate (a) with your employer, (b) your employer's colleague, and (c) a peer employee, **demonstrate** your understanding of the format and the ability to write correct, clear, and complete memorandums. (Ap-

proval of all memorandums by a committee of classmates.)

5. Given unorganized notes from which to compose two informal reports of progress, needs, results, or recommendations, **judge** how to organize the material and present the main points and type a usable one-page report. (Logical organization, appropriate side headings, usable reports as judged by the instructor.)

6. Given a simple office task such as stuffing envelopes or opening the mail, **construct** a step-by-step procedure that can be followed successfully by a classmate as you explain the steps orally from the instructions in the written procedure.

7a. While listening to oral or taped directions for performing an unfamiliar office task, **demonstrate** your ability to follow directions that are given orally. (Successful completion of the task.)

7b. Given a one-page article from a business magazine, **analyze** for important points and write a summary of no more than 75 words. (Main points extracted to the instructor's satisfaction, no errors in mechanics.)

8. Given a taped 15-minute speech, **analyze** the content in a typewritten summary of no more than two typed pages. (Main points extracted to the instructor's satisfaction, no errors in mechanics.)

9. After listening to an assigned committee discussion of a controversial topic, **assess** the validity of the arguments and draw conclusions which are expressed in a typed report. (Decisions must conform to consensus of the class expressed in an evaluation session.)

10. Choosing your own topic, in a five- to eight-minute talk to the entire class or group of peers (as your teacher directs), **assess** the main arguments and persuade your classmates to take an action you want. (Criteria for evaluation established by class prior to the speech.)

11a. Given three days to plan a panel discussion of a business topic chosen by the members of the panel in cooperation with the teacher, while interacting with other committee members during planning and with the audience during the discussion, **decide** on the topic, each person's responsibilities, organization of the discussion, and form of summary; and **consistently demonstrate** the type of interpersonal behaviors acceptable in business. (Evaluation of process by Figures 4.8 and 4.9.)

11b. Using the results of committee planning in 11a, **defend** the positions taken during the panel discussion and the written summary of the discussion. (Audience evaluation and teacher evaluation of written statement.)

12. Using library sources and interviews with office employees, cooperatively **assess** the importance of communication skills in the office in a written report based on the contributions from each member. (Evaluation of affective behaviors while working on

the project by use of instruments in Chapter 4, pages 79–86.) Evaluation of the written reports by instructor, following the points listed on a checklist handed to students prior to the project.

These performance goals are, of course, only suggestions and should be modified by every instructor before adoption. Situations establishing possibilities for group interaction are emphasized. If such experiences are available in other courses in which business communication students are enrolled (such as office simulation or other strategies in the clerical program), they should be deemphasized here. See Figure 7.7, page 143, for opportunities to build communication skills into other courses; then find out what is actually being done in these classes.

Evaluation is not always a one-time test. Some of the performance goals involve several days of controlled observation and continued writing efforts.

## Identifying and Sequencing Subcompetencies

Because it would take too much space to identify and sequence the subcompetencies required to achieve all the performance goals listed in the preceding section, only one goal is developed here. (See Figure 11.3.)

## Identifying Student Characteristics and Present Competencies

Many of today's business students have already been underachievers in communication. Although such underachievers need to develop new competencies in this area, they also need remedial work that will appeal to them. Until now many of them may have seen no reason for learning in the communication area. They can speak and be understood by their peers; isn't that enough? They do not need to write very often, and the television screen rather than written materials is the source of outside information. They do not read, they "tune out" what they do not want to hear, they have few occasions to write, and they are satisfied with their speech.

These students are usually unaware that communication skills required in business differ from those they already possess. They come into the business program anxious to learn new subjects such as typewriting or data processing, but they are quite unconvinced of either the pervasiveness of the need for communication competencies in office work or of their own deficiencies in this area.

Telling them that they need additional experiences in reading, speaking, listening, and writing is not enough. The differences between their present patterns and those essential to success in entry-level jobs must be demonstrated and experienced many times before a favorable climate for learning can exist. Fruehling gives four reasons for apathy toward business writing instruction in terms that are equally applicable to instruction in business reading, listening, and speaking: students (1) have never

Figure 11.3   Sequencing of subcompetencies for performance goal 3A

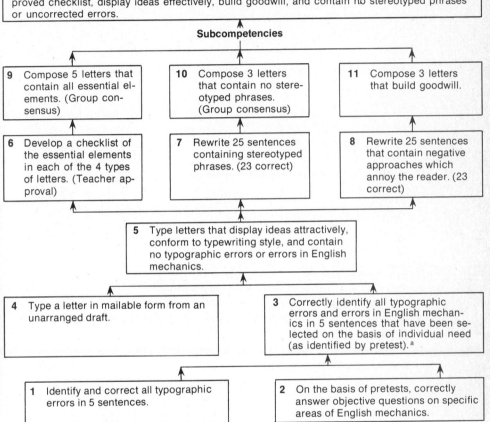

**Performance goal 3A**

Given a case problem requiring the writing of four types of letters (requests, acknowledgements, transmittal of materials, and orders for goods), **demonstrate** that you can compose and type communications that contain all essential information when evaluated against an approved checklist, display ideas effectively, build goodwill, and contain no stereotyped phrases or uncorrected errors.

**Subcompetencies**

9   Compose 5 letters that contain all essential elements. (Group consensus)

10   Compose 3 letters that contain no stereotyped phrases. (Group consensus)

11   Compose 3 letters that build goodwill.

6   Develop a checklist of the essential elements in each of the 4 types of letters. (Teacher approval)

7   Rewrite 25 sentences containing stereotyped phrases. (23 correct)

8   Rewrite 25 sentences that contain negative approaches which annoy the reader. (23 correct)

5   Type letters that display ideas attractively, conform to typewriting style, and contain no typographic errors or errors in English mechanics.

4   Type a letter in mailable form from an unarranged draft.

3   Correctly identify all typographic errors and errors in English mechanics in 5 sentences that have been selected on the basis of individual need (as identified by pretest).[a]

1   Identify and correct all typographic errors in 5 sentences.

2   On the basis of pretests, correctly answer objective questions on specific areas of English mechanics.

[a]This subcompetency, which is used with individually prescribed or small-group learning, must be worked on throughout the achievement of other subcompetencies and performance goals until it is achieved.

been required to develop writing ability, (2) have enjoyed little success in their first writing experiences because they cannot distinguish between good and bad models, (3) are uncertain about precise English and the mechanics of style, and (4) have not been challenged by the methods used in teaching.

It is imperative, then, that pretesting be done to determine the needs of the learner before he or she ever attempts any assignments in Business Communication.

Many school systems have a test consultant who can make recommendations and has a file of standardized tests in spelling, punctuation, usage, and English mechanics that are available for examination. In addition, the teacher should consult the current catalogs of business education publishers for tests in Business English. There are also tests included in programmed textbooks and transparencies that the teacher can use to measure the present levels of competency of entering students. With ingenuity and a bit of teaching experience, any teacher can develop a resource file in this area.

Standard tests that measure writing ability are harder to find. The teacher can, however, assign a writing exercise that will provide the information sought.

## Matching the Learner With Appropriate Performance Goals

Although large- and small-group activity characterizes much of the Business Communication course, the able students naturally achieve higher levels in performance goals. They are the moderator of the panel discussion, the reporter for the committee, the leader in developing the questionnaire, the researcher who locates more and better information, the one who invites and introduces the guest speaker, the organizer who influences the decisions about who does what in completing the project—just by a process of natural selection. The instructor must be very careful to rotate the positions of responsibility so that the less able members of the class, too, become involved in the activities and receive maximum benefit from participating in them. Even so, the better students will, and should, perform at a higher level than the others.

In written communication, pretests will uncover learning needs. A student weak in punctuation might be required to complete an entire six-hour programmed instruction unit covering the 27 rules for punctuation, possibly as homework so that he or she is free to engage in class activities. Another student might take the tests in the Perkins programmed instruction unit without completing the exercises. If this learner could not identify an appositive and punctuate it, only the frames covering appositives would be assigned. A laboratory day a week—or sometimes even two if needed—might be set aside for individually prescribed instruction, with differentiated assignments for each learner. While one student is assigned instruction in punctuation, either using the framed instruction or a programmed textbook, another would be rewriting a letter that did not contain all of the essential elements or did not meet the criteria for the assignment (Brendel and Near 1). Two other learners working as a committee might prepare the instrument they plan to use in interviewing a recent graduate. Others might be typing special assignments in English usage, punctuation, and spelling to meet their personal needs (Brendel and Leffingwell and Brendel and Near 2).

## Applying Learning Principles

Learning principles 1, 2, and 6 apply particularly to business communication.

## Principle 1: Learning Must Be Perceived as Relevant

Any program in business communication must be perceived by the learner as important to success in business. Since interpersonal relations is the most important component of entry-level office work, the teacher, too, must appreciate its importance. By assigned readings, discussions, and contacts with business, every business teacher in every subject can and should stress its relevancy. Traditional Business English courses that emphasize correctness in writing only have not seemed to learners to be tied up with their future in business. There must be reorganization of the subject matter in terms of communication competencies and of methods by which the competencies are developed before students will realize the importance of effective communication. Also, if the course is fun, apathy toward it will disappear.

## Principle 2: Learning a New Behavior Results from the Learner's Interaction with His or Her Total Environment

Competency in business communication has not been essential to many students' present environment. If, however, the learner's self-esteem is developed through ability to meet realistic, relevant performance goals not only in writing but also reading, speaking, and listening, the new, desired behaviors will emerge—behaviors that not only constitute adequate preparation for the new environment of business but will also enable the learner to function better in the present one.

## Principle 6: Students Should Be Aware of Progress Toward Goals

The learner has a right to know how each en route goal contributes to the performance goal. Nothing is to be included in the course that does not contribute to established objectives. Feedback of results at every step is possible. For instance, oral performance is evaluated immediately. First drafts of written assignments are evaluated during the class session, and rewrites based on this feedback are evaluated by the teacher without delay. At every point the learner knows whether a goal has been met or whether recycling is necessary.

## Using Appropriate Teaching-Learning Strategies

Activities that enable learners to achieve the fifteen performance goals for a suggested one-semester business communication course are summarized on page 256, in each of the four aspects of communication, before specific teaching strategies are suggested for each one of the performance goals.

## Reading

- Textbooks and supplementary textbooks containing models of the communications to be written or discussions to be held.
- Newspapers, business periodicals, and business books that students locate through reference to *Reader's Guide to Periodical Literature* and *Business Periodicals Index.*

## Listening (Live or Taped)

- To directions for completing assignments.
- To teacher explanations.
- To other students and reacting to their ideas.
- To authorities.
- To discussions among other students.

## Speaking

- To the class (prepared speeches and summaries of group discussions).
- To peers in small groups.

## Discussing (Listening *and* Speaking—Interacting)

- Process evaluation as well as product evaluation of such things as courtesy, respect for the opinions of others, sharing responsibility, extent of involvement with the group.
- Case problems in human relations—Developing principles that can be used in future situations in which the same problem occurs.
- Case problems resulting in the composition of a written communication. Assessing the situation and deciding on the course of action to be taken in completing assignments. Understanding the function of the communication to be written.
- Group interviews eliciting needed information.
- Committee activities, including group discussions of issues (panels or debates) and committee activities or projects such as organizing, executing, and summarizing the information as a group working toward a common goal.

## Writing

- Letters in four situations requiring *application* of cognitive skills.
- Letters in four situations requiring *evaluation* or decision making in the cognitive domain.
- Memorandums.
- Informal reports from unorganized notes.
- Office procedures.
- Summaries of written and oral business information.
- Informal reports of committee discussions and projects.

## Performance Goals 1 and 2: Affective Behaviors

Before students can master these two affective goals, it is important for them to understand the meaning of the "you" attitude, effective communications, and improvement of communication skills. A group discussion is an effective way to introduce these concepts. It is also helpful for students to listen to taped or live discussions that exemplify both good and bad affective behaviors. Unless a student recognizes an existing difficulty, it will be impossible to correct it.

## Performance Goals 3 and 4: Writing Letters and Memorandums

Strategies for learning English mechanics and for composing are discussed separately.

ENGLISH MECHANICS. Each learner's deficiencies in English mechanics should first be revealed through pretests. If all students are seriously deficient in the same area, group drill is indicated. If only a few learners need help, small-group instruction or programmed learning would be appropriate. The teacher must develop a resource file of specialized materials for each kind of deficiency—new drills, additional en route goals (either new ones or more tests of the old ones after a student has completed recycling), minipacs, transparencies, portions of programmed materials cataloged as to coverage, Educational Developmental Laboratories programs, or workbooks.

Strategies for learning English mechanics are different from those used for learning to write well. The lowest levels of cognitive learning are required. The learner who has acquired *knowledges* (such as the meaning of the word "clause"), can then achieve *comprehension* (what an introductory clause is) and is ready for *application*. Through drill, responses to introductory clauses are developed to the extent that they are always punctuated with a comma. This automatization is accomplished in much the same way that psychomotor skills are developed. That is why the mechanics of English can be taught well by using programmed materials, workbooks, and other kinds of drill materials, followed by evaluation and recycling if necessary until the subject matter mastered through isolated drill can be recognized when included with other subject matter.

An effective evaluation instrument is the proofreading exercise, and many, many of them should be used both for learning and for evaluation of the learner's ability to detect errors in typing, punctuation, and word usage.

Learning the mechanics of English can be facilitated by the use of committees of two. Students exchange written assignments with other student proofreaders. They mark all errors in mechanics and return them to the author, who has the privilege of correcting all errors before submitting them to the instructor. Proof that this strategy works is evidenced by the fierce debates between the students as to a particular construction.

Another successful strategy individualizes remedial work. Every student paper receives two grades: one for content and the other for mechanics. The grade on mechanics is coupled with assignment of additional work. The student is to write at the bottom of the paper the rule and two sentences illustrating correction of the error. If a word is misspelled, the student writes the word correctly in two original sentences. All papers are resubmitted to the teacher regularly.

A study of English mechanics should not dominate the course, however. Correctness is an important aspect of communicating, of course; but the office worker must also become an accomplished composer of the materials in which English mechanics are applied.

BUSINESS COMPOSITION. Probably the next recommended step is learning to write sentences. Practice exercises are assigned in rewriting sentences containing stereotyped phrases, in changing negative statements to positive ones, and in building goodwill. When students feel that they are ready for tests measuring en route performance goals in these areas, they attempt them and are ready to begin studying letters if they meet the standards. If not, they are recycled through additional writing practice and retested.

For a long time teachers have thought that students learn to compose by composing. Most of them would be shocked to learn the results of Inman's study to determine the effect of varying the frequency of writing upon student achievement in business correspondence (Inman, p. 38). Four classes at Western Kentucky University were taught the same content by the same teacher using the same teaching procedures for two consecutive semesters. The only variable was the number of writing assignments completed: Group A, 24; Group B, 15; Group C, 10; and Group D, 6. The groups were tested at the beginning and at the end of each semester using three tests: the Missouri College English Test (a standardized college English test), the Principles of Business Writing Test (an objective test developed by the researcher), and a Written Letter Test, which measures actual writing ability. Achievement was significantly higher for the second-semester students, as would be expected. The big surprise, though, is that students who completed only six writing assignments achieved significantly better than the groups who completed 24, 15, and 10 writing problems.

These results confirm the hypothesis that there is little value in doing something until you know what you are trying to do and that a writer needs to recognize "good" writing in the category in which he or she is to write. As Fruehling says,

. . . give the students an opportunity to read the smooth, easy flow of a model. . . . It certainly won't take them very long to recognize that they may have to develop certain skills. In any event, they will soon become aware of their strengths and weaknesses (and so will you). This individualized approach makes the whole writing experience more meaningful because you are now able to prescribe and direct learning activities that will help the student correct his weaknesses, whatever they may be, and polish his strong points. This approach makes the student aware of the real value of understanding the mechanics of style because they are presented in a realistic context—as new tools for expressing himself. He is motivated . . . for he knows that he can learn to communicate better. . . . This approach . . . would encourage more purposeful reading if many model letters were provided and real correspondence were used for work assignments. Critiquing many, many letters with the guidance of an experienced instructor could provide the students with some ability to distinguish between good and bad correspondence. . . . (Fruehling, p. 23)

A teaching cycle that has proved effective in helping students learn to write forceful business communications is as follows:

1. Use a communication textbook and supplementary textbooks such as typewriting and shorthand textbooks as well as other business communication textbooks, lectures, and discussion for identifying the elements of good writing in each of the eight letters to be written.

2. Locate and discuss models that contain the elements thus identified. The more resources available, the better. Ask students to select model communications and to justify their choice to the group. Test the student's ability to identify good and poor models.

3. If a student is not an accomplished typist, and many enrollees in Business Communication are not, choose the en route goal requiring a typed letter that meets business standards. Recycle if necessary.

4. Discuss the problem to be solved by writing the communication assigned so that the learner identifies with the situation. Questions such as these may be used to set the stage: What action do you want to influence the reader to take? What is the first thing the reader wants to know when reading your letter? How can you close the letter to secure action? What are the essential elements to be included? If you say no, how can you soften the blow? How can you build goodwill in the letter? (The teacher explains that the solution must conform to company policy in the organization being studied. The writer cannot grant a 15 percent discount if a 5 percent discount is the policy.)

5. Have the students write the communication. In some situations it might be advantageous for two students to work together. Sometimes letters should be written in class; at other times, as homework.

6. Discuss sample first attempts either in small groups or with the entire class, projecting the letter on the overhead projector screen. (Making the transparency is a simple matter.) Students make most of the comments, with the teacher offering suggestions at the end of the discussion. It is a good idea to evaluate these first drafts and permit their writers to rewrite before the communication is

graded (if a grade is required other than the evaluation of a performance goal). After all, there is still truth in the saying "Writing is rewriting," even if the learner has adopted a model. This strategy usually results in a student's asking, "May I read my letter?" or "May the transparency of my letter be discussed?" rather than trying to avoid presenting a composition.

7. Rewrite if necessary or if the student feels that a second attempt would result in a better product.

8. Exchange papers with proofreading partner for location of errors. Correct. (As a performance goal, the writer, not the partner, proofreads the product, but this is an evolving standard.)

9. Evaluate for grading purposes and, more important, for determining whether the teaching strategies worked or should be modified.

The use of the overhead projector in presenting communications for evaluation causes students to give attention to display and correctness just because their products may be chosen for evaluation. Sometimes, however, a student who has not had time to put a draft into satisfactory form may ask to read an effort aloud so that he or she may benefit from criticism.

Of course, no one strategy should be used so exclusively that learners become bored with it. One assignment on selecting model letters as a way of emphasizing the pattern of the expert would be challenging; the next one might not work at all. Interest in learner-teacher evaluation sessions may begin to pall if they are used continuously. The alert teacher will observe learner reaction to strategies used and try new ones when student efforts lag.

## Performance Goals 5 and 6: Writing an Informal Report from Unorganized Notes

After a textbook assignment, the class discusses the kinds of informal reports (progress, needs, results, or recommendations) and the purposes they serve. Students locate and present models of informal reports they think effective and defend their choices. They then develop guidelines for the preparation of informal reports.

Sample unorganized notes upon which reports are to be based are provided the learners. During either a teacher-led discussion or in a small group which has access to teacher assistance, one set of notes is analyzed and a report planned. Each student then plans a format that is approved by the teacher before the report is typed. (A learner with a typing problem completes the en route goal requiring the production of a usable informal report with subheadings.) An evaluation session is held either with the teacher or with a committee of peers who have access to teacher guidance before another report is attempted.

If learners have difficulty in organizing their ideas into logical order, it is wise to spend time in small groups in identifying and sequencing main ideas rather than in typing reports in which this weakness is compounded.

If a teacher prefers traditional class organization in which all students are working on the same performance goal, it is still possible to individualize instruction so that more competent students are given more complicated notes and produce reports requiring a higher level of decision making.

If the teacher organizes the course so that each learner works alone or in a small group organized for students with the same problems until Performance Goal 5 is achieved, the student then tackles Performance Goal 6 regardless of the accomplishments of the rest of the class.

## Performance Goal 7a: Writing and Following Procedures

Following procedures written or given orally by somebody else is a component of office simulations and of other clerical courses. *Writing* procedures is suggested for inclusion here because of the difficulty of such precision writing. By having the writer orally instruct another student who performs the operation while referring to the written procedure, three types of business communication are integrated (writing, speaking, and listening).

One strategy for demonstrating the difficulty of writing procedures and of following unorganized oral instructions is to ask volunteer role players to attempt the performance goal before the unit is started. Usually such a demonstration results in chaos and emphasizes the need for learning.

Small-group instruction is especially suitable in procedures writing and in giving and listening to oral instructions. Students can try out the written procedures on each other until they feel that they are ready to ask for the evaluation instrument.

## Performance Goal 7b: Abstracting Business Information

The competencies learned in Performance Goal 5 in organizing notes are transferable here, and the same strategies can be used. The teacher may want to collect materials from business to supplement magazine articles, such as directives to employees or reports of a committee meeting.

Of course, en route goals on not-yet-mastered English mechanics will be included.

## Performance Goal 8: Analyzing Oral Presentations

For the first attempt a committee may listen to a report (and relisten if necessary) and compose a summary, which is projected on the overhead projector screen for comparison with the summaries of other groups. Tapes should be progressively longer and more difficult.

One way of enlivening a unit like this is to assign summaries of speeches being made in the school assembly or on television.

### Performance Goal 9: Analyzing Committee Discussion

The reader should review the section dealing with listening for ideas. (Recycle to Chapter 7, pp. 129–130.) A student listening for the group consensus and discussing the validity of the arguments on which it is based must operate on the highest level in the cognitive domain. It is highly possible that this performance goal should be restricted to the better students in the class. At any rate, so far as most learners are concerned, success will come only after considerable experience.

### Performance Goal 10: Giving an Oral Talk to Persuade

After a reading assignment on preparing and presenting a talk and a review of textbook discussion of letters that persuade, the class discusses the material and develops criteria by which each speech will be evaluated. In consultation with the teacher, each student's topic is decided and sources of information are discussed. As preparation for the talk that meets the performance goal, preliminary attempts are tape recorded and critiqued by the speaker and at least one other student, possibly several times before the performance goal is attempted.

### Performance Goals 11a, 11b, and 12: Committee Planning, Executing, and Reporting

This book has emphasized the value of group interaction and the teacher's responsibility for developing good interpersonal relationships throughout; it has also outlined in detail the techniques for organizing and conducting such activities and for evaluating both the product and the interaction process that result. (Recycle to Chapters 4 and 7.)

This chapter will not repeat this material. This does not mean that it is considered any less important in business communication. In fact, it is *more* important. Performance Goals 11a, 11b, and 12 require application of the material in Chapter 7.

All strategies included here conform to the most recent trend in business communication, the organization of a communication laboratory in which all components of communication are integrated as committees plan and execute projects. The advantage of this plan is that students learn when they need to know. Strong students help weak ones. (Never underestimate the power of students to teach each other!) The disadvantage is that various types of communication may not receive the in-depth treatment that is needed.

## Evaluating the System

The competencies, performance goals, and strategies presented in this chapter differ considerably from those found in traditional Business Communication courses.

One class may have so many deficiencies in English mechanics that a great deal of time must be given to remediation—although it is usually possible to improve mechanics at the same time that composition competencies are being developed. One teacher may decide to include sales letters and credit letters, although the business needs of most of the students hardly justify the decision. Another teacher may use telephone communication as the mode for building speech competencies and may drop formal speeches. Still another may want to include writing Mailgrams. One teacher may find that another whole course in the business department is built around group interaction and will give minimal attention to discussion techniques.

All right, this chapter contains one set of competencies and performance goals. The teacher chooses the ones that can be defended for a particular school, revises some, and substitutes new ones according to needs. The same comments apply to the suggested teaching strategies. They represent one way of conducting the course. It is hoped that they provide a fresh approach. The question after they have been tried, though, is: Did they work? Are they the performance goals that *you* want for *your* class? Do they meet the employment needs of your students? Which of them did your students actually attain? How many students actually demonstrated by their affective behaviors and the quality of their communication that they value effective communication and that they continually attempt to improve their communication skills?

Answers to these questions will determine the modifications made in the system next time around.

## LEARNING ACTIVITIES

**1.** During all small-group activities used in reaching the performance goals in this chapter, demonstrate your ability to achieve consistently satisfactory ratings by your instructor and peers on the evaluative instruments in Chapter 5, p. 79–84. Your instructor will assign evaluation committees on a rotation basis. The standard, "consistently satisfactory" ratings, implies a number of evaluations. (Performance goal 1)

**2.** Given 10 situations requiring business communication, differentiate, to your instructor's approval, among those in which process evaluation is appropriate, those in which product evaluation is appropriate, and those in which both evaluations should be used. (Performance goal 1)

**3.** Select one letter from a typewriting, shorthand, and an office practice textbook that you would use either positively or negatively in developing the concept of good business writing. To what points would you call attention? Estimate the time taken from other competencies to develop this concept and defend this practice. (Performance goal 2)

**4.** In a small group, develop criteria for evaluating a teaching demonstration whose objective is the development of a model to be used in writing some type of business communication. (Performance goal 3)

**5.** After preparing an overall plan for meeting one of the performance goals requiring written communication, microteach a 15-minute segment live or on videotape that meets Flanagan's criteria or those developed in learning activity 4. (Performance goal 3)

**6.** In a small group, develop criteria for selecting a pretest in English mechanics and decide from among the tests available the one that most nearly meets your criteria, defending your choice to your instructor's satisfaction. (Performance goal 4)

**7.** After examining all available tests of English mechanics according to your instructor's plan, take one test and self-score it. Prescribe en route goals for yourself in conference with your instructor, achieve them, and retake the test. Appraise your ability to identify needed subcompetencies. (Performance goals 4, 5, and 7)

**8.** As a member of a small group, contribute to the development of criteria that meet your instructor's approval for evaluating a speech that will be given in performance goal 6.

**9.** Tape record a five-minute speech on a topic of your own choice. With one colleague, evaluate it in terms of learning activity 8. Retape, reevaluate, and repeat until you and your partner are satisfied. (Performance goal 6)

**10.** According to your instructor's plan, familiarize yourself with available teaching resources through examination, demonstration, personal use, and written descriptions for your kit of teaching materials. (Performance goals 5, 7, and 8)

**11.** As a member of a small group, check three textbooks in business communication against the competencies listed in this chapter. Recommend one book for adoption, indicating the level and type of student for which it is suitable. Prepare a written composite report indicating areas that would require supplementary learning materials and indicate specific sources of these materials. (Performance goals 7 and 8)

## SELECTED READINGS

ANDREWS, ANNE, "All Within Earshot," *From Nine to Five,* Vol. 2, No. 21.

BONNER, WILLIAM H., "The Teaching of Business English and Communication," *National Business Education Yearbook,* Washington, D.C., 1971, pp. 105–113.

BRENDEL, LEROY, AND ELSIE LEFFINGWELL, *English Usage Drills and Exercises, Programmed for the Typewriter,* Gregg Division, McGraw-Hill Book Company, New York, 1968.

BRENDEL, LEROY, AND DORIS NEAR (1), *Punctuation Drills and Exercises, Programmed for the Typewriter,* Gregg Division, McGraw-Hill Book Company, New York, 1970.

_____ AND _____ (2), *Spelling Drills and Exercises, Programmed for the Typewriter,* Gregg Division, McGraw-Hill Book Company, New York, 1974.

ENGERRAND, DORIS A. D. (1), "A Content Survey Analysis of Oral Communication Taught in Business Education Classes in the Public High Schools of United States Office of Education, Region IV," unpublished doctoral dissertation, Georgia State University, Atlanta, Ga.,as reported in the *Journal of Business Education,* December, 1971, p. 120.

_____(2), same study as reported in *Business Education Forum,* October, 1971, p. 34.

ERICKSON, LAWRENCE W., *Basic Components of Office Work—An Analysis of 300 Office Jobs,* Monograph 123, South-Western Publishing Company, Inc., Cincinnati, 1971.

FRUEHLING, ROSEMARY, "A Job-Oriented Approach to Business Correspondence," *Business Education World,* January-February, 1972, pp. 22–23.

INMAN, THOMAS H., "A Study to Determine the Effect of Varying the Frequency of Writing Upon Student Achievement in Business Correspondence," unpublished doctoral dissertation, Northern Illinois University, DeKalb, Ill., 1970, as reported in *Business Education Forum,* October, 1971, p. 38.

KEEFE, W. F., *Listen, Management,* McGraw-Hill Book Company, New York, 1971.

LAWRENCE, NELDA R., "Innovations in Teaching Business Communications," *Delta Pi Epsilon Journal,* February, 1969, pp. 9–16.

NICHOLS, RALPH G., AND LEONARD A. STEVENS, *Are You Listening?* McGraw-Hill Book Company, New York, 1959.

PERKINS, W. E., *Programmed Punctuation,* South-Western Publishing Company, Inc., Cincinnati, 1971, based on dissertation entitled "The Development and Evaluation of Programmed Punctuation Materials for Secondary School Transcription Classes," University of California, Los Angeles, Calif., 1970.

STEAD, BETTE, "Communication: The Way to a Relevant Curriculum," *Delta Pi Epsilon Journal,* November, 1969, pp. 27–32.

STODDARD, TED D., AND S. ELVON WARNER, "A Competency-Based Approach for Teaching Business Writing Concepts and Skills," *Journal of Business Communication,* Summer, 1973, pp. 7–15.

TREECE, MALDRA C., "Business Communication Practices and Problems of Professional Secretaries," *Journal of Business Communication,* Summer, 1972, reporting dissertation entitled "Written Communication Responsibilities and Related Difficulties Experienced by Selected Certified Professional Secretaries," University of Mississippi, University, Miss., 1971.

VAN RENS, MARETA, "A Study of Business English Instruction in the Wisconsin Public Schools for the Academic Year 1967–68," unpublished master's thesis, University of Wisconsin, Madison, Wisc., 1969, as reported in *Business Education Forum,* October, 1970.

VON IGNATIUS, BERYL, *Survey of Selected Firms in the Los Angeles Area to Determine Communication Skills Needed for Entry-Level Clerk Typists, Stenographers, and Secretaries,* unpublished master's thesis, California State University, Los Angeles, Calif., 1972.

WILLIAMS, CHARLOTTE A., "An Experimental Instructional Approach Utilizing the Small Group Concept," *American Business Communication Association Bulletin,* March, 1973, pp. 9–14.

ZAUGG, MARGARET D., as reported in "Committee Report, Views of Business Representatives," *American Business Communication Association Bulletin,* June, 1973.

## PERFORMANCE GOALS

**1.** Given details on students in a typical accounting class (high school or two-year college), including reading levels, cumulative grade averages, occupational goals, computational competencies, and other relevant data, and using this chapter and learning activities 1, 2, and 3, analyze the data, group the students, and recommend minimum competencies for each group and **defend** your recommendations in terms of the material in Chapter 12 and class discussions.

**2.** Using a competency from performance goal 1 which is appropriate for performance on the job, the material in this chapter, and learning activities 4, 5, 6, 7, and 8, **construct** a performance goal, an evaluation, a model similar to Figure 12.4, and a model similar to Figure 12.6. Evaluation will be based on inclusion of all components of the performance goal, appropriateness of the evaluation, logical sequence of the subcompetencies, and inclusion of multiple learning activities and self-evaluations to enable all students to achieve.

*Subcompetencies*

a. **Construct** an acceptable performance goal for a given competency.

b. Plan and **construct** an evaluation appropriate for measuring achievement of one goal.

c. **Analyze** a performance goal for subcompetencies and sequence the subcompetencies to illustrate their relationships.

d. **Construct** a model of learning activities, self-evaluations, and teacher evaluations similar to Figure 12.6 which illustrates different paths a learner may take.

# CHAPTER 12

# Accounting

Business is increasingly dependent on reports of financial transactions to improve daily operations as well as to forecast future costs and profits. Emphasis is on the systematic flow of data so that accepted accounting concepts and principles function to provide data to monitor financial activities. While the major responsibility for financial decision making lies with top management, executives are dependent on the supportive staff of accounting and clerical employees to collect, sort, classify, record, store, and summarize data.

Accounting is the preparation and interpretation of financial records. It begins when a transaction is recorded on a source document, which is some form of business paper such as a sales slip, an invoice, a time card, or a check. The data from these source documents must then be processed to produce the financial information required by management. But accounting does not stop with the preparation of records—it also involves the use, or interpretation, of this information. (Freeman, pp. 5–6)

No definition of accounting is complete without identifying the ways by which data are processed. Four such procedures are manual (by hand); mechanical (by use of posting machines, adding machines, and cash registers); punched card (by automatic equipment which reads holes in punched cards); and electronic (by entering data into a computer system and processing it automatically according to instructions which direct computer operations).

## Needs of the Learner

Economic activities of individuals, business, and government create an aggregate impact which cannot be caused by individuals or business operating alone.

Accounting and economics studied simultaneously enable an individual to view his or her financial activities in terms not only of the family but also of the national economy.

## Needs of Business

As more spendable income is generated, a growing demand for goods and services is created. A business operating for profit, as well as a nonprofit organization, maintains a system of accounting in order to use its financial records in planning for increased profits or optimum reduction of costs or both. It is not surprising, then, that the demand for workers in accounting continues to expand. The Bureau of Labor Statistics predicted the increases shown in Figure 12.1 in each of the accounting categories between 1970 and 1980 ("Tomorrow's Manpower Needs," see Selected Readings).

While the greatest increase is forecast among the professional accountants (63 percent), the growth among accounting clerks and hand bookkeeping clerks is also to continue.

The accounting occupational cluster is divided into two major segments—professional and clerical. Within the professional categories are the auditor, chief accountant, and five categories of *accountant*. Since professional accountants generally hold a baccalaureate degree and also have accounting experience, only the description of Accountant I, the lowest level within the professional category, is presented here (*National Survey . . .,* pp. 40–41)

*Accountant I.* At this beginning professional level, the accountant learns to apply the principles, theories, and concepts of accounting to a specific system.
. . . works under the close supervision of an experienced accountant whose guidance is directed primarily to the development of the trainee's professional ability and to the evaluation of his potential for advancement.

Tasks performed by Accountant I include:

. . . examining a variety of financial statements for completeness, internal accuracy, and conformance with uniform accounting classifications or other specific accounting requirements; reconciling reports and financial data with financial statements already on file, and pointing out apparent inconsistencies or errors; carrying out assigned steps in an accounting analysis, such as computing standard ratios; assembling and summarizing accounting literature . . . preparing relatively simple financial statements, not involving problems of analysis or presentation; and preparing charts, tables and other exhibits . . . .

## Clerical Groups in Accounting

Four classifications of clerical workers fit into the second category of accounting occupations—the Accounting Clerk I, Accounting Clerk II, the Full-Charge Bookkeeper, and those engaged in related occupations (*National Survey . . .,* see Selected Readings).

*Accounting Clerk.* Performs one or more accounting clerical tasks such as posting to registers and ledgers; reconciling bank accounts; verifying the internal consistency, completeness, and mathematical accuracy of accounting documents; assigning prescribed accounting distribution codes; examining and verifying for clerical accuracy various types of reports, lists, calculations, posting, etc.; or preparing

Figure 12.1   Increases in accounting categories between 1970
              and 1980

| | Number employed, 1970 | Estimated number to be employed, 1980 |
|---|---|---|
| Accountants | 490,000 | 800,000 |
| Accounting clerks | 480,000 | 530,000 |
| Bookkeeping clerks (hand) | 860,000 | 970,000 |

Source: U.S. Department of Labor.

simple, or assisting in preparing more complicated, journal vouchers. May work in either a manual or automated accounting system. The work requires a knowledge of clerical methods and office practices and procedures which relate to the clerical processing and recording of transactions and accounting information (*National Survey* . . ., p. 72).

*Clerk, Accounting I.* Under close supervision, following detailed instructions and standardized procedures, performs one or more routine accounting clerical operations, such as posting to ledgers, cards, or worksheets where identification of items and locations of posting are clearly indicated; checking accuracy and completeness of standardized and repetitive records or accounting documents; and coding documents using a few prescribed accounting codes.

*Clerk, Accounting II.* Under general supervision, performs clerical accounting operations which require the application of experience and judgment, for example, clerically processing complicated or nonrepetitive prescribed accounting codes and classifications, or tracing transactions through previous accounting actions to determine sources of discrepancies.

*Bookkeeper (clerical), full-charge bookkeeper, general bookkeeper.* Keeps records of financial transactions of establishment: Verifies and enters details of transactions as they occur or in chronological order in account and cash journals from items, such as sales slips, invoices, check stubs, inventory records, and requisitions. Summarizes details on separate ledgers, using adding machine, and transfers data to general ledger. Balances books and compiles reports to show statistics, such as cash receipts and expenditures, accounts payable and receivable, profit and loss, and other items pertinent to operation of business. Calculates employee wages from plant records or time cards and makes up checks or withdraws cash from bank for payment of wages. May prepare withholding, Social Security, and other tax reports. May compute, type, and mail monthly statements to customers. May complete books to or through trial balance. May operate calculating and bookkeeping machine (*Dictionary* . . ., Vol 1, p. 66).

*Related accounting employment.* Related occupations are listed under the *Dictionary of Occupational Titles* classification of "computing and account-recording occupations." These include cashiers, tellers, automatic data-processing-equipment operators, billing-machine operators, bookkeeping-machine operators, computing-machine operators, account-recording-machine operators, and computing- and accounting-recording operators (*Dictionary* . . ., Vol. 1, p. 7).

## Sources of Employees in Accounting

The four-year college tends to be the major source of professional accountants, many of whom begin work at the Accountant I level and work up the occupational ladder, possibly becoming Certified Public Accountants. State requirements for the Certified Professional Accountant vary somewhat, although the majority of states require a baccalaureate degree.

Major sources of accounting clerks, full-charge bookkeepers, and those in related employment are two-year colleges and high schools, although frequently these workers need considerable on-the-job experience before they are promoted to the ranks of full-charge bookkeepers or accounting clerks.

Research provides guidelines for schools to plan curricular changes in accounting programs. The research analyzed below is subdivided into accounting in two-year colleges and in high schools.

TWO-YEAR COLLEGE ACCOUNTING GRADUATES. Ozzello, Kelly, and Yandoh provide evidence that key functions in accounting can be performed adequately by graduates of two-year colleges. Kelly verified that such positions are open to these graduates. Generally these positions require higher-level competencies than those for which the high school graduates are hired, but considerably lower level than those required of professional accountants.

The American Accounting Association found that one-third of the graduates of the two-year college accounting programs studied entered the labor force in accounting and accounting-related positions (*Report* ..., p. 21). On the other hand, there is evidence that some of these graduates delay entry into business and attend four-year colleges. For example, Yandoh studied 207 two-year graduates of accounting programs in 13 community colleges and found that approximately half of them entered four-year colleges.

Job titles filled by two-year college accounting graduates studied by Yandoh include the following in descending order of the number reporting: bookkeeper, account clerk, accounting clerk, junior accountant, accountant, cost accountant, staff accountant, payroll clerk, accounting analyst, accounting manager, accounting specialist, accounts receivable clerk, assistant bookkeeper, assistant manager of accounts, auditor, clerk, credits and collections clerk, mortgage clerk, pay-disbursing specialist, personnel accounting clerk, remittance adjuster, accounts examiner, and various tax titles (Yandoh, p. 62).

Generally speaking, graduates of two-year career accounting programs begin work in related clerical tasks rather than as accounting clerks or accountants.

HIGH SCHOOL ACCOUNTING GRADUATES. Although research indicates that there are jobs in which tasks taught in high school accounting are performed, much depends upon the needs of companies within the geographic areas served. The majority of jobs open to high school accounting graduates are of a general clerical nature, requiring performance of some accounting tasks in addition to filing, typewriting, and the operation of business machines (Clow).

EMPLOYMENT POSSIBILITIES. Research indicates that accounting graduates of two-year colleges who also have work experience may find employment at the lowest professional level, Accountant I; as accounting clerk at various levels; or as full-charge bookkeeper. Graduates of high school with accounting experience and/or post-high school education may procure jobs as accounting clerk in various categories such as accounts receivable, accounts payable, payroll, billing, inventory control, cash receipts, or as full-charge bookkeeper.

## Identifying and Classifying Competencies

Limited research is available identifying competencies of workers in accounting, and much of that available concentrates on accounting-related tasks performed by clerical workers.

Figure 12.2 illustrates selected competencies identified for entry-level workers and combines the findings of Lanham, Erickson, and West. (Recycle to Chapter 3.) In the second column of the figure each competency is classified by dominant domain and level. Six of the nine cognitive competencies are at the application level. While the three competencies at the analysis-synthesis and evaluation levels may not be performed by entry-level workers in larger companies, it is possible that these competencies are essential in entry-level positions in smaller firms. Five of the fourteen competencies are affective, revealing the importance of these behaviors.

Also, each competency in Figure 12.2 is analyzed for the action required of the student so that the appropriate verb may be selected. The next steps reveal the result of the performance—a product or a controlled observation process, the conditions under which the student will perform, and the criterion to be used to judge the performance. All teachers in a given school make the decisions regarding the conditions and the criteria, so that all students will perform under the identical conditions and be judged according to the same standards.

Figure 12.3 on page 274 shows competencies essential to second-level workers. (Recycle to Chapter 3, p. 52.) Comparison of these competencies with those shown in Figure 12.2 reveals a greater proportion of the cognitive competencies at the analysis-synthesis level or higher for the second-level employee. While most of the competencies are not likely to apply to the student being graduated from a high school or a vocational-technical school, they may apply to selected students completing accounting programs at the two-year college level.

Little research evidence exists to guide the accounting teacher in integrating punched card and electronic data processing with accounting instruction. (See Chapter 13). Moon substantiates the need for accountants to know the capabilities of the computer as a tool in solving problems and

Figure 12.2  Competencies of entry-level workers analyzed for components of performance goals

| Competency | Dominant domain & level | Verb | Result of performance | Conditions of performance | Criterion |
|---|---|---|---|---|---|
| Make routine decisions according to operations manual or written policies. | Cognitive: evaluation | Defend | Product: essay | Given case study and statement of company policy. | Two decisions made in keeping with policy stated. |
| Analyze and interpret data in accounting records correctly as requested by management. | Cognitive: analysis | Analyze | Product: short answer | Using complete set of books student prepared; given 10 questions. | All 10 answered correctly. |
| Explain reasons for actions or decisions logically. | Cognitive: analysis | Analyze | Product: essay | Given five management cases (name types). | Logically as evaluated by teacher. |
| Locate errors and correct them so that work is correct. | Cognitive: application | Demonstrate | Product: correct trial balance | Given trial balance which has errors and accompanying journals and ledger. | Trial balance in balance and correct and all corrections made according to instructions. |
| Classify source documents according to company's classification system. | Cognitive: application | Classify | Product: short answer | Given 10 source documents and instructions for classification. | All 10 classified correctly, according to instructions. |
| Compile accurate data from records and prepare summary reports in form requested for planning by management. | Cognitive: application | Demonstrate | Product: completed report | Given correct trial balance and instructions. | In acceptable form with data correct. |
| Maintain accurate records for source documents in form desired by management. | Cognitive: application | Demonstrate | Product: completed journals | Given 15 source documents and the necessary journal forms. | Each transaction correctly entered in appropriate journal. |

Figure 12.2 (Continued)

| Competency | Dominant domain & level | Verb | Result of performance | Conditions of performance | Criterion |
|---|---|---|---|---|---|
| Maintain file of source documents and records produced so that they may be retrieved within seconds. | Cognitive: application | **Demonstrate** | Product: short answer | Given a file of source documents which has been maintained by students, 20 questions, and 10 minutes. | Nineteen questions answered correctly from data, within time limit. |
| Follow written instructions accurately. | Cognitive: application | **Demonstrate** | Product: corrected flowchart | Given a flowchart illustrating flow of purchases on credit and written instructions. | Procedures followed according to instructions. |
| Take pride in all work performed. | Affective: high-level responding | **Demonstrate consistently** | Product: work submitted | In all work prepared in class or at home. | Accurate work submitted according to instructions. |
| Adhere to schedule given. | Affective: high-level responding | **Demonstrate consistently** | Product: work submitted | Given verbal instructions on deadlines for reports for accounting applications. | Work submitted according to instructions and on date due. |
| Tolerate routine work without revealing frustrations. | Affective: high-level responding | **Demonstrate consistently** | Controlled observation of process | While being observed doing routine work. | Work consistently without wasting time or exclaiming or complaining. |
| Work effectively as a member of a team which contributes to company's success. | Affective: high-level responding | **Demonstrate consistently** | Controlled observation of process | While being observed at work as a member of a team on an accounting application. | Contribute to the work of the team in the opinion of team members and instructor. |
| Write all numbers, letters, and words legibly. | Affective: high-level responding | **Demonstrate consistently** | Product | In all work prepared in class or at home. | Readable to teacher. |

Figure 12.3    Competencies of second-level workers in accounting and account-ing-related positions classified by domain and level

| Competency | Domain | Level |
|---|---|---|
| 1. Review output to determine and correct errors of information systems. | Cognitive | Analysis/synthesis or evaluation |
| 2. Summarize output from system for the purpose of presenting management with concise reports which are accurate. | Cognitive | Analysis/synthesis |
| 3. Construct basic flow charts for projects, systems, or subsystems for the purpose of planning, analyzing, implementing, controlling, and budgeting. | Cognitive | Analysis/synthesis |
| 4. Analyze the needs, attitudes, motivations, and actions of others to facilitate desired outcomes. | Cognitive | Analysis/synthesis |
| 5. Ascertain and analyze the capabilities and functions of data reproduction equipment. | Cognitive | Analysis/synthesis |
| 6. Determine what happened to produce errors in information system and how system may be changed to produce fewer errors. | Cognitive | Analysis/synthesis |
| 7. Assemble and arrange input for processing. | Cognitive | Application |
| 8. Convert data to appropriate coding schemes. | Cognitive | Application |
| 9. Adjust quickly to new equipment, procedures, and work changes. | Affective | High-level responding |
| 10. Communicate effectively with management, coworkers, and subordinates. | Affective | High-level responding |
| 11. Appreciate how inaccurate data affects own work and that of other workers. | Affective | High-level responding |

Source:  Competencies developed from tasks in Huffman and Gust, *Business Education for the Emergent Office*, USOE Grant No. OEG 0-0-080414-3733 (083), Center for Vocational and Technical Education, Ohio State University, Columbus, Ohio, June, 1970.

manipulating data. Source documents and other forms processed by accounting employees differ in a business which utilizes a computer. One study revealed 90 percent of 600 companies studied handled accounting applications by computer (*Management . . .*, p. 25). Such applications as general accounting, sales analysis, and inventory control were named most frequently as being handled by computers.

In a computerized system the accounting tasks performed by entry-level workers differ from those performed in manual systems, particularly in general ledger work, accounts receivable and payable, payroll, sales forecast, and inventory records. From the scanty evidence available, it seems imperative that anyone entering accounting work be familiar with the various forms of input and output, the origins of data, and how the computer processes data as well as the kinds of output generated by the computer. It is likely that the higher the level of accounting job held, the greater the need for understanding the computer's capabilities.

## Constructing Performance Goals

Four of the fourteen competencies analyzed in Figure 12.2 are the bases for a performance goal below. Comparison of each goal with the components in Figure 12.2 illustrates how these components serve as the basis for goal construction.

---

COMPETENCY 4
Locate errors and correct them so that all work is accurate.
PERFORMANCE GOAL
Given a trial balance that has errors and the accompanying journals and ledger, **apply** the steps in locating errors and correct each so that all work is completely accurate.

---

COMPETENCY 5
Classify source documents according to company's classification system.
PERFORMANCE GOAL
Given ten source documents and instructions, **classify** each document correctly according to the instructions.

---

COMPETENCY 6
Compile accurate data from records and prepare summary reports in form requested by management for use in planning operations.
PERFORMANCE GOAL
Given a correct trial balance and instructions, **demonstrate** the ability to prepare summary reports of a balance sheet and an income statement in the form requested with data correct.

---

COMPETENCY 7
Maintain accurate records for source documents in form desired by management.
PERFORMANCE GOAL
Given 15 source documents including checks, invoices, credit memorandums, purchase requisitions, purchase orders, statements of account, and the appropriate journal forms, **demonstrate** the ability to journalize by recording each transaction correctly in the appropriate journal.

---

COMPETENCY 8
Maintain file of source documents and records produced so that they may be retrieved within seconds.
PERFORMANCE GOAL
Given a file of source documents maintained by student, 20 questions, and a time limit of ten minutes, **demonstrate** the ability to retrieve the information by answering 19 out of 20 questions accurately.

---

COMPETENCY 9
Follow written instructions accurately.
PERFORMANCE GOAL
Given a flow chart illustrating the flow of papers related to purchases on credit and written instructions, **demonstrate** the ability to follow the written instructions in correcting the flow chart.

---

---

COMPETENCY 10
Take pride in all work performed.
PERFORMANCE GOAL
When preparing class work and homework, **demonstrate** pride in all work by consistently submitting accurate work according to instructions.

---

COMPETENCY 11
Adhere to schedule given verbally so that work is completed on time.
PERFORMANCE GOAL
When making accounting applications for which deadlines are given verbally, **demonstrate** the ability to adhere to the schedule by submitting work according to instructions and on date due.

---

COMPETENCY 12
Tolerate routine work without revealing frustrations.
PERFORMANCE GOAL
While being observed by the teacher as you perform routine accounting tasks such as posting or checking, **demonstrate** the ability to tolerate routine work by working without wasting time, exclaiming, or complaining.

---

COMPETENCY 13
Work effectively as a member of a team that contributes to company's success.
PERFORMANCE GOAL
While being observed by team members and instructor or while at work as a member of a team on an accounting application, **demonstrate** the ability to contribute a fair share of output.

---

COMPETENCY 14
Write all numbers and words legibly.
PERFORMANCE GOAL
In all work prepared in class or home, **demonstrate** the ability to write numbers and words legibly so that they are readable by the teacher.

---

## Identifying and Sequencing Subcompetencies

After the teacher identifies the competencies needed for entry-level employment and uses them to construct performance goals, the next step is to determine the subcompetencies needed to achieve the performance goal. Competencies identified as those performed on the job are usually at the application level or above, yet the student must master facts and develop understanding before he or she can apply knowledge. At the other extreme, evaluation is dependent upon knowing facts; understanding concepts, principles, and rules; discovering relationships; and formulating generalizations. Each of these is a subcompetency of "the ability to make simple decisions based upon data."

A simple goal such as that in Figure 12.4 involves multiple subcompetencies, some of which must be performed in sequence and some of which

Figure 12.4 Sequencing of performance goal for accounting competency 4

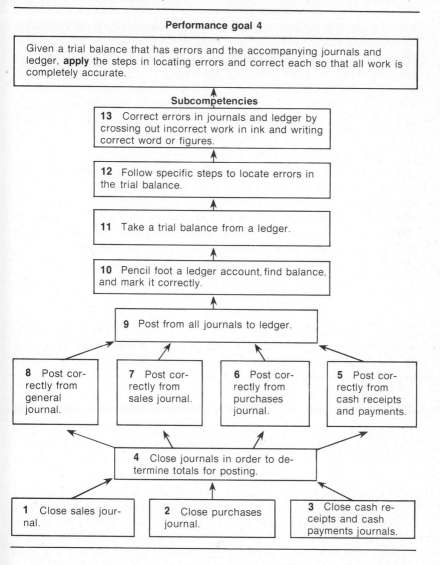

**Performance goal 4**

Given a trial balance that has errors and the accompanying journals and ledger, **apply** the steps in locating errors and correct each so that all work is completely accurate.

Subcompetencies

**13** Correct errors in journals and ledger by crossing out incorrect work in ink and writing correct word or figures.

**12** Follow specific steps to locate errors in the trial balance.

**11** Take a trial balance from a ledger.

**10** Pencil foot a ledger account, find balance, and mark it correctly.

**9** Post from all journals to ledger.

**8** Post correctly from general journal.

**7** Post correctly from sales journal.

**6** Post correctly from purchases journal.

**5** Post correctly from cash receipts and payments.

**4** Close journals in order to determine totals for posting.

**1** Close sales journal.

**2** Close purchases journal.

**3** Close cash receipts and cash payments journals.

can be performed in any order. (Recycle to page 97.) For example, No. 9 is dependent upon mastery of Nos. 8, 7, 6, and 5. Subcompetencies 1, 2, and 3 and 5, 6, 7, and 8 may be performed in any order.

## Pretesting and Matching Learner With Performance Goals and Subcompetencies

What basic abilities should a student possess to succeed in an accounting course and progress on the job?

Historically, no other single area of business education has had students with as diverse aptitudes and interests as accounting. For this reason many schools have stratified their offerings, using the course titles of accounting, bookkeeping, and recordkeeping. Theoretically, these titles provide a logical basis for developing student competencies, but problems have ensued. Frequently, this practice has led to frustration, for students recognize the labels and fear that enrolling in a lower-level course may label them as slow learners. In an effort to overcome this stigma, Stewart provided a more flexible plan by offering a three-level spectrum. A student could begin at the lowest level and progress as far as he or she desired; or possibly a student with sufficient interest and ability might enter at either of the two higher levels and progress upward.

Schultheis analyzed such jobs as cash, invoice, account, payroll, and cost clerks to determine what tasks a slow learner might perform (Schultheis, pp. 60–77). He found that the greatest obstacle to the potential employability of slow learners for many recordkeeping positions is the general complexity of the positions—a variety of tasks to be performed, decisions to be made, and the application of rules and principles to various situations (Schultheis, pp. 92–99). Only one-quarter of the positions studied offered employment potential to the slow learner; payroll and cost-clerk positions offered the fewest opportunities.

Webb found that not only intelligence level but reading level, listening ability, writing skill, and quantitative ability all contributed significantly to success in the study of high school accounting. Webb's findings seem to confirm suspicions of many accounting teachers that even a student with basic skills needs to be motivated.

Henderson studied intelligence of former students who had or had not studied bookkeeping. Students in the 90–99 I.Q. range who had studied bookkeeping and who were working in business performed twice as many bookkeeping duties as their counterparts working in business who had never studied bookkeeping. The implication is that for those with scores in the 90-99 I.Q. range, a high school bookkeeping course is beneficial.

In a study of almost 600 New York City accounting workers, West reinforced the fact that entry-level accounting employees perform extremely narrow job duties. He found that although half of the workers surveyed had received some accounting instruction in high school, a number of these workers also took post-secondary courses to improve and expand their knowledges. Apparently the employee who senses a need for additional training seeks it. This is in keeping with the concept of continuing education throughout life. (West, pp. 176–181).

However, the above research is based on traditional recordkeeping courses. Slower students can learn but are often hampered by time constraints in traditional one-year classes. The wisest course for a teacher confronted with students of mixed abilities is to match a student with goals which are attainable and relevant and to provide a flexible time structure, particularly for the slow student.

Pretesting enables the accounting teacher to assess (1) retention of previously learned facts and terms and (2) the ability to read and follow written instructions; perform simple arithmetic functions; and read, interpret, and execute written problems.

Once the results of the pretest are available, the teacher analyzes the results to determine kinds of competencies the student is ready to work toward. Often an individual student may need to be routed toward subcompetencies or even remedial instruction in computations, reading, and writing. Because accounting instruction moves from the simple to the complex, a student need not be pretested at the beginning of each performance goal because success on one goal reveals readiness for a higher one.

Because of the diversity of learning levels and learning patterns, no teacher can assume that all students will complete the fourteen performance goals on pages 272–273. Some students may complete only a few; others may demand higher-level goals. How does a teacher decide upon the minimum any one student must attain? Since accounting and general clerks' jobs are likely to require a wide range of competencies, even a student who progresses no further than completing the following competencies is likely to find employment related to accounting: (1) locate errors and correct them so that all work is accurate; (2) maintain file of source documents and records produced so that they may be retrieved in seconds; (3) follow written instructions accurately; (4) take pride in all work performed; (5) tolerate routine work without revealing frustration; (6) work effectively as a member of a team; and (7) write all numbers, letters, and words legibly.

## Identifying and Applying Appropriate Learning Principles

The accounting teacher who utilizes a textbook accompanied by a teacher's guide and follows the learning system in this book automatically applies the seven principles of learning, which are directly related to learning accounting.

## Choosing Appropriate Teaching-Learning Strategies

Because each segment of learning in accounting provides a foundation for what follows, each learner must master basic principles. It is essential to identify and use learning activities that enable students with varying levels of reading, general aptitude, and interest patterns to meet one competency-based performance goal before attempting the next one.

## Allocation of Time

Undoubtedly the prevalent pattern of accounting instruction is one year for high schools and for many two-year colleges. However, many students who begin accounting do not complete the requirements during the one year. Some schools (high schools and two-year colleges) are experimenting with open-ended programs, enabling a student who has achieved the required goals to complete the course at any time ranging from six months to two years.

Evidence of Erickson, Lanham, Spanswick, West, and Luxner leads one to question the need for two years of accounting for typical high school students. Those students who are bright, quick, and intensely motivated, however, can benefit from advanced accounting, particularly if it embraces concepts and practical experience in processing data by computers. Those who are likely to find advanced accounting beneficial are workers on the job. Generally, the two-year college provides advanced courses for part-time students.

Instead of advanced accounting, some schools offer innovative programs for the second year in applied accounting: programs designed to develop competencies in using posting machines, processing data by punched-card equipment and computers, and providing some form of supervised cooperative work experience.

## Organization Patterns

Until a few years ago, the dominant pattern in accounting was large-group instruction. Although this is still used in many classes today, more teachers now utilize small-group and individual instruction.

LARGE-GROUP INSTRUCTION. Students in homogeneous accounting classes do learn in the teacher-dominated class, provided all students are present and want to learn. The problem of absences compounded with lack of motivation, however, makes large-group instruction ineffective for many students. Even students who are grouped according to ability have different learning patterns and learning rates. Rapidly accumulating evidence leaves little doubt that the high school or two-year college accounting class taught as one group fails to meet the needs of many students, particularly after the first few days of instruction. Many accounting teachers now begin instruction to a large group and reorganize as students reveal learning problems and erratic attendance patterns.

SMALL-GROUP INSTRUCTION. Alert teachers employ small groups regularly. Students receive instruction, interact among themselves, read and discuss material, and solve problems in groups. Teachers who recognize that students can learn from each other provide multiple experiences for group activities. It is not unusual to find three or more groups in an accounting class, each functioning with some teacher assistance but proceeding on their own initiative at other times. Use of the growing number of learning resources permits small groups to engage in multiple learning experiences with limited teacher direction.

INDIVIDUAL INSTRUCTION. Because almost all accounting classes include students with a wide range of abilities, interests, motivation, and attendance patterns, individually paced and individually prescribed instruction provides opportunities for effective use of both student and teacher time. (Recycle to Chapter 7, pp. 100–101.)

## Teacher Presentations

Some students in small or large groups look to the teacher to provide instruction on new concepts. These students may expect and need leadership from the teacher for each step of their accounting instruction. Basically, there are three approaches a teacher may employ in presenting new accounting concepts: teacher demonstration, developmental, and problem solving.

DEMONSTRATION. (Recycle to Chapter 7, pp. 137–138, for steps in demonstrations.) All new material is explained by the teacher, who actually does the work on the chalkboard or a transparency. Usually this type of lesson precedes any reading of the textbook by the student. For instance, a teacher whose immediate goal is for the students to post five entries from the general journal to the ledger explains that the journal is a book of original entry and that, in order to accumulate information concerning the business in an orderly way, accounts are used to summarize data. Then, he or she flashes a blank ledger form on the screen and examines the number of accounts needed by looking at the journal. When a glance at the journal reveals the need for six accounts, the teacher then writes the names of the six accounts on the ledger form on the transparency. The students imitate by opening six ledger accounts. Next, the teacher examines the first journal entry and explains that all debits are posted first. The first debit to cash is posted—the amount first, followed by the posting reference and the month, day, and year. Finally, the teacher posts the ledger page in the posting reference column of the journal. The students then imitate by posting the same debit.

Immediately after the students post the first debit, the teacher directs each student to check the data posted with that on the teacher's transparency. A student who has errors then corrects each one. Eventually, the teacher posts the second debit, the students imitate, and then they evaluate. Then the teacher follows the identical steps for the next five credits. After all items are posted, the teacher directs the students to check their ledgers with the transparency. At this point, the teacher walks about the room, determining which students need help.

After all the steps in posting are completed, the teacher asks the students to review the steps, as they are listed on a transparency or the chalkboard.

A demonstration is appropriate for teaching a concept which is learned by following a model rather than by rationalizing. It is inappropriate for a concept which requires understandings of "why." Demonstrations are suitable for presenting the forms of the trial balance, statements, and special journals, taking a trial balance, totaling and ruling journals, writing checks, and posting.

DEVELOPMENTAL METHOD. This approach engages students, through questioning, in thinking about what is being done and why. The same lesson on posting may be taught through a developmental method. The teacher intersperses developmental questions throughout the presentation of the posting process. As students watch the projected transparencies of the journal and ledger, the teacher posts the debits, asking such questions as: "How many different accounts are involved in the five journal entries?" "How many accounts will be in the ledger?" "How many account titles must I write in the ledger?" "Should the accounts be in any order?" "Why?" (It is explained that debits are posted first; that the amount is posted first, then the date, and then the posting reference to lessen the danger of error.) "How can I know by looking at the journal that an item has been posted?" "What are the steps just completed?" Students post first debit and check with transparency, then continue. The teacher then presents the posting of credits, asking, "To which account should I post the first credit?" "On which side?" "Why?" "In what order should I post?"

Finally, the teacher asks the students to summarize by listing the steps in posting, which are placed on a transparency or the chalkboard.

Such presentations are appropriate for almost any subject matter in accounting, for the questions direct thinking toward the desired answer. The teacher must include all members of the group in the discussion, encouraging participation by even the most reluctant.

PROBLEM SOLVING. This approach places the student in a position where a logical solution must be found. While the mechanical steps of posting cannot be taught by problem solving, the entire concept of posting can be developed by this approach.

The teacher places the transparency of the journal on the screen and begins asking such questions as, "How much cash do we have after these transactions are completed?" "How much is owed us in accounts receivable?" "What is the value of furniture at the end of this period?" The students add and subtract to reach the correct answers. The teacher asks, "Why are you taking so long?" The answer is, "The amounts are not in any one place, and we must gather them for computation." *The student identifies the problem.* The teacher then says, "Well, why not figure out a way the amounts could be in one place for addition or subtraction?"

After a few moments, the students offer solutions. One student may volunteer, "We could use T accounts." The teacher accepts the answer and records it on the chalkboard and says, "Anyone have another idea?" Another student may suggest multiple columns in the journal. Each suggestion is accepted and recorded. No response is discouraged, no matter how remote it seems; for the chief purpose is to get students to analyze the problem for solutions. *Students offer possible solutions, which the teacher accepts and records.*

After all suggestions are recorded, the teacher asks developmental questions about each suggestion without indicating whether it is correct or incorrect. Eventually, students reject one solution, test and reject another, and someone finally emerges with one solution which appears to be the best. *Identify best solution.* Students then test that solution and accept or reject it. *Test best solution.*

Sometimes a teacher finds that although the best solution given approximates that desired, some element is lacking. He or she then uses that solution and develops it into the appropriate one.

Since teachers of accounting should emphasize the *why,* students who learn by the problem-solving approach are involved in thinking. They can rationalize to the point of envisioning a process by which the solution is accomplished. They are not learning by rote; they are learning by thinking. In the developmental method, the teacher guides students in their thinking process, but in problem solving the teacher encourages creative thinking.

Not all students learn by the problem-solving approach, just as not all students learn by the developmental method or the demonstration.

Each teacher perfects the three presentations so that another type may be used for a student who has not learned by the first method or even the second.

Some teachers videotape presentations for viewing more than one time. Once a good presentation is on tape, a teacher who identifies a student having difficulty with a concept reruns the tape for that student. Teachers who use tapes find them flexible, for the viewing may be stopped momentarily while a student asks questions.

## Homework

Homework should be a learning experience during which the student applies what has been learned. After a new concept is presented, the teacher assigns an application to be done individually or in small groups so that students who have difficulties can be identified. Unless a student is successful in the class application, a similar problem should not be assigned for homework. The wise teacher simply reteaches the concept to those who reveal a need, perhaps the next day, then tests those students on its application before assigning homework again.

Unless the teacher has identified each student's reading comprehension and knows the student can comprehend the textbook, homework reading on a new concept is assigned only after the material has been presented in class.

Problems given for homework should be directly related to a subcompetency toward which each student is working; and the student, too, must be aware of the purpose; otherwise, the student regards homework as busywork.

Evaluation of homework is a challenge even to the experienced teacher. Four different methods enable students and teachers to evaluate assignments. First, the teacher may collect the homework, check it immediately, and return it *no later than the next day.* If correct, it is accepted and so marked; if incorrect, it is returned so that the student may seek assistance from

Figure 12.5   Check sheet for analysis of a homework problem

**Name** _____

Using your homework from Problem 7, page 207, answer the following questions.

1. How many sales credits are in the Cash Receipts Journal? _____
2. From whom did Swanson receive payment on account on October 28? _____
3. What was the total cash debit for October? _____
4. How many entries do you have in the General Journal? _____
5. Indicate the balances of the following accounts as of October 31:
   a. Cash _____
   b. Accounts receivable/Cross Corp. _____
   c. Land _____
   d. Terry Swanson, capital _____
   e. Sales _____
6. What are the totals of your trial balance? _____

either the teacher or another student to determine how to correct the errors. All unsatisfactory work should be corrected and returned to the teacher, who eventually accepts it.

Second, the teacher may assign one or two students whose homework has been approved the task of auditing the homework of several other students and helping them make corrections.

Third, many teachers vary the checking of homework, letting students audit their own work against a transparency containing correct work.

Fourth, Thompson recommends a simple procedure of an "Audit Check Sheet" (Thompson, p. 174). On the date each problem is due, a check sheet is distributed similar to the one in Figure 12.5, and ten minutes of the class time is used for students to complete their own check sheets. Later, the teacher spot checks the sheets. Or the students may check their own papers against answers projected on a transparency. Thus they will know immediately how well the work has been done.

Any of these four methods of homework focuses on student learning and removes the harassment many students feel when they hand in homework.

## Accounting Applications

Accounting applications, sometimes called practice sets, vary from complete sets of books including journals, ledger, subsidiary ledgers, and forms for worksheets and statements accompanied by printed transactions to more elaborate applications complete with actual source documents. A rationale for using accounting applications is that the student views the whole cycle and work flow from the original source documents to the statements, outgoing papers, and multiple reports emerging from the system. Some applications include flow charts which illustrate the flow of papers through the system, enabling the student to check the steps through which information should be processed. Accounting applications are a form of simulation. The applications provide the opportunity to apply concepts and principles learned and to gain an overview of the entire accounting cycle. Published accounting applications range from those requiring simple recordkeeping duties for service businesses to the more complex activities involved in handling financial information for a merchandising business. Applications are also available for punched-card systems as well as accounting systems integrated with computers.

Since research shows that few, if any, high school or two-year college accounting graduates begin work as full-charge bookkeepers, some teachers question time spent on accounting applications. However, the consensus is that accounting applications are a vital ingredient in bridging the gap between the contrived atmosphere of the classroom and the reality of business. Much of the effectiveness of any accounting application depends upon its applicability to the performance goals sought, the caliber of the students and their interests, the way the teacher uses the application as a teaching device, an integrating device, or a testing device, and the quality of the application.

**GUIDELINES FOR THE TEACHER.** The following guidelines are especially helpful for beginning teachers who wish to use accounting applications effectively:

1. Analyze the performance goals and identify an application which will contribute to the achievement of an individual student's ultimate goal.
2. Before giving the application to the students, complete it to determine that it fulfills the goal for which it is selected.
3. Once an application is identified as a learning activity, construct a goal for it. The goal should be compatible with the performance goals each student is seeking.
4. Construct the evaluative instruments to be used for each accounting application. These may include:

   *a.* Periodic accuracy checks for work done at a given date using such questions as those in Figure 12.5. Such checks permit the student to ascertain whether all work to a given point is correct. Students may help each other here in identifying and correcting errors, or the teacher may give the help.

   *b.* Audit the complete application. A better technique than a teacher audit is to identify one student's application as correct and let that be the model against which students may audit their own or a classmate's application. Several students may be appointed auditors. Grading accounting applications on accuracy only places the emphasis on the recording aspects rather than on interpretations of the data, on application-level competencies rather than on analysis or evaluation-level competencies.

        *c.* Evaluate the learner's interpretation of the application by posing questions that emphasize the use of the books as sources of information about the state of a business. Questions such as the following may be used: How many customers purchased merchandise on account during the period? To whom was check #34 issued? For what was check #41 issued? What was the cost of goods sold? How much do we now owe the government for FICA? What were the total sales on account? What were the total sales? When was Sampson's invoice of December 1 paid? How many creditors owe us money?

5.    Structure the teaching strategies for each application to meet individual needs. The following strategies are most often used:

    *a.* Individual applications selected for each student on the basis of subcompetencies of goals may be done by the individual (1) working alone, (2) in a small group of students working the same application, or (3) working in a group as the teacher goes over each transaction or batch of transactions before they are entered.

    *b.* One application for a small group, with each student assigned a responsibility such as cash clerk (cash receipts and cash payments), sales clerk, or purchases clerk. Students may rotate jobs at stated intervals.

6.    Make decisions before applications are begun, such as:

    *a.* Should work be done in class only, or should applications be taken home? The answer depends upon the goal. If the application is a learning experience, students working together outside of class may teach each other.

    *b.* What will be the final disposition of the completed application? Again, teachers may not agree on the answer. If the student can refer to the application after completing the course, it may serve as a review on the job. The fear that students will share applications with next year's class may be averted by varying them each year.

    *c.* Should the teacher's key be in evidence during class? Many teachers prefer to check students' problems against a completed application. Some teachers, however, have no hesitation about letting students use the published key in auditing their books.

    *d.* How shall the application be graded? Much depends upon the performance goal toward which the application contributes. Experienced teachers frequently require that the application be audited and corrected just like accounting records for a business. The student thus realizes that actual accounting work is demanding and requires limitless patience. If all students are ultimately required to have correct applications, grades are frequently based upon the student's interpretation of the completed application, asking questions similar to those in 4*c* above.

## Identifying and Applying Learning Activities

New learning resources enter the market regularly, adding to the vast collection now available. Textbooks, workbooks, study guides, programmed materials and printed modules, audiotutorial modules, films, the computer, and television are all resources from which teachers and students select learning activities.

**WORKBOOKS AND STUDY GUIDES.**   Workbooks include study guides as well as business forms and papers to be used in solving textbook problems. Most teachers find workbooks an invaluable aid, for the papers are correlated with the textbook problems and eliminate the necessity of duplicating and distributing forms. Generally, problems in workbooks are solved individually or in small groups in class or at home. Since the workbook provides for learning, not testing, teachers need not fear copying. When the student is evaluated on a goal, it is obvious who has learned from workbook exercises and who has not. Workbooks also may provide valuable sources of forms for product evaluations. The day before the test, students remove forms to be used and the teacher retains these to distribute with the evaluation.

Study guides are used in various ways. Some teachers use them as pretests; others use them for student self-evaluations. When they are used as self-evaluations, students complete them in class, check their solutions, and—with the cooperation of the teacher—isolate those areas requiring further study.

Wunsch analyzed three methods of using study guides:

1. Learning devices and self-evaluations which students check for accuracy, correct, and keep for reference.
2. Tests which are collected at the beginning of the year and parts are distributed periodically as evaluations.
3. A combination of learning device and test, sometimes for self-evaluations and at other times for teacher evaluations.

Wunsch found that students in the upper socioeconomic groups used the study guides for self-evaluation as effectively as any of the other two methods, whereas students in the lower and middle socioeconomic groups performed more effectively when the study guide was used for testing.

Accounting teachers should experiment with various ways of using these materials and measure their effectiveness in preparing students to meet performance goals.

**PROGRAMMED MATERIALS.**   Evidence is available that the effectiveness of programmed materials in accounting depends upon student learning patterns and the quality of the materials. (See Askins, Cloud, Gibbs et al., Glover, Halverson, Huffman, and Orefice, Selected Readings.) Generally, such materials are as effective as conventional teaching for some students. In some areas such as problem solving, they have been found to be more effective. Also, there is evidence that some students permitted to work at their own pace toward relevant goals on programmed materials do exceedingly well because of the flexibility of time; others need constant prodding and do not benefit as much from programmed materials as they do from teacher instruction. Because the reading comprehension level is an important variable, teachers must match the reading level of the student with the level of the material.

While some published programmed instructional materials are available for high school students, many are geared for the two-year college student. However, if the high school student is able to read the material and it contributes toward the individual's achievement of stated goals, there is little reason for withholding such materials from a high school student.

**MODULES OR PACKETS.** Modules for individualizing instruction are frequently created by the teacher and may be used by individuals or small groups working together. A module usually contains (1) a model such as Figure 12.6 illustrating the path a student should take to initiate the work and branching steps, depending upon the success or failure to meet a given subcompetency; (2) an instruction sheet containing the performance goal and either the various subcompetencies needed or specific en route goals; and (3) self-evaluations by which students may check their own progress. While the student must be able to follow the model and read the instruction sheet, the learning activities included are usually those involving different kinds of learning activities—observing, reading, listening, discussing, and so on, as illustrated in Figure 7.2 on page 125.

In Figure 12.6, for example, the subcompetency dealt with is "Retrieve selected data from inventory cards." A large group may view the introductory film, and from that point on the students might work in small groups or individually. The teacher may bring the small groups into a larger group whenever a need is indicated. Figure 12.6 provides multiple self-assessments for the subcompetency so that a student who needs more learning opportunities has access to them. On the other hand, the student who learns quickly and is able to perform at the first self-assessment simply moves to the next subcompetency.

**AUDIOTUTORIAL MODULE.** One major advance in accounting instruction is the use of modules presented on a filmstrip and coordinated with an audio cassette. Each module covers one topic and may be used alone or as a supplement to the textbook and teacher presentations. One unresolved problem is that the available modules may not parallel any existing accounting textbook. When they are used as individual teaching materials, the student progresses through steps illustrated in Figure 12.7.

The advantage of the professionally prepared audiotutorial module over the teacher-prepared ones is obvious. The audiotutorial modules are usually pretested and revised before production, and the quality of the filmstrips and tapes is frequently considerably better than that of those prepared in many schools. However, despite their high quality, they are useful only when they contribute to a stated goal.

Trainer's experiment with 30 of the 50 audiotutorial modules in the system revealed that students who achieve the most between pre- and posttests proceeded at their own speeds, used the modules more than once, did homework assignments, participated in self-quizzes, sought assistance from either the teacher or laboratory assistants, and were exceedingly active in the learning process. Further evidence emphasizes that students who are not sufficiently motivated to particpate in a self-instructional program

Figure 12.6 Multiple learning activities used in different organizational patterns for one subcompetency

**Performance goal:** Given inventory cards, completed purchase requisitions, purchase orders, and invoices, and requests for data retrieval from the forms, **demonstrate** the ability to retrieve correct data by answering 13 of the 15 questions posed.

**Subcompetencies needed:** Differentiate among various forms; answer questions regarding data on various forms; retrieve data from each of the forms; analyze questions in terms of data needed.

**Subcompetency:** Retrieve data from inventory cards:

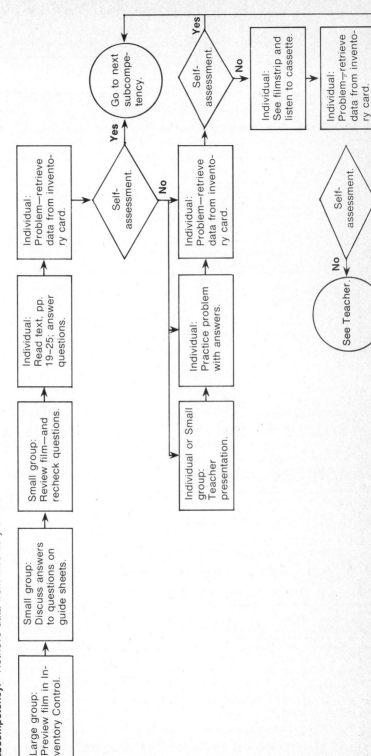

Figure 12.7   Self-paced instruction for an audiotutorial module

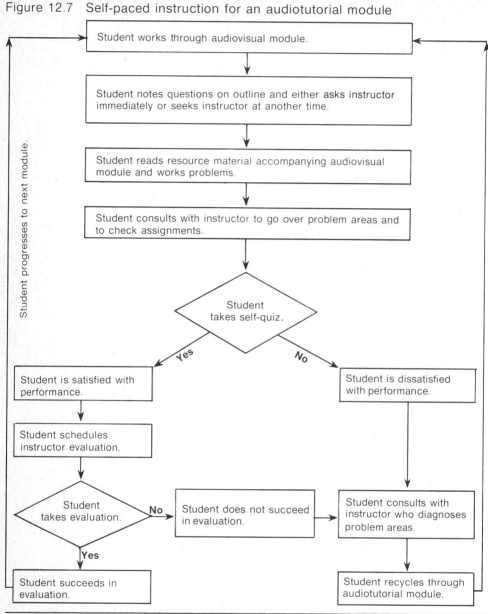

Source: Jaimie L. Trainer, "Flexible Learning Program for Accounting," unpublished article, 1973.

need the discipline which comes from teacher direction and planned student-teacher conferences or learning-teaching experiences involving the teacher.

**TRANSPARENCIES.**   Many teachers who establish goals relating to accounting and data processing rely heavily on commercially prepared or teacher-made transparencies. One example of the use of transparencies to expand the scope of the accounting course is a set of transparencies made available by the New York State Department of Education for use in differentiating among various ways of processing data involving accounts receivable, purchases, inventory control, and payroll. (*Automatic Data . . .*, see Selected Readings.)

Transparencies may be supplemented with tape recordings which explain the principles or concepts illustrated. Students who are absent or need additional exposure to a concept already presented may listen to the tape and view the accompanying transparencies as many times as needed.

TELEVISION.  Accounting taught by television is a reality, particularly in two- and four-year colleges. Television is emerging as a resource for high school accounting. Evaluation of TV instruction has been favorable, particularly where the instructor's presentation is accompanied by professionally prepared visuals. Moreover, schools which have the greatest success with instructional TV follow a formal presentation with small-group discussions and applications. Many systems permit students to interrogate the lecturer-instructor during or immediately following the presentation. This permits automatic feedback as to the success with which the lecturer is communicating. If several students answer the question incorrectly, the lecturer is immediately aware of the need to clarify the concept.

Some colleges and universities are equipped with dial-access systems by which the student who wants to view a videotaped presentation which was missed or wishes to see the tape for a second time simply dials the number of the tape and the presentation is transmitted to the television screen before the viewer at any hour of the day or night. The benefits of televised instruction are unexplored in many schools, however, because of the technical problems involved.

THE COMPUTER.  The basic question of whether it is preferable to follow accounting with a course in data processing or integrate data processing with accounting from the beginning is unresolved. Werner experimented with teaching high school accounting integrated with data processing and compared the effectiveness of this combination with the teaching of accounting followed by data processing. He found that his students achieved higher scores in data processing concepts when accounting and data processing were integrated.

The basic decision depends on how data is processed in businesses in the area served by the school. As minicomputers are used more widely or as offices utilize time sharing of facilities (see Chapter 13, pp. 302–303), the processing of data by computers is inevitable. There is a sound basis for teaching the accounting student to use the computer as a tool for making accounting computations. Accounting students taught BASIC (see Chapter 13, pp. 306, 321) learn quickly to use the computer to (1) compute hourly wages and print out gross earnings, each specific deduction, and net earnings; (2) calculate the stock turnover rate for several businesses and prepare a printout to spread the cost over the entire life of the asset; (3) prepare daily cash reports; and (4) calculate two methods of determining depreciation and identify circumstances under which each would be used.

In integrating the computer with accounting, the major objective is to enable the student to use the computer as a tool like the adding machine, only a much faster one. The accounting clerk need not be proficient in programming, but he or she should understand how data fed into the computer is processed and how to interpret the data emerging from the computer.

Frequently it is possible, through terminals, to prepare programs and data on punched cards for conversion onto tape for computer input. Generally, the two-year colleges have access to both terminals and punched-card input, while many high schools must rely on input through terminals only.

Highly motivated students often become so involved that they establish their own goals for problem solving. Also, the challenge of the computer frequently activates students who normally display little motivation.

SIMULATION.   In accounting, simulation may be as simple as a model office using an accounting application. (Recycle to pp. 284–286 of this chapter.) Students may be assigned recordkeeping and auditing functions as well as end-of-the-period activities requiring summaries and simple analysis of the records. Another simulation may be designed to develop those competencies essential to entry-level jobs. The activities are performed in an environment which demands that the students establish a work flow, work under pressure, make routine decisions, and interact with others in jobs which are directly related (Davis, pp. 43–45).

A well-designed simulation places the student in a realistic problem-solving situation where the decisions made affect the business and the work of the other employees. Simulations may be created for students of varying levels of ability. For example, a more complex problem-solving situation might be established for a college accounting student involving decisions as to which system is most effective for handling cash, processing sales, controlling inventory, and other business functions implementing the system (Perritt, pp. 18–22).

ELECTRONIC CALCULATORS AND ADDING-LISTING MACHINES.   For years teachers' opinions differed as to whether calculators and adding machines should be used in the accounting class. *Nobels* reported 969 entry-level tasks classified as numerical clerical records . . . including the computing and checking of data. (Recycle to Chapter 3, pp. 49–52.) Obviously mechanical computational skills must be developed. With adding machines or electronic calculators found in every office and the electronic calculators available at less than $100, there is substantive evidence that entry-level workers use the equipment. In accounting, students add columns and check tapes for errors as well as compute interest and discounts on calculators, just as workers in an office do.

SUPERVISED COOPERATIVE WORK EXPERIENCE.   Because entry-level jobs for graduates of high schools and many two-year colleges are clerical rather than professional, supervised cooperative work experience in accounting is rare for those below the four-year college. If high school and two-year college students perform accounting-related tasks on a job, work experience may, however, be valuable. Some schools send two students, working as a team, for one job. The students discuss how tasks should be performed, work together, and learn from each other as well as from the work experience. In addition, they tend to strengthen affective behaviors as they complete assigned work together.

## Evaluating Students and the System

Accounting, unlike shorthand and typewriting, has no specific standard measurements to guide in evaluation. Evaluation rests on attainment of performance goals that determine whether required competencies in the cognitive and affective domains have been achieved.

### Criterion-Referenced Measures (Recycle to pp. 67–68, 152–153)

Publishers' tests supplied when a textbook is adopted are generally excellent measures of comprehension, application, and even some analysis if they relate directly to established goals. Generally, publishers' tests are more appropriate for subcompetencies than for performance goals, for they may evaluate fragments of a competency rather than performance of competencies found on the job. Many teachers find them especially useful for determining readiness for evaluations on performance goals; in fact, some teachers use them only as such self-evaluations.

### Norm-Referenced Measures (Recycle to pp. 67–68, 152–153)

Although norm-referenced measures have no place in grading, there are times when it is desirable for accounting teachers to compare students' achievements. One instrument available in high school accounting is the National Business Entrance Test in Bookkeeping (National Business Education Association). The two-hour test evaluates (1) understanding of principles and practices, (2) ability to follow instructions, and (3) neatness. Certificates of proficiency are awarded to successful students.

Data from such tests provides input for individual teachers in terms of their effectiveness in working with students of varying abilities.

ADVANCED PLACEMENT AND/OR CREDIT BY EXAMINATION. Although advanced placement of college freshmen who have studied accounting in high school is not new, the practice is not universal. Some colleges relied on specially constructed tests or grades earned in college accounting to measure achievement. (See Barbour, Smith, Margulies, and *Factors* . . . in Selected Readings.) Tambrino compared the achievement of selected high school and college students on the American Institute of Certified Public Accountants (AICPA) Level I Accounting Achievement Examination. High school students who participated studied college placement accounting, a course especially designed for students who expressed an interest in college accounting, and they were taught by teachers who had been trained to teach college accounting during a teachers' workshop. College-level textbooks were used by the students at both levels. When results of the tests were compared with the norms established for the 80 four-year colleges, the high school students compared favorably with the college students.

Although they are not yet available, the AICPA is establishing norms for the two-year college accounting student. In the future these norms will guide colleges in evaluating a student's readiness for advanced placement and may assist students in receiving credit for competencies they can demonstrate.

Since people may learn as much from experiences outside school as from formal courses, the College Level Examination Program (CLEP) has been developed by the College Entrance Examination Board and the Educational Testing Service, Princeton, New Jersey. Accounting is one of dozens of subjects for which CLEP offers an examination, success in which may lead to either advanced placement or college credit, or both.

The CLEP accounting test has two parts. One is an 80-question multiple-choice examination to be completed within 90 minutes, and the other an optional essay which tests the candidate's ability to apply accounting concepts and procedures to various problems. The test is described this way:

More than half of the examination deals with financial accounting topics such as: concepts and principles, rules of double-entry accounting, the accounting cycle, presentation of and relationships between general-purpose financial statements, valuation of accounts and notes receivable, valuation of inventories, initial costs of plant assets, depreciation, long-term debt, capital, cash and stock dividends, treasury stock, purchase and sale of merchandise, revenue and cost apportionments, financial statement analysis, and partnership accounting. (*CLEP* . . ., p. 24).

Norms have been established by administering the test to 2,284 full-time undergraduates toward the end of their first-year accounting. Interestingly, the ages of those who performed best ranged from 26 to 55, an indication that experience in accounting, rather than formal courses only, may be a major factor contributing to their success.

## Grading

Grades are given in most schools, and the accounting teacher must develop an equitable means of assessing achievement, whether the student has performed on lower- or higher-level goals. It is highly desirable that students in all classes in the same institution be graded similarly. One system is to analyze the levels of goals and grade in terms of the levels attained. (Recycle to Chapter 8, pp. 156–160.) Theoretically, only students who attain goals involving analysis/synthesis and evaluation might receive "A." This method is an improvement over giving "extra credit" for additional problems at the same level as those completed successfully. Not all students are capable of attaining at the higher levels though, nor is it expected that they will do so.

Since affective goals are included among performance goals, these should then become a part of the grade.

## System Evaluation

The students' success in achieving the performance goals set is the criterion by which the system is evaluated. The teacher must always be alert for modifications needed to help even one student.

## Learning Activities

1. Visit an office employing first- and second-level accounting employees and observe for half a day two employees at each of the two levels, listing the tasks performed by each group. Report your findings to your subgroup and, from the reports of all members of your group, construct a list of tasks performed by workers at each level, duplicate them, and present them to your large group for discussion. What are the more commonly performed tasks at the entry level? Is there an overlap in tasks performed at the two levels? How do the tasks your groups found compare with those in this chapter? What standards would you add to the tasks? (Performance goal 1)

2. Using the tasks resulting from learning activity 1, convert each task your group agrees upon into a competency and for each competency construct a performance goal. You may wish to work in groups of two or three to construct the competencies. (Performance goal 1)

3. Visit a local high school or two-year college and talk with the teachers to determine the *minimum competencies* each accounting student is expected to have at the end of the first year of accounting. Report your findings to your class and discuss how the competencies you identified relate to those developed in learning activity 2. (Performance goal 1)

4. Arrange to observe a first-year accounting class for a minimum of four times. Prior to the first visit, work with your group and prepare an observation sheet to collect information to be used later in class discussions. The following are suggestions to which your instructor may wish to add:

   a. Instructional organizational patterns employed—large- or small-group and individual.
   b. Goals for students—are they actual performance goals? Are they clearly stated for students? What are the minimum goals? What provisions are made for students of diverse abilities?
   c. Teacher presentations—fact, problem solving, or demonstration.
   d. Variety of instructional resources—what variety do you observe?
   e. Types of homework and use of homework. What is the purpose? What disposition is made of homework?
   f. Is data processing integrated into the accounting instruction? How? What are students expected to be able to do as a result of the integration?
   g. Are calculators or adding-listing machines available for students? Is a sufficient number available? (Performance goal 2)

5. Using the data collected in learning activity 4, discuss the findings with members of your subgroup and prepare a one- or two-page report from your group on (a) your reactions to your findings in terms of the

philosophy in this chapter, (*b*) your reactions in terms of the philosophies of members of your group, (*c*) what changes you might make were you teaching the particular class and why you believe them necessary, and (*d*) how the goals of the class observed relate to the competencies your group constructed from tasks in learning activity 2. (Performance goal 2)

6.  Select one performance goal you constructed for learning activity 3, analyze it for subcompetencies, and sequence your subcompetencies as in Figure 12.4. Construct an actual evaluation for the goal and administer it to high school and two-year college students who are now taking accounting. Analyze the results and determine which subcompetencies each student lacks. Arrange a small-group discussion, report your findings to your peers, and make a brief report to the entire class. (Performance goal 2)

7.  Using the performance goal in learning activity 6, analyze it for the various learning experiences possible and construct a model to illustrate multiple teaching-learning experiences, self-evaluations, and opportunities for recycling. (Performance goal 2)

8.  Compile an up-to date annotated list of instructional materials, including as many kinds of those discussed in this chapter as you can, by consulting the teacher's source books or manuals provided by publishers of textbooks, publishers' catalogs, suggestions from professional magazines, and other sources you identify. Your large group may wish to break into small groups, each having an assignment for one type of resource—films and filmstrips, simulations, applications, etc. Compile and duplicate the final list, including the following information about each item: title, source with address, approximate cost, and a brief description (annotation). (Performance goal 2)

9.  Construct a criteria sheet to be used while observing a peer teach a developmental lesson. One group may be assigned the task, or several small groups may wish to construct criteria sheets which can be evaluated and from which one acceptable for use may be designated. Use the six points a through f in learning activity 10. (Performance goal 3)

10.  For any portion of learning activity 7 in which you recommended a developmental lesson, use the subcompetency and prepare a plan you might use to teach a small group using a format your instructor recommends. Submit the plan to two of your peers for their evaluation according to the following points:

    a.  Does the teacher state the goal(s) to be achieved?
    b.  Are key questions stated for easy reference?
    c.  Are the questions so stated that they will elicit a response other than "yes" or "no"? Are the questions developmental?
    d.  Is provision made for a *student summary* at the end?
    e.  Are there activities included which will enable the students to apply what they learned from the presentation?
    f.  What provisions are made for student reinforcement—knowing whether he is right or wrong? (Performance goal 3)

11.  Construct a criteria sheet to be used while observing a peer teach a problem-solving lesson, using the five points (a through e) in learning activity 12 as a guide and adding those your peers and instructor may suggest. (Performance goal 3)

**12.** For any subcompetency selected from those identified in learning activity 6, prepare a problem-solving plan to be used in teaching a group—small or large—using the format your instructor suggests. Submit it to two of your classmates for evaluation in terms of ease of use and the following criteria:

   a.  Does the plan as constructed call upon the student to do something he or she does not know how to handle?
   b.  Does the teacher have the student state the problem?
   c.  Once the problem is clarified, does the plan provide for accepting alternative solutions to the problem?
   d.  Does the plan provide for analytical questions to assist students in examining the soundness of each alternative which may be suggested?
   e.  Does the plan provide for student testing of the best alternative once it is selected? (Performance goal 3)

## SELECTED READINGS

*A Statement of Basic Accounting,* American Accounting Association, Evanston, Illinois, 1966.

ASKINS, BILLY E., "Determining the Effectiveness of Programmed Instruction—A Training Course Example," *Accounting Review,* January, 1970, pp. 159–163.

*Automatic Data Processing Supplement to Bookkeeping and Accounting I and II Syllabus,* The University of the State of New York, The State Education Department, Bureau of Secondary Curriculum Development, Albany, N.Y., 1971.

BARBOUR, EDNA H., "The Effects of the Study of High School Bookkeeping Achievement in Elementary College Accounting," unpublished doctoral dissertation, Ohio State University, Columbus, Ohio, 1955.

BOYNTON, LEWIS D., ROBERT M. SWANSON, PAUL A. CARLSON, and HAMDEN L. FORKNER, *Century 21 Accounting,* South-Western Publishing Company, Cincinnati, Ohio, 1972.

BOYNTON, LEWIS D., *Methods of Teaching Bookkeeping and Accounting,* South-Western Publishing Company, Cincinnati, Ohio, 1970.

*CLEP General and Subject Examinations,* Educational Testing Service, Princeton, N.J., 1973.

CLOUD, CHARLES DOUGLAS, "An Experimental Study Comparing the Effectiveness of Programmed Instruction and the Conventional Method of Teaching First-Semester Principles of Accounting," unpublished doctoral dissertation, Arizona State University, Tempe, Ariz., 1971.

CLOW, JOHN E., "A Study of the Duties and Qualifications of Bookkeepers and Accountants in Manufacturing Firms in the DeKalb-Sycamore, Illinois Area," unpublished doctoral dissertation, Northern Illinois University, DeKalb, Illinois, 1967.

DAVIS, ROSE ANNE, "SOLE Stimulates Students," *Business Education Forum,* May, 1971.

*Dictionary of Occupational Titles,* Vol. 1, "Definitions of Titles," 3d ed., U.S. Department of Labor, Washington, D.C., 1965.

DOUGLAS, LLOYD V., JAMES T. BLANFORD, AND RUTH I. ANDERSON, *Teaching Business Subjects,* 3d ed., Prentice-Hall, Inc., Englewood Cliffs, N.J., 1973.

*Factors That Affect Performance in Accounting Classes,* San Mateo Junior College, Office of Research, San Mateo, Calif., 1968.

FREEMAN, M. HERBERT, J. MARSHALL HANNA, GILBERT KAHN, and DAVID H. WEAVER, *Accounting 10/12,* 2d ed., Gregg Division, McGraw-Hill Book Company, New York, 1973.

GIBBS, W. E., D. L. HUNT, and W. F. FAHRNER, "Comparative Study of Conventional and Programmed Instruction in Bookkeeping," *Journal of Educational Research,* March, 1968, pp. 320–323.

GLOVER, MILDRED W., "An Experiment in the Use of Programmed Instruction in Elementary Accounting," unpublished doctoral dissertation, University of Georgia, Athens, Georgia, 1970.

HALVERSON, G. L., "The Development and Evaluation of Programmed Instruction for Use in Supplementing the Teaching of High School Bookkeeping," *National Business Education Quarterly,* October, 1964, p. 25.

HARMS, HARM, B. W. STEHR, AND E. EDWARD HARRIS, *Methods of Teaching Business and Distributive Education,* South-Western Publishing Company, Cincinnati, Ohio, 1972.

HENDERSON, BRAXTON C., "A Comparative Analysis of Post-High School Bookkeeping Experiences of Selected Business Students," unpublished doctoral dissertation, Stanford University, Stanford, Calif., 1960.

HUFFMAN, HARRY, "Using Principles of Programmed Instruction," *Business Education World,* December, 1971, pp. 18–20.

KELLY, RICHARD L., "A Job Analysis of Tasks of Selected Semi-Professional Accountants in New York State," unpublished doctoral dissertation, Pennsylvania State University, State College, Pa., 1970.

LUXNER, LOIS A., "Factors Affecting the Employability of Vocational Bookkeeping Students," unpublished doctoral dissertation, University of Pittsburgh, Pittsburgh, Pa., 1970.

*Management and the Computer,* Dow Jones & Co., Inc., New York, 1969, p. 25.

MARGULIES, LIBBY DOMSKY, "A Comparison of the Topical Achievement in Elementary Accounting between Students Who Had Bookkeeping in High School and Those Who Did Not," unpublished master's research, Temple University, Philadelphia, Pa., 1972.

MC KITRICK, MAX O., "An Instructional Model for Training Accounting Clerks," *Business Education Forum,* January, 1973, pp. 43–44.

MOON, JAMES E., "An Inquiry into the Objectives and Implementation of Methods of Accounting Computer Education," unpublished doctoral dissertation, University of Alabama, Tuscaloosa, Alabama, 1970.

MUSSELMAN, VERNON A., AND H. MARSHALL HANNA, *Teaching Bookkeeping and Accounting,* McGraw-Hill Book Company, New York, 1960.

*National Survey of Professional, Administrative, Technical, and Clerical Pay,* Bulletin 1742, Bureau of Labor Statistics, U.S. Department of Labor, Washington, 1972.

OREFICE, DOMINICK, S., "An Experiment to Determine the Effectiveness of Programmed Instruction in Elementary Accounting," unpublished doctoral dissertation, Rutgers University, Rutgers, N.J., 1971.

OZZELLO, LAWRENCE M., "An Analysis of Accounting-Type Activities Performed by Technical Accountants in Firms Manufacturing Durable Goods with Implications for the Evaluation of Post-Secondary Terminal Accounting Programs," unpublished doctoral dissertation, Michigan State University, East Lansing, Mich., 1967.

PERRITT, ROSCOE D., "Simulation-Computer Age Teaching Method," *The Journal of Data Education,* January, 1972.

*Report of the Conference on Junior College Curriculum,* 1971–1972, ED 065-112, American Accounting Association, New York, 1972.

SCHRAG, ADELE F., "A Systems Approach for Curricular Revisions in Bookkeeping," *Business Education Forum,* April, 1972, pp. 45–46.

SCHULTHEIS, ROBERT A., "The Potential Employability of Slow Learners in Record-keeping Positions," unpublished doctoral dissertation, Indiana University, Bloomington, Indiana, 1966.

SHOOK, JAMES L., "A Study to Determine the Qualifications, Duties, and Practices of Bookkeepers in Selected Kewanee Manufacturing Firms," unpublished doctoral dissertation, Northern Illinois University, DeKalb, Illinois, 1967.

SMITH, JOHN W., "Articulation of High School Bookkeeping and College Elementary Accounting," unpublished doctoral dissertation, The University of Oklahoma, Norman, Oklahoma, 1968. (An abstract appears in *Delta Pi Epsilon Journal,* August, 1970, pp. 2–9.)

SPANSWICK, RALPH S., "An Investigation to Determine the Qualifications and Skills Desired, Accepted, and Actually Used in Manual Bookkeeping Jobs Which Were Listed in Chicago and New York City Newspapers During the Months of May and August, 1966," unpublished doctoral dissertation, Northern Illinois University, DeKalb, Illinois, 1967.

STEWART, JEFFREY R., JR., *Pilot Programs in High Schools to Prepare Students for a Wide Spectrum of Computing, Recording, and Bookkeeping Occupations,* ED 012-389, Virginia Polytechnic Institute College, Blacksburg, Virginia, 1967.

SWANSON, ROBERT M., "Evaluation of Accounting Instruction," *Business Education Forum,* December, 1972, p. 20.

TAMBRINO, PAUL A., "An Evaluation of Student Achievement in College Placement Accounting Taught in Selected High Schools on Long Island," unpublished doctoral dissertation, Temple University, Philadelphia, Pa., 1973.

THOMPSON, WILLIAM P., "What Should I Do about Accounting Homework?" *The Journal of Business Education,* January, 1972, p. 174.

"Tomorrow's Manpower Needs," Vol. 4, *The National Industry Occupational Matrix and Other Manpower Data,* Bulletin 1737, U. S. Department of Labor, Bureau of Labor Statistics, Washington, D.C., 1971.

TRAINER, JAIMIE L., C.P.A., former instructor at Clarion State College, Clarion, Penn., "Flexible Learning Program for Accounting," unpublished article, 1973.

WEAVER, DAVID H., "The Whys in High School Accounting—Concepts, Principles, and Controls," *Business Education World,* November-December, 1971, pp. 22-23, 53; September-October, 1972, pp. 26-27.

WEBB, HAROLD QUENTIN, "The Prognostic Potential of Selected Factors for Predicting Achievement in the Study of High School Bookkeeping and Accounting," unpublished doctoral dissertation, Ohio State University, Columbus, 1971.

WERNER, DONALD A., "A Comparison of Two Methods of Teaching Business Data Processing and Accounting," unpublished doctoral dissertation, Arizona State University, Tempe, Arizona, 1971.

WEST, LEONARD J., ET AL., "Survey of Entry-Level Bookkeeping Activities in Relation to the High School Bookkeeping Curriculum," Research Report 73-1, Institute for Research and Development in Occupational Education, Office of Teacher Education, The City University of New York, N.Y., November, 1973. Also in *Delta Pi Epsilon Journal,* entire issue, November, 1974.

WUNSCH, MICHAEL R., "A Comparison of Effects of Achievement of Three Methods of Study Guide Use in First Semester Bookkeeping," unpublished doctoral dissertation, University of California, Los Angeles, Calif., 1969.

YANDOH, KEITH T., "The Upstate New York Community College Career Accounting Graduate," unpublished doctoral dissertation, State University of New York at Albany, Albany, N.Y., 1971.

## PERFORMANCE GOALS

**1.** Given a description of students in a typical school and using the information in this chapter and learning activity 1, describe the computer literacy and problem-solving competencies you would recommend, and **defend** your recommendations in terms of this chapter and your instructor's presentations. Evaluation will be based on the substantiation of your arguments in terms of information presented in this chapter and by your instructor.

**2.** Given a description of students, including their general aptitudes and abilities and their vocational goals, describe the cognitive and affective vocational competencies you recommend for each group you identify, and **defend** your recommendations with data provided in this chapter and by your teacher. Evaluation will be based on substantiation of your arguments in terms of information presented in this chapter and by your instructor.

**3.** Select one terminal cognitive competency from either performance goal 1 or 2 and for it **construct** a performance goal, an evaluation, a model illustrating the relationships among the subcompetencies (see Figure 13.5), and a model illustrating the teaching-learning strategies and self-evaluations (see Figure 13.7). Evaluation will be based upon the components of the performance goal, the appropriateness of the evaluation for the goal and subcompetencies, the completeness and logical arrangement of the subcompetencies, and the inclusion of multiple learning activities and self-evaluations to enable all students to achieve.

*Subcompetencies*

a. **Construct** an acceptable performance goal for a given competency.

b. Plan and **construct** an evaluation which measures the performance stated in the goal.

c. **Analyze** a performance goal for subcompetencies and arrange the subcompetencies in sequence to illustrate their relationships.

d. **Construct** a teaching-learning strategy model with multiple learning activities and self-evaluations.

**4.** From the strategy model constructed for performance goal 3, select any activity which involves a teacher presentation to a small group (fact or demonstration), plan it in detail, and **demonstrate** your ability to meet the criteria developed in learning activity 7 by videotaping before a minigroup.

*Subcompetencies*

a. **Plan** a demonstration or fact lesson according to the criteria presented in Chapter 7 and those recommended by your instructor.

b. **Present** the demonstration or fact lesson according to criteria developed in learning activity 7.

**5.** Using a performance goal which you constructed for a problem-solving competency, **decide** on an appropriate evaluation and construct it, and, using either batch processing or a terminal, develop two learning activities students may use to prepare themselves to achieve the stated goal.

# CHAPTER 13

# Business Data Processing

Activities in business, government agencies, and social organizations generate pyramids of data essential to effective operations. The handling of this paperwork is called *data processing*. *Data* is unorganized facts, and *processing* consists of multiple operations in manipulating data to provide information to guide immediate and long-range activities.

Data may be either scientific or business in nature. Unlike scientific data which involves high-level mathematical operations, business data requires few mathematical operations. Whether data is scientific or business, processing includes the functions of collection of data, input, manipulation, filing, and output. Specifically, the data processing cycle involves recording, classifying, sorting, computing, storing, retrieving, reproducing, reporting, and communicating.

All these operations may be done manually, mechanically, by punched card, or by computer. Regardless of the method employed, the steps in the cycle remain constant, as illustrated by Figure 13.1. The amount of human intervention is great as data is processed manually and mechanically; it diminishes somewhat when data is handled by punched-card equipment. When the computer is used for processing data, human intervention ceases at the point at which data and instructions are fed into the system.

Punched-card data processing (PCDP) is based on the representation of data by holes punched in cards to enable the data to flow through the necessary operations with a minimum of human intervention. *Electronic data processing* (EDP), the term used for computer processing, involves operations that are performed in millionths, billionths, and even trillionths of a second.

This chapter focuses mainly on electronic data processing, which is rapidly emerging as the most economical means of data processing. To a lesser extent, it discusses punched-card data processing as well.

Figure 13.1   Comparison of data processing methods

| Functions | Manual | Mechanical | Punched card | Computer |
|---|---|---|---|---|
| **Collection of data** | Sheet of paper | Typewriter | Punched card | Card, tape, or technical device |
| **Input** | Handwritten forms | Adding machines | Collator | Card reader into magnetic tape |
| **Manipulation** | Mental arithmetic | Calculator | Sorter, reproducer, and accounting machine | Central processing unit |
| **Filing** | In-file | In-file | Tub (revolving drum) | Magnetic tape |
| **Output** | Handwritten documents | Bill or sales slip | Printed copy | Printed copy Video display |

The reader of this chapter who has no background in data processing is directed to Selected Readings at the end of the chapter for specific items that provide an introduction to the subject.

## The Computer

A *computer* is an electronic device that houses a stored program to direct processing, an internal storage unit to accept data and instructions, and an arithmetic-logic unit for processing data and making logical decisions. The computer cannot function alone. It requires an input device, which receives the data to be manipulated; it requires instructions to direct its operation; and it must have an output device, which produces, in either printed or punched form, the results of processing. A computer system with one input device and one output device is illustrated in Figure 13.2;

Figure 13.2   A computer system

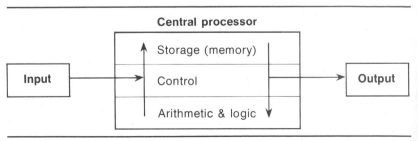

Source: Irving Phillips, "Business Machine and Computer Manufacturing Career Opportunities," *Occupational Outlook Quarterly*, U.S. Department of Labor, Bureau of Labor Statistics, Summer 1971, pp. 14–19, 70.

but note that most computer systems have multiple input and output devices. The control unit monitors all operations as data is stored, handled by the arithmetic-logic unit, and stored before output.

Computer systems are classified as mini, small, medium, and large, depending upon the capacity of the internal storage, the speed of operation, and the cost.

Minicomputers are compact in size and have limited internal storage. Both factors make them attractive to businesses which plan to abandon manual and mechanical systems of processing data. A minicomputer is relatively low in cost and may be rented or purchased at prices ranging from $10,000 to $50,000. Some projections estimate that between 200,000 and 300,000 minicomputers will be in use within ten years. Digital Equipment Corporation's PDP 6 is an example of a minicomputer. Next in size, the small computer has a slightly larger internal storage than the minicomputer, and its purchase price ranges from $60,000 to $300,000. Models 20 and 30 of the IBM System 360 and IBM System/3 are examples of the small computer. Businesses now using punched-card equipment are strongly attracted to the minicomputer and small computer because of their flexibility and versatility.

Medium-sized computers have larger storage capacities and operate considerably faster than small computers. They are especially adaptable to time-sharing systems. *Time sharing* is the term used to describe a system by which one computer at a remote location is interconnected with multiple terminals (typewriterlike keyboards) through telephone lines. This data communications system enables a person at a terminal to type data on the keyboard, enter it into the computer system, and receive output through printed copy at the terminal. Another form of data communication is the Touch-Tone device or voice-response unit that can be connected to a computer. Medium-sized computers are available at $100,000 and up.

A typical large computer system costs several million dollars and operates at nanoseconds (billionths of a second) and even picoseconds (trillionths of a second). Both the medium- and large-size computers rely on magnetic tape input/output as well as printed output.

The 100,000 computer systems now in operation are expanding rapidly, and by 1980, according to some forecasts, 300,000 will be in operation in the United States and 800,000 around the world. The proliferation of computer systems affects the tasks performed by employees at multiple levels as more and more applications are handled by computers. Originally, computers were programmed to handle both tasks involving large quantities of paperwork and repetitive tasks formerly done manually; today, computers are solving problems that could never be solved before. For instance, were it not for computers, the millions of telephone calls made each day would not be possible, and the compilation of telephone directories for large metropolitan areas would consume so many months that they would be obsolete when published.

Gigantic strides in computer technology have forced people to develop new ways of thinking and to formulate more efficient working patterns. Only recently have specific competencies been identified for those performing computer jobs. The Data Processing Management Association (DPMA) and other professional groups are continually analyzing occupational needs and tasks to provide guidelines for training on the high school and post-high school levels. Developments in computer design accelerate, demanding a continuous reevaluation of the education and training needs of those in data processing jobs and those planning to enter them. Education for the computer age involves preparing students and workers for unpredictable situations a decade hence as well as for retraining on or off the job.

No other teacher of business subjects is forced to update competencies more frequently than the teacher of data processing. Short-term summer programs, college courses, and work experience all assist teachers in evaluating current developments. Also, because of the trend in the use of computers for instructional purposes, there is increasing need for all teachers to understand programming languages, which are explained later in this chapter, so that they may communicate with those who are preparing computer programs.

## Needs of the Learner

Computers increase people's efficiency in every segment of society. Computers—once used only for scientific and business functions—now diagnose illness in people and malfunctions in automobiles and equipment, determine traffic patterns, analyze census figures, transmit data over long distances, construct graphs and charts, plot the performance of stocks and forecast future performances, print books, monitor patients suffering from cardiac and respiratory disorders, sort mail, write music, communicate with depositors by recorded voice, guide learning, and provide information for the management of government, industries, and nonprofit institutions so that intelligent decisions can be made.

Computers affect the life of everyone—the depositor whose checking and saving accounts are handled by computer, the shopper whose purchases are scanned at the checkout counter by a magnetic reader connected to a computer so that an itemized list of items and total may be prepared, the consumer whose federal income tax return is examined by computer. Students' lives are even more directly affected by computer-managed instruction (CMI) and computer-assisted instruction (CAI). (Recycle to Chapter 7, p. 158.)

Vocationally, the computer offers diverse opportunities. A student is involved in analyzing, synthesizing, and creating both new programs and new systems to increase worker and and dollar productivity. Also, a student who enjoys repetitive work finds satisfaction in preparing data for input into the computer system. This field also offers wide promotional opportunities.

## Needs of Business

Accelerated installation of computers is accompanied by a growing demand for competent people to prepare data for input into the system, to operate the system, and to utilize data emerging from the system.

New systems of office procedures, the use of terminals for data inquiry and retrieval, and increased emphasis on technical vocabulary in reports and the preparation of data to be processed through the system affect all office workers. Multiple jobs in distribution are also affected by computers, particularly those involving cash registers, which capture information at the point of sale to validate the customer's credit. Computers are also used to update accounts receivable; route shipments and prepare shipping instructions; prepare sales slips and monthly statements, analyze and manage inventory; prepare purchase requisitions; provide data for multiple sales item analysis; improve efficiency of sales force; provide data on which managerial decisions are made; and produce daily billings by account, area, and article, daily balance sheets, and daily income statements.

The lowest-level job in the data processing occupational ladder is the position of data-entry clerk. The data-entry clerk can train to become a data-entry supervisor, a tape librarian, and a computer operator; some data-entry clerks move directly into the computer operator position. Alternatively, the data-entry clerk can train to become a punched-card equipment operator, handling equipment such as the sorter, collator, reproducer, interpreter, calculator punch, and accounting machine. A computer operator can be promoted to the positions of junior programmer, applications programmer, systems programmer, systems analyst, and data processing manager, in that order.

DATA PROCESSING MANAGER.    This is a highly responsible position attained only after successful experience at lower levels. Typical tasks include the following: confer with management about data needs; identify applications; plan, coordinate, and direct all data processing activities; communicate with operating personnel; supervise the system and all activities; evaluate work performance of supervisees and arrange training and retraining as needed.

SYSTEMS ANALYST.    An analyst determines efficient patterns of information flow based on analysis of specific needs. He or she structures the computer processes, and plans for processing and distributing data. Selected tasks include the following: test, debug, revise, and retest new programs; analyze adequacy of system in terms of company requirements; prepare documentation including formats and layouts; collect, organize, and evaluate the system and business environment within company; prepare systems flowcharts; and design report formats.

PROGRAMMER.    A programmer uses a language acceptable to the computer and writes instructions (program) for the manipulation of the data to be fed into the system. Programmers may be classified as systems programmers or applications programmers. The systems programmer's job requires previous satisfactory work experience, whereas the applications programmer may be a recent graduate of a two- or four-year college. A junior programmer may be promoted from a lower-level job after completing in-service computer training. A *systems programmer* communicates with data processing personnel and with other employees who provide input data and use output from the system, tests new programs, and prepares general and detailed flowcharts. An *applications programmer* writes programs for flowcharts, following documentation; revises existing programs and tests revisions; isolates and corrects program errors; and coordinates programming requirements with the equipment.

A *junior programmer* codes routine programs, maintains and updates the library of programs, and selects and mounts tapes.

Data processing managers tend to select programmers on the basis of previous work experience and programmer trainees by their scores on an aptitude test such as IBM's "Programmer Aptitude Test," which measures mathematical and verbal aptitudes and logical thinking ability.

Computers communicate in different languages called *programming languages.* Gigantic strides in programming languages have been made. Originally, the programmer had to write an instruction for each operation to be performed and assign specific storage locations for data and instructions (machine language). Today's high-level programming languages require no such detailed steps. There are two categories of high-level programming languages: first, procedure-oriented languages such as FORmula TRANslator (FORTRAN) and COmmon Business Oriented Language (COBOL) and, second, problem-oriented language such as Report Program Generator (RPG). A *procedure-oriented* language is one designed for the solution of a problem. It consists of a system of computational procedures resulting in a problem's solution. A *problem-oriented* language (RPG) describes the report(s) to be created. RPG is the primary programming language used with small computer systems such as IBM System/3, although some medium- and large-size systems may accept RPG when processing selected business applications.

FORTRAN is used mainly for scientific applications, and COBOL and RPG are used for business applications.

There are hundreds of programming languages. Two languages used primarily for students engaged in problem solving are Beginners' All-Purpose Symbolic Instruction Code (BASIC) and A Programming Language (APL), both of which are discussed under Teaching-Learning Strategies in this chapter.

COMPUTER OPERATOR.   The following are selected tasks of the computer operator: review the job request form for instructions to the computer operator, estimate computer time, and determine the availability of the appropriate equipment (the computer and peripheral equipment such as the card reader and printer, the input devices, and the output devices); select the magnetic tapes; load the magnetic tapes on tape drives; monitor the console light to see if operations are moving smoothly and make necessary adjustments; maintain a log with program name and time run began and ended; make routine decisions to expedite computer run; and communicate with consultant and programmers when the need arises.

In a small operation, the programmer may also be the computer console operator; in a large installation, the operator may be assisted by the tape librarian and need possess no knowledge of programming languages. Since this job is one of major responsibility, employers tend to prefer to train or retrain their own handpicked employees.

Requisites for the job of computer operator are usually a high school education; analytical ability to diagnose trouble as it occurs and take necessary action in correcting the problem; calmness under stress, so that the operator may resolve crises without compounding them; and dexterity in handling tapes, punched cards, and console controls.

TAPE LIBRARIAN.   While the title of tape librarian suggests that the sole responsibility of librarian is to maintain tapes, put them on tape drives, and remove them for storage, studies reveal that most tape librarians have other responsibilities such as operating a card-punch machine or other punched-card equipment. Basically, this is a clerical job that requires no education beyond high school and little or no job training. The person selected should be painstakingly careful in handling tapes and maintaining accurate records on the condition of the tapes and the jobs on which they are being used. Most tape librarians are skillful in splicing magnetic tape when accidents occur and tapes must be repaired.

PUNCHED-CARD EQUIPMENT OPERATOR.   Although many large companies no longer use sorters, collators, reproducers, and accounting machines because of the availability at reasonable cost of minicomputers or small computers, some companies continue to use such equipment. Also, larger companies often use the equipment as backup. Operators of punched-card equipment are usually high school graduates who were trained either in vocational schools or on the job. Minimum competencies are speed and accuracy in selecting and inserting wired panels and decks of cards. Today most panels for the accounting machine are prewired by the manufacturer, although panels for the collator, reproducer, and interpreter must be rewired as the applications change. The operator's basic tasks are as follows: insert and remove cards for sorter, collator, reproducer, interpreter, and accounting machine; operate all machines in the punched-card system; make minor adjustments on the equipment; wire control panels; check each job to see that minimum steps are performed.

Estimates of future needs for punched-card operators are not reliable because of the rapid conversion to computers. Community needs should be surveyed constantly, using techniques such as those described by Bonarti.

DATA-ENTRY CLERKS.   Jobs in this category, both at the entry level, include the card-punch operator and the direct-entry clerk. Such an operator scans the original document and either punches the card or types the data for input into the system. The punched card served as the major computer input until 1966, when key-to-tape input was perfected. There is now a distinct trend toward key-to-tape or key-to-disk equipment. With key-to-tape input, the direct-data-entry clerk enters the data and edits it for accuracy. He then presses a key to send the data directly onto magnetic tape.

Direct-entry equipment is approximately 50 percent faster than card-punch equipment because errors can be corrected within seconds. Tasks performed by data-entry clerks include these: identify data from original documents, extract data from code sheets, punch or type data, edit the visual of the data typed (on small TV screen) or verify the card punched.

## Opportunities in the Computer Field

The present demand of skilled programmers who have work experience exceeds the supply by approximately 100,000. In fact, the president of the American Federation of Information Processing Societies (AFIPS) says, "There are distressingly large numbers of poorly qualified people at all levels" in the computer field. ("If Computers . . .," p. 86)

Multiple factors affect any projections of work force needs. One of these is the rapid rate at which minicomputers and small computers are replacing punched-card equipment.

Although employment projections are subject to economic fluctuations, they provide some guidance in designing education and training programs for the data processing occupations (see Figure 13.3).

The rapidly accelerating pace at which minicomputers and small computers are being installed in businesses is affecting the competencies needed for entry-level employment in data processing. More opportunities are available for applications programmers, and the two-year college data processing graduate who has acquired work experience during college is frequently considered for these jobs. The two-year college data processing graduate without experience is more likely to begin a data processing career as a junior programmer or a computer operator. From these jobs, many work their way into applications programmer jobs by performing successfully in their entry-level jobs and by taking either in-service or in-school courses in data processing. High school graduates who have developed

## Figure 13.3   Projected growth of jobs in data processing

| Job category | Average annual need | Projected total for 1980 |
|---|---|---|
| Systems analysts | 27,000 | 425,000 |
| Programmers' | 23,000 | 400,000 |
| Computer operators | 18,000 | 420,000 |
| Punched-card equipment operators | — | 15,000 |
| Data-entry clerks | 80,000 | 1,500,000 |

Source: Irving Phillips, "Business Machine and Computer Manufacturing Career Opportunities," *Occupational Outlook Quarterly,* Department of Labor, Bureau of Labor Statistics, Washington, D.C., Summer, 1971, pp. 14–19, 70.

competencies in programming are sometimes hired as junior programmers, from which post they may aspire with additional education to applications programmers. Motivated high school graduates who understand data processing concepts and who possess the characteristics of accuracy and pride in work may be hired as tape librarians and eventually become junior programmers by completing additional computer training.

The data-entry clerk, the lowest-level worker on the data processing occupational ladder, provides a key link between the company and the computer because of the high degree of accuracy required in performing data-entry tasks.

Cooperative planning by high schools, vocational-technical schools, and two-year colleges—particularly those located close to computer jobs—is essential before sound programs in data processing can be developed and implemented. The local chapter of the Data Processing Management Association (DPMA) and advisory groups from industry can be very helpful in planning new programs and revising existing ones.

## General Objectives of Data Processing

Objectives in data processing instruction may be classified under *computer literacy, problem solving,* and *vocational* (those for employment). Although the competency-based education approach places the emphasis on vocational data processing, this chapter also focuses on computer literacy and problem-solving objectives relevant to general education.

## The Computer in General Education

Pertinent elements of computer applications and effects should be integrated into all courses to which they relate at all educational levels.

COMPUTER LITERACY. The objectives of computer literacy are to provide the following:

- Understanding of the role of the computer in society—government, business, and the life of the individual as well as the computer's social and economic impact
- Understanding of key concepts associated with computers
- Understanding the differences in manual, mechanical, punched-card, and electronic data processing
- Opportunity to apply computer concepts through programming problems relevant to the student

While the argument for computer literacy for all high school students is strong, it is imperative for the 65 percent who do not go directly to college from high school.

PROBLEM SOLVING. The use of the computer as a tool in problem solving provides opportunities for developing and/or strengthening logical thinking abilities. The effects of alternative solutions may be examined and logical decisions made. The Conference Board of the Mathematical Sciences recommends the development of proficiency in the use of computers as a tool for all high school students. Tiedeman found that in addition to improving decision-making skills, computer use motivates students and also stimulates interest in careers in the computer field. In high school, problem-solving competencies may be developed by business students by using the computer as a tool in solving problems in mathematics, general business, accounting, consumer economics, and distribution. In the two-year college, use of the computer in problem solving may or may not be presented through a separate data processing course. Instructors of accounting, finance, management, and statistics frequently employ the computer as a student tool in problem solving. Multiple recommendations are now available to the teacher planning a separate course in data processing or the integration of data processing within an existing course.

## The Computer and Education for Employment

While the primary objective of data processing courses in the vocational-technical schools is to prepare students for jobs in data processing, students are also expected to develop problem-solving abilities through use of the computer. Advanced data processing courses at the two-year college are also geared toward employment in data processing. Both the vocational-technical school and the two-year college work closely with business to assure the relevance of their data processing courses. Also, the two-year college is likely to require supervised cooperative work experience for its data processing students. Some comprehensive high schools also provide training for data processing jobs, particularly when there are no accessible vocational-technical schools to assume this role.

Regardless of the educational level, all data processing teachers have multiple opportunities to assist students in developing attitudes which will enhance their effectiveness in data processing installations and enable them to adjust to technological changes which may affect their jobs.

At the high school level, the purpose of data processing instruction is largely general education, although preparation for entry-level jobs is included among objectives in some schools. High schools (1) develop computer literacy, (2) encourage the use of the computer as a tool in problem solving, (3) develop problem-solving abilities, (4) provide an appreciation of the computer's role in society, (5) provide opportunities for career exploration, (6) prepare students for entry-level jobs in computer installations.

Vocational-technical schools (1) prepare data-entry clerks, (2) prepare operators of punched-card equipment, (3) provide an understanding of the computer and the ability to use one or more programming languages so that students may enter jobs as computer operators or programming trainees.

Both high schools and vocational-technical schools prepare individuals to go on to two- or four-year colleges. Two-year colleges prepare people for higher-level entry jobs and enable students to develop problem-solving competencies applicable to other business courses. Two-year colleges (1) provide technical knowledges and skills to enable graduates to procure jobs as computer operators, junior programmers, or programmer trainees, and to seek retraining when necessary; (2) provide foundation to enable graduates to adapt to new systems, equipment, and languages on the job; (3) provide understanding of what the computer can do to enable a student of accounting, business mathematics, consumer economics, general business, finance, insurance, or management to use the computer in solving problems and making decisions.

Four-year colleges prepare students for management jobs in data processing and in applications of computers to solve management problems. Four-year colleges provide broad business and data processing education to enable graduates to move to positions of systems programmers, system analysts, data processing managers, and other specialized data processing jobs in government and industry. The goal is to (1) prepare graduates who can communicate with personnel at all levels and who can interpret and use data produced by computers in making intelligent decisions, and (2) prepare students who will become junior executives in analyzing problems and applying them while establishing computer routines to assist in their solution.

## Identifying and Classifying Competencies

Although research provides some insight into the competencies needed to perform entry-level and second-level jobs in data processing, the actual competencies needed by all students have not been pinpointed.

## Competencies for All Students

The following competencies are suggested as guides in meeting the general purposes of computer literacy and problem solving by computers:

---

COMPUTER LITERACY

1. Explain how the computer affects an individual's activities such as banking, paying bills, and income tax reports.
2. Explain the social and economic changes resulting from electronic data processing which have emerged during the past five years.
3. Explain how a digital computer operates, including all components.
4. Explain the capabilities of a computer system and the limitations of the computer in handling a specific application.
5. Identify multiple applications appropriate for a computer system based upon observations in industry.

6. Differentiate between input data and output data of a computer system.
7. Defend vital issues such as "a cashless society" and "the infringement of the computer on the rights of the individual" by giving pros and cons which can be substantiated.
8a. Write and run a computer program with accompanying data and interpret the output correctly. (A competency for higher-ability students only.)
8b. Study printouts and identify input, computer processing of data, and output.

---

PROBLEM SOLVING

9. Analyze problems and use the computer as a tool in decision making by testing alternatives and seeking solutions according to specified criteria.
10. Use the computer as a tool in solving problems for other subjects— business mathematics, accounting, general business, etc.—so that the problem is solved logically and in as few steps as possible.

## Competencies Essential for Employment

Despite several studies based on opinions of data processing supervisors and workers, considerably more research is needed. Too often, research concentrates on the backgrounds of those holding various jobs and on the opinions of those in data processing installations rather than on the actual competencies really needed by workers. Today employers recognize that motivation of the individual, interpersonal behaviors, and the ability to perform on the job are all related to job success.

While the trend toward analysis of tasks is a fairly recent one in business education, basic data processing tasks have been identified and may be used in creating competencies. Lanham and his team for NOBELS (recycle to Chapter 3) classified 152 tasks under the electronic data processing category and identified the ten most frequently used verbs used in describing data processing tasks as *receive, punch, deliver, place, obtain, check, remove, write, record,* and *insert.* However, the study concentrated on lower-level clerical tasks such as receiving input, listing input and output, checking output for completion and accuracy, and communicative skills involved in obtaining input-output and working with supervisors rather than on tasks performed by workers in data processing installations.

ENTRY-LEVEL COMPETENCIES. Borcher and Joyner were the first to identify tasks performed by workers in data processing, from the computer operator to the manager. The following competencies, developed from tasks from Borcher and Joyner, and Erickson, might be demanded of a student working toward the goal of entry-level employment in data processing.

## COGNITIVE: EVALUATION

1. Decide when supervisor must be called to avert problems on equipment.
2. Screen reports and instructions for obvious errors and either correct them or refer them to supervisor for correction.

## COGNITIVE: ANALYSIS/SYNTHESIS

3. Communicate problem to supervisor so that it is clearly understood.
4. Monitor console during operations so that program runs correctly.

## COGNITIVE: APPLICATION

5. Decipher handwriting of others correctly.
6. Maintain a correct log of daily jobs so that it is up to date at any moment.
7. Punch cards to correct input or for input.
8. Check wiring on control panels and make necessary adjustments to enable machine to execute problems correctly.
9. Operate sorter, interpreter, collator, reproducer, and accounting machine so that output is usable for next step of system and is free from errors.
10. Search tape library and select precise programs and/or data called for by job description.
11. Use correct tapes for program and data and mount them on tape drives so that they operate efficiently.
12. Operate console so that computer run emerges.

## COGNITIVE: COMPREHENSION

13. Follow oral instructions correctly as stated.
14. Follow written instructions on job description correctly as stated.
15. Match similar and dissimilar items correctly.

## AFFECTIVE: HIGH-LEVEL RESPONDING

16. Show interest in improving self and job.
17. Reveal initiative by requesting new assignments when work is completed.
18. Exert extra effort by helping others when assistance is needed.
19. Demonstrate pride in work by doing it accurately.
20. Appreciate that work created by you affects the output of the entire system.
21. Inquire and explore to seek help when needed.
22. Keep work organized while coping with interruptions.
23. Show respect for workers of all ages—same age, older, and younger.

24. Show interest in adhering to procedures and schedules by following them to the letter.
25. Maintain good work pace by meeting schedules even though it involves working beyond stopping time or working without breaks.
26. Work effectively as a member of a team by assisting others to meet deadlines whenever necessary.
27. Tolerate tedious work without complaining.
28. Demonstrate flexibility by trying new procedures as they are suggested by supervisor.
29. Seek help when needed so that valuable time is not lost.
30. Exercise care so that products handled are not lost or damaged.

**SECOND-LEVEL COMPETENCIES.** Huffman and Gust concentrated on the tasks performed by second-level workers, from which the competencies listed here are constructed. (Recycle to Chapter 3, p. 52.) A comparison of entry- and second-level competencies reveals that second-level workers engage primarily in analysis and evaluation (decision making), while entry-level workers perform more tasks at the application level of the cognitive domain.

---

COGNITIVE: EVALUATION

---

1. Analyze company's needs and design a system for handling information which meets those needs.
2. Identify alternative combinations of equipment, procedures, and staff and decide upon that which meets needs of system.
3. Formulate plans for collecting, processing, storing, and retrieving information to meet company's needs.
4. Formulate standards for measuring performance and comparing results with standards.

---

COGNITIVE: ANALYSIS/SYNTHESIS

---

5. Summarize output and convert into usable reports which are acceptable according to standards established.
6. Convert program written in one language to a different language which performs the same steps.
7. Develop program logic charts for machine routines.
8. Analyze programs and make modifications which enable them to run accurately or faster.
9. Analyze problems for which there are no programs and construct flowcharts which are detailed and provide for each step.
10. Determine cause of errors in information system and correct data as necessary to permit a correct run.
11. Analyze inputs by test runs and revise until correct.
12. Construct programs from tested flowcharts and test run until correct.
13. Communicate with those who request computer analyses and develop flowcharts and programs to meet their needs.

14. Analyze system for errors; edit and correct all programs to enable system to function effectively.
15. Analyze information system and make suggestions to management which will provide additional data needed for effective operations.

## AFFECTIVE: HIGH-LEVEL RESPONDING

16. Adjust quickly to new routines, equipment, procedures, and work sequences by following new routines in daily work.
17. Communicate effectively with management and other personnel.
18. Reveal flexibility in moving from one system to another and back.
19. Accept all people without revealing hostility or impatience. (Plus all affective competencies for the entry-level, pp. 313, 314.)

## PSYCHOMOTOR: APPLICATION

20. Manipulate all equipment with ease.

## Constructing Performance Goals

The teacher should be thoroughly familiar with the procedures presented in Chapters 3, 4, and 5 before proceeding with the conversion of the identified competencies into performance goals.

Figure 13.4 illustrates the components needed to convert competencies into performance goals. A computer literacy competency, a problem-solving competency, a cognitive entry-level competency, an affective entry-level competency, and a second-level competency illustrate the procedures in converting a competency into the following performance goals:

## Computer Literacy

COMPETENCY 1
Defend vital issues such as "a cashless society" and "the infringement of the computer on the rights of the individual" by giving pros and cons.
PERFORMANCE GOAL 1
Given a topic for research and appropriate sources, gather the information; and, while working as one member of a debate team, develop your arguments for and against the topic; and, while performing during debate, **defend** your stand for the position assigned to you (for or against) according to the criteria your class uses for critiquing debates.

## Problem Solving

COMPETENCY 2
Analyze problems and use the computer as a tool in decision making.

**315**

Figure 13.4 Selected competencies analyzed for components of performance goals

| Competency | Verb | Evaluation & result of performance | Conditions | Criterion |
|---|---|---|---|---|
| **Computer literacy** | | | | |
| 1. Defend vital issues such as "a cashless society" and "the infringement of the computer on the rights of individuals" giving pros and cons. (Cognitive: evaluation) | 'Defend | Process: using controlled observation and criteria sheets | Given topic for research; working as one member of a debate team; take a stand to defend; while being observed by peer evaluators. | According to criteria your debate teams are using. |
| **Problem solving** | | | | |
| 2. Analyze problems and use the computer as a tool in decision making. (Cognitive: evaluation) | Decide | Product: computer printout | Given a business problem and access to terminal, and using BASIC. | Computer printout and flow-chart of program which solved the problem. |
| **Entry level** | | | | |
| 3. Operate sorter, interpreter, collator, reproducer, and accounting machine so that output is usable for the next step of the system and free from errors. (Cognitive: application) | Demonstrate | Product: printed report emerging from accounting machine and decks of cards | Given correctly punched decks of cards for an application such as payroll or sales analysis; given equipment needed. | Printed report is complete and accurate and all decks are complete and error free. |
| 4. Keep work organized while coping with interruptions. (Affective: high-level responding) | Demonstrate | Process: controlled observation using criteria sheets | While being observed in work situation during which three or more interruptions occur. | Reveals organization by locating piece of work asked for immediately with no hesitation. |
| **Second level** | | | | |
| 5. Construct programs from tested flowcharts and test run until correct. (Cognitive: analysis) | Analyze | Product: computer printout | Given tested flowcharts for each of four business problems, data for each, and access to computer. | Test and revise until each program runs, using printouts as evidence. |

PERFORMANCE GOAL 2
Given a problem to be solved while using BASIC and a terminal, analyze the problem, **decide** on the solution, and construct the flowchart; code the program before running it, presenting the flowchart and desired printout as evidence of your decision.

## Vocational (Entry Level; Cognitive)

COMPETENCY 3
Operate sorter, interpreter, collator, reproducer, and accounting machine so that output is usable for the next step of the system and free from errors.

PERFORMANCE GOAL 3
Given correctly punched decks of cards for an application such as payroll or sales analysis and access to punched-card equipment needed, **demonstrate** your ability to operate the sorter, interpreter, collator, reproducer, and accounting machine by producing a printed report which is complete and accurate and accompanied by the decks of cards emerging from the processes.

## Vocational (Entry Level; Affective)

COMPETENCY 4
Keep work organized while coping with interruptions.

PERFORMANCE GOAL 4
While being observed by teacher and peers during work situations in which you will be interrupted three or more times, **demonstrate** your ability to keep your work organized despite interruptions by locating specific items on request.

## Vocational (Second Level)

COMPETENCY 5
Construct programs from tested flowcharts and test run until correct.

PERFORMANCE GOAL 5
Given tested flowcharts for each of four business problems, data, and access to a computer, **analyze** the flowcharts and code for each a COBOL program, testing and revising until each program produces the desired printout.

### Identifying and Sequencing Subcompetencies

Numerous subcompetencies are needed to meet almost every performance goal in data processing. Figure 13.5 illustrates the analysis of subcompetencies for a goal for problem solving. A teacher using such a model may identify other subcompetencies pertinent to individual students. Each of these would be an en route goal for a student working toward the stated goal.

**317**

Figure 13.5   Problem-solving performance goal
              analyzed for subcompetencies

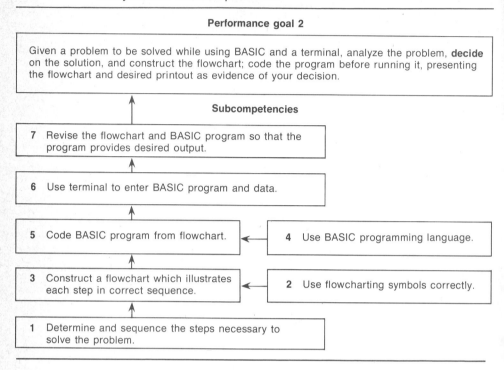

**Performance goal 2**

Given a problem to be solved while using BASIC and a terminal, analyze the problem, **decide** on the solution, and construct the flowchart; code the program before running it, presenting the flowchart and desired printout as evidence of your decision.

**Subcompetencies**

7   Revise the flowchart and BASIC program so that the program provides desired output.

6   Use terminal to enter BASIC program and data.

5   Code BASIC program from flowchart.        ←        4   Use BASIC programming language.

3   Construct a flowchart which illustrates each step in correct sequence.        ←        2   Use flowcharting symbols correctly.

1   Determine and sequence the steps necessary to solve the problem.

## Applying Learning Principles

Virtually all the principles of learning apply to data processing. Those which are especially important to all data processing students follow:

LEARNER MUST PERCEIVE THAT WHICH IS TO BE LEARNED AS RELEVANT. Data processing provides exciting opportunities for students in all areas, whether the student's goal is computer literacy or vocational training, many elements are relevant to students.

LEARNER IS AN ACTIVE PARTICIPANT IN THE PROCESS. So much of data processing involves student activity that this principle is automatically applied.

LEARNER KNOWS IMMEDIATE GOAL TOWARD WHICH HE OR SHE IS STRIVING. Since one goal is a computer program that will run, the student recognizes that anything which contributes to the production of a program is useful.

LEARNING PROCEEDS FASTER WHEN LEARNER IS AWARE OF PROGRESS. Whether the student is preparing input data or writing a program, it will soon be apparent whether or not the work is correct. This principle is automatically provided for in all vocational data processing and in problem solving using the terminal for input/output.

## Pretesting and Matching Learner with Performance Goals and Sub-competencies

Because of the vast differences in ability required for the data-entry clerk and the applications programmer, data processing offers various goals. Some of these are attainable by any student who is capable of understanding and following instructions and is willing to learn.

Pretesting enables the teacher to pinpoint students who have difficulties in interpreting and following instructions, solving simple problems, and thinking logically. Also, vocational data processing teachers frequently use the IBM "Programmer Aptitude Test" to identify students who are likely to succeed in programming. Pretesting helps each student to select appropriate performance goals. Results of pretests help the teacher to discover the subcompetencies a student lacks and for which en route goals must be established.

In many data processing classes students work toward different goals, depending on interests and aptitudes.

## Selecting Teaching-Learning Strategies

The instructor in data processing will find it most effective to use a wide range of learning activities—presented in accordance with appropriately varied organizational patterns–in order to help students achieve their stated goals.

### Organizational Patterns

Data processing lends itself to all three organizational patterns. Large-group instruction is effective only for the introduction of concepts, watching a film, or listening to a guest speaker. Small-group organization offers greater flexibility. A major advantage of the small group is that individuals working in teams are forced to interact; thus positive affective behaviors may be strengthened. Performance goals for affective behaviors almost dictate this organizational pattern.

Once the teacher determines the specific goals toward which students are working, the formation of small groups is natural. One group may be solving problems which require use of the terminal; another group may be discussing the construction of a flowchart for a given problem; another group may be receiving audiotutorial instruction in the operation of a card-punch machine.

Individually prescribed instruction enables each student to select relevant goals. Individually paced instruction is essential even for students working in small groups, for some students take substantially longer to succeed in achieving a performance goal than others.

The teacher is likely to find that groups are forming, expanding, and terminating with regularity as students progress. The activity approach necessitates students moving around the room, talking over problems, working together, and observing each other.

## Learning Activities

Every type of activity illustrated in Figure 7.2 is applied in data processing. (Recycle to Chapter 7, p. 125.) In addition to activities involving reading, listening, and writing, students also perform, observe, speak, and discuss. Multiple learning activities appropriate for data processing include the following:

- *Listening* to instructions by teacher, by other students who may be demonstrating equipment, and to audiovisual presentations
- *Observing* operation of equipment, construction of a flowchart using flow-charting symbols; demonstrations of coding in programming languages from flowcharts, field trips to computer installations, and bulletin board displays
- *Discussing* (listening and speaking) in groups solving a problem, deciding on multiple approaches to programming, and identifying the files for input and output
- *Performing* while solving problems in study guides, games, and simulations; while preparing reports on research of social and economic consequences of automation, analyzing observations of field trips, and analyzing job opportunities in the community; and in operating equipment and constructing flowcharts, coding programs, and solving problems at the terminal or preparing for batch processing by the computer

The data processing teacher must be aware of new learning resources. Long before he or she plans learning activities, three basic decisions must be made: (1) the hardware to be used for instructional purposes, (2) the programming language(s) (software) to be taught, and (3) whether programming is to be accomplished by batch processing or by a terminal or both. *Batch processing* refers to the grouping of data for input into the system. Punched cards are generally used. Both the program and data are punched, the cards are assembled into a deck, and the entire deck is presented for input and read into the system as a package.

HARDWARE. What hardware (physical equipment) is most desirable for developing goals involving computer literacy and problem solving? vocational competencies? There is no one answer. Much depends upon the resourcefulness of the teacher and the cooperation of local industries.

Ideally, computer literacy and problem-solving goals are met by student use of terminals for solving problems in business mathematics, mathematics, accounting, general business, or other subjects. Use of the terminal places the stress on concepts rather than on the computations themselves. Should a school have no terminals available, the data processing teacher may find one or more local businesses willing to run student programs. While such a setup may not be ideal, the program run outside nevertheless enables a student to examine the output, to identify errors, to make corrections elsewhere, and to have the program rerun.

Hardware for business data processing for vocational purposes varies according to schools. Because schools rushed to purchase punched-card equipment some years ago, many schools have it available today. The card-punch machine is the basic equipment in most schools. It can be used effectively combined with: (1) a sorter, (2) a sorter and an accounting machine, (3) a sorter, collator, reproducer, interpreter, and an accounting machine, (4) a card reader connected to a computer located elsewhere, or (5) a card reader and computer on the premises. Also, some schools have a terminal connected to a computer at another location.

More recently the minicomputer has become available for student use in some schools. Kleiner sought to identify a low-cost computer system useful for teaching programming in high school and reached the following conclusions:

1. The basic computer should cost under $10,000 except when the computer can meet some special education requirement.
2. The computer must have at least one higher-level language, preferably BASIC, in addition to assembly language.
3. The computer manufacturer should be able to provide adequate maintenance from a nearby service center.
4. The computer manufacturer should provide adequate software (programs) support in order to utilize his equipment.
5. The computer should support a multiuser system as well as a single-user system.

Use of such a minicomputer would be appropriate for achieving goals involving computer literacy and problem solving as well as some goals associated with vocational competencies.

SOFTWARE. The second decision involving learning activities is the software (the programming language) to be employed. Naturally the language used must be compatible with the hardware. A programming language used for problem solving should be sufficiently easy to learn to enable the student to proceed speedily to meaningful applications. A language which has a minimal number of commands is BASIC. Although a bit more complex to learn than BASIC, APL is considerably simpler than FORTRAN. APL is especially useful for problem solving in mathematics, although BASIC may also be used. Fingar studied educational uses of APL and found that it had been successfully taught to junior high students and could be used in applying business problems.

COBOL is widely used and is recommended as the language for advanced programming work for those who desire to enter business as junior programmers. RPG is the language selected by many schools preparing business data processing workers. It is frequently used as the initial language, and students later learn COBOL.

With the current trend toward computer literacy and problem-solving competencies, many high schools defer the teaching of the higher-level languages such as COBOL and FORTRAN to the vocational-technical schools and two-year colleges and concern themselves with teaching BASIC or APL.

Students apparently learn programming equally well whether by terminals in a time-sharing system or through batch processing.

TIME SHARING. Time sharing is a technique which enables several users at terminals remotely located from the computer to communicate on-line with the computer and receive what appears to be instantaneous feedback from the computer. For example, twenty terminals may be connected to one computer by telephone lines, and the computer accepts programs and input data from several terminals at the same time that it is processing data from another terminal and sending output to other terminals. Terminals may produce hard copy (printed output), or they may display the output on a televisionlike screen.

Time-sharing systems are ideal for problem-solving activities, but most vocational-technical schools and two-year colleges offer hands-on-computer experiences for students preparing for such jobs as computer operator and programmer. In such instances, batch processing is generally used.

## Selecting Learning Activities

In addition to computers and terminals, the teacher of data processing has a vast selection of resources to employ for student learning activities.

VIDEOTAPES. Because demonstrations must be repeated as various students exhibit readiness for goals, some teachers record a master demonstration on videotape which students may play back at any time needed.

COMPUTER-ASSISTED INSTRUCTION. Computer-assisted instruction is used successfully in teaching both introductory aspects of data processing and programming. One program tested at Ocean County Community College, Toms River, New Jersey, serves as an example. There are no formal classes, and students arrange their own hours. During these hours they may receive instruction via terminals by interrogating the computer for various phases of the first-semester course. Hard copy produced by each student becomes the textbook. The course consists of more than ninety programs in nonsequential order, for no two students take the same path. In addition to the basic concepts, the objectives of the course include the ability to use the terminology intelligently, write brief programs, and distinguish among several computer languages. Students are tested while at the terminal, and the computer records their progress, analyzes each response, and feeds the next part of the program for which the student has shown readiness. A student who encounters a problem is recycled through a given program, perhaps by a different route.

**PROBLEM SOLVING AT THE TERMINAL.**　Students' interest in grades prompted one teacher to develop a problem for students to apply at the terminal. Figure 13.6 presents a flowchart and two possible solutions to the problem. The problem given students follows.

---

Below are the names of students in two classes with their respective grades for a given test. Use the data and prepare a flowchart and code and run via terminal a BASIC program that will determine the highest, lowest, and average grade within each class.

---

Students working with the problem may reach the solution with slightly different programs. Later students may compare the programs created and determine whose program solved the problem in the fewest steps.

Any teacher who plans for problem-solving activities may develop a battery of problems from which students may select those which appeal to them.

**SIMULATIONS AND GAMES.**　Both simulations and games offer opportunities for involving students in decision making. There is a growing body of materials to employ in simulating situations by computer. One list presents about two hundred articles and publications related to both simulations and games (Peterson). One computerized management simulation demands that students make all decisions within a hypothetical organization. Data is punched into cards which can be mailed to the company for processing with results returned in ten days. Therefore no computer need be available. One positive aspect of this experience is that students who drive the "company" into bankruptcy receive a memo indicating that the students should start a new company, reanalyze, and remake decisions in order to put the business on a profitable basis.

Some colleges are testing simulations in which students operate a corporation during periods of inflation or depression or during "normal" periods. Data is fed into the computer and students receive the results of their decisions. They may then analyze the outcomes of their decisions in terms of income and losses.

For simulations the teacher should refer to Peterson, McNair and West, and Huntington Two in the Selected Readings at the end of the chapter.

**OTHER LEARNING RESOURCES.**　Audiovisual materials such as films and filmstrips as well as audiotutorial materials, programmed books, textbooks, pamphlets, posters, pictures, transparencies, and educational kits including practice materials and facsimiles provide challenging learning activities.

**SUPERVISED COOPERATIVE WORK EXPERIENCE.**　Growing numbers of two-year colleges and some vocational-technical schools require data processing students to spend a prescribed period in a work situation for which they are paid. The actual experience combined with parallel in-school work

Figure 13.6   Two BASIC programs with flowchart for Method 1

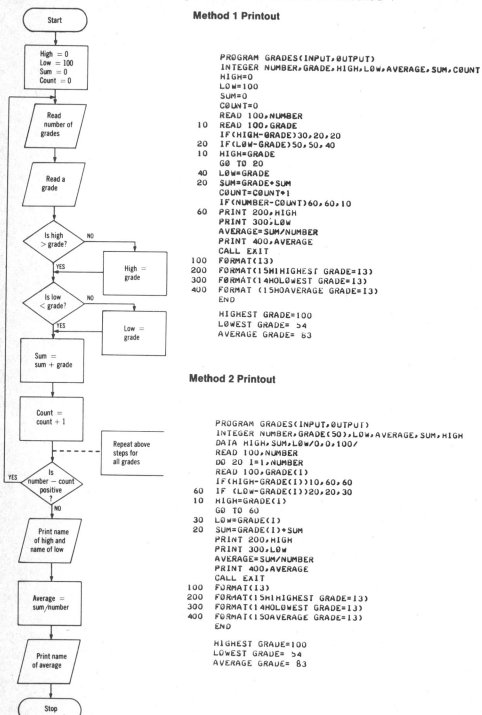

**Method 1 Printout**

```
      PROGRAM GRADES(INPUT,OUTPUT)
      INTEGER NUMBER,GRADE,HIGH,LOW,AVERAGE,SUM,COUNT
      HIGH=0
      LOW=100
      SUM=0
      COUNT=0
      READ 100,NUMBER
10    READ 100,GRADE
      IF(HIGH-GRADE)30,20,20
20    IF(LOW-GRADE)50,50,40
10    HIGH=GRADE
      GO TO 20
40    LOW=GRADE
20    SUM=GRADE+SUM
      COUNT=COUNT+1
      IF(NUMBER-COUNT)60,60,10
60    PRINT 200,HIGH
      PRINT 300,LOW
      AVERAGE=SUM/NUMBER
      PRINT 400,AVERAGE
      CALL EXIT
100   FORMAT(I3)
200   FORMAT(15HIHIGHEST GRADE=I3)
300   FORMAT(14HOLOWEST GRADE=I3)
400   FORMAT (15HOAVERAGE GRADE=I3)
      END

      HIGHEST GRADE=100
      LOWEST GRADE= 54
      AVERAGE GRADE= 83
```

**Method 2 Printout**

```
      PROGRAM GRADES(INPUT,OUTPUT)
      INTEGER NUMBER,GRADE(50),LOW,AVERAGE,SUM,HIGH
      DATA HIGH,SUM,LOW/0,0,100/
      READ 100,NUMBER
      DO 20 I=1,NUMBER
      READ 100,GRADE(I)
      IF(HIGH-GRADE(I))10,60,60
60    IF (LOW-GRADE(I))20,20,30
10    HIGH=GRADE(I)
      GO TO 60
30    LOW=GRADE(I)
20    SUM=GRADE(I)+SUM
      PRINT 200,HIGH
      PRINT 300,LOW
      AVERAGE=SUM/NUMBER
      PRINT 400,AVERAGE
      CALL EXIT
100   FORMAT(I3)
200   FORMAT(15HIHIGHEST GRADE=I3)
300   FORMAT(14HOLOWEST GRADE=I3)
400   FORMAT(15OAVERAGE GRADE=I3)
      END

      HIGHEST GRADE=100
      LOWEST GRADE= 54
      AVERAGE GRADE= 83
```

in data processing provides realistic applications of in-school learning. Some companies are reluctant to assume responsibility for students who are not yet graduated from high school; for unless they are bright, quick, and vitally interested and have a sufficient background, they may consume precious time which the supervisor might use in performing assigned tasks. However, if companies are agreeable and if the students are sufficiently trained, the benefits far outweigh the disadvantages. Moreover, the experience provides the student with another asset to use when applying for a job after graduation, for more and more companies hire only experienced people in data processing jobs.

**PLANNING LEARNING ACTIVITIES FOR PERFORMANCE GOALS.** No other class provides more opportunities for student activities than does one in data processing. Whether students are working toward computer literacy and problem-solving goals or preparing for entry-level positions in data processing, the classes are alive and activity-oriented. For example, students working toward goals of computer literacy are constantly interacting with the teacher and each other in group planning and group discussions. Small groups preview films and filmstrips in order to construct guidelines for observers to use; individuals lead discussions of what has been viewed in a film; small groups plan questions to pose to guest speakers and later interact with the speaker. Small groups visit installations and later report to the larger group concerning what was observed. Some teacher-directed presentations are essential, but the wise teacher involves students to the greatest extent possible and limits lecturing to essential knowledges. Simple games or simulations enable students to determine precisely what the capabilities of a computer are.

Those students involved in developing problem-solving abilities have a narrower range of activities, for they work individually or in teams on programmed materials on decision making and flowcharting and view films and filmstrips related to the construction of flowcharts. Either a teacher presentation or programmed materials would enable them to grasp BASIC in order that it may be applied for programming. Eventually, each student or team has multiple opportunities at the terminal, feeding in programs and data and receiving the results. More complex games and simulations may be used, particularly those which provide feedback which students can use in examining the consequences of actions taken.

Figure 13.7 presents a model of learning activities which might be used as students work toward the entry-level performance goal 3. The model presents multiple self-evaluation points for the student to use in selecting relevant learning activities. While the group would begin together by viewing a film on all types of punched-card equipment and their uses, each student would soon branch into those learning experiences needed. A teacher who prepares such a model and distributes it to students encourages students to pursue self-evaluation and also provides guides for students to follow in moving from activity to activity.

Figure 13.7 Learning activities for performance goal for entry-level employment

**Performance goal 3:** Given correctly punched deck of cards for an application such as payroll or sales analysis and access to punched-card equipment needed, **demonstrate** your ability to operate the sorter, collator, reproducer, and accounting machine by producing a printed report which is complete and accurate and accompanied by the decks of cards emerging from the processes.

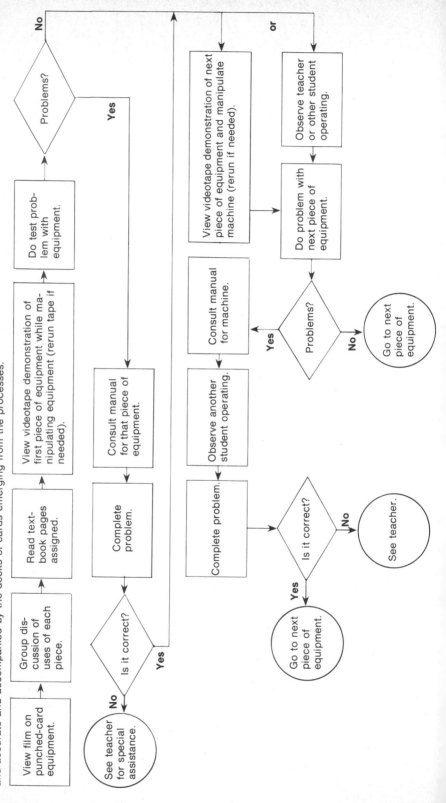

## Evaluating Performance of the Student and the System

Since the criterion is selected at the time the performance goal is constructed, the teacher is responsible for evaluating student performance against stated criteria. If the student achieves the goal, the system works for that student.

There is difficulty in grading students on the basis of goals attained. Guidelines in Chapter 8 direct the teacher in establishing equitable means of grading students according to the levels of goals attained. No matter what grading pattern is used, students should be informed of the grading procedures at the time they enter a course. Also, the grading plan should be defensible to both students and parents, school administrators, and admissions officers of two- and four-year colleges.

## Certification of Data Processing Workers

A trend today is for higher-level data processing employees to seek professional status by passing the Certification in Data Processing (CDP) Examination offered by the DPMA. The content of the examination is geared to the person who has substantial work experience in EDP and an educational background which qualifies him or her for leadership in this rapidly changing field. (See MacGowan and Henderson in Selected Readings at the end of this chapter.)

The American Federation of Information Processing Societies (AFIPS) recognizes the lack of criteria for accreditation of data processing workers and is planning proficiency examinations at multiple levels within data processing installations.

Teachers who meet the standards of the CDP are entitled to use the letters after their names. The distinguishing feature of a CDP is the professional recognition within the data processing field.

## College-Level Examination Program

The College Level Examination Program (CLEP) developed by the College Entrance Examination Board, Educational Testing Service, Princeton, New Jersey, and administered by many two- and four-year colleges, enables a person who possesses competencies in data processing gained through work experience to demonstrate them and thereby earn college credit. Two separate subject examinations are offered in data processing: Computers and Data Processing and Elementary Computer Programming; FORTRAN IV.

## Certification of Teachers

Although most states have their own requirements for certifying teachers of data processing, the Society of Data Educators (SDE) initiated the development of the Certified Data Educator (CDE) examination, and it is now offered by the Certification Councils. Successful completion of the examination and substantiating evidence regarding academic work and teaching proficiency entitle the teacher to the CDE diploma. The CDE provides a uniform standard for teachers of data processing, whereas certification requirements vary from state to state.

In addition to the CDE Basic Proficiency examination, applicants may either take an examination to demonstrate proficiency in programming or submit evidence of programming competencies.

CDE substitutes successful achievement on either the CDP examination or the CLEP Examination in Computers and Data Processing for its own examination.

## Learning Activities

1.  Arrange to visit two or three people who have been out of school several years and who have no formal training in data processing. Discuss with them the competencies suggested in this chapter for computer literacy and identify those you find most important. Report your findings to a small group and decide which computer literacy and problem-solving competencies you as a group recommend for all students regardless of vocational interests. (Performance goal 1)

2.  Divide into two groups and arrange to visit (1) a punched card equipment installation and (2) an electronic data processing installation. Using the competencies in this chapter, prepare for the visits. Duplicate lists of competencies so that they may be used during the industry visit. Validate the competencies within the two types of installations, making notes for later discussion. Return to your subgroup [(1) or (2)] and report your findings. Determine how the original list may be verified for your community and make revisions before duplicating and distributing to other members of your class. Establish a large group and, after reports from the small group, discuss the findings. (Performance goal 2)

3.  Arrange to visit as often as needed a class in data processing in a nearby school other than your own and collect information regarding the (a) goals toward which students work, (b) characteristics of students, (c) ways in which individual differences are met, (d) types of learning activities students engage in, (e) follow-up of students who are prepared for vocations in data processing. Return to your small group and report your findings, and then make a group report to the larger group, before discussing the findings of all of the groups. (Performance goal 3)

4.  Plan a strategy for identifying data processing equipment that is appropriate for classroom use and for gathering material on all types of instructional resources the students might use—books, pamphlets, transparencies, filmstrips, films, and simulations. The collection may be done by individuals or small groups. For the learning materials, provide each member of the class with a duplicated list of the item, its cost, and the source. (Performance goal 3)

**5.** Using the information collected in learning activity 3, divide into small groups and discuss (a) the positive aspects of the observations and (b) the negative aspects. What are the group's judgments on the meeting of individual needs, relevance of goals to students, learning activities students completed, and the follow-up conducted? Make your group report to the larger group and have an individual in the larger group summarize the group reports. (Performance goal 3)

**6.** Using the results of learning activities 1, 2, 3, 4, and 5, divide the large group into small groups. Within each small group select competencies with which you wish to work. Then proceed to (a) construct performance goals, (b) plan evaluations, (c) analyze and sequence subcompetencies, and (d) construct a teaching-learning strategy model utilizing the resources identified in learning activity 4. Transmit each subgroup's efforts to other members of the class and schedule a discussion following each group's presentation. Make modifications resulting from the group's reactions. (Performance goal 3)

**7.** Using the guidelines for demonstrations and developmental lessons, Chapters 7 and 12, divide into groups and construct criteria to evaluate presentations. Have your instructor respond to your sheets and make the necessary modifications so that they are usable. Duplicate them in quantity sufficient for each observer and each performer to use in Performance goal 4)

**8.** Work as a member of a team of four to identify a problem-solving goal appropriate for students you may teach. Once the goal is constructed, break into two groups of two students each and work separately: (a) Use the terminal or batch processing to construct an evaluation appropriate for the goal. Test-run it and make the necessary corrections until it runs error free. (b) Construct two learning activities using the terminal or batch processing to enable the student to achieve the goal. Test these until they run. Present your printouts of the evaluation and the two learning activities to the other team for evaluation. Which team's evaluation is most appropriate? Why? Which team's learning activities are better? Why? Can the students follow the instructions for the learning activities? (Performance goal 4)

## SELECTED READINGS

### Background

The first section of these readings is for the teacher who is uninitiated in data processing and who desires to build a background.

AWAD, ELIAS M., *Automatic Data Processing,* Prentice-Hall, Inc., Englewood Cliffs, N.J., 1973.

CASHMAN, THOMAS, AND WILLIAM KEYS, *Data Processing: A Text and Project Manual,* 2d ed., McGraw-Hill Book Company, New York, 1974.

DOCK, V. THOMAS, AND EDWARD ESSICK, *Principles of Business Data Processing*, 2d ed., Science Research Associates, Inc., Chicago, 1974.

FUORI, WILLIAM A., (1), *Introduction to American National Standard COBOL*, McGraw-Hill Book Company, New York, 1975.

————(2), *Introduction to Computer Operations*, McGraw-Hill Book Company, New York, 1973.

LA FAVE, LAWRENCE, GEORGE D. MILBRANDT, JR., AND DAVID W. GARTH, *Problem Solving: The Computer Approach*, McGraw-Hill Book Company, New York, 1973.

LAURIE, EDWARD J., *Modern Computer Concepts*, South-Western Publishing Company, Incorporated, Cincinnati, 1970.

SCHNAKE, M. A., *Data Processing Concepts*, McGraw-Hill Book Company, New York, 1973.

SILVER, GERALD A., AND JOAN B. SILVER (1), *Simplified Basic Programming*, McGraw-Hill Book Company, New York, 1974.

————(2), *Computer Algorithms and Flowcharting*, McGraw-Hill Book Company, New York, 1975.

WANOUS, S. J., E. E. WANOUS, AND GERALD E. WAGNER, *Introductory Data Processing*, South-Western Publishing Company, Inc., Cincinnati, 1973.

**Additional**

BOBCOCK, S. S., AND E. O. SCHILD, *Simulation Games in Learning*, Sage Publications, Beverly Hills, Calif., 1968.

BONARTI, ANTHONY M., "Report of a DP Justification Survey," *Journal of Data Education*, February, 1972, pp. 12–16.

BORCHER, SIDNEY D., AND JOHN W. JOYNER, *Business Data Processing Occupational Performance Survey*, The Center for Vocational and Technical Education, The Ohio State University, Columbus, March, 1973.

*Data Management*, January, 1972, p. 25.

FAIRBANKS, ROSWELL E., AND CHARLES P. PETITIJEAN (EDS.), *Processing Data in Business Education and Government*, The Eastern Business Teachers Association Yearbook, Somerset Press, Somerville, N.J., 1972.

FINGAR, PETER, JR., "The Use of APL in Modern Business Curriculum," *Business Education Forum*, October, 1972, pp. 64–67.

HURST, DELBERT B., "Knowledges and Skills Necessary for a Career in Electronic Data Processing," unpublished doctoral dissertation, Georgia State University, Atlanta, 1970.

Huntington Two, a federally funded project, Polytechnic Institute of Brooklyn 333 Jay Street, Brooklyn, N.Y.

"If Computers Can Learn to Talk Simple English—," *U.S. News & World Report*, June 24, 1974, pp. 86–87.

KLEINER, GENO, "Development of Specifications for a Low-Cost Computer System for Secondary Schools," Final Report, Stevens Institute of Technology, Hoboken, N.J., May, 1971, ED 061 768, 76 pages.

MACAULEY, THOMAS, *CAL/APL Computer Assisted Learning: A Programming Language* Author's Manual, Coast Community College District, Costa Mesa, Calif. 1971.

MACDOUGALL, JOHN M., "Current Trends in Self-Instruction for Data Processing Training," *Journal of Data Education*, October, 1973, pp. 18–25.

MACGOWAN, ROGER, AND REID HENDERSON, (EDS.), *CDP Review Manual: A Data Processing Handbook*, Auerbach, Philadelphia, 1972.

MCBRIEN, ROBERT J., "Simulation Games for Computer Concepts Instruction," *Journal of Data Education*, March, 1974, pp. 4–7.

MCNAIR, DOUGLAS, AND ALFRED WEST, "Development and Testing of a High School Business Game," Final Report, ED 040 606.

PETERSON, NORMAN D., "Literature Relating to Simulation," *Journal of Data Education*, May, 1973, pp. 4–12.

PHILLIPS, IRVING, "Business Machine and Computer Manufacturing Career Opportunities," *Occupational Outlook Quarterly*, Department of Labor, Bureau of Labor Statistics, Washington, Summer, 1971, pp. 14–19, 70.

"Recommendations Regarding Computers in High School Education," Conference Board of the Mathematical Sciences, April, 1972, Washington, D.C., ED 064 136.

SCHRAG, ADELE F., "Computer Terminals in the Classroom," *Business Education Forum*, February, 1972, pp. 48–49.

SKELTON, JOHN E., "Time Sharing versus Batch Processing and Teaching Beginning Computer Programming: An Experiment," *AEDS Journal*, June, 1972, pp. 103–110.

SPEEDIE, STUART, "Elements of Computer Careers," *AEDS Monitor*, November, 1973, pp. 14–15, 18.

SWANSON, A. K., "The Computer as a Tool of Instruction," *AEDS Journal*, Winter, 1973, pp. 56–64; Winter, 1974, pp. 92–96.

TIEDEMAN, DAVID V., "An Information System for Vocational Decisions (ISVD) Cultivating the Possibility for Career through Operation," Harvard University, Graduate School of Education, Cambridge, Mass., December, 1966, ED 062 655.

## PERFORMANCE GOALS

**1.** Given details on students in a typical business mathematics class (high school or two-year college), including reading levels of individuals, results of business mathematics pretests, occupational goals, and other relevant data and using this chapter and learning activities 1 and 2, analyze the data, group the students described, and for each group recommend minimum competencies and **defend** your recommendations in terms of material presented in Chapter 14 and in class discussions.

**2.** Selecting from those constructed for performance goal 1 one competency which is appropriate for performance on the job and using the material in this chapter and learning activities 3, 4, 5, 6, and 7, **construct** a performance goal, an evaluation, a model similar to Figure 14.3, and a model of learning activities to be employed for each subcompetency (see Figure 14.4). Evaluation will be based on all components of a performance goal, the appropriateness of the evaluation for the goal, the logical sequence of the subcompetencies, and the inclusion of multiple learning activities and self-evaluations to enable all students to achieve.

*Subcompetencies*

a. **Construct** an acceptable performance goal for a given competency.

b. Plan and **construct** an evaluation appropriate for measuring performance on a goal.

c. **Analyze** a performance goal for subcompetencies and arrange the subcompetencies in sequence to illustrate their relationships.

d. **Construct** a teaching strategy model, including learning activities, self-evaluations, and teacher evaluations which illustrate different paths a learner may take.

**3.** Using any subcompetency you designate, plan a short presentation of either a demonstration of a new concept in business mathematics or a drill to enable students to meet an en route goal, and **demonstrate** your ability to present it to a minigroup according to specific criteria you construct for your evaluators (observers) to employ. (See learning activity 8.) Videotaping equipment should be used whenever possible so that the performer, instructor, and peers may evaluate the performance as the tape is rerun. When videotaping equipment is not available, the lesson may be taped, and a minigroup may participate as students while two other people evaluate the presentation.

# CHAPTER 14

# Mathematics for Business

Most entry-level business positions require competencies in solving business mathematics problems and in operating computing equipment. In fact, preemployment tests frequently include items to measure an applicant's ability to solve business problems manually.

Great numbers of office workers engage in manual, mechanical, and electronic computations each day. The argument for the inclusion of business mathematics in the high school or two-year college programs is particularly sound in terms of reactions of business employers, who indicate that their employees lack the cognitive skills essential for performing simple computations. Some students need business mathematics; some do not. It is not a question of requiring all business students to take a separate course in business mathematics but of evaluating each student's computational abilities to determine specific goals that will enable each student to perform effectively on the job or as a consumer.

A basic question is, "How effective are business mathematics courses that are currently being taught?" Findings of research studies done over a span of 24 years (1945–1969) provide the disappointing answer that they are not effective enough. (Polishook; Gamble; Hantjis) The average student evaluated on Polishook's business applications test in 1945, 1965, and 1969 had only 5½ problems out of 10 correct.

Business mathematics is the application of the fundamental arithmetic processes to solving business problems. Since each business's demands for problem solving differ, no one set of goals can possibly meet every contingency the entry-level worker may meet. Therefore, the responsibility of the school is to provide the student with multiple business applications likely to be found in the majority of businesses. Moreover, no one set of goals can possibly meet the individual needs of all students. Such a subject as business mathematics, whether in a single course or integrated as part of an existing course, lends itself nobly to the learning systems approach, whereby each student works toward goals selected particularly for him or her.

## Needs of the Learner

Each citizen is confronted with understanding federal, state, and local tax structures, combating inflation, and determining costs of borrowing as interest rates fluctuate. Solving problems within these areas requires the individual to understand the problem, set it up, and compute the desired answer manually or with the assistance of mechanical devices.

Most business employees are required to compute amounts that provide data which management analyzes for decision making. The clerk whose tasks include auditing invoices engages in computations, as does the successful executive who plans for company expansion and intelligent investment of company capital.

A student's earlier mathematical education affects computational abilities. Until the new mathematics permeated grades 1 through 9, most students who entered business mathematics classes had spent at least two years in mathematics classes geared to sharpening their computational skills in solving general and consumer mathematics problems. All of that is changed, and students who have been exposed to the new mathematics handle algebraic and geometrical concepts long before entering a business mathematics class. Depending upon the program, students of new mathematics are involved in game theory, sets, and logic as well as in using the computer as a tool. Their mathematics learnings are geared largely to conceptual learnings with little emphasis on performing simple computations. These students are educated to question mathematical operations—why fractions are divided the way they are, what would happen if the denominators and numerators were added. Basically, they are taught to explore and analyze the theory of mathematics. Because of this emphasis, they are likely to be more agile in working with concepts but are frequently ill prepared to perform calculations encountered in business and consumer activities.

A study involving opinions of mathematics educators recommends the development of creative learning materials and the redesign of subject matter in mathematics toward needs of individuals preparing for multiple occupations. (*Wyoming* . . . , Selected Readings).

While the business student needs to be involved in solving business problems, the industrial student needs to solve mathematical problems related to production control or tension needed on some piece of equipment involved in manufacturing. Their needs are different.

In addition, students enter their educational programs with varying mathematical backgrounds as well as diverse levels of ability in performing the basic computations. Thus, any school must provide opportunities for students to be pretested as a means of determining their computational abilities and opportunities for them to apply computational skills to problems relevant to their occupational goals, whether these be office, distribution, trade and industrial, or health occupations. In fact, the basic question is whether there should be a vocational mathematics course or laboratory into which students planning for a variety of occupations may enter with the dual purpose of sharpening computational skills and applying these skills to problems they are likely to encounter on the job.

## Needs of Business

Although little research is available to guide the teacher in deciding what computational skills a business worker should have, one study identified both the mathematical processes and the business computations that are needed in five basic office occupational groups (Perkins, pp. 39, 91, 110, 128, 147, and 162). There is evidence that almost all office workers perform addition, subtraction, multiplication, and division. (See Figure 14.1.)

Smaller percentages of workers perform manipulations with decimals and fractions, and even fewer perform such specific computations as those involved in interest charges, dividends, etc. (See Figure 14.1.) No evidence is presented in Perkins's study regarding how the processes are performed—manually or mechanically. From the data, only a generalization can be made that to prepare future business workers, the school should provide training in the basic processes of arithmetic as well as on equipment.

The business teacher must be aware that even students who achieve specific goals in performing the mathematical processes lose substantial degrees of these cognitive skills over a period of nonuse. Thus, if students are to enter employment with computational skills, some type of refresher program is needed immediately prior to graduation, whether it be a formal course or application of the arithmetic processes in a simulated or real office situation. Detailed data on the kinds of computing equipment used by most businesses is scant. In fact, the most recent study on kinds of calculators used in business was conducted in 1968. Since that time the electronic calculator has literally revolutionized the market to the point where the rotary calculator, full-keyboard calculator, and the key-driven calculators are no longer manufactured. The electronic calculator with its miniaturized solid-state circuitry is the only computing equipment now available. By the time students of today enter business, they will probably use the electronic calculator exclusively. They are so low in price that many students in high schools and colleges now request their teachers' permission to bring them to class to use in both classwork and during tests. It is common to see students in accounting, finance, marketing, management, statistics, and other subjects use these calculators as tools.

Several sophisticated palm-sized calculators now available are preprogrammed to handle many separate business operations, each in split seconds.

Figure 14.1  Percentage of 663 respondents reporting mathematical tasks performed in offices

| Mathematical processes & business computation | All office workers | Secretarial & stenographic | Clerical | Bookkeeping & accounting | Business machine operators | Data processing |
|---|---|---|---|---|---|---|
| **Mathematical processes** | | | | | | |
| Add | 95 | 96 | 94 | 98 | 90 | 90 |
| Subtract | 93 | 94 | 89 | 97 | 90 | 90 |
| Multiply | 89 | 92 | 83 | 97 | 79 | 85 |
| Divide | 87 | 91 | 78 | 96 | 78 | 68 |
| Add long columns of figures | 81 | 82 | 75 | 92 | 76 | 75 |
| Use decimals | 77 | 80 | 65 | 92 | 72 | 65 |
| Use fractions | 68 | 69 | 56 | 86 | 72 | 41 |
| Convert fractions to decimals | 53 | 51 | 40 | 74 | 57 | 31 |
| Convert decimals to fractions | 47 | 45 | 32 | 70 | 57 | 21 |
| **Business computations** | | | | | | |
| Compute percentages | 46 | 43 | 31 | 69 | 42 | 35 |
| Compute sales tax | 37 | 27 | 29 | 66 | 39 | 26 |
| Compute trade and cash discount | 26 | — | — | 47 | 23 | — |
| Compute interest charges | 23 | — | — | 37 | 30 | — |
| Compute amount and percent of markup or loss | 16 | — | — | 24 | — | — |
| Compute insurance premiums | 12 | — | — | 22 | — | — |
| Compute property and/or income taxes | 11 | — | — | 23 | — | — |
| Work with reciprocals | 9 | — | — | 22 | — | — |
| Compute dividends | | | | | | |
| Compute foreign monies figures | 7 | — | — | — | — | — |
| Convert figures to metric system | 4 | — | — | — | — | — |

Source:  Edward A. Perkins et al., Clusters of Tasks Associated with Performance of Major Types of Office Work, Final Report, pp. 39, 91, 110, 128, 147, 162.

Selected operations include the following used in business:

1. Constant storage
2. Selective roundoff
3. Percentage calculation
4. Percent difference
5. Square foot
6. Powers (exponentiation)
7. Running total (summation)
8. Mean (arithmetic average)
9. Standard deviation
10. Number of days between two dates
11. Future date given number of days
12. Future value of an amount compounded
13. Present value of an amount compounded
14. Remaining principal on a mortgage
15. Accrued interest (360- and 365-day year)
16. Discounted notes (360- and 365-day year)

While the older types of calculators continue to be used in some offices, as equipment is replaced, the newer electronic calculators are purchased.

Such an illustration alerts the business teacher to the need for keeping abreast of technological developments affecting classroom instruction as well as to the accelerating rate of obsolescence of office machines purchased for classroom instruction.

## Identifying and Classifying Competencies

Analysis of the needs of business alerts the business teacher to gear instruction not only toward computational processes but also toward using emerging data in making decisions for business operations. Needless to say, the basic computational skills of addition, subtraction, multiplication, and division cannot be overestimated for any student who plans to enter business and move from entry-level to higher-level jobs.

Most business teachers and students encounter situations in which the student computes an incorrect percentage, although a glance should indicate that the answer is illogical. Too often the student is not even aware of the error. Frequently, this situation is a direct outcome of concentration upon the process rather than an understanding of the relationship of the data involved. Three principles involved in business mathematics follow:

1. Determine relationships among numbers.

    *Examples:*
    Does $5 + 10 = 10 + 5$?
    Does $6 \times 18 = 18 \times 6$?
    Is 15 $33\frac{1}{3}\%$ of 45?

2. Think inductively. Students make choices in the application of mathematical processes and apply them to a given situation. Because the process selected must yield the desired data, students must select the appropriate process and test it.

    *Example:*
    Workers A, B, and C each earn the same hourly rate and, during

the week of October 3, they each worked the same number of hours, yet their net pay differed.

A received $29 more than B

B received $16 less than C

C received $9 more than D

How much more (or less) did D receive than A?   B?

3. Think deductively. Students use data computed from which to draw conclusions.

*Example:*

Jason Keel is interested in purchasing a color television set. He found one for a down payment of $75 and monthly payments of $34.44 for one year. Another dealer offered him the identical set for a down payment of $50 and 18 monthly payments of $26.22. Was the rate of interest charged by these two dealers (*a*) the same or (*b*) more or less for one than the other?

Because problem solving is essential to deductive thinking, the teacher must be aware of the components of problem solving. Subcompetencies essential to problem solving include the following:

1. Read the material so that the thoughts can be explained accurately.
2. Follow vocabulary involving quantitative data so that the logical steps may be identified.
3. Discern relationships between parts of the problem in order to identify the computational steps involved.
4. Apply computational skills with accuracy.
5. Apply essential facts, rules, or formulas.
6. Set the problem up correctly for computation.
7. Interpret the answer in relation to the problem.

Students entering a business mathematics class or a business class in which business mathematics is an essential tool may or may not possess all of these basic competencies. Thus, the business teacher may be confronted by the task not only of developing the computational skills of the students but also the need to assist them in determining relationships among numbers, thinking inductively, and developing problem-solving competencies.

No research study has identified specific computational competencies needed by various business workers for successful performance on the job. Until such time as the precise competencies are available, the following, derived from multiple sources, serve as guides as to the typical competencies. While not all students can attain all of these competencies, the teacher anxious to prepare students for jobs may use selected competencies as the basis for planning.

1. Compute accurately: trade discounts; cash discounts; interest costs; investment return on capital; price-earnings ratio, turnover rates; bank discount rates. (Cognitive: application)

2. Compute accurately: taxes; payrolls; measurements using English measures; measurements using the metric system; mean, median, and mode. (Cognitive: application)

3. Analyze numbers from various forms and decide correctly which are to be used in computing correct information. (Cognitive: application)

4. Audit data and compute corrections. (Cognitive: application)

5. Follow verbal and written instructions. (Cognitive: application)

6. Use ten-key adding machine and electronic calculator to compute correctly. (Cognitive: application)

7. Convert numbers: decimal to binary, binary to octal, octal to binary. (Cognitive: application)

8. Use data computed to decide as to the lowest-cost items. (Cognitive: evaluation)

9. Explain verbally or in writing the answer to a problem so that its meaning may be understood by another person. (Cognitive: analysis)

10. Discriminate between logical and illogical answers and recompute answers which are illogical to logical ones. (Cognitive: evaluation)

11. Produce accurate work at all times. (Affective: high-level responding)

12. Tolerate routine work without exhibiting frustration or anger. (Affective: high-level responding)

13. Work well with others involved in same or related tasks. (Affective: high-level responding)

14. Interpret, extract, and report data revealed on line, bar, and circle graphs. (Cognitive: analysis and synthesis)

15. Use data in reports as a basis for constructing bar, line, or circle graphs to reveal relationships. (Cognitive: evaluation)

16. Compute metric and English measurements accurately. (Cognitive: application)

## Constructing Performance Goals

Once identified, these competencies and others a teacher may add form the basis for the next step of the learning system, that of constructing performance goals.

Careful analysis of the sixteen competencies reveals that on the job many are performed in combination with others. The teacher examines the list and selects those which measure a competency performed on the job. For example, the teacher may have several goals in mind for the end of the learning experiences, one of which is to compute by calculator many of the items in Competency 1 or 2. However, in business it is likely that the student will extract the data to be computed from reports or business forms (Competency 3), follow verbal and/or written instructions (Competency 5), and audit the data and compute corrections (Competency 4) until all are correct (Competency 11). Thus, the competency the teacher seeks is as follows: Manually compute trade and cash discounts, interest, and bank discount, using source documents, following the verbal or written instructions given, and audit work and correct errors. (Competencies 1, 3, 4, 5, 6, and 11.) (See Figure 14.2.)

The teacher simply asks, "Which of these competencies should be combined to evaluate in a situation similar to that found on the job?" Thus, the teacher provides for the integration of multiple behaviors.

Figure 14.2 reveals that the most appropriate evaluation is the product performance. The student produces a tangible product which may be evaluated.

Because the level of the dominant domain determines the verb selected, the teacher uses Figure 5.1 to guide in verb selection. The result of the performance was identified when the evaluation was planned. It is either a product or a controlled observation process. A parallel step is determining the conditions of performance. Some teachers believe that time should be a factor in the conditions. If so, the time limit is stipulated as a condition. (Any teacher may take the test, recording the time needed to complete it and double the time allowed the student.) Teachers more concerned with quality may omit a time constraint. Another major decision of conditions which must be stated is whether or not calculators will be used during performance.

The last decision involves how well the student must perform. Since business demands accuracy, particularly in this day of high-speed computer operations, a teacher cannot justify 70 percent accuracy on computations as the minimum. The error tolerance for performance goals must be in keeping with the demands of business; therefore, each criterion in Figure 14.2 is stated "with no uncorrected errors." Students moving through the learning system may be recycled until they attain that level, particularly if the atmosphere is conducive to student self-evaluations.

---

COMPETENCY
Compute trade and cash discounts, interest and discount on notes, and salesmen's commissions from source documents with electronic calculator; follow instructions; and audit until all work is correct (1, 3, 4, 5, 6, 10, 11).
PERFORMANCE GOAL
Given 20 business papers such as invoices, notes, memorandums on notes discounted, and sales reports and instructions for proceeding, **demonstrate** the ability to extract data from the business papers, compute with electronic calculator, follow instructions, and audit and correct all work according to instructions.

---

COMPETENCY
Compute with electronic calculator trade and cash discounts from source documents; follow verbal and written instructions; and audit until correct (1, 3, 5, 6, 10, 11).
PERFORMANCE GOAL
Given data on 20 employees and payroll forms, electronic calculator, and instructions, **demonstrate** the ability to use the correct data, compute with

electronic calculator, and follow instructions by having all work correct and according to instructions.

---

COMPETENCY
Convert numbers accurately: decimal to binary, binary to octal, octal to binary, and audit until correct (7, 4).
PERFORMANCE GOAL
Given 10 numbers in decimal, binary, and octal and instructions for conversion, **demonstrate** the ability to convert all numbers accurately and according to instructions.

---

COMPETENCY
Make decisions on data in terms of facts given; audit and correct errors (9).
PERFORMANCE GOAL
Given data on various costs from problems computed, an electronic calculator, and instructions, **defend** decision as to the best method according to criteria given.

---

COMPETENCY
Explain verbally to another the answer and its meaning so that it is understood (8).
PERFORMANCE GOAL
Given data already computed such as interest, discounts, payroll, or percentages and while being observed by teacher, **demonstrate** the ability to explain the precise meaning of the answer to another student with explanation correct and nothing omitted according to teacher's controlled observations.

---

COMPETENCY
Tolerate routine work without exhibiting signs of frustration or anger (12).
PERFORMANCE GOAL
While performing some repetitious tasks such as checking computations, adding, subtracting, multiplying, dividing, or making extensions on invoices, **demonstrate** the ability to work with no verbal outburst, no grumbling, and no wasting time during work period, during controlled observations.

---

COMPETENCY
Work well with others involved in same tasks without revealing resentment or irritation (13).
PERFORMANCE GOAL
While being observed performing assignment of business mathematics, **demonstrate** the ability to work with others without revealing frustration or resentment toward others.

---

COMPETENCY
Interpret, extract, and report correctly data on line, bar, and circle graphs (14).
PERFORMANCE GOAL
Given three graphs (line, bar, and circle) and specific instructions, **analyze** the data and prepare a simple statement for each graph, explaining precisely what the graph shows, with all data correctly reported and analyzed.

Figure 14.2 Competencies analyzed for components of performance goal

| Competency | Dominant domain & level | Result of performance | Verb | Conditions of performance | Criterion |
|---|---|---|---|---|---|
| Compute from source documents with electronic calculator for trade and cash discounts, interest and discount on notes, and salespeople's commissions; follow verbal and written instructions; and audit until correct (1, 3, 4, 5, 6, 10, 11).[a] | Cognitive: application | Product: invoices, etc., with amounts | **demonstrate** | Given 20 invoices, notes, and instructions and a ten-key adding-listing machine or electronic calculator. | No computation errors and instructions followed. |
| Compute with ten-key adding machine or electronic calculator for all payroll from source documents; follow instructions and audit all work until correct (2, 3, 5, 6, 11).[a] | Cognitive: application | Product: payroll register | **demonstrate** | Given 20 employees' payroll data and tax tables; given instructions and forms and using ten-key adding-listing or electronic calculator. | No computation errors and answers placed according to instructions. |
| Convert numbers accurately; decimal to binary, binary to octal, octal to binary, and audit until correct (7, 4).[a] | Cognitive: application | Product: answers to problems | **apply** | Given 10 numbers in decimal, binary, and octal; given instructions. | No errors and as instructions indicate. |
| Make decisions on data in terms of facts given; audit and correct errors (8).[a] | Cognitive: evaluation | Product: decision and defense in writing | **defend** | Given data already computed; given verbal instructions; using electronic calculator. | Defend in terms of instructions. |
| Explain verbally to another the answer and its meaning so that it is understood (9).[a] | Cognitive: analysis | Process: controlled observation | **demonstrate** | Given data already computed and instructions as to what should be explained to another; while being observed. | All explanations correct and nothing omitted according to teacher's controlled observation. |

[a]See pp. 339–340 for competencies referred to in parentheses.

Figure 14.2 (continued)

| Competency | Dominant domain & level | Result of performance | Verb | Conditions of performance | Criterion |
|---|---|---|---|---|---|
| Tolerate routine work without exhibiting signs of frustration or anger (12).[a] | Affective: high-level responding | Process: controlled observation | **demonstrate** | While performing some repetitious tasks such as checking computations or performing simple additions, subtractions, or multiplications and observed by teacher. | No verbal outburst, no grumbling, and no wasting of time. |
| Work well with others involved in same tasks without revealing resentment or irritation (13).[a] | Affective: high-level responding | Process: controlled observation | **demonstrate** | While being observed by teacher; while working with others in performing task. | Gives equal credit to other performer and displays no resentment or irritation. |
| Interpret, extract, and report correctly data on line, bar, and circle graphs (14).[a] | Cognitive: analysis | Product: report | **analyze** | Given a line graph with data plotted (same for bar and circle); instructions. | With all data reported accurately and analyzed. |
| Use data in reports to construct bar, line, or circle graphs to represent relationships (15).[a] | Cognitive: evaluation | Product: graph | **decide** | Given business reports such as earnings statements or sales figures; given graph paper and instructions to decide on type of graph and plot. | Data plotted on graph is correct and reveals what instructions requested. |
| Compute metric and English measures accurately (16).[a] | Cognitive: application | Product: recorded measurements | **demonstrate** | Given 15 measurements in English and metric systems and instructions. | Compute all measurements accurately and according to instructions. |

[a]See pp. 339–340 for competencies referred to in parentheses.

COMPETENCY

Use data in reports to construct bar, line, or circle graph to represent relationships (15).

PERFORMANCE GOAL

Given business reports on earnings and/or sales and instructions, **decide** on the appropriate graph and plot the data on the graph, labeling correctly so that it corresponds with instructions and is meaningful to reader.

COMPETENCY

Compute metric and English measurements accurately (16).

PERFORMANCE GOAL

Given 15 measures, some metric and some English and instructions, **apply** knowledge by computing each measurement accurately and as instructed.

## Identifying and Sequencing Subcompetencies

Before the teacher analyzes the performance goals for subcompetencies, it is essential to identify the *prerequisite* competencies needed to perform computations and work with business problems. These fall into three groups. The student must be able to first, use numbers; second, compute by adding, subtracting, multiplying, and dividing; and third, read and analyze word problems. A student who is unable to perform adequately in any of these three areas is not ready to tackle the performance goals set forth on pages 340–341, 344.

To assist the teacher in analyzing the subcompetencies in each of the three areas above, the subcompetencies are listed and each is converted into an en route goal which a student lacking the competency might work toward.

## Using Numbers

SUBCOMPETENCY

Comprehend similarities and differences.

EN ROUTE GOAL

Given five business forms—purchase requisitions, invoices, and/or statements and a copy of a machine tape on which all computations are listed, **match** the answers with each form, identifying all answers with the correct forms.

SUBCOMPETENCY

Differentiate between logical vs. illogical answers.

EN ROUTE GOAL

Given the answers for 20 problems of addition, subtraction, multiplication, and division, some of which are obviously illogical, **identify** all illogical answers correctly.

SUBCOMPETENCY
Describe the meaning of answers.
EN ROUTE GOAL
Given three interest problems and answers, **describe** in writing the meaning of each answer in terms of one effect on each business's financial condition: (1) the company paying interest and (2) the company receiving interest, with the effects described correctly.

## Computing

SUBCOMPETENCY
Add correctly whole numbers, decimals, fractions, and mixed numbers with like and unlike fractions.
EN ROUTE GOAL
Given 10 problems set up for computation comprised of four digits, six digits including decimals, like and unlike fractions, and mixed numbers, **compute** the problems and place the answers in the blocks indicated with no more than one arithmetic error.

SUBCOMPETENCY
Subtract correctly whole numbers, decimals, fractions, and mixed numbers with like and unlike fractions.
EN ROUTE GOAL
Given 10 problems set up for computation comprised of six digits including decimals, like and unlike fractions, and mixed numbers, **compute** the problems and place the answers in the blocks indicated with no arithmetic errors.

SUBCOMPETENCY
Multiply correctly whole numbers, decimals, fractions, and mixed numbers with like and unlike fractions.
EN ROUTE GOAL
Given 10 problems set up for computation comprised of six digits including decimals, like and unlike fractions, and mixed numbers, the student will **compute** the problems and place the answers in the blocks indicated with no arithmetic errors.

SUBCOMPETENCY
Divide correctly whole numbers, decimals, fractions, and mixed numbers with like and unlike fractions.
EN ROUTE GOAL
Given 10 problems set up for computation comprised of six digits including decimals, like and unlike fractions, and mixed numbers, **compute** the answers and place them in the blocks indicated with no arithmetic errors.

An en route goal may also have subcompetencies. For example, each of the en route goals in computing has subcompetencies which may be stated as follows: Add (subtract, multiply, or divide) (*a*) four-digit numbers,

Figure 14.3   Application-level performance goal sequenced according to subcompetencies

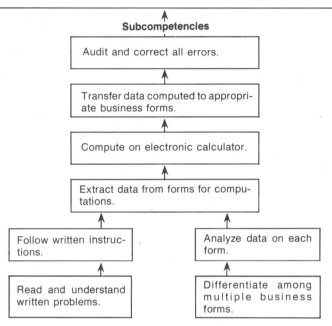

**Performance goal: application level**

Given 20 business papers such as invoices, notes, memorandums on notes discounted, sales reports, an electronic calculator and instructions, **demonstrate** the ability to extract data from the appropriate papers, compute, follow instructions, and audit all work so that it is correct and according to instructions.

Subcompetencies

Audit and correct all errors.

Transfer data computed to appropriate business forms.

Compute on electronic calculator.

Extract data from forms for computations.

Follow written instructions.

Analyze data on each form.

Read and understand written problems.

Differentiate among multiple business forms.

(*b*) six-digit numbers with decimals, (*c*) fractions (like and unlike), and (*d*) mixed numbers with like and unlike fractions.

## Identifying Subcompetencies of Performance Goals

It is important that the teacher know the precise behaviors needed to achieve a stated goal. The analysis of performance goals and their sequencing from simple to complex guide both student and teacher in building the subcompetencies needed for attainment of the goal. One performance goal selected for analysis of subcompetencies is illustrated in Figure 14.3. Eight different subcompetencies are directly related to the goal. A student who is unable to perform any one will not achieve the goal.

## Matching Each Learner With Performance Goals and Subcompetencies

Just as students entering any class have various levels of previous learning, so do those entering business mathematics. Some students have deficiencies in computing, in reading and understanding problems, and in following written or verbal instructions. The teacher who pretests each student to determine strengths and weaknesses is forestalling later problems. A pretest comprised of the three areas (1) using numbers, (2) computing, and (3) reading and analyzing word problems enables the teacher to pinpoint those who need remedial work before tackling business application computations. (Recycle to pp. 344–345.) In addition, the teacher may wish to test higher-level subcompetencies such as determining relationships among numbers and engaging in inductive and deductive thinking. (Recycle to pp. 337–338.) Teacher analysis of the pretest results identifies students who need to perfect subcompetencies before tackling business mathematics problems. Any subcompetency a student lacks then becomes an en route goal for that student. En route goals provide immediate attainable goals toward which the student works before confronting more complicated competencies.

After pretesting, the teacher is likely to find a minimum of three groups of students in the typical class. The first group will be those who achieved admirably on the pretest and are qualified to begin work on performance goals. The second group will probably need remedial work in several areas, and specific en route goals should be established for each of the lacking subcompetencies. The third and last group will likely have serious deficiencies to be overcome before they can proceed to performance goals. They, too, should be directed to en route goals to prepare them for success later.

Teachers who encourage students to select performance goals which are relevant and attainable to them usually establish a minimum which all students are expected to attain. For example, in addition to the subcompetencies required to progress to the performance goals, a teacher may decide that the first three goals on page 342 are required. Thus, the student who must spend time retooling on the subcompetencies required to progress to the performance goals must attain only three to achieve the minimum for business mathematics. Student decisions as to performance goals provide incentive to students, particularly those who have the ability and interest to strive toward higher-level goals. On the other hand, some students who lack motivation are satisfied to achieve at the minimum number required.

## Identifying and Applying Appropriate Learning Principles

The examples given in this chapter, of matching each learner with goals, reveals these principles at work:

Principle 1: Learner perceives the relevance of that which is to be learned.

Principle 2: Learning new behavior results from interaction with total environment.

Principle 3: Learning is facilitated when learner can associate past learning.

Principle 4: Learner is an active participant.
Principle 5: Learning is more effective when learner knows goal toward which he is striving.
Principle 6: Learner is aware of progress being made.

Because so much of computing is a cognitive skill, the principles of skill building also apply in some instances. Principle 8 (To make a response the learner must have behavior in repertoire) relates particularly to computations. The student who cannot perform the computations cannot relate mathematical abilities to business problems.

Principle 11 (Isolated practice on unmastered components may be preferable to practice on the final task) applies. A student who cannot compute simple interest problems needs to master the process before being asked to make decisions based on data resulting from the computations and comparison of various interest rates.

## Selecting and Implementing Teaching-Learning Strategies

Before the actual teaching of business mathematics may be planned, several questions must be analyzed and answered by school administrators and business teachers:

**Are business math goals to be met in a separate course, or should they be integrated into existing courses in mathematics, accounting, clerical practice, retailing, etc.?**

What are the basic organizational patterns a teacher is likely to encounter? In the two-year college, high school, and vocational-technical school, the teacher may be asked to teach a separate business mathematics class to students in the ninth grade or above. Or, all students may be required to take a general mathematics or algebra course which includes some business mathematics. In many high schools no general or business mathematics course is offered, and the teachers of accounting, distribution, consumer economics, and office practice may find that some of their students do not possess the basic computational skills needed for the particular subject; thus, each teacher becomes a teacher of business mathematics. Eirich compared the business mathematics achievement of students from three different mathematics courses and found that those who had taken the business mathematics course rather than the general mathematics or algebra achieved higher scores on the posttest. While these findings argue in favor of a separate course, Polishook found that student achievement on a business mathematics test was about the same for those who had taken a separate business mathematics course as for those whose business mathematics was integrated into general business. Also, neither group revealed mastery of business mathematics.

Obviously there is no one answer, for student needs differ. Some students who lack the prerequisite subcompetencies and need additional practice in computational skills may benefit greatly from a separate course. Other students who need quick review and retooling may progress best by applying the mathematics in a class in accounting, data processing, or retailing.

When a separate course is offered, grade placement makes little difference in student achievement. Gamble compared achievement in business mathematics for students in the ninth, tenth, eleventh, and twelfth grades and found the greatest increase in the ninth grade and overall achievement poor for all groups.

Because students tend to forget how to interpret and compute business problems during periods of nonuse, many schools provide a means of retraining graduating seniors. Before students are exposed to employment aptitude tests involving logical decisions based on mathematics and general computations, some schools offer minicourses. Other schools establish open laboratories for student testing and upgrading, and still other schools place students in simulated or actual work situations in which they apply their mathematical abilities. The important thing is for schools to provide students who need to retrain with the opportunity to do so before applying for jobs which require applications of business mathematics.

## Large-Group, Small-Group, or Individualized Instruction

After pretesting, the group may be subdivided according to their levels of achievement. Whether the teacher has pretested students in a business mathematics class or in another class—accounting, general business, etc.—the varying levels of mathematical learning are likely to occur.

Large-group instruction in business mathematics may not be feasible, but small-group instruction may be highly productive. Generally, large-group instruction neglects the needs of students at the two extremes of the continuum—those who need much remedial work and those who are capable of solving higher-level problems.

Instruction may take the form of individually prescribed instruction for the few students who are highly competent and wish to proceed alone. The teacher has a responsibility to these students to provide not only the basic computational skills for job entry but opportunities to engage in decision making.

Teachers who have employed individually paced instruction and left students to work completely alone report mixed results. Generally, those students who are unmotivated and conscious of their own computational inadequacies need considerably more teacher direction and attention than individually paced instruction alone permits. Some individually paced instruction punctuated with teacher-directed small-group instruction usually produces results for students who do not work well alone.

Another type of class organization is emerging, particularly in the vocational-technical schools. All vocational students—health, distributive, automotive, small-appliance repair, office, etc.—are scheduled for one mathematics class. Students who need special instruction to achieve the subcompetencies needed before applying their mathematics to problems in their field may be taught as a group. Once the goals of students involve applications in their special area, small groups are formed. The instructor's role is to develop instructional materials for each occupational group and move from group to group helping students as needed.

## Teachers of Mathematics for Business

No single preparation equips a teacher to teach mathematics for business. Ideally, the decision of who is to teach is dependent upon interest in mathematical applications as well as on the teacher's competencies in mathematics. Generally, the beginning teacher is assigned to the business mathematics course. This teacher may be a business teacher or a mathematics teacher, and some schools even employ a team approach, using the two teachers (business and mathematics) to develop the course and each to teach the part in which special competency is shown. Whether a single business or mathematics teacher or several teachers teach business mathematics or whether business mathematics is integrated into existing business courses, a coordinated planning effort is essential. Not only should the teacher or teachers of a separate course be involved, but so should all teachers who teach subjects in which business mathematics is applied. Only through concentrated team effort can the course be planned to meet relevant goals effectively.

## Use of Calculators

While the effect of using calculators to enhance learning has been investigated, there is a paucity of evidence to guide the teacher. Two studies strengthen the beliefs of many teachers as to the positive effects of calculators on student achievement in business mathematics. Page studied the gains in student achievement between two groups, those who used the calculators as tools in solving business problems and those who studied business mathematics and calculators as separate entities. Students who used the calculators as tools achieved greater gains in computational activities. Haga's work concentrated upon students' performances on decimals, fractions, and percentages, three essential components of business mathematics. After pretesting 500 students, Haga selected 123 whose scores in computational skills were exceedingly low and placed these students in classes where they used electronic calculators as tools in solving problems involving decimals, fractions, and percentages. Students who lacked skill in handling these mathematics components improved their skills perceptibly and solved problems rapidly. Office workers do use computing equipment as tools, and these two studies support the thesis or contention that realistic use of equipment by students solving mathematical problems in business classes may affect student achievement positively. Also it may enable students to develop the competencies needed for employment.

The philosophies of teachers and administrators responsible for establishing goals for business mathematics determine to what extent equipment is available for use. Certainly the availability of funds for equipment is a major factor in the decision; however, when the evidence is presented forcefully, funds frequently are forthcoming. Once a decision is made to provide computational equipment, the teacher is likely to require students to demonstrate manual mathematical competencies prior to giving them access to the equipment. Increasing numbers of teachers believe, however, that the calculators are a motivating force and should be used simultaneously with the development of manual computational competencies. Electronic calculators lend a more exciting and professional aura to business mathematics in high schools and two-year colleges. Also, they offer promise of greater student achievement in both computational and analytical competencies. Ideally, one calculator should be available for each student.

## Learning Activities

Some teachers of business mathematics tend to think they must explain a concept at the chalkboard, while other teachers who seek to involve students recognize that teacher explanations tend to stifle student involvement. The multiple learning activities available to today's business mathematics teacher produce a different learning environment than that of the teacher who had to rely only on the textbook and chalkboard. Many resources may be combined to involve a student in multiple learning activities using textbooks, workbooks, transparencies, modules, filmstrips, cassettes, programmed materials, simulations, calculators, and the computer.

**TEXTBOOKS AND WORKBOOKS.** Textbooks are available for every level of student learning and are supplemented by workbooks as well as transparencies, cassettes, and filmstrips.

Textbook authors anticipate that the teacher will employ the content effectively for each student, so they include all related topics in the hope that the teacher will select specific content and problems applicable to each student working toward a stated goal.

Teachers use textbooks differently, but a growing trend is use of the textbook as one source of learning activities and combining it with others which involve activities in addition to reading and drills.

**MODULES.** Modules or learning packets are rapidly appearing in many business mathematics classes. They may be as simple as instruction sheets accompanying textbooks or as sophisticated as synchronized tape and filmstrip presentations which the student listens to and watches. Regardless of their simplicity, they enable each student to engage in learning activities to meet an immediate and relevant goal or subcompetency.

There is a decided trend toward teachers creating their own modules for business mathematics students. Such teachers rely heavily on the textbook and supply each student with (1) instruction sheets, (2) a textbook, (3) self-evaluations, and (4) answers to the self-evaluations. Students may use the materials while working alone or in small groups. Some teachers who have created their own modules are delighted with results; others are disappointed. Much depends upon the quality of the instructional materials created by the teacher, the appropriateness of the textbook for the student's reading level, and the motivation of the student using the materials.

PROGRAMMED MATERIALS.    Multiple research evidence shows that programmed instructional materials enable students of business mathematics to achieve more in less time. Huffman and Myers both confirm these facts. Greatsinger's experimental group, using programmed materials to learn fractions, progressed much faster than those who used the conventional textbook and teacher-directed activities. The promise of programmed materials becomes even more attractive when the Jenkins's study is examined, for such materials were especially effective in sharpening computational skills and developing problem-solving abilities among educable mentally handicapped students. Such findings offer hope that the slower student may benefit from programmed instructional materials provided they are written at a level which can be read and understood.

As with modules, the effectiveness of programmed materials varies with the reading level of the student, the reading level of the materials, the quality of the program, and the availability of other learning activities to a student who does not learn from programmed materials. They are not a panacea for all ills in the business mathematics class. Each business teacher will want to identify various programmed materials and employ those which are appropriate for remedial instruction, enrichment, or simply as a change of pace, and to select those appropriate for students.

COMPUTERS.    The computer offers multiple learning activities for students in using mathematics for business problems. First, computer-assisted instruction has proved effective in drilling lower-grade students in the fundamental processes and can be used as a learning activity for students who must develop computational and conceptual subcompetencies before tackling business problems. Programmed Logic for Automated Teaching Operation (PLATO, University of Illinois, Urbana, Illinois) includes segments on arithmetic drills which may be employed by the business teacher with access to terminals. PLATO utilizes slides as well as an electronic chalkboard in presenting concepts by means of a television screen. Second, the computer may be used as a tool in decision making. Students develop habits of logical thinking as they solve mathematical problems at the terminal. Once the teacher locates a terminal and verifies that it handles a simple language students can learn quickly (BASIC, for example; see Chapter 13, pp. 321, 322), construction of problems is relatively easy. Students must identify the steps to be performed by the computer and enter them into the computer in a language acceptable to the computer. The output is the computer program and the answers; thus, the student receives immediate feedback and knows whether the problem answer is correct or incorrect. Moreover, the computer identifies the precise point at which the error occurs so that the student may correct the error and complete the problem correctly.

More sophisticated problems are possible, depending upon how deeply the teacher wishes to become involved in using BASIC. Its relative simplicity makes it so easy to learn and use that most students respond enthusiastically.

What are the benefits of using the computer? First, the student recognizes that the computer does only that which it is programmed to do; a mistake in the program results in errors in output. Second, the computer is a natural tool for involving students in experiences which develop critical thinking abilities. Third, the computer is a powerful motivating device for slower students who have difficulties mastering a basic computational process as well as for the more able student capable of creating original problems and solving them.

**DRILLS.** Drills play a major role in learning business mathematics concepts. Although some students need daily drills, others need only occasional ones. The chief purpose of drills is for the student to apply that which has just been read or presented. Drills may be oral or written. Oral drills may originate with the teacher, a cassette, flash cards, or a tachistoscope (filmstrip projector which controls the speed at which the filmstrip moves); written drills may be in the form of quizzes from duplicated sheets or transparencies.

Four principles guide the teacher in selecting material for drills:

1.  The only meaningful drill is practice on some element not mastered; thus, all drill work must provide for individual differences. It is not likely that an entire class will benefit from the same drill.
2.  Each student must be aware of the purpose of the skill he or she is striving to attain so that practice is relevant.
3.  Short, intensive drills are more meaningful; for once the work becomes routine, the student may no longer concentrate on it.
4.  Because the student needs to know if he or she is correct, answers to practice problems should be made available so that each student may self-check his or her work.

Regardless of the sources of oral drills, they are usually conducted with small groups or an individual. If several students have need for the same drill, oral group response may strengthen a student's confidence. After a few minutes it is essential for the teacher to identify students who are not responding correctly. This may be done by close observation or by calling on individuals to respond orally.

The tachistoscope has the advantage of pacing student responses, for the teacher can set the instrument to control the speed at slightly above that of the student responses in order to elicit faster responses. Oravetz experimented with the tachistoscope by contrasting achievement gains on a test of one group using the tachistoscope and another whose audio-oral drills were presented by the teacher. Although both types of drills were effective in increasing achievement, the group using the tachistoscope increased their scores more than the teacher-led group. Also, such differences in achievement were retained six weeks after the experiment ended.

Written drills are offered in the form of short quizzes which some teachers give regularly. The purpose of a quiz is to ascertain whether the student has mastered a given process or concept, so it is not graded. After the written quiz, some teachers flash a transparency containing the answers onto the screen and either have students check their own answers or check each other's. Or, some teachers prefer supplying students with duplicated answer sheets to be used in the same way.

Regardless of whether the drill is oral or written, the teacher uses the results as the basis for diagnosing individual needs. Some students may have performed satisfactorily; others may not. Those who do not succeed on drills are directed to additional learning activities; those who are successful then go to the next appropriate goal or subcompetency.

SIMULATIONS. Many commercially prepared simulations are available to use in placing students in situations where they are forced to make decisions as to various business matters and, in the process, to use business mathematics. These experiences are particularly valuable for students who have demonstrated computational abilities and show readiness for more challenging experiences involving analysis and decision making (evaluation).

One simple simulation is frequently used as a capstone experience in applying mathematics to business forms. A student may listen to a tape or read instructions which state the individual's responsiblities in an accounting department of the XYZ Company and that any invoices received marked "Okay for payment" are to be paid within the discount period and the discount taken. Oral or written instructions inform the student what is to be done with the invoice once the check is written for the employer's signature. A student must analyze the data on each form, select that which applies, make decisions, compute the data, and follow the stated instructions.

PLANNING FOR COMBINATIONS OF LEARNING ACTIVITIES. Figure 14.4 illustrates how a teacher plans to combine various learning activities to enable a student to achieve a performance goal. When analyzed, the performance goal in the figure involves at least three subcompetencies:

1. Differentiate among multiple business forms, extract correct data, and compute accurately.
2. Determine dates for discounting notes and compute net proceeds correctly.
3. Analyze data from sales reports and compute correctly.

The teacher using the model is providing for individual needs. For example, Student A is pretested and needs all three subcompetencies. Student A may work in a small group or alone and sees the film, reads the text, does the problems, and is successful on the self-evaluation for Subcompetency 1. At that point Student A moves to Subcompetency 2. Student B performs so well on the pretest that he or she is scheduled for Subcompetency 3 initially. That student proceeds through the learning activities for 3 and if successful on the self-evaluation, takes the posttest on the goal.

A student who performs unsatisfactorily on the self-evaluations for

Figure 14.4 Learning activity combinations

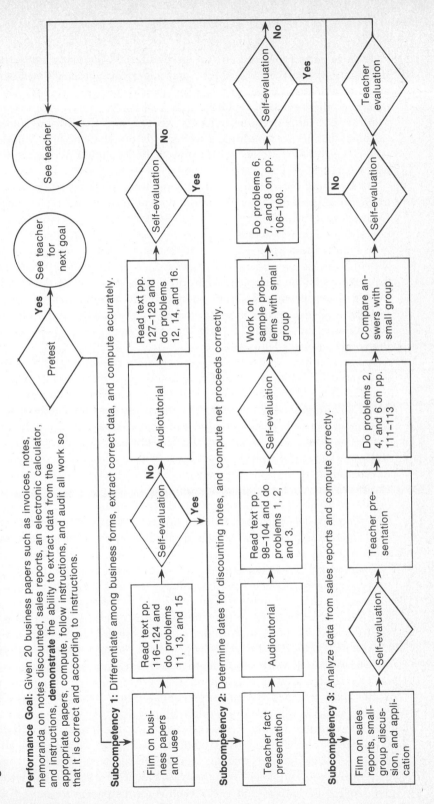

**Performance Goal:** Given 20 business papers such as invoices, notes, memoranda on notes discounted, sales reports, an electronic calculator, and instructions, **demonstrate** the ability to extract data from the appropriate papers, compute, follow instructions, and audit all work so that it is correct and according to instructions.

**Subcompetency 1:** Differentiate among business forms, extract correct data, and compute accurately.

**Subcompetency 2:** Determine dates for discounting notes, and compute net proceeds correctly.

**Subcompetency 3:** Analyze data from sales reports and compute correctly.

Subcompetency 1 proceeds to the audiotutorial (filmstrip and cassette presentation), does the text problems, and engages in another self-evaluation on 1. If still unsuccessful, the student goes to the teacher. The teacher diagnoses the student's problems and either prescribes other learning activities or assumes responsibility for working directly with the student.

Some students need multiple learning activities; some do not. A student who succeeds after one or two learning activities should not be required to use another.

What should the teacher do if students from all three groups require attention at the same time? Of course, this can be a problem, particularly for the teacher who is inexperienced in working with the groups simultaneously. Sometimes teachers involve better students in helping with Group 2 or 3 until the teacher can meet with them. Teachers who utilize this system find that as students and teacher gain experience, problems that arise are minor and a teacher can move from group to group quickly. Such a system presupposes that the models and accompanying materials selected from the textbook and prepared by the teacher are easily read and followed by students. Should the instructional resources be poorly prepared, problems will result.

Another problem which discourages teachers from adopting such a system is the need for building a file of model and supplementary instructional materials. Happily some school systems pay teachers for work on curriculum materials during the summer months, and any teacher who plans to employ this model approach should propose lead time with pay in order to prepare usable materials. Also, many colleges and universities offer independent study courses for credit, and the teacher who wants to develop supplementary materials may do so under the supervision of a qualified person who will check the materials for validity and ease of use. Unless a teacher has prepared usable materials to give to students working in groups, the best approach is to spend part of each period teaching each group before having them do drills by themselves. Even then, duplicated sheets are needed to save time in giving assignments.

HOMEWORK. To be meaningful to the student, homework must be planned as a carefully structured sequence of activities. Basically, homework in business mathematics has two purposes: to provide (1) drills on concepts which have been learned so that the student may strengthen learning to retain it and (2) opportunities for self-diagnosis by the student whose homework relates directly to his or her needs.

Generally, homework assignments to an entire class are meaningless to many students, and for that reason alone some students simply do not do the work assigned. When assignments are individualized to provide drills to students who need the additional practice, they may be analyzed the following day in any of several ways. First, the teacher may flash a transparency on the screen so that students check their own answers against the correct ones; second, students working on the same assignment may exchange papers and check each other's work for accuracy; third, the teacher may collect the papers and check each student's papers to analyze the kinds of errors made. Regardless of which of the three methods is employed, the main purpose is to diagnose each student's learning problems and prescribe remedial learning and/or practice to reinforce that which has been learned.

Each student has the responsibility for his or her own learning through self-checking and self-diagnosis of homework. It is imperative that a student doing homework in business mathematics have some direct access to correct answers as soon after the homework is completed as possible.

Generally students do homework they perceive to be of value. Therefore, since a few carefully selected homework problems can benefit students, the teacher should limit the number in each assignment. By keeping the assignment short and individualizing it according to student needs, the teacher may motivate the student to complete the assignment. Of course, homework on a new concept or principle should be assigned only after the student has had opportunities to apply the principle under the teacher's observation. Few gains result if a student flounders through an especially difficult assignment with no knowledge of how to proceed.

No teacher should worry about copying of homework assignments, for the student who does so will probably not be able to solve the problems on an evaluation. There is much to be gained when students work together to prepare homework, for the session may be one of learning rather than copying.

## Ideas to Motivate Students

A new world of mathematics can be opened to students by involving them in problem-solving situations in which they use mathematics as a tool. While the primary purpose of business mathematics is to solve problems likely to be found in business, some students may be motivated by applications closer to their life experiences. Teachers who have worked with students who are educationally or economically disadvantaged have found that the structures of drills (oral and written) do not always motivate students sufficiently. Efforts to find challenging experiences for these students have frequently resulted in projects students engage in without being conscious that their adventures will develop their mathematical skills, their skills in using numbers, or even decision-making abilities.

SHOPPING EXPEDITION. Students construct their own shopping lists and select the stores in which the items will be priced. With guidance from the teacher, the students may engage in comparison shopping to identify stores which charge lower prices and to determine on which day food prices are lower, and they may compare unit prices on multiple sizes of the same item.

A TRAFFIC SURVEY. At stipulated intersections, count the cars going in specific directions. This may be combined with timing traffic lights in order to determine how long the green light is on and how many cars may go west, east, etc., during one light.

EFFICIENCY OF CARS. Analyze two or three cars one would like to purchase someday. Students in one class brought in pictures of cars they would like to own and then began gathering data to determine the prices of the cars, the mileage per gallon of gasoline, data from test runs, costs of financing, insurance costs, and cost of operation. Research as well as mathematics is involved, and students engage in competition to prove that one car is superior to another.

COMPARISON OF BORROWING COSTS. Compare borrowing costs at banks versus loan companies. Students collect data on rates and then compute the rates to determine the actual dollar costs to the borrower. They then make decisions based on whether they should make a purchase if borrowing is necessary.

ANALYZE RENTED VERSUS OWNED LIVING QUARTERS. Students capable of tackling aspects of this problem involve themselves in critical analyses of newspaper advertisements for homes and study neighborhoods in terms of transportation facilities, commercial properties, schools, etc., and mortgage costs.

STUDY CAREER OPPORTUNITIES. One teacher found that the study of occupations and the average annual earnings of jobs within the occupational field enables students to project lifetime earnings for one job as compared to another.

ANALYZE PRODUCTION COSTS. Students might analyze the costs of producing an item that they find interesting. This would involve the learning of mark on, transportation costs, percentage of profit, and other costs passed on to the consumer.

CALCULATE AN ENTRY-LEVEL WAGE EARNER'S INCOME. Use gross income and compute withholding taxes, state and local taxes, and prepare a simple form for income tax returns.

While application of the mathematical skills to business problems is the major goal in business mathematics, the student who needs special motivation to remedy mathematical deficiencies may respond more positively to projects designed to capture interest than he or she will to remedial drills. Once the teacher knows the students and what "turns them off," activities may be designed to "turn them on."

## Evaluating the Student and the System

Student achievement in business mathematics can be determined by comparing the pretest and posttest scores of an individual. Contents of the test depend upon what the school and its business teachers view as the business mathematics competencies a student should exhibit.

The use of self-evaluations is illustrated in Figure 14.4. Students have multiple opportunities to evaluate their own progress toward the goal before submitting themselves to teacher evaluation of the goal. Evaluation is a daily activity in any business mathematics class or laboratory. A teacher who elects not to use models to guide groups must still provide multiple opportunities for students to engage in introspective self-evaluation. Many students tend to overestimate their learnings in mathematics; unless they are encouraged by the teacher to test themselves critically, they will attempt the final evaluations before they can meet the goal.

A self-evaluation is never used for grading. It enables both student and teacher to judge an individual's readiness for the formal evaluation on a specified goal.

Because of the tremendous pressure to meet individual needs, virtually all instruction in business mathematics is criterion-referenced. Only one strong argument can be found for norm-referenced evaluations. Because of the research findings and criticisms that students who take business mathematics do not achieve at sufficiently high levels, use of a test which measures those business competencies demanded on the job and has norms against which to compare students emerging from business mathematics programs can provide evidence of a teacher's success. The results of the test are completely unrelated to grades but alert the teacher as to how his or her students compare with those taught by other teachers.

Because tests of competencies reveal what a student is capable of doing, the ideal procedure is to issue to each student a printout of those competencies attained. (Recycle to Chapter 8, pp. 158.) In a system where a "pass" or "no pass" is used, no further grading is necessary.

In schools where grades are required, the business mathematics teacher should work with other teachers of the same subject to develop a grading system to accompany adopted performance goals and then share the system with the students. Each student then knows from the beginning of the year how he or she will be evaluated and graded. For example an "A" may require two goals at the analysis level.

A profile for each student's attainments on various competencies or subcompetencies (see Figure 14.5) enables both students and parents to examine the precise accomplishments of a given student.

The system may be evaluated by the numbers of students who achieve the minimum performance goals. While each teacher may view the number of goals required differently, some consensus must be achieved by two or more teachers in a school if their students are to be compared prior to their job entry. Evaluation of the components of the system is made each time a student was tested on a given performance goal; thus, the teacher has multiple opportunities to evaluate the effectiveness of the learning activities as student after student utilizes them and meets with success or failure. Failure reveals to the teacher that something is wrong in the system for that student not achieving and the feedback should result in modifications within the system.

## Learning Activities

1. Arrange to visit a business office and observe two clerical workers who perform computations as part of their jobs. Identify the computational tasks performed, the conditions under which performed (with equipment or without), and how often they perform these computations in the course of the average work day. Select what you believe to be the three most important competencies and prepare to discuss them with members of your

Figure 14.5 A profile of business mathematics competencies and level of accuracy achieved

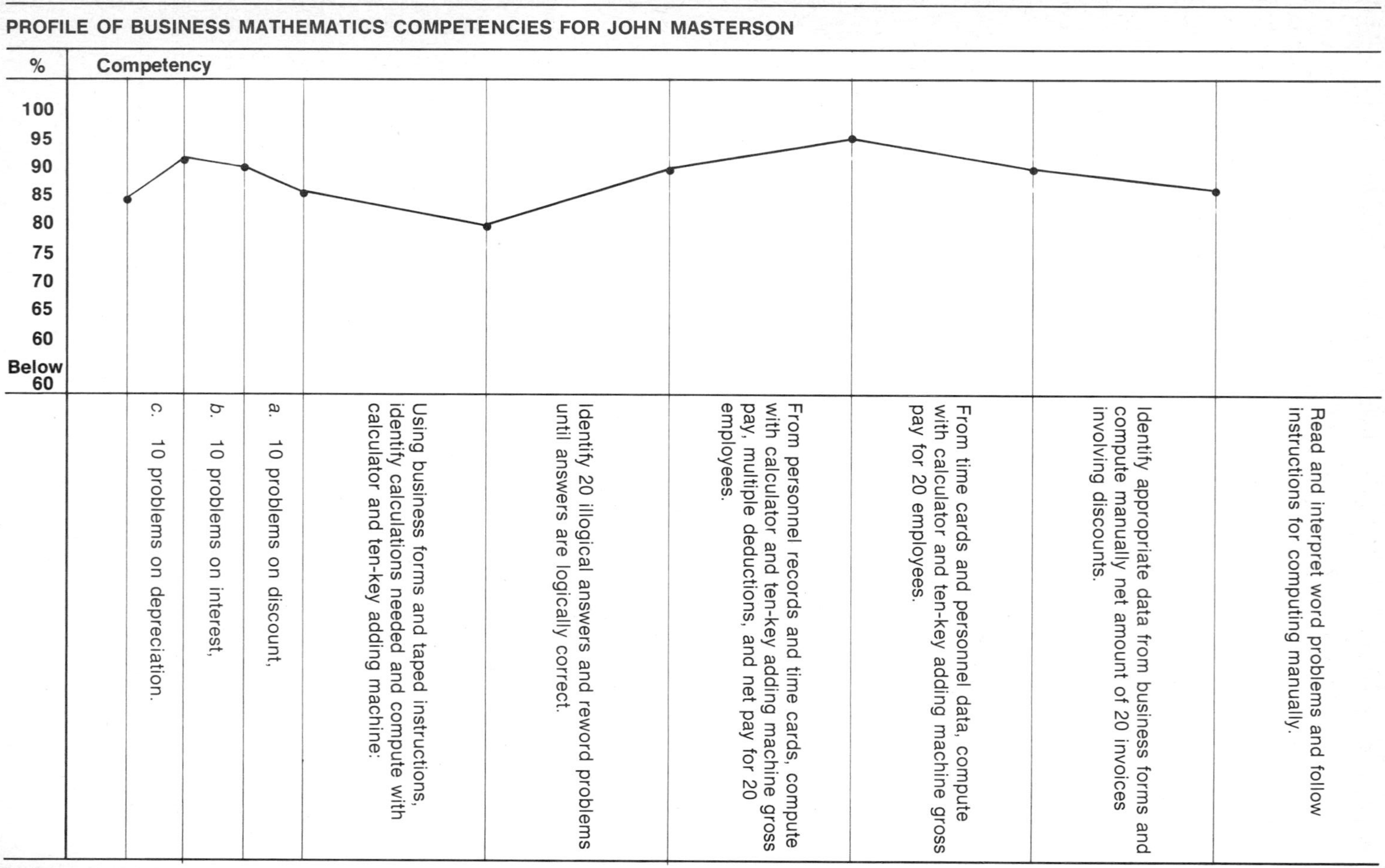

PROFILE OF BUSINESS MATHEMATICS COMPETENCIES FOR JOHN MASTERSON

| % | Competency |
|---|---|
| 100 | Read and interpret word problems and follow instructions for computing manually. |
| 95 | Identify appropriate data from business forms and compute manually net amount of 20 invoices involving discounts. |
| 90 | From time cards and personnel data, compute with calculator and ten-key adding machine gross pay for 20 employees. |
| 85 | From personnel records and time cards, compute with calculator and ten-key adding machine gross pay, multiple deductions, and net pay for 20 employees. |
| 80 | Identify 20 illogical answers and reword problems until answers are logically correct. |
| 75 | Using business forms and taped instructions, identify calculations needed and compute with calculator and ten-key adding machine: |
| 70 | a. 10 problems on discount, |
| 65 | b. 10 problems on interest, |
| 60 | c. 10 problems on depreciation. |
| Below 60 | |

group in class. From the various reports by class members, what conclusions can be drawn about computational competencies needed for entry-level office workers? Working with your group, construct a list of competencies you agree upon as those likely to consume the greatest proportion of time of the clerk engaged in computations. (Performance goal 1)

**2.** Assume that the competencies your class members identified in learning activity 1 are representative of the community. Work in subgroups of two or three to construct performance goals you believe would measure the attainment of these competencies, duplicate your goals, and distribute them for discussion in your class. From all of the subgroups reporting, select those goals which seem most desirable in terms of the competencies needed as identified in learning activity 1 and duplicate them so that each class member has a copy. (Performance goal 1)

**3.** Select one performance goal constructed for learning activity 2 and analyze it for subcompetencies, preparing a model similar to Figure 14.3. Present the model to your subgroup for discussion and revise any part as needed. (Performance goal 2)

**4.** Arrange three or four visits to a business mathematics class or a class in which business mathematics is being taught as a part of accounting, clerical practice, or some other related subject. Before your visits, work with your group to construct an observation sheet to collect data for class discussion on:

    a.  Instruction employed—large- or small-group, individualized, or a combination.

    b.  Diverse goals for students of varying abilities in mathematics.

    c.  Strategies used—programmed materials, teacher demonstrations, packets, or other.

    d.  Types of homework and purpose of homework as well as its disposition.

    e.  Use of computing equipment as well as teacher's philosophy on equipment.

    f.  Kinds of drills employed.

    g.  Types of evaluations—student self-evaluations and teacher evaluations.

    h.  Grading system. (Performance goal 2)

**5.** For one performance goal from learning activity 3, construct an evaluation which is appropriate as a pretest and posttest for the goal and test it to determine that it does measure the performance sought. Make any modifications necessary and submit it for evaluation to two peers. (Performance goal 2)

**6.** Compile an up-to-date annotated list of instructional materials you may use to teach business mathematics, including the many kinds discussed in the chapter, by consulting sources identified by your instructor, publishers' catalogs, professional magazines, and ERIC (Recycle to Chapter 7, pp. 145–146.) Compile and duplicate the final list for distribution to each member of your entire group, including the kind of item (filmstrip, module, etc.) with date it was released or published, source with address, approximate cost, and a brief description (annotation). (Performance goal 2)

**7.** Using the performance goal selected for learning activity 5 and Figure 14.4 as a guide, construct a teaching strategy model illustrating the use of multiple learning activities and self-evaluations as well as diverse paths to meet student needs. (Performance goal 2)

**8.** Visit a local school and offer your tutorial services for one or two business mathematics students or students whose business mathematics needs improving for another subject such as accounting. Teach the students by either (*a*) a demonstration of a method of solving a problem or (*b*) a drill on a particular concept. Tape or videotape the presentation and submit it to a small group of your peers for evaluation in terms of the following:

    a   Was the presentation or drill appropriate for the goal sought by the students? Why or why not?

    b.  Did the presentation or drill assist the students in learning? How or how not?

    c.  Were the students given an opportunity to practice the work? (Performance goal 3)

**9.** Construct a performance goal to use for students who are to use the computer either at a terminal or by preparing punched cards for a program run. Construct the program in BASIC or another language your instructor may designate and run it. Utilize your printout of the program and the results of the run for discussion in your group as to the use of the computer as a tool in business mathematics.

## SELECTED READINGS

BORMANN, THOMAS M., "Instruction for Electronic Calculators," *Journal of Data Education,* February, 1973, pp. 23–26.

CARAVELLA, JOSEPH R., "Metrification Activities in Education," *Business Education Forum,* December, 1973, pp. 14–16.

DOUGLAS, LLOYD V., JAMES T. BLANFORD, AND RUTH I. ANDERSON, *Teaching Business Subjects,* 3d ed., Prentice-Hall, Inc., Englewood Cliffs, N.J., 1973.

EIRICH, WAYNE M., "A Comparison of the Business Mathematics Achievement of Business Mathematics Students, Algebra Students, and General Mathematics Students," unpublished doctoral dissertation, Arizona State University, Tempe, Ariz., 1968.

GAMBLE, HARRY T., "A Study of Business Arithmetic Achievement in Selected Grades, 9 to 12," unpublished doctoral dissertation, Temple University, Philadelphia, 1965.

GREATSINGER, CALVIN, "An Experimental Study of Programmed Instruction in Division of Fractions," unpublished doctoral dissertation, Colorado State College, Greeley, Colo., 1966.

HAGA, ENOCH J., "Improving Mathematical Skills Electronically," *Journal of Data Education,* May, 1971, pp. 239-241.

HANTJIS, ANTHONY W., "A Study of Business Arithmetic Errors in Relationship to Selected Student Factors," unpublished doctoral dissertation, Temple University, Philadelphia, 1969.

HARMS, HARM, B. W. STEHR, AND E. EDWARD HARRIS, *Methods of Teaching Business and Distributive Education,* South-Western Publishing Company, Inc., Cincinnati, Ohio, 1972.

HUFFMAN, HARRY, *Report on Programmed Business Mathematics,* McGraw-Hill Book Company, New York, 1962.

JENKINS, O. H. L., "A Study of the Effect of Three Methods of Teaching Arithmetic to Mentally Handicapped Students," unpublished doctoral dissertation, University of Michigan, Ann Arbor, Mich., 1967.

KILPATRICK, JEREMY, "Analyzing the Solution to Word Problems: An Exploratory Study," unpublished doctoral dissertation, Stanford University, Palo Alto, Calif., 1967.

KLINE, MORRIS, "New Math + Confusion," *The New York University Alumni News,* April, 1974, p. 2.

LEWIS, HARRY, "The New Business Mathematics," *Business Education World,* March-April, 1968, pp. 4–5.

MYERS, GEORGE G., "An Experiment in Programmed Learning in Business Mathematics at East Tennessee State University," unpublished doctoral dissertation, University of Tennessee, Knoxville, Tenn., 1965.

NAMETH, JAMES J., "Performance Objectives for the Office Machines and Office Procedures Program," ED 048 448, San Mateo High School and Electa Phohle, Aragon High School, June, 1970.

ORAVETZ, ROBERT F., "An Experimental Study to Determine the Effectiveness of Various Drill Patterns in Business Mathematics-General Mathematics Instruction," unpublished doctoral dissertation, University of Pittsburgh, Pittsburgh, 1966.

PAGE, CHARLES W., "Teaching Business Arithmetic and Calculators as an Integrated Subject," unpublished doctoral dissertation, University of Northern Colorado, Greeley, Colo., 1970.

PEACOCK, R. L., AND A. G. MOODIE, "An Evaluation of a Business Machines Course for General Mathematics Students," ED 059 252, Vancouver Board of School Trustees, British College, July, 1971.

PERKINS, EDWARD A., ET AL., *Clusters of Tasks Associated with Performance of Major Types of Office Work, Final Report,* ED 018 665, Grant OEG 4-7-070031-1626, Washington State University, Pullman, 1968, pp. 39, 91, 110, 128, 147, and 162.

POLISHOOK, WILLIAM M., "The Effectiveness of Teaching Business Arithmetic as a Separate Subject and as an Integrated Part of Junior Business Training," unpublished doctoral dissertation, New York University, New York, 1945.

ROSENBERG, R. ROBERT, "Taking Inventory in Business Mathematics," *Business Education World,* December, 1969, pp. 24–25.

SUYDAM, MARILYN N., *Teaching Mathematics to Disadvantaged Pupils: A Summary of Research,* ED 049 934, Mathematics Education Reports, April, 1971.

TENER, MORTON, "Teaching Business Mathematics by Differentiated Methodologies," unpublished doctoral dissertation, Temple University, Philadelphia, Penn., 1968.

*Terminal Performance Objectives for Selected Programs in Business Education, Distributive Education, and Career Guidance,* ED 048 448, San Mateo Union High School District, San Mateo, Calif., September, 1970.

TONNE, HERBERT A., "A Critique of Bookkeeping Instructional Content," *The Journal of Business Education,* December, 1970, pp. 106–108.

WOOD, MERLE W., "Business Data Analysis—A Student Project," *Business Education World,* November-December, 1971, pp. 22–23.

*Wyoming Mathematics Curriculum Guide,* Grades 7–12, ED 050 071, Wyoming State Department of Education, Cheyenne, Wyo., 1970.

**363**

## PERFORMANCE GOALS

**1.** Given five competencies, select one and **construct** a teaching-learning system which includes an acceptable performance goal, four subcompetencies, an actual evaluation which measures the performance goal, a discussion of how appropriate principles of learning apply, and a teaching-learning strategy (organizational patterns and instructional resources appropriate for each subcompetency).

**2.** Using the classifications of clerical competencies in this chapter and given a description of students' abilities, reading rates, and career objectives, determine which competencies are appropriate for each student or subgroup of students, and **defend** your decision based upon this chapter.

**3.** Develop a ten-minute presentation for a subcompetency constructed for performance goal, and submit a detailed plan for teacher approval. Use the plan as the basis for a performance to **demonstrate** your ability to teach a small group while being recorded or videotaped. Evaluation by peers and instructor will be based upon criteria developed in learning activity 5.

# CHAPTER 15

# Clerical Program

For many years vocational business education has recognized the need for providing capstone experiences requiring the application of office skills in an office environment, learning situations in which the student performs interrelated office tasks while interacting with other workers.

Traditionally these learning experiences were provided in a limited way in "practice" courses in office practice, secretarial practice, and bookkeeping practice. Office practice is for high-level students who are completing a nonstenographic business program. Secretarial Practice is for stenographic students. Bookkeeping Practice is for students who simulate buying, selling, and banking activities while they learn to keep records. The traditional Clerical Practice course is usually restricted to unrelated and simplified office tasks that can be completed in one period, often with little carryover from one day to the next. Little attempt is made to integrate these tasks into real office situations or to include the more complex activities.

Traditional courses are often restricted to the following components:

- Subject matter that has not been learned in other courses (filing, telephone and receptionist duties, the use of reference sources, and office machines other than the typewriter).
- Facts and concepts about business organization and a worker's relationship with other workers, with emphasis on acceptable office behavior. (More attention is given to the affective domain than in most other business courses.)
- The integration of previous learnings. (The learner is brought to the level of competencies required to meet actual business standards.)
- Remedial work in fundamental skills in which the learner is deficient (grammar, spelling, punctuation, vocabulary, handwriting, and arithmetic).

In some schools cooperative office work experience is provided as the final course. The experiences vary from those in which learners work in school offices or prepare materials for outside community agencies to formal programs meeting strict requirements for reimbursement.

Recently attempts have been made to bring clerical experiences even more in line with the needs of business and of the learner. Few areas of office education are undergoing more innovation and experimentation than is the clerical program. One of the major reasons is the provision of funds through the Vocational Education Act of 1968 and its amendments.

## Needs of the Learner

Although highly motivated and academically competent students are enrolled in traditional courses in Office Practice, Secretarial Practice, and Bookkeeping Practice, the typical student in clerical programs has limited academic ability, a poor self-image, limited interest in school, and a culturally different background from students of 25 years ago. Clerical courses are often prescribed for low-ability students by academically oriented guidance counselors, not because the students are really expected to secure clerical positions but because there seems to be no other place for them. The potential dropout and the potentially unemployable are frequently registered in a clerical course, for here at least is a class involving activity, a suitable dumping ground. Difficulties in the learning situation are often further compounded by language problems of foreign-language-speaking learners and by reading disabilities of many enrollees.

Many learners come from homes in which neither parent is gainfully employed, and they are unfamiliar with the work ethic. Students have few opportunities to learn the requirements for office employment in either the home or the community.

Yet these learners make up the very group on which business and government are expending large sums for out-of-school office training. Schools, too, have the responsibility to initiate experimental programs or to reorganize existing courses to meet the needs of disadvantaged students, so that they can become gainfully employed.

## Needs of Business

The needs of business were formerly defined in general terms, but qualitative and quantitative standards were never readily available. Neither were the tasks to be performed identified. Considerable progress has been and is being made, however, in analyzing the tasks performed in the clerical job cluster.

Most teachers would agree that the first five categories of office tasks performed by beginning office workers studied by Erickson (recycle to p. 50) should be included in any clerical program: communicating with others (90 percent); sorting, filing, and retrieving (71 percent); typewriting (49 percent); and checking, computing, and verifying (47 percent). These tasks are the basis of the clerical procedures course developed in this chapter.

An analysis of tasks requiring effective communication indicates the necessity for establishing situations that develop competencies in the affective domain: telephoning; receiving callers; acting with courtesy, tact, and calmness; coping with pressures of simultaneous tasks and contacts; showing good judgment; explaining and discussing procedures with other workers; and cooperating with others in a common effort. Learnings in the cognitive domain that are necessary in communicating with others include writing messages and routine letters, listing and scheduling activities, and using office sources of information.

Tasks involving sorting, filing, and retrieving documents indicate that papers must be handled in volume and that the transfer of daily assignments between teacher and learner will not develop the skills required for office employment. Experiences must be provided that require sorting, filing, and retrieving a large number of papers within office time limits and without error.

Typing usable office papers is an important requirement of office jobs. Basic typewriting skill must be applied, then, in processing office papers used in the classroom. West states:

If there is to be the remotest chance of satisfying employment needs, production training must be begun much earlier than is common, so that a broad spectrum of tasks and a wide range of task complexity can be included in the training. Particularly to be redressed is the disservice to low-ability students in those clerical training programs aimed at little more than success at the 5-minute straight copy employment test. Such students more than others need large amounts of practice at realistic typing tasks, and such an instructional focus appears to be at no cost to the copying skills measured in Civil Service and other employment tests. (West, p. 35)

Checking, computing, and verifying are the final category of Erickson's tasks. The importance of these activities dictates that at last the burden for evaluating work produced in the classroom must be shifted from the teacher to the person on which it should rest, the learner.

Fruehling classifies the broad objectives of any clerical program as (1) developing the capabilities needed to succeed in a work environment, (2) acquiring the necessary technical skills, and (3) finding a satisfying worker role (Fruehling, p. 17). The first two of these objectives are based on the competencies identified by Erickson and also conform to the objectives of career education (Chapter 1, pp. 14–15). The third objective is equally important, for if a worker does not fit a job in terms of interests and temperament as well as in technical and environmental competencies, limited success will accrue. This relatively new dimension, so important to the career education concept, has been added so that the learner can match interests and temperament to capabilities.

The performance goals in this chapter match Fruehling's three objectives. The reader is then shown how to reach these goals in a greatly modified traditional clerical practice course and also in a simulated office. If these or similar performance goals are not presently met in the clerical curriculum, any one of them can be incorporated into existing courses, regardless of their names. The point is that instruction in these categories is essential to entry-level workers. It is up to the individual school to work out plans for including it someplace.

Possible competencies needed to meet the three objectives in most clerical programs are listed in Figure 15.1 on pages 370–371. After the competencies are categorized into the three groups, they are analyzed as to dominant domain, level to be achieved within the domain, type of evaluation to be used, and verb that best describes the level of performance expected. (Recycle to Chapter 5, pp. 91–104).

In some competencies, such as No. 9 (placing and answering telephone calls) two evaluations are necessary. The student must demonstrate proper techniques while telephoning, but he or she must also achieve the cognitive competency of decision making so that the type of service that is chosen is appropriate in a given situation.

A glance at the whole table of competencies indicates the importance that is placed on the higher levels of achievement. All affective behaviors must be developed to the highest level. No psychomotor behavior appears as the dominant type of learning, for the learner must apply not only psychomotor skill but primarily cognition in typing a usable product. Even in the cognitive domain the higher levels of behavior are stipulated. In all competencies except one part of No. 7, the learner is to achieve the application level (seven competencies) or reach the highest possible level, evaluation (eight competencies).

Before writing performance goals, the teacher needs specific information about business production standards, but this is hard to find and varies widely. Sometimes a specialist provides it. Goodman, for instance, lists business filing standards and suggests classroom standards as well (Goodman, p. 258). See Figure 15.2 on page 372.

Another point should be made about Figure 15.2. Many of the process evaluations involve the affective domain: how the learner reacts to other workers. This is a new area requiring new tools and new understandings of office requirements.

## Planning Evaluations and Constructing Performance Goals

A performance goal for each clerical competency listed in Figure 15.1 follows. (Recycle to Chapter 5 for how to write performance goals.)

### Interpersonal Relations

1. Given at the beginning of the program a chart showing the eight competencies in interpersonal relationships, and in cooperation

with the teacher, list at each marking period situations in which you **demonstrate** the expected behavior and other situations in which you do not **demonstrate** the expected behavior. For a satisfactory rating at the end of the program, the cumulative report must reflect increasing levels of competency in interpersonal relations as rated by the teacher and the learner. It must also contain at least five process evaluations of group behavior, individual behavior in the group, or product-process evaluation that met the standards agreed upon by class for instrument in Chapter 7, pages 79–84.

## Composing

2. Given all essential information to be included (address, quantity, price, terms, problem, etc.) **decide** on content and form while composing, editing, and typing five letters: order, payment, complaint, acknowledgment, and cancellation of an appointment. Criteria: all essential data, helpful tone, no uncorrected errors, attractive appearance.

## Recognizing Interrelationships

3a. While performing a simple office task (such as arranging materials in a file folder or requisitioning materials from central files), **analyze** and flowchart the procedure, using the appropriate symbols. Instructor approval.

3b. Given ten requests for specific information and an organization chart, **analyze** the chart and list the person to whom each inquiry should be referred. Nine correct.

3c. Given a demonstration of a modern electronic cash register, **analyze** the flow of information generated by a sales record by listing the operations affected. All correct.

## Recording

4. Given the beginning inventory, the information for preparing ten sales slips and packing slips, and ten purchase invoices to be paid today, **demonstrate** ability to prepare the sales slips, compute purchase discounts to which the company is entitled, and to summarize the sales and purchase information in alphabetic form to show the final inventory. No uncorrected errors and correct inventory figure.

## Typing

5. Given a project requiring the typing of letters and envelopes, tabulations, manuscript from rough draft, and fill-ins on form

Figure 15.1   Competencies to be developed in the clerical program classified as to level of domain and verb to be used in evaluation

| Competency | Dominant domain & level | Evaluation | Verb |
|---|---|---|---|
| **Developing the capabilities needed to succeed in a work environment** | | | |
| 1. Exhibit interpersonal skills that are acceptable in business | Affective: whenever possible, high level | Process: controlled observation | **Exhibit** |
| Act with tact, courtesy, and calmness | Affective: whenever possible, high level | Process: controlled observation | **Exhibit** |
| Cope with pressures | Affective: whenever possible, high level | Process: controlled observation | **Exhibit** |
| Listen attentively | Affective: whenever possible, high level | Process: controlled observation | **Exhibit** |
| Speak courteously | Affective: whenever possible, high level | Process: controlled observation | **Exhibit** |
| Respect other people's ideas | Affective: whenever possible, high level | Process: controlled observation | **Exhibit** |
| Discuss work problems | Affective: whenever possible, high level | Process: controlled observation | **Exhibit** |
| Tolerate routine work | Affective: whenever possible, high level | Process: controlled observation | **Exhibit** |
| Work harmoniously for a common cause | Affective: whenever possible, high level | Process: controlled observation | **Exhibit** |
| 2. Express written ideas in letters, memos, and reports so that they are understood and accepted | Cognitive: evaluation | Product | **Decide** |
| 3. Recognize the interrelationships of office jobs by reading departmental organization charts, flowcharting an office task, and analyzing the dependency of various functions on sophisticated equipment | Cognitive: evaluation | Product | **Analyze** |
| **Acquiring needed technical skills** | | | |
| 4. Record sales, purchases, and inventory transactions | Cognitive: application | Product | **Demonstrate** |
| 5. Type letters, memos, and forms that meet office standards of usability | Cognitive: application | Product | **Demonstrate** |
| 6. Duplicate and copy by mimeograph, copying machine, or spirit duplicator to meet office standards | Cognitive: application | Product | **Demonstrate** |
| Choose appropriate process in terms of product, cost, and use for which copy is intended | Cognitive: evaluation | Essay | **Decide** |
| 7. File materials in office file or send material to central files so that it can be retrieved easily and quickly | Cognitive: application | Product | **Demonstrate** |
| Sort, file, and retrieve for the alphabetic and subject file systems | Cognitive: application | Product | **Demonstrate** |

Figure 15.1 (continued)

| Competency | Dominant domain & level | Evaluation | Verb |
|---|---|---|---|
| Understand how and why numeric and geographic files are used | Cognitive: comprehension | Short-answer and completion tests | **Differentiate** |
| Develop concepts about central files organization and management until student can solve simple problems | Cognitive: evaluation | Essay | **Decide** |
| 8. Apply skills in computing and verifying to handling petty cash, checkbook, payroll, and bank reconciliation until answers check against each other | Cognitive: application | Product | **Demonstrate** |
| 9. Place and answer telephone calls that give and receive business information that is complete and in acceptable business form | Cognitive: application | Process: controlled observation | **Demonstrate** |
| Select appropriate type of telephone service | Cognitive: evaluation | Essay | **Decide** |
| 10. Meet callers courteously and direct them to the appropriate person | Cognitive: evaluation | Process: controlled observation | **Demonstrate** |
| 11. Locate business information sufficiently well to find every item called for by referring to the appropriate source among the reference materials available | Cognitive: evaluation | Product | **Decide** |
| 12. Use mail services so that communications and materials are sent by the appropriate method in terms of importance, time factor, and cost | Cognitive: evaluation | Short-answer and completion tests | **Decide** |
| **Finding a satisfying worker role** | | | |
| 13. Investigate the requirements of jobs in the Clerical Cluster such as clerk-typist, file clerk, office machine operator, switchboard operator, post office clerk, or receptionist to the point where intelligent vocational choices can be made within the cluster in terms of self | Cognitive: evaluation | Essay | **Decide** |
| Analyze technical skills, interpersonal relations, and temperament so that vocational choice made will provide a satisfying worker role | Affective: highest level | Process: controlled observation | **Decide** |
| 14. Develop interviewing skills that peers agree will enable interviewee to be considered for the job of his choice | Affective: highest level | Process: controlled observation | **Demonstrate** |

Figure 15.2  Typical filing standards from business offices
with suggested standards for classroom use

| Activity | Business pieces per hour | School pieces in ten minutes |
|---|---|---|
| **Alphabetic filing** | | |
| Indexing letters | 150 | 25 |
| Sorting letters: alphabetic sequence | 275 | 45 |
| Sorting cards: alphabetic sequence | 300 | 50 |
| Sorting letters: first alphabetic character only | 850 | 140 |
| Sorting cards: first alphabetic character only | 900 | 150 |
| Filing letters in captioned folders | 200 | 35 |
| Filing cards: alphabetic | 250 | 40 |
| Retrieving letters: alphabetic | 40 | 15 |
| Retrieving cards: alphabetic | 60 | 20 |
| **Numeric filing** | | |
| Sorting letters: strict numeric sequence | 325 | 55 |
| Sorting cards: strict numeric sequence | 350 | 60 |
| Sorting letters or cards: terminal digit | 1,500 | 250 |
| Filing letters: strict numeric sequence | 230 | 40 |
| Filing cards: strict numeric sequence | 300 | 50 |
| Filing letters or cards: terminal digit | 500 | 90 |
| Retrieving letters: strict numeric sequence | 50 | 15 |
| Retrieving cards: strict numeric sequence | 75 | 20 |
| **Subject filing** | | |
| Coding and filing letters | 100 | 15 |
| Filing papers previously coded | 150 | 25 |
| Retrieving letters in subject file | 30 | 10 |

Source: Goodman, *Eastern Business Education Yearbook*, p. 258.

letters, **demonstrate** ability to plan and type three 100-word arranged letters and envelopes, fill in addresses and salutations on ten form letters, type a one-page manuscript from rough draft, and type a five-line three-column tabulation without columnar headings within one hour. No more than one unmailable item. (To allow for test conditions, a one-item tolerance is permitted.)

## Duplicating

6.   Given a letter containing a body of four lines, **demonstrate** ability to duplicate it on the copying machine, the mimeograph, and the direct-process duplicator within 20 minutes. Office standards of legibility. Work area left clean.

6a.  Given ten problem situations involving choices of duplicating process, **decide** which process to use, defending the decision in an essay.

## Filing

7a. Given a situation in which only a personal subject file is maintained (no central files) and 30 office communications, **demonstrate** filing competencies by disposing of certain papers in ways other than filing and, using a relative index, file the rest. No misfiles.

7b. Given a file of 500 letters correctly filed alphabetically, **demonstrate** filing competencies by retrieving 30 letters in 20 minutes.

7c. Given 40 index cards on which personal names are typed, **demonstrate** filing competencies by filing the cards within ten minutes with no more than one misfile.

7d. Given a case problem involving an office filing system that does not function well, **decide** on recommendations for change and write an essay defending the choices made.

## Verifying and Checking

8a. Given check stubs for 23 checks (including deposit notations) and 20 canceled checks, **demonstrate** computing and verifying skills by reconciling the bank statement on a bank form.

8b. Given 15 vouchers for petty cash withdrawals and the petty cash record book, **demonstrate** ability to keep petty cash records by updating the records and requesting a check to renew the fund. No errors.

8c. Given payroll time records for five hourly workers, their rates of pay, and all data about withholdings, **demonstrate** ability to compute the weekly payroll. No errors.

## Telephoning

9a. Given five problem situations in which two students, using classroom equipment, initiate and receive business telephone calls, **demonstrate** ability to place and answer calls, terminate the calls, record names and numbers given in a conversation, record and deliver messages, transfer calls to a more appropriate person, and locate business services in the *Yellow Pages*. Criteria: Group evaluation using written criteria that have been developed through group discussion.

9b. Given five problem situations, **decide** upon the appropriate telephone service and in an essay defend decisions made. Four correct.

## Meeting Callers

10a. Given data about the purpose of ten office callers' visits and an organization chart of the company, **demonstrate** understanding of office organization by preparing a log of callers.

10b.   Given three problem situations involving troublesome office callers, **demonstrate** skill as a receptionist to the satisfaction of a small group of peers who have previously developed written criteria.

## Locating Information

11.   Given access to a dictionary, the *Yellow Pages,* ZIP Code directory, company manual, atlas, *World Almanac and Book of Facts, Business Periodicals Index,* and *Books in Print,* **demonstrate** ability to locate answers to ten questions. No errors.

## Mailing

12a.   Given a list of 20 items to be mailed, **decide** the appropriate class of mail to be used. Nineteen correct.

12b.   Given a list of ten problems involving poorly handled office mail, **decide** how the company can expedite the mail and answer completion questions relating to each problem. Nine correct.

## Learning Job Requirements

13.   Given access to the *Dictionary of Occupational Titles* and oral information obtained through class interviews with graduates employed in jobs in the Clerical Cluster and through individual interviews with clerks throughout the clerical program, **decide** which two jobs would provide the most satisfying worker role and write an essay of at least 200 words defending choices made. Criteria: The writer indicates an understanding of the tasks involved and the nature of the work as well as recognition of his or her competencies, temperament, and aspirations. Written expression meets office standards.

## Interviewing

14.   Given a choice of one of the two jobs chosen in No. 13, **demonstrate** ability to apply for a job during an interview with the teacher, a personnel director, or the school principal. Criterion: Meets standards of a minigroup which has developed a checklist for the evaluation with which the interviewee is familiar.

While performance goals are being written, the teacher also plans the evaluation instruments used to measure their achievement. It might also be a good idea to construct an alternative form of the instrument that can be used with students who must be recycled through one or more subcompetencies that prevented achievement of the performance goal the first time around.

In Performance Goal 2 (Composing Letters), the teacher would list the essential information to be included in each letter to be written. With this list no problem occurs and no time is wasted in filling in fictitious names and information for the tests. This same list is used, of course, in grading the letters; and only the element of tone and courtesy are left to the teacher's discretion.

If affective behavior and interaction with others are being evaluated, the reader should consider using the instruments in Chapter 7, pp. 79–84, or, with students, devise similar ones for guidance during controlled observations.

## Identifying and Sequencing Subcompetencies and Writing En Route Goals

Subcompetencies for the performance goals on pages 368–374 are listed next. Also included are possible en route goals, although a student may already possess the required subcompetency and skip over all listed en route goals. An experienced teacher of clerical procedures can anticipate, though, problem areas and develop a collection of en route goals to meet most possible needs of students with different learning problems. For instance, three en route goals are listed for Performance Goal 2B, since each student's problems with spelling and English mechanics are different from those of others.

### Performance Goal 1: Interpersonal Relations

SUBCOMPETENCY A.  Participate in a group effectively as measured by evaluations using Figures 4.8 and 4.9 in Chapter 4.

EN ROUTE GOAL A.  In discussion groups, **demonstrate** in at least six evaluations that you can meet the criteria in Figure 4.10.

SUBCOMPETENCY B.  Demonstrate expected behaviors at each marking period.

EN ROUTE GOAL B.  In an analysis by learner and teacher, **demonstrate** improvement in categories in which weakness is shown.

### Performance Goal 2: Composing

SUBCOMPETENCY A.  Include essential information.

EN ROUTE GOAL A.  After writing each of the five types of letters required, **demonstrate** that you included the essential information contained in a checklist prepared by the class.

SUBCOMPETENCY B.  Write without errors in spelling, English mechanics, or grammar. (Roger Landroth presented these en route goals for a New York City clerical group of low ability at the Gregg Shorthand Teachers Association of New York City and Vicinity on November 3, 1973.) Depends on individual needs on pretests.

EN ROUTE GOALS B. Given a paragraph of 100 words containing ten misspelled words, **demonstrate** ability to spell by circling each misspelled word and writing it correctly in the margin within five minutes and with 90 percent accuracy.

Given ten unpunctuated compound sentences, **demonstrate** ability to punctuate compound sentences by inserting all necessary commas in five minutes with 100 percent accuracy.

Given a rough draft of a business letter of 120 words containing ten errors in capitalization, **demonstrate** ability to work from rough draft by typing one copy, a carbon copy, and an envelope that are mailable in 20 minutes.

## Performance Goal 3: Recognizing Interrelationships

SUBCOMPETENCY A. Flowchart so that operations comprising a task are shown in proper sequence.

EN ROUTE GOAL A. Given a model flowchart, **demonstrate** understanding of the symbols used by answering 23 of 25 multiple choice test questions correctly.

Given a simple office task, as a member of a minigroup, **construct** a flowchart showing the sequence of operations. Teacher approval.

SUBCOMPETENCY B. Read an organization chart to see who is responsible for what.

EN ROUTE GOAL B. Given an organization chart of a department, **demonstrate** understanding of the interrelationships of jobs by answering nine of ten multiple choice questions correctly.

SUBCOMPETENCY C. Analyze the capabilities of data information machines to understand the effect of each worker's effort on total production.

EN ROUTE GOALS C. **Define** the following terms: unit record, magnetic ink character recognition, integrated data processing, common machine language, electronic printing calculator, rotary calculator, audit tape, memory, magnetic disk, input, and output. Nine correct.

After a visit to a computer installation, **list** the uses made of source data. Teacher approval.

Given a case problem for preparation of payroll, **analyze** in written form the capabilities of each machine involved in the preparation of the final paycheck.

## Performance Goal 4: Recording

SUBCOMPETENCY A. Solve addition, subtraction, multiplication, and division by longhand and on a ten-key adding machine.

EN ROUTE GOAL A. Given five problems in addition, each of which contains four addenda of three digits, **demonstrate** skill in addition by accumulating the sums in ten minutes with 90 percent accuracy. (Similar problems in other three processes.)

SUBCOMPETENCY B.   Identify like and different names and numbers.

EN ROUTE GOAL B.   Given the Minnesota Clerical Ability Test, **demonstrate** ability to check figures and names by scoring 95 percent.

SUBCOMPETENCY C.   Verify multiplication, addition discounts, and subtraction on sales slips and invoices.

EN ROUTE GOAL C.   Given 50 sales slips and invoices, **demonstrate** ability to verify them by locating *all* errors in computations.

## Performance Goal 5: Typing

SUBCOMPETENCY A.   Follow directions as to number of copies, to whom sent, and supplies to be used.

EN ROUTE GOAL A.   Given oral directions for preparing five communications, **demonstrate** ability to listen to directions by answering 15 of 20 questions about the directions correctly.

SUBCOMPETENCY B.   Proofread.

EN ROUTE GOAL B.   Given a series of ten business papers with the number of errors stated, **demonstrate** proofreading competency in locating typographic, spelling, and punctuation errors by finding 15 errors. (Later the number of errors will not be specified.)

SUBCOMPETENCY C.   Correct errors.

EN ROUTE GOAL C.   Given a typed page containing five typographic errors requiring erasing, crowding, and spreading letters for correction, **demonstrate** erasing ability by making corrections. Four acceptable.

SUBCOMPETENCY D.   Develop standards of mailability.

EN ROUTE GOAL D.   Given five letters prepared by a peer, **decide** which ones are mailable. Agreement with the teacher.

SUBCOMPETENCY E.   Meet office production time standards.

EN ROUTE GOALS E.   Given two 100-word letters and envelopes to be typed from unarranged copy with one carbon within ten minutes, **demonstrate** ability to meet office production standards. Both letters mailable.

Given a one-page report with a title and margin headings that is in rough-draft form, **demonstrate** ability to meet office production standards by typing a usable copy in ten minutes.

Given a four-column table of ten items to be typed with a title in ten minutes, **demonstrate** ability to plan and type tables.

## Performance Goal 6: Duplicating and Copying

No en route goals unless student has difficulty in interpreting reading assignments.

## Performance Goal 7: Filing

SUBCOMPETENCY A.   Inspect for release mark so that no unauthorized papers are filed.

EN ROUTE GOAL A. Given ten letters (originals and carbon copies), **demonstate** ability to reject *all* papers not released for filing.

SUBCOMPETENCY B. Index by reference to relative index listing all headings and subheadings so that uniform captions are used.

EN ROUTE GOAL B. Given ten items for subject filing, **demonstrate** ability to assign caption by referring to a relative index. No errors.

SUBCOMPETENCY C. Code so that filing instruction is recorded.

EN ROUTE GOAL C. Given the ten items above after they have been properly indexed, **demonstrate** ability to code the items. No errors.

SUBCOMPETENCY D. Cross reference so that item called for under another caption can be located.

EN ROUTE GOAL D. Given 15 items ready for placing in the files, **demonstrate** ability to use the relative index and cross reference items likely to be called for under another caption. Fourteen correct.

SUBCOMPETENCY E. Sort into alphabetic groups.

EN ROUTE GOAL E. After typing 100 names on cards with surname first, **demonstrate** ability to sort them into alphabetic sequence. No errors.

SUBCOMPETENCY F. Locate proper file storage (drawer or file).

EN ROUTE GOAL F. Given simulated shelf or drawer labels and a list of names sorted into alphabetic groups, **demonstrate** ability to match labels and alphabetic groups on matching test. No errors.

SUBCOMPETENCY G. Arrange materials in the folder.

EN ROUTE GOALS G. Given five items to be filed in a folder, **demonstrate** ability to arrange them in proper sequence.

Given four sets of items to be sequenced in four folders, **decide** on their proper order by answering 19 of 20 multiple-choice questions correctly.

SUBCOMPETENCY H. Place folders in file.

EN ROUTE GOAL H. **Demonstrate** inserting and removing folders from equipment available in classroom. Instructor approval.

SUBCOMPETENCY I. Charge materials to borrowers.

EN ROUTE GOAL I. Given five requests for filed materials, **demonstrate** filing competence by completing charge-out slips correctly. Instructor approval.

SUBCOMPETENCY J. Refile materials.

EN ROUTE GOAL J. Given five folders to be returned to the file, **demonstrate** ability to refile them. No errors.

SUBCOMPETENCY K. Make decisions about what to file.

EN ROUTE GOAL K. Given ten items (important letters, unimportant letters, announcements, appointments, advertising, etc., **decide** which items to record and destroy, to post on the bulletin board, and to file. Instructor approval.

SUBCOMPETENCY L. Retrieve filed materials.

EN ROUTE GOAL L. **Demonstrate** ability to locate filed materials by retrieving seven letters from an alphabetic file in five minutes.

SUBCOMPETENCY M. Apply understanding of numeric and geographic filing.

EN ROUTE GOALS M.   Given 25 multiple choice questions about numeric and geographic filing, **decide** which situations are appropriate for their use. 23 correct.

SUBCOMPETENCY N.   Develop records management concepts.

EN ROUTE GOAL N.   Given two problem situations, as a member of a minigroup, **decide** on recommendations for changes in records management and defend decisions. Instructor approval.

## Performance Goal 8: Computing and Verifying

Given petty cash, bank reconciliation, and payroll problems, **demonstrate** ability to solve them before attempting the terminal goal.

## Performance Goal 9: Telephoning

SUBCOMPETENCY A.   Place and answer calls that meet business standards.

EN ROUTE GOAL A.   Given three problem situations, **demonstrate** correct telephone technique to meet the standards of peers using a checklist which they developed.

SUBCOMPETENCY B.   Choose appropriate telephone service.

EN ROUTE GOALS B.   **Define** message unit, WATS, station-to-station call, person-to-person call, leased wire, button telephone, Touch-Tone telephone.

Given three problem situations requiring the choice of appropriate service, as a member of a minigroup, **decide** what service to use and defend choice to the satisfaction of the instructor.

## Performance Goal 10: Meet Callers

Additional role plays until student meets criteria.

## Performance Goal 11: Locate Information

Given 12 problems requiring use of the eight references, **demonstrate** ability to locate business information. Ten correct.

## Performance Goal 12: Mail

If student cannot achieve the terminal performance goal, give additional tests of the same type.

## Performance Goal 13: Job Requirements

SUBCOMPETENCY A.   Identify relevant information.

EN ROUTE GOAL A.   Given a term-long assignment in learning clerical job requirements, as a member of a minigroup, **construct** a checklist to be used during class and individual interviews that represents the consensus of the group and is approved by the teacher.

**379**

Using the checklist, **demonstrate** listening skill by listing the usable information from a sample interview. Teacher approval.

SUBCOMPETENCY B. Analyze competencies.

EN ROUTE GOAL B. Given your term record, **construct** a chart covering all units of the course and self-evaluate competencies in each area as Unacceptable, Minimal, Average, Good, or Superior. After an instructor conference, the ratings may be modified.

SUBCOMPETENCY C. Analyze skills in interrelationships.

EN ROUTE GOAL C. Given your evaluations for each marking period, **construct** a chart listing the eight interpersonal relationships in Competency 1 and self-evaluate your competency in each one. After an instructor conference, the ratings may be modified.

## Performance Goal 14: Interview

Sample interviews may be held in minigroups, which have developed a list of possible questions.

### Identifying Present Levels of Competency

Pretests are recommended in typewriting, calculating, composition, English mechanics (punctuation, spelling, grammar, vocabulary, and usage), and clerical aptitude in matching numbers and names. Results of these tests can be recorded on a master profile sheet for each student such as the one shown in Figure 15.3. This profile of Mary Gonzales shows pretests used, en route goals from which she was exempted, weaknesses requiring special attention, en route goals prescribed, the grading period in which she attained each en route goal, and the date on which she met each performance goal. This record forms the basis for teacher-learner conferences and individualization of instruction. Areas may be added for attendance, grooming, work habits, and reading scores. All master profiles should be updated regularly and used constantly in deciding on individualized assignments if normal instruction does not yield satisfactory results.

Since the student's perceptions of office work are an important factor in determining training needs, the teacher may want to administer the **Office Work Perceptions instrument (50 questions) reported by Huffman** (Huffman, pp. 78-81). The teacher can evaluate success in changing perceptions at the end of the course.

Brower substantiates the importance of pretesting students' perceptions of office work (Brower, pp. 1-12). When he compared the perceptions of high school students with those of office supervisory personnel in such areas as entry-level job titles, beginning salaries, rates of advancement, fringe benefits, methods of securing employment, working conditions, and personal traits required for success, he found that office employment expectations of business students are not generally in agreement with

Figure 15.3   Clerical program profile sheet

| Student<br>Area | En route goal<br>pretest exemptions | Weaknesses | En route goals<br>prescribed | Oct. | Nov. | Dec. | Jan. | Performance<br>goals completed |
|---|---|---|---|---|---|---|---|---|
| Interpersonal relations | | LETS OTHERS DO WORK; DOES NOT ACCEPT CRITICISM | A, B1, D1, F, G | | # | B | | |
| Composing: content mechanics | GRAMMAR (B2) ✓✓ | SPELLING | A, B1, B3, B4 | A, B1 | B3 | B4 | | 12/18 |
| Job inter-relationships | | | A, B, C | | | A | BC | 1/5 |
| Recording | ✓ | HANDWRITING | A, B, C, D | | | A, B | C, D | 1/20 |
| Typing | ✓ TABULATION (E3) | PROOFREADING | A, B, C, D, E1, E2 | A, B | C, D | E2 | E1 | 1/5 |
| Duplicating & copying | ✓✓ | | | | | | | |
| Filing | | | A-N | | | A-N | | EXEMPT |
| Computing & verifying | PETTY CASH (A1) ✓ | ADDITION PERCENTAGE | A2, A3 | A2, A3 | | | | 12/17 |
| Arithmetic skills | ✓ | | | | | | | 10/20 |
| Checking | ✓ | | | | | | | |

Source: Michigan State University, Block Time Simulation, Vol. 2, p. 9.

those of office supervisory personnel. Greater differences occur among the students in the clerical subjects than among the students in other business curriculums.

## Identifying and Applying Appropriate Learning Principles

In planning clerical programs, the teacher finds two principles of learning particularly applicable.

RELEVANCY. Although most business teachers prefer that the final "practice" course should be a culminating experience open only to students with at least average grades, English skills, good attendance records, and basic typing skill, some school administrators have, more or less in desperation, enrolled students who have previously demonstrated little academic promise, just because of the activity component, with considerable success. One productive program was a one-year funded Senior Intensified Program (SIP) in Detroit public schools, which was initiated for inner-city seniors who had studied no previous business courses (Brown, pp. 255-264). Training in four office areas was included: clerk-cashier, clerk-typist, clerk-stenographer, and data processing console operator. Instructional packages were prepared for daily periods of 80–120 minutes, and one semester of part-time work experience (15 hours a week) was required. The goal was preparation for entry-level office jobs. A follow-up of SIP graduates showed that 57 of 200 enrollees were employed. Depth interviews were held with these 57 SIP students and with their supervisors as well as with 57 graduates of the traditional program and their supervisors. (The SIP graduates had taken only half as many semesters of business subjects as the traditional graduates.) The full-time work patterns of both groups were basically the same. The supervisors' ratings showed no significant difference. (A *significant difference* indicates that the data has been subjected to statistical treatment that insures that there is a real difference that cannot be due to errors in sampling.) The success of this program demonstrates clearly the importance of using methods and materials relevant to the learner's needs.

INTERACTION WITH TOTAL ENVIRONMENT. Students who react negatively to the school environment may respond to an office environment positively when the learning environment is extended into the business community. Learning experience must include interaction also with other learners in a work situation and with persons employed in offices. In a recent study, Levin found that students working for specific goals individually prescribed to meet their learning needs were absent less than half as frequently as other students. In other words, it was possible for them to react favorably to the environment as they experienced successes that improved their self-images.

## Teaching Strategies

Woodward analyzed the performance of high school seniors enrolled in two-hour office practice courses in eleven Utah schools by comparing their clerical skills with those of other high school students who participated in the General Office Practice Clerical Tests and the Typewriting Tests from the National Business Entrance Tests series. (The General Office Practice Test employs multiple choice questions to measure clerical skills in filing, computing, checking, and verifying and cognitive comprehension of office procedures. It does not purport to measure communication skills and other affective behaviors. The typewriting test is a timed production test of different types of office papers.) The results were discouraging. Ninety percent of the Utah students fell below the tenth percentile of national norms on the General Office Clerical Test and 80 percent fell below the fiftieth percentile of national norms on the Typewriting Test of production. Changes were effected by revising the course and equipping a mobile model office which can be moved from school to school throughout this sparsely populated state, so that more high school students have access to materials and equipment that simulate the modern office.

## The Traditional Course

If revised, the traditional classroom course in which the only learning resources are office machines and a textbook-workbook can accomplish the performance goals listed on pages 368–374.

ROTATION PLAN.   The battery plan, which allows every student access to a machine so that the whole class can be instructed in its operation at the same time, is expensive. Because of equipment costs, the rotation plan is used in many traditional classrooms. Instruction is organized around a limited number of machines to which students are rotated.

A rotation schedule must, of course, provide for working on performance goals other than those involved in operating office machines. A machine rotation schedule is only the teacher's guide to assure each learner access to equipment. If the learner meets the designated performance goals in using the equipment in a shorter time, the equipment may be released to another student who has not met the goals in the designated time.

## Meeting Performance Goals

Suggestions are given below for handling each of the fourteen suggested performance goals on pages 368–374. The reader should turn to these pages in following the suggestions.

PERFORMANCE GOAL 1 (INTERPERSONAL RELATIONS).   At the beginning of instruction, the teacher discusses the goal with the entire class, indicating ways in which learners may exhibit the desired behaviors. A conference with each learner is required at each marking period.

PERFORMANCE GOAL 2 (COMPOSING).   See Chapter 11, "Communication," pages 241–265, for a complete discussion of teaching strategy.

PERFORMANCE GOAL 3 (JOB INTERRELATIONSHIPS).   Instruction in reading and constructing flow charts may be given the entire class or minigroups. Organization charts should be obtained from cooperative office education students or students in a simulation class if possible.

PERFORMANCE GOAL 4 (RECORDING). Individually prescribed instruction modules should be assigned learners whose pretests show deficiencies. Applications are then made in completing sales slips and computing discounts by using workbook problems. If students are not proficient in checking numbers and names, additional drills should be given until they can meet the en route goal.

PERFORMANCE GOAL 5 (TYPING). Individually paced instruction should be used as learners achieve the necessary en route goals that are based on both quality and quantity standards and that evolve finally to reach office requirements. (See also Chapter 9, Typewriting, pp. 165–197.)

PERFORMANCE GOAL 6 (DUPLICATING). The teacher instructs one student in the operation of each duplicating machine. This live presentation may be supplemented by taped instructions and a written procedure at the work station. When the learner finishes the assignments on one machine and also feels capable of meeting the time standard imposed in the performance goal, he or she instructs the next student before moving to the next machine. (The new learner is also to listen to the tape and read the procedure.)

Large- or small-group discussion is the most economical strategy for preparing learners to choose the appropriate process in reproducing copy.

PERFORMANCE GOAL 7 (FILING). The filing goals are met while the learner completes laboratory assignments, which include workbook exercises and filing actual letters and cards (either miniature letters or letters salvaged from a typewriting class). In addition, learners should work with real filing equipment, inserting full-size letters into folders, removing and reinserting a folder. Filing operations can be covered best by using individually paced instruction. The material on filing systems can be taught in one-time class discussions, with those unable to achieve the performance goal recycled into a small group for discussion, teacher reinstruction, and possibly audiovisual presentations.

PERFORMANCE GOAL 8 (COMPUTING AND VERIFYING). Individually paced learning is suggested while students complete the workbook exercises.

PERFORMANCE GOAL 9 (TELEPHONING). After the textbook is read and discussed and workbook assignments are completed, small groups are organized. As two students complete assigned telephone calls on whatever intercommunication equipment is available, the other students evaluate the conversations, using checklists which they have developed. Teletrainer, classroom telephone training equipment, which provides two interconnected telephones on which a conversation can be heard by the group, is available, along with learning exercises, from the local telephone company in most communities. Sample booklets recommending telephone techniques, explaining various services, and describing various business telephones are also usually available. Representatives welcome the opportunity to describe the positions available with the telephone company. If telephone equipment is limited, the telephone unit may be included in the rotation schedule.

PERFORMANCE GOAL 10 (MEETING CALLERS). The roleplays follow the pattern used in No. 9.

PERFORMANCE GOAL 11 (LOCATING REFERENCE MATERIALS). Because of the limited supply of source materials, this activity should be included in the rotation schedule. A small group may work together in locating the information in the first assignments, with the individual later assuming responsibility for independent work.

PERFORMANCE GOAL 12 (MAILING). Students can probably meet the goals after reading, completing workbook assignments, and asking questions at individually paced rates.

PERFORMANCE GOAL 13 (JOB REQUIREMENTS). This activity extends throughout the course. It provides many opportunities for developing skills in interpersonal relations included in Performance Goal 1. The entire class engages in the group interviews with graduates employed in various jobs in the Clerical Cluster. (See Chapter 7, page 130.) The whole class listens to the teacher's explanations of the *Dictionary of Occupational Titles,* which should be available in all clerical classrooms. Small groups interview workers in different categories (after a group has developed the interview guide) and present their findings to the class. Students discuss their occupational choices in small groups and solicit peer evaluation of their temperamental suitability for them. Students may bring in newspaper and magazine articles for the bulletin board about various jobs and present the information in class. Such articles may be used in duplicating projects so that they are available to every student. Before a field trip to a local office, students develop questions they will be expected to answer in writing. Appropriate topics for special committee reports are Kinds of Jobs in Which Entry-Level Workers Are Employed; Tests Given for Entry-Level Jobs; Opportunities for Continuing Education; Standards for Dress, Speech and Office Behavior; and Employee Evaluation Plan. At the end of the course each student might make an oral three-minute presentation from the final essay.

PERFORMANCE GOAL 14 (INTERVIEWING). Following a reading assignment and class discussion, the entire class may develop a checklist or revise an existing one for evaluating a job interview, or each small group may develop its own evaluation instrument. Using possible questions, practice interviews are conducted between members, evaluated, and polished before the final evaluation.

ACTIVITY DAY. One suggestion is to set aside one day a week for enrichment activities involving either the whole class or small groups. Friday should not be chosen because business cooperation is less likely to be obtained on the busy Fridays. Activities might include group interviews, case problem discussions, field trips, oral presentations and demonstrations, show-and-tell presentations when each student displays some type of business information not included in the textbook, or a film.

When learners have been working alone, they welcome these sessions, which give a sense of belonging to a group and give experience in interaction. Spacing activities a week apart is desirable, for learners can use the intervening week for preparations that would not be possible on consecutive days.

## Block-Time Scheduling

Because traditional 28- to 50-minute class periods may not give the learner enough time to finish jobs started and to integrate office activities, one of the first research projects authorized under the Vocational Education Act of 1963 was conducted by Michigan State University in cooperation with high schools in five states to study block-time instruction in vocational office education.

Poland found that 36 state supervisors reported existing block-time programs in their states, more than half of them vocationally reimbursed. The emerging values were flexibility to meet individual student needs; preparation for immediate, gainful, or even technical positions; a closer simulation of actual business experiences; better instruction; and integration of all office education subjects. Block clerical programs can be either organized for (1) classes meeting for two or more class periods for learning activities that combine or replace two or more required subjects or for (2) subjects that are unified or fused around a central theme, units of work, or problems stemming from one or more subject fields.

## Job-Related Modules

With the general acceptance of the block-time concept, various teaching strategies evolved that include integrated activities. A pioneer project of this type is the Office Job Training Program (Gregg) consisting of tasks required on fifteen entry-level clerical jobs. In developing the materials, "the authors first identified the clusters of tasks associated with each job, then they identified the particular skills needed to perform each task, and they proceeded to design a training program around just those skills . . . it integrates the teaching of skills in the way that skills are integrated in the performance of actual jobs" (Hodges, p. 18).

The fifteen jobs included in the series are the most common entry-level, limited-function jobs available: file clerk, mail clerk, typist, office cashier, stock control clerk, payroll clerk, billing clerk, clerk-typist, credit clerk, accounts receivable clerk, order clerk, purchasing clerk, accounts payable clerk, personnel clerk, and traffic clerk. Learners work independently on jobs of their choice and in the sequence they choose. They may complete all the jobs, as many as they can, or as many as they and their teacher agree on as optimal. Instruction is given through on-the-job conversations and conferences with the teacher-office supervisor, the learner realizing the value of asking for help when necessary.

Students move at their own pace, knowing through detailed previews the work expected at each stage and, through self-checks, the quality of their performance of it. The learner who completes unit after unit develops a broad range of basic clerical skills found in a variety of office job experiences. The student also senses the kind of job he or she would prefer and would perform best in. The modules can be used for exploratory motivational experience; for a core of job-training experiences that will prepare for employment; and for preparation for office simulation or cooperative work experience.

## Simulation

Driska found in 1967 that 80 percent of the state business education supervisors indicated a need for more simulated office education materials. Successful simulations are being used in many high schools, learning resources are becoming available for such classes, and summer workshops for teachers are offered in which teachers may plan simulations.

Simulation is employed in its simple form in discussions of case problems, role playing, and using classroom telephone systems, discussed earlier in the chapter.

A second kind of simulation involves the work done at one work station only. The activities in the Office Job Training Program are examples. Another example is the college secretarial procedures course in which the learner performs work done by the secretary and copes with the human relations problems encountered. The simulation may be based on situations requiring reference to the textbook, which is used as a resource only. (See *Practicum,* Selected Readings.) Or the simulations may be closely related to the textbook, a simulation project at the end of each section of the textbook requiring reference to that one section only for completion. (See *Simulated Office Situations,* Selected Readings.)

The third type of simulation more nearly approximates reality. An office containing a number of work stations is organized along functional lines with managers in the various departments and with work flowing between stations. As input comes into this office (in the form of orders, payments, inquiries, and so on), it generates a flow of work through the various job stations so that at each stage some form of output is produced. Students rotating through all the jobs experience the interrelationships of the different functions and the frustrations occasioned by workers who do not carry their part of the load. They hold staff meetings regularly to plan work and to change procedures. In other words, the affective dimension is accentuated.

There are two kinds of model office simulation—one in which all input is created in the office and one in which already-prepared business documents are available from which output is prepared. An example is an input-originating automobile insurance office, developed by Beverly

**387**

Funk in close cooperation with the insurance industry in the state of Washington. Applications for automobile insurance with the classroom insurance agency are made by students in the automobile safety class and processed in the model office, which is advised constantly by a local insurance company. A similar simulation is taught by Julius Milkes in Northport High School in New York State.

The other kind of office simulation provides prepared input documents. The pioneer effort in this type is the Lester Hill Office Simulation, in which learners in four departments (Sales, Warehouse, Traffic, and Accounting) process business documents relating to relationships with customers, suppliers, and the bank. Students complete orientation exercises and then rotate through the departments and the outside agencies and verify transactions regularly with both the internal and external components. The teacher adapts the systems to the number of learners involved, their abilities, and the time allotted to the project (from 45 to 90 hours). Advantages claimed by Sabin for office simulations are (1) fast feedback so the learner quickly sees the consequences of his actions and can modify or change them; (2) the control factor by which the teacher can adapt the complexity of a job to the level of the learner and match performance goals to the capabilities of the individual learner; (3) the low-risk factor, as the learner in a simulation, in contrast with the learner on a real job, can make a mistake without its costing him his job; and (4) the cost factor, as simulation is less expensive than a work-experience program (Sabin, p. 6).

Originally, simulations were conceived as terminal training, but they have proved to be such strong motivational devices that they may well be used early as a way of helping students improve their self-image while giving relevancy to school learnings and keeping students in school.

The following discussion indicates how the teacher using an office simulation project would develop the fourteen competencies suggested for the clerical program. The performance goals might, however, be revised as the teacher sees fit. For instance, no time standards are set in a simulation project, as built-in pressures are included in the time schedules for the flow of work. One teacher may, however, wish to retain them in the performance goals adopted, especially for the student who does not yet "measure up," but another teacher would drop them.

PERFORMANCE GOAL 1 (INTERPERSONAL RELATIONSHIPS). In the simulated office, students *must* work together in performing the designated tasks. Work reports are kept that include evaluations of affective behaviors for a weekly teacher-manager's grade. The general manager and department managers are expected to assist with these evaluations as part of their responsibilities, a factor that is expected to improve worker performance because of a possible greater desire to meet peer expectations than teacher expectations.

PERFORMANCE GOAL 2 (COMPOSING). The students write the types of communications required as a regular part of the jobs at their work stations. Because they understand the uses to which their communications are put, they probably perform better in the simulation project than in the regular classroom. A student who does not meet the competency standards in composition or English mechanics, though, should be recycled through the necessary en route goals outside the simulation project. There is a danger that this step could be overlooked if the simulation is not competency-based.

PERFORMANCE GOAL 3 (JOB INTERRELATIONSHIPS). Each worker depends on other workers for the input into each job. If a worker is absent or incompetent, a heavier burden falls on coworkers.

PERFORMANCE GOALS 4-12 (RECORDING, TYPING, DUPLICATING, COMPUTING AND VERIFYING, TELEPHONING, MEETING CALLERS, LOCATING BUSINESS INFORMATION, AND MAILING). Learners work with a large enough volume of business papers to develop considerable competence in organizing them. Also, each learner's work is verified at the next work station to which the solutions flow. The activities are integrated rather than isolated, as they are in a workbook.

The success of a simulation project depends on the teacher's ability to evaluate whether a particular competency has been developed to office standards, to modify work assignments in terms of the learner's needs, and to reschedule the successful learner into new responsibilities and the unsuccessful learner into individually prescribed learning modules.

PERFORMANCE GOAL 13 (JOB REQUIREMENTS). While students who have completed an office simulation will understand the requirements of the limited number of clerical jobs, they will not have as broad an understanding of job opportunities as the learner who meets Performance Goal 13. Here the teacher could provide additional learning experiences outside the simulation project.

PERFORMANCE GOAL 14 (INTERVIEWING). The student applies for a job in the simulated office. If interviewing skills are unsatisfactory, additional interviews may be required as the learner moves to each new work station.

## Evaluation

But is simulation really a better teaching strategy than traditional methods? When Horwitz compared students who had completed a simulation project with those of similar expectations and clerical abilities who had completed traditional courses after at least six weeks of actual employment, she found no difference in job satisfaction, but the members of the simulation group received significantly higher job performance ratings by their supervisors. In other words, the simulation students met only two of Fruehling's objectives: acquiring the necessary technical skills and developing the capabilities needed to succeed in a work environment, but they were no better satisfied with their worker roles or more able to choose a job for which they were temperamentally suited than the students from traditional classes. This research suggests the desirability of adding this new dimension to simulated office instruction.

Nelson compared Utah high school students using Mobile Office Education materials with students in daily two-hour traditional office education classes. The simulation students ranked significantly higher in motivation, cooperativeness, ease in making friends, self-centeredness, and logical thinking and were significantly better in filing and checking than nonsimulation students. There were no significant differences between the groups in 26 other skill and personality areas. Additional research is obviously needed to evaluate office simulation.

Effective use of the simulated office as a teaching strategy demands that performance goals be available to the learner. There must be built-in checkpoints at which the learner is stopped and recycled through additional en route goals if unsuccessful. A real danger exists that a student may be rotated to a new work station before meeting the criteria in the present one, a danger that can be averted if the teacher constantly revises the work schedules in terms of learners' needs.

The teacher who is trying to develop standards for a clerical program (either simulated office or traditional course) will be helped by selected criteria developed by Luke for evaluating the office production laboratory (Figure 15.4).

## Equipment

Clerical workers cannot be trained without access to at least the essential equipment they will use on the job. In some schools equipment must be kept to a bare minimum because of limited budget. The equipment selected, however, must be capable of producing work that meets office standards, and competencies required to operate additional equipment can be learned on the job or in a cooperative office work-experience program.

Recommended equipment and supplies for both the simulated office and the traditional classroom are shown in Figure 15.5.

Many materials are available to supplement or even supplant the traditional textbook-workbook. Enrichment or remedial learning resources are appearing in large numbers, probably because of the current emphasis on competency-based business programs, and the teacher is confronted with the problem of keeping abreast of developments. (Recycle to Chapter 7.)

The business community provides the strongest support service available to the clerical program. A competent and active advisory committee strengthens the program and keeps it up to date about business developments. The community as well as the school is the laboratory in which learners achieve employability.

## Cooperative Office Work Experience

Work experience is highly regarded as a strategy in office education at all levels, including the community college. (Recycle to Chapter 7, pp. 140–141.)

**Figure 15.4** Selected portions of criteria for the evaluation of the office production laboratory at the secondary level

A. The instructional content of each work station in the Office Production Laboratory is realistic and equivalent to the tasks performed in actual offices.

**Instructional content**                                                                                    **Check list**

1. included in work stations ranges in difficulty (low entry-level positions to high entry-level positions) to meet the needs of all students    _____

2. has built-in pressures (workloads) and conditions (environmental) commonly found in business offices in the community    _____

3. is individualized so that each student can progress according to his own level of ability    _____

4. is based on objectives stated in behavioral terms to enable students to better understand what is expected of them    _____

5. is based on sound psychological principles of learning    _____

**Tasks**

6. performed at each work station simulate actual office work    _____

7. performed at each work station require students to integrate skills and knowledges previously learned    _____

8. and situations requiring flow of work from one person to another and teamwork to complete a job are built into each work station    _____

B. Work habits, personality traits, and attitudes necessary for success in an office occupation are incorporated.

**The students**                                                                                             **Check list**

1. are encouraged to use good work habits and good housekeeping conditions at their work stations    _____

2. are taught to follow oral and written directions    _____

3. are given situations in which they are expected to determine priorities, plan and organize their work, coordinate their activities, and evaluate their own work    _____

4. are provided opportunities to work together as a team    _____

5. are encouraged to practice good human relations in the Office Production Laboratory    _____

6. are taught to increase productivity while maintaining quality in their work    _____

7. are made aware of good grooming habits, good health habits, and personal cleanliness expected of employees    _____

8. are expected to demonstrate loyalty to and respect for their employers and/or employing firms (represented by the work station) by:
   • striving always to turn out high-quality work
   • having a positive attitude toward the company    _____
   • fully utilizing the time spent at the work station    _____
   • recognizing matters that should be kept confidential and maintaining these confidences    _____

Source: Adapted from Cheryl Luke, "Criteria for the Evaluation of the Office Production Laboratory at the Secondary School Level," unpublished doctoral dissertation.

Formal cooperative office education programs are usually organized to qualify for reimbursement under the Vocational Education Act of 1963 (recycle to Chapter 1) and its amendments by meeting three criteria:

1.  Students must receive instruction, including required courses and related vocational instruction, by alternating study with a job in their major fields. They receive the minimum wage for their employment.
2.  These two experiences must be planned and supervised by a school coordinator and an employer representative so that each contributes to the learner's education and employability.

## Figure 15.5 Recommended equipment and supplies

| Simulated office | Traditional classroom |
| --- | --- |
| Office desk with work space and storage space for each worker | Desk, preferably an office desk |
| Typewriter for each work station, preferably an electric one | Same |
| Electronic calculator or ten-key adding machine on each desk | Battery of electronic calculators and/or ten-key adding machines to support each rotation group |
| A photocopy machine, a spirit duplicator, and a mimeograph machine | Same |
| A drawer or shelf file for each department in which materials are already stored | One drawer or shelf file, in which materials are already filed, for demonstrations by teacher and learners |
| File folders, file guides, labels, sorter | Same |
| | A miniature filing set for each student or a series of letters produced by typewriting class (one for each student) |
| Standard reference materials (one: atlas, sample pages from the telephone directory and *Yellow Pages* (available for each student from the telephone company in several locations), *World Almanac and Book of Facts,* zip code directory, *Books in Print* and *Business Periodicals Index* available in the library, *Dictionary of Occupational Titles.* Several dictionaries and style manuals | Same |
| Interoffice telephone on each desk | An interconnected set of at least two telephones—possibly Teletrainers from the local telephone company |
| Business forms and stationery of sufficiently high quality to enable the worker to produce usable work | Same |
| Other supplies: a postage scale, rubber fingers, a mail register, a visitors' register, a stapler, erasing shields, erasing materials, rubber cement, plastic letter-size covers, and a desk name-plate for each learner | Same |
| Teacher-dictated tapes and cassettes of job instructions which the student can play as many times as necessary | Same |

3. Work periods and school attendance are alternated, with half a day in school and half in the office, one week in school and the next in the office, or a sustained period in the office followed by an equal time in school.

After a feasibility study to determine whether a school should inaugurate a cooperative office work-experience program and it is decided to go ahead, a steering committee including business representatives is formed that continues in an advisory capacity. A step-by-step training plan is then formulated and a school coordinator chosen. The coordinator must be qualified by education, work experience, and personality for a leadership role. A primary responsibility is selection of students who will profit from work experience and have potentiality to perform the tasks expected of them. (One criticism of work experience is that sometimes students are rejected who would profit most from inclusion in favor of those who are already employable and might better remain in the academic environment.) The coordinator next solicits work stations in offices whose supervisors will assist learners in adjusting to work patterns and learning job disciplines and whose stations provide a variety of learning experiences. When agreement is reached that a student is to work in a specific station, a contract is drawn up and signed by all parties (the school, the student, the employer, and the parents), identifying their respective roles.

During employment, training is given by both the office supervisor and the school supervisor, who holds formal classes in which the subject matter is dictated by the worker's deficiencies on the present job and also by the learner's special interests and abilities. Both teacher-coordinator and training supervisor make controlled observations periodically of the worker's technical skills, human relations skills, ability to interact with other workers to achieve a common goal, and ability to use background business information.

When assessing the effectiveness of office-work experience programs, Kingston collected data from high school principals, coordinators, employers, and graduates of both cooperative and traditional business programs in New Jersey who had been working a year or two. She found significant differences in favor of cooperative students in getting first office jobs at higher levels, in current salaries, in job performance ratings, and in attitude toward work and other people. No significant differences were found in beginning salaries, job stability, reasons for changing jobs, or job satisfaction. Clemons investigated the strengths and weaknesses of cooperative office education in high schools in Kentucky by personal interviews with present enrollees, teacher coordinators, and employers. Strengths were personal appearance and strong character. Weaknesses were lack of decision-making abilities, work organization, interest, knowledge, and understanding of the business world. Business representatives cited inadequate preparation in the communication skills as *the* major weakness. Students viewed poor job placement as a major weakness and complained that job placements often had little relevancy to their interests and abilities. This reaction parallels teacher-coordinators' statements that locating appropriate job stations was their major problem.

## Clerical Programs at Other Levels

While this chapter has focused on terminal high school instruction, teachers at other levels can without too much difficulty adapt these competencies and performance goals to their needs. In a two-year college or independent business school course in Secretarial Procedures, for example, the teacher would add dictation-transcribing equipment and at least one MT/ST and one Executive typewriter to essential equipment. Units of instruction on the organization of a word-processing center, how to make travel arrangements, and how to expedite meetings might be added. Case problems would become much more complex, since higher-level decision making would be required. The learner would be expected to plan and execute work with increasingly less supervision. Supervisory duties and problems would be added, for the college-trained person would be expected to be promotable within a relatively short time.

## Evaluating the Clerical Program

With so many options open and with evidence accumulating as to the effectiveness of new strategies, the teacher *must* periodically reexamine the needs of business and of students to see whether the present system is working. Did clerical students meet Fruehling's three objectives? What new competencies and performance goals should be added? Which deleted?

## Learning Activities

1. Work with a committee in classifying instructor-supplied lists of competencies to be achieved in the clerical program into appropriate categories, domains, levels of domain, and type of evaluation until your instructor approves your decisions. (Performance goal 1)

2. While working in a group, establish criteria to use in evaluating the effectiveness of instructional resources and have it approved by the instructor.

3. Using the criteria developed in learning activity 2, work in a small group to identify instructional resources for any of the following: a traditional clerical procedures class, an office simulation, a cooperative office education program, or an individualized class or laboratory. Prepare and duplicate a resource list which includes type of resource, title, a brief description, source, approximate cost, and intended use. (Performance goal 1)

**4.** As a member of a small group and according to your instructor's plan, construct a list of questions to which you expect to find answers and visit a class involved in a simulation project, in an individually prescribed instruction project, or in the activities in a traditional clerical, office, or secretarial practice class. Your group will present to the class your evaluation of the strengths and weaknesses of the strategies used. (Performance goal 1)

**5.** After informing your group of the topic chosen for your teaching demonstration, develop with them the criteria for evaluation of your performance and have the criteria approved by your instructor.

**6.** As a committee member following your instructor's plan and given performance goals, evaluate at least three films, filmstrips, cassettes, or in baskets (from *The Secretary* magazine) according to criteria developed in learning activity 5. Each committee will prepare and distribute a teaching plan for one item which it recommends, indicating the goals for which it is appropriate and the levels of students for whom it is most appropriate. (Performance goal 1)

**7.** Using the criteria sheet developed in learning activity 5 and the plan for teaching, practice your presentation to a small group. (Performance goal 3)

## SELECTED READINGS

BROWER, EDWARD B., "Office Employment Expectations of Business Students," *Delta Pi Epsilon Journal,* November, 1971,pp. 1-12 (reporting unpublished doctoral dissertation entitled "A Study of Office Employment Expectations of White and Nonwhite Business Education Students," Temple University, Philadelphia, Penn., 1970).

BROWN, FRANCIS J., "A Final Outcome Analysis to Compare the Effectiveness of an Experimental Business Education System versus a Traditional Business Education System to Prepare Students to Secure Entry Jobs in Office and Retail Occupations," unpublished doctoral dissertation, Wayne State University, Detroit, Mich., as reported by Frank W. Lanham and Fred S. Cook in "Preparing Students for Office and Distributive Occupations—The Intensified Approach," *National Business Education Yearbook,* Washington, D.C., 1970, pp. 255-264.

CLEMONS, ELAS MERLE, "An Assessment of the Cooperative Education Programs in the Secondary Schools of Kentucky," unpublished doctoral dissertation, University of Kentucky, Lexington, Ky., 1971, as reported in *Business Education Forum,* October, 1972, p. 35.

DOUGLAS, LLOYD V., JAMES T. BLANFORD, AND RUTH I. ANDERSON, "Teaching Clerical Practice and Stenographic Practice," *Teaching Business Subjects,* 3rd ed., Prentice-Hall, Inc., Englewood Cliffs, N.J., 1973, pp. 216-266.

DRISKA, ROBERT, "A Critical Analysis of Office Education on the Secondary Level," unpublished doctoral dissertation, Arizona State University, Tempe, Ariz., 1967.

FRUEHLING, ROSEMARY, "The Whole Worker: A Clerical Program Goal," *Business Education Forum,* February, 1972, p. 17.

GOODMAN, DAVID, "Filing and Records Management," *Eastern Business Teachers Association Yearbook*, Somerville Press, Somerville, N.J., 1971.

HARMS, HARM, B. W. STEHR, AND E. EDWARD HARRIS, "Office Practice," "The Cooperative Plan," " 'In-School' Laboratory Instructional Plans," *Methods of Teaching Business and Distributive Education*, 3d ed., South-Western Publishing Company, Inc., Cincinnati, Ohio, 1972, pp. 179-220, 411-470, 471-522.

HODGES, GAIL, " 'On-the-Job' Training in the Classroom," *Business Education World*, January-February, 1972, p. 18.

HORWITZ, RUTH KAFRISSEN, "The Effectiveness of the Simulated Office," unpublished doctoral dissertation, Temple University, Philadelphia, Penn., 1973.

HUFFMAN, HARRY, "Trends in Clerical Instruction," *Business Education Forum*, December, 1972, pp. 24-27.

HUFFMAN, HARRY, CLYDE WELTER, AND MARIA PETERSON, *Modifying Disadvantaged Students' Perceptions of Office Work*, The Center for Vocational and Technical Education, Ohio State University, Columbus, Ohio, pp. 77-81.

KELLER, LOUISE, "The Teaching and Coordination of Cooperative Office Education," *National Business Education Association Yearbook*, Washington, D.C., 1971, pp. 114-130.

KINGSTON, CARMELA C., "A Study of the Status and Effectiveness of Cooperative Office Education in New Jersey, 1968-9," unpublished doctoral dissertation, Temple University, Philadelphia, 1970, as reported in *Business Education Forum*, October, 1971, p. 40.

LEVIN, HERBERT A., "An Analysis of Selected Characteristics of Students in Clerical Skill Laboratories Compared to Students in Traditional Skills Training Classes," unpublished doctoral dissertation, Temple University, Philadelphia, Penn., 1973.

LUKE, CHERYL, "Criteria for the Evaluation of the Office Production Laboratory at the Secondary School Level," unpublished doctoral dissertation, Indiana University, Bloomington, Ind., 1973.

"Meeting Individual Needs of Office Clerical Students," *Business Education Forum*, February, 1969. Each year, the February issue of *Business Education Forum* focuses on the clerical program.

NELSON, FRANK E., "Evaluating Office Practice Simulation Programs in Utah," unpublished doctoral dissertation, Utah State University, Logan, Utah, 1972, as reported in *Business Education Forum*, October, 1973, pp. 49-50.

POLAND, ROBERT, "Block-Time Approach in Office Education," *National Business Education Yearbook*, Washington, D.C., 1970, p. 264.

POLAND, ROBERT, (ED.), "Part IV: Types of Secretarial Office Training," *National Business Education Association Yearbook*, Reston, Va., 1974, pp. 128–156.

*Practicum* to accompany *The Administrative Secretary*, Gregg Division, McGraw-Hill Book Company, New York, 1970.

SABIN, WILLIAM H., "Simulation in the Seventies: An Overview," *Business Education World*, September-October, 1971, p. 6.

*Simulated Office Situations* to accompany *Secretarial Procedures and Administration*, 6th ed., South-Western Publishing Company, Inc., Cincinnati, 1973.

STEWART, JEFFREY, AND WALTER L. SHELL, (EDS.), "The Office Practice Program in Business Education," *Eastern Business Teachers Association Yearbook*, Somerville Press, Somerville, N.J., 1969.

WEST, LEONARD J., "Reversed Instructional Procedures for Vocational Typing Tasks," *Delta Pi Epsilon Journal,* February, 1972, p. 35.

WOODWARD, LYNDA MAE H., "An Analysis of Performance of Utah High School Senior Students in Office Practice Courses as Compared with National Norms for National Business Entrance Tests," unpublished master's thesis, Brigham Young University, Provo, Utah, 1970, as reported in *Business Education Forum,* October, 1971, p. 57.

## PERFORMANCE GOALS

**1.** Given a list of topics in consumer education, **identify** ten tasks, standards, and then competencies, in terms of Chapters 3 and 16.

**2.** Select one competency from those identified for performance goal 1 above, and **develop** a teaching-learning system including classification of competency into domain and level, construction of performance goal, identification and sequencing of subcompetencies, planning of an evaluation, and selection of teaching-learning strategies.

**3.** Given a description of four students in a consumer education class including such things as grade level, reading level, economic background, and the like, **decide** on four competencies appropriate for each student, and defend your answer in terms of Chapter 16.

# CHAPTER 16

# Consumer Education

"Understanding conspicuous consumption and compensatory consumption," "Getting the most for the least money," and "Learning how to budget,"—all are responses to the question, "What is consumer education?" Each response, however, reveals only one facet of consumer education.

What *is* consumer education? It is preparing individuals with cognitive and affective learnings required in day-to-day living, learnings that will enable them to get maximum satisfaction from limited resources consistent with a personal value system.

In discussing the role of consumer education in occupational preparation, the California State Department of Education defined consumer education this way:

Consumer education, as an integral part of vocational education, is the development of the individual in skills, concepts, and understandings required to develop sound decision making for: (1) Achieving maximum utilization of and satisfaction from resources, (2) Evaluating alternatives in the marketplace, (3) Understanding rights and responsibilities as a consumer in society, and (4) Fulfilling role as a participant in a free enterprise system. (*Role of Consumer Education in Occupational Preparation*, p. 1)

Consumer information, in contrast to consumer education, deals with specifics such as size, weight, color, and use rather than value relationships. Consumer information enables the individual to meet an immediate need or solve an immediate problem such as deciding which electric ice cream freezer to buy. Consumer education enables the individual to practice wise buymanship regardless of what is being purchased—a camera, a carton of cola, or a car.

Consumer education is taught in grades K–12, in junior and community colleges, in senior colleges, at graduate levels, and in noncredit adult education programs. Recently six books—each directed at a particular level of consumer education (early childhood, elementary, secondary, junior and community college, teacher education, and continuing education)—were published; they collectively provide guidance and insight for consumer educators at all levels (see Schoenfeld et al.). Consumer education may be taught in the elementary school or in the middle school or high school within a business department, home economics department, or social studies department. It may also be taken up in driver education, industrial arts, mathematics, health, science, and English courses. This chapter is primarily concerned with consumer education taught in grades 9–12 within a business department. Some schools offer modules in consumer education topics; others offer a one-semester course or a one-year course; and still others offer consumer education as a unit in courses other than business. Consumer education is most often categorized in the social business area (the nonvocational area); however, in response to an acute need, state departments of education are increasingly including consumer education as a part of vocational preparation.

## History of the Consumer Movement

The current focus on consumer problems is the third such mass movement during this century. As it did in the early 1900s and during the 1930s, the public is now again responding to dwindling natural resources, shortages, rising prices, shoddy merchandise, and other consumer abuses with boycotts, marches, and demands for new protective legislation. All three eras of consumer concern within this century have been periods of social unrest and economic upheaval. In each era critics of the social system were alarmed at the human costs of industrialization and the uneven distribution of income. In each period inflation spiraled, causing economic hardships on the masses, particularly those on fixed incomes. Exposé journalism focused attention on injustices in each period.

Along with the benefits that industrialization brought during the early 1900s came major problems, including child labor, slums, immigrant abuse, hazardous working conditions, and municipal corruption. Because the turn of the century had seen purchasing power declining, the labor movement made rapid gains as it appealed to persons who acutely felt rising prices. The public in general regarded the labor movement and the giant corporations as the culprits. This period of consumer concern saw the enactment of the Pure Food and Drug Act of 1906, the Clayton Antitrust Act of 1914, and the Federal Trade Commission Act of the same year, and the breaking up of monopolies such as Standard Oil.

World War I and the prosperity of the 1920s saw the cry for consumer protection diminish to a mere whisper, and then the 1929 stock market crash and subsequent Depression spurred new interest in consumer problems. "Use it up, wear it out, make it do, or do without" became the rallying cry; and for the first time consumer education topics began to find their way into school curricula. The need for grade labeling and quality testing of products was apparent in the bleak Depression years, and two consumer testing organizations emerged: Consumers' Research and then Consumers Union. After a hundred people died from taking an untested liquid form of sulfa, Food and Drug Administration control was extended, in 1938, to ensure the safety of products before they reached the market.

Interest in the consumer movement waned in the 1940s, as national attention was focused on World War II and postwar adjustments. The present interest in consumer affairs was given impetus by President Kennedy's 1962 message to Congress, the first message by a President of the United States specifically on consumer affairs. President Kennedy advocated a Consumer's Bill of Rights including the right to choose, the right to be informed, the right to safety, and the right to be heard.

Renewed interest in consumer protection resulted in new legislation in the 1960s, including the Highway Safety Act, the Truth in Packaging Act, and the Truth in Lending Act. At the same time Part F of the Vocational Education Amendments Act of 1968 authorized funds for consumer and homemaking education programs; in so doing, it relegated consumer education to homemaking. Even though business education per se was not included in the authorization, business education has participated in funded interdisciplinary programs. The Vocational Education Amendments of 1972 encouraged and supported the development of new and improved consumer education curricula and authorized a Director of Consumers' Education within the U.S. Office of Education.

What does the future hold for consumer education? It seems clear that concern for consumer problems and consumer protection will continue and will fluctuate in intensity with the social and economic climate.

## Needs of the Learner

Consumer "education" begins for most young people as children in front of television sets watching commercials in which animals, cartoon characters, or TV personalities extol the features of toys or food products. If you overhear a four- or five-year-old child singing, you are likely to hear the current TV commercials rather than the songs which are our country's musical heritage. Those commercials are translated into action at the supermarket, when children pressure their parents to buy the advertised products; here also, the products are within easy reach, silently shouting "Buy! Buy!"

The scale is tilted in favor of corporations spending vast sums of money to entice teenagers to buy, but relatively little is spent on teaching them to buy wisely or perhaps not to buy at all. Prosperous times have also prompted the attitude, "Don't worry if it breaks; just throw it away and buy another one." This attitude causes concern not only from a consumer viewpoint but also from an environmental position.

The crux of the problem of satisfying individual needs lies in the fact of scarcity. Human wants and needs are infinite in number and manifestations, but resources to fulfil those needs and wants are finite. Fleck says that individuals have many other needs, but these eight seem unusually important (Fleck, p. 38):

1. To belong
2. For achievement and recognition
3. For economic security
4. To be free from fear
5. For love and affection
6. To be free from intense feelings of guilt
7. For self-respect
8. For an understanding of the world in which one lives

Psychologist Maslow's hierarchy of needs is conceptualized below as a pyramid, with basic needs at the bottom and higher-level needs disposed in ascending order.

Figure 16.1   Maslow's hierarchy of needs

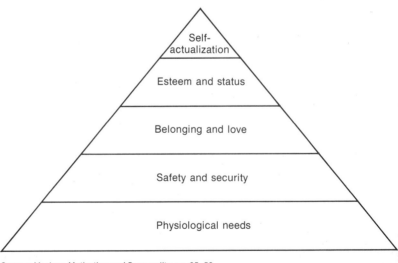

Source: Maslow, *Motivation and Personality*, pp. 35–58.

Learner needs are compounded in the case of the poor. Caplovitz and others have documented the fact that the poor, who can least afford to pay high prices, in fact pay dearly for merchandise which may be available for less in other neighborhoods. For many reasons—including lack of transportation, child care, credit, and confidence—the poor do not leave their neighborhoods to shop. They tend to be easily influenced by advertising and salespeople, and—unfortunately—deep human needs drive the poor into a commercial jungle in which exploitation and fraud are often the norm rather than the exception.

## Needs of Business

Cartoonists sometimes portray business on one side of a compound, separated by barbed wire from the consumer on the other side; and both sides are shown with weapons drawn. Such portrayals erroneously picture business and consumers in opposite camps. Legitimate businessmen hate shysters and hucksters as much as do consumers. Such shysters not only drain business away from legitimate business firms but cause a pale of mistrust to settle over the entire business community. Since World War II, business firms have widely embraced the marketing concept, the philosophy that all the resources of an organization are mobilized to create a product, stimulate demand, and satisfy the customer at a profit. Business is increasingly accepting social responsibility for its stake in consumer education.

## Identifying and Classifying Competencies

The first step in the teaching-learning system is to identify and classify competencies to be attained. Instead of dealing with tasks to be performed on the job, consumer education involves tasks performed in the marketplace or the using of goods and services provided in the marketplace. Several major studies have identified competencies in vocational education, but as yet no definitive studies identifying competencies in consumer education have been published. Since we do not have the same kind of data from which to work in consumer education, we must rely on professional judgment as to what constitutes necessary competencies. The standard in consumer education is not the same kind of precise measurement as in the vocational area because the competency is linked to the uniqueness of the individual learner and his or her value system. The responsibility, however, falls on the consumer education teacher or the local school district to identify appropriate competencies, including standards.

Consumer education is geared toward the attainment of those competencies needed in acquiring and using goods and services. Since in our society most people purchase goods and services rather than make their own (food, shoes, dry cleaning, and so on), consumer education focuses on buying and using rather than making and using.

At this point consumer education teachers must identify their own competencies in consumer education. Some teachers start with a list of topics or a published list of objectives deemed appropriate in consumer education and use these as a basis for identifying competencies. One such list will be used to identify competencies which will then be carried through the teaching-learning system.

The *Suggested Guidelines for Consumer Education* identify the following eight topics as appropriate to consumer education (President's Committee on Consumer Interests, p. 2): (1) making consumer decisions, (2) examining quality, (3) consumers' rights and responsibilities in the marketplace, (4) consumers' right to safety, (5) examining personal values, (6) psychological influences on the consumer, (7) sharing costs, and (8) sharing risks.

More detailed lists of consumer education topics are given in Figure 16.2.

If a teacher chooses to use published objectives as a starting point for identifying competencies, then the following examples might be useful—one from a state level and the other from the federal level.

*Suggested Guidelines for Consumer Education* say objectives for a consumer education program might be those which enable the student to:

- Exercise his rights more actively as a consumer
- Contrast responsible and irresponsible transactions in the marketplace
- Identify cultural influences on personal values
- Differentiate wants from needs
- Compare budgeting procedures of different families
- Distinguish quality from nonquality products

The State of Illinois has mandated that pupils in the public schools in grades 8 through 12 be given courses which include instruction in consumer education, including but not necessarily limited to installment purchasing, budgeting, and comparison of prices. The Illinois *Guidelines for Consumer Education* (Office of the Superintendent of Public Instruction) say that essentially, problem-solving consumer education objectives should include helping the students to do the following:

- Become an informed consumer
- Understand the role of the consumer in our society
- Develop a sound decision-making process based upon one's individual goals and values
- Utilize resources to facilitate greater satisfaction in making consumer decisions
- Understand the rights and responsibilities of the consumer in society

The topics from *Suggested Guidelines for Consumer Education* are used to identify tasks, standards of performance, and competencies as shown in Figure 16.3.

Once competencies have been identified, the teacher must determine the domain and level within the domain. The domain, level, evaluation,

## Figure 16.2 Topics in consumer education

| Uhl list[a] | Campbell list[b] |
|---|---|
| 1. The consumer in the economy | 1. The consumer and the economy |
| 2. Consumption, production, and income | 2. Values and goals |
| 3. Management and family income | 3. Occupation and income |
| 4. Saving and investment | 4. Management of resources |
| 5. Credit | 5. Economic choices |
| 6. Planning for consumer risk and uncertainty | 6. Consumer information |
| 7. Community consumption and taxes | 7. Advertising, selling aids, and motivators |
| 8. Consumers in the market | 8. Buying goods and services |
| 9. Consumer aid and protection | 9. Housing |
| 10. Consumption of food | 10. Consumer credit |
| 11. Clothing and household soft goods | 11. Insurance protection |
| 12. Housing and shelter | 12. Savings and investments |
| 13. Durables—Equipment, appliances, and furniture | 13. Taxes |
| 14. Transportation | 14. Consumer grievances |
| 15. Consumer services | 15. Consumer protection |
| 16. Leisure | 16. Consumer rights and responsibilities |
| 17. Education | 17. The consumer and the environment |
| 18. Consumer health | |
| 19. Consumer organization | |
| 20. Consumer information | |

[a] Joseph N. Uhl, "The Purdue Consumer Education Study." See Selected Readings.
[b] Sally R. Campbell, *Consumer Education in an Age of Adaptation.* See Selected Readings.

verb, conditions of performance, and criteria for evaluation are shown in Figure 16.4 on pages 408–409.

## Planning Evaluations

At the time performance goals are constructed, the evaluations to measure those performance goals are planned. Evaluations from previously constructed examinations or from publishers can be utilized if they are available. Otherwise, the teacher will construct examinations to measure the attainment of the performance goal.

For example, a checklist like the one in Figure 16.5 on page 410 could be used to evaluate psychological influences upon the consumer with reference to competency 5 (Correctly recognize psychological influences upon the consumer).

## Constructing Performance Goals

The next step in the teaching-learning system is to construct performance goals. The seven competencies are shown on pages 406–407, with their corresponding performance goals.

**Figure 16.3   Consumer education tasks converted to competencies**

| Topic | Task | Standard of performance | Competency |
|---|---|---|---|
| 1. Making consumer decisions | Make buying decisions | Wise according to teacher | Make buying decisions which the teacher judges to be wise for the student, based on wise buying principles and the student's consumer profile |
| 2. Examining quality | Arrive at a conclusion regarding quality of a product | Recognized criteria for judging quality | Arrive at a conclusion regarding quality of a product by applying recognized criteria for judging |
| 3. Consumer's rights and responsibilities in the marketplace; consumer's right to safety | Identify four consumer rights known as the Consumer's Bill of Rights and show evidence of each right being exercised or violated | Correctly | Correctly identify four consumer rights known as the Consumer's Bill of Rights and show evidence of each right being exercised or violated |
| 4. Examining personal values | Analyze personal values | Student-prepared checklist | Analyze your personal values against a student-prepared checklist which includes items such as income, goals, culture, lifestyle, ethnic background, religious beliefs, and the like |
| 5. Psychological influences on the consumer | Recognize psychological influences on the consumer | Correctly | Correctly recognize psychological influences upon the consumer |
| 6. Sharing costs | Describe how consumers share costs for public services | Correctly | Correctly describe how consumers share costs for public services |
| 7. Sharing risks | Identify ways in which consumers share risks through insurance | Correctly | Correctly identify ways in which consumers share risks through insurance |

COMPETENCY 1

Make buying decisions which the teacher judges to be wise for the student based on wise buying principles and the student's consumer profile.

PERFORMANCE GOAL

**Defend** your purchasing decision for the last four purchases of $3 or over by describing the item purchased, reason for purchasing that brand, and alternative uses for the money spent. Evaluation criterion is the teacher's judgment of the reasonableness of your purchases consistent with both the principles of wise buying and a consumer profile, such as Campbell's (Campbell, p. 61).

COMPETENCY 2
Arrive at a conclusion regarding quality of a product by applying recognized criteria.
PERFORMANCE GOAL
Given four garments (four shirts, for example), examine each garment and **judge** quality according to recognized criteria and accurately reach a conclusion as to whether each garment is excellent, good, or poor in quality.

COMPETENCY 3
Decide when consumer rights are being violated.
PERFORMANCE GOAL
Correctly **identify** the four rights known as the Consumer's Bill of Rights and prepare a portfolio which includes newspaper and magazine clippings which show a right being exercised or violated and defend your choice before your small group of six students.

COMPETENCY 4
Analyze your personal values against a student-prepared checklist which includes items such as income, goals, culture, life-style, ethnic background, religious beliefs, and the like.
PERFORMANCE GOAL
Working with a group of three or four other students, **develop** a checklist of factors which influence consumer values and then analyze your own values by responding to the items on the checklist.

COMPETENCY 5
Recognize psychological influences upon the consumer.
PERFORMANCE GOAL
Given a list of 20 magazine and newspaper advertisements which reflect psychological influences on the consumer, in all cases **identify** the human need appealed to.

COMPETENCY 6
Recognize how consumers share costs for public services.
PERFORMANCE GOAL
Given dialogue concerning public services for a community, write an essay in which you correctly **describe** three levels of government which levy taxes and explain the major types of taxes each level levies.

COMPETENCY 7
Correctly identify ways in which consumers share risks through insurance.
PERFORMANCE GOAL
Given six case studies, correctly identify ways in which consumers share risks through insurance, **list** ten hazards against which insurance can be obtained and identify the type of insurance coverage which protects against each hazard.

## Identifying and Sequencing Subcompetencies

Since almost every performance goal involves the mastery of several subcompetencies, those subcompetencies must be identified and sequenced. If attaining one subcompetency depends on the mastery of another, the

Figure 16.4 Consumer education competencies analyzed for components of performance goals

| Competency | Dominant domain and level | Results of performance | Verb | Conditions of performance | Criterion |
|---|---|---|---|---|---|
| 1. Make buying decisions which the teacher judges to be wise for the student based on wise buying principles and the student's consumer profile | Cognitive: evaluation | Product | **Defend** | Having made four purchases of $3 or over | Teacher judgment of reasonableness of your purchases consistent with both the principles of wise buying and consumer profile |
| 2. Arrive at a conclusion regarding quality of a product by applying recognized criteria for judging | Cognitive: evaluation | Product | **Judge** | Given four garments | No errors consistent with recognized criteria |
| 3. Decide when consumer rights are being violated. | Cognitive: knowledge and application | Product | **Apply** | After identifying Consumer's Bill of Rights, prepare a portfolio | According to Consumer's Bill of Rights |

Figure 16.4 (*continued*)

| Competency | Dominant domain and level | Results of performance | Verb | Conditions of performance | Criterion |
|---|---|---|---|---|---|
| 4. Analyze your personal values against a student-prepared checklist which includes items such as income, goals, culture, lifestyle, ethnic background, religious beliefs, and the like | Cognitive: analysis/synthesis | Product | **Analyze** | Analyze own values against student-prepared checklist | Consistent with checklist |
| 5. Recognize psychological influences upon the consumer | Cognitive: knowledge and application | Product | **Recognize and apply** | Given a list of 20 magazine and newspaper advertisements | Each psychological influence correctly |
| 6. Describe how consumers share costs for public services | Cognitive: comprehension | Product | **Describe** | Given dialogue concerning public services for a community | Correctly |
| 7. Identify ways in which consumers share risks through insurance | Cognitive: knowledge | Product | **Identify** | Given 6 case studies | Correctly |

## Figure 16.5 Checklist for competency 5

Each statement exerts a psychological influence upon a consumer. Place a check mark in the column describing the need to which the statement appeals.

| | Physiolog-ical needs | Safety & security | Belonging & love | Esteem & status | Self-actual-ization |
|---|---|---|---|---|---|
| 1. Miss America chooses | | | | | |
| 2. Stock market hits new low | | | | | |
| 3. Subcompact Whizzer averages 26 mpg | | | | | |
| 4. Alive Bible sells 14 million copies | | | | | |
| 5. Fresh tomatoes only 18¢ a pound | | | | | |
| 6. Worst plane crash kills 346 | | | | | |
| 7. Own 102 great books | | | | | |
| 8. The shoes the champions wear | | | | | |
| 9. Your family deserves the best | | | | | |
| 10. Beauty is a joy forever | | | | | |
| 11. The way to a man's heart | | | | | |
| 12. Everybody is going | | | | | |
| 13. Solid comfort | | | | | |
| 14. The key to success | | | | | |
| 15. The road to wealth and happiness | | | | | |
| 16. An apple a day | | | | | |
| 17. Disaster may be around the corner | | | | | |
| 18. The finest made | | | | | |
| 19. First choice of movie stars | | | | | |
| 20. Be one of the crowd | | | | | |

subcompetencies must be sequenced in proper order. Identification of the subcompetencies necessary to mastery of performance goal 1 is shown in Figure 16.6.

## Pretesting and Matching Learner With Performance Goals and Subcompetencies

Since all students come to the classroom with some background in consumer education, the purpose of pretesting is to determine the extent of prior learnings in order to identify realistic performance goals for the individual student. A variety of assessments may be used to determine the present level of competency. The evaluations planned and developed to measure the competencies may also be used as pretests, or alternative forms may be used.

Since consumer education is inextricably tied to the uniqueness of the individual and his or her value system, it is helpful to have relevant information on each student, such as the Campbell consumer profile or an attitude inventory. Once the student's present level of competency is determined, then he or she is matched with appropriate performance goals and subcompetencies.

## Applying Appropriate Learning Principles

The next step in the system is to identify and apply appropriate learning principles. Selected learning principles follow.

**RELEVANT.** Consumer education can be the most exciting study in the entire curriculum because it relates so directly to the student's day-to-day living. The student who perceives the relationship of consumer education to the ability to plan for and get a motorbike or used car will be eager to learn provided the student is a suburban, urban, or rural youth whose family has a car. Study of the acquisition and care of an automobile would be almost meaningless to an inner-city teenager who does not personally know anyone who owns a car. The teacher must structure the learning situation so that the learner will see the relevance of what is happening in the classroom to everyday life outside the classroom. Achieving this relevance is easier in consumer education than in many other classes; however, it is not automatic.

Figure 16.6    Sequencing of subcompetencies for performance
goal 1

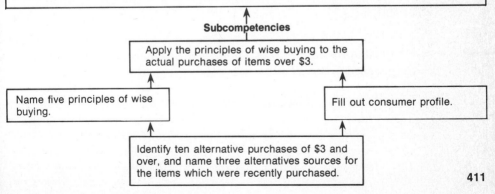

**Performance goal 1**

**Defend** your purchasing decision for the last four purchases of $3 or over by describing the item purchased, reason for purchasing that brand, and alternative uses for the money spent. Evaluation criterion is the teacher's judgment of the reasonableness of your purchase consistent with both the principles of wise buying and your consumer profile.

**Subcompetencies**

Apply the principles of wise buying to the actual purchases of items over $3.

Name five principles of wise buying.

Fill out consumer profile.

Identify ten alternative purchases of $3 and over, and name three alternatives sources for the items which were recently purchased.

411

INTERACTION WITH ENVIRONMENT.   A student who is grappling with the problems of learning wise buymanship principles will learn more easily by solving simulated problems in the marketplace. The "real" problems in the marketplace may involve actually comparing and reporting back to the class but not actually making the purchase.

LEARNER ACTIVE.   Learning proceeds more effectively when the learner is an active participant in the learning process; for example, when he or she actually goes into the marketplace to gather data about bank services, to survey prices at local drug or food stores, and to investigate the services of the local fire or police department rather than merely hearing facts. When it is not feasible to go into the community, the process can be simulated in the classroom.

GOAL DIRECTED.   The era of accountability has forced teachers and students alike to verbalize goals—both en route goals and terminal goals. In the past a student could spend a year in a consumer education class and leave the class thinking that the goal was to determine the unit price of a supermarket product without ever understanding that this was only a subcompetency to the competency of ability to do comparison shopping.

EXPANDING PATTERN OF BEHAVIORS.   Learning proceeds more effectively when the learner participates in a continuously expanding pattern of behaviors. Learning might be initiated by asking students to record for one day everything they eat. Later this could be expanded to include the cost of food (no small calculation when all costs are included, such as salt and pepper). Costs for one day for one person could be expanded to one week for one person, then one week for a family, then a month, and then a year. Later, shelter and clothing could also be calculated. The calculations, from the simplest to the most complex, could be used to analyze spending.

## Selecting and Using Appropriate Teaching-Learning Strategies

Selection of teaching strategies should include consideration of large-group, small-group, and individual instruction. Many activities and media are appropriate for all three types of instruction; others, for only one or possibly two. The list of activities and media in Figure 16.7 can serve as a stimulus to the teacher who is developing strategy in consumer education.

Strategies appropriate to use in connection with performance goal 1 might include the following:

1.  Brainstorm purchases teenagers might make where the cost of the good or service is $3 or over.
2.  Discuss how one's value system affects what he or she buys; for example, one teenager might give the $3 to a church's special building fund; another might buy a sack of hamburgers to take home to younger brothers or sisters for a special treat; another might buy an eight-track tape; another might go bowling; and another might put $3 in a savings account for vocational school tuition.

Figure 16.7   Use of activities and media

| | Type of instruction | | |
| --- | --- | --- | --- |
| | Large-group | Small-group | Individual |
| **Activities** | | | |
| Guest speaker | x | x | |
| Demonstration | x | x | x |
| Interviews | x | x | x |
| Field trips | | x | x |
| Learning packets | | | x |
| Comparison shopping | | x | x |
| Panel discussion | x | x | |
| Plays and skits | x | x | |
| Games | | x | |
| Brainstorming | x | x | |
| Questioning | x | x | |
| Simulation | x | x | x |
| Projects | x | x | x |
| Lecture | x | x | |
| **Media** | | | |
| Transparencies | x | x | x |
| Graphs, charts, diagrams, posters, maps | x | x | x |
| Newspapers and magazines | x | x | x |
| Films | x | x | |
| Television | x | x | x |
| Flip charts | x | x | |
| Collages and montages | x | x | x |
| Outdoor advertising | x | x | x |
| Audiotapes | | x | x |

3. Working in groups of not more than six students, draw up a list of wise buying principles and then verify the list against a library reference supplied by the teacher.

4. View a movie in a large group or, in a study carrel, view a filmstrip on wise buying.

5. In order to analyze personal attitudes, fill out a consumer profile or consumer attitude inventory supplied by the teacher.

6. Prepare a checklist with wise buying principles down the left column and the four items purchased at over $3 across the top. Place a mark in the column next to each wise buying principle if it was adhered to in making the purchase.

   a. For each item bought, write out a short statement as to why the item was purchased, reasons for selecting that brand, and names of goods or services which you considered buying instead of the one you did buy.

   b. Review your checklist and statements and defend them in a small group of four students.

413

The *Suggested Guidelines for Consumer Education* identify activities by four grade levels for the topics which were the basis for the seven competencies carried through the teaching-learning system. Activities for grades 10-12 for topics relating to the seven competencies are shown:

MAKING CONSUMER DECISIONS. Buying a used car: (1) Use overhead transparencies to demonstrate how to buy a used car. (2) Help students develop a checklist on how to shop for a used car. (3) Visit a used-car lot or have a dealer bring a used car to school. (4) Have students do a study of the costs of running a car. Consider depreciation, insurance, gas and oil, parking and registration fees and costs, tires, repairs and maintenance. Those who intend to buy a car should make plans for income to support it. (5) Visit the automotive shop in the industrial arts department. Have the students demonstrate simple maintenance and repair techniques: how to adjust a choke, change the oil and oil filter, clean the air filter, change a tire, polish a car, adjust spark plugs, start a stalled car with jump cables.

EXAMINING QUALITY. Divide the class into three groups. Have each group conduct a scientific experiment on the following: identity of artificial color on oranges, rapid identification of margarine and butter, qualitative analysis of cold tablets.

CONSUMER'S RIGHTS AND RESPONSIBILITIES IN THE MARKETPLACE. (1) Collect and display newspaper or magazine articles about fraudulent practices affecting consumers. Discuss laws that protect the consumer—national, state, and local. (2) Ask student "roving reporters" to interview a supermarket manager on how he tries to protect the consumer. (3) Show medical quackery films, such as *Health Fraud Racket* (FDA). (4) Invite local Food and Drug Administration consumer specialist to speak on laws pertaining to food, drugs, and cosmetics. (5) Have class draw up a list of questions to ask FDA specialist after each student takes a personal inventory of all food, drugs, and cosmetics he or she ordinarily uses.

EXAMINING PERSONAL VALUES. (1) Encourage each student to select an imaginary salary. Have student deduct taxes and plan a budget for the rest of his or her income. (2) Each student analyzes his or her proposed spending pattern for class discussion. (3) After the class develops a survey sheet and using a tape recorder, students interview three families on how they spend money.

PSYCHOLOGICAL INFLUENCES ON THE CONSUMER. (1) Encourage students to make a list of all their clothing and equipment needs for a full year. Students should list clothing and equipment they already have, along with those they intend to purchase. Supply students with catalogues and ads to help with prices. Ask students to explain why they chose their particular items. (2) Have discussions of quality versus quantity. Student reports should reflect the cost per month of being appropriately and attractively dressed.

SHARING COSTS. (1) Students form teams to debate question, "Does our community need an increase in local taxes?" (2) Discuss federal and local tax return forms. (3) Invite an attorney to class to answer questions drawn up by students. (4) Make a bulletin board of all tax forms used by local citizens.

SHARING RISKS. (1) Class discussion on functions of insurance (protection or savings) and costs of types of policies. (2) Students discuss case studies to determine whether or not insurance would offer the kind of protection or savings program needed for the family situation presented in each case. (3) Encourage students to do individual reports on social security, Medicare, workmen's compensation.

Strategy includes resources as well as activities. The federal government, state and local governments, school districts, business firms, and others have developed materials in consumer education. Teachers should recognize that consumer education classes are attractive targets for organizations who wish to promote a particular point of view, and materials from nonprofit organizations should receive the same careful scrutiny given to materials from publishers. Consumer organizations and professional associations may have current materials. Organizations of particular interest to consumer educators include national consumer organizations such as Consumer Federation of America and National Consumer's League, Inc.; professional associations such as American Council on Consumer Interests, American Home Economics Association, and National Business Education Association; and periodicals such as *Consumers' Research, Consumer Reports, Journal of Consumer Affairs, Journal of Consumer Research,* and *Media and Consumer.* Information concerning these and other organizations can be found under Resources (p. 475).

Consumers Union publishes a monthly loose-leaf teaching aid called "Teaching Tools for Consumer Ed" which includes discussion items, new and current resources, a clearinghouse for developments in consumer education, and a current listing of professional meetings, seminars, and workshops. Teachers may order *Consumer Reports* magazine in bulk at less than half the usual cost, and "Teaching Tools" is free with bulk orders. One issue of "Teaching Tools" said that a particular issue of the magazine should provide the teacher with ample information and ideas for a unit on automobiles, and students can be encouraged to do follow-up research and reports on many of the topics covered in the magazine. Their research efforts may be as simple as clipping articles from current newspapers and magazines on topics such as auto safety, auto pollution, car maintenance and repair, warranties, and auto recalls. These articles could then form the basis for a class discussion, debate, presentation, individual research project, and/or bulletin board display.

*Consumer Update* is published by Gregg and Community College Division of McGraw-Hill as a professional service to help consumer educators focus on current issues. The premier volume carried articles on topics such as product safety, the Better Business Bureau, unfair sales practices, the courts as an effective deterrent to consumer fraud, and nutritional labels. Some issues have inserts which can be used to make transparencies, such as the one on nutritional labeling shown in Figure 16.8.

**415**

Figure 16.8

# FROZEN DELIGHT
# BRAND CASSEROLE

## NUTRITION INFORMATION

(Per Serving)
*Serving size = 8 oz*
*Servings per container = 2*

| | |
|---|---:|
| **Calories** | 560 |
| **Protein** | 23 g |
| **Carbohydrate** | 43 g |
| **Fat** | 33 g |

(PERCENTAGE OF CALORIES FROM FAT = 53%)

| | |
|---|---:|
| Polyunsaturated* | 22 g |
| Saturated | 9 g |
| Cholesterol *(18 mg/100 g) | 40 mg |
| Sodium (365 mg/100 g) | 810 mg |

PERCENTAGE OF U. S. RECOMMENDED DAILY
ALLOWANCE (U. S. RDA)

| | | | |
|---|---:|---|---:|
| **Protein** | 35 | **Niacin** | 25 |
| **Vitamin A** | 35 | **Calcium** | 2 |
| **Vitamin C** | 10 | **Iron** | 25 |
| **Thiamin** | 15 | Vitamin $B_6$ | 22 |
| **Riboflavin** | 15 | Vitamin $B_{12}$ | 15 |

\* Information on fat and cholesterol content is provided for individuals who, on the advice of a physician, are modifying their total dietary intake of fat and cholesterol.

Note: Values for nutrients listed in bold face are required.

Source: *Consumer Update*, Vol. 1, No. 2.

## Evaluating Student Achievement

Throughout the learning process the student and the teacher have had regular feedback of progress in meeting en route goals and acquiring subcompetencies. The student who did not meet en route goals recycled to alternative learning activities that dealt in a new way with the subcompetencies. The final step in the system is to evaluate mastery of performance goals using the evaluations planned at the outset. The student who meets the terminal goals is ready to go to other competencies and performance goals; however, if the terminal goals are not yet met, then the student recycles to activities which will enable him or her to meet the goal. The student's success is a reflection of the effectiveness of the teaching-learning system.

## Learning Activities

**1.** Visit your college or university library or curriculum resources center and look up consumer education materials to find state plans for consumer education, courses of study, resource units, modules of learning, or suggested topics in consumer education, and prepare a list of such materials. This task may be divided so that members of a group may each research one aspect and pool the findings in a group report which will be evaluated for completeness. (Performance goal 1)

**2.** Working in small groups, prepare a list of types of data about students such as grade level, reading level, and socio-economic background, which the teacher should have in order to determine competencies in consumer education for those students. (Performance goal 3)

**3.** Since consumer education is tied to students' value systems, working in small groups, construct an instrument which indicates values. The instrument might be a check sheet for students to check preferences, interests, and values, or it might be an open ended questionnaire. (Performance goal 3)

**4.** Given a description of students with diverse learning abilities and present level of each, and a list of competencies appropriate for consumer education, decide on the competencies you would suggest for each student, defending your choices with reasons that reveal your understanding of student needs. (Performance goal 3)

**5.** Given six competencies in consumer education, construct performance goals for each, consistent with material in Chapter 5. (Performance goal 2)

**6.** Given a competency in consumer education which can be developed using all three patterns of instruction, construct a plan to develop that competency using (a) large-group instruction, (b) small-group instruction, and (c) individualized instruction. (Performance goal 2)

## SELECTED READINGS

ANDERSON, CHARLES A., "The Effectiveness of a Simulation Learning Game in Teaching Consumer Credit to Senior High School Students in Comparison to a Conventional Approach to Instruction," unpublished doctoral dissertation, University of Maryland, College Park, Md., 1969. Also *Business Education Forum*, vol. 25, October, 1970, pp. 24–25.

BAKKEN, MELVIN R., "Money Management Understandings of Tenth Grade Students," unpublished master's thesis, University of Alberta, Calgary, Alberta, 1966. Also *National Business Education Quarterly*, vol. 36, October, 1967, p. 6.

BEATTIE, A. DONALD, "Relationships Between High School Pupils' Information and Attitudes Toward Personal Finance," *Delta Pi Epsilon Journal,* vol. 7, no. 4, July, 1964, p. 97.

BIBB, FRANCES G., "A Comparative Study of the Knowledge of Three Aspects of Consumer Information Possessed by Selected Indiana, Illinois, and Wisconsin University Freshmen," unpublished doctoral dissertation, Northern Illinois University, DeKalb, Ill., 1971. Also *Business Education Forum,* vol. 27, October, 1972, p. 33.

BERGHAUS, NONA ROSE, "A Developmental Sequence of Content Essential to Personal Money Management," unpublished doctoral dissertation, University of Oklahoma, Norman, Okla., 1966. Also *Journal of Business Education,* vol. 42, March, 1967, p. 253, and *National Business Education Quarterly,* vol. 36, October, 1967, pp. 8-9.

BODUCH, THEODORE J., "Consumer Economics," *NBEA Yearbook,* vol. 10, 1972, pp. 11-23.

BONNICE, JOSEPH G., "Consumer Rights—and Responsibilities," *Business Education World,* vol. 52, January–February, 1972, p. 23. See also Bonnice in each issue of *Business Education World.*

BROWN, RICHARD D., "Teaching for Consumer Conscience in Business Education," *American Vocational Journal,* vol. 46, May, 1971, pp. 22-23.

BURTON, JOHN R., "Teachers' Attitudes toward Consumer Issues and Their Appraisal of the Educational Relevance of These Issues," unpublished doctoral dissertation, University of Connecticut, Storrs, Conn., 1970. Also *Delta Pi Epsilon Journal,* vol. 13, August, 1971, pp. 37-40, and *Journal of Consumer Affairs,* vol. 6, Winter, 1972, pp. 223-228.

CAMPBELL, SALLY R., *Consumer Education in an Age of Adaptation,* Sears, Roebuck and Co., Chicago, 1971.

CAPLOVITZ, DAVID, *The Poor Pay More,* The Free Press, New York, 1967.

"Consumer Education: Its New Look," *Bulletin of the National Association of Secondary School Principals,* vol. 321, October, 1967.

*Consumer Update,* Gregg and Community College Division of McGraw-Hill, New York, vol. 1, nos. 1 and 2, 1974.

ENGLISH, DONALD E., "Relationship of Teacher and Student Attitudes to Consumer Education Instruction in the Secondary Schools of Illinois," unpublished doctoral dissertation, University of North Dakota, Grand Forks, N. Dak., 1971. Also *Business Education Forum,* vol. 27, October, 1972, pp. 37-38.

FLECK, HENRIETTA, *Toward Better Teaching of Home Economics,* The Macmillan Company, New York, 1968.

HAAS, MARY HELEN, AND MARCILE WOOD, "Consumers on the Alert," *American Vocational Journal,* vol. 45, November, 1970, pp. 36-37.

HAWAII BUSINESS EDUCATION ASSOCIATION TAB Project, "Teaching Aids for Business Teachers, General Business and Consumer Economics," University of Hawaii, Honolulu, 1970.

HERRMANN, ROBERT O., "Consumerism: The Past Is Prologue," *Business Education World,* vol. 54, November–December, 1973, pp. 24, 30.

HOPKINS, CHARLES (ED.), "Consumer Education in: Junior High School, Senior High School, Junior College, Vocational School, at the Adult Level," *Business Education Forum,* vol. 27, March, 1973, pp. 15-28.

INACKER, CHARLES J., "Personal Finance Attitudes and Understandings of Selected Camden County, New Jersey, High School Seniors: A Comparative Study," unpublished doctoral dissertation, Temple University, Philadelphia, Pa., 1972, also *Business Education Forum,* vol. 28, October, 1973, p. 44.

JELLEY, HERBERT M., "Measurement and Interpretation of Money Management Understandings of Twelfth-Grade Students," *Delta Pi Epsilon Journal,* vol. 3, no. 1, November, 1960, p. 1.

LARSON, EVELYN R., "A Comparison of Personal Finance Understandings of High School Students," unpublished doctoral dissertation, University of Minnesota, 1969. Also *Business Education Forum,* vol. 25, October, 1970, pp. 40–41.

LOWE, ROSS E., "Varying the Routine in Consumer Education Classes," *Journal of Business Education,* vol. 45, November, 1969, pp. 73–74, December, 1969, pp. 115–116.

MAGNUSON, WARREN G., AND JEAN CARPER, *The Dark Side of the Marketplace,* Prentice-Hall, Inc., Englewood Cliffs, N.J., 1968.

MASLOW, ABRAHAM H., *Motivation and Personality,* Harper and Row, Inc., New York, 1970.

MAXWELL, GERALD W., "What to Teach about the New Truth-in-Lending Law," *Business Education Forum,* vol. 24, January, 1970, pp. 30–32.

NADER, RALPH, AND JEAN CARPER, *The Consumer and Corporate Accountability,* Harcourt, Brace & Jovanovich, New York, 1973.

ODOM, JEFFREY V., "The Effect of Metrication on the Consumer," *Business Education Forum,* vol. 28, December, 1973, pp. 10–13.

OFFICE OF THE SUPERINTENDENT OF PUBLIC INSTRUCTION, *Guidelines for Consumer Education,* State of Illinois, Springfield, 1972.

MURPHY, PATRICIA D., "Modules for Consumer Education: A Spiral-Process Approach to Curriculum Development," *American Vocational Journal,* vol. 48, October, 1973, pp. 52–54.

POLICIES COMMISSION FOR BUSINESS AND ECONOMIC EDUCATION, "This We Believe about the Role of Business Education in Consumer Education," *Business Education Forum,* vol. 27, April, 1973, pp. 14–15.

PRESIDENT'S COMMITTEE ON CONSUMER INTERESTS, *Suggested Guidelines for Consumer Education, Grades K–12,* U.S. Government Printing Office, Washington, D.C., 1970.

*Role of Consumer Education in Occupational Preparation,* Vocational Education Section, California State Department of Education, Sacramento, Calif., 1972.

SCHOENFELD, DAVID, ET AL., *Consumer Education Materials Project,* (six books on consumer education at the levels of early childhood, elementary, secondary, junior and community college, teacher education, and continuing education) Consumers Union of United States, Inc., Mount Vernon, N.Y., 1973.

SMITH, CARLTON, RICHARD PUTNAM PRATT, AND THE EDITORS OF TIME-LIFE BOOKS, *The Time-Life Book of Family Finance,* Time-Life Books, New York, 1970.

STANTON, WILLIAM R., AND E. THOMAS GARMAN, "A Creed for Consumer Educators," *Balance Sheet,* vol. 55, December, 1973–January, 1974, pp. 150–151.

UHL, JOSEPH N., "The Purdue Consumer Education Study," *Journal of Consumer Affairs,* vol. 4, Winter, 1970, pp. 124–134. See also ERIC Document No. ED 038–549.

VAN HOOK, BARRY, "The Contributions of Gladys Bahr to Consumer and Economic Education at the Secondary School Level," unpublished doctoral dissertation, Northern Illinois University, DeKalb, Ill., 1973.

VAN TASSEL, HARRIET, "Consumer Protection Begins with Education," *American Vocational Journal,* vol. 45, February, 1970, pp. 38–41.

## PERFORMANCE GOALS

**1.** Given a broad topic in general business such as insurance or consumer protection, identify a subtopic such as automobile insurance or consumer protection at the federal level, and then identify eight tasks a student should be able to perform relative to the topic; add standards to the tasks, and **identify** competencies.

**2.** Given a competency in general business, **construct** a teaching-learning system for the competency. Evaluation will be based on the following components: a performance goal which meets the criteria; subcompetencies identification; an evaluation for measuring the competency sought; learning principles applied; learning activities and resources selected; and flexibility of materials in different organizational patterns.

**3.** Given a description of four diverse students with differing socioeconomic backgrounds, learning problems, reading levels, and present competency levels, **decide** on ten competencies for each student defending your choices with reasons that reveal your understanding of student needs according to instructor approval.

**4.** Given a description of students and a list of six competencies along with present level of competencies possessed by students, **decide** on teaching-learning strategies which include all three teaching-learning patterns—large-group, small-group, and individual.

**5.** Using one competency identified for performance goal 4 above that is appropriate for large-group instruction, **demonstrate** your ability to microteach or on videotape live a 10-minute segment as your instructor directs until a committee of your peers and your instructor approves your performance.

**6.** Using one competency identified for performance goal 4 above that is appropriate for small-group instruction, **demonstrate** your ability to structure and teach a small group as your instructor directs until a committee approves the instruction.

**7.** Using one competency identified for performance goal 4 above that is appropriate for individual instruction, **construct** a learning package to develop the competency, and field test it on a ninth- or tenth-grade student (neighbor, sibling, or through cooperation of a general business teacher), and revise the package until it meets the approval of your instructor and a committee of your peers.

# CHAPTER 17

# Basic Business

The purpose of basic business education is economic education, in contrast to the career preparation objective of the vocational business subjects. Education *about* business is achieved through the social business subjects; in contrast, education *for* business is achieved through the vocational business subjects. One goal is to prepare students to function intelligently in a business society and the other is to prepare them for jobs in business.

In "This We Believe about Business Education in the Secondary School," the Policies Commission for Business and Economic Education includes both the vocational and nonvocational goals of business education, holding that business education is an effective program of occupational instruction for secondary students desiring careers in business. Business education has an important contribution to make to the economic literacy of all secondary school students. Business education is desirable for students who plan programs requiring postsecondary and higher education in the field of business. The statement goes on as follows:

**Roles as Consumers, Workers, and Citizens**

The consumers, workers, and citizens should know how to interpret economic issues which affect them and how to manage their economic affairs efficiently.

*We Believe That*

Opportunities must be provided for secondary school students to develop an understanding of how our business system operates. . . .

Programs that develop economic understanding should be planned cooperatively with other departments of the school that are concerned with economic education. . . .

Any requirements relating to the development of personal and social economic competencies should be reciprocally recognized by the respective departments of the school. . . .

In the *Encyclopedia of Education,* DeBrum points out that the two distinct but equally important objectives of business education have as their ultimate aim to improve the economic system. He says the social business area can be divided into two kinds of economics: (1) social economics, which lays a foundation on which to build an understanding of the structure and the operation of the economic and business system, and (2) consumer economics, which provides each student with skills and understandings that will enable him to conduct his own business affairs effectively (DeBrum, p. 565).

Sluder says the objective of basic or general business education is the providing of general business information of value to everyone conducting his or her own business affairs. He suggests its introduction-to-business function includes prevocational objectives in addition to its economic and consumer literacy function.

## History of General Business

General business is the most popular of the social business subjects. In fact, among all business subjects offered at the high school level, it ranks second in the number of students enrolled, typewriting obviously being first (Malsbary, p. 11). Over its long history, general business has had several major shifts in direction. Originally it was a vocational course called *junior business training,* which prepared potential school dropouts for jobs as clerks or messengers. When jobs became scarce and the age for compulsory school attendance was raised, the goals of general business training changed. It became an exploratory course, along with exploratory courses in math and science. Each was designed to teach students a little about several different phases of each discipline. In general business, students explored typewriting, shorthand, and recordkeeping. Another era saw courses justified on their personal-use value; business filing became personal recordkeeping, and postal and shipping services became mailing and shipping for personal use.

General business is now divorced from the old junior business training image, and business educators agree that economic literacy is the primary goal of general business.

## Content

The broad area of basic business education encompasses courses such as general business, basic business, consumer economics, business law, business principles, economics, economic geography, and introduction to business. General business is usually taught at the ninth- or tenth-grade level and the other courses anywhere from the ninth to twelfth grades. The following topics are usually included in general business:

1. Understanding the free enterprise system
2. What business is and does

3. Money and banking
4. Credit
5. Effective money management
6. Consumer information and protection
7. Saving and investing
8. Insurance
9. Career exploration
10. Labor-management relations
11. Citizenship responsibilities

McKitrick compared the contents of general business, economics, and consumer economics textbooks. He found that the following topics received major emphasis in two leading textbooks in general business and in consumer economics:

*General Business Textbooks*

1. American business and the student
2. Money and banking activities
3. Wise use of money
4. Credit
5. Sharing economic risks through insurance
6. Savings and investments
7. Organization of business
8. Occupational information
9. Government, business, and societal relationships
10. Citizenship responsibilities

*Consumer Economics Textbooks*

1. The consumer and the economy
2. Money management
3. Banking services
4. Wise use of credit
5. Protection through insurance
6. Principles of buying
7. Savings and investments
8. Investing in a home
9. The consumer and the law
10. Consumer protection: government and private sources
11. Advertising and the consumer

Wolters submitted a list of over 70 topics gleaned from textbooks, research, and professional publications to a national panel of college and university experts whose background included supervising student teachers in general business, teaching general business methods, and high school teaching experience in general business. The panel of experts felt that 15 out of the 70 topics should be stressed in general business classes. The 15 topics are grouped into topical areas.

*Business System*
1. You and the business economy
2. Characteristics of a free enterprise system

*Career Education*
3. Planning your future

*Consumer Education*
4. Consumer buying

    5.  Services for the consumer
    6.  Problems of the consumer
    7.  Sources of consumer information
*Credit*
    8.  Establishing credit
    9.  Kinds of credit
  10.  Cost of using credit
*Citizenship*
  11.  Citizenship responsibilities
*Insurance*
  12.  Automobile insurance
*Money*
  13.  Borrowing money
  14.  Planning a savings program
  15.  Planning the use of your income

Irving determined the status of general business in Wisconsin's public secondary schools by focusing on the overall pattern of instruction emerging from administration of the course, students in the course, subject matter and instructional materials used in the course, and backgrounds of the teachers of the course. Considerations of subject matter and instructional materials included topics which received highest and lowest priority and use of textbooks, workbooks, field trips, films, overhead transparencies, and the blackboard.

## Needs of the Learner

A basic axiom in economic theory is the law of scarcity which applies to governments, business firms, and individuals. Unlimited wants are clamoring to be satisfied, and yet only limited resources are available for want satisfaction. In order to get the most satisfaction from available resources, the learner must acquire cognitive and affective learnings which will enable him or her to make the most intelligent decisions possible as a consumer, producer, and citizen.

The philosophy of basic business education is that general business has something for all students, boys and girls, regardless of major concentration, ability level, reading level, or age. All students are presently consumers and as time goes on will make decisions of ever greater magnitude in the marketplace. All students will become eligible to vote and will make decisions at the ballot box. Most students already are or will become producers of goods and services.

The specific contribution of today's general business is to explain the role and purpose of business in our economic system, according to Price.

An economic system, after all, is simply an arrangement for satisfying human wants. In the United States business firms produce 90 percent of the goods and services people buy to satisfy their wants. Business provides employment for roughly seven out of eight workers. Other subjects in which economic topics are integrated often overlook the significant role of business in our society. (Price,.Musselman, Hall, *Teacher's Source Book,* p. 2)

The free enterprise system depends on a well-informed citizenry to function most effectively, and yet studies have shown that individuals in our country generally are not well informed on economic matters. Perhaps the best-known study was one conducted under the auspices of the Joint Council on Economic Education which included the development of a standardized 50-item dual-form test, the Test of Economic Understandings, to measure the concepts deemed essential for economic citizenship. About a third of each test covers microeconomics (the branch of economics dealing with particular aspects of an economy); one-third covers macroeconomics (that branch of economics dealing with the broad and general aspects of an economy); and the remaining third deals with applications and special topics such as international trade, comparative economic systems, and the farm problem. The Test of Economic Understandings was administered to 6,500 high school seniors selected to include a cross section of high school seniors from large and small schools and cities, different sections of the country, and varying income levels. The seniors comprised two groups, those who had taken no course in economics and those who had completed a one-semester course. The average mean score was 24.2 for those without a course in economics and 29.7 for those with an economics course, a statistically significant difference in favor of those students who had taken an economics class. Even so, both groups scored shockingly low (Bach and Saunders).

## Needs of Business

Although the basic business subjects do not prepare workers for business, the needs of business cannot help but be more nearly met by workers who understand the interaction of forces within the business system. Workers who understand the interrelationship and interdependence of individuals, businesses, and units of government will be better workers within the business system. It is easy for individuals and business firms to complain about taxes, for example; but those same individuals and business firms would not be willing to give up police or fire protection or good roads for a lower tax bill. That is not to say that all tax money is wisely spent; however, not all money spent by individuals or business firms is wisely spent either.

Price summarizes the need for today's general business as follows:

No one could honestly deny the need for economic education in a nation like ours where the economic decisions each of us makes as an individual has such far-reaching effects. As consumers, our choices help to determine how the valuable productive resources of this country are used. As producers, we help to determine how efficiently our productive resources are used. As workers, we also help to determine wages and prices. As voting citizens we help to decide issues that serve to modify our free economy in some way. Taxing policies, Medicare, the minimum wage, farm price supports, the war on poverty, and antipollution programs are examples. Our daily papers devote more space to economic problems—inflation, deflation, economic growth, employment, unemployment—than to any other single topic. (Price, Musselman, Hall, p. 2)

## Identifying and Classifying Competencies

The first step in the teaching-learning system is to identify competencies, no small task in the social business area. Major studies have done this in the vocational business area, but thus far no such studies have pinpointed necessary competencies in general business. Thus the teacher or curriculum consultant must use professional judgment in determining tasks and standards and then competencies in general business. The teacher can approach the problem of identifying tasks from several different positions, such as using topics identified by research as essential in general business, topics from general business textbooks, or topics identified by others. For example, the National Task Force of the Joint Council on Economic Education identified seven important areas of which every high school graduate should possess an understanding. These are:

1. What economics is all about, why it is important, and how one thinks about economic problems.
2. The nature of the persistent economic problem faced by all societies: wants, scarce resources, the need for decision making, and the need for an economic system of some kind.
3. The market economy of the United States: how it is decided in the United States today (*a*) what goods and services will be produced, (*b*) how they will be produced, (*c*) what total level of production will be maintained, and (*d*) how what is produced will be shared among the American people.
4. Economic growth and stability, the long- and short-run performance of the American economy: (*a*) economic growth—the long-run problems associated with increasing the total production of goods and services faster than the rate of population growth so that living standards can rise, and (*b*) economic stability—the determinants of the level of income and employment in the short run *or* how to manage our economy so that we can have full employment without inflation.
5. The distribution of income: the factors determining the distribution of income among individuals and groups in the United States and thus determining who will get the goods and services produced.
6. The United States in the world economy: the importance of world trade and finance to the United States and the ways in which the achievement of our economic goals is related to world economic developments.

7.  Other economic systems: how other societies organize economic life to achieve their economic goals—not only the Communist countries but also the democratic societies of the West and the developing nations of Asia, Africa, and Latin America. (Calderwood, p. ix)

The topic receiving the highest priority in Irving's study was credit. Three of Wolters's fifteen topics pertained to credit—establishing credit, kinds of credit, and cost of using credit. McKitrick found that credit received major emphasis in both general business and consumer economics textbooks. Credit is a major institution in our economic society and relates indirectly to several of the important areas identified by the Joint Council on Economic Education. Credit, therefore, will be used to illustrate the teaching-learning system in general business, beginning, in Figure 17.1, with identifying the tasks, adding standards, and then defining competencies.

## Planning Evaluations

After the competencies are identified and classified, evaluations are planned which will be used to measure whether or not a student has attained the competencies. In an evaluation asking for a description or explanation, it is not necessary to give a test item other than simply asking for the description or explanation. For low-level cognitive learning, objective or short-answer items can be used; for example, with reference to competency 1, an item might be stated:

1.  Three groups who use credit in a free enterprise system are:

    *a.* _____

    *b.* _____

    *c.* _____

**or**

1.  In a free enterprise system, which use credit?

    *a.* governments
    *b.* businesses
    *c.* consumers
    *d.* all of the above

Often performance within a group is measured by means of a check sheet. Recycle to Chapter 4 for more complete discussion on evaluation.

## Constructing Performance Goals

The next step in the teaching-learning system is to develop goals which state (1) a measurable behavior, (2) the conditions under which performance will be conducted, (3) the product to merge from the performance, and (4) the criterion or standard on which performance will be based. Realistic performance goals provide the basis for the learner and the teacher to know exactly what is to be accomplished.

Figure 17.1   Converting basic business tasks to competencies

| Task | Standard | Competency |
| --- | --- | --- |
| 1. Identify the three groups who use credit in a free enterprise system. | Textbook discussion | Identify the three groups who use credit in a free enterprise system, consistent with textbook discussion. |
| 2. Explain the purposes for which credit is used by each of the three groups. | Correctly | Correctly explain the purposes for which credit is used by each of the three groups. |
| 3. Identify the three bases on which consumer credit is granted. | Correctly | Correctly identify the three bases on which consumer credit is granted. |
| 4. Describe credit rating. | Teacher judgment | Describe credit rating to satisfaction of teacher. |
| 5. Differentiate between installment and noninstallment consumer credit. | Accurately | Accurately differentiate between installment and noninstallment consumer credit. |
| 6. Determine under what circumstances the use of consumer credit is advantageous or disadvantageous. | Peer judgment | Determine under what circumstances the use of consumer credit is good and under what circumstances it is bad to the satisfaction of peers in a small group. |
| 7. Conclude whether the use of credit is free. If not, determine who pays. | Correctly | Correctly conclude whether the use of credit is free, and if not, determine who pays. |
| 8. Determine the effect on our economy if the use of credit were banned. | Peer judgment | Determine the effect on our economy if the use of credit were banned, according to criteria established by peer group. |

The basic business competencies are analyzed in Figure 17.2, and performance goals for the eight competencies on credit are shown below.

1. Given a work sheet correlated with a textbook, in the space provided **state** the three groups who use credit in a free enterprise system, and then check your response against the key provided.
2. Working in a small group, **explain** the purposes for which credit is used by each of the three groups while the other students evaluate your explanation in light of assigned reading and a check sheet created by your group.
3. Given essay questions in an individual learning packet, correctly **identify** the three bases upon which consumer credit is granted (sometimes called the "three C's" of credit).
4. After viewing a film on credit rating, **describe** credit rating in a brief paragraph that you give to your teacher for evaluation.

Figure 17.2 Analysis of basic business competencies for components of performance goals

| Competency | Dominant Domain and Level | Result of Performance | Verb | Conditions of Performance | Evaluation |
|---|---|---|---|---|---|
| 1. Identify the three groups who use credit in a free enterprise system, consistent with textbook discussion. | Cognitive: knowledge | Product | State | Given a worksheet correlated with a textbook | Key provided |
| 2. Correctly explain the purposes for which credit is used by each of the three groups. | Cognitive: analysis/ synthesis | Product | Explain | Working in a small group, using check sheet developed by group | Group consensus |
| 3. Correctly identify the three bases on which consumer credit is granted. | Cognitive: knowledge | Product | Identify | Given essay questions in an individual learning packet | Teacher judgment against learning packet information |
| 4. Describe credit rating to satisfaction of teacher. | Cognitive: comprehension | Product | Describe | After viewing a film on credit ratings | Teacher judgment |
| 5. Accurately differentiate between installment and non-installment consumer credit. | Cognitive: comprehension | Product | Differentiate | Given five situations involving both types of credit | Teacher judgment against learning packet information |
| 6. Determine under what circumstances the use of consumer credit is advantageous or disadvantageous. | Cognitive: evaluation | Product | Determine | Working in small group | Group consensus |
| 7. Correctly conclude whether the use of credit is free, and if not, determine who pays. | Cognitive: evaluation | Product | Conclude | Working in small group which includes teacher | Teacher judgment |
| 8. Determine the effect on our economy if the use of credit were banned according to criteria used by peer group. | Cognitive: evaluation | Product | Determine | Working in small discussion group | Small-group judgment |

5. Given five situations involving both types of credit, accurately differentiate between installment and noninstallment consumer credit.
6. Working in a small group of students, **determine** under which circumstances the use of consumer credit is advantageous and disadvantageous, to the satisfaction of peers in the small group who use an instrument similar to that shown in Figure 4.5, page 80, for self-evaluation.
7. Working in a small group which includes both students and teacher, correctly **conclude** whether the use of credit is free, and, if not, determine who pays.
8. Working in a small discussion group of students, accurately **determine** the effect on our economy if the use of credit were banned.

## Identifying and Sequencing Subcompetencies

The next step in the teaching-learning system is to identify and sequence subcompetencies. Performance goal 8 illustrates this step in Figure 17.3.

## Pretesting and Matching Learner With Goals

In planning for any class and particularly for general business, the teacher should attempt to analyze who the students are. Otherwise, the teacher may be attempting to teach how to invest in stocks and bonds to students whose families are grappling with how to stretch a welfare check to the end of the month. Students will come to the general business class with a limited background in economic understandings, particularly since evidence shows that even adults have limited knowledge in this area. Nevertheless, at this step in the system, it is necessary to determine student characteristics and present level of competency.

Since general business is for all students, a typical class might have students with a wide range of abilities, interests, and motivation. The characteristics of a particular class will depend to some extent on the attitudes of the counseling staff and the administrators toward general business and on what the grapevine has had to say about previous classes. Most classes will have some students who are motivated and some who are not, both boys and girls, students who are concentrating in business and others who are not. In schools where general business is particularly popular, you will find a teacher who is committed to students and to general business. In the past general business has sometimes been referred to as a dumping ground, and this could be true even today at one or more of the 27,000 secondary schools in this country. Even if general business in a particular school should happen to get more than its share of less able students, the teacher should remember that these students too are consumers of the goods and services of business, they either are or likely will be workers in business, and all are citizens in a free enterprise system. They too have a right and a need for the basic economic understandings taught in general business.

Figure 17.3  Sequencing subcompetencies for basic business performance goal 8

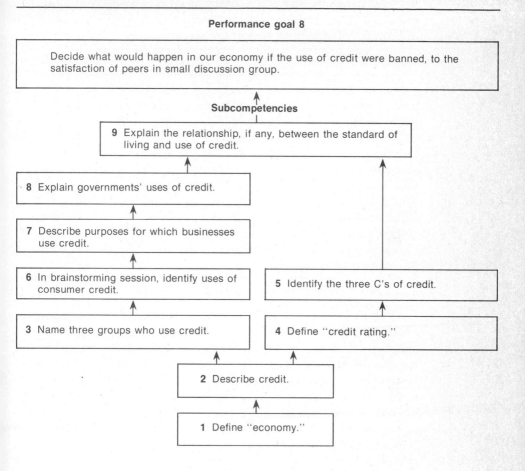

**Performance goal 8**

Decide what would happen in our economy if the use of credit were banned, to the satisfaction of peers in small discussion group.

**Subcompetencies**

9 Explain the relationship, if any, between the standard of living and use of credit.

8 Explain governments' uses of credit.

7 Describe purposes for which businesses use credit.

6 In brainstorming session, identify uses of consumer credit.

5 Identify the three C's of credit.

3 Name three groups who use credit.

4 Define "credit rating."

2 Describe credit.

1 Define "economy."

In fact, in some cases the need may be more acute and more persistent because of the possibility of such students being victims of a failure syndrome.

Student characteristics will affect the teacher's decisions regarding performance goals, level at which to start a topic, depth of treatment, and variety and extent of teaching-learning activities. Factors such as the following can be considered: age level, maturity level, reading level, attention span, socioeconomic home conditions, environmental limitations, study habits, motivation, and the like.

In addition to general characteristics of students, the teacher needs to know the specific competencies of individual students. Such data is ascertained by pretesting, using either test items identified at the time performance goals were written or alternative forms of test items. In a typical class, some students will already possess some or all of the competencies and others will lack all of them. Students should bypass those competencies they already possess and begin to work on those they do not yet possess.

## Applying Appropriate Learning Principles

The next step in the system is to relate the appropriate learning principles to the particular performance goal. Let us look at some of the principles of learning in relation to general business.

---

**Principle 1. The learner must perceive what is to be learned as relevant.**

---

Probably the major reason for the lack of economic understandings among citizens today is the fact that they cannot see the relationship between dry economic theory and everyday living. Although it is easier today for the teacher to help students see their relevance by using the excellent instructional materials which are available, it is still up to the teacher to utilize the materials in an effective manner. If learners can be shown that their understanding of the economic system gives them an edge over persons who do not understand the system, they will be more willing to learn than if the proposed learning is simply memory exercises. Since the heart of general business is the cognitive and affective learnings that are necessary to function intelligently in a business economy, it has built-in relevance just waiting to be tapped.

---

**Principle 2. Learning results from the learner's interaction with his or her total environment.**

---

The learner in general business not only interacts with the textbook, other written material, filmstrips, transparencies, films and other media but also with the business world. A trip to the grocery store, service station, bowling alley, bank, or other place of business provides an opportunity to relate theory to practice in the "real" world. Learning will be facilitated when the learner uses his or her own income and expenses for preparing a budget rather than doing a sterile workbook assignment. An examination of an annual report of a company in an industry currently in the news—oil or transportation, perhaps—will help a learner to understand profit and the profit motive better than would the use of outdated materials. A discussion of competition centering around competitive products used by ninth- and tenth-grade students will be more meaningful than discussing competition in isolation from what is happening today.

---

**Principle 3. Learning is facilitated when the learner can associate new behaviors with previously learned behaviors.**

---

Learning is related to prior learnings in general business, but the relationship may be indirect. Even though the concept of gross national product may be new, students do have prior learnings, including how to read, how to listen, and how to analyze. In general business, the student's understanding of comparison shopping will be facilitated if it builds on an experience the student has had in buying a product on the basis of comparison shopping and another product without comparison shopping.

---

**Principle 4.** Learning proceeds more effectively when the learner is an active participant in the learning process.

---

The learner should be involved in the planning as well as the performing of the process of learning. When students are actively involved, they will get more from the learning than if they are passive. Strategies which employ doing—making, reacting to, speaking, collecting, interacting, writing, constructing, and the like—will facilitate learning more than passive activities such as listening or even reading. General business courses today provide ample opportunities for students *to do;* for example, to reinforce business vocabulary by working crossword puzzles.

## Selecting and Using Teaching-Learning Strategies

How are students to be grouped? This question must be answered before teaching-learning strategies can be selected—and it is really a matter of choice, because general business lends itself to all three organizational patterns: large-group, small-group, and individual instruction. A large group might be construed as an entire class of 28 students or a group of four or five classes with over 100 students meeting together to hear a guest speaker. Students might brainstorm possible guest speakers, and invariably they will think of some that have not been thought of before. Possibilities include a representative from the county weights and measures office; a consumer advocate; a representative from a cooperative explaining the co-op form of organization; an insurance adjuster telling how claims are evaluated and damages assessed for an automobile accident or for a windstorm, flood, or other natural disaster; a representative from a credit bureau discussing how a credit rating is established; a representative from a law enforcement agency discussing the effect of shoplifting on the cost of goods; and so on. Provision can be made in the large group for questions to be written out and handed to a monitor, who sorts them and gives them to the speaker; or a question-and-answer period can be conducted simply by having a student stand and ask a question. In addition to guest speakers, large-group instruction in general business might include viewing movies, filmstrips, or other media; subject matter might include the stock exchange, the Federal Reserve System, how buying decisions are made, forms of taxation, some facet of insurance, and the like.

Even though guest speakers and use of media would also be appropriate for small groups, other strategies, such as those which develop listening and speaking skills and affective behaviors, are particularly suited to them. Discussions, projects, field trips, visual displays—all discussed in more detail below—can be effectively handled by small groups.

Individual instruction in general business is increasingly being recognized as a viable strategy. Certain teachers throughout the country have developed and implemented individually paced and individually prescribed learning for their general business students. Individual learning packages are being used, and no doubt this trend will not only continue but accelerate.

Numerous modes of instruction in addition to the above are useful in general business. These include case problems, role playing, projects, slides, committee work, demonstrations, dramatizations and skits, reading, films, transparencies, bulletin boards, audiotape and videotape, lectures, games, and simulations.

For the performance goals relative to the topic of credit, goals 3 and 5 indicate the use of individual learning packages. Those goals might also incorporate the use of transparencies and teacher guide notes provided by a publisher or a school district or prepared by the teacher; use of transparencies is appropriate for other goals as well. Brief lectures illustrated with already prepared charts or illustrated on the chalkboard would be appropriate to introduce any of the concepts relative to credit. A subcompetency of performance goal 8 is to define "economy." In order to explain "economy" or "economic system," the teacher might indicate that we have an economic system because we have unlimited wants and limited resources and must have a way to balance these. The teacher could use a balancing scale of justice or even a seesaw or teeter-totter with "wants" on one side and "resources" on the other. Initially, wants outweigh resources; but as the demonstration progresses, students see that some wants have to be cast off in order to balance the available resources. In lieu of actual scales, a flannel board or chalkboard could be utilized for the illustration. A student or small group of students might prepare bulletin boards relative to one or all the performance goals. Performance goals 2, 6, 7, and 8 indicate the use of small groups. Recycle to Chapter 7 for handling of small groups.

Some strategies appropriate for general business are discussed in more detail below.

## Transparencies

Transparencies shown on an overhead projector have come to be a mainstay of general business teachers. A few years ago media specialists recommended an overhead projector for every thirty teachers, and now they recommend an overhead projector for every classroom. Transparencies are popular because they offer advantages not available with other methods or media. They are usable by teacher or by the learner and can be used in large groups, small groups, or individual instruction. Prepared color transparencies and teacher guide notes as well as transparency masters for general business are available from publishers. In using the masters, the teacher runs the master and special transparent film through an indirect-heat-processing copying machine, a process which is fast and efficient. The teacher can use his or her own copy for making such transparencies too. The same copy that is used to make the transparency can also be used to make a spirit duplicator master, so that the teacher can give the learners a copy if desired.

Examples of teacher-prepared transparencies for general business include the following:

- Transparency made from data taken from the newspaper every January when the President presents his annual budget to Congress. Circle or bar graphs can be used to show where the federal dollar comes from (federal income tax, etc.) and where it goes. When the topic of taxation is studied, then the teacher has the current information. The same information may be obtained from the *Teaching Taxes* unit issued annually by the Internal Revenue Service.
- In a consumer module, transparencies of magazine advertisements of goods and services can be used to show the relationship of buying to human needs and wants.
- Magazines or newspapers may provide statistical data on such topics as current gross national product figures, dollar loss from fires in the local county, tax rate for the local community, average annual wages by industry and type of jobs, number of business failures within the first year, number of qualified voters who actually vote in the local community, and so on.

Transparencies can be correlated with sound on cassette tape for use by individual students.

## Slides

A series of slides can be developed on almost any topic in general business, such as credit, for example. A series could show places of business displaying credit cards that are accepted there, and students can deduce the universal acceptance of credit cards. Or a series could be developed around local establishments which lend money, including savings and loan institutions, banks, small loan companies, credit unions, and so on. The student who sees on a slide the local bank at Fifth and Main is much more interested than if he or she hears the teacher say "Banks lend money." For a lesson on insurance, a series of slides could be developed around types of coverage with one or more slides illustrating each type of coverage. Slides could also depict local insurance companies or agencies to help the student see that the textbook information is really what is happening in his or her own community. In a unit on taxes, a series of slides could show goods or services provided by tax dollars. Pictures of post offices, internal revenue forms, federal courthouses, military installations or even recruiting pictures for the military services, social security cards, passports, and Veterans Administration hospitals could be used. A similar series could be developed for the state in which you live. It might include the capitol, highway patrol, motor vehicles department, highways, state college and/or university, and so on. Still other series could be developed for the county or town.

Once the slides are developed, they can be used from year to year with occasional updating of particular slides.

## Slides and Sound

The synergistic effect of a slide/sound presentation is greater than either medium used alone because the presentation gets attention, holds attention, and is current. Slide/sound units can be developed for use in introductory, developmental, or culminating activities, and can be used with a large group, small group, or single student in a study carrel. Ten to fifteen minutes seems to be an optimal time span. The developer may choose a rapid-fire pace or a slower, more deliberate pace. The following steps may be used in developing slide/sound presentations in general business.

DECIDE ON TOPIC AND OBJECTIVE. The objective can be an introduction to a broad topic such as credit, or it can be a narrow topic such as merits of no-fault insurance. It is important to clearly define the topic and purpose at the outset.

WRITE THE SCRIPT. Start with an outline of important points to be covered, and develop the script from the outline. If the unit is to be more than a bunch of pictures shown together, the script must cover key ideas in a logical manner.

OUTLINE PROPOSED SLIDES. Sometimes done simultaneously with script writing, the decisions on proposed pictures may be readily apparent as the script is developed. Other pictures will have to be thought out at length.

TAKE THE SLIDES. Group the proposed pictures so you do not have to make repeated trips to one location. You will need permission to take shots within business establishments, and some business firms may refuse or be reluctant to grant permission for security reasons. Reasonably good photography must be employed. This means proper framing, proper focusing and lighting, and some imagination. If does not mean professional photography or expensive equipment.

PREPARE TITLE AND CREDIT SLIDES. The title slide sets the stage for what is to follow, and the credit slide gives credit to the person(s) who developed the unit. This becomes especially important if a unit is shown by someone other than the person who made it.

DECIDE ON SOUND. Sound probably should include some narration but not so much that it overwhelms the listener. Key points can be narrated at the time the same points are presented on the slide. Sound effects might include a ticker tape, sirens, fog horn, train whistle, jet engines, traffic noise, and the like. Any music used should contribute to the overall theme and in addition should be music with which students can identify.

RECORD SOUND. Usually more than one person is involved in recording because of various sounds being combined. It may be feasible to record narration on one tape, sound effects or music on another tape, and finally to use a third tape combining the two. Cassette tapes are especially easy to handle. The narrator should have a pleasant voice on tape, because an accent, twang, or raspy voice will spoil an otherwise good unit. The narrator should be thoroughly familiar with the material so it comes out naturally, not as though he or she were reading.

**SYNCHRONIZE SLIDES AND SOUND.** The presentation can be developed to utilize the automatic feature of slide projectors so that slides will change at regular intervals, say ten seconds; or the slides can be changed manually in response to a bell or click on the sound track. Another alternative is to manually change the slides in response to a cue on an accompanying script. While there is much to be said for the automatic change, it does mean that every picture must be on the screen the same length of time. With the audio or script signal, some pictures can be on the screen five seconds and others for fifteen or twenty seconds. Naturally, the slides should appear on the screen at the time the appropriate sound appears on the sound track. Equipment is available on which the sound can be recorded on the frame of the slide. This has certain advantages, but it precludes background music or other uninterrupted sound.

**EVALUATE AND REVISE.** Once developed, the unit should be critiqued by professional colleagues and students and revisions made as necessary (Blockhus, "Slide/Sound Media").

It would probably not be feasible for a single teacher to develop several slide/sound presentations at once, but he or she might develop two or three a year. Several teachers in a school or school district could develop units, perhaps during workshops or in-service training sessions, and share the completed units. Schools which have an audiovisual department or camera club offer a plus incentive for teachers.

## Filmstrips

Filmstrips are not a new medium for the classroom; however, good filmstrips designed specifically for the general business class are of fairly recent origin. Filmstrips correlated with sound on records or cassette tapes are especially effective and lend themselves either to group instruction or individual instruction. Most general business teachers will probably utilize commercially available filmstrips such as the *Business and You* series available from Gregg. However, some teachers and some students may develop their own. Textbooks in audiovisual methods or workshops designed specifically for this medium would benefit developers of their own filmstrips. One method of development is to cull from a series of slides those you want in the filmstrip and send the slides to a special laboratory to be made into a filmstrip. A second method is to arrange all material consecutively, number each piece, and after preparing a shooting schedule corresponding to the numbers, shoot the film in sequence.

In audiotutorial labs, students work individually at study carrels equipped with a filmstrip projector, cassette player, and study guide. A series of filmstrips correlated with audio cassettes and study guides enable the student to progress at his or her own rate. A lab assistant or paraprofessional is usually on hand to help if needed. The student may meet with the teacher at specified times individually or in a small or large group. **437**

## Films

Films are an excellent teaching medium, and good films are available for the general business class. Films are positive motivators because they combine sight, motion, and sound and enable students to "visit" places they would not otherwise see. School media coordinators will help the general business teacher locate current, appropriate films for specific competencies. Audiovisual departments of teacher training institutions, state or county boards of education, and business education periodicals are all sources of information on film availability.

A word of caution is in order. Films lose their effectiveness if they are not shown at the time the student is studying the topic of the film; therefore, films should be ordered well in advance of the screening date. Many general business teachers place their orders in May for the following year.

## Field Trips

The lists below, of possible field trips for the general business class or small group of students, are meant to stimulate the teacher to think of field-trip sites in his or her own community. In most areas one may find, close to home, the following: a commercial bank, Federal Reserve or branch bank, savings and loan institution, post office, department store or other merchandising firm, regional shopping center, merchandise mart, wholesale produce or fish market, truck terminals, dock facilities, railroad facilities, and public utilities.

It may be necessary to go somewhat farther afield to visit a stock or commodity exchange, airport (maintenance, marketing, and/or control tower facilities), industrial firm (such as a cannery, refinery, bakery, or bottling plant), industrial museums and exhibits (e.g., automobile or oil museums), government installations (testing facilities, courts, laboratories), trade fairs, cooperatives, farms and/or ranches, or flea markets.

Every community has business establishments which might provide appropriate field trips for general business classes. Manufacturing firms located in large and small communities throughout the country include factories which make candy, pencils, books, fortune cookies, lawn mowers, tarpaulins, kitchen utensils, automobiles, bicycles, clocks, locks, paper, bathing suits, school jewelry, newspapers, cereals and other foods, toys, and thousands of other products. Companies sometimes provide standard tours which might not meet your goals. Explain to the tour director exactly what your objectives are. Otherwise, your secondary school students might get a canned tour geared to elementary-age children. At the outset, determine what your students' experiences and interests are. Perhaps your regional post office provides an excellent tour, but it would not be too meaningful for your general business students if most of them have been there before.

Sometimes the logistics of arranging transportation and taking students out of other classes make a field trip for the entire class unfeasible. Some teachers have found that taking a committee of six to ten students on a field trip is a good solution to the logistics problem. Sometimes one group will go one place and another group will go another place, and all groups will report to the entire class on what they saw and learned. Such trips are sometimes recorded via videotape, slides, movies or stills, and these are shown to the rest of the class. Sometimes it is not feasible for even a small group of students to visit a site as a body; therefore, some teachers assign a student to prepare a report on a business and the student may visit the business on his or her own. The report may either be a required or an optional assignment.

## Projects

In preparing a report on a business establishment, students can gather information by visiting the company individually or writing the company or by finding published material in newspapers or magazines. Students may have access to business establishments which teachers do not have. Through a relative or neighbor, a student can sometimes arrange to visit a business and get annual reports, advertising brochures, and either products or mockups of products. As an example, one student prepared a report on a company which manufactures blue jeans and brought to class the particular brand of blue jeans and pointed out distinguishing features, including three trademarked labels. Another student prepared a report on a company which manufactures a heart pacemaker, and he was able to show the class a simulated model of the pacemaker. Another student might do a project on services provided by labor unions, perhaps using material furnished by someone he or she knows.

In addition to library research or visiting business firms or labor halls, other projects provide meaningful learning experiences for students. Some projects are particularly well suited to students who may not possess well-developed verbal skills and consequently do not do very well on written reports. Such students might prepare a visual type of project such as a bulletin board or mobile.

## Bulletin Boards and Other Visual Media

Consider the starkness of a classroom which has nothing but a calendar to break the monotony of the bare walls in contrast to a classroom which has attractive bulletin board displays which correlate with the topic being learned. Such attractive bulletin boards not only stimulate interest but also are a learning medium. Bulletin board displays should be planned around a theme and coordinated with other learning activities. Because bulletin board space may be at a premium, it is a good idea to develop a tentative calendar for bulletin boards for the year. Such a plan stimulates ideas for bulletin boards and ensures that the appropriate materials will be on hand at the time the topic is being discussed. Given time to plan and some guidance, students themselves will be able to develop attractive bulletin boards which will appeal to other students.

Articles by Marlow and Oeser and by Eckert, listed in the Selected Readings, are especially helpful in planning and constructing bulletin boards.

A mobile is a free-hanging art object characterized by a theme. Each part hangs from a central core by a thin wire or string. A mobile depicting types of federal taxes might show the central core as "federal taxes" with four separate parts, one each for income, social security, excise, and tariff. Another mobile might have "forms of money" for its theme, with parts for coins, paper bills, checks, and credit cards. Naturally each part would be simulated, not real money. Labels, seals of approval, government publications, and data taken from magazines and newspapers might be potential parts for mobiles on sources of consumer information. Mobiles prepared by students can be displayed in the classroom, hanging out of easy reach of students but not out of sight. Mobiles or other visual media should be changed regularly so that the visual will correlate with the topic under discussion.

Posters, collages, montages, and dioramas are other visual art forms which may lend themselves to the general business classroom. Such visuals have an added value beyond the general business class. They stimulate questions and arouse the interest of students who are not in the general business class, thus providing a natural recruiting opportunity for the business department.

## Guest Speakers

Guest speakers can be an effective strategy if a few basic guidelines are followed, such as those discussed in Chapter 7. The guest speaker should have some expertise in the topic under discussion and should be briefed beforehand on what is expected of him or her and how to handle unexpected questions. When a successful businessman was asked by a general business student how much money he made, he quickly replied—in a light vein—more than the company thought he was worth but not as much as he thought he was worth. Students too should be briefed beforehand.

## Crossword Puzzles and Hidden-Word Puzzles

General business teachers use crossword puzzles to teach vocabulary. Already prepared crossword puzzles in general business are available, or a teacher may develop them. Hidden-word puzzles feature vocabulary words on a grid similar to that used in crossword puzzles; however, nonsense letters fill in all the empty blocks and the student must seek out the appropriate words. Crossword puzzles teach word definition while hidden-word puzzles teach word recognition.

## Resources

An abundance of free and inexpensive materials is available from many sources in addition to complete published learning systems which have features such as textbooks, student activity guides, transparencies, and filmstrips. Teachers' source books, speakers at conventions and workshops, and business education periodicals are all sources of information on current materials. In addition, business firms, trade associations, and labor unions provide materials. It is imperative that the teacher evaluate available materials and choose carefully those which will assist the student in attaining the performance objective he or she is seeking.

## Evaluating Student Achievement

As the student progresses through the system, he or she engages in self-evaluations and evaluations of subcompetencies, finally culminating in the evaluations identified in step 2 to measure achievement of the performance goal. If the evaluations reveal mastery of the performance goal, then the student goes on to another competency and peformance goal. If the performance goal is not achieved, however, then the student recycles through other teaching-learning strategies to enable him or her to achieve the goal satisfactorily. The evaluations also show whether or not the teaching-learning system has been successful. If the student does not achieve, it might indicate that an adjustment needs to be made in the system; if so, the system should be modified.

## Learning Activities

1. As a member of a small group and according to your instructor's plan, observe a general business class and interview the teacher to obtain answers to questions which your group has developed, such as competencies expected of general business students, evaluations used to measure the competencies, teaching-learning strategies found most effective, maturity level of students, reading level of students, interests of students, and the like. Your group will present a report to the class on your findings. (All performance goals)

2. Until your instructor approves your decisions, work with a small group to classify into appropriate domains, levels of domain, and type of evaluation. Instructor-supplied lists of competencies to be achieved in general business. (Performance goal 2)

3. Identify from general business textbooks or research, topics usually taught in general business, and then identify subtopics for the broad topics. Working in committee and using your instructor's plan, evaluate the topics in terms of importance to a given group of students, until you achieve group consensus and instructor approval. (Performance goal 1)

**4.** Based on observation of a general business class and description of students in the class and using a topic mutually agreed upon between you and your instructor, identify competencies appropriate for students in that class. (Performance goal 3)

**5.** Based on observation of a general business class and given a list of six competencies, identify appropriate teaching-learning strategies including all three patterns of instruction wherever appropriate. Prepare and duplicate a report for your peers. (Performance goals 4, 5, 6, and 7)

**6.** Using your instructor's plan for evaluating published materials for general business such as textbooks, workbooks, transparencies, films, and filmstrips, including the effectiveness of the materials in achieving pre-identified competencies, prepare a report to be distributed to your class indicating students with whom you would use the materials, the length of time estimated for use, equipment or supplies required, source, and the like. (Performance goals 2, 4, 5, 6, and 7)

**7.** For one general business competency, construct a subcompetency to be developed to the indicated level within each domain: cognitive (comprehension, application, analysis/synthesis, and evaluation) and affective (consistently exhibiting). (Performance goals 1 and 2)

**8.** Working in a small group and using materials supplied by your instructor such as old evaluation sheets, develop criteria for evaluating a microteaching segment. (Performance goal 5)

**9.** Using evaluation instruments supplied by your instructor or one developed by a committee of peers, evaluate the effectiveness of small-group instruction. (Performance goal 6)

**10.** Given ten competencies in general business, write a performance goal for each until each goal meets criteria for performance goals as set forth in Chapter 5. (Performance goal 3)

## SELECTED READINGS

ATWOOD, ILLA W., "A Case for Case Problems," *Business Education Forum,* vol. 23, no. 6, March, 1969, p. 5.

BACH, G. L., and PHILLIP SAUNDERS, "Economic Education: Aspirations and Achievements," *American Economic Review,* vol. 55, June, 1965, p. 332.

BLOCKHUS, WANDA, "Basic Business Education in the Future," *Delta Pi Epsilon Journal,* vol. 13, no. 4, August, 1971, p. 28.

————, "Media Mix in General Business," *Business Education World,* vol. 52, no. 2, November–December, 1971, p. 5.

————, "Slide/Sound Media in Basic Business Classes," *Business Education Forum,* vol. 27, no. 2, November, 1972, p. 55.

————, "Structure and Use of Small Groups in Basic Business," *Business Education Forum,* vol. 29, no. 1, October, 1974, p. 27.

BROWER, WALTER A., AND J. E. GRATZ (ED.), *Socio Business Economic Education,* Eastern Business Teachers Association, Yearbook 41, 1968.

BROWN, BETTY JEAN, "The Relationship between Supervisor and Student Evaluations of Teaching Effectiveness of General Business Teachers," unpublished doctoral dissertation, University of Tennessee, Knoxville, 1971, also "Delta Pi Epsilon Research-Award Study," *Delta Pi Epsilon Journal,* vol. 15, no. 3, May, 1973, p. 1.

CALDERWOOD, JAMES D., "Teacher's Guide to Developmental Economic Education Program," Joint Council on Economic Education, New York, 1964.

CRAWFORD, MAURICE L., "A Comparative Study of Basic Business Education in California Junior and Senior High Schools," unpublished doctoral dissertation, University of California at Los Angeles, Los Angeles, Calif., 1962.

CREWS, JAMES W., "The Teaching of General Business and Economic Education," *National Business Education Yearbook,* no. 9, 1971, p. 87.

DAUGHTREY, ANNE SCOTT, *Methods of Basic Business and Economic Education,* South-Western Publishing Company, Inc., Cincinnati, 1974.

DE BRUM, S. JOSEPH, "Social Business Education in the Secondary Schools," *Encyclopedia of Education,* The Macmillan Company, New York, 1971, p. 565.

ECKERT, SIDNEY W., "A Dark Horse Medium in Basic Business," *Business Education Forum,* vol. 28, no. 6, March, 1974, p. 21.

———, "The Effect of the Use of Overhead Transparencies on Achievement and Retention in General Business," unpublished doctoral dissertation, University of Minnesota, Minneapolis, 1967.

GARRISON, LLOYD L., "A Syllabus for Teaching Economics in the High School General Business Course," Joint Council on Economic Education, New York, 1964, pp. 1–52.

HAIRSTON, JAMES W., "An Operational Definition of a 'Good' Teacher of Basic Business Classes Based upon an Analysis of Critical Incidents," unpublished doctoral dissertation, Colorado State University, Greeley, Colo., 1965.

HALL, J. CURTIS, "Better Basic Business for the Secondary School," *Business Education Forum,* vol. 24, no. 8, May, 1970, p. 6.

———, "A Systems Approach to the General Business Course," *Business Education World,* vol. 52, no. 1, September–October, 1971, p. 14.

HANSEN, ETHEL D., "A Comparison of the Teaching Behavior of Creative and Less Creative Basic Business Teachers," unpublished doctoral dissertation, University of Minnesota, Minneapolis, 1969.

HOPKINS, CHARLES R., "A Measure of Economic Understandings and General Business Knowledge of Tenth-Grade Students," *National Business Education Quarterly,* vol. 28, Fall, 1969, p. 17.

———, "Textbook Reading Levels," *Business Education Forum,* vol. 28, no. 8, May, 1974, p. 40.

IRVING, LEROY G., "A Survey of General Business Courses in Wisconsin Secondary Schools, 1971," unpublished master's thesis, University of Wisconsin, Madison, Wis., 1972.

JONES, EUGENE, "A Critical Look at Basic Business Education," *Delta Pi Epsilon Journal,* vol. 13, no. 4, August, 1971, p. 10.

KOURILSKY, MARILYN, "Learning through Advocacy, An Experimental Evaluation of an Adversary Instructional Model," *Journal of Economic Education,* no. 3, Spring, 1972, p. 86.

MALSBARY, DEAN R., "Basic Business Research Improves Instruction," *Business Education Forum,* vol. 28, no. 6, March, 1974, p. 11.

MARLOW, CLAUDIA C., and ETHEL A. OESER, "Bulletin Boards for Basic Business," *Business Education Forum,* vol. 28, no. 6, March, 1974, p. 19.

MC KITRICK, MAX O., "Building Business Teacher Competencies," speech at NBEA Convention, Chicago, Feb. 22, 1973.

MINTZ, HERMAN, *General Business Skits,* Monograph 124, South-Western Publishing Company, Inc., Cincinnati, 1971.

MUSSELMAN, VERNON A., *Methods in Teaching Basic Business Subjects,* Interstate Printers and Publishers, Danville, Ill., 1971.

————, "Using Subjective Examinations in Basic Business Classes," *Balance Sheet,* vol. 52, November, 1970, p. 102.

NANASSY, LOUIS C., "From Junior Business Training to General Business—Five Decades of Development," *Balance Sheet,* vol. 52, April, 1971, p. 296.

NELSON, ROBERT E., "A Comparison of Teaching Methods in General Business," unpublished doctoral dissertation, Northern Illinois University, DeKalb, Ill., 1970, also *Business Education Forum,* vol. 26, no. 1, October, 1971, p. 46.

POLICIES COMMISSION FOR BUSINESS AND ECONOMIC EDUCATION, "This We Believe about Business Education in the Secondary Schools," *Business Education Forum,* vol. 25, no. 1, October, 1970, p. 8.

POLLOCK, CARL H., JR., "Identification, Classification, and Ranking of Problems Encountered by Teachers of General Business," unpublished doctoral dissertation, Colorado State University, Greeley, Colo., 1967, also *Delta Pi Epsilon Journal,* vol. 10, no. 2, February, 1968, p. 30.

PRICE, RAY G., "Business Education: Innovations and Needs," *Delta Pi Epsilon Journal,* vol. 13, no. 2, February, 1971, p. 18.

————, "Developing Economic Concepts through General Business," *Business Teacher,* vol. 44, no. 3, January-February, 1967, p. 17.

————, "Multimedia in General Business?" *Business Education World,* vol. 54, no. 4, March-April, 1974, p. 21.

————, VERNON A. MUSSELMAN, AND J. CURTIS HALL, *Teacher's Source Book and Key, General Business for Everyday Living,* Gregg Division, McGraw-Hill Book Company, New York, 1972.

SCOTT, JAMES CALVERT, "Reading Rate—A Neglected Factor in the Basic Business Classroom," *Business Education Forum,* vol. 28, no. 7, April, 1974, p. 32.

SLUDER, LESTER, "An Analysis and Synthesis of Research Findings Pertaining to General Business," unpublished doctoral dissertation, Indiana University, Bloomington, Ind., 1965.

TORRANCE, E. PAUL, AND ETHEL HANSEN, "The Question-Asking Behavior of Highly Creative and Less Creative Basic Business Teachers Identified by a Paper-and-Pencil Test," *Psychological Reports,* vol. 17, 1965, p. 815.

VAN HOOK, BARRY, "The Contributions of Gladys Bahr to Economic Education," unpublished doctoral dissertation, Northern Illinois University, DeKalb, Ill., 1973.

WARMKE, ROMAN F., "The Conceptual Strand Approach to Economic Education," *Business Education Forum,* vol. 22, no. 4, January, 1968, p. 8.

WEST, LEONARD J., "Business Education," *Encyclopedia of Educational Research,* 4th ed., The Macmillan Company, New York, 1969, p. 105.

WOLTERS, MARY J. B., "A Study of General Business Content Based on Nationwide Authoritative Opinion and Practices in California Public Schools," unpublished master's thesis, San Jose State University, San Jose, Calif., 1972.

WYLLIE, EUGENE D., "Basic Business Education—Is There Hope?" *Delta Pi Epsilon Journal,* vol. 13, no. 4., August, 1971, p. 3.

## PERFORMANCE GOALS

**1.** Given details on students in a marketing class—high school or two-year college—including reading levels, cumulative grade averages, occupational goals, and other relevant data, and using this chapter and learning activities 1, 3, 4, and 5, **analyze** the data, group the students, and recommend minimum competencies for each group, defending your recommendations in terms of this chapter and Chapter 3.

**2.** Using one competency identified for performance goal 1 above which is appropriate for performance on the job, **construct** a teaching-learning system including identification and classification of the competency, planning of an evaluation, construction of a performance goal, identification and sequencing of subcompetencies, application of learning principles, and identification of appropriate teaching-learning strategies. Evaluation will be based on all components of the system including multiple teaching-learning activities and self evaluations that enable all students to achieve.

**3.** Select any subcompetency identified for goal 2 above which is appropriate for teacher presentation, and **demonstrate** your ability to teach the subcompetency by teaching either live or on videotape for ten minutes. Evaluation will be by peers on criteria previously developed.

**4.** Given an outline of topics included in a marketing class for learners of specified abilities and information about tasks performed by marketing and distributive workers, list those topics you would retain, those you would drop, and those you would add and **defend** in writing your decisions. Evaluation will be based on whether the topics achieve the competencies listed in the chapter.

# CHAPTER 18

# Marketing and Distribution

The marketing field employs one out of every three people in the work force—including proprietors, managers, and employees—and continues to grow faster than most occupational fields. The American Marketing Association defines *marketing* as the performance of business activities that direct the flow of goods and services from producer to consumer or user. Activities include packaging, selling, pricing, servicing, storing, transporting, advertising, and research. Often "marketing" and "distribution" are used synonymously.

Retailing—selling directly to the ultimate consumer—is the largest single area of employment within distribution and the most visible. Especially visible are salespeople, cashiers, and delivery people. Less visible personnel include purchasing agents, shipping clerks, and copywriters. Wholesaling includes any nonretail sale such as sales by farmers to processors and sales by manufacturers to other manufacturers, wholesalers, or retailers.

Industrial marketing is that segment which markets products that are used to make consumer goods or other industrial goods or to operate a business or nonprofit organization. The industrial market includes government agencies at all levels. Samson says that industrial marketing is consistently overlooked in writings on distributive education and often in distributive education programs, and yet it accounts for sales nearly equal to the total sales of retailers and wholesalers combined. (Samson 2, p. 42.)

Distributive education is the study of marketing, including retailing, wholesaling, and industrial marketing. The U.S. Office of Education describes distributive education as follows:

Distributive education includes various combinations of subject matter and learning experiences related to the performance of activities that direct the flow of goods and services, including their appropriate utilization, from the producer to the consumer or user. Distributive education is comprised of programs of occupational instruction in the field of distribution and marketing. These programs are designed to prepare individuals to enter, or progress or improve competencies in distributive occupations. Instruction is offered at the secondary, postsecondary, and adult education levels and is structured to meet the requirements for gainful employment and entrepreneurship at specified occupational levels. Distributive occupations are found in such areas of economic activity as retail and wholesale trade, finance, insurance, real estate, services and service trades, manufacturing, transportation, utilities, and communications. (*Standard Terminology* . . .)

Distributive education encompasses all facets of the study of marketing. It includes courses with titles such as Retailing, Marketing, Advertising, and Sales or Salesmanship. A high school course in selling and an adult education course in merchandising are both distributive education, as are cooperative distributive education programs. Although funded cooperative and project plan programs (see p. 461) are a major part of distributive education in high schools and community colleges, they are not the only forms of distributive education. Preparatory instruction prepares students, both young people and adults, to enter employment in distributive jobs. Supplemental instruction is also given for persons already employed who desire to gain additional competencies in order to update, retrain, or advance on the job.

Figure 18.1 shows the relationship between preparatory and supplemental distributive education.

Distributive education at the K–8 level is part of total career awareness education whereby children on a continuous basis learn about the world of work, the variety of jobs, and the importance and interrelationship of all jobs. The career exploration phase of distributive education at the ninth- and tenth-grade levels includes courses aimed at economic understandings, more in-depth introduction to the business world and the world of work in marketing and distribution. At the eleventh- and twelfth-grade levels, students receive actual training which can be used in entry-level jobs in marketing. In addition to classes such as sales and retailing, some schools also offer the cooperative plan or project plan programs in distributive education which may or may not be federally funded programs. At the postsecondary level, distributive education in community colleges, vocational schools, or other schools includes both beginning and advanced courses such as sales, supervision, fashion, and the like. The cooperative and project plans are part of some postsecondary programs but not all.

Distributive education at the adult level includes courses similar to those at the postsecondary level; however, these do not include funded cooperative or project plan programs. Training may be given by business firms as part of in-service training or at evening vocational and technical schools or other special training programs for adults. Courses may be preparatory or supplemental. College-level supplemental education includes a wide variety of courses aimed at giving an employee additional skills related to his job. The college courses might be at night or employees might be released from work during the day to take the courses. In addition, some colleges and

Figure 18.1 Relationship between preparatory and supplemental education

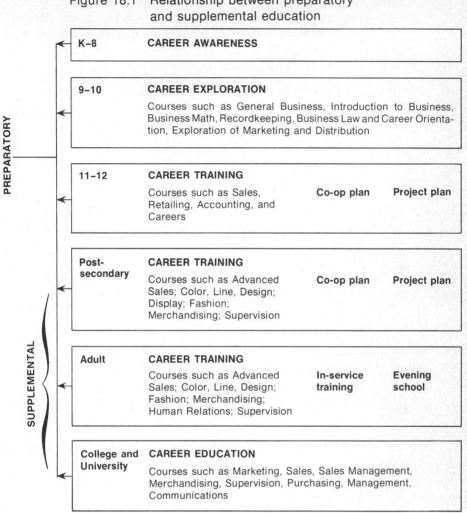

universities offer nonfunded cooperative training either half days or on alternative weeks or months. Colleges and universities offer preparatory distributive education, including courses such as Marketing, Management, Human Relations, Merchandising, and Personnel Management.

The content of distributive education might include the same subject at three different levels: high school, community college, and senior college. For example, courses in sales are offered at all three levels, with basic treatment in high school and more sophisticated treatment in college. The content of such a course at any level might include the preapproach, approach, presentation, handling objections, and closing. The senior college course might go at greater depth into careers in selling and sales management as well as product knowledge, knowledge of people, and ethics in selling. Human relations is another subject which is taught at several different

**449**

levels. A high school might concentrate on how to get along—no small task—while a more advanced college course might include employee attitudes and management philosophy, factors influencing organizational patterns, supervision and leadership, interviewing, and training methods.

## Aims and Objectives of Distributive Education

As part of her major study "A Competency Pattern Approach to Curriculum Construction in Distributive Education," Crawford identified the primary goal of distributive education—preparation for gainful employment and for advancement in distributive occupations—and the following subgoals: (1) engender an understanding and appreciation of the American private enterprise system as a cornerstone of the American democracy; (2) foster an awareness of the civic, social, and moral responsibilities of business to society; (3) encourage and promote the use of ethical standards in business and industry; (4) stimulate the student's interest in his chosen distributive career field by providing an understanding of the opportunities it offers him to be a contributing member of society; (5) prepare distributive personnel to analyze consumer demand and to satisfy the needs and wants of consumers intelligently, efficiently, and pleasantly; (6) provide training that results in increased efficiency in distribution and marketing; (7) contribute to the improvement of the techniques in distribution and marketing; (8) be sensitive to changes in distributive and marketing practices and procedures as they are affected by societal, economic, technical, and educational developments and adapt to such changes; (9) advance the objectives of the total education program; and (10) strive to develop among employers, employees, and consumers a wider appreciation of the value of specifically trained personnel in distribution.

Distributive competencies may fall into one or more of these areas: economic, basic skill, marketing, technical competency, or social competency. The economic competency refers to basic understandings of the free enterprise system including competition, profits, role of government, and how price is affected by supply and demand. Basic skills are those mathematical, computation, and communications skills necessary in distributive jobs. "Marketing" refers to such functions as buying, selling, sales promotion, marketing research, and operations. Technical competency is specific knowledge or skill related to a particular product or service. Social competency, so important in distribution, refers to attitude, appearance, and personality traits in human relations.

## Principles of Distributive Education

Eight principles of distributive education were evident when Warmke found complete agreement among education leaders on these eight statements:

- Distributive education identifies a program of vocational education designed for the preparation, adjustment, and advancement of management, supervisory, sales, and service personnel in marketing and distribution.

- When post-high school (thirteenth and fourteenth years) instruction is available and the community is large enough, cooperative part-time distributive education instruction should be provided in both the high school and in the post high school.
- Adult distributive education should be promoted wherever the need is apparent.
- The primary objectives of state and national distributive education clubs' contests should be educational.
- Coordination in a school system with more than one cooperative distributive education program should be done by the person who teaches the student.
- For their on-the-job experiences, cooperative part-time students should receive the prevailing wage for the type of work they are doing.
- Class time should sometimes be devoted to distributive education club activities.
- Assuming that experience in a distributive occupation is required, the experience must be coordinated by a teacher-coordinator or coordinator.

## Issues in Distributive Education

Weatherford found complete lack of agreement among distributive education leaders on thirteen statements. These issues include the following: (1) whether the present activities of DECA are effectively accomplishing the stated goals of the organization, (2) how local programs should be financed, (3) whether a state-supported college or university should provide a distributive teacher education program without additional financial support from the State Department of Education, (4) whether classroom instruction with simulated in-school laboratory job experiences is adequate preparation for a secondary school student who plans a career in a distributive occupation, (5) who should make the final selection of students for the program, (6) what percentage of classroom time in the cooperative program should be devoted by the student-trainee to the study of his specific job, (7) who should have the responsibility for establishing distributive education teacher certification standards, (8) whether an occupational or career objective in a distributive occupation should be required of all distributive education students, and (9) whether the teaching contract of the teacher-coordinator should specify responsibility in the area of adult education.

## Taxonomy of Distributive Education and Distributive Occupations

Instructional programs in distributive education may comprise any combination of the following areas from the U.S. Office of Education taxonomy, universal classification system, in distributive education. Each classification includes organized subject matter and learning experiences and usually applies to distributive employees and management personnel.

**451**

| | | | |
|---|---|---|---|
| 4.01 | Advertising services | 4.11 | Hotel and lodging |
| 4.02 | Apparel and accessories | 4.12 | Industrial marketing |
| 4.03 | Automotive | 4.13 | Insurance |
| 4.04 | Finance and credit | 4.14 | International trade |
| 4.05 | Floristry | 4.15 | Personal services |
| 4.06 | Food distribution | 4.16 | Petroleum |
| 4.07 | Food services | 4.17 | Real estate |
| 4.08 | General merchandise | 4.18 | Recreation and tourism |
| 4.09 | Hardware, building materials, farm and garden supplies and equipment | 4.19 | Transportation |
| | | 4.20 | Retail trade, other |
| | | 4.31 | Wholesale trade, other |
| | | 4.32 | Distributive education, other |
| 4.10 | Home furnishings | | |

## Needs of the Learner

Our society has shifted from a production-oriented society to one which is distribution-oriented. The industrial revolution brought an era of major emphasis on the production of goods and services; however, new technology has enabled us to produce goods and services not only at a phenomenal rate but with an ever-decreasing number of worker-hours per unit. Thus emphasis is now on the distribution of those goods and services. In fact, our society as we know it depends on an efficient distribution system. Learners are part of this society and their needs and wants are influenced by it. The teacher must identify the needs of a particular learner and then utilize the teaching-learning system to meet those unique needs. This is equally true whether students are preparing to enter the distributive field or advancing in the field.

## Needs of Business

Research in distributive education has identified competencies necessary for the distributive worker. Although the main purpose of Crawford's study was to construct a competency pattern for the distributive education teacher-coordinator, she also identified 983 tasks performed by distributive workers. Critical tasks performed by workers included specific job tasks and related job tasks having to do with display, stock, advertising, merchandise knowledge, store policies and procedures, interpersonal contacts, supervisory responsibilities, and requirements concerning equipment and materials. Crawford organized the 983 tasks performed in distributive jobs into nine areas, a classification used later by other researchers: (1) advertising, (2) communications, (3) display, (4) human relations, (5) mathematics, (6) merchandising, (7) operations and management, (8) products and/or service technology, and (9) selling.

Ertel used a task analysis approach in identifying tasks essential for retail distributive employees working in department stores, variety stores, and general merchandise stores. He used the following work categories in distributive education: selling, stockkeeping, cashiering, receiving-marking merchandise, display, advertising, delivery, recordkeeping, pricing, buying, controlling merchandise, and customer relations. Task analysis inventories were administered by trained interviewers to 609 employees who comprised a stratified random sample of supervisory and nonsupervisory employees, with the percentage of stores and employees in each stratum matching the national percentages. Tasks were shown in rank order as performed by supervisory and nonsupervisory personnel. Substantial percentages of nonsupervisory personnel reported selling, stockkeeping, cashiering, receiving, display, and recordkeeping as major tasks within their jobs; substantial percentages of supervisors reported that they performed these tasks plus advertising, pricing, buying, and controlling merchandise.

The Inter-State Distributive Education Curriculum Consortium operating through the Wisconsin Department of Public Instruction used Crawford's 983 tasks to determine those tasks which were required in 75 percent of 69 distributive occupations. The Consortium found that fewer than 100 of the 983 tasks were required in 75 percent of the 69 occupations. In the area of communications, the Consortium found seventeen tasks necessary in *all* distributive occupations. These are paraphrased below.

*Knowledge of*
1. How to address customers, supervisors or management, and other employees in a businesslike manner.
2. When to keep communications confidential.
3. How to speak so that correct interpretations can be made by the listener(s).

*Skill in*
4. Listening and following directions.
5. Effectively using speech and vocabulary.
6. Communicating with customers, coworkers, and supervisors.
7. Talking clearly and pleasantly, conveying spirit and enthusiasm in one's speech.
8. Assisting with training or teaching others.

*Attitude that*
9. The ability to communicate skillfully in good English is essential to a person's business advancement.
10. In distributive occupations the "spoken word" is an important tool.
11. Fashion and style information, product knowledge, and business trends can be obtained by reading trade and business journals and publications.
12. The voice can be used to express conviction and convey confidence.
13. The tone of voice can express sincere welcome and eagerness to be of service.
14. Nothing is quite so important or contagious as an enthusiasm—for the store, for the merchandise, and for customers.

15. First impressions are important to the business and last impressions are longest remembered.
16. Certain thoughtlessly used terms or words can be misinterpreted by the listener.
17. Attending departmental or storewide meetings is a good way to keep informed of promotions, changing methods, and operating picture.

Region V of the U.S. Office of Education—comprising the states of Illinois, Indiana, Michigan, Ohio, and Wisconsin—conducted a study to determine employer preferences and teacher-coordinator practices as they relate to the organization and operation of cooperative-plan distributive education programs at the secondary school level. Findings included competencies which (1) coordinators indicated that students who graduate from the distributive education program do possess and (2) employers indicated that individuals employed full-time should possess at a significantly higher level than those competencies students entering the cooperative phase of the distributive education program possess (Harris (2), p. 17).

| *Employers*<br>*N=474* | *Coordinators*<br>*N=492* |
|---|---|
| Working with people | Knowledge of products or services |
| Written communication | Advertising |
| Oral communication | Public relations |
| Salesmanship | Nonselling duties |
| Display | Distribution in the free enterprise system |
| Buying | Understanding of how goods and services get from the producer to the consumer |
| Decision making | Mathematics in business |
| Job opportunities in marketing and distribution | Following directions |
| Acceptance and adherence to company policies | |

## Identifying and Classifying Competencies

Since human relations tasks were identified by researchers including Crawford, the IDEC Consortium, and Region V of USOE as essential to success in marketing and distribution, selected human relations tasks are used to illustrate the teaching-learning system. Selected tasks are listed, standards added, and competencies identified in Figure 18.2.

## Planning Evaluations

At the time the teacher constructs the performance goal, the evaluation is planned to measure that goal. In some cases the evaluations will have

Figure 18.2  Distributive and marketing tasks converted to competencies

| Task | Standard | Competency |
| --- | --- | --- |
| 1. Handle a difficult customer. | Effectively | Effectively handle a difficult customer so that the customer leaves the station in good humor. |
| 2. Dress appropriately for the job. | Store policy on dress | Dress in accordance with store policy for appropriate dress. |
| 3. Practice the policies and procedures of management. | Satisfaction of supervisor | Practice the policies and procedures of management to the satisfaction of supervisor. |
| 4. Identify the factors which usually affect employee morale. | Correctly according to key | Correctly identify the factors which usually affect employee morale. |
| 5. Explain instructions to someone selected to do a job. | Clearly | Clearly explain instructions to someone selected to do a job. |
| 6. Exhibit appropriate personality traits and attitudes. | Successful job performance | Exhibit personality traits and attitudes necessary for successful job performance. |
| 7. Conduct self during interview. | Favorable impression | Conduct self during interview so as to make favorable impression. |

to be constructed, and in other cases the teacher can select appropriate evaluative instruments which are part of learning activity packages, are furnished as supplementary materials to a textbook, or are available from some other source.

## Constructing Performance Goals

Now the teacher is ready to construct performance goals for the competencies which have been identified and classified. Sample goals are shown in this chapter; however, only the teacher can determine the performance goals needed by his or her students. Some of the goals apply if the student has on-the-job training in addition to class work or performs in a simulated store. Competencies are analyzed in Figure 18.3.

COMPETENCY 1
Effectively handle a difficult customer so that the customer leaves the station in good humor.
PERFORMANCE GOAL
Without notice that you are being observed in handling a difficult customer, **exhibit** effective behavior which results in the customer leaving your work station in a good frame of mind. The peer or supervisor who observes you will write a short description and date of the episode.

COMPETENCY 2
Dress in accordance with store policy for appropriate dress.
PERFORMANCE GOAL
Without notice that you are being observed at random intervals over a period of a month, **exhibit** appropriate dress for your work station which is in accordance with store manual.

COMPETENCY 3
Practice the policies and procedures of management to the satisfaction of supervisor.
PERFORMANCE GOAL
Satisfactorily **apply** the policies and procedures of management as recorded on check sheet filled out weekly by your supervisor (or teacher).

COMPETENCY 4
Correctly identify the factors which usually affect employee morale.
PERFORMANCE GOAL
Given an individual learning packet, correctly **identify** the factors which usually affect employee morale.

COMPETENCY 5
Clearly explain instructions to someone selected to do a job.
PERFORMANCE GOAL
Given a task to explain to someone else, clearly **explain** the task so that the person receiving the explanation can correctly do the task.

COMPETENCY 6
Exhibit personality traits and attitudes necessary for successful job performance.
PERFORMANCE GOAL
Consistently **exhibit** personality traits and attitudes necessary for successful job performance, such as punctuality, loyalty, honesty, dependability, enthusiasm, ability to accept criticism, willingness to work, friendliness, and helpfulness. Evaluations will be recorded by supervisor and peers on a checklist at periodic intervals over the semester.

COMPETENCY 7
Conduct self during interview so as to make favorable impression.
PERFORMANCE GOAL
In a real or simulated interview, **demonstrate** your ability to make a favorable impression on the interviewer by exhibiting such qualities as poise and composure, good speech techniques, enthusiasm, and resourcefulness as recorded by the interviewer on a rating form.

## Identifying and Sequencing Subcompetencies

The next step in the teaching-learning system is to identify and sequence subcompetencies. Performance goal 7 illustrates this step in Figure 18.4.

Figure 18.3 Marketing and distributive competencies analyzed for components of performance goals

| Competency | Dominant domain & level | Result of performance | Verb | Conditions of performance | Evaluation |
|---|---|---|---|---|---|
| 1. Effectively handle a difficult customer so that the customer leaves the station in good humor. | Affective: low-level responding | Process | **Exhibit** | While being observed on the job | Observation |
| 2. Dress in accordance with store policy for appropriate dress. | Affective: low-level responding | Process | **Exhibit** | While being observed | Observation |
| 3. Practice the policies and procedures of management to the satisfaction of supervisor. | Cognitive: application | Product | **Apply** | Apply the policies and procedures of management | Supervisor's checklist |
| 4. Correctly identify the factors which usually affect employee morale. | Cognitive: knowledge | Product | **Identify** | Given individual learning packet | Key |
| 5. Clearly explain instructions to someone selected to do a job. | Cognitive: analysis | Process | **Explain** | Given task to explain to someone else selected to perform the task | Satisfaction of person receiving explanation |
| 6. Exhibit personality traits and attitudes necessary for successful job performance. | Affective: high-level responding | Process | **Consistently exhibit** | Observation of peers and supervisor over period of time | Checklist |
| 7. Conduct self during interview so as to make favorable impression. | Affective: low-level responding | Process | **Demonstrate** | While being interviewed | Rating sheet |

Figure 18.4 Sequencing of subcompetencies

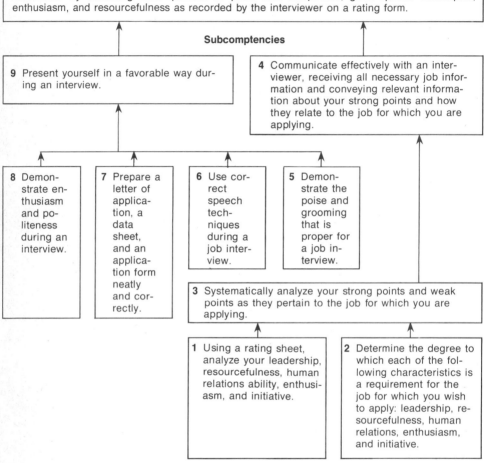

**Performance goal 7**

In a real or simulated interview, **demonstrate** your ability to make a favorable impression on the interviewer by exhibiting such qualities as poise and composure, good speech techniques, enthusiasm, and resourcefulness as recorded by the interviewer on a rating form.

**Subcomptencies**

9 Present yourself in a favorable way during an interview.

4 Communicate effectively with an interviewer, receiving all necessary job information and conveying relevant information about your strong points and how they relate to the job for which you are applying.

8 Demonstrate enthusiasm and politeness during an interview.

7 Prepare a letter of application, a data sheet, and an application form neatly and correctly.

6 Use correct speech techniques during a job interview.

5 Demonstrate the poise and grooming that is proper for a job interview.

3 Systematically analyze your strong points and weak points as they pertain to the job for which you are applying.

1 Using a rating sheet, analyze your leadership, resourcefulness, human relations ability, enthusiasm, and initiative.

2 Determine the degree to which each of the following characteristics is a requirement for the job for which you wish to apply: leadership, resourcefulness, human relations, enthusiasm, and initiative.

## Pretesting and Matching Learner With Performance Goals and Subcompetencies

After competencies and their subcompetencies have been identified, the student must be tested to determine whether he or she already possesses the competency. It is probable that the student already possesses some of the subcompetencies. At any rate, the results of the testing determine where the student must begin in pursuit of the competency. At this point in the system, the learner is matched with the performance goals appropriate for him or her.

## Applying Appropriate Learning Principles

Some of the learning principles in Chapter 6 are discussed in more detail here.

### Principle 1: Learning Must Be Perceived as Relevant

Although it is often easy for a student in marketing and distribution to see the relevance of the learning to what is done on the job, the teacher cannot assume that a student will automatically see the connection. The student may be enrolled in the class through a scheduling expediency rather than a motivation stemming from an understanding of the total marketing field and its opportunities. It is up to the teacher to aid each student in recognizing the relationship of distributive education to personal career goals. The teacher must help the student to get an overview of the entire field of marketing as well as its various sectors and then relate the student's career goal to the competencies needed for that goal.

### Principle 2: Learning Results from the Learner's Interaction With the Total Environment

Students have opportunities in either real or simulated stores to experience the activities which make up the field of marketing—selling, packaging, pricing, servicing, and advertising. Students integrate these activities into their experiences as consumers. Activities of a distributive education or marketing club afford the student opportunities to develop leadership abilities as well as to perfect abilities to interact with a group.

### Principle 4: Learning Proceeds More Effectively When the Learner Is an Active Participant in the Learning Process

Responsibility for learning must pass from the teacher to the student, and when the learner becomes an active participant in the learning process through whatever strategies are employed, learning proceeds more effectively. Classroom work which is supplemented with work experience usually is more meaningful than classroom work alone. If the student has an opportunity to participate in a cooperative plan program, so much the better. The cooperative plan is the most effective method of distributive education when implemented correctly because the learner is not only learning in the classroom but also on the job. In cases where training stations and/or training sponsors are not available, the project plan becomes a feasible alternative.

### Principle 5: Learning Is More Effective When the Learner Knows the Immediate Goal

Clearly defined performance goals are available for both student and teacher, and therefore both are aware of the immediate and terminal goals toward which the student is striving. Since the subcompetencies are sequenced, the learner knows what must be accomplished and in what order.

### Selecting Teaching-Learning Strategies

Nowhere in the teaching-learning system is the professional judgment of the teacher more apparent than in the selection of appropriate teaching-learning strategies. The teacher must decide upon organizational patterns, learning activities, and resources. Strategies are selected on the basis of the competency being sought, the conditions under which performance will take place, and the characteristics of the individual learner.

## Organizational Patterns

Marketing and distribution lends itself to all three organizational patterns—large-group, small-group, and individual instruction. Likely more than one organizational pattern will be utilized to develop a group of competencies, because no matter how effective an organizational pattern is, it loses some effectiveness if it is the only pattern ever used. Some teachers may feel more comfortable with one pattern than another; however, they should make deliberate attempts to include other patterns to meet specific performance goals. Some teachers, for example, feel that they are not teaching if they have directed a student to an individual learning activity packet which the student completes without further assistance from the teacher.

A master teacher will perfect her or his own skill in handling all three organizational patterns, because each pattern has a place in the repertoire of strategies for marketing and distribution. The teacher who is a natural performer in front of large groups ranging in size from 30 to 300 and who receives excellent receptions from such groups may be tempted to utilize large-group instruction exclusively. However, that teacher must realize that certain competencies can only be developed where there is one-to-one interaction between teacher and student or between student and student, and that therefore small-group work must be utilized. The teacher who is not comfortable in front of a large group of perhaps 50 students, and there are some such teachers, may want to avoid large-group instruction altogether; however, he or she must realize that certain competencies can be achieved most expeditiously through large-group instruction. Another teacher may have acquired excellent learning activity packets for a particular course and therefore decide to abandon large- and small-group instruction in favor of a total individual program. However, that teacher must understand that as good as learning activity packets are for achieving certain competencies, they are not effective for achieving others, such as the ability to work with others or the ability to influence a small group.

Figure 18.5

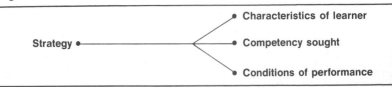

An example of the use of the three organizational patterns for competency 4 ("Correctly identify the factors which usually affect employee morale") is shown.

- Individual: Individual learning packet on aspects of employee relations including employee morale.
- Small group: Based on reading, research, and discussions with family, students could discuss in small groups the factors which often affect employee morale in a work situation.
- Large group: Large group could see a film on manpower development, leadership, or the like and/or hear a personnel manager or union representative speak on the topic of employee relations and employee morale.

## Cooperative Plan

The cooperative plan in distributive education, as in office education, consists of an in-school class of related instruction and placement of students in training stations where they work, are paid, and practice their class-learned skills under the direction of a training sponsor. This plan is considered ideal because the student not only has related class work but also has on-the-job training and remuneration. The coordinator of a cooperative program is the distributive education teacher, often called a teacher-coordinator, in the local school who provides the distributive education and related instruction and also coordinates the on-the-job training with the training sponsor. It is beyond the scope of this book to tell in detail how training stations are selected, placements are made, and the like; entire books are devoted entirely to the cooperative plan.

Crawford and Meyer suggest that consideration be given to the following variations of the cooperative plan: (1) Curriculum covering two school years, providing an average of at least one regular class period a day of vocational instruction in distributive subjects, and providing scheduled periods of cooperative training both years (formerly called Program A). (2) Curriculum covering one school year providing an average of at least two regular class periods a day of vocational instruction in distributive subjects and providing scheduled periods of cooperative training throughout the year (formerly called Program B). (3) A program covering one school year, providing an average of at least one regular period a day of vocational instruction in distributive subjects, providing scheduled cooperative training, and enrolling only those students who have completed two or more semesters of vocational instruction in a related occupational curriculum (formerly called Program C).

In comparing the subject-matter achievement of senior students from Plan B and Plan C programs, Hoffman found no difference in students' learning in ten instructional areas: human relations, job skills and product knowledge, marketing, salesmanship, orientation to distributive education, sales promotion and advertising, retail mathematics, job knowledge and job adjustment, merchandising, and economics of distribution.

Samson determined the critical requirements for performance of secondary school distributive education teacher-coordinators. He collected 1,548 critical incidents which were classified into these categories: student discipline and control, direction of club program and projects, administration and operation of the program, instructional activities, coordination, and personal and professional relationships. Critical behaviors were classified differently by four observer groups—student-learners, supervising school administrators, faculty members, and training sponsors. Samson found differences among all comparisons of personal and professional characteristics, with differences favoring coordinators who were younger, in lower salary range, having less educational preparation, with less experience in distributive education, and those with greater experience in distributive occupations.

Harris determined the effective and ineffective critical requirements for office education and distributive education teacher-coordinators. He delineated sixty-one critical requirements in eight categories, including forty-five effective and sixteen ineffective behaviors, for distributive education teacher-coordinators.

## DISCIPLINE AND CONTROL OF STUDENTS

THE EFFECTIVE DE COORDINATOR.   Recommends dropping students who violate cooperative program rules. Secures cooperation of training station personnel and guidance department or administrative staff members in assisting students. Penalizes assignments which are late, improperly prepared, or not completed.

THE INEFFECTIVE DE COORDINATOR.   Warns, threatens, or pleads with students in an attempt to gain a change in behavior. Allows students to change training stations for minor reasons.

## SELECTION OF TRAINING STATIONS AND PLACEMENT ACTIVITIES

THE EFFECTIVE DE COORDINATOR.   Secures the cooperation of understanding employers and training sponsors in order to place students in stations where they will receive adequate instruction. Changes training stations for students who are not making progress they are capable of or would benefit by a different training station.

THE INEFFECTIVE DE COORDINATOR.   Places students in training stations where the training received is not consistent with the program or student career objectives. Places students who are lazy, indifferent, or poorly adjusted in another training station.

## EVALUATION AND SELECTION OF STUDENTS

THE EFFECTIVE DE COORDINATOR.   Accepts students with known limitations if the deficiency can be compensated by other factors. Utilizes the services of professional staff members to aid in understanding student applicants for the cooperative program.

**THE INEFFECTIVE DE COORDINATOR.** Accepts students who have little chance for success. Accepts students without securing sufficient background information about them. Accepts students whose reasons for enrolling are not consistent with the objectives of the program.

## PERSONAL AND PROFESSIONAL RELATIONSHIPS

**THE EFFECTIVE DE COORDINATOR.** Utilizes conferences, rating sheets, and other devices to keep staff members informed about the program, and discusses student problems with appropriate staff. Consults with employers, training sponsors, and parents in order to avoid or solve problems. Informs students and employers of necessity for following school regulations. Works effectively with individuals in the community.

**THE INEFFECTIVE DE COORDINATOR.** Does not follow school policy. Does not provide adequate supervision and control of student activities. Does not make good use of coordination time. Does not keep administrators adequately informed about students and the program. Does not have an effective working relationship with businessmen. Does not provide assistance to students to help them adjust to their occupation.

## ADJUSTING STUDENT TRAINING STATION PERFORMANCE PROBLEMS (Employer-suggested)

**THE EFFECTIVE DE COORDINATOR.** Holds conferences with students, employers, and other employer representatives to clarify and solve problems. Holds conferences with students who are suspected of performing dishonest acts on the job, and works cooperatively with training station personnel to gain a better understanding of dishonest act performed. Holds conferences with employer prior to time student is actually discharged. Provides students who are having difficulty with guidance and constructive suggestions.

**THE INEFFECTIVE DE COORDINATOR.** Warns students to improve personal appearance or action will have to be taken. Warns or drops students from the cooperative program who do not improve.

## ADJUSTING STUDENT PROBLEMS (Student-suggested)

**THE EFFECTIVE DE COORDINATOR.** Works closely with training sponsors, parents, and counselors to help students who are having difficulty in adjusting to the responsibilities of being cooperative trainees. Helps students gain confidence in themselves. Removes student from a training station when convinced that it would be beneficial to the student.

## DIRECTION OF IN-SCHOOL LEARNING ACTIVITIES

**THE EFFECTIVE DE COORDINATOR.** Effectively utilizes resources of local business establishments to supplement the instruction facilities of the school. Provides students with guidance and direction in a variety of cocurricular activities.

DEVELOPMENT AND PROMOTION OF PROGRAM

THE EFFECTIVE DE COORDINATOR.   Effectively utilizes a variety of techniques to inform students, teachers, administrators, and local businessmen about the program. Works with retail merchant and advisory groups resulting in a better cooperative program status.

In studying the relationship between certain personality characteristics of distributive teacher-coordinators and job satisfaction, Olson found seventeen variables which helped predict job satisfaction in the areas of achievement, coworkers, creativity, social status, supervision-human relations, and general job satisfaction. The seventeen personality variables were outgoing, intelligent, emotionally mature, submissive, conscientious, venturesome, sensitive, artless, self-controlled, relaxed, easy-going, extroverted, responsive, dependent, stable, aggressive, and creative.

## Project Plan

The project plan is the process by which classroom instruction is correlated with a series of learning activities and projects related to a student's occupational goal. The real world of work is simulated in the classroom through a sequence of projects which the student undertakes and completes. Crawford and Meyer suggest these alternatives for the project plan: (1) Curriculum covering one school year two periods a day or two school years one period a day of vocational instruction in distributive subjects and providing scheduled periods for project/laboratory training throughout the year(s). (2) Curriculum covering one school year one period a day for students who expect to enroll in the cooperative curriculum the following year; or an accelerated curriculum for above-average students who plan a career in distribution requiring preparation beyond high school or who plan full-time employment above the entry level upon graduation from high school; or for students planning careers in specialized fields such as fashion merchandise, food distribution, petroleum distribution, agridistribution, and the travel industry.

When Ferguson compared the effectiveness of the project and cooperative plans of teaching high school distributive education, specifically economic understandings and sales comprehension, he found no difference between the distributive education students and the control students. Four groups of students from ten high schools were included, an eleventh-grade English or social science control class, an eleventh-grade project plan distributive education class, a twelfth-grade cooperative plan distributive education class, and a twelfth-grade English or social science control class. When he compared the two groups of distributive education students, he found no difference between the two groups on economic understandings; however, he did find a difference in sales comprehension in favor of the cooperative students.

Rowe used eleven high schools and 1,200 students in comparing the achievement of project plan and cooperative plan distributive education students. Each school contained an eleventh-grade project class, an eleventh-grade nondistributive control class, a twelfth-grade cooperative plan class, and a twelfth-grade control nondistributive class. In addition, three schools also included a twelfth-grade project plan class. Rowe found no correlation between students' socioeconomic status, age, sex, and scores attained on standardized tests measuring economic understanding and sales comprehension and likewise no difference between scores on the test of economic understanding and sales comprehension. There appeared to be a difference between the twelfth-grade cooperative students and project students on the test of economic understanding.

## DECA

Distributive Education Clubs of America (DECA), an integral part of reimbursable distributive education, is the program of youth activity designed to develop future leaders for marketing and distribution (recycle to Chapter 2, p. 31). DECA is the only national youth organization operating through the public schools to attract young people to careers in marketing, merchandising, and management. Its purposes are to develop a respect for education in marketing and distribution which will contribute to occupational competence and to promote understanding and appreciation for the responsibilities of citizenship in our free competitive enterprise system. Although members have opportunities to serve as leaders *and* followers, DECA's major thrust is to develop leadership. In so doing, DECA members have opportunity for state and national recognition that they would not have otherwise.

As part of the instructional program, DECA is cocurricular, and its activities take place during school time like any other instructional activity. DECA has successfully motivated both high school and community college students toward careers in distribution primarily because of the competitive activities and conferences.

Distributive education students, comprising a local school chapter, elect officers with the distributive education teacher serving as adviser. Under the leadership of the state DECA adviser, all chapters within the state comprise a state association with its own elected officers. National officers are elected by each of the five national divisions: high school, junior collegiate, collegiate, alumni, and professional. Overall control of DECA lies with DECA, Inc., its legal sponsoring group, composed of one representative from each state plus the District of Columbia and Puerto Rico.

## School Store

The school store provides teaching-learning opportunities in some schools. Marketing and distributive students perform some or all of the merchandising functions connected with operating a school store with work being performed on school time and no wages paid. Such stores handle staple school supplies, soft goods such as T-shirts and sweatshirts, and novelties. Depending on the school and space available, the store might carry record albums, eight-track cartridges and cassettes, paperbacks, magazines, cards, candy, and the like. A store with about 400 square feet of selling space provides space for each item to compete with other merchandise for the customer's attention and gives students the opportunity to change displays and locations in order to determine which items sell best where.

Learning opportunities include all phases of store operations, merchandising, sales promotion, and financial control. Levinson lists the following specific activities (Levinson, pp. 14–16):

*Store Operations*

1. Handling and controlling merchandise, from receiving through final sale.
2. Handling space utilization (including the layout of merchandising units), maximizing the flexibility necessary to accommodate changes in the store.
3. Finding improved ways to present, display, and promote the products carried, using the available store fixtures.
4. Controlling pilferage.
5. Handling personnel schedules, training, and performance evaluations.
6. Developing necessary systems and procedures for "paper" control of merchandise and recordkeeping.

*Merchandising*

1. Determining what, how much, and when to buy.
2. Locating and evaluating sources of supply.
3. Placing orders and handling pricing.
4. Maintaining stock control records of performance for analysis, evaluation, and future planning.
5. Handling clearance of slow-moving merchandise.
6. Reordering.
7. Planning space allocation, determining where certain items should be displayed and how much space should be devoted to individual categories, new items, etc.

*Sales Promotion*

1. Planning promotional events.
2. Arranging for the use of media (school paper, etc.) for publicity.
3. Preparing promotional materials.
4. Handling window displays.
5. Increasing sales of various items via more effective in-store presentation.

*Financial Control*

1. Handling cash.
2. Managing financial recordkeeping and auditing.
3. Handling financial planning (both short-term and long-term).
4. Taking inventory, pricing, and evaluating age, turnover, and profitability of items.
5. Evaluating cash flow and preserving credit and solvency.
6. Preparing financial reports.

## Brainstorming

Creative thinking is the life blood of marketing and distribution. In the last twenty-five years extensive research has focused on how to foster and develop creative thinking. One of the oldest and most useful exercises is brainstorming, provided that it is carefully structured. (Recycle to Chapter 7, p. 131.) Although brainstorming can be fun, it is not for fun; it is a means for producing high-level creative ideas. In brainstorming the quantity of ideas is the key purpose, because research has consistently shown that the more ideas produced, the more likely the session will produce high-quality ideas. If a hundred ideas are produced, it is more likely that five of these will be high-quality ideas than if only five ideas were produced in all. Wild ideas are encouraged because an element from one idea can be combined with another element from someone else to ultimately produce an innovative, useful solution. Participants are encouraged to hitchhike on the ideas of others. Judgment is ruled out during a brainstorming session; criticism and evaluation of ideas come later. Leventhal suggests the following plan for structuring brainstorming sessions (Leventhal, p. 14-15):

1. The brainstorming group should be larger than ten. The class should be divided with one group observing while the other participates. (An experienced leader could use the whole class as one group.)
2. The . . . teacher . . . serves as group leader and appoints one or two observers to serve as recorders on the blackboard.
3. A specific question or problem is chosen so that there is complete understanding.
4. The group is asked to provide solutions, answers, or ideas to the question or problem. All ideas, no matter how extreme, are recorded. There is no evaluation or opinion about any of the ideas.
5. All participants are encouraged to think of ideas as wild as possible and as many as possible and to build upon or modify the ideas of others.
6. The following day (or on a later date) the group evaluates the ideas one by one and the best five or six are selected.
7. From these selections, the best one is agreed upon.

## Word Puzzles

Word puzzles can be used to teach low-level cognitive skills such as word recognition or word definition. To construct a hidden-word puzzle or crossword puzzle, determine the words to be included, define the outer borders on graph paper, and, letter by letter, place the words across, up, down, diagonally, and backward. Aria suggests that in advertising, for example, a puzzle could be used for types of media, a more detailed puzzle for periodical advertising, and an even more comprehensive one for magazine advertising. A few lines from her puzzle reviewing vocabulary for a fourteen-week term are shown in Figure 18.6.

Figure 18.6   Aria's vocabulary reviewing puzzle

| S | U | H | L | T | D | F | F | I |
|---|---|---|---|---|---|---|---|---|
| L | N | E | C | U | I | G | I | W |
| O | P | A | I | O | S | P | E | C |
| G | A | D | M | Y | P | L | T | N |
| A | C | L | P | A | L | Y | S | E |
| N | E | I | U | L | A | B | V | E |
| G | D | N | L | R | Y | I | M | F |
| O | L | E | S | A | L | E | D | E |
| E | D | R | E | T | T | U | L | C |

1  Items purchased without intentionally planning on buying them are called _____ **im-**

   **pulse**      .

2  Showing merchandise on mannequins either inside the store or in windows is called

   _____ **display** _____ .

3  In the mechanical makeup of an advertisement the four parts are illustration,

   logotype, _____ **headline** _____ , and _____ **copy** _____ .

4  Commercials and public service announcements placed at the end of a show are

   called _____ **clutter** _____ .

5  A brief, striking phrase that is used in sales promotion and advertising is a

   _____ **slogan** _____ .

6  A commercial can be broadcast on the air either _____ **live** _____ , filmed, or video

   taped.

7  An abbreviation for the national, state, and local youth organization of distributive

   education is _____ **DECA** _____ .

Source:  Maria Zak Aria, "Puzzle Fun Aids Learning," *Business Education Forum,* December, 1973, p. 44.

## Games

Games are being used successfully in business to train managers, supervisors, and buyers. One such game teaches inventory control and buying for manager-trainees who must maintain adequate inventory and purchase goods when appropriate. Other marketing games are played by groups, each group deciding what to produce, the volume produced, and the selling price. Data is fed into a computer for analysis, and each group improves its market position or suffers a setback based on its own decisions in relation to decisions made by competitors. Because games have proved successful in business and in education, no doubt their use will continue to increase because they contribute to acquisition of competencies at high levels of the cognitive and affective domains.

## Self-Instruction

Roberson compared the relative effectiveness of teaching specific related information in distributive individual self-instruction with that of teaching by a combination of teacher lectures and class discussions. The basic assumption was that if either the lecture-discussion method or the individual study method were superior or more effective, it must be superior in terms of informational achievement and the effort, time, and costs involved in attaining these outcomes. Experimental findings were measured and the groups compared on the basis of (1) informational achievement, (2) amount of time required for all students to receive instruction, (3) approximate time required for initial preparation of teaching materials, (4) amount of time for the instructor to present the instruction, (5) student attitudes toward a unit of instruction when taught by a particular method, and (6) cost of teaching materials. Roberson found no significant difference in informational gain of students taught by lecture-discussion versus individual study. The lecture-discussion method requires more time for students to receive instruction than the individual study method; however, initial preparation of materials for teaching by the individual study method requires more time than to prepare materials for the lecture-discussion method. Use of individual study will result in a substantial saving of time required for the coordinator to present related information. When taught by different teaching methods, student attitudes toward a unit may differ. Roberson concluded that both individual study and the lecture-discussion method of teaching should be used to present related information to distributive education students.

## Resource Materials

Materials for marketing and distribution are available from publishers, state and federal governments, and school districts. Hirschfeld and Leventhal catalogued information on distributive education materials, each entry containing the name of the publication, author, date, publisher, whether student or teacher material, cost, length, grade level, suggested time of use, objectives, summary description, and availability of materials and tests.

The Program for the Improvement of Distributive Education (PRIDE) is a four-level learning system developed at Michigan State University under the direction of Lorraine Furtado, project director, and Peter Haines, consultant. The four levels of learning follow on page 470.

- Basic knowledge and facts relevant to distributive occupations
- General application of knowledge and facts that apply to a number of distributive jobs
- Specific application of knowledge and facts in each student's vocational objective
- Logic and problem solving in the specific job selected by the student

PRIDE was pilot-tested in twenty-three Michigan schools including traditional high schools and area skills centers, incorporating a cross-section of socioeconomic levels, school sizes, racial/ethnic students, and school plant facilities. The PRIDE system includes thirty-three modules of instruction which contain goal statements, basic reference and instructional materials, teaching-learning activities, and evaluation instruments. The materials are available to teachers who participate in a workshop on the system.

## Evaluating Student Achievement and Effectiveness of System

The final step in the teaching-learning system is administration of the evaluation instruments to assess student achievement. A student who meets each of the performance goals is considered successful, and the system is also considered successful. The system is geared toward success because each student successfully masters sequenced subcompetencies which in turn lead to mastery of the competency. A student who does not master a subcompetency is recycled through other teaching-learning strategies to master the subcompetency. Because of the emphasis on en route evaluations by teacher and student, rarely does a student not achieve the competency after achieving the subcompetencies. Because the nature of marketing and distribution makes it a "people business," the interactions among people are crucial; therefore, the learnings in the affective domain are especially important. Self-evaluations are important to focus attention on the student's progress in meeting goals, particularly affective goals.

If students do not meet terminal performance goals, then the teacher must search for a breakdown somewhere in the system. Were competencies carefully identified to apply to the student's career objective? Were performance goals and evaluations structured realistically to reflect those competencies? Were subcompetencies objectively identified and accurately sequenced? Did pretests reveal unusual learning difficulties for the student? Were the strategies appropriate for the performance goal and for the particular student? An analysis of each step in the system should reveal where the breakdown occurred, and modifications can then be instituted.

## Learning Activities

1. As a member of a small group and according to your instructor's plan, construct a list of questions to which you expect to find answers and visit a marketing class at either a high school or two-year college. Visit the class, observe the teaching-learning strategies employed and interview the teacher. Your group will present to the class your findings

including the strengths and weaknesses of the strategies used. (Performance goals 1, 2, and 3)

**2.** As a member of a small group and using lists of competencies supplied by your instructor, classify the competencies into appropriate categories, domains, levels of domain, and type of evaluation until your instructor approves your decisions. (Performance goals 2 and 4)

**3.** Using an instructor-supplied outline, plan and execute a committee or individual report based on actual interviews with students now enrolled in a cooperative distributive education class, in a project class, and/or a traditional class. Your report will be evaluated on completeness and techniques used in getting data. (Performance goals 1 and 2)

**4.** As a member of a small group, follow your instructor's plan for evaluating published materials for marketing and distributive classes, by checking them against the competencies listed in this chapter. Present a group report to the class describing the materials, indicating the students with whom you would use them, length of time estimated for use, physical facilities required, sources, and strengths and weaknesses. Duplicate the report for each student. (Performance goals 1, 2, and 4)

**5.** For one marketing and distributive competency, construct a subcompetency to be developed to the indicated level within each domain: Cognitive: comprehension, application, analysis/synthesis, and evaluation; and Affective: consistently exhibiting. (Performance goal 1)

**6.** Working in a small group, develop the criteria for evaluation of a teaching strategy indentified by you as the one you plan to microteach. (Performance goal 3)

**7.** Given 10 sample performance goals in the marketing and distribution program, identify those that meet the criteria for performance goals and rewrite those not acceptable until they do meet the criteria. (Performance goals 2 and 4)

## SELECTED READINGS

ARIA, MARIA ZAK, "Puzzle Fun Aids Learning," *Business Education Forum*, December, 1973, pp. 43–44.

ASHMUN, RICHARD D., "Improving the Content of the Postsecondary Distributive Education Program," *NBEA Yearbook*, no. 8, 1970, p. 237.

BUREAU OF BUSINESS EDUCATION, *Programmed Instruction: Distributive and Office Education*, California State Department of Education, Sacramento, 1969.

CARTER, K. KENNETH (ED.), "Focus on (Evaluation of Components in) Marketing and Distribution," *Business Education Forum*, April, 1972, p. 13.

*Challenges and Perspectives for Distributive Education*, Washington. American Vocational Association, 1972.

CRAWFORD, LUCY C., *A Competency Pattern Approach to Curriculum Construction in Distributive Teacher Eduction*, vols. I–IV, Virginia Polytechnic Institute, Blacksburg, Va., 1967, Grant OE-6-85-044.

———, AND WARREN G. MEYER, *Organization and Administration of Distributive Education*, Charles E. Merrill, Inc., Columbus, Ohio, 1972.

*Distributive Education in the High School*, U.S. Department of Health, Education, and Welfare, Office of Education, U.S. Government Printing Office, Washington, D.C., 1969.

ERTEL, KENNETH ARTHUR, "Identification of Major Tasks Performed by Merchandising Employees Working in Three Standard Industrial Classifications of Retail Establishments," unpublished doctoral dissertation, Washington State Univeristy, Pullman, Wash., 1967.

————, "Clusters of Tasks Performed by Merchandising Employees in Three Standard Industrial Classifications of Retail Establishments," University of Idaho, Moscow, Idaho, 1968, Grant OE 7-0031.

FERGUSON, EDWARD T., JR., "A Comparison of the Effectiveness of the Project and Cooperative Methods in Distributive Education at the Secondary Level," unpublished doctoral dissertation, Michigan State University, East Lansing, Mich., 1967.

GILLESPIE, KAREN R. (ED.), "Focus on (Projects in) Marketing and Distribution," *Business Education Forum,* April, 1972, p. 17.

HARRIS, E. EDWARD (1), *Employer Preferences and Teacher-Coordinator Practices in Distributive Education,* Region V—U.S. Office of Education, 1971.

————(2), "Office Education and Distributive Education Teacher-Coordinators: Critical Requirements and Reasoned-Judgment Comparisons," unpublished doctoral dissertation, Northern Illinois University, 1965; also Monograph 115, *Requirements for Office and Distributive Education Teacher-Coordinators,* South-Western Publishing Company, Incorporated, Cincinnati, 1967.

HARRISON, WAYNE J., "Learning Manager Coordinates Individual Instruction," *Business Education Forum,* November, 1972, p. 57.

————, AND TOM HEPHER, "Learning Activity Packages: An Innovative Approach to Distributive Education," *DE Today,* Fall, 1972, p. 3.

HIRSCHFELD, MARVIN, AND JEROME I. LEVENTHAL, *A National State of the Art Study of Curriculum Instructional Materials for Distributive Education,* Temple University, Philadelphia, 1973, Grant O-72-4839.

INTERSTATE DISTRIBUTIVE EDUCATION CURRICULUM CONSORTIUM (IDECC), *Competencies in Distribution,* Wisconsin Distributive Education Resource Center in Cooperation with Dept. of Public Instruction, Madison, Wisc., mimeo. n.d.

LAW, GORDON F., *Cooperative Education Handbook for Teacher-Coordinators,* American Technical Society, Chicago, 1970.

LEVENTHAL, JEROME I., "Problem Solving and Creative Thinking in Distributive Education," *Business Education Forum,* April, 1970, pp. 14–16.

LEVINSON, LAWRENCE, "The School Store: Learning by Involvement," *DE Today,* Part I, Spring, 1974, p. 1, p. 7. Part II, Summer, 1974.

MASON, RALPH EDWARD, "An Analysis of Related Instruction for Cooperative Part-Time Programs in Distributive Education in Illinois," unpublished doctoral dissertation. University of Illinois, Urbana, Ill., 1961.

————, AND PETER G. HAINES, *Cooperative Occupation Education and Work Experience in the Curriculum,* Interstate Printers and Publishers, Danville, Ill., 1972.

MEYER, WARREN G. (1), "Reevaluation of Distributive Education," *Business Education Forum,* January, 1968, p. 13.

————(2), "Retailing Classes in Comprehensive High Schools," *DE Today,* Spring, p. 6, Summer, p. 4, Fall, p. 6, 1971.

————, AND RICHARD D. ASHMUN, "Media in Distributive Education;" *AV Instructor,* April, 1970, p. 33.

————, AND PATRICIA MINK RATH, "Marketing: Capstone or Foundation?" *Business Education World,* May-June, 1970, p. 12.

_____, AND HAROLD O. TOUPIN, "A Career in Marketing and Distribution," *Business Education Forum,* May, 1972, p. 9.

NORTHWEST REGIONAL EDUCATION LABORATORY, *Vocational Instructional Materials for Distributive Education Available from Federal Agencies,* superintendent of Documents, Washington, D.C., 1971, HEW Contract O-7-4480 (357).

OLSON, HARRY J., "Relationships Between Certain Personality Characteristics of Distributive Education Teacher-Coordinators and Job Satisfaction," unpublished doctoral dissertation, University of Minnesota, Minneapolis, Minn., 1967.

*Program for the Improvement of Distributive Education (PRIDE),* Michigan State University, Department of Secondary Education, East Lansing, Mich., 1973.

ROBERSON, ROY PARKER, "An Experimental Comparison of Two Methods of Teaching Related Information in Distributive Education at the High School Level," unpublished doctoral dissertation, University of Missouri, Columbia, Mo., 1967.

ROWE, KENNETH LEROY, "Development of Selected Marketing Competencies through Utilization of Two Methods of Teaching in the Secondary School," unpublished doctoral dissertation, Michigan State University, East Lansing, Mich., 1969.

SAMSON, HARLAND E. (1), "Critical Requirements for Distributive Education Teacher-Coordinators: A Study of Observed Effective and Ineffective Behaviors of Iowa Secondary School Distributive Education Teacher-Coordinators Based upon an Analysis of Critical Incidents," unpublished doctoral dissertation, University of Minnesota, Minneapolis, Minn., 1964.

_____ (2), "Objectives of Career Education for Distributive Occupations," *NABTE Review,* 1974, p. 42.

*Standard Terminology for Curriculum and Instruction in Local and State School Systems,* U.S. Department of Health, Education and Welfare, Office of Education, U.S. Government Printing Office, Washington, D.C., 1970, Bull. OE-23052.

VIVIAN, NEAL E. (ED.), "Focus on (Systems Approach in) Marketing and Distribution," *Business Education Forum,* April, 1973. p. 17.

WALSH, LAWRENCE A. (1), "The CCEM Matrix and Distributive Education," *DE Today,* Fall, 1972, p. 11.

_____ (2), "Individualizing Instruction: the DE Learning System," *DE Today,* Spring, 1972, p. 11, and Summer, 1972, p. 11.

_____ (3), "Keeping the Program Individualized," *American Vocational Journal,* April, 1973, p. 46.

WARMKE, ROMAN F., "Distributive Educaton Issues in 1959: A Study of Current Distributive Education Issues, Based upon Opinions of Education Leaders," unpublished doctoral dissertation, University of Minnesota, Minneapolis, Minn., 1960.

_____, *Distributive Education Issues,* Monograph 102, South-Western Publishing Company Inc., Cincinnati, 1961.

WEATHERFORD, JOHN WILSON, "Identification and Analysis of the Current Issues in Distributive Education," "unpublished doctoral dissertation, Ohio State University, Columbus, Ohio, 1972.

**473**

# Resources

The following are selected sources a teacher may use to locate appropriate instructional materials for business education classes. The various periodicals listed are a good place to begin a search and frequently provide up-to-date references on specific materials. Because of the dynamic state of the educational publishing industry, the teacher is cautioned to verify the organizations and addresses listed below before contacting them directly.

## Periodicals

Initials given in parentheses after each periodical refer to the publisher in the selected list of organizations following.

Abstracts of Instructional Materials (CVE)
Advertising Age (AA)
AEDS Journal (AEDS)
AEDS Monitor (AEDS)
American Business Communications Association Bulletin (ABCA)
American Vocational Journal (AVA)
Annual Buying Guide (CUUS)
AV Communications Review (AECT)
Balance Sheet (S-WPC)
Business Education Forum (NBEA)
Changing Times (CTES)
Consumer Bulletin (CR)
Consumer Reports (CUUS)

DE Today (GCCD)
Delta Pi Epsilon Journal (DPE)
Educational Technology (ETP)
Infosystems (HPC)
Journal of Business Communication (JBC)
Journal of Business Education (JBE)
Journal of Consumer Affairs (ACCI)
Journal of Consumer Research (JCR)
Journal of Date Education (SDE)
Journal of Economic Education (JCEE)
Journal of Marketing (AMA)
Media and Consumer (MCF)
The Secretary Magazine (NSA)

## Organizations and Companies

Abacus Computer Corp., 110 East Granada Ave., Ormand Beach, FL 32074.

Addison-Wesley Publishing Co., Reading, MA 01867.

Advertising Age (AA), 740 Rush St., Chicago, IL 60611.

AFL-CIO Publications, 815 Sixteenth St., N.W., Washington, DC 20206.

American Advertising Federation, 1225 Connecticut Ave., N.W., Washington, DC 20036.

American Bankers Association, 1120 Connecticut Ave., N.W., Washington, DC 20036.

American Business Communications

Association (ABCA), Department of Business Communication, University of Illinois, Urbana, IL 61801.

American Council on Consumer Interests (ACCI), 238 Stanley Hall, University of Missouri, Columbia, MO 65201.

American Federation of Information Processing Societies, 210 Summit Ave., Montvale, NJ 07645.

American Home Economics Association, 2010 Massachusetts Ave., N.W., Washington, DC 20036.

American Marketing Association (AMA), 222 South Riverside Plaza, Chicago, IL 60606.

American Stock Exchange, 86 Trinity Pl., New York, NY 10006.

American Vocational Association (AVA), 1510 H Street, N.W., Washington, DC 20005.

Association for Computing Machinery, 1133 Ave. of the Americas, New York, NY 10036.

Association for Educational Communications and Technology (AECT), 1201 16th St., N.W., Washington, DC 20036.

Association for Educational Data Systems (AEDS), 1201 16th St., N.W., Washington, DC 20036.

William C. Brown, Publishers, 2460 Keiper Blvd., Dubuque, IA 52001.

Canfield Press, Division of Harper & Row, 850 Montgomery St., San Francisco, CA 94133.

The Center for Vocational Education (CVE), The Ohio State University, 1960 Kenny Rd., Columbus, Ohio 43210.

Changing Times Education Service (CTES), 1729 H St., N.W., Washington, DC 20006.

Computer Games, Inc., P.O. 544, Chicago Hts., IL 60411.

Comspace Corp., 350 Great Neck Rd., Farmingdale, Long Island, NY 11735.

Conference Board, Information Service, 845 Third Ave., New York, NY 10022.

Consumer Federation of America, 1012 14th St., N.W., Suite 1105, Washington, DC 20005.

Consumers' Research (CR), Inc., Washington, NJ 07882.

Consumers Union of United States (CUUS), 256 Washington St., Mount Vernon, NY 10550

Council of Better Business Bureaus, 1150 17th St., N.W., Washington, DC 20036.

Council for Family Financial Education, Twin Towers, Silver Spring, MD 20910.

CUNA International, Inc., 1617 Sherman Ave., Madison, WI 53701.

Data Processing Management Association, 505 Busse Highway, Park Ridge, IL 60068.

Delta Pi Epsilon National Office (DPE), Gustavus Adolphus College, St. Peter, MN 56082.

Distributive Education Clubs of America, Inc., 200 Park Ave., Falls Church, VA 22046.

Dow Jones & Company, P.O. Box 300, Princeton, NJ 08540.

DYMAX, P.O. Box 310, Menlo Pk., CA 94025.

Educational Technology Publications (ETP), 140 Sylvan Ave., Englewood Cliffs, NJ 07632.

Enterlock, Inc., Newburyport, MA 01950.

Eye Gate House, Inc., 146–01 Archer Ave., Jamaica, NY 11435.

Fearon Publishers, 6 Davis Dr., Belmont, CA 94002.

Federal Reserve Banks: *Atlanta*—104 Marietta St., Atlanta, GA 30303; *Boston*—30 Pearl St., Boston, MA 02106; *Chicago*—230 South La Salle St., Chicago, IL 60690; *Cleveland*—East 6 & Superior, Cleveland, OH 44101; *Dallas*—Station K, Dallas, TX 75222; *Kansas City*—Federal Reserve Station, Kansas City, MO 64198; *Minneapolis*—73 South 5, Minneapolis, MN 55440; *New York*—Federal Reserve P.O. Station, New York, NY 10045; *Philadelphia*—925 Chestnut St., Philadelphia, PA 19101; *Richmond*—100 North Main, Richard, VA 23261; *St. Louis*—P.O. Box 442, St. Louis, MO 53166; *San Francisco*—400 Sansome St., San Francisco, CA 94120.

Future Business Leaders of America-Phi Beta Lambda, P.O. Box 17417, Dulles Airport, Washington, DC 20041.

Ginn & Company, Division of Xerox, 191 Spring St., Lexington, MA 02173.

Glencoe Press, Division of Macmillan Co., Riverside, NJ 08075.

Gregg and Community College Division (GCCD), McGraw-Hill Book Co., 1221 Ave. of the Americas, New York, NY 10020.

Hayden Book Co., Inc., 50 Essex St., Rochelle Pk., NJ 07662.

Health Insurance Institute, 277 Park Ave., New York, NY 10017

Hitchcock Publishing Co., (HPC), Hitchcock Building, Wheaton, IL 60187.

**475**

Institute of Life Insurance, 277 Park Ave., New York, NY 10017.

Insurance Information Institute, 110 William St., New York, NY 10038.

Richard D. Irwin, Inc., 1818 Ridge Rd., Homewood, IL 60430.

Joint Council on Economic Education (JCEE), 1212 Ave. of the Americas, New York, NY 10036.

Journal of Business Communication (JBC), Department of Business Communication, University of Illinois, Urbana, IL 61801.

Journal of Business Education (JBE), 15 South Franklin St., Wilkes-Barre, PA 18701.

Journal of Consumer Research (JCR), 222 South Riverside Plaza, Chicago, IL 60606.

Kiewit Computation Center, Dartmouth College, Hanover, NH 03755.

Media & Consumer Foundation (MCF), P.O. Box 1225, Radio City Station, New York, NY 10019.

Money Management Institute, Household Finance Corporation, Prudential Plaza, Chicago, IL 60601.

National Association of Manufacturers, 277 Park Ave., New York, NY 10017.

National Association of Real Estate Boards, 155 East Superior, Chicago, IL 60611.

National Association of Secondary Principals, 1904 Association Dr., Reston, VA 22091.

National Book Co., Education Research Associates, 1019 S.W. Tenth Ave., Portland, OR 97205.

National Business Education Association (NBEA), P.O. Box 17402, 1906 Association Dr., Reston, VA 22091.

National Consumer Finance Association, 1000 16 St., N.W., Washington, DC 20036.

National Consumers League, 1029 Vermont Ave., N.W., Washington, DC 20005.

National Council of Teachers of Mathematics, 1904 Association Dr., Reston, VA 22091.

National Foundation for Consumer Credit, Inc., 1819 H St., N.W., Washington, DC 20006.

National Industrial Conference Board, 845 Third Ave., New York, NY 10022.

National Secretaries Association (NSA), 2440 Pershing Rd., Kansas City, MO 64108.

New York Stock Exchange, 11 Wall St., New York, NY 10005.

Office of Consumer Affairs, Executive Office of the President, Washington, DC 20402.

Office Education Association, 1120 Morse Rd., Columbus, OH 43229.

J. C. Penney Co., Consumer Relations, 1301 Ave. of the Americas, New York, NY 10019.

Pitman Publishing Co., 6 East 43 St., New York, NY 10017.

Quantra Development Corp., 15 Whitfield Ter., New Rochelle, NY 10801.

Savings and Loan Foundation, Inc., 1111 E St., N.W., Washington, DC 20004.

Science Research Associates, Inc., Division of IBM, 1540 Page Mill Rd., Palo Alto, CA 94304.

Sears, Roebuck & Company, Consumer Information Services, 303 East Ohio, Chicago, IL 60611.

Society of Data Educators (SDE), 983 Fairmeadow Rd., Memphis, TN 38117.

South-Western Publishing Co., (S-WPC), 5101 Madison Rd., Cincinnati, OH 45227.

Tecnica Education Corp., 1864 South State St., Suite 100, Salt Lake City, UT 04115.

United States Government: *Teaching Taxes Program*—contact your regional office of Internal Revenue Service. For a guide to federal agencies, see *Guide to Federal Consumer Services* (1971), Office of Consumer Affairs, available from Superintendent of Documents, Washington, DC 20402, or *Annual Buying Guide* published by Consumers Union.

United States Savings & Loan League, 111 East Wacker Dr., Chicago, IL 60601.

John Wiley & Sons, Inc., 605 Third Ave., New York, NY 10016.

# Index